National Children's Bureau series

Editor: Mia Kellmer Pringle

This new series examines contemporary issues relating to the development of children and their needs in the family, school and society. Based on recent research and taking account of current practice, it also discusses policy implications for the education, health and social services. The series is relevant not only for professional workers, administrators, researchers and students but also for parents and those involved in self-help movements and consumer groups.

Caring for Separated Children
R. A. Parker (editor)

A Fairer Future for Children
Mia Kellmer Pringle

Adoption and Illegitimacy: a Study of the Effects of Changing Families
Lydia Lambert and Jane Streather

Report of the National Children's Bureau working party established:

'to consider the care, welfare and education of children separated from their families for recurrent or long periods. In particular, to examine the means of planning for these children so as to promote continuity and quality in their care, education and welfare.'

Professor R. A. Parker (Chairman)

Professor Hugh Bevan
Mary Evans
Michael Fitzgerald
Dr Robert Holman
Dr Iris Knight
Martin Manby
Dr Mia Kellmer Pringle
Jane Rowe
George Thomas
Baroness Young

Dr Judith Unell (Secretary)

Caring for Separated Children

Plans, procedures and priorities

Edited by

R. A. Parker

A report by a working party established by the National Children's Bureau

First published 1980 by
THE MACMILLAN PRESS LTD
London and Basingstoke
Associated companies in Delhi Dublin
Hong Kong Johannesburg Lagos Melbourne
New York Singapore and Tokyo

Filmset in Great Britain by
VANTAGE PHOTOSETTING CO LTD
Southampton and London
Printed in Hong Kong

British Library Cataloguing in Publication Data

Caring for separated children.
1. Child welfare – Great Britain
2. Parental deprivation
I. Parker, Roy Alfred
II. National Children's Bureau
362.7′3′0941 HV887.G5

ISBN 0–333–26893–8
ISBN 0–333–26894–6 Pbk

Contents

Part II Planning

Part III The Future

Membership of the Working Party

Chairman

Professor R. A. Parker
Department of Social Administration, School of Applied Social Studies, University of Bristol.

Members

Professor H. K. Bevan, JP, LLM
Faculty of Law, University of Hull.

Mrs Mary Evans
Lately Inspector of Special Education with ILEA. Now Co-director of the Schools Council Project, 'The Education of Disturbed Pupils'.

Mr Michael Fitzgerald, MBE
Child Care Adviser.

Dr Robert Holman
Community Social Worker, Church of England Children's Society.

Dr Iris Knight
Senior Clinical Medical Officer, Essex Area Health Department.

Mr Martin Manby
Assistant Director (Field Work), Islington Social Services Department.

Dr Mia Kellmer Pringle, CBE
Director of the National Children's Bureau.

Miss Jane Rowe
Formerly Director of the Association of British Adoption and Fostering Agencies. At present researcher on the 1975 Children Act and freelance worker.

Mr George Thomas
Director of Social Services, London Borough of Harrow.

The Baroness Young
Former Chairman of Oxford City Children's Committee.

Government Observer

First Miss Joan Vann and then Miss Pam Thayer
Department of Health and Social Security.

Secretary

Dr Judith Unell

Preface

by Lord Wolfenden of Westcott
President of the National Children's Bureau

Background to the working party

The fate of children whose own parents are unable or unwilling to care for them has long been one of the major areas of the National Children's Bureau's concern. For this reason it reviewed the state of knowledge regarding residential and foster care in this country, the United States and Western Europe.[1] When a decade later both these reviews were brought up to date[2] it was found that, regrettably, very little had changed; even the number of children in care had not been reduced despite the more community-orientated philosophy enshrined in the 1969 Children and Young Persons Act.

In fact, so closely did the present state of knowledge resemble the situation of ten years ago that the major conclusions and recommendations reached then were reprinted in the later volumes. In particular the emotional and educational consequences, and hence the long-term psychological ill-effects and social costs, did not seem to have been ameliorated during the intervening years. Thus lower than average levels of language, and of intellectual and scholastic performance, were all too prevalent. These findings were also confirmed by the Bureau's longitudinal National Child Development Study. The proportion performing poorly in general knowledge, ability to express themselves in conversation, reading and arithmetic was twice or three times as high among children 'in care' as among their peers.

However, where fostering and adoption practice is concerned, a recent Bureau enquiry has disclosed a state of transition and signs of change.[3] Conventional attitudes and cautious policies are being challenged and the question is being raised of whether family placement should be considered as an option for all children who, for long or short periods, cannot live with their own families.

The Bureau has also been concerned to increase public understanding of the needs of children in care. To do so it set up a working party which produced a guide for the intelligent layman on long-term substitute care.[4] A similar aim prompted another project, which gave the opportunity to young people growing up in residential care to voice their feelings and concerns.[5] This innovative venture, which is still continuing, is now beginning to influence public opinion and professional thinking.

Origins of the working party

In 1973 the then Chairman, Tony Rampton, and the then Director, Jane Rowe, of the Association of British Adoption Agencies (ABAA) expressed to the Bureau their concern about the quality of public care for children who are separated from their families. This concern was shared by several of the Bureau's member organisations. Subsequently, ABAA wrote formally suggesting that a working party should be set up to consider the subject. The Bureau's Executive Committee accepted this proposal and drew up preliminary terms of reference. A wide-ranging brief was proposed:

> To consider the nature of complementary, compensatory and substitute parental care, the nature and degree of adequacy of services for children and families needing such care and to make proposals about the development of such services and any further action which is required.

The Gulbenkian Foundation made a generous offer of financial support. Roy Parker, Professor of Social Administration at the University of Bristol, agreed to chair the working party.

The scope of the enquiry

It was clear from the beginning of the enquiry that the original terms of reference needed to be limited. The working party had a planned life-span of eighteen months and it did not possess the resources necessary for a comprehensive review of services. Thorough investigations into particular aspects of the child care services were being carried out by other committees (such as the DHSS working party on foster care practice and the Court Committee on the child health services) and we realised that any attempt to duplicate their work would be wasteful and superficial. In the light of such considerations, and with the Bureau's approval, the terms of reference were reformulated as they appear on p. ii (opposite the title page).

Acknowledgements

The Bureau is extremely grateful to all those who made it possible for this work to be undertaken: the organisations who asked for the working party to be set up, in particular the then Association of British Adoption Agencies; the Gulbenkian Foundation, who made it financially possible; the various organisations and individuals who provided evidence; and the selected local authorities who gave a great deal of information to enable case studies to be made of current practice. Dr Sula Wolff, Consultant Psychiatrist at the Royal Hospital for Sick Children in Edinburgh, participated in the discussions which led to the writing of this report and her contribution was very much appreciated.

Above all, the Bureau is deeply indebted to the members of the working party, who gave so generously of their knowledge, experience and time; and in particular to the chairman, Professor Roy Parker, whose wise, able and close guidance, as well as detailed editorial work, enabled the task to be brought to a fruitful conclusion. Very special thanks are due to Dr Judith Unell, the secretary to the working party, to Penny Harrington and Myra Soons of the National Children's Bureau, and to Lynda Vyvyan-Jones of Bristol University, who behind the scenes typed and retyped different parts and revised versions of the report.

February 1979

Part I

Background

1

Introduction

This report is about the well-being of children who are cared for over long periods of time by people other than their parents. More especially, it is concerned with a group of children for whose care corporate bodies, such as local authorities or voluntary children's societies, have a significant measure of responsibility. Their parents do not have day-to-day responsibility for them nor are such parents usually in a position to exercise firm and active control over those who do care for their offspring. In some cases, indeed, their rights have been specifically curtailed by a court of law.

Typically, no one *person* has complete and comprehensive responsibility for the child's present care and future welfare in the way that is usually expected of a parent. Consequently, these children are dependent upon adults whose responsibilities are often ambiguous and who are themselves liable to be replaced. In particular, they are likely to feel uncertain and unsure about the future since it has no obvious or foreseeable pattern. As a result they may face particular difficulties in acquiring, or retaining, a sense of their identity. Often they can provide no answers for themselves to the questions: who am I? where do I belong? or where am I going? They are, in every sense of the word, *vulnerable* children.

It is hard, nevertheless, to draw up a list of all the children who fall into the category that we have described. Many of them are in the care of local authorities; others are looked after by voluntary societies. Some are long-stay patients in hospitals, particularly the very severely mentally or physically handicapped. There are others in special boarding schools and some of the older ones are in penal establishments. However, it can be misleading to point to these settings in order to identify the children with whom we are concerned. There are, for example, children who spend only a short period in local authority care and who are not separated from their parents again. Likewise, many children spend some time in hospital, but only a small proportion stay there for long and in fewer cases still are parents unable or unwilling to maintain contact. The great majority of children in boarding schools return home at holiday times and parents exercise continuing responsibility.

For reasons like these we cannot say exactly how many children experience long-term separation. We do know, however, that they exist and that, as well as being the responsibility of corporate bodies, some misfortune has befallen them which was severe enough to deprive them of the ordinary experiences of life in their own family. Some have suffered because their parents have been unable to provide consistent and affectionate care. In some cases they have been neglected or abused. Others will have parents whose capacity for child-rearing has been temporarily or permanently impaired by illness, or by the lack of adequate social support or material resources. Again, there are those who will have experienced problems like these as well as others such as physical or mental handicap.

The group we are describing comprises some of the most seriously disadvantaged children in our society. Of course, they are not the only ones. They are, however, especially dependent upon corporate bodies to ensure their day-to-day care and to make constructive and appropriate plans for their future. Having assumed a measure of *public* responsibility the bodies concerned have a particular obligation to provide as good a care and planning service for those children as is possible.

This is not easy, despite the fact that there is considerable agreement about what should be done. The problems arise in actually realising the goals of good child care; of converting exhortation and good intentions into solid achievements. We have tried to take account of this simple fact by devoting particular attention to the identification and analysis of these problems rather than providing a detailed guide to practice. In doing so we believe that our discussion will be of value to those at central and local levels who are responsible for the formulation of policy and the management of resources, as well as to those who are actively engaged in providing services for individual children and their families.

We are deeply conscious that our report does not fully meet the request of those numerous people who greatly assisted our enquiry in the spoken hope that, when published, it would give clear-cut advice on practical routes towards better performance in child care. The social terrain we are all exploring is not only different in different areas but changing so rapidly that we have found it possible only to indicate compass points and, by posing the questions that need to be answered, allow care-givers to map their own routes.

In approaching our task we have been aware that the standards of services for protecting and caring for children have been called seriously into question by the suffering and death of children like Maria Colwell. More generally, uncertainty has grown about the effectiveness of social work with children in the new social services and social work departments. For example, it has been claimed that many children stay in residential homes when they could be better placed in foster homes or adopted. By contrast, it is also maintained that with more support and help from their families a substantial number of children could be restored earlier to their parents. There is also a widely held conviction that by providing timely and appropriate services much long-term separation of children from their parents could be prevented. Certainly, it was concerns like these which prompted the setting up of this working party.

It goes without saying that services for vulnerable children and their families could be better. That is different, however, from the contention that standards have declined. This is the particular fear that has disturbed many of those involved with, or responsible for, these services. Hence, we have been at pains, first, to examine the question of deterioration and then, second, to consider ways in which, in general, improvements might be made. Whether or not services were better a decade ago we can still learn from the experience of the intervening years. This learning must be applied to correcting what is considered to be wrong now and to creating conditions in which the risks of child suffering and unhappiness are minimised and opportunities maximised.

In our special concern for separated children we are liable to rely too heavily upon administrative and legal classifications which serve to mark these children off from other children. Of course, children with different types of handicaps, disadvantages or disorders call for different kinds of help and treatment. However, there is a danger that we may overlook important aspects of the environment which are required by *all* children, relating to the general quality of life, their rights, their responsibilities and their status in our society. It seems to us that what happens to children living away from home also reflects what happens to many other children. In some ways it is a sad commentary that it was necessary for the United Nations to designate 1979 as *the* Year of the Child. How much better were every year the year of the child.

Whilst children 'in care' have certain characteristics as a group which distinguish them from other children in terms of their social and family circumstances, they share with all children the characteristics of immaturity and, like all children, they require an environment that meets certain basic needs for adequate physical, intellectual and emotional development. Part of the answer to improving the quality of our services for separated children is to be found in achieving *general* improvements in the quality of life that all children experience. And that, in its turn, is related to the quality of life of their parents or other adults upon whom they are dependent in various ways.

The idea of children being 'in care' is apparently simple. There is, furthermore, a comfortable ring about the phrase. It conveys an impression of security and benevolence. There is also a kind of administrative tidiness involved which can reassure those who are anxious about the well-being of certain children. Alternative arrangements may lack this tidiness but yet be preferable.

The first aim of the statutory and voluntary child care services should be to enable the families of vulnerable children to provide adequate care themselves. To achieve this they will often require additional help which gives them respite or relief by augmenting the care which they can give their children. Such a partnership is generally accepted in the educational field but less readily so where actual care is concerned. The dearth of day care provision bears ample witness to the fact. Prevention of family breakdown entails the identification and active support of overburdened or handicapped parents so that they are not left to cope with insuperable problems unaided, and crises which result in the child being suddenly received into care are avoided. If prevention fails, and the separation of the child from his family becomes necessary, then foster care or residential care should be offered as another means of sharing responsibility for the child with his own parents. This implies that the parents should be involved in planning and that special social work guidance is available to both the parent and the substitute care-givers to manage their inevitably difficult and demanding relationship. The rehabilitation of the child with his family will, in part, depend upon the success of this work.

It must be recognised, however, that there will be children who lose contact with home or who need protection from damaging parents. 'Total' substitute care in the setting of an adoptive home, foster home or a residential unit will continue to be needed for such children and special skills will be required in its provision. But we anticipate that this group of children will be significantly smaller than the group which has viable links with home and parents and for which the 'shared care' approach will be appropriate.

Whether a child lives at home or is placed in some form of substitute provision the overriding aim should be high quality care. In setting that aim, however, we must not ignore the fact that the children with whom we are particularly concerned are likely to have suffered not only by virtue of separation but also because of the events which made it necessary and which may have been affecting their development for some time. These circumstances may themselves impose limitations on the kind of care which it is possible to provide.

Similarly, all the conceivable choices may have some serious disadvantages beyond a certain point in a child's history of disruption or deprivation. Overlooking this fact creates three dangers. First, the morale of residential child care staff and of foster parents who are struggling with the day-to-day care of separated children may be severely undermined. What they are able to achieve will rarely match theoretical standards of perfection. Second, it may lead professional workers to reject the care which can be offered by parents or foster parents with whom the child has formed a close bond because they are judged to fall short of a high standard. Third, in the process of waiting for the 'best' form of care for a child, time passes and this in itself may cause still further problems. If the preferred course of action cannot eventually be realised the 'next best' arrangement may also have been lost in the waiting.

We have endeavoured to take account of these realities in a way which is helpful to the children and to those bearing the burden of decision, without losing sight of the pressing need to raise standards.

We must aim high but, in doing so, we must be sure that the gradient is not so impossibly steep that most of the movement is downwards rather than upwards.

Part I of this report contains three more chapters. The first examines briefly the legal and administrative framework within which services for separated children are set. Since we felt that it was necessary to draw some preliminary conclusions about the present sense of disquiet and controversy surrounding these services we devoted the next chapter to identifying the main trends and background factors which have shaped that concern. Although our terms of reference, as set out on p. ii (opposite the title page), focus upon children once they are 'in care' and apart from their families we felt, none the less, that no treatment of this subject would be satisfactory without at least some consideration of how this might be prevented. Hence, Chapter 4 raises some of the issues about prevention as well as indicating what needs to be done.

Our terms of reference also place a special stress upon planning for the individual child. We wished to maintain that central emphasis in the report and to that end Part II is devoted to a consideration of the key people in the decision network surrounding separated children (Chapter 5), followed by an examination of the key decisions which are, or have to be, made (Chapter 6).

The evidence we received, as well as our own deliberations over many months, encouraged us, in Part III of the report, to look forward and to offer certain general suggestions which may help in fashioning the future development of services for separated children. In Chapter 7 we look at some new ways of regarding available resources and at the possibility of somewhat different solutions. Finally, in Chapter 8 we gather together some of the unanswered questions which might provide the framework for a research agenda.

We have not included case studies of individual children to capture and convey the vivid nature of the problems before us: but they *are* personal and passionate. We should not leave this introduction, therefore, without impressing upon the reader that in the final analysis it is not law, administration or policy which matter in themselves but how they can be used to create high-quality services for *particular* children and their families. In order not to lose sight of the importance of this we have included, from time to time in the report, quotations from the National Children's Bureau publication *Who Cares?* This was produced by a working group of young people who are, or were, in long-term care and who came together to discuss their experiences. We are grateful to them for talking with members of our working party and for enabling us to preface some of our remarks with such moving and apt words.

2

The Legal and Administrative Framework

People think that if you're in care you're some kind of freak like you popped down from Mars. But a kid who's in care isn't any different from anybody else. It's just that he wants to be noticed – that he's not just a name, a number and a little bit of print on some paper . . .

In this chapter we present an outline of the legal and administrative arrangements which shape the care of separated children. We also indicate the number of children receiving different forms of care and note the trends which these figures have followed in recent years. Further information is provided in Appendix C.

We begin by considering children who are in the care of the local authorities. Then we turn to children who are separated from their parents and live in accommodation not directly provided by local authorities. However, this is not an entirely separate category since some children who are in local authority care are placed in such accommodation. Where possible we have indicated this overlap and assessed its size. With this precaution we end by estimating the number of separated children.

Children in local authority care

Voluntary admission to care

A child may be received into care in England and Wales under section I of the Children Act, 1948, if he is abandoned or lost, if he has no parents or guardian, or if his parents or guardian are prevented by some specific reason from caring for him. The voluntary basis of this procedure means that the child can be removed from care at the discretion of his parents or guardian and, indeed, it is written into the Act that the local authority has a positive duty to ensure, wherever appropriate, that the child is returned home. The Children Act, 1975, has placed some limits on parental discretion in respect of children who have been in care for more than six months. Now they have to give twenty-eight days' notice of their intention to remove the child, although this requirement may be waived by the local authority.

Under certain conditions specified in section 2 of the Children Act, 1948, and section 57 of the Children Act, 1975, the social services committee of a local authority may pass a resolution in respect of a child already in care in order to assume parental rights. Over the years approximately 20 per cent of children in care under the provisions of the 1948 Children Act have been subject to such resolutions. If the child's natural parents object to a resolution being made it automatically lapses unless the local authority lays a complaint before the juvenile court, in which case the court hears the evidence of both parties and decides either that the resolution shall not lapse or, alternatively, that the resolution be set aside. The Children Act, 1975, contains new rights of appeal for parents at this stage.

In Scotland voluntary admission to care is facilitated by section 15 of the Social Work (Scotland) Act, 1968. Overall arrangements are broadly similar to those in England and Wales.

Table 2.1[1] (overleaf) summarises the main statistics covering voluntary reception into local authority care. It shows comparatively little change over the last twenty years, although fewer admissions are occurring now than ten years ago but more children are in care at a particular date. This indicates that they are staying longer. They may remain in care until the age of 18 or 19 in certain circumstances.

Committal to care

In England and Wales a child may be committed to the care of a local authority by a juvenile court under the provisions of the Children and Young Persons Act, 1969. Two main procedures are involved. First, the local authority, the police or the NSPCC may initiate *care proceedings* if there is evidence that a child is not receiving adequate care, protection or control. This would cover

TABLE 2.1 *Children received into care under voluntary provisions of the Children Act, 1948, and Social Work (Scotland) Act, 1968, during certain years and the numbers in care on certain dates in those years*

England and Wales

	1956	1966	1976
Received into care during the year	35032	49755	39516
In care on 31 March (30 November for 1956)	43621	46793	54028*

Scotland†

	1957	1966	1974
Received into care during the year	4825	5994	5037
In care on 31 December	–	–	9385

SOURCES See note 1 to this chapter.
* Figure includes a rounded element.
† Figures for Scotland are not available for the same years as for England and Wales and certain data are not published for earlier years.

circumstances of neglect, ill-treatment and so on. Second, *criminal proceedings* may be instituted against children or young persons who are of an age (10 years and up to 17) to be prosecuted as juveniles for criminal offences.

Under both these procedures if the case is proven the court may make a care order. This gives the local authority substantially the same powers and duties in respect of a child or young person as have hitherto been exercised by his parents or guardian. A care order continues until the child reaches the age of 18 or, in some cases 19, unless he, his parents on his behalf, or the local authority applies to the court for it to be discharged and the court decides to do so or to vary the order. An interim care order has the same effect but lapses after twenty-eight days, although it may then be renewed.

In the case of criminal proceedings only, the court may commit a child or young person into the care of the local authority on remand until he is to appear in court, usually whilst reports are awaited. Also, if a child between 10 and 17 years is arrested but cannot be immediately brought before a juvenile court to be charged, a senior investigating police officer may make arrangements for him to be taken into the care of a local authority. However, he must be brought before a court within seventy-two hours.

There are also cases in which, as a matter of urgency, children need to be removed from home immediately for their protection. In such circumstances a constable may detain a child in a 'place of safety' for up to eight days. The local authority or the NSPCC may take similar steps but must apply to a justice for an order. In this case the maximum period is twenty-eight days. Most children will be detained in a place of safety controlled by a local authority, such as a community home. But hospitals or police stations may also serve the purpose. Thus, strictly speaking, children who are subject to place of safety orders are not 'in care' but many do become the responsibility of a local authority.

In addition to these provisions, certain powers exist under matrimonial and other legislation for the committal into care of children involved in wardship proceedings and children whose parents have been engaged in divorce proceedings where the issue of custody has not been resolved.

The position in Scotland is different.[2] Part III of the Social Work Act, 1968, established children's hearings. They replaced juvenile courts. At each hearing the child and his family meet with a panel of three lay people from the local community who have been selected and trained for the task. The hearings are served by a reporter who is appointed by the local authority. Hearings are held in cases where children may require compulsory measures of care. They may be offenders or in need of care or protection because of ill-treatment, neglect and in certain other circumstances. Any person (but most often the police) may give information to the reporter if they believe that a child is in need of compulsory care. The reporter is responsible for investigating the facts and for deciding whether there are grounds for action. If there are he may conclude that voluntary help is required or that the child and parents should attend the hearing. If child and parents accept the grounds for a hearing the panel proceeds to consider the case in consultation with them and with a social worker. They may then decide to discharge the referral or make a supervision order (section 44(1)). This places the child under the supervision of the social work department. In many cases the child is supervised at home but the requirement may impose conditions about where he shall reside. A specific residential establishment may be named. Regular review hearings are held for children under supervision. In cases where the parents or child dispute the grounds for a referral the matter is considered by the Sheriff for a determination. There is also appeal to the Sheriff from the decision of a hearing. Furthermore, grave offences are not dealt with by the hearing system but are referred to the Sheriff court.

Hence, since this system came into operation in 1971 it is difficult to present comparable figures for compulsory admission to care for England and Wales and for Scotland. Children living at home but subject to a supervision requirement in Scotland are not 'in care' in the accepted sense of the term. They resemble more closely children subject to supervision orders in England and Wales, who are not regarded as being 'in care'.

Tables 2.2, 2.3 and 2.4 summarise information for several years. Comparisons over time are complicated by the changes in Scotland which we have described and by the implementation of the Children and Young Persons Act, 1969, in England and Wales. As from 1971 this abolished approved school orders. Hence, children under 19 in approved schools or supervised under after-care procedures became, at a stroke, part of the 'in care' population. So too did those in remand homes. Subsequently, many children who might have been committed to approved schools in the past have been dealt with by means of care orders placing them in the care of local authorities. Table 2.2[3] shows the number of children committed to care in England and Wales by the courts in various years. For purposes of accurate comparison, the approved school and remand home figures for earlier years have also been included.

Even after making this adjustment to take into account the changes introduced by the 1969 legislation, it can be seen that there has been a marked increase in the number of children committed to care by the courts: a growth of 97 per cent over the twenty years 1956–76. In particular, the balance between offenders and non-offenders has shifted. In 1966 about twice as many offenders as non-offenders were committed to care; in 1976 the non-offenders exceeded the offenders by several hundred. The raising of the age of criminal responsibility from 8 to 10 hardly provides an adequate explanation. The increase in non-attendance at school may be a somewhat more important cause, as may be concern about non-accidental injury.

TABLE 2.2 *Children committed by courts to the care of local authorities or approved schools in England and Wales during certain years*

	1956	1966	1969	1972	1976
Fit person orders					
–as offenders	3088	1395	1541	–	–
–as non-offenders		3153	3433	–	–
Approved school orders*	3235	5435	5394	–	–
Care orders†					
–as offenders	–	–	–	9559	5621
–as non-offenders	–	–	–		6379
Various matrimonial causes	–	168	145	259	860
Total	**6323**	**10151**	**10513**	**9818**	**12860**

SOURCE See note 3 to this chapter.

* Includes interim orders.

† Strictly, these figures are for approved school admission. A large majority would be on approved school orders. They do not include recalls and readmissions.

If we examine information about committed children actually in care rather than that describing admissions (Table 2.3) we see a similar picture. The number of children in care in England and Wales at a particular time as a result of court orders rose by 53 per cent between 1956 and 1976 even when an allowance is made for the changes brought about by the 1969 Act. To this end, the numbers in approved schools and remand homes have been included again for the earlier years as well as an estimate for the number under 19 who were discharged from approved schools on licence or supervision. This is important because in 1976 about 35 per cent of all committed children were allowed to be in the charge of a parent, guardian or friend and were, therefore, hardly 'separated'. This is a real and significant development as can be seen from Table 2.5 where the manner of accommodation for all children in local authority care is set out.

A rather different picture emerges from the Scottish statistics (Table 2.4). As far as supervision with a residence requirement is concerned, offenders now outnumber non-offenders by about three to one. This also appears to hold true for supervision without residence requirements, although the difference is less pronounced.

TABLE 2.3 *Children in the care of local authorities or approved schools in England and Wales at certain dates who have been committed by the courts*

	1956	1966	1968	1972§	1976§
Number of committed children in care of local authorities on 31 March*	18726	22364	22569	40100	46600
Other court orders	n.i.	n.i.	n.i.	2400	5000
Number in approved schools on 30 June	6667	8140	7380	–	–
Number on licence or supervision from approved schools†	4400	5372	4871	–	–
Number in remand homes on 31 December‡	565	1172	1257	–	–
Total	**30358**	**37048**	**36077**	**42500**	**51600**

SOURCE See note 3 to this chapter.

* For 1956, 30 November.

† This is an estimated figure for those on supervision under 19. It is based on 66 per cent of the resident approved school population.

‡ These figures are estimates based upon occupancy rates applied to the number of places available.

§ Figures for 1972 and 1976 are rounded.

TABLE 2.4 *Children committed to the care of local authorities in Scotland during certain years: for 1972 and 1974 the numbers subject to supervision with a residence requirement (Children and Young Persons Act, 1937 and Social Work Act, 1968)*

	1966	1972	1974
Children committed to care on fit person orders	303	–	–
Approved school orders	1117	–	–
Supervision with residence requirement			
–offenders	–	1377	1301
–non-offenders	–	523	397
Total	**1420**	**1900**	**1698**

SOURCE See note 3 to this chapter.

The placement of children once in care

Well before a child enters local authority care, important decisions should be made about his placement, based on a detailed assessment of the child himself, his parents and his general family and social background. In the case of emergency placements, such decisions need to be taken as soon as possible after the child has left his own home. In making such placements, the authority has a duty to act as a good parent would and the new 'welfare principle' of the 1975 Children Act obliges local authorities to give first consideration to the interests and welfare of the child in care when taking decisions about him, whatever his route into care. A wide variety of placements is potentially available. A child may be placed in a foster home; a community home (that is, a residential unit providing group care for children); a community home with education on the premises, known in Scotland as a 'list D' school; a registered voluntary home; a private home; a hospital; a special school for handicapped children; or, as we have noted, he may be returned home to his parents or relatives. Following their admission some children may spend a period in a community home with observation and assessment facilities or attend daily for the purposes of assessment.

Table 2.5 indicates some important changes in the manner of accommodation of children in the care of local authorities in England and Wales. Although more children are in foster homes than at any time since the Second World War, the proportion has declined. So too has the proportion in residential nurseries, but in this case there is also a marked reduction in absolute numbers. There are more children in community homes with observation and assessment facilities on the premises, although for 1976 those who were formerly in remand homes or in classifying schools within the approved school system would be incorporated in the new category. Even so, this still indicates some 1500 more children in such accommodation at the end of March 1976 than at the same time in 1966. The single most notable change however, as we have already suggested, is in the number of children allowed to be in the charge of a parent, guardian or friend. In the ten years between 1966 and 1976, the number has risen by some 8000 and proportionately from 11 per cent of all children in care or on licence from approved schools to 18 per cent.

TABLE 2.5 *Number and proportion of all children in care accommodated in various ways at certain dates in particular years (30 November 1956, 31 March 1966–76) in England and Wales*

	1956		1966		1971		1976	
	No.	%	No.	%	No.	%	No.	%
Boarded out with foster parents	27098	37	31816	38	30217	33	33064	33
In LA residential home/community homes	15812	21	15008	18	16457	18	20259	20
In LA residential nurseries	4443	6	3032	4	2500	3	1889	2
In reception/ assessment/ observation centres	1429	2	1949	2	2627	4	4976	5
In lodgings/ residential/ employment/hostel	3413	5	2796	3	3243	3	3718	3
In voluntary homes	4584	6	4895	6	5480	6	4189	4
In special schools/ homes for handicapped	2206	3	2127	3	2301	2	2789	3
Approved schools/ community homes with education	6667	9	8140	10	7654	8	6784	7
Remand homes	565	1	1172	1	1291	1	–	–
On licence/ supervision from approved schools	4400	6	5372	6	5052	5	–	–
In the charge of parent, guardian, friend	n.i.	n.i.	4387	5	12269	13	17950	18
Other accommodation	3362	4	3147	4	3338	4	5010	5
Total	**73979**	**100**	**83841**	**100**	**92429**	**100**	**100628**	**100**

SOURCE See note 3 to this chapter.

Children in accommodation not directly controlled by social services or social work departments

Children in private foster homes

A child may be placed privately in a foster home by his own parent or guardian. He then becomes subject to the protection afforded by the Children Act, 1958, as amended by the 1969 and 1975 Acts. The local authority must be notified and then has a duty to visit. Certain people can be prohibited from acting as foster parents.

There is evidence in official figures that the number of children supervised in private foster homes in England and Wales has declined somewhat in the past four years from a peak of 11 180 in 1973 to 8707 in 1976.[4] But the total number of children living in private foster homes is impossible to estimate accurately since not all private foster parents register with the local authority. Even when supervised, this group of children remains especially at risk since the attention it receives from local authorities appears to be markedly less than that devoted to children in local authority foster homes.[5]

Children in private residential homes and hostels

A child in the care of a local authority may be placed in a private home or hostel. He will then be visited by an officer of the authority and a general appraisal of standards of care provided may be carried out through inspection of the home and children by a member of the Social Work Service of the DHSS or, in Scotland, the Social Work Services Group. However, registration of the home, either with the central department or the local authority, is not required. If a child is placed privately in such a home by his own parents, however, he does become a foster child within the meaning of the Children Act, 1958 (as amended) and the local authority has the same responsibilities towards him as towards a child in a private foster home.

However, as the Harvie Report pointed out,[6] a mentally handicapped child who is not in care but who is placed by a local authority in a private or voluntary home registered under section 19 of the Mental Health Act, 1959, is not afforded protection under the Children Act, 1958. He is placed instead under the provisions of the

Health Services and Public Health Act, 1968, and this means, in effect, that no local authority has any statutory responsibility for his supervision.

No reliable figures are available for the total number of children in private homes. The Harvie Committee (reporting in 1974) suggested that there were 300 severely mentally handicapped children accommodated in this way who were not 'in care'. Current figures from the DHSS indicate that another 450 children who are 'in care' in England and Wales are accommodated in private boarding homes and hostels for maladjusted children.

Children in hospital

Many children spend some period in hospital. Only a few stay for protracted periods. Amongst them the severely mentally handicapped form the single most numerous group. They rarely need to be in hospital because of an acute medical condition, but continuous nursing care is needed by some who are multiply handicapped.

A child who is in the care of a local authority and who is admitted to hospital must be supervised, visited and his progress reviewed at six-monthly intervals by local authority social workers. However, his day-to-day management and care are in the hands of the hospital consultant. The hospital will be managed by the area health authority in which it is located.

A child in hospital who is not in care remains the responsibility of his parents. If a child appears to have lost all contact with his parents he may be judged to have been abandoned, in which case the hospital should inform the local director of social services who may decide to receive him into care.

Figures provided by the DHSS indicate that at the end of 1975 there were 5140 children under 16 in mental handicap hospitals and units in England and Wales.[7] This number does not differentiate between those in care and those who are not. The official admissions figures reveal that there was a small rise in the total number of children and young people admitted to mental handicap hospitals between 1970 and 1973, but that the number of *first* admissions showed an encouraging and fairly sharp decline during this period. The same child may be admitted on more than one occasion for 'holidays' or to give parents a break.

Children in voluntary homes

Certain of the former voluntary approved schools have elected, under the provisions of the Children and Young Persons Act, 1969, to become integrated into the local authority community home system as controlled or assisted community homes. Other voluntary homes must be registered with the DHSS under section 29 of the Children Act, 1948. Like statutory homes, they are subject to guidance by officers of the DHSS Social Work Service (Social Work Services Group in Scotland) and they must aim to provide the same standards of care.

Children living in a voluntary home must be visited by officers of the local authority in which the home is sited. If a child in care is placed by his local authority in a home run by a voluntary organisation (such as Barnardo's or the Church of England Children's Society), the authority makes payment to the organisation but, subject to agreement, retains the responsibility for planning his care and treatment and for visiting him. A child who is not in local authority care but who is admitted independently to a voluntary home remains the responsibility of his parents, although there is provision (not yet implemented) in the 1975 Act for local authorities to pass a resolution under section 2 of the 1948 Act vesting parental rights and duties in a voluntary organisation looking after a child in its care.

The larger voluntary children's societies offer a range of day care, fostering and adoption services in addition to residential homes. Before placing a child for adoption or arranging for him to be boarded out, a voluntary society is required to consult the local authority about the prospective foster or adoptive parents and, when the child is placed, to notify the local authority so that an entry may be made in the register of boarded-out children.

The scale of the provision of substitute child care services within the voluntary sector has declined considerably in the post-war period, in part because the societies have turned their attention to preventive work and day care. Table 2.6 sets out the main features of this change in England and Wales and in Scotland.[8] As can be seen, a substantial proportion of children who are accommodated in voluntary homes are in the care of local authorities. There is, therefore, an overlap between these figures and those in Table 2.1. Indeed, the actual role of voluntary bodies in caring for children in local authority care is even greater than these figures suggest since children in voluntary community homes with controlled status (and in some cases assisted status) are enumerated as if they were in local authority facilities. Thus, they do not appear in Table 2.6. Were they to do so, about 75 per cent of children cared for by voluntary bodies would be seen to be the responsibility of local authorities.

TABLE 2.6 *Children cared for in assisted community homes and voluntary homes registered under section 29 of the Children Act, 1948, or boarded out by voluntary organisations in England, Wales and Scotland and the proportion of these in local authority care*

	England and Wales		Scotland	
	No.	% in LA care	No.	% in LA care
1958	21868	19	3695	32
1962	18403	20	3464	45
1966	15734	30	2708	68
1970	12475	43	n.i.	n.i.
1974	9507	54	2108	n.i.
1976	10035	42	n.i.	n.i.

SOURCE See note 8 to this chapter.

Children in special boarding schools for handicapped pupils

Local education authorities are required to make provision for the education of children suffering from a defined range of handicaps. Special education in day schools, special units attached to ordinary schools and residential schools is provided directly by local education authorities or in independent units registered with the Department of Education and Science under section 70 of the Education Act, 1944. Independent day and boarding schools are run either by private individuals or by voluntary societies. Both statutory and independent schools are liable to inspection by Her Majesty's Inspectors and local authority inspectors may also make visits.

Children are placed in special residential schools when a combination of behavioural and learning difficulties is associated with family tensions necessitating partial separation from home, or when the special educational needs of the child cannot be met locally; for example, in a rural area where no suitable day school is available.

Since the passing of the Education (Handicapped Children) Act, 1970, responsibility for the education of severely mentally handicapped children has passed from the health authorities to the education authorities. These children may be taught in hospital schools or may be placed in one of the available range of special day and boarding schools. In addition, moves have been made by some local education authorities to integrate severely mentally handicapped children into normal educational provision.

Parents of a handicapped child placed in a boarding special school by the local education authority retain their full parental responsibilities unless the child is in the care of the local authority, in which case the authority must arrange for his supervision and must review his care and treatment at the statutory six-monthly intervals.

DES statistics show that the number of children accommodated in maintained and non-maintained boarding special schools in England and Wales was 21 326 in 1974, having remained fairly steady since 1972. There had been a sharp rise between 1971 and 1972, reflecting the implementation of the Education (Handicapped Children) Act, 1970. Of these 21 326 children, 2218 (or about 10 per cent) were in local authority care.

Children in 'other accommodation'

Even now we have not exhausted all the arrangements and provisions for separated children. For example, the 1971 census[9] tells us that there were more than 200 children in homes for the disabled and more than 3200 in places of detention in Great Britain; that is, detention centres, borstals, remand centres, prisons and special hospitals. In addition, there are probably more than 1300 children who are in local authority hostels in England and Wales but not in care.

The total population of separated children and concluding remarks

Arriving at an estimate of the total population of separated children from the different official sources described above is a hazardous undertaking. It is even more difficult to determine their ages. There is considerable risk of double-counting because of the large number of children in care who are living in accommodation not directly under local authority control. Also, the dates in the year on which local education authorities, social services departments and area health authorities submit their returns often differ. And it is impossible to estimate accurately the number of children in private residential homes and hospitals, and private foster homes. It is difficult to assemble aggregate statistics for the United Kingdom (or even Great Britain) as a whole.

Fortunately, our guesses on this subject can be better informed by an excellent, if slightly dated, independent source. In 1971, Moss carried out a census of children in residential establishments in England and Wales. He concluded that 275 000 children (including those in local authority foster homes) were living away from home.[10] If we subtract from this total the number of children in ordinary boarding schools and acute non-psychiatric hospitals who are not dealt with in our report, we arrive at a figure of about 120 000 separated children on any one day.

Moss's figures lend support to our own rough calculations which suggest that there were some 133 000 separated children in England and Wales in 1976, other than children in ordinary boarding schools and non-psychiatric hospitals. About 22 000 of these children are actually living with relatives, guardians or friends or were boarded out with relatives. An adjusted total, therefore, might be 111 000. However, it must be re-emphasised that this is a figure calculated on a particular day. More children than this will experience separation and forms of substitute care. We do not know how many, nor do we know the number of occasions when this happens for individual children.

We are aware that we have provided only a cursory description of the legal and administrative frameworks which shape the lives of separated children.[11] In general, however, we wish to emphasise several points:

1. the legislation is extensive and complex;
2. many of the provisions are open ended. Both care orders and voluntary admissions may continue until the child is 18 unless deliberate steps are taken before then;
3. the distinction between compulsory committal to care and voluntary admission is legally quite clear but in practice it may be difficult to draw in terms of a child's circumstances. For example, a neglected child may be brought before a court or a children's

hearing (leading to a care order or supervision) or be received into voluntary care. It is likely that whether the child comes into care through compulsory measures or voluntarily will have important implications for the parents and their future involvement in planning for the child. Furthermore, the existence of a compulsory order may force local authorites to plan more deliberately than in 'voluntary' cases;

4. the legislation lays down many requirements and offers a variety of discretionary and permissive powers to local authorities. Just how these are implemented and interpreted varies in different parts of the country. It is dangerous, therefore, to assume that a common legislative framework gives rise to common policy and practice;
5. none the less, the children's legislation does provide a basis for planning for children in care, albeit a complicated one. No comparable framework exists for separated children who are not in local authority care;
6. the distinction between being 'in care' and not being in care is becoming more clouded. Changes following the 1969 Children and Young Persons Act and the Social Work (Scotland) Act, 1968, in particular, are leading to more 'intermediate' arrangements.

Having described the administrative boundaries and the diverse informal arrangements that have shaped the provision for separated children, we must question their appropriateness and flexibility. What we have is a series of public and private child care systems which sometimes compete and overlap but which hardly comprise a comprehensive service. Children of similar age and similar needs may be treated differently because they find themselves in different systems. Serious child care inequalities have arisen as a result. For example, mentally handicapped children have not benefited from some of the progressive developments in planning and caring for separated children and, despite sympathetic statements from central and local government, are often consigned to large hospitals and a bleak future of unending institutional care. It must be noted, however, that the national development group set up by the Secretary of State is now particularly concerned with the care of those children. Children in private residential establishments and private foster homes have received inadequate protection in law and practice. The 1975 Children Act does contain welcome provisions to improve the statutory protection of this latter group. Finally, we must note that information about certain children appears to be difficult to obtain once they enter prisons, mother and baby homes or accommodation designed for adult handicapped people.

We could not fully explore in this summary the massive issues of child care organisation and law but we hope that we have indicated the labyrinth of different provisions and divided responsibilities. This is the context for subsequent chapters. Although we have been at pains not to forget the wide range of children involved, often in small administrative categories, we have paid most attention to children in local authority care. They are certainly a vulnerable group since they have sometimes lost contact with their parents or have parents who are unable to ensure their welfare. These same parents tend to be under-privileged themselves, geographically scattered and hence in no position easily to form the parental interest groups that we have seen spring up in other settings. Nor, with the exception of the 'Voice of the Child in Care', have we discovered any general pressure group which is devoted entirely to the interests of children in public care.

3

Causes of Concern

There is undoubtedly a widespread concern about a decline of standards in the services for separated children. In this chapter we discuss the four reasons that are most commonly advanced to explain this change. They are: the loss of specialised skill; increased rates of staff turnover; rising demand; and shortage of resources. Whilst we take most seriously the need to improve the quality of services for separated children, we have also been anxious to bear in mind that the country is not enveloped by a blanket of low standards. There are noticeable differences between areas, as there are between organisations and between the different spheres of work with children and their families. Some of the provisions we saw impressed us as being of a high standard; whether they were previously even better we cannot judge. However, particular examples of good practice do not justify general complacency. Much remains to be done and in considering four causes of concern we have also sought ways in which such improvements might be achieved.

The loss of specialised skills

It's not just 'looking after kids'.

It is widely believed that the special skills possessed by the staff of the former children's departments are fast disappearing. This is usually attributed to three principal causes. First, to the rise of the generic social worker. This led to social workers having to grapple with such diverse case loads that adoption, foster care and similar work were infrequently encountered. There is now, some maintain, so little regular experience of certain situations and procedures that expertise cannot be developed. Second, fewer training courses are specifically geared to producing expert child care staff except in the residential field. As a result, it is contended, newly trained recruits lack the special knowledge necessary for doing good work with children and their families. The third reason advanced for the erosion of specialist skills is the promotion or retirement of the experienced staff from the old children's departments. Anxiety is expressed about the future when this diminishing pool of experienced workers eventually disappears. Together with this, promotion in general continues to be tied to a shift from practice to management, a process in which accumulated skill and experience are lost to the field.

This account of what is happening, however, must be set alongside certain other observations. Specialisation has not vanished completely. Adoption officers, for example, appear to be reasonably numerous. Other staff specialise in foster home finding and selection or in court work, and individual case loads do not always span the whole range of work undertaken by social service departments. In recent years several of the larger voluntary child care organisations have become *more* specialised, not less.

On the residential care side, the recent organisational changes have not led to more general forms of provision. Community homes still admit children, and old people's homes continue to look after the elderly. Having said that, however, the field social work support for both children and staff in residential care appears to be less specialised, except perhaps at the senior level. Many would also contend that field social workers now visit residential homes less frequently, although it must be pointed out that as a result of the 1969 Children and Young Persons Act they probably pay more visits to those community homes which were formerly approved schools.

Since so many of the children with whom we are concerned are living in residential settings of one kind or another, these considerations are directly relevant to the 'loss of skill' argument. Of course, there have been changes in the nature of specialisation in residential care (for example, by age, sex and problem) but there is no uniform pattern.

The part played by foster parents (who, on any one day in 1976, looked after about 40000, or approximately 40 per cent, of the children in the care of local authorities in Great Britain) should not be overlooked in this matter of specialisation. Organisational changes have not substantially altered their special role. In fact, experiments with 'professional' fostering and with fostering hard-to-place children, as well as the emergence of foster parent groups, all point in the opposite direction. However, the social workers who recruit foster parents, help them and advise about the children almost certainly possess less experience than before.

The fear about 'loss of special skills' also seems to overlook the professions other than social work which are involved in providing various services for children. In the health field there continues to be considerable specialisation in children's problems and the report of the Court Committee recommends its further development.[1] The educational system stands as the single largest service devoted to work with all kinds of children, and the police in many areas have moved towards a more specialised administration for dealing with the children and young persons who come to their notice, particularly through the juvenile bureaux. Thus, viewed more broadly, a considerable degree of specialisation in child care remains.

In the narrower context of field social work the reorganisation of the personal social services which occurred in the wake of the Seebohm Report, and earlier in Scotland, has led to a loss of the particular experience and skill generated by special and separate local children's departments. How far this is the result of the administrative changes themselves or of the secondary changes (such as increased staff movement) which they caused is hard to tell. Nor is it clear whether these are temporary or permanent changes. It must also be borne in mind that there may well be a somewhat idealised view of the extent to which special skills existed in the children's departments of the past; a past liable to be eulogised by those who worked in departments with a high proportion of trained staff and outstanding leadership. It is certainly worth recalling that the percentage of trained field staff varied enormously between areas and that overall it stood at only 37 per cent in 1966. Even fewer residential child care staff were trained. In the same year, no more than 10 per cent of them held the appropriate certificate. What may have been important to feelings of confidence, however, was the steady increase in the proportion of trained staff: from 27 per cent trained in 1963 to 47 per cent in 1969.[2]

Whatever the skills of child care workers in the past, it is now essential to be clear about which skills need to be developed or created in the future. In our view, the main deficiencies in child care skill and knowledge relate to:

1. insufficient acquaintance with the relevant law and detailed procedures;
2. lack of a close knowledge of children's past and present circumstances;
3. a lack of up-to-date information about the nature and quality of possible resources;
4. an inadequate understanding of the developmental aspects of childhood; and
5. too little first-hand experience with children and insufficient skill in communicating with them.

Improvements in these spheres are essential if better standards of practice amongst social workers dealing with children are to be achieved. This is not incompatible with a more general and community-based approach. Indeed, the repair of some of these shortcomings (such as 3 and perhaps 2 above) depends upon such an emphasis. Other improvements will rely more on training and particularly upon staff development programmes. But the shortcomings themselves are in part a product of another factor altogether: that is, staff turnover. The rapid change of staff creates havoc for young children who need substitute care throughout their childhood; it makes the provision of long-term support for foster parents and others a hopeless quest and it impedes the acquisition of experience and skill. We deal with this issue next but consider it a crucial factor in any analysis of 'loss of skill' or 'declining standards'.

High rates of staff turnover

> *My brother and I had more social workers than I can remember. They'd see us once and then disappear for six months, then we'd have a new one. And it's been going on all the time I've been in the home. They've been leaving or they've been going ill.*

Recent years have seen high turnover rates amongst social service staff. The detailed pattern is hard to discern, but it appears to correspond with a more general trend which is perceptible amongst the white-collar and professional sections of the working population as a whole.[3] However, it is possible to gain a general picture of the extent of social worker mobility in recent years from several sources.

The DHSS statistics about social service departments' staff in England paid special attention to turnover in 1973.[4] Between 1972 and 1973 there was an 11 per cent increase in the number of whole-time equivalent social workers. If each part-timer were counted separately then the increase in people taking up new posts would be higher. These were the *extra* newcomers. At the end of September 1973, 8 per cent of social workers (excluding trainees) were seconded for training. These were the *temporarily absent.* Leaving aside secondment, changes of job within the same department and the whole of the residential field, a 20 per cent turnover of social work staff (managers, supervisors, social workers, trainees and assistants) occurred in 1973. These were the *leavers.* But this overall figure for England disguises marked variations. The turnover of staff was highest in Greater London (24 per cent). It varied considerably by age, with the highest rate in the 25–34 age group (28 per cent) and the lowest (7 per cent) amongst those between 55 and 59. Mobility was fairly low amongst management and supervisory staff (9 per cent) but equally high amongst both qualified and unqualified field social workers (28 and 29 per cent respectively). Regions with high rates of turnover also seemed to have high rates of secondment for training.

Of those who left field social work during the year up to September 1973, 8 per cent went to undertake training without secondment; 35 per cent went to other social work jobs in other departments or areas; 16 per cent left because of marriage, pregnancy or retirement and a massive 42 per cent departed for 'other reasons'.

The DHSS working party on *Manpower and Training for the Social Services*[5] advocated more research on this whole issue. As it is, their report only deals with the limited concept of 'wastage', showing that in 1973 the rate stood at 9 per cent for both qualified local authority fieldwork staff and for the residential child care sector. By wastage, however, the report means the movement of staff out of *all* forms of social service employment. This is a key consideration for the manpower planners but with respect to the acquisition of special experience and continuity of contact with children the crucial issue is the level of crude turnover. This would add to the wastage figures the circulation of staff within and between social services, as well as those seconded for full-time training. The Butterworth Report provided this kind of information for 1970–1. It indicated a turnover rate of nearly 19 per cent for local authority social workers of main grade and above in England and Wales, and slightly less in Scotland.[6]

A conservative estimate of the movement rate for social work staff involved with separated children is around 20 per cent a year in recent years; much more in certain areas, less in others. Add in staff coming to fill newly created posts as well as the coming and going for training and one gains an idea of the real scale of mobility. Were we to trace the individual histories of children in care, an even more vivid picture of the succession of staff concerned with them over *several* years would be available.

These figures are disturbing because high turnover undermines commitment to individual children and their families; it hinders the acquisition and reassessment of information; makes difficult the pursuit of any kind of plan as well as the monitoring of, and reflection upon, what has happened. It is also liable to impede the development of certain kinds of skills which evolve from fairly long spells of work with *particular* children and their families. For the child and his family, it removes a known figure who can be contacted, taken to task, appealed to or shunned. It is significant that frequent staff changes figured prominently in the criticisms that children, parents and foster parents expressed to the working party about the services. They were also quick to point out that each change has *two* aspects; there is the person who leaves and the new one who comes. In these circumstances, a tendency not to bother much about the new social worker because 'she will soon be leaving anyway' is not surprising.

There is also the likelihood that high rates of turnover themselves sustain and even generate further turnover. Job satisfaction depends on being around long enough to see the effects of one's interventions. It also depends upon reasonable stability amongst one's colleagues. High rates of movement may be a kind of contagion. Once they are reversed a similar but opposite effect may reduce turnover more than expected.

The figures discussed above concern the turnover of social workers in social service departments. Information is less readily available about the voluntary sector but the working party was told that voluntary organisations experienced less movement than that which occurs in the public sector. However, there do appear to be high turnover rates amongst other groups of social service personnel concerned with children at risk; for example, nursery nurses, the Supplementary Benefits Commission's officers, teachers, police constables and so on. By contrast, general practitioners and consultants tend to stay put. Despite such exceptions, groups of staff who need to collaborate on child care matters are markedly mobile. It should surprise nobody, therefore, when co-ordination and liaison break down.

When one adds to staff mobility the fact that the families of the children themselves are frequently on the move, the difficulties of planning are further exacerbated. The mobile family, for example, may fail to register with a doctor, and in any case various records take time to be transferred. More localised social services may have accentuated the problem of short-distance family movement within a city or town if 'cases' have to be passed across from one office to the next.

Yet it would be short-sighted to assume that all movement is undesirable. Mobility may offer a fresh start; the chance to challenge assumptions about children and their families; the opportunity to change a stressful environment or to replace a sick or overwhelmed member of staff. Conclusions about the impact of mobility may also depend upon whether it involves the replacement of an unqualified by a qualified person or vice versa.

There are also differences between the effect of staff mobility in residential and non-residential settings. A year's *daily* (and nightly) care is qualitatively different from a year's social work on a once-monthly basis. The time dimensions are different. Likewise a year spent with a foster family cannot pass unnoticed by a child; whereas four visits by the social worker during the same period may well be hard to recall. To the child the most important person is the one he sees daily. In this respect turnover amongst residential staff or the breakdown of foster placements are matters of great concern. Turnover amongst social service field staff who have less contact with the child but carry major responsibilities for his future is also disturbing but for somewhat different reasons. In this case continuity of support, planning and review are placed in jeopardy.

In the light of these considerations, the proposal that residential staff and foster parents should carry more responsibilities to match their *daily* involvement with children seems worthy of serious examination, although bearing in mind that such close daily contact can lead to a rather narrow perspective.

Even when staff stay in one place for a reasonable time, child mobility may still give cause for great concern. Some children come in and out of care; parents under stress may make a variety of temporary private arrangements for their children; children in care are moved around; they change schools and some go home for short or long periods. There is almost certainly a problem of children who move as well as of 'children who wait'. Perhaps the most disturbing situation is where children are moved around whilst they wait upon the firm decisions of a constantly changing array of adults.

Whilst continuity of care staff is essential, especially for young children and children who have no other permanent parent figure in their lives, continuity of place and surroundings (including nursery school or school, personal possessions, friends and neighbourhood) must not be underestimated. The need for continuity applies with equal force to the styles and principles of child-rearing to which children are subject. Whatever its form, movement is liable to create more discontinuities than appear at first sight.

Extensive movement of staff must give cause for grave disquiet. However, economic stringency may now be reducing the rate. If this is so it may now be more feasible for recruitment policies to take account of the likely levels of mobility amongst applicants; but beyond factors such as age, surprisingly little is known about what determines who leaves and who stays. Is it job satisfaction; job specification; marital status; being part-time or full-time; being trained or not trained? And how do these factors vary at different times depending, for instance, upon the prevailing economic climate, or upon how organisations treat their staff? How far is frequent movement a reaction to professional autonomy being incompatible on the one hand with what is required and permitted and, on the other hand, with what responsibility the individual is capable of assuming?

Mobility adversely affects standards, but it only partly explains the present wave of concern. We must turn to a third cause. This is the rising tide of demands upon the personal social services in general and upon services for children in particular.

Rising demand

They have got to have a break, like we've got to have a break.

'The personal social services cannot measure up to all that is now expected of them, nor can they develop at the anticipated rate.'[7] So begins the DHSS report on manpower and training in the social services. As in that report, this discussion is mainly concerned with the work of the local authorities' social services departments. But its relevance to children who are the responsibility of other departments, or who fall outside the statutory system, should be evident. It is often argued that children in hospitals, boarding schools, private hostels and private foster homes need greater social work support. Yet unless the social services departments discover some means of controlling their current volume of work, it is difficult to see how these responsibilities can be properly discharged.

The fact that there has been a dramatic increase in the demands made upon social services departments (social work departments in Scotland) is undisputed. Quite how large that increase has been, and what kinds of work have expanded most, remain to be accurately charted. Demand, for example, is not adequately reflected in 'number of places provided' or people served. Much of the bombardment never appears in these figures, although its management consumes a large slice of scarce resources. Leaving aside those demands which are *not* met, dealing with various kinds of short-term demand is now the most characteristic feature of local authority social work. This is borne out by the studies undertaken by the National Institute of Social Work. Looking at a year's intake of clients in one area office of a social services department Goldberg and her colleagues found that 52 per cent of the cases were closed within one week of referral; 65 per cent within a month and 82 per cent before three months had elapsed. 'By six months', they explain, 'only 10 per cent of the referrals were estimated to be open but thereafter the closure rate slows down . . . among those long survivors are the very young and the very old.'[8]

A few further statistics will illustrate the point in another way. In 1973–4, social services staff in England and Wales assisted with nearly 20 000 telephone installations; provided close upon 150 000 different aids for the elderly and the handicapped as well as overseeing some 32 000 adaptations to their dwellings. These figures do not include all the enquiries which did not lead to the provision of a service. In addition, it needs to be emphasised that approaching 450000 children were referred to English social services departments in the same year for possible admission to care or preventive work; of whom only some 50000 were actually received into care.[9] Although there are no means of knowing what happened to the bulk of the referred children who did not enter care, many of them must have been dealt with in the space of one or two interviews.[10] There is no way in which 20000 social workers, trainees and welfare assistants, carrying responsibilities for the elderly, handicapped and mentally disordered as well, could do anything else. The *increase* in demand which these figures indicate is apparent when it is noted that the comparable 'bombardment' figure for the child care referrals in 1965–6 was only 150000, but leading to about the same number of admissions as in 1973–4.[11]

High standards of performance in any work presuppose a regulated flow: inundation brings skimping in its wake. Many considered this to be the crux of the present problem of standards. Several good reasons are adduced for this situation. They correspond broadly with those discussed in the DHSS manpower and training report.[12] Four explanations are considered below which refer more directly to the children's field.

Administrative reorganisation arising from the Local Authority Social Services Act, 1970 and the Social Work (Scotland) Act, 1968. When welfare, children's and health departments were separate and undertook different work, there were undoubtedly some cases which slipped through the net. The more complicated structures which then existed were often difficult for the public to understand. A single all-purpose department, more often organised at an area level, offers easier access. At the same time the staff within it are less able than before to refuse or redirect work by pointing to clearly defined departmental boundaries. It is easy to guess but difficult to prove just how far the amalgamation of the early 1970s has created or released demand, or how far this has altered the referring patterns of other organisations.

The Children and Young Persons Act, 1969. In England and Wales the Children and Young Persons Act, 1969, exposed the new social services departments to an extra surge of work with children and their families. Care orders replaced fit person orders and approved school orders; and probation orders for those under 17 were superseded by supervision orders. As a result, a so far uncalculated amount of work with older children and the courts shifted from the probation service to social services departments. Responsibility for negotiating placements for children committed on care orders was also transferred to them. In terms of crude numbers the flow of children from the courts has increased steadily. In 1969, the total of approved school orders and fit person orders amounted to about 10 000 in England and Wales. The number of care orders made in the year ending March 1976 stood at 12 000, an increase of 20 per cent.[13]

There has been a related growth in social service departments' responsibility for the preparation of social enquiry reports for the courts and in the Scottish social work departments for the children's hearings. Residential assessment facilities also appear to be more frequently used in providing reports for the courts. Intermediate treatment has had to be developed in collaboration with the new regional planning bodies. In addition, notifications from the police about children at risk or 'coming to notice' have reached high levels (6 000 a year in one metropolitan district visited by the working party, only 20 per cent of which could be followed up).

Raising the school-leaving age. The raising of the school-leaving age appears to have added to the pressures in certain areas where rates of truancy are high, where truants are likely to be brought to court and where the courts decide to make a supervision or care order. A number of social services staff resent the diversion of resources this entails, especially where older children in their last year of school are involved. Although detailed national figures are not readily available it must be observed that whereas the *total* number of children before the courts for non-attendance hardly varied between 1969 and 1973, the number of supervision orders made fell by nearly 30 per cent whilst the number of care orders rose by 87 per cent. It is also important to see that, in 1969, 35 per cent of the non-attending children subject to these orders were 14 years or older but that by 1973, the first full year after the leaving age was raised, this proportion had reached 55 per cent.[14] Of course, this first year was special in that children who had *expected* to leave school were obliged to stay on. In subsequent years that expectation would be less important. During the transitional period, however, some field workers feel that this older age group has captured a disproportionate amount of attention at the expense of potentially more valuable work with younger children.

Divorce reform. The year 1969 also saw the passing of the Divorce Law Reform Act and in 1971 it began to operate. Between that year and 1975, the number of petitions filed annually rose from roughly 70 000 to 140 000. It is hard to estimate the impact of these changes on the child care work of social services departments but the number of children coming into care under the Matrimonial Causes Acts, 1965 and 1973, might provide one indication. In 1970 there were 127 but by 1976 the figure had multiplied fivefold to 623.[15]

These four changes – social service reorganisation, the 1969 Children and Young Persons Act, the raising of the school-leaving age and divorce law reform – appear to have had a fairly direct effect upon the demand for services for children. That, however, is only part of the story, as has already been suggested. Other legislation, such as the Chronically Sick and Disabled Persons Act of 1971, increased the demands upon social services departments from other directions. All these changes, moreover, have occurred against the backcloth of local government reorganisation. Little is known about the costs of these administrative rearrangements but, in the short term at least, they are liable to create unavoidable and largely unspecified extra work. There may be less obvious consequences as well. Social services departments are, in many circumstances, dependent upon resources controlled by other departments and organisations in planning for separated children: for example, places in special schools, adolescent psychiatric units, voluntary homes or hostels. Faced with financial stringency and, in some circumstances, actual cuts, such agencies are anxious to control the flow of demand upon them. If this is so, and it would need further testing, then it is perfectly predictable that the social services departments, with more general and ultimate responsibilities, will become increasingly overburdened. Even within the social services departments there is some suggestion that heads of homes have exercised greater authority in the matter of admissions than existed prior to the reorganisation of the early 1970s.[16]

An overwhelming flood of work leads to loss of morale and brings the threat of chaos. The possibility of formulating and controlling policy recedes, and the headquarters of the social services departments are then obliged to delegate the task of rationing services to the area teams. Basic grade social workers and their seniors may, in the end, be forced to bear a heavy burden of this responsibility. In our view this should not happen. There is no excuse for leaving staff to make priority choices unaided, and it is here that effective dialogue between social services departments and elected members is vital. Even so, where social workers feel uncertain about their effectiveness and judgement, the problem of priorities is likely to loom especially large.

When a department lacks the power to regulate its own boundaries, or finds itself in a weak position to secure the help of other organisations, it loses the initiative in planning and providing services. It assumes an essentially defensive posture, responding to crisis after crisis but never getting to grips with the demands that are being made. Social workers lose the chance to learn and practise those skills which make sustained contacts with children and families rewarding and fruitful. The very atmosphere of emergency and crises militates against longer-term work – why start it if you cannot carry it through?

Standards of work with children who are, or who are liable to be, separated from their families are undoubtedly related to the total volume of demands competing for attention. If the volume can be better controlled and classified this must improve the chances of raising standards. But these things depend upon an accurate appreciation of what is happening as well as clear leads about priorities from elected members, management committees and senior staff. They also demand the discerning use of the talents and skills of the personnel available, and careful negotiation with the sources of referral.

The force of the tide of rising demands has been considerable. It accounts in some part for the disappointing standards of child care provision. However, it is closely related to the question of available resources. Shortage of resources is, indeed, one other explanation offered for the present 'crisis'. We consider it next.

Insufficient resources

The things we want to change don't cost money . . . it's people . . .

The personal social services have been the fastest growing sector of public expenditure. But the pattern is uneven. As Judge points out, 'the annual growth rate between 1963–9 was 7.3 per cent: and between 1969–73, 11.8 per cent . . . This acceleration,' he continues, 'reached its height between the Seebohm and local government reorganisations when the average growth rate was 16 per cent per year. Since then the growth rate has declined.'[17] The 1976 public expenditure review showed provision for expenditure on the personal social services to rise 2 per cent a year until 1979–80. It contended that 'this provision should be sufficient to maintain standards of service for the whole population, including the rapidly increasing numbers of old people and children in care'.[18] Whether this was a reasonable assumption or not it is now plain that the 2 per cent increase is unlikely to be met. Indeed, the 1977 expenditure plans suggest that the effect of the changes proposed will be to bring down public expenditure *below* the levels for 1975–7. The report concludes that although 'a modern civilised society needs an adequate level of public services . . . at this juncture further social improvements must depend on the prior achievement of our economic and industrial objectives'.[19] Reductions in some standards or in the coverage of services seem inevitable unless there is a deliberate change in national priorities.

A lack of relevant information makes it impossible to determine how the 'children's services' as a whole fared during recent years by comparison with other personal social services. However, it is possible to make some estimates with respect to capital spending. Although there are variations between different areas, the general picture for 1974–5 is of both local authority applications and central government approvals of loans running at some 75 per cent above the DHSS guidelines. These suggested that children's provision, plus day nurseries, should receive 20 per cent of the cake; in the event they obtained 34 per cent. The approvals for all other client groups fell below the guidelines.[20] This, at least, does not support the view that children's services are the cinderella of local government spending. Indeed, they seem to have been accorded a higher priority at the local level than by the DHSS. It must be emphasised, however, that this is mainly spending on residential provision and, to a large extent, upon children who cause 'trouble'. The more resources we invest in bricks and mortar the less able shall we be to change direction or balance.

The cry for 'more resources' to shore up unsatisfactory child care services is often heard despite the unprecedented increase in expenditure on the personal social services of the early 1970s. It seems reasonable to assume that services for children did not suffer to such an extent that they received no share of the growth. Yet resources are still in short supply. The key to this puzzling situation is almost certainly to be found in the growing imbalance between resources and the demands made upon them. Bearing this in mind, we offer several observations in summarising the question of resources.

Existing child care resources are heavily concentrated in the residential sector. Residential care is ill-equipped to deal with sudden or erratic changes in demand. Although the marginal cost of placing extra children in existing units is fairly low, the costs of new building to increase (or replace) the stock are now staggeringly high and may become prohibitive for some authorities. A commitment to capital investment in the past also pre-empts a considerable proportion of the current budget of the personal social services. McCreadie argues that it may actually be necessary to cut some services in the future, simply in order to accommodate the costs generated by the high levels of capital expenditure in 1971–2 and 1973–4.[21]

We need not recapitulate the discussions to be found in the DHSS manpower report about the desirability of more training and the more efficient use of social workers. None the less these issues are of the utmost importance. Certainly, more careful consideration needs to be given to the most appropriate and economical use of staff at all levels, although they are not the only resources to be taken into account.[22] Given a 'no growth' prospect, at least to the end of the decade, it becomes imperative to consider the possibility and desirability of tapping different kinds of resources outside the ambit of the conventional services. It is, of course, already happening in an apparently *ad hoc* fashion as children who are committed to the care of local authorities are sent home pending a suitable residential place or as a prelude to their permanent return. As we noted in the previous chapter, the ten years between 1965 and 1976 saw the proportion of children 'committed to care but allowed to be under the control of a parent, guardian or friend' jump from 17 per cent to 35 per cent, an increase only partly accounted for by the inclusion in these figures of children who were formerly subject to approved school orders but home on supervision. Even so, if only half of these children were in community homes instead, the additional public cost would be at least £23 million a year, assuming that the social work offered in both contexts was roughly the same.[23]

Throughout this report we argue for a shift towards a more fluid network of community-based and community-supplied resources, directed at the whole family rather than at children in isolation. It would be irresponsible to claim that resources of this kind will necessarily be more economical, but there seems to be at least some prospect that this would be so.

The preoccupation with how resources are shared between major social service sectors is understandable and timely. New style documents like the DHSS *Priorities for Health and Social Services in England* and *The Way Forward* are starting to grapple with this complex issue.[24] However, there are equally pertinent questions to be asked about allocations *within* the children's services. As has already been pointed out, there appears to have been a disproportionate shift of resources away from the younger children in need towards an older age group. The trend could be more pronounced still were the intentions of the 1969 Act actually fulfilled. As it is, some 2000 boys between 15–18 are in borstals and more again in detention centres.[25] In 1971 there were 165 children over 15 who were removed from the care of local authorities in England and Wales to borstals. This is generally regarded as a 'last resort' measure. By 1973 the figure had risen to 767 but has since dropped back to just over 200. Such 'shipping out', as it has been called, is saving local authorities money as well as relieving them of some of the most troublesome older children.

It is hard to know how far the present allocation of resources appropriately reflects the age structure of children in need. Although the proportion of under-fives in local authority care has fallen from about 20 to 12 per cent in the last five years there are no comparable figures to tell us what is happening as far as preventive work is concerned or in the private sector. If our general impression is correct, however, the shift of resources from younger to older children is disturbing because the greater hope of successfully engaging in prevention and good planning must rest with the younger ones. Even amongst them the stress upon 'at risk' children may have caused a further shift of attention away from the *majority* of younger children in care. The Association of Directors of Social Services expressed a similar fear in their evidence to the Select Committee on Violence in the Family, arguing 'that a comparatively small number of children had been receiving intensive coverage, diverting resources from the very much larger group of children who might be lying on the margin of child neglect, and possibly suffering more than some victims of violence'.[26]

Questions abound about the allocation of resources within the children's field. Practitioners may be tempted to view them as not being their major concern. Yet much of the *final* allocation, although not the guiding policy, has to be at the discretion of the staff actually involved. It is their judgements which help to decide the matter, as it is their skill and sensitivity (or lack of it) which ultimately determine the quality of service.

Conclusion

The assertion that the quality of services for children has declined is hard to prove or disprove *in general*; not least because of changes in values, expectations and standards of living. There are many indications, however, that in certain areas, and in particular aspects of the work, standards are too low and may have been eroded. We have, in the previous paragraphs, endeavoured to set this situation into a broader context. In particular, we have been at pains to consider both the positive and the negative aspects of the present position.

When a recent public expenditure review tells us that in the personal social services 'the programme does not allow for any general improvements in standards of service',[27] we must take seriously the problem of discovering ways of doing so which do not depend upon more money. That is not to say that pressure for more generous expenditures should be relaxed, but account must be taken of political realities.

In the light of this and the other issues discussed in this chapter, we recommend that special attention be paid to the general problems of:

1. using the available manpower and other resources more appropriately, economically and efficiently;
2. reducing the mobility of staff and minimising the ill-effects when it does occur;
3. improving the input of instruction about child care law in training programmes and devoting more attention to knowledge about child development and skill in communication with children;
4. better regulating and classifying the flow of referrals;
5. utilising more unconventional and community-based resources, and
6. devising better ways of forestalling the circumstances which lead to children's long-term separation from their parents. This is the subject of the next chapter.

4

Prevention

I don't know why I was put into care.

We now know enough about the disadvantages to the child of long-term separation from parents, and about the difficulties of providing substitute care, to place a high value on prevention. The fact that the chances of restoring a child to his family decline with the increasing duration of the separation also points to the need to prevent short stays in substitute care becoming long. Logically, our priority should be to stop circumstances arising in which children can no longer be cared for by parents. Indeed, this has been stated unequivocally by the DHSS in its 1976 priorities document: 'It is a key objective of the personal social services', they say, 'to support the family. Where children are concerned the main objective is to help families provide a satisfactory home for the child, and to enable children to stay with their families except where it is against the child's interest.'[1] The proviso reflects an important dilemma. In order to forestall suffering and, in extreme cases, death, some children must be removed from their parents' care. Hence, a general commitment to 'prevention' may call for several quite different courses of action depending upon *what* it is that we wish to prevent. Avoiding admission to care, for example, is not an end in itself. Under certain circumstances good quality substitute care may well be the best form of prevention that can be achieved.

Prevention must be an objective at *all* stages of intervention. The nature of preventive action depends upon what has gone before. Prevention of permanent family breakdown as a result of temporary incapacities of the parents or a temporary disturbance in the child will differ from the intervention needed when a child is at risk of physical injury, distorted emotional development or death. The conventional threefold medical classification of prevention is one way of portraying these differences.

Varieties of prevention

'Primary' prevention is thought of as comprising those services which provide general support to families and reduce the levels of poverty, stress, insecurity, ill-health or bad housing to which they may otherwise be exposed. We ought not to have to repeat yet again the importance of adequate income, especially for one-parent or large families and at periods when there is only one earner. Nor should we have to explain once more the value of good housing, although we would draw particular attention to the ill-effects of overcrowding and shared family homes as well as to the anxieties caused by insecurity of tenure. Even when it appears secure, reliable tenure may be vested in the husband and not enjoyed by wives and children.

'Secondary' prevention is more specific. Once problems have actually arisen help of various kinds may supply a remedy or at least forestall something worse. At this stage services are liable to be restricted to those who are assumed to be at 'special risk' or whose circumstances warrant special priority. The allocation of day care provision is one example and the payment of temporary financial help under section 1 of the 1963 Children and Young Persons Act is another.

'Tertiary' prevention, at least in the context of our concerns, would aim at avoiding the worst consequences of a child actually having to spend long periods in substitute care. At the very least it would ensure that no *further* harm was done the child and, at best, that his well-being was enhanced in every way possible. It would include preventing his remaining in care unnecessarily or in forms of care which were not appropriate to his needs.

These are rough classifications which simplify a complicated matter. Yet they do serve to highlight the pitfalls of advocating prevention without being clear what it is that we have in mind. They also help in considering just which forms of prevention should be accorded priority. This is especially important when resources are scarce and questions about the economic return on various forms of prevention are being more sharply posed.[2] Not everyone is convinced that general preventive measures, either in health care or social work, are the best ways of spending public monies. Some argue that allowing a degree of urgency or crisis to develop is a valuable way of settling priorities and not wasting time or resources where risk has not yet become reality. To that is added the fact that, without compulsion, those at greatest risk seem least likely to avail themselves of preventive services.

Similarly, it is hard to demonstrate conclusively which preventive policies are successful. What actually works? In many instances, as the Seebohm Report admitted in its discussion of prevention,[3] we are still unsure. Prevention may sometimes only defer an unpalatable decision: is the delayed removal of a child from his home good prevention or not? We also have to face the possibility that certain conventional forms of 'preventive' help may create greater dependency and incapacity, not less. In that respect it may be vital to consider how far preventive measures should be directed towards the community more generally rather than at families and particular individuals. Looking at the question more broadly still one must ask whether really fundamental prevention can be achieved other than by changes in the character and organisation of certain economic and social institutions.

It is tempting to extol the virtue of preventing children coming into care simply because many children in care are known to be unhappy, to have an excess of emotional and behavioural difficulties, to be underfunctioning educationally and at risk of adult personality difficulties. On the other hand, we are also aware that to allow children to remain in or return repeatedly to homes in which the basic ingredients for child care are lacking has similar results. More remains to be done, by way of obtaining better evidence and clearer ideas, in order to answer some of the questions about prevention and substitute care that we have noted above. What kinds of prevention are needed; at what time; for which people; to what avail and in which order of priority? How can social workers and others be helped to distinguish between those children who would be better helped by removal from those who will benefit from support at home?

We can do little more here than acknowledge the need for better answers. Two things we can say. First, there is a ladder of preventive measures and, somewhat paradoxically, that which we strive to prevent at one level may well, in its turn, become a preventive measure at the next. We want to prevent separation of the child, but such separation may, in altered circumstances, be the best means of avoiding even worse things happening to him. Second, there is unlikely to be any *one* thing that has to be done to reduce the risks of permanent separation for children. As in the health field it is the combination over time of *many* entangled measures that is most likely to take us forward: clean water plus better nutrition, plus improved housing, plus medical discovery, plus reduced working hours, plus improved incomes – and so the chain continues. With conviction, steadily accumulating evidence and numerous different endeavours (often unspectacular in themselves) we may substantially reduce the risks of children being placed in jeopardy.

Notwithstanding the difficulties surrounding the concept and practice of prevention there are several issues which are especially relevant to reducing the risk of children being placed in long-term care away from their parents. They are discussed below.

Day care

There is now a sizeable body of literature, many ideas and practical schemes concerned with the provision of day care, especially for the under-fives.[4] Even so, 'what is provided . . . both full-time and part-time, is inadequate, uneven and uncoordinated'.[5] Alongside these deficiencies there are problems in determining how day care does or should fit into a pattern of services helping to prevent permanent separation. One problem is that day care serves a variety of purposes. A second difficulty is that it is desired by some and not by others. The evidence from Margaret Bone's study, for example, tells us that whilst 32 per cent of children under five in England and Wales in 1974 were receiving some form of day care 'it was wanted for a further 33 per cent'. The mothers of another 33 per cent did not want it although some of them were using it.[6] Were those who were not receiving day care (or for whom it was not being sought) in less 'need' than those who were?

Much of the debate about day care looks at its 'purposes' from the standpoint of the child: how his or her emotional, intellectual and social development may be affected for good or ill. We would wish to endorse those concerns but, seen from a preventive perspective, it is equally important to view day care as a means of assisting parents in their tasks of child care. This is a somewhat under-emphasised aspect but one which is crucial in the interests of forestalling long-term separation.

Parents under stress, as well as those who are bringing up handicapped or disturbed children, may well be able to surmount periods of special crisis, avoid reaching breaking point and replenish their energies and patience if they can be assured of some respite from the demands of constant care. In this respect it would be helpful to have a clearer view of when mothers or fathers feel in most need of support and relief: when, for example, does child abuse most often occur? We may be lulled into misleading assumptions by nomenclature. Evening, night or weekend care may be needed as much as day care by some families.

Attaching importance to the contribution that day care can make to sustaining parents is not to deny the needs of the child. At best day care should offer additional and compensatory experiences of a high order. But that which falls somewhat short of these high standards may still provide much needed relief to parents and thereby *indirectly* bring some benefits to the child. Even where mothers work full-time and their children receive daily care elsewhere there continue to be many opportunities for contact between parent and child: bathing, putting to bed, care in the night, waking and dressing. In this respect it is necessary to bear in mind not only that 74 per cent of mothers of children under five do not work, but also that of the 26 per cent who do, only 6 per cent work more than thirty hours a week.[7] Most still spend a considerable part of each day with their children.

In considering the contribution of day care to prevention (rather than its general purposes) *two* questions must be borne in mind. First, how and in what ways does it directly benefit the child and, second, does it enable parents to cope better when they resume the care of the child? An affirmative answer to the second question may depend upon the involvement of fathers and mothers, for day care can then potentially engage them in a learning, integrative and sharing experience. Where this happens there is an opportunity to convey some of the skills of parenting to those who are uncertain or inept and to build up confidence where it may be at a low ebb.

Part-time or occasional day care may well be sufficient to fulfil some of the purposes that we have outlined: through pre-school play groups, mother and toddler clubs, lunchtime arrangements and so on. Although these examples emphasise the pre-school group, older children and their families as well may benefit from occasional arrangements; for example, schemes in the school holidays. In other circumstances day care will need to provide a substantial period of 'alternative' care.

There is an important preventive role for such full-time day care, especially where there are single parents who have to work or, temporarily, when families are without a second parent through illness or other circumstances. About 6500 of the under-fives admitted to care in England and Wales in 1976 were received because of 'death of mother, father unable to care'; 'deserted by mother, father unable to care'; 'child illegitimate, mother unable to provide'; and 'short-term illness of parent or guardian'. These categories accounted for about a third of all the admissions in that age group.[8] We *must* ask how many of these children could have been as well or better cared for in full-time day care and with less risk of long-term separation. As a start it would be valuable to find out what alternatives parents themselves would have preferred.

Certainly many of the social workers to whom we spoke maintained that a proportion of admissions to care could have been avoided had there been the appropriate forms of day care available at the right time. But there were waiting lists to be joined or negotiated and a lack of jointly planned provision by social services, health and education departments. The separate administration of nursery education on the one hand and day nurseries on the other was regarded as an impediment to the best use of resources. Indeed, it was widely felt that only through the existence of day care 'programmes', incorporating many forms of provision as well as assistance to voluntary groups, and stretching across departmental jurisdictions, could the full potentialities of such schemes begin to be realised. This sentiment was forcefully expressed in the Bureau's journal *Concern* in 1975 which proposed integrated multipurpose pre-school centres and found little theoretical or practical justification for 'perpetuating the artificial distinction between pre-school care and education'.[9] Such centres could provide flexible programmes and more appropriately meet the needs of a variety of children. A falling birth-rate offers a particularly favourable situation in which such a reorganisation and development could occur. Several more recent publications have also called for greater integration.[10]

We know that there were at least 12 000 'priority' children on the waiting lists for local authority day nurseries in 1974,[11] and that this represented merely the tip of much greater general demand. We know that the variations in day care provision between authorities, and within areas too, is great. There are also marked variations in its use by children's ages: 4 per cent of those under one; 8 per cent of one-year-olds; 19 per cent of two-year-olds; 47 per cent of those who were three and 72 per cent of those aged four.[12] Given such shortages and variations we ought to record systematically how many admissions to care could have been avoided, in the view of the social workers and the parents, by the use of day care. To put the issue in proper perspective, however, it should also be recorded how many and which children are admitted to full care whilst receiving day care; this may, for example, be more likely to happen where private child-minding occurs rather than in other forms of day care.

The question of payment is an important matter. Social work staff to whom we spoke were often critical of the scale of charges for day care, disturbed by the implications of a comparatively cheap private child-minding sector and perplexed by the fact that, alongside these provisions, stood a free nursery education system. Charging arrangements and their implications require more careful examination than they have so far been accorded.

It may also be illuminating and helpful in the development of day care policy to consider the *full* extent and nature of contemporary day care provisions. Middle-class families, for example, employ mothers' helps and au pairs. How far this model could be reproduced for families at known risk seems a reasonable question. There is also daily 'baby sitting' to be considered. When there is already an extensive and mixed system of day care being provided in this country it is imperative to take account of *all* its features and, wherever possible, build upon, support and improve what is already there. This holds true especially for private child-minding[13] – an unfortunate term which hardly conveys a sense of positive child-caring.

Home help

Housework and child care are hard work. Where parents, particularly mothers, are unwell, disabled, mentally disordered or greatly overburdened, help in the home may make the difference between managing and despairing. However, especially with the reduction of births at home, there has been a shift in the allocation of home helps away from families and towards the elderly. In 1963 some 75 per cent of the cases attended by home helps were elderly; in 1973 the proportion had risen to 86 per cent.[14] Nevertheless, within this general trend it is evident that in some areas the home help service has been extended to provide support for vulnerable families with children. Again, it would be valuable to check on the number of admissions to care where it was considered that the provision of a home help could have made a preventive contribution; and at what juncture. Some social workers with whom we discussed the matter felt that the actual *amount* of such help (and its regularity) was an important variable.

Home helps can make several different kinds of contributions as well as assisting with the housework to be done. First, they may provide company and thereby a safety valve for mothers who feel too hostile and aggressive towards their children. Second, they may 'take over' temporarily and thereby allow mothers to get out of the house and away from the children for a while. Third, they may provide play and language stimulation for the child and, in some instances, for the mother as well. Fourth, a home help may act as a role model for some mothers. Fifth, they can provide a link with other services so that other help can be mobilised, quickly if necessary.

There are, of course, limitations upon what they can do in these directions. Much will depend upon who they are and what support they receive in their turn. They are not in the home all the time. They have conventionally been seen as working with and relating to mothers. How they might work with fathers or with couples is not generally explored. The service is still predominantly a matter of women working with women.

The difficulties facing the imaginative development of a home help service with a preventive orientation should not be allowed to detract from its potential. Quite modest changes may go a long way. For example, in the Schaffers' Scottish study of admissions to care because of mothers' confinements in maternity hospital it was noted that 'few families availed themselves of this service . . . this may be partly a lack of communication . . . about the existence of such provision but partly also a matter of the rigid hours worked by the home helps'.[15] This may be an important factor but, in addition, we know little about the willingness of husbands and wives to receive a home help into their home or about the effect of charges. An enquiry to consider the steps required in order to create a *preventive* home help service and to assemble experience gained from different local experiments is much needed.

The schools

Our schools are the most extensive yet local set of child-centred resources. They offer largely unrecognised opportunities for contributing to the task of prevention. There is a sense in which education offers substitute care to all children providing, as it does during the day, a safe environment, food and a wide spectrum of rewarding and challenging activities. The school group may indeed be seen as an extended family group where teachers are the controlling and caring adults and where fellow pupils form a sibling group. Furthermore, and increasingly over the past two decades, ordinary and special schools have seen it as part of their work to provide compensatory education for groups of children who appear to have had insufficient or inadequate care during their early years. To give a comprehensive account of the various ways in which this is attempted is not possible here but, in broad terms, one can see such a pattern of provision in nursery schools, special day schools and in ordinary schools where there are nurture groups for younger children and, for older pupils under stress, special withdrawal groups and quite extensive pastoral and counselling services. All these provisions exist with the declared aim of giving children an intensive experience of being specially regarded, provided for and helped. Most of them also offer warmth, comfort, the provision of food, a domestic setting, and opportunities for making close links with professionally concerned adults, hand in hand with an individual teaching programme. This programme is a planned attempt to give environmental and sensory experiences which lead to good language development, social skills and an appetite for learning. All this has in it a very considerable amount of both supplementary and complementary care which, at its best, provides a model of what may be done for children in special need. It is the character of these models which needs to be conveyed in a sensitive fashion to parents.

Alongside these activities it must be recognised that compulsory education is one of the most important influences upon the patterns of family life. It can provide respite for mothers as well as for their children; it enables mothers to take paid work outside the home for limited periods without anxiety about their offspring; it sets the need for certain routines and then, in the holidays, requires substantial readjustments to be made. It makes regular and irregular calls upon a mother's purse as well as stretching her patience in battles about the 'right' clothes or actual attendance. Schools exert powerful influences upon the patterns of children's friendships and these, in turn, affect their behaviour. Meeting at the gates or inside the school enlarges the circle of acquaintances that mothers make. Just how schools are organised, when they are open and shut, and their rules and regulations are factors which make a steady, if unspectacular, impact upon most families, especially mothers, but which remain less than fully appreciated. Where the children of one family attend different schools the effects are liable to be more complicated. Compulsory school attendance may both ease and exacerbate family difficulties and tensions.

The possibility of schools making a preventive contribution will be increased not only when the special provisions described above actually exist but also by their being flexible across a range of issues: from the community use of school space and equipment to matters of daily routine. It is plain that schools could be used more extensively as places for the social care of children of working mothers during school holidays and after school hours. However, the value of flexibility will in part depend upon the extent to which the schools' staff are aware of children at risk and how much they know, both about the children *and* their families; indeed upon whether they identify them at all, either as individuals or groups. There is no doubt that as teachers in daily contact with the children they are in as good a position as any to try.

Like most institutions, therefore, the schools can both accentuate and mitigate some of the problems with which families wrestle. When children stay away, for example, how the school responds largely settles which of them return to school or eventually go to court. When schoolchildren do appear in court (for whatever reason), what the teacher or headteacher has to say becomes part of the documentation upon which decisions about their futures rest. Schools can adhere firmly to a policy that 'no-child-is-turned-away' and pride themselves on incorporating and helping those who are very handicapped or disturbed. Or, by contrast, they may readily suspend (or decline to admit) difficult children or children with difficulties. Some schools seem to foster behaviour that gets children into trouble whilst others, hardly a stone's throw away, seem able to prevent it.[16]

The education system offers a variety of alternatives to permanent separation. In particular, boarding schools of many kinds can provide an intermediate solution for older children which, sensitively managed, does not sever links between parent and child and is widely regarded as 'legitimate', carrying a lesser stigma than going into care. Weekly or occasional boarding, unconventional holiday dates and community location all potentially add to the role that residential schools, or residential provision in day schools, might play in the preventive process.

The health services

By comparison with the schools and the personal social services our health services have a long-standing, impressive and explicit concern with prevention. The admirable DHSS consultative document on the subject brings the issue to the forefront once more.[17] However, the preventive concerns of the health services are, understandably, primarily directed at forestalling ill-health. Although there is a connection between ill-health and long-term separation of children from their families, the significance needs to be highlighted. For example, the treatment of a child or parent, although not regarded as a preventive measure in health terms, may well be a vital step in the prevention of separation. As in previous sections, however, we cannot examine this issue as fully as it deserves, and the recent report on child health services covers a great deal of the ground.[18] Nevertheless, there are several illustrations of what we have in mind.

The health services are undoubtedly in a good position to secure the early identification of children at risk of impaired physical, emotional and intellectual development within their own families. Throughout the country, for example, there seems to be a fair degree of uniformity in officially notifying the birth of each child to a health visitor, so that caring health supervision may be instituted from the outset. Most health visitors are either directly attached to general practitioners or linked with them and with the hospital services. They provide, therefore, a direct channel of communication between family and medical services from the very beginning and a source of advice, support and information to mothers. As a health visitor's involvement with a family is renewed with the birth of each child and extends over the years to school age and often beyond, she should have a good knowledge of individual families and the relations within them. But as the Auckland Report indicated,[19] health visitors move and so do families. In some cases this may prove to be a major drawback to realising the full potential of the services. As we have said before, high mobility has a bearing upon the extent to which the necessary interprofessional collaboration and consultation can be achieved.

We know that children 'at risk' of impaired growth and development are less likely than other children to have contact with the child health services.[20] None the less, research has shown that attendance rates at clinics rise when health visitors actively encourage the use of a developmental pediatric service. This may be one means to the more extensive early recognition of handicap or distress. However, although such early recognition is essential it will be nullified if lack of resources or geographical variations of provision within the health service create delays and long waiting lists for treatment. Even with encouragement some mothers will not take their children to clinics on a regular basis. We need to appreciate how these services are seen by such mothers and what costs are involved for them in attending; for example, in terms of their fears, difficult and costly public transport, taking time off work, or overcoming fatigue and depression.[21]

These discussions tend to concentrate (and rightly so) upon the health needs of *children* and the recognition of risk. The treatment of many childhood conditions can help to reduce pressures on families. However, the treatment of serious handicap in childhood is often arduous and stressful, and can *add* to the burdens of parents.

Alongside these considerations it must be remembered that in the 'reasons for admission to care', *parental* illness looms large in the returns. Even though classifications are crude and oversimplified the fact remains that the ill-health of the parent was involved in 25 per cent of all admissions of children to care in England and Wales in 1976 (33 per cent if one considers only voluntary admissions under section 1 of the Children Act, 1948).[22] Although the figures do not tell us what proportion of these admissions was due to mothers' illnesses and what to the fathers', it is likely that in most cases it was the mothers'. It would also be helpful to know how many of the short-term admissions due to parental illness became long stay.

On the face of it, more careful attention to the health of the parents of children at risk may hold out an important hope of reducing the need for separation. Even where admission to care does not occur we know that there are many health problems amongst the parents of children at risk. If a child is thought to fall into this category, then one priority should be to give special heed to the health of the parents. We recognise the importance of this during pregnancy but somehow seem to lose sight of it as the child grows older, and we hardly include the health care of fathers as part of the network of possible preventive measures. That is not to say that their health care is ignored but that it is not so often considered in *this* context.

The relationship between sickness and the income maintenance system is also important to note when prevention is being considered. Although sickness benefit is available for the ill person no provision exists whereby the healthy man or woman in employment can receive any benefit in order to stay at home to look after a sick spouse and the children. As a result some may not be able to afford to care for the children themselves when sickness strikes. This particularly applies when the mother is ill.

Improving parental care

So far, we have highlighted some of the resources and services that might be developed to facilitate prevention. In this last section we consider what might be done to improve the capacities and skills of parents themselves where a risk of long-term separation exists.

Parents who have spent part of their own childhood in care, or whose early lives have been disorganised or disturbed, are likely to have missed the good ordinary experiences of parental care. Their own skills as parents may be damaged as a result. In a few cases this damage is irrevocable and the parents will never be able to provide a satisfactory home. But there are parents, presently regarded as 'inadequate', who could be helped to provide 'good enough' care. Sympathetic advice from health visitors which extends beyond the simple physical needs of babies; group care for depressed mothers with young children, as well as the provision of home helps who offer models of confident and sensitive child care and also support for the mother herself, could all be useful aids to improving skills. Much is now known about the needs of developing children[23] but, by contrast, less attention tends to be given to the parallel development of adults in meeting these needs. One of the problems is that more notice has been paid to 'parental pathology' than to ordinary and successful parenting.

The grave difficulties involved in intervening to improve parenting were clearly outlined in the DHSS paper *Preparation for Parenthood*.[24] We do not claim to have agreed upon or resolved these issues. However we would make three particular points with respect to the quality of parenting and the prevention of the need for substitute care.

First, all children receive less than perfect parental care. There is an almost infinite number of variations in the parenting that children experience and yet reach adulthood physically and emotionally intact. Child-rearing practices vary by class, culture and even region. For many social workers who are confronted with the task of deciding when removal is really called for in the child's interest, the most crucial skill is to be able to judge that care is no longer 'good enough'. To err on the side of undue caution or undue confidence is to incur unnecessary risks for the child. Little professional advice and guidance seems to deal with the *marginal* family situations that social workers encounter. Where the question of court action is considered, for example, the available facts may be circumstantial and leave room for doubt. Yet it is in these families that prevention might prove most effective; where the scales can actually be tipped because they are finely balanced. More consultation, information and research might well be devoted to improving abilities in recognising such a situation; but that will not alter the fact that prevention often implies taking risks, since the decisions which have to be taken are reached by weighing advantage against disadvantage in highly complex circumstances.

Our second point is that how children are treated by their parents, and whether or not they eventually have to be admitted to long-term care, is likely to be affected as much by the relationships between the key adults as by those between adult and child. In particular, marital conflict and violence, sometimes associated with excessive drinking, involve children in ambivalent relationships in which they fill the role of scapegoat. Similarly, one is conscious of the detrimental impact that wider conflicts within the extended family may have on the child. All these factors emphasise that a truly preventive policy must devote as much attention to adult relationships within (and around) families as to those between children and adults. That places marital counselling and marital social work squarely within a framework of preventive services.

Third, it is shortsighted to concentrate solely upon the mother–child relationship or even upon how this is affected by the mother's other relationships. How fathers treat their children and are seen by them is also important. The father's role in the family and the mother's view of him have demonstrable effects on children, especially boys and particularly at adolescence. Having said that, however, it is necessary to recognise that the father figure may not be the child's natural father. Little attention seems to have been accorded to the impact of step parents or the effect of a series of 'step' parents. This seems to us an area of potentially valuable investigation. Much theory and counselling practice appear to rest, at least implicitly, upon the assumption that couples are married and that both are the parents of the children for whom they care.

The division or sharing of roles between men and women may also be relevant to the genesis of family problems and to their solutions. When fathers are disabled or hospitalised or desert their families, mothers are expected to provide both maternal and paternal care for their children. By contrast, fathers are not usually expected or encouraged to assume the maternal role when mothers leave home or are severely handicapped. Our tax and social security systems reflect this view and the labour market is not organised to permit the combination of paid work with child care. Although there is a category in the official statistics for children admitted to care entitled 'deserted by mother, father unable to care' there is no comparable heading for 'deserted by father, mother unable to care'. Similarly, 'death of mother, father unable to care' appears without a parallel classification 'death of father, mother unable to care'. Where parental illness is the factor precipitating separation it is almost certainly mothers' illnesses. 'Parental care' is frequently a synonym for maternal care. A commitment to improving and encouraging parental care needs to face critically the prevailing assumptions about the roles of men and women in caring for their children and the policies based on these assumptions.

In our preventive endeavours we must beware of viewing families as undifferentiated units ('policies to support the family'). Each is composed of unique individuals who interact in various private and public ways and who have their own interests, strengths and weaknesses.

Conclusion

There are other suggestions and ideas about what would contribute to successful prevention. The task, however, is extremely complex and progress will be by trial and error, experiment and evaluation. It will also depend upon what *precisely* we wish to prevent, where our sights are set, the extent to which different situations are distinguished, and just how remediable conditions really are. However, we believe that only by a firm preventive orientation and commitment can the potentialities be discovered. Despite this conviction words may still ensnare us. We may, for example, actually make more progress in prevention if we think less about prevention but more about enablement.

At present prevention is a tree of stunted growth. This is sometimes blamed upon the reluctance of the relevant local committees to spend money on support services, where the benefit is hard to demonstrate, preferring instead to create visible assets such as purpose-built homes. Senior social work staff can feel trapped by a pattern of expenditure which has been imposed from above and by numerous past decisions. (In the words of one director, referring to an 'excessive' commitment to capital projects, 'we are building a future we don't want'.) In a time of economic stringency, moreover, some preventive services may easily come to be regarded as unnecessary or dispensable frills. At the same time a climate of public criticism about the laxity of social services in safeguarding children in hazardous family situations can encourage expenditure on 'safety': and clearly, many preventive services, by their very use, imply some risk, some marking time.

Those responsible for planning a range of preventive services have to identify the blend of practical help and professional skills needed in order to work preventively with *various* kinds of families and different family members. There are rarely detailed measures of the need for the various services or evidence of how they can best be fitted together. Only by building up a comprehensive yet classified picture of these needs will local areas be able to select the mixture most suitable to their particular setting.[25] If prevention is better developed it should help to provide the extra information upon which *subsequent* preventive policies can be more appropriately built.

For preventive policies to be relevant to particular needs they must also take account of major changes in the social structure. More single parents are bringing up children on their own. Women's refuge centres help mothers to care for hundreds of children, many of whom might otherwise be in local authority care. More children now experience parental divorce and subsequent remarriage. The school-leaving age has been raised and more children are staying on beyond that point. Unemployment amongst school-leavers is high. Other changes may be equally important for the ways in which we *think* about 'prevention'. Television ownership and coverage is almost universal. A system upon which an Open University can be developed successfully or a literacy campaign supported ought to be seriously considered as a way of helping to improve child care. A start has been made in the child-minding field. Likewise telephone ownership, though less widespread, is growing. Supplying free or subsidised telephones, together with an answering support service, may be both a cheap and effective way of ensuring consumer-controlled preventive help. The principle has been largely accepted for the old and infirm and the severely disabled.

The very scarcity of preventive services provides a unique opportunity for imaginative and bold schemes. There is no burdensome legacy of old commitments and out-dated resources.

Part II

Planning

5

Key People

In the previous chapter we discussed the support services to families that can prevent children having to be looked after away from home. However, some children need alternative care and for some of them this needs to be on a long-term basis. Placement may be arranged privately and informally within families or amongst friends. In this chapter, though, we focus on the network of key people who are involved when a child passes from the care of his parents to the care of a public or semi-public body. For the child, and for those around him, many things change when this happens. We consider below four in particular.

Transferring care

> *Being in care you feel you've got a cross on your back. You feel marked.*

First, when children 'come into care' certain rights and duties become vested in corporate organisations rather than private individuals. Yet many of the essential parental responsibilities which corporate bodies assume can only be exercised in practice by individual people working with the child concerned. Full responsibility, however, is rarely assigned to them; attachments tend to be partial and open to disruption as the professionals and the children come and go. In sharp contrast parenthood in our society depends upon personal, comprehensive and continuing commitments to children, reinforced by mutual emotional attachments between them and their parents. Once a child enters substitute care there is a separation of actual care from formal responsibility. We suspect that this is one of the major obstacles to the provision of satisfactory substitute care.

A second change which occurs when an organisation assumes a child's care is that its responsibilities are discharged by dividing them into a number of activities performed by different groups of people. The processes of arranging the care, lending support and implementing subsequent plans, are usually undertaken by field social workers. Then there are the tasks of actually looking after the child from day to day: feeding, clothing, protecting, comforting and teaching appropriate social behaviour within a framework of an emotional commitment to the child. These are performed by substitute parents – be they foster parents, residential child care workers, nurses or domestic helpers. In addition, there are the tasks of formally educating, treating or assessing a child: work which is usually carried out by acknowledged professionals, who do not normally have a physical care relationship with the child. Then there are those who supply or control the support and facilities upon which these other activities rely: notably elected members and senior administrators. Finally, the provision of substitute care is also beginning to include 'representation of the child's interests' as a separate category of responsibility.[1]

Thus, the more or less comprehensive role which is assumed by parents in our society is, in practice, divided amongst a number of people when certain rights and duties pass to corporate bodies. Such differentiation, of course, occurs in part for all children once they enter the day school system; more so for those at boarding school. Similarly, a division of care is reflected in day care arrangements as well as in the employment of nannies or au pairs. The difference for the child in care is not only a matter of degree but arises from the fact that the parent or parents no longer carry the responsibility for maintaining overall continuity of care for him. It seems inevitable that responsibilities for children in care will continue to be divided between a number of people and hence pose problems of collaboration and primary responsibility.

It is interesting to note that in the 1940s the Curtis Committee clearly thought that the new children's officers it was recommending would themselves carry personal and long-term responsibility for the child in care.[2] Now (and perhaps from the start in all but the smaller authorities) the scale of operations precludes this kind of personalised responsibility at a senior level for all children in care.

There is a third change which is linked with the two we have already noted and which introduces further complexity into the position of the child in care. Although certain 'rights and duties' are transferred, the process is in many respects both vague and incomplete. The meaning of parental 'rights', for example, is obscure. A recent *Justice* report concluded that 'although the term is often used and the concept is apparently well enough understood to be the subject of litigation, hardly anyone has attempted to define the *legal* interest, if there is one, of a parent in a child'. Later, the report adds for good measure that 'the concept of parental rights . . . is really a chimera'.[3] Parental 'duties', although more precisely defined in some respects (for example, maintenance and the provision of education), remain uncodified in many others (such as health care). Likewise, there are only limited spheres in which the rights and duties of a child vis-à-vis his or her parents are legally defined.

Parental care of a child is normally provided in a satisfactory fashion without reference to any legal definitions. Unless things go seriously wrong it is mostly assumed that an implicit understanding exists about the duties and responsibilities of parents and children towards each other. When these relationships are replaced by others for a considerable period of time, but not broken completely, the question of what *precisely* is transferred by way of rights and duties becomes a crucial issue. What exactly are the duties and rights of a care authority acting *in loco parentis*?[4] Only with adoption, when all previous legal rights and duties are extinguished, are the uncertainties packed away once more into a single box labelled 'parenthood'. Any partial transfer necessitates that the box be opened, left open and the ambiguities and confusions within exposed to view.

Whether done on a voluntary or on a compulsory basis, therefore, the transfer of the care of a child is not an exact process. It is not an act of total severance either legally or physically, and never emotionally. Visits are made, letters are written and things are remembered. Feelings of interest, guilt, love, anger and curiosity are not expunged; and when the pattern of daily relationships is drastically changed, new and lasting attachments are inevitably formed.

These facts bring us to the fourth change. Substitute care involves more than making alternative arrangements and settling legal status. New attachments are made. They are liable to conflict with or, in the case of very young children, supersede the old and, because of this, to create special tensions for the children, their parents and the care-giver. How are the new and important attachments and interests to be reconciled with those that exist already?

Over the last twenty years much evidence has accumulated that socialisation, as well as the learning of language and other skills in early childhood, depends on mutually reinforced interactions between infants and care-givers, which may be biologically based and which depend upon the development of specific affective bonds between the child and his parents or substitute parents.[5] When separations between parents and young children are brief, reunion is less disturbed by anger on the part of the child if, during the separation, his needs for specific bonds have been met by a strictly limited number of care-givers.[6] Moreover, the care given is likely to enhance the child's sense of identity if the care-giver is allowed to become fond of and attached to the child and to know and react to him as an individual person. It is known that when child care staff have autonomy in planning their caring functions in children's daily lives they are better able to interact with them in such a way as to stimulate their language development.[7] Where groups of pre-school children are cared for in the same room social skills are liable to be lost and aggression to develop. The importance of well-organised activities has been stressed as a way of minimising these risks.[8] There is increasing recognition that parents and substitute parents serve as role models for children from two or three years onwards and that this has profound effects on the child's behaviour and later personality.[9] Not only do substitute parents need to provide affection and security but they need to know how to foster impulse control and the development of conscience in the children they look after. These important aspects of child development need to be integrated into planning for individual children and the organisation of substitute care.

Different strategies, of course, must be used for children at different development levels and with different parenting needs. In young children requiring long-term substitute care, decisions which arbitrate between the claims of different parent figures must be based on the principle that the child's needs are paramount, a principle now incorporated in the 1975 Children Act. In the case of older children, substitute care must take full account of the firm attachments that they may already have to their parents.

Complexity, diversity and ambiguity are familiar features of substitute care. For the child in particular they accentuate the conflict between the claims of a 'lost' past and a new present; but the adults involved also experience and have to live with that tension.[10] It is not easy to duplicate the 'natural' rights, duties and sentiments which are widely believed to be the proper basis of parental care. No amount of reassurance, for example, will entirely convince parents that when a young child becomes deeply attached to a substitute parent it is easy to transfer his strongest feelings back again to them: and especially so when there has been little opportunity to form a bond with them during the early months of life. In short, good substitute care is liable to provoke considerable anxiety in natural parents. Without careful selection and preparation for their task, foster parents, and houseparents too, are likely to develop feelings of rivalry and even hostility towards the natural parents which often persist until the child either returns home or is adopted.[11] Yet unless such mutual tensions between parent figures can be resolved the children themselves will not be helped with their own feelings of divided loyalty, and these may prejudice their later personality development. The allocation of 'rights and duties' to corporate bodies tends to obscure many of these problems which arise directly from the fact that the actual care of a child *can* only be provided in essentially personal ways.

We have drawn attention to only four of the changes which occur when a child enters care. There are others; but the ones we have selected seem to us to contain the essential elements of the problem of transferring care. A better understanding of that problem will help in discovering ways of improving policies and practices. But however good the administrative arrangements and the legal provisions, the actual care provided for children by public organisations depends on the interactions, and hence on the personal qualities, experience and conditions of work, of their substitute care-givers. These, in their turn, depend upon the professional qualities of the individual social workers who assess the children and their families, formulate plans for the future, support the care staff and work with natural parents.

Since substitute child care is, in our society, a complicated version of what most people regard as a simple and natural task we need to be especially aware of the complexities and clear about the components of good care. We would certainly include: affection; comfort; nurture; the provision of role models; exerting control; stimulation;

protection; and meeting the child's need to be 'needed'. These objectives are difficult, but not impossible, to realise in substitute arrangements where the aim is the child's return to his parent or parents. Where this is not the aim then these components of good care are likely to be more readily achieved. The gravest difficulties arise where it remains unclear which of these plans is being followed. A special responsibility rests upon social workers and others to *have* a plan and to make sure that those who are affected know what it is. We turn now to consider each of the main people (or groups of people) involved with the separated child.

Children

> *I want to know where I'm going to be living and what's going to happen to me.*

It is misleading to refer *generally* to children in care. They range from newborn babies to young adults; they are boys and girls, black and white. Some are healthy and some are sick. Educational retardation may be a problem in some cases but not in others. The list of differences is almost endless. Although the unique needs of each child must be considered in planning his or her care and treatment, some form of classification is also required for the development of appropriate policies. Ideally, we should discuss each category separately, but that is impossible in a report of this kind. However, we do provide an example of the kind of classificatory system which we have in mind in Appendix B. Three important dimensions are emphasised in that scheme: age, state of physical and emotional health, and educational abilities. Other variables might well include legal status, past history or current forms of care or treatment. Such a system would, in our view, serve to sharpen and improve practice as well as better inform the policy debates about provision for children in care.

Relevant and differentiated information is indispensable to good planning and we shall discuss this matter further in the following chapter when we consider key decisions. Here we wish to look at the role of the child in planning and deciding about his or her future. We recognise that much will depend upon his age, his health and whether he suffers a degree of handicap. Nevertheless, certain principles should be enunciated.

Older children should be involved in the key decisions about their future. There are three reasons. First, it is *their* life and well-being which is at stake; they have strong feelings and an incontrovertible central interest. They also have certain legal rights to be consulted under the 1975 Children Act and previously under adoption legislation.[12] A second reason for ensuring their involvement is because they possess information which is relevant to planning decisions. The third is because they are, and should be helped to be, in a position to influence their own futures. Having said that, there remain at least three problems which have to be faced. There is the question of age; the issue of communication; and the child's location in a field of conflicting social forces.

It is unrealistic to think that a particular age can be prescribed at which children should be consulted or rules laid down for precisely how they might be heard. The formula in adoption proceedings could be used as a general guideline; namely, that if the child is of an age to appreciate the nature of the decision, he or she should be consulted. Such a requirement is obviously open to differing interpretations, but it would be a valuable start were this principle to become part of accepted practice.

Children of, say, 10 years and above should certainly be capable of participating in planning and in key decisions. But in order to be able to form some opinion about the future they need information about the past, supplemented by a simple account of the current difficulties facing their parents and possible options for the future. In many cases this information might be given by parents themselves with the help of a skilled social worker. However, if children are to be involved and given truthful and straightforward information this must be a regular and accepted part of their experience; suddenly to burden them with new and often distressing information at the time of key decisions is likely to be traumatic and harmful. Involvement in the way that we have suggested presupposes established practices whereby children are provided with information about their past. Separated children have usually experienced more than their fair share of disruption and change; but they can be helped to understand the past if important events and people are kept alive by photographs, letters, autobiographical stories and if a sympathetic and trusted adult is there to explain some of the reasons for painful upheavals. Some items of information may be too damaging to be helpful, at least at particular ages and stages of a child's development: but in principle, children should have a right to simple, honest and sympathetic information about their past. As a guideline, we might take the range and kind of information unseparated children would acquire or be given in the normal course of events.

Various proposals were submitted to the working party whereby the interests of handicapped and young children who are isolated could be better represented when decisions are taken. The basic idea in most of these schemes required the creation of a panel of lay people, with special training or competence in child development and law, to act as independent representatives for children in assessments and reviews. Doubts were expressed, however, that this would introduce yet another person into the procedures and one who had limited contact with the child and no special authority. Others felt that children who were incapable of articulating their needs to a stranger would be better served by befriending schemes in which adults in the community are encouraged to share in the care of isolated children. People who have invited separated children into their own homes and who have earned their trust are in a better position than strangers to help them express their own interests when key decisions come to be taken. Likewise, staff in residential homes could probably fill this role, especially those who do not carry major responsibilities towards the child on behalf of an authority. Another view was that 'representing the child's interests' was a primary responsibility of the social worker concerned. Just how, when and by whom young children are involved in the major decisions about them remains a difficult issue which deserves more study. Much depends upon the skills available for communicating with children.

The common reaction of many children who are asked to express themselves when a decision is to be made is silence. The child in court rarely says anything when asked to explain his behaviour or to offer an interpretation: court utterances are almost entirely adult. Even in less formal and daunting surroundings, silence (or 'dunno') is a typical reaction of children invited to say what they want or why they want it. In such circumstances children are liable to be dismissed as stupid, indifferent or truculent. What seems fairly clear, however, is that it is frequently the setting which inhibits, overawes or frightens them. This is a challenge that has to be faced if we are to achieve a greater involvement of children.

This aim notwithstanding, we need to accept that only children in middle childhood can begin to voice clear decisions and that no child under the age of adolescence should be made to carry the responsibility for vital decisions about his own future. Moreover, it is important to realise that whilst it is essential to make clear decisions about a child's substitute care and his future placement, such decisions will inevitably be associated with ambivalent and at times conflicting emotional reactions in the mind of the child and often in the minds of his parents and even his care-givers. Situations in which such decisions are made inevitably arouse anxiety and evoke irrational responses in children and adults. This should not cause surprise but needs to be recognised if misunderstanding of the child's actual communications or his lack of communication are to be avoided. Only those who know a child well or who are particularly perceptive and experienced will know how to interpret communications, both verbal and non-verbal.

Children may remain silent or monosyllabic when they find themselves forced into situations where they are expected to choose between people; their parents; their relations; their friends or those who care for them. There are, indeed, widespread conventions in our society that such choices *should* be avoided. We share with the authors of the recent DHSS circular, referred to earlier,[13] the conviction that the involvement of children should not oblige them to make these kinds of choices (implicitly or explicitly), although some children will indicate spontaneously and firmly their preferences. To advocate a child's involvement is not to advocate the abdication of adult responsibilities.

Parents

I was put into care just after I was born . . . I don't know why I was put into care. I go and see my mother every weekend. I don't know what happened to my Dad.

We have pointed out the need for classification with respect to children in care. In a similar way the circumstances and predicaments in which parents find themselves vary considerably but can be grouped into a number of categories. There are healthy parents and sick parents; separated parents and those who are still together; remarried parents with step-children; single parents; parents who have disappeared and parents who visit regularly. Again the possible divisions are numerous. Across-the-board generalisation is the ever-present pitfall. The pitfall is more likely to be seen, and thus avoided, if contact is maintained with parents and if they are engaged in the main decisions about their children.

The three reasons which we adduced for involving children in key decisions are also powerful with respect to the parents. First, they retain certain rights and duties as parents unless these are proscribed by a court of law. Second, they, like their children, possess information which is relevant to planning. Third, parents are in a position to exert influence on their child's future. They also have to come to terms with their future roles in relation to the child they have relinquished. This is always attended by emotional upheavals but involvement in decision-taking will help parents face and survive this ordeal.

There are, as we have said, few clearly codified parental rights and duties. If anything, however, these appear to be *more* carefully specified once a child has passed 'into care'. The difference is that the definition of rights and duties tends to be couched in terms of the regulation of the relationship between the parents and the *authority* rather than between them and the child. A new requirement in the 1975 Act, for example, obliges the parents to give the *authority* twenty-eight days' notice that they wish to exercise their right to remove a child who has been voluntarily in care for more than six months.

Some information which is relevant to planning for the separated child is available in records or through direct observation; albeit interpretations may vary. Other important information, however, is held only in the private possession of parents: facts about the child's early history; their own backgrounds; their present circumstances and future intentions. To help parents disclose their feelings and discuss emotionally charged aspects of their past and present lives, requires a high degree of skill and experience on the part of the social worker. Professional skill is also needed to assess how capable or likely parents are to follow through their intentions. Many parents will feel that in surrendering their caring role they have surrendered parts of themselves: their sense of adequacy; self-esteem; self-confidence or personal worth. Under such circumstances they may well be disinclined to share further information in the planning process, choosing instead to maintain a reserved distance. It will depend upon the trust and confidence which exists and upon their perception of the value of the information in question. Some will be cautious lest it be used against them later. This should not be surprising because parents often view local authorities as hostile and punitive. The local authority's evidence, for example, may have been an important contributory factor in persuading the court to make a care order; and if the parent later applies for the order to be discharged against the advice of the local authority, a variety of evidence will be offered in order to oppose the application, some of which will be about the parents' capacities and reliability.

It is essential that the views expressed by parents are taken into full account and that, if they conflict with the views of the local authority, the issue as it affects the child is set against a detailed professional assessment of the child, of his parents, and of the substitute care-givers. The obvious difficulties which face both authorities and parents in exchanging information is no reason to ignore the parents or deliberately keep them at arm's length.

There may be a few parents who are too sick or too disturbed to be able to express a view or provide information. Some others may be considered to be 'untraceable' although, as Rosamund Thorpe's research shows,[14] many of them can be found by reasonably determined searching. The Harvie Report on residential care for mentally subnormal children reminds us that a child is more likely to be abandoned in care by its parents 'where the parents are effectively abandoned by the placing authority'.[15]

Even where parental rights are severely curtailed they may be reinstated upon appeal and certain duties, like financial contribution, do continue. Unless they are specifically prohibited by a court order, parental meetings with their child, visits or correspondence cannot actually be prevented. Nor is there any way, short of arrest or imprisonment, in which parents can be stopped from intervening illegally to re-establish or maintain their sphere of parental influence. In these senses it is the parental ability to influence the child's future which makes it essential to plan *with* them: at the very least to be able to appreciate the nature and extent of that influence.

It is easy to fall into the habit of talking about parents in general. As we have already pointed out, however, there may be circumstances in which children are either the target of parental conflict or the vehicle by means of which it is conducted. One should not assume, therefore, that both parents have the same interest in their children or that they have reconcilable plans and aspirations. That is one of the *facts* that has to be ascertained. There may be no way in which agreement between parents can be secured: witness the intervention of the courts in matters of custody and access connected with divorce. We do not know how many parents of children in care are single, separated, divorced or remarried. We do know that in 1975 alone nearly 250 000 children under 16 throughout England and Wales had parents who divorced that year.[16] Divorce is likely to be more common amongst parents of children in care. But it is not only parental separation or divorce which creates complexity in planning for the child in care; it is re-marriage and cohabitation as well. In 1975 in Great Britain, almost 30 per cent of all marriages were re-marriages, although it is not clear how many of them involved children under 16.[17] The figure for the parents of children in care is, again, likely to be even greater. Thus, we should be constantly aware that the rights, duties and interests of each parent (or parent figure) may not be identical. Consulting or considering only one of them is unsatisfactory; indeed it may lead to worse decisions than if neither is contacted.

There are formidable problems in enlisting parental involvement, both for authorities and for parents. However, this ought not to detract from the *principles* which should guide planning endeavours, namely:

1. That parental rights and duties as legally defined should only be extinguished by due process in a court of law and not by the *de facto* application of administrative rules or professional practices. (Since a court hearing is obligatory if there is parental objection to a local authority passing a resolution assuming rights and duties, we include this in our definition of 'due process'.) All concerned should have a clear appreciation of what rights and duties do or do not continue to reside with the parents (and which parent) whilst the child is in care.
2. Both parents should always be given printed and verbal information which clearly differentiates between their particular rights and duties and those of the authority whilst their child is in care. It might well include 'reasons for admission' as well as what needs to be done before a child returns home. We have been impressed by the model documents set out in the annex to the DHSS circular on the implementation of the 1975 Act.[18]

3 In general, parents should be consulted at points of major review or decision and informed of the outcome. If this is not done the reasons should be recorded and form part of the review process, and be carefully examined on *each* occasion. Although parental views should be taken into account there will be times when their preferences are overridden. There may be occasions when it is not in the interests of the child to trace parents or reinvolve them if contact has been broken, especially when young children have been placed in permanent substitute families. Much harm may be done by arousing feelings of regret and potential hope in parents when they are, in fact, unable to make a long-term commitment for care to their child. Their reappearance at arbitrary moments in his life serves only to interfere with his current relationships and may cause so much anxiety and conflict in the child and his care-givers that his behaviour becomes more difficult and his place in his substitute home is threatened. While such circumstances may not be common, they are extremely important and require to be fully documented.

Children and parents – some conclusions and general remarks

> *Social workers don't always tell children what a Care Order or Section 1 is. They don't say, 'Oh, your mother can come back any time and take you away'. They should explain what your real situation is in care.*

We recommend that clear and simply written statements should be prepared for parents and older children in order to help them know where they stand and what they can or cannot do as well as what responsibilities fall to the caring authorities. This will not be easy; not least because of the variety of situations which arise (and hence the danger of misleading generalisations) and because of the lack of a comprehensive codification of parents' and children's rights and duties in the first place. Once more, however, we maintain that the principle is clear, and that difficulty and complexity are no defence for not moving as far as we can towards its realisation. Certain simple standard documents, indeed, could probably be produced nationally.

Such documents would not deny the individual variations in life-style, circumstances or personality of children, parents and care-givers. Nor would they curtail proper professional discretion.

There are 'rules' or 'agreements' which fall short of legal rights and duties but which nevertheless need to be understood and often carefully negotiated. Visits by parents to foster homes; visits home by children who are subject to care orders; systems of complaint; financial assessment procedures, and many other things besides fall into this category. It is fashionable to talk of 'contracts' in social work practice and although these rarely have the force of law they do stress the need for minimum agreements between the parties whose views may differ about what is to be done, when, by whom and how. We doubt whether all these circumstances can be covered in a published 'guide'. Some could be. Others should be set out in letter form to particular parents and children. We return to a fuller and more general consideration of 'contracts' at the end of this chapter.

Parents and children sometimes need to enlist a 'second opinion' about difficult decisions. There are few simple decisions about the entry to and exit from substitute care, about the particular form it should take or whether it should be provided at all. Ambiguity, doubt and uncertainty are common features of the decision process. Just as authorities are often wise to seek second opinions, parents and children may also consider it necessary. The possibility of easily and conveniently obtaining a second opinion should not be restricted to professionals. A wider application of the principle is incorporated in the notion of a 'child's representative' but there are other cases too (for example, ascertainment of maladjustment, educational potential, severity of handicap) where the good parent considers it prudent to seek reassurance through a second opinion. We should be sure that this opportunity is available when children are in care. There is, for example, an argument for parents and children having some say about which social worker is allocated to them. Requests for changes of social worker (or, in the case of a child, doctor or teacher) should be taken seriously.

Parents and children are likely to be helped by support groups. The value of self-directed support groups for foster parents has been demonstrated by the National Foster Care Association. Group work with parents and separated children is in its infancy but promising schemes are beginning to emerge. Certainly, support is much needed by the parents of children in care. They often feel isolated from relatives and friends with children, since there is no acknowledged role in our society for the parents separated from their child. They are likely to feel that their own experience of surrendering their child is unique. Contact with other parents in similar circumstances is the only way in which they can compare and share their experiences, as well as consider the practices of caring agencies more generally and press for change.

Support groups can also be set up to carry out specific tasks, as the National Children's Bureau sponsored working group of young people in care has demonstrated. This group set itself the task of preparing a report on the experience of residential care from the child's point of view. This has now been published by the Bureau as *Who Cares?* The group not only helped to fill a major gap in our knowledge about residential care: it also seems to have enlarged the social experience of its members and set a precedent for group work with separated children.

The discussion so far in this chapter covers contentious and sensitive areas. It is almost certainly impossible to lay down firm rules about all categories and conditions. Hard and fast 'rules' are inappropriate where the uniqueness of individual experience and need must be allowed to weigh in decisions about children's lives. None the less, the elucidation of principles or guidelines is important since only then can the appropriate direction of any changes be determined, and the *case* for exceptions be made clear.

Residential care staff

> *We think residential staff should have more say, in everyday things, after all they're the ones who are looking after you.*

Just over half, or some 55 000, of the children in the care of public and voluntary bodies in Great Britain are currently accommodated in residential homes or schools of one kind or another.[19] The care staff who look after them number some 20 000, about 14 per cent of whom are trained.[20] Little is known about this group of people, about the patterns of their work or the quality of the care that they are able to provide.

This adds to the danger that in the enthusiasm for 'community-based' care, the residential sector will be arbitrarily devalued and its potential overlooked, despite the new terminology of 'community homes'. We share the concern of the DHSS Social Work Service Development Group that present economic stringencies should not be used as a reason 'for relegating residential care to second best status again', or for saying 'that we do not need it. That would be unrealistic and damaging to an aspect of our services only recently emerging from twenty years of under valuation'.[21] If we ignore this warning we are liable to find ourselves acting as though residential care were *already* a small fraction of total provision. As a result, even less attention than now might be paid to the detailed consideration of which kinds of residential care are required for which children, for what purposes and at what time. Yet without answers to these kinds of key questions no basis exists upon which to decide about issues of recruitment, training and organisation. Parenthetically, it may be noted that if residential care were *actually* a minor and scarce resource it might be used more selectively and deliberately.

Whatever the longer-term future may hold, the quality of care received by many of today's separated children depends upon the standards of residential provision. These vary considerably, although it is common for policy debates to refer to such provision as if it were a uniform commodity. Differences between homes (and in certain cases within them) are as great as some of those between residential and other forms of care. However, it will be hard to draw upon the experience of the best whilst such major differences are not openly acknowledged.

Having made these general observations there remains an enormous task of exploration and review upon which it is impossible for us to embark. We are unable to do more than elaborate a few of the more specific issues which impressed us on our visits or which were conveyed in the evidence submitted.

One set of such issues centres upon the question of who should work with the parents of children in residential care. The staff we met expressed considerable uncertainty about the proper extent of their involvement in this respect. Their hesitation usually sprang from a fear of trespassing upon the field social worker's territory. The situation looked even more complicated to residential staff in voluntary agencies who were unclear about where the social work responsibilities of the 'placing' local authorities and their own organisation began and ended.

Yet we were told by residential staff in both sectors that where they relied upon field staff for information about the social backgrounds and current family circumstances of the children in their care, they often received little or none. This may reflect the diversion of social workers' time and energy to various other forms of short-term and crisis work, as a result of which contact with families may become sporadic once their children have been admitted to care and 'safely' lodged in a residential home. We had no way of testing the accuracy of these perceptions or interpretations, but they did exist.

We also gained the impression that residential staff would have welcomed the chance to work more directly with parents, especially where younger children were concerned who came from reasonably local areas. In virtually all the community homes we visited, staff expressed a positive and largely accepting attitude towards parents. In some cases they had gone to considerable lengths to encourage visits, to host group meetings with mothers and to set up activities within the home in which parents could be involved. Some senior staff had also taken it upon themselves to visit parents.

We do not know how widespread such developments are but the fact that they exist at all highlights important questions about the division of responsibilities between field and residential staff; especially in matters connected with parents, potential foster parents and the child's school. Who goes to the school on the various parents' evenings? Who introduces the child to his new foster home? Who takes him to hospital? Who goes to collect him if he runs away? These and other similar questions were posed by residential staff in their endeavour to clarify where their role ended and the social worker's began.

On a number of occasions residential staff suggested that responsibility for monitoring the family circumstances of children in their care and liaising with outside bodies should be transferred to them, where appropriate, from the field social workers. Although such proposals raise many difficult questions they do warrant serious consideration. There are many factors to be taken into account.

1. Which staff in the residential homes might be responsible for this 'outside work'? Should it fall to the more senior; the trained; those who volunteer; to someone filling a specially created role or, perhaps, a person chosen by the child?
2. Is this an appropriate time for such a change in light of the small proportion of trained staff in the residential field? Given the recommendation of the Central Council for Education and

Training in Social Work working party on residential social work that there should be a single pattern of training for field and residential social workers, as well as pleas that an increase in the proportion of trained staff in residential work should have high priority, the proposal may become more attractive as time passes.[22]

3. What happens where the child is placed elsewhere, in another home or foster home? If the residential staff continued to be involved how would this affect the allocation of responsibility for newcomers to the home?
4. Would the case for a transfer of responsibility be different in short-stay residential provision?
5. Could the aims of the proposal be as well or better met by attaching some field staff to homes? Those who sought to 'specialise' in children and were prepared to mix fieldwork with direct daily caring might find the prospect attractive. There are some similarities in the position of social workers in hospitals and probation officers in prisons.
6. How far is the feasibility of changes in either of these directions (residential staff moving out or field staff moving in) dependent upon limited catchment areas, size of homes, their location, the turnover rates of staff and children, and staffing ratios? Community-based units serving one or two area teams, and containing fifteen to twenty children, might provide the kind of arrangement in which such changes could be made.
7. How is the proposal affected if a closer integration is achieved between residential provision and other community resources, which together support mixed patterns of day, night and weekly usage? Would this not, in any case, challenge the existing division of work between field and residential staff?
8. Could the suggestion be applied to the staff who look after children in long-stay hospitals? Such hospitals often rotate nursing staff from ward to ward so that no one is committed to planning for specific children. Until this practice is stopped and until these staff are offered the chance to carry out the principles implied by good child care practice and child development theory, it would seem irresponsible to enlarge further their responsibilities by asking them to undertake work with parents. We are sure that the Jay Committee will be considering such issues.[23] Children in hospitals especially raise questions about the similarity or differences between nursing care and social care.[24]

We suspect that there is greater similarity than is currently reflected in the respective training programmes or professional self-images.

9. In some cases, particularly in special boarding education, it will be relevant to consider how far teachers could or should also assume responsibilities for work with the parents of the children they teach.

There are no ready answers to these questions; but if we are to think in inventive and constructive ways about securing the best interests of the child we cannot ignore the problems which may be created by the conventional division of responsibilities. It is certainly conceivable that local variations are so great that no national blueprint can be satisfactorily produced.

One issue, then, in considering the role of residential staff concerns the division of responsibility for working with parents. Another is the question of specialisation *within* the residential child care sector. There are at least two overlapping aspects: first, the nature of the intake (especially in terms of children's ages, sex, ethnic background, behaviour problems, handicap and previous experience) and, second, the degree of specialisation amongst staff. Both matters are influenced by other factors, especially the size of the home, the rate of turnover and the amount of discretion that the head is able to exercise over admissions. Although the issue was widely acknowledged, ideas about what should happen varied considerably. We were told, for example, of the problems which were encountered when rather difficult adolescents were cared for together with younger children. On the other hand some successful experiments have relied upon grouping together children of various ages who have particular problems or needs. By contrast, other staff were at pains to advocate and demonstrate the desirability of avoiding such specialisation in residential care.

Many kinds of arrangements can work successfully and much depends upon the commitment, skill, sensitivity and enthusiasm of the staff and upon the 'atmosphere' that they are able to create. Changes in structures or admission policies will be of little avail if a residential home lacks these ingredients. How they can be engendered and sustained is a matter of the utmost importance and one which again depends upon the detailed study and understanding of varieties of residential life.[25]

The most pressing issue is, of course, the need for increased training for residential care staffs. All institutions in which children are cared for away from home on a long-term basis, whether run by social workers, by educationalists or by doctors, need to include among their staff people who, whatever else they contribute to the child's welfare, have two kinds of special expertise. First, pedagogic skills based on a knowledge of child development and consisting of special abilities in communicating with children and for creating a child-centred environment in which children can develop physically, emotionally and intellectually. The second special expertise is interpersonal skills which enable staff to foster helpful interactions between children and their parents; to provide relief for parents in distress; and to help other professionals concerned with the child's care or education to interact helpfully with each other, with the child and his parents, and to make plans for the child's future which treat him as a whole person. Such skills must be taught; they are rarely acquired without special training.

We recommend that every institution for children should aim to have on its staff at least one fully-trained child care worker in a position of influence with the personality attributes which fit him or her for the tasks outlined above. Furthermore, in the training of residential staff special emphasis should be given to three aspects of child care: the promotion of the child's physical, emotional, social and intellectual development; the structuring of his environment in order to foster both emotional and intellectual growth; and the creation of conditions and methods for effective and helpful communication with the child's parents and with other people concerned with his welfare.

Foster parents

I don't think our Mum would want us to be fostered.

Some 75 000 foster parents look after children placed by local authorities and voluntary bodies in Great Britain. Roughly another 15 000 act in a private capacity and are supervised under the child protection legislation. These numbers may strike the reader as surprisingly large for we have deliberately counted wives *and* husbands rather than adopt the convention of counting couples as 'one'. But, whichever way they are enumerated, the fact remains that foster parents far outnumber any other single category of care-providers for separated children. In England and Wales about 40 per cent of children in care are boarded out and in Scotland a comparable figure stands at about 45 per cent.

We cannot comment in detail upon the many issues connected with the use of foster care. The recently published DHSS working party's report has elaborated many of them.[26] But there are certain features of the *role* of foster parents that have attracted our attention and which are pertinent to the discussion of the interests and responsibilities of care-givers.

Before considering these in more detail, however, there is one basic point to be made. Like residential care, foster care is a highly varied service which is often treated and discussed as if one foster home were like another. There can be a vast difference between the 'best' and the most marginal foster home which an agency continues to use only because a child has already formed roots there or because nothing else is available. It is noteworthy that nearly 13 per cent of children boarded out by local authorities in England and Wales in 1976 were placed with relatives.[27] As the DHSS foster care report points out this is often a very different situation from that in which the child goes to strangers.[28] Various studies have endeavoured to develop classifications of fostering based upon styles or motivation.[29] It is also appreciated that some foster parents like to look after babies and toddlers whilst others are good with teenagers; some like to undertake short-term and contract fostering whereas others want an indefinite commitment, perhaps with adoption as a final aim. Schemes are now being introduced which recruit specialised, 'professional' foster parents for sibling groups, black children, the handicapped or for disturbed adolescents.[30] At least one important and clear division of foster parents will arise in the near future as some seek and obtain custodianship orders.[31]

Notwithstanding these important variations some general points about the foster parent role call for attention. Several research reports, particularly those which explore the views of foster parents directly, confirm a strong impression that we gained from meeting foster parents.[32] Namely, that they do not readily distinguish between the roles of ordinary parent and foster parent. Their emphasis is upon what might be regarded as the 'normalisation' of the child's position in their family. Treating the foster child as 'one of our own' is a common approach to the task of providing loving care and is embodied in the formal agreements which local authorities make with foster parents based upon the boarding-out regulations. As a result, those features of fostering which challenge or throw doubt upon such attitudes tend to be resented or denied. Relations with and feelings towards the child's own parents are consequently often tense. Although some foster parents are able to welcome and work with natural parents, many are content that they visit only infrequently, and some are openly hostile.

The foster parent's role is ambiguous, ill-defined and is liable to vary in different circumstances. Many have to act as parents yet acknowledge that their position is temporary and circumscribed in various ways by the policies of the placing agency and the interests of the child's own parents. Yet, as Shaw concludes from his study, to most foster parents 'successful fostering means loving children and being good at looking after them, the ultimate objective being the foster child's absorption into the family'.[33] The contradiction between this popular perception of the fostering role and the desire on the part of authorities to retain contact with natural parents, in order to facilitate the child's eventual return, is now widely recognised. But it does little to reduce the countervailing pressures to which many foster families and foster children are exposed. We probably overestimate the extent to which these conflicts can be lessened by the encouragement of 'professional' fostering, the greater security foster parents will be afforded by the 1975 Act and the growth of foster parent groups. Indeed, the two latter developments may increase them.

The conflict that foster parents commonly see between their rights and those of the natural parents can prove a serious barrier to satisfactory care. For example, the foster care study carried out by the Social Services Research and Intelligence Unit in Hampshire revealed that 40 per cent of foster mothers and 60 per cent of the fathers believed that they were taking over the rights of the natural parents with respect to the children in their care.[34]

We doubt whether these conflicts and ambiguities can be entirely resolved, although there are several ways in which the position could be eased:

1. Foster parents should always be provided with a clear written statement of their rights and duties, together with a similar statement describing the position of the natural parents and the

authority involved. Discussion will be needed to explain the implications and to give tangible examples.

2. Some members of the working party consider that this should go further and provide a more detailed and contractual basis to the foster placement. But there are limits to how far these very personal services can be specified by rules and regulations. If social workers can convey an openness of practice and generate confidence in their help and advice, foster parents may be helped to use their role in imaginative ways. For example, some foster parents do not communicate with natural parents, not because they do not wish to do so, but because they are somehow afraid that this might not be approved by the placing agency. The same thing also happens with natural parents. It must be conceded that there seem to be instances where this is an entirely accurate conclusion: where agencies wish to preserve contact but on their terms and under their control.
3. Were there a more detailed contract it might indicate both what was expected in these matters and also protect foster parents (and thereby the children) from unrealistic expectations. Social workers do not deliberately overburden or exploit foster parents but when they are desperate for a place for a child they may be tempted to ask foster mothers to take 'just one more'. Or they may press her to take a child she feels unsure about or before there has been time for a full consultation with everybody in the family. Placements like these are in no one's longer-term interest.
4. In these and other circumstances some social workers fail to give foster parents much information about the natural parents. Such information could best be given by the parents themselves before the fostering begins and from time to time later on. This highlights the value of natural parents being taken to meet foster parents before the child is placed. It is not a matter of satisfying idle curiosity but of ensuring that foster parents have a realistic basis for working with and caring for a child. The risk, of course, is that acquaintance with parents and their circumstances may confirm foster parents in their unfavourable view. On the other hand the technical skills of social workers should serve to enhance mutual understanding between parents and foster parents.
5. If children were fostered in their own neighbourhoods, as often

happens where private fostering is arranged, it would cast foster care in a somewhat different mould. Geographical distance makes it that much more difficult for parents to visit or for the foster parents fully to appreciate the child's earlier environment; it may reinforce class or cultural differences.

6. Many children are not placed in foster homes directly from their own homes; they frequently go to a residential home first. Indeed, there is evidence to suggest that this arrangement gives a better chance of success than immediate placement.[35] Yet there is little discussion of how the child and his foster parents might be supported by residential staff. After all, these are people who have cared for *this* child and with whom he or she may have formed an attachment. They will have bathed him, read to him, dealt (or not dealt as the case may be) with temper tantrums, sorted out battles, offered comfort and been roused to anger. It is often the lack of these personal (and passionate) experiences which foster parents cite in their criticism of the ability of social workers to help.
7. The need for skilled and sympathetic support for foster parents must be emphasised, especially at certain times and with certain kinds of children. What information is available indicates rather infrequent visiting by social workers. Given the other pressures on them it may be valuable to gain a clearer impression of when and where support is most needed and not rely upon the eruption of a crisis before substantial help is forthcoming. It is also important to enlist the regular help and assistance of local doctors, health visitors and teachers. The foster status of the child is not always fully appreciated by these other professionals.
8. If we could more accurately estimate the chances of a child returning to his family then it might be possible eventually to create two categories of foster care. One would aim to provide *alternative* temporary care, the other prolonged *substitute* care, possibly leading to custodianship or adoption. Something of this kind already exists with the distinction between short- and long-term fostering. But this suggestion does turn upon our ability to assess accurately future prospects.
9. Lastly, we must beware of regarding foster families as units in which interests are broadly compatible and shared. Foster mothers do not necessarily speak for the rest of the family or for the foster child. Help, support and attention may, for example,

> be most needed by the foster parents' own child. The roles of *all* the members of these families are altered and complicated by the presence of a foster child. Like the foster parents, their own children are cast into an ambiguous and often uneasy role which they have to live with and, given help, sort out.

As with residential care we know that some foster homes are much better than others, yet there seems to be a reluctance to identify the most marginal for what they are until a crisis develops. What evaluative research has been undertaken tends to concentrate on breakdown and failure.[36] We might, with considerable profit, endeavour to learn from the most successful foster parents as well, involving them in recruitment campaigns and encouraging the mutual support of neighbouring foster parents. We treat foster parents as a care resource for individual children but rarely regard them as a resource for general experience, information and ideas. The National Foster Care Association is one valuable channel through which such help might be sought and developed by organisations responsible for child care.

Field social workers

> *What I can't stand is some young bird breezing in who you've never seen before in your life and saying, 'Hi, I'm your new social worker . . . tell me what you feel about things.'*

In most areas of the country social workers carry the major day-to-day responsibility for ensuring that the long-term well-being of the separated child is considered and advanced. As we have seen, however, it is by no means a complete or unambiguous responsibility. But for practical purposes it is the social workers who arrange admissions, placements and discharges. It is they who often enlist the help of other professionals; attend courts in connection with children; work with the parents; select, support and supervise foster parents and visit children in a variety of residential homes. The list could be further elaborated, but is sufficient to indicate how much of the social worker's time is spent covering the 'spaces in between'. In the complicated circumstances of many separated children these, regrettably, are often numerous.

Partly because of this, social workers face special problems of maintaining the network of interests and collaboration upon which the quality of care and planning depend. This obviously requires skill and adaptability but it also requires reasonable permanence. That is why, in Chapter 3, we have placed such emphasis upon the problem of social worker mobility.

The question of movement, however, is only part of a broader issue concerning the tempo of social work. Many social workers are unable to devote as much time or attention to matters associated with children in care as they wish or as is needed. Nor are they always able to have sufficient direct and regular contact with the children themselves. We suggest below several courses of action which might help to ease these problems:

1. The establishment of career grades for social workers might be further encouraged. The career structures that commonly exist in social services departments link promotion with increasing administrative responsibilities. Direct contact with children and families may cease quite early in the career of the ambitious and able social worker. There is a good case for a separate administrative grade within departments in parallel with career practice grades, but with certain crossing points.
2. More use might be made of part-time social workers who are often quite experienced and trained. People who are married and with children appear to move less often than the single or the newly married.[37] The majority of social workers continues to be women; but many mothers are only able to work part-time. Were they recruited (or retained) more often then greater stability might be introduced into social work. The same argument is likely to apply to residential staff. It might be noted that long-term work, which makes fairly predictable demands, is particularly suitable for part-timers.
3. More appropriate use might be made of the help given by social work assistants. The content of the duties undertaken by social workers with mixed case loads should be scrutinised in order to discover how much routine work could be usefully carried out by social work assistants. A more discriminating division of work between trained and untrained staff ought to allow social workers to give more time to those decisions which require complex judgements and thorough investigation. The difficulty in doing so springs, perhaps, from the fact that these 'key decisions' cannot always be separated from the less dramatic work of

maintaining the network which we referred to above and to ensuring that a variety of both small and large decisions fit together smoothly. 'Pairing' social worker and assistant on particular cases or groups of cases may help by making it possible for the latter to do some of the 'network' jobs whilst enabling the former to be available for crucial decisions.

Measures like these may help, but departments will always have to contend with the movement of staff. White-collar workers in our society move home more frequently than manual workers, and social workers are no exception to this general rule.[38] However enthusiastic the efforts to prevent the 'waste' of talent and skill and to create more satisfying working conditions, ways must still be devised of lessening the harmful effects of social worker movement. The following paragraphs note some ideas that may be of help:

1. Crucial decisions about children in care might more often be made by a small *group* of key people. The juvenile courts and the hearings in Scotland provide examples. Responsibility for and experience of the decision would thereby be shared, although responsibility for the implementation of the decision would have to be assigned to an individual, albeit acting with or through others.
2. By extension of this argument it will be important to consider carefully who is most likely to remain, and secure their particular involvement.
3. If an increasing part of the role of social work comes to be seen as enabling a variety of *other* people to discharge the responsibilities of the community towards deprived children, then again some of the continuing responsibilities and commitments could be shared. Yet because of the *public* aspect of responsibility for separated children there is an understandable reluctance to move in that direction. It is also difficult because of the disputation and conflicting interests which often surround the child in care. None the less, the balance between individual professional responsibility and some form of shared responsibility should be examined alongside the problem of mobility.
4. We have argued earlier that the introduction of career grades for some social workers might prevent the erosion of special skills and experience. The kinds of career grade social workers we have in mind would probably be older and unlikely to make

> frequent moves. Having said this, however, it must be noted that if too much comes to depend upon senior staff with special skills in the children's field then there may be an even greater upheaval when they *do* move; especially if they are not easily replaceable or if other staff have not extended *their* skill and experience of this aspect of work.

It is difficult to decide which social work 'specialisms' should be developed. The needs vary between areas, with the character of the population covered and with the staff resources available. What is appropriate now may not be appropriate in ten years' time. Rather than a national review of the issue of specialisation, therefore, local solutions should evolve in response to local analyses of the problem; at least for the present. However, we would make one recommendation now which is that there should be a post of special responsibility in social services and social work departments for overseeing the planning for isolated children in care, a category in which we would include those in hospitals and special schools who lack any home base.

Central government

Before completing our review of some of the groups of people involved in the care of separated children we must pause to consider the role of central government. Obviously in budgetary and legislative terms it creates the general framework in which services are developed and provided, as local government does in its turn. However, these are not the issues upon which we wish to comment here. They are the questions of regulation and inspection.

The disappearance of the former Children's Department inspectorate seems to be widely regretted amongst experienced social workers. The Regional Social Work Services Officers of the DHSS were said to be very responsive to demands for help and information but insufficiently active in enforcing standards or in contacting local departments. It was felt by some local authorities' staff that they experienced a weakened control now compared with previous arrangements. Although the DHSS Social Work Service still have inspectorial authority they do not conduct full-scale evaluative reviews of departments' work as, from time to time, the children's service inspectorate did.

The scale of social work activity has increased so much in recent years that the costs of re-introducing an inspectorate along the old Home Office lines would probably be prohibitive. Central–local government relations have also changed with the reform of local government. Local authorities are larger, have unified social services departments, possess their own research capabilities and, in many places, there are strong and independently-minded social service committees. Central government departments are larger and cover a wider range of services. New semi-independent bodies, like the Central Council for Education and Training in Social Work, have assumed special responsibilities and both professional bodies and the relevant trade unions now have to be considered by central and local governments. They provide their members with channels of communication to policy centres and, in the case of bodies like the British Association of Social Workers, are publishing codes of practice. All these developments preclude simply stepping back to past systems of inspection. Even so, we must report the frequently expressed view amongst the staff to whom we spoke that some guidance and monitoring of an 'inspectorial' kind was required.

The Centre for Studies in Social Policy (now the Policy Studies Institute) has produced an excellent paper which looks at the prospects and problems of quality control in the health and personal social services. We cannot improve upon their analysis, and share their belief that 'the development of inspection – in the sense of quality monitoring rooted in professional self-policing and self-criticism – could in time provide the required basis of information for educated public debate about professional standards, priorities and policies'.[39]

Working together – the case for contracts

There are so many people discussing your future and disagreeing . . .

One of the themes running through this chapter has been the proliferation of interests which occurs when a child passes into care and the difficulty of achieving the kind of central co-ordinating role which concerned parents provide for their children. Added to which many children coming into care need a wider variety of services than other children: special medical care and treatment; work to improve educational achievement; vocational guidance and help to develop social skills. We were told repeatedly that planning for deprived children was hindered by failures of collaboration and inadequate trust between professionals.

Some of the exhortation to strive for better collaboration overlooks the fact that there may well be conflicting interests and opinions amongst those involved with a child and that clear-cut responsibility, plus the necessary authority capable of settling differences, do not always exist. Much can be achieved by close working relationships and by familiarity, although in some cases that may actually serve to expose differences that had previously not been realised. There are ambiguities and contradictions that cannot be glossed over. If the child is not to suffer from the indecision or the constant skirmishing that these tend to produce then means have to be found to affix responsibility, take decisions and check that things needing to be done are done.

We believe that the idea of 'contracts', which was touched upon earlier, holds some promise in this respect. They are already in use in a few places: for example, in the special fostering project being run in Kent. If corporate bodies are to care responsibly for other people's children then everyone involved must understand the various levels of accountability and who is responsible for what is happening (or not happening) at any one time; and that includes parents and children. Everyone must also understand their expected commitment and, where possible, how long it will last. By failing to have a *written* agreement (contract) about these things we fail to specify commitments, relying instead upon goodwill and presumed understandings. Although helpful, they can be hard to sustain sufficiently to see a plan through. The caring agencies have a responsibility to the child, in its own right, to be able to say at any time what has been done, is being done and will be done, plus who carries the responsibility. The nature and level of 'contracts' will, of course, vary; but we can indicate the kind of thing we have in mind by considering briefly what a contract might include in a case where a 7-year-old child is being reunited with his family from whom he was removed to foster parents because of non-accidental injury two years before.

1. The child to spend weekends, first at fortnightly, then at weekly intervals in his biological mother's home. After this has been

happening for two months, that is about six such weekends, his adjustment to be reviewed. Evidence to be considered must include an up-to-date medical and health visitor's report; an up-to-date school report of his behaviour; a detailed description of his behaviour given by the foster parents so that their views and observations can be taken into account; his family's observations, as well as a report by himself given to the social worker *or* teacher (whomever he has the closest and longest relationship with) about his views. These to be obtained without either the parents or foster parents being present.

2. If he is returned to his mother, supervision to continue for at least one but preferably two years. This must include regular visits as well as the right to see him by himself.
3. The foster parents to have the right to see him at least once a month but, in turn, to undertake to help him accept the situation rather than win him back.
4. The parents to agree to allow these contacts with the foster parents and not to criticise them in the child's hearing. The child also to be permitted to write to his foster parents should he wish to do so.
5. The parents to agree to regular check-ups for him during the first two years after his return home: after three months, six months, twelve months and twenty-four months; the child to be given a physical check-up as well as a psychological/psychiatric examination. Refusal to let him be examined to be regarded as a ground for taking the case back to court.
6. The social services department to be responsible for initiating these re-examinations and for collecting and collating all the necessary reports, including an up-to-date school report, covering his behaviour and appearance.

There are other aspects of 'working together' which we shall consider later; but we must reiterate the complexity of substitute care and the great demands which are made upon collaborative endeavour if the child's well-being is to be pursued as successfully as possible. But realistically, it is hard to reproduce the co-ordinative impact made by a vigorous, self-confident, partisan and single-minded parent, short of adoption or an adoption-like situation. That being so we have to be at special pains to *secure* commitments. Putting them on paper for all to see and remember is a beginning.

6

The Key Decisions

There are certain key decisions that have to be made when a child is separated from his or her parents. These decisions assume special importance because they are the ones which more or less settle the character of the next stages and guide thinking and expectations in particular directions. In stressing them, we do not underestimate the impact of a host of other daily decisions upon a child's well-being. Nevertheless there are major turning points: legal, administrative and emotional. The timing of these key decisions may be crucial. We cannot ignore the fact that in some cases they are allowed to emerge by default, partly because the occasion for firm choices has been allowed to pass or simply because it has not been recognised.

In this chapter we have selected four such major decisions. We comment upon the processes involved and explain why we consider their improvement to be a basis for better care and sound planning.

Reception into substitute care

When I first came into care I just couldn't understand that my Dad couldn't have me. I used to get really funny ideas – I used to wonder why I was in care because I've got parents.

Obviously the initial decision to admit a child to care, to special boarding education or to hospital is of the utmost importance. Even where the ostensible reason for admission suggests a short stay, we know that it may become protracted: the reasons for *coming* into care may be rather different from the reasons for *staying* in care. It is at the point of admission that inadequacies in the preventative services become most apparent. Yet we know comparatively little about what actually occurs at this vital stage: who contributes to the decision; what negotiations take place with the existing care-takers; what information is available; why there are wide variations between apparently similar areas;[1] what are the untried or discarded alternatives; what happens to the applications that are refused and who makes the final formal decision?

For the social workers who deal with applications for voluntary admission there are dilemmas and uncertainties. We were told on several occasions, for example, that there was a 'loss of nerve' amongst inexperienced and often untrained staff who felt under great pressure to safeguard themselves against the public criticism which follows mistaken child care decisions, and who therefore sometimes acted too hastily and erred on the side of admission. Alongside this is the difficulty of knowing when to initiate care proceedings in cases of neglect or cruelty. Where apparently neglectful mothers or fathers themselves *request* the admission of their children, it may be thought best to proceed on this voluntary basis rather than seek a court order. Whether or not this is an appropriate course of action will depend upon the health and mental state of the parents as well as their circumstances. It will also depend upon whether court action is considered feasible, and that may turn upon the involvement and advice of a local authority's legal department.

Each of these courses of action has different implications for the child's future, some of which may be of cardinal importance. We consider below a number of issues which bear upon the quality of decisions about reception as well as the terms of admission.

Supervision

Junior staff in particular impressed upon the working party the importance they attached to good supervision in the reception decision. There were complaints that supervision was sometimes inadequate and not always available when needed, as well as observations that the quality of their own child care case work was governed in a random and accidental fashion by the previous child care experience of their seniors. Rapid changes among supervising staff were felt to be highly disruptive.

The internal regulations of many social services departments specify that a decision about the reception of children into care may be taken only after consultation, but they are not always strictly observed. In at least one authority, basic grade social workers were sometimes given no assistance when taking this critical step. They felt that this gave them a responsibility that was beyond their experience and competence to handle. They thought it anomalous that they were required to refer to headquarters decisions about the expenditure of small sums of money under preventive legislation, whereas, even in financial terms, reception into care was a decision of incomparably greater significance.

We agree with the tenor of such criticisms and echo the statements made by the British Association of Social Workers (BASW) in their evidence to us:

> Decisions which affect the allocation of resources, the placement of a child or legal proceedings concerning a child should *never* be made without consultation [our emphasis].
>
> All social workers dealing with children need to have machinery whereby they can consult with colleagues, share their concerns and receive an objective evaluation of their work.

There are, of course, problems about what is done in emergencies but a useful parallel may be observed in the compulsory hospital admission of psychiatric patients where *two* doctors have to sign the certificate. There are other examples in medicine and the law of the kind of shared decisions which BASW is advocating: termination of pregnancy and decisions taken by juvenile court and children's hearings all require that decisions be shared.

Although guidelines for minimum standards of practice during reception into care and checklists for completing social histories are essential, they should not be allowed to become substitutes for detailed consultations between social workers and their senior colleagues, as well as with other professions whenever necessary. Otherwise it would be too tempting for the authorities to believe that they had discharged their responsibilities by issuing instructions, and the blame for mistaken decisions would fall too readily upon junior staff.

Intake teams

More or less specialised intake teams, rather than the duty rota system, now exist in many social services departments. Their job entails dealing with a wide range of initial applications and enquiries. Evidence about the general effect of intake teams indicates that fewer cases than before are accepted for further work. More are dealt with quickly, referred on elsewhere or encouraged to make other arrangements. As one commentator has put it, 'seniors spoke about their relief as the files to be allocated "dwindled mercifully"'.[2] We have been unable to discover the particular impact of these changed ways of working upon the reception into care decision but see opportunities for improved practice, particularly with respect to greater standardisation in the collection of information.

Information

Given skill and sensitivity, good decisions about reception will rely heavily upon good information. It is widely accepted that there should be a full picture of the child, the family circumstances and the events precipitating the request for care. There are circumstances in which this is impossible to obtain and others in which the sense of urgency telescopes the search for information to the barest minimum. Where a court is responsible for the formal decision, however, it is automatically deferred until the called-for information is assembled. This may be a procedure to be copied at other entry points. There may be parallels to be drawn with such options as place of safety orders, interim care orders and remand.

Likewise, the extent to which prior information about a child and his family is available will depend partly upon the extent and kind of preventive involvements discussed in Chapter 4. Although prevention may fail to forestall admission to care, the fact that it has existed, and information has been collected, may facilitate better decisions at a later time.

Good information is required at the point of deciding about reception for at least two distinct purposes. First, as a basis for deciding whether or not reception is necessary and, second, because information collected at this time will help to construct a prognosis and aid subsequent plans and decisions.

Whether or not a child *should* be received into care is a matter of judgement about need or risk on one hand and the alternatives which are available on the other. It is the second of these considerations which we feel receives too little attention in the assembly of information. In that respect, an inventory of 'community resources' would be invaluable if kept up to date. What is needed is detailed knowledge of voluntary groups and organisations, day facilities, play groups and so on. Local offices of the social services departments should know the *people* who are the community resources: the child-minders, private foster parents and good neighbours. Where the extent and character of these resources are unknown the conclusion that admission to care is necessary will be based upon inadequate information.

What is actually recorded at the time of reception (and the care with which it is done) creates an invaluable baseline as well as conveying a sense of concern to both child and parents. If a child's family circumstances are not described at the time of his or her removal, and if there is no clear statement about the aims to be achieved by a period in care, then there is no way of measuring progress or of later evaluating the appropriateness of the decision: in short, there is no way of learning. Likewise, recording what the different people involved expect of the future may help later in assessing whether the picture has changed.

We would emphasise especially the importance of careful recording at this time as one means whereby the child's right to a full biography is protected. Reception may be (but should not be) the last opportunity for gathering information about parents, previous history, feelings and places. Details about the point at which separation occurred, and the reasons why, will be much sought after by the permanently separated child as he gets older. In this, as in so much else to do with reception and planning, it is vital to possess a well-founded means of assessing the likelihood of the child remaining in care for a long period. If a child really is going to return to his parents in a month then some would contend that it is unnecessary to collect a great deal of information. This view, however, ignores the facts that without enough information it may be difficult to judge whether the child *will* return and that coming into care for the first time is not a random event but should be treated as a warning sign that the child and family are 'vulnerable'.

The regulation of reception into care under section 1 of the Children Act, 1948

In the course of gathering our evidence, several suggestions were advanced about ways in which a greater degree of regulation could be introduced into the voluntary admission process. We believe that some of these ideas warrant serious consideration.

The circumstances in which children may be admitted to care under section 1 of the 1948 Act might be more fully elaborated. For example, and following BASW policy, it could be made clear that homelessness did not normally justify the reception of children into care. As it stands, the first section of the 1948 Act is so broad that almost any family problem could be regarded as cause for admission. We recognise that scope for discretion is required but do not see that this removes the need for firm guidance, both nationally and locally. It might take the form of memoranda or an amendment to the 1948 Act which extended the 'welfare principle' (introduced by the 1975 legislation with respect to children *in* care) to the decision about admission *to* care. Section 59(1) of the 1975 Children Act might achieve this, were small changes made. These are indicated below, in italics:

> In reaching any decision relating to a child in their care, *or about the admission of a child to their care*, a local authority shall give first consideration to the need to safeguard and promote the welfare of the child throughout his childhood; and shall so far as practicable ascertain the wishes and feelings of the child regarding *those* decisions and give due consideration to them, having regard to his age and understanding.

Where reception is necessary it may still be useful formally to offer it for a limited duration in the first instance. It may not be possible to endow such arrangements with the force of law but at least a reapplication could be required (and hence a review of any changed circumstances) upon expiry. Such a development might form the first rung of a ladder of decisions which make clear to all concerned the likely duration of a child's separation, culminating, if necessary, in the assumption of parental rights by the local authority or in adoption.

Rowe and Lambert[3] have demonstrated the importance of making firm plans for children soon after they come into care. Their work suggests that if steps are not taken to restore children to their parents early, then they are likely to face permanent separation. Once a child leaves his home his place in the family is liable to close up unless he is visited frequently or visits his family, and is remembered in present activities and future plans.

In certain circumstances, time-bound agreements with parents would help to emphasise their continuing involvement and responsibilities. We are conscious, of course, that such arrangements may lead children to believe that they will be taken home at the end of a fixed period. If parents do not or cannot do this, the child's feelings of being let down may be intense. On balance, however, we feel that care offered for limited periods is to be commended. It would, for example, help to compress the time during which decisions had to be made about the child's likely future. It would also give an extra urgency to the work carried out with parents immediately after separation.

We recognise, of course, that such arrangements will contribute little to the problem of children who are in and out of care repeatedly and in quick succession. It is also plain that a time-limited admission could lull staff into a feeling that, since the child will soon be returning home, he or she warrants only minimum attention. The same assumption may also lead to the child being placed where he cannot remain if the expected return does not materialise. He will then be moved unnecessarily. Despite the danger of these possibilities, we consider that the suggestions for time boundaries deserve careful examination and we would recommend comparative studies in this field.

We are encouraged in this by the provisions for various time limits which have been included in the 1975 Children Act. These impose limitations on the rights of parents to *reassume* the care of their children. For example, they will not be able to remove their child from the care of people who have looked after him for five years or more, or have applied to adopt (or notified the local authority of their intention to do so) pending a hearing. Nor will they be able to resume looking after him without giving twenty-eight days' notice once he has been in care under section 1 of the Children Act, 1948, for six months or more. The local authority will be able to assume parental rights on the additional ground that a child has been in continuous care for three years or more and that it is not in his or her interest to be removed from care at that time. All these changes introduce the notion of time boundaries.[4]

What we have in mind, however, is the introduction of boundaries which limit the duration of a child's stay in care. Quite how long such time-bound admissions should run is a matter for debate. It might be for a maximum of six months, although there may well be a case for shortening the period (say to six weeks) especially for young children or where there is a temporary family crisis with a foreseeable end. Upon any reapplication at expiry another short-term agreement might be concluded, day care provided instead or open-ended admission offered as now. There may need to be a restriction placed upon the number of consecutive short-term admissions before alternative steps have to be taken.

There would be, therefore, two kinds of status for the child in care under section 1 of the 1948 Act: the contractual short-term admission and the open-ended arrangement as at present. The latter would remain appropriate where a child was, for example, abandoned or orphaned. However, in these kinds of cases there would be a *prima facie* assumption that parental rights would be taken by the local authority.

Undoubtedly, there would be real difficulties in deciding how the conditions of a short-stay agreement could be enforced. There would also be problems about *which* parent is party to the agreement, and if both, how they may best be consulted. There would be problems too with the parent who is in long-stay hospital care. Despite these difficulties and the difficulty of applying any sanctions if the agreement is broken we do feel that the very existence of an 'agreement' would serve the purposes we see for it. There is also the other side of the coin: difficulty has been experienced by some parents in 'recovering' their children from care, and aspects of the new legislation which we have described may actually heighten apprehension on this count. An 'expiry date' would help to lessen these fears. It will doubtless be argued that there are occasions when it is in the child's best interest to remain in voluntary care against the parents' wishes. If that situation arises a care order or the assumption of parental rights is indicated. Voluntary admission under the 1948 Act should not become *de facto* compulsion.

So far we have applied the notion of a time-limited 'contract' only to those children who enter local authority care on a voluntary basis. However, the principle underlying the proposal might be applied, with appropriate modifications, to other circumstances in which children are exposed to the risk of long-term separation as a result of the waning interest and commitment of adults; for example, in hospitals for the severely subnormal.

We should also note that the age for children being discharged from care presently stands at 18 (with provision for extension to 19

…ases). This too is a time limit, albeit crude and arbitrary. …y be a case (with the reduced age of majority and the … school-leaving age) for moving this ceiling either upwards or … wards. Greater provision might be made for variations in individual needs. We do not necessarily advocate altering maximum ages but neither do we feel that they should be taken for granted or be the same for all children.

Committal to care under a care order

The old approved school orders were more circumscribed and contractual in character than the present care orders and supervision orders in Scotland. There is, however, a statutory requirement that they be reviewed after six months but this interval is often extended. We are uncertain how much more regulation is desirable or possible. It is, however, necessary to consider the fact that care orders span children of all ages and children involved in both care and criminal proceedings. The admirable desire to dispel the aura of criminality around the older delinquent may have unnoticed consequences for the younger neglected or abused child. We are not convinced that the terms of care orders should be identical for both categories or that they should all run until the child is 18 irrespective of his age when they are made, or the different problems that bring him to court.

In care proceedings, the onus of proof is on the authority initiating the case. Some proceedings are contemplated but not pursued for want of hard evidence. How they differ from those which are brought to court is a matter of great importance, affecting as it does the whole question of improving the regulation of reception into care. We still know little about such decisions although the variations between areas remain substantial.[5]

Other forms of long-term care

So far we have been concerned with children received or committed to public care because of family breakdown or delinquency. But in 1971, for every three children in children's homes or approved schools, one was in a hospital for the psychiatrically ill or mentally subnormal; one in a hospital for the physically ill; more than one in a residential school for handicapped children and ten in other kinds of boarding schools.[6] A minority of these 'other' separated children were *also* in public care but most were not.

There is likely to be an overlap between children in these different institutions in terms both of their problem behaviour and of the difficulties experienced by parents. It is known, for example, that the psychiatric disorders of children in residential schools for the maladjusted have much in common with those of children in approved schools;[7] and children with chronic or recurrent physical ill-health are known to be predisposed to psychiatric disorders, as are children with mental handicaps.[8]

The questions of why and how children are admitted to these other forms of long-term provision are pertinent to our exploration of the key decision to transfer full-time care from the parent to an organisation. At one end of the social and economic spectrum parents with personality disorders who experience marital discord or disruption may send their children to independent boarding schools, while at the other end of that spectrum they depend on the child care facilities of the social services. Despite these differences, the problems attaching to children living away from home for long periods are similar and so, for a variety of interacting reasons, are those of their parents. The separation itself and the contact with institutional life, whatever the reason for it, make their impact both on children and on their parents. Hence, we should look as carefully at these 'reception' decisions as we have at those in the local authority sphere. Unfortunately, this is extremely difficult to do in a comprehensive fashion because of the wide variety of provisions and the semi-private nature of many of them.

In this discussion, we have concentrated upon aspects of the reception decision. We have not considered the processes by which children are actually received; what and who accompanies them; what information is available to those initially responsible for their care; or what impact different kinds of experience make upon them. This omission is in no way intended to dismiss the profound significance of these matters for the child and for the quality of care he or she receives.

Assessment

> *You can have the situation where the child's in care and doesn't want to see his parents. And yet the social worker can force you to go home, even if things are bad and you . . . know it's not right.*

Assessment may be regarded as a way of describing a child's needs and how these can best be met by the different resources of care, education or treatment which are available. It constitutes a prelude to placement and, if completed early enough, a basis for deciding whether substitute care is necessary. If possible, assessment should be done before a child is removed from the home in which he is currently living.

Assessments vary enormously in their degree of formality; in the people making them; in their timing; in their setting; and in how they are conducted, as well as their outcomes. Some placements may have to be arranged at short notice with little consultation or information, but even here some rudimentary assessment has to be made. At the opposite end of the scale, assessments may take several weeks to complete, involve a wide range of people, assemble a wealth of information and make precise recommendations about what needs to be done. Those who are responsible for making an assessment may be able to implement the preferred course of action directly. More often they advise other people or bodies (which then accept or reject what they have to say), or negotiate with yet others who control the chosen resources. For these reasons, there is likely to be a discrepancy between the 'ideal' placement, what is recommended in the light of the available options, and what actually happens.[9]

'Assessment' thus covers a multitude of different ways in which placement decisions are influenced by a calculation of what is best for the child based upon information about his needs, the resources to hand and future prospects. It tends to be seen, however, as occurring at a particular time when choices *have* to be made because an interregnum has occurred (or been created) between a child's past and his future. However, as we point out later, ideally assessment should be a continuing process, which is probably most effective when conducted by those responsible for subsequent action.[10]

Residential assessment

At any one time about one in twenty children in care in England and Wales are accommodated in 'community homes with observation and assessment facilities'.[11] However, it must be noted that not all children in assessment centres will be subject to assessment. A study of admissions to assessment centres in the South West region in 1975 showed, for example, that on average 74 per cent of the 'beds' in such establishments were occupied on any one day and that of these, 48 per cent would be used for assessment purposes. An additional 33 per cent would be filled by children whose assessments were complete but for whom no placement was yet available. The remaining 19 per cent would be used to 'hold' children for other reasons.[12]

It is important to point out that the change in nomenclature from remand homes and classifying schools to 'community homes with observation and assessment' which followed the 1969 Children and Young Persons Act did not substantially alter the actual homes involved. They continue to be used to provide reports for the juvenile courts and for the children's hearings in Scotland. Thus there is a substantial minority of children in such homes who are on remand pending reports. There are others who, having been committed to care by the courts, spend a period in such centres in order to determine where they should best be placed. The regional study mentioned above showed that 30 per cent of the children passing through such centres in the year ending March 1975 (or still in residence at that time) were subject to place of safety orders, interim care orders or on remand.[13] Unfortunately, the report does not distinguish between interim care orders and remand but the great majority would fall into the latter category. One might estimate, therefore, that about a quarter of all children dealt with in assessment centres are not yet 'in care', although some will be committed upon reappearance in court. We also know that many children return home upon leaving assessment centres; the regional study puts the proportion at 28 per cent.[14] Most of these will be in care but allowed to be in the care of a parent or relative.

Children in assessment centres are predominantly adolescent boys. The study already quoted discovered that boys between 12 and 17 accounted for 54 per cent of all the children accommodated in a full year. Those aged 14 or 15 were the most numerous, being 29 per cent of the grand total. Boys significantly outnumbered girls at all ages, and overall by two to one.[15] Taking boys and girls together it is noteworthy that only 12 per cent of all children passing through the assessment centres in that region were under 10 years of age. A similar pattern emerges from a study of assessment undertaken by the Wessex Children's Regional Planning Committee.[16] This picture, of course, reflects the situation which existed prior to the 1969 Act and the continuing close relationship of assessment centres with the juvenile court system. Delinquency still remains a common reason for children to be admitted for residential assessment (the South West regional study puts it at two-thirds).[17]

The changes initiated by the 1969 legislation make it difficult to judge precisely how the 'observation and assessment' system differs from what went before. It was presumed that residential assessment resources would become available more generally to children at risk or already in care. Our impression is that they continue to be much used in connection with the courts and as a waiting facility once recommendations are made but before the required placement becomes available. Costly assessment resources are, then, still primarily devoted to adolescents, particularly boys.

We do not suggest that more young children should be placed in residential assessment centres instead, but that some of the resources consumed by such centres might be redirected towards these age groups. This is an important issue; but it should not obscure the fact that there are special problems and shortcomings in residential assessment whatever the child's age, sex or legal status. 'Waiting' is one of the most commonly observed drawbacks of this system. There are two aspects.

First, since places in assessment centres are often in short supply, children who are recommended for admission sometimes have to wait in alternative temporary arrangements.[18] We certainly gained the impression, however, that the greater the presumed 'crisis' the easier it was for a child to be advanced to the head of the queue. The Association of Directors of Social Services, for example, told the Expenditure Committee that they had experience 'in some authorities, particularly in the London area and urban centres, of very great difficulty in having children assessed. Sometimes there can be a delay of months rather than weeks'.[19]

Second, there is ample evidence that once the assessment is completed some children have to wait for long periods until the recommended placement materialises. Adolescent girls, for instance, present a particular problem. The South West regional study examined the speed with which different options could be mobilised and, by implication, what that indicated about shortages at the next stage in the chain. It showed that children who are to go home stay for the shortest time, whereas those waiting for foster homes or residential special education remain in the centres for the longest period after assessment is completed.[20] Delays appear to occur for a mixture of reasons: no vacancies, the refusal of heads of other establishments to accept certain children and, in some cases, a lack of clarity about who is responsible for implementing recommendations.

The unattractive but accurate administrative term 'silting-up' describes the situation in many assessment centres.[21] What this means for the child is a matter of serious concern. Regimes are geared to short stays; some children do move on rapidly (for example, those not being assessed, those returning to court and those going home). We can only guess at the uncertainties, anxieties and doubts which a prolonged state of limbo causes the child who remains behind. We were told of some who, when the time came, pleaded not to be moved because they had spent such a long time in a centre. A minority of children stay a year and more, and others may have no idea when the next move will take place. We are obliged to question the value (and cost) of eventually arriving at the 'best' placement in this way.

There is another major problem in the process of residential assessment: namely the fact that children are in an unfamiliar setting, often remote from their local communities, away from their usual schools and, of course, separated from their families or those who last looked after them. In the centres we visited parents were not involved in assessment meetings although, of course, they were seen. Given all these circumstances, we cannot but be doubtful about the extent to which the child's social situation (and his behaviour in it) can be adequately appreciated or how far the potentialities and plans of the key adults in his world are properly taken into account. However warm, skilled and caring the staff may be, the children are being assessed in an alien setting. Reports of outcomes are not often received, so that the staff have virtually no means by which to judge the correctness of the decisions that were made during assessment.

One further limitation is inevitable when 'good' placements are in short supply. It arises because recommendations cannot always be fulfilled. When second, third or fourth choices have to be used, one is led to question the justification for creating elaborate residential provisions for the purposes of careful assessment. That is not to deny that there are other reasons for residential placement. But the call for more *assessment* places makes little sense without an adequate supply of the placements indicated by the assessment process. And if more such placements *were* readily available, the flow of children through these centres would be increased and the need for more places reduced accordingly. We must bear in mind, however, that for some adolescents a period of residential assessment, even without subsequent placement, may be helpful if it provides them with an opportunity to take stock and a chance for their parents to do the same, temporarily relieved from the pressures of stressful behaviour or relationships.

Together with the problems we have noted (of waiting, the alien setting and the lack of places for children to go to next), there is the fact that, except in the cases of remand, other interim orders and in Scotland referral for reports for the hearings, assessment centres are almost always used after the decision to admit the child to care has been taken. As a result, the task of assessment for this group is narrowed and limited to selecting those forms of care which are then possible. This encourages a restricted focus which is liable to miss detailed information about the family and community from which the child comes. Less emphasis is then given to what the family and community might offer, or be helped to offer, and more attention is devoted to what the formal care system has available. For these reasons, as we have said, assessment should be carried out whenever possible before a decision is made to remove a child from home. It must be integrated with preventive work if it is to serve to strengthen care within the family and the community rather than act as an introduction to the public care system. Indeed, early voluntary admission to an assessment centre for a fixed period might be offered for some children.

We do not wish to dispute the value of residential assessment in certain circumstances; indeed such occasions are admirably described in the MIND report on assessment.[22] Yet we must consider whether the value of residential assessment is not being overemphasised and, perhaps more fundamental still, whether the reason for a child being placed in such centres is always because assessment is essential at that point. The centres are already used, as we have seen, for other purposes. But it may be that a 'spell away for assessment' also serves unstated purposes; in particular, to provide a place when alternatives break down and to satisfy everybody that something positive is being done.

In the light of all these considerations, we feel that it would be helpful to the younger child in particular if the emphasis on formal assessment could be repositioned both in place and time; back to where the 'problem' arose and back to a time before it had reached crisis proportions. We believe that the fuller development of day or domiciliary assessment is the way to do it. Whether this is equally appropriate for the adolescent before the court is less clear.

Domiciliary and day assessment

The education and health services have quite well-established arrangements whereby formal assessments are carried out in the child's own home, especially where they are physically or mentally handicapped. In many authorities, all such assessments would be conducted at home unless circumstances prevented it. By comparison the personal social services have not developed their assessment procedures along these lines, although the social workers involved with families at risk will be assessing the situation informally. They are, of course, also more likely to encounter circumstances which do not lend themselves to domiciliary assessment. Nevertheless, we would wish to see comprehensive home assessment more often considered and more often used.[23] This may not necessarily be in the child's own home; it could be in a foster home or the residential home where the child is living. It may be in conjunction with child guidance or child psychiatric clinics. In some circumstances the local school may be the appropriate place. Obviously, not all situations call for the same arrangements.

Day assessment centres also offer a promising way forward. They can be informal, local enough to know about the schools, the doctors, the police, other key figures and organisations, as well as being in a position to make observations over a number of attendances. When residential assessment centres are locally based it is clearly valuable if they can offer day arrangements as well, as some are already doing. And the child guidance clinics constitute a valuable local resource which already exists.

A combination of day and domiciliary arrangements may be an appropriate means of assessment in certain instances; not least in order that all the professions involved share common first-hand experience of the child *and* family at home. That is not to detract from the importance of the careful recording of the life histories of the parents and the child but to place these crucial data in the context of present circumstances.

In any of these settings, however, it is still essential to recognise that formal and 'comprehensive' assessments introduce a powerful factor into the situation. Even assessment at home gives no guarantee that a picture of 'how it really is' will be obtained. Although we tend to favour assessment at home or in day facilities, we recognise that much turns upon the child's age and the circumstances of his or her care.[24]

The information

Assessment is about collecting, testing and weighing information. What we say below is general and applies both to the residential and non-residential situations. We have selected those aspects of the 'information question' which we regard as of special importance in ensuring good decisions.

The processes of assessment need to facilitate the involvement of parents and children (where they are old enough) at the earliest possible stage. There is a danger that reliance will be placed upon second-hand information or upon reports derived from observations made about the behaviour of parents or children during highly selective or unusual circumstances.

There are at least two good reasons for seeking the closer involvement of parents and children wherever possible. The first is that both have a right to a say in what is to happen. (This is formally recognised, of course, in the court hearing.) What the respective parents want may be different and may in any case not be judged to be in the child's best interests. None the less their views need to be taken into account. So do the child's preferences, hopes and fears. These things in themselves are highly relevant information; and in turn introduce the second good reason for parent and child involvement. Both retain a considerable ability to upset plans of which they disapprove. The likelihood of that happening can only be determined if parents and children are consulted. Certainly, if more than lip-service is to be paid to the aim of restoring separated children to their families, parents must be treated in ways which, from the start, emphasise their continuing responsibilities; even care orders do not extinguish all rights and duties. It is also desirable in most cases for the child to feel that his parents understand and approve of the steps that are taken to safeguard his welfare, although we recognise that this may not always be possible.

We heard the argument that parents and children could not be involved in planning because they would be ill at ease and overwhelmed by the formality of assessment meetings. But if that is so (and it almost certainly is), the onus should be on the assessment team to arrange opportunities in which they do feel able to participate. The members of the working group of young people in care set up by the National Children's Bureau probably spoke for many such children when they described the resentment they felt during large case conferences, as it became clear that the assembled strangers had discussed the most intimate details about their lives.

While subscribing, therefore, to the principle of parental involvement we recognise that its effective accomplishment is not always easy. Care needs to be given to creating circumstances in which parents feel able to express themselves. Some members of the working party believe that this usually requires the privacy of a professional interview; others consider that the more public context of a decision-taking meeting is necessary, though probably more distressing. Nevertheless, if the principle is clear and accorded priority then ways have to be found for adhering to its spirit. For example, it is essential that the consideration of possible placements is accompanied by the opportunity for parents and children to know what is involved. Actually going to *see* a possible home or school will make a world of difference, often enabling them to speak out when otherwise they would have remained silent for want of information. Exactly how or where parents and children express their views is unimportant as long as an opportunity exists and their participation does not degenerate into a token gesture.

There will always be cases in which decisions have to be taken in opposition to the parents' or children's views. But they still have the right to know the grounds for these decisions. The parents of children in care who met members of the working party were adamant that the pain caused by an honest and forthright explanation of such a decision in terms they understood would be infinitely preferable to the frustration and uncertainty that come from being denied information.

There are also people other than parents who have had, or will have, responsibility for the daily care of a child. We were impressed to see how much recognition their contribution to assessment is generally accorded.

However well the assessment process is organised there remains the problem of knowing just what information is required in order to make a good decision. At any one time the child's file contains the known 'facts' about him and his situation. Documents and reports pass to and fro, are amended, reproduced or elaborated. Most decisions rely to some extent upon documentation. It is therefore of paramount importance that the facts recorded are accurate, up-to-date, relevant and comprehensible. There is no doubt that the quality of written reports varies enormously. From our scrutiny of a small selection of recorded material and from what we were told[25] we would pick out several points which require constant attention. There is certain basic information needed for successful assessment. We would draw attention to the following:

1. Knowledge of the stresses experienced by children in the past is essential. For example, children who have been repeatedly removed from home or who have suffered from more than one breakdown in a foster home are unlikely to be able to cope with a new foster home in which they are expected to form trusting relationships with their care-givers. Such children may, at least initially, adapt more readily to life in a children's home where the demands for intimacy will be less. At the same time, a child who enters care during a crisis in his previously stable family, will be helped by admission to a foster home where he is likely to form adequate emotional relationships with his substitute care-givers and can be prepared for a smooth return to his own family when the crisis is over. Provision that is suitable for one child may compound the damage that has been done to another by disturbances in his past.
2. Information is needed about deficiencies in the child's education and health. Placements away from the natural family do not always meet the most basic emotional needs of a child, but alternative care under 'public' supervision does offer opportunities for repairing gaps in a child's physical and intellectual development. For example, the self-image of an insecure child

may well be improved by first-class dental or orthodontic care, speech therapy, remedial reading or weight reduction. It is vital to identify those problems which *can* be rectified with reasonable certainty and which will strengthen the social skills and confidence of deprived children. Careful examination which covers points like these should, without fail, be part of every assessment procedure, as should an account of the child's strengths, special interests or gifts which could be developed and built on.

3. Information is needed upon which to judge the likely length of a child's separation from home. The introduction of time-limited arrangements is likely to help. But other factors, particularly the quality of knowledge about the parents, are crucial. In this respect the inclusion of up-to-date information about the social and material circumstances of the family needs particular attention. Many of the difficulties that parents, especially poor parents, face in bringing up their children cannot be related to problems of personality and background alone. They are social in origin. Great pressures can be imposed on the most stable parents by an inadequate income, poor housing, isolation from friends and relations, long-term unemployment, chronic illness and so on. We know from several studies how much the 'stacking' of problems occurs amongst parents of children coming into care.[26] We need to be able to judge which of these is susceptible to amelioration, either by deliberate intervention or with the passage of time, and what difference that might make.
4. Conversely, not all problems can be detected and understood by reference to present social conditions. Parents' life histories will be needed to gauge their capacities and likely future behaviour. Without such histories, serious illness and personality disorder (if they exist) may fail to be recognised and major errors made in decisions. Concern not to ignore the strengths, capabilities and rights of natural parents should not obscure the fact that there are some who suffer from long-term personality difficulties which jeopardise their children's well being and some who find themselves unable to undertake the task of child rearing without a degree of hostility that they find intolerable. Sufficient and relevant information is urgently needed if such parents are to be identified.
5. When recommending what placement is most suitable for a child, the everyday and ordinary features of his life need to be known. For the younger children this now seems to be standard practice:

> feeding routines, toilet habits, bed-times and toys. In the case of older children, we suspect that similar kinds of items are more easily overlooked, perhaps because it is assumed that they can tell us about their preferences and familiar routines.

In addition to suggesting what basic information is necessary if assessment is to be done well, we wish to highlight certain weak spots that seem to occur in recorded information. One is that descriptions of problem behaviour are frequently not precise enough: for example, where, when and how does pilfering take place, and with whom? What exactly was the nature of the theft or violent episode and just where did the child run to? Added to this is the risk of imprecise words being differently interpreted by different people. Adjectives such as aggressive, lazy, quiet or troublesome, spring to mind as examples. Pejorative words need to be avoided in favour of objective descriptions of behaviour. It helps if parents or children are quoted verbatim.

It is hard to practise careful discrimination. Reports tend not to be ordered by any consistent plan and then there is the risk that a ragbag of facts is assembled; possibly because they might 'eventually' prove to be relevant or simply because they happen to be available. Undisputed and proven facts are not always distinguished from hearsay and allegation. The 'facts' contained in files and reports are liable to assume a life of their own and to be repeated or paraphrased time and again without the reliability of the source being re-examined or changing circumstances being recorded. For example, we suspect that minor though dramatic details about the behaviour of the child or his parents get reproduced (albeit parenthetically) in each fresh document. Similarly, social workers' reports to consultants are liable to reappear in a condensed fashion when they in turn commit their opinions to paper. Differences in interpretation or perceptions amongst members of assessment teams are always in danger of disappearing in the homogenisation of the single report or committee decision.

Reports serve a variety of purposes. Amongst these is the aim of 'negotiating' with other controllers of resources. Reports like these seek to 'make a case' rather than to give an accurate picture of the child. Indeed, that alone may prejudice his chances of being accepted by the recommended placement. If he is accepted, however, a less than frank report may lead to wrong decisions or approaches when he gets there. It will also sour future relations between the agencies concerned.

A distinction should always be drawn between the information that is needed in order to make a decision about a child and the information that is needed by people who are providing day-to-day care. Ignorance of a child's past will usually hinder the care-taker in providing optimal care.

It may be misleading to have completely standardised checklists or forms as a basis for collecting information. As we have already suggested, a much greater differentiation of children and their circumstances (by age, problems, past history, handicap, parental history and so on) will create a sharper awareness of what needs to be known about *specific* kinds of conditions. But those conditions have, of course, first to be identified.

Several people involved in assessment impressed upon us that they did not always receive crucial information or were unable to obtain it. There was special mention of delay and the lack of good medical histories. This was not only a problem where information needed to be transmitted between organisations, it also appeared to happen within them.

Finally, we might note that recorded recommendations tend not to explain precisely what the preferred placement has to offer a particular child or to give information about its strengths and weaknesses. Indeed, as we noted earlier, details about placement options are less likely to be available than details about the child himself.

In conclusion, it must be emphasised that probably no more than a third of children in care are ever subject to a process of comprehensive residential assessment, although this would happen on almost all occasions for those admitted to special boarding education or hospitals for the mentally subnormal. Just how many children *should* be assessed in this way is hard to say. Many children are boarded out for a short term immediately upon reception whilst others go straight to a children's home. Some of them are being assessed informally and placed effectively and economically. We do not know how many. That being so, we should be at least as concerned about how placement decisions are made for this 'unobserved' two-thirds as we are in the case of the others who pass through residential assessment. Assessment for these young children who are not 'troublesome' needs to be as thorough and undertaken with the same sense of gravity as the assessment of older troublesome children before the courts.

Review

What's a review? I don't think I've ever had one.

Although the distinction between assessment and review is somewhat artificial it does serve to draw attention to the need to take stock of placement arrangements, plans and a child's general progress. We do not suggest, of course, that the child be needlessly disturbed in order to see that all is well. Indeed, constant reconsideration may engender such anxiety in foster parents and others that they are discouraged from making a proper commitment to the child. It may also have the effect of disrupting ties which were 'good enough'.

A recent unpublished study in one area of the country, which examined a sample of children in residential care, concluded that 44 per cent were considered by the social workers involved to be 'appropriately placed'.[27] There is a danger, however, that without regular reviews it is all too easy for many 'inappropriately placed' children to become regarded as 'settled'. Settled, that is, to the extent that any change of placement is traumatic. The tide of events may eventually force reconsideration and reassessment. Such events too often constitute a crisis which is brought about by the child's 'troublesome' behaviour; because caring staff issue some form of ultimatum or as a result of mounting pressure from natural parents about what they feel should happen next. Many admissions (and readmissions) to assessment centres, for example, appear to be the outcome of breakdowns in other forms of substitute care.[28] In a strangely perverse way, therefore, the sense of crisis and urgency which often makes it difficult to reach sound decisions when a child first comes into care is liable to be reproduced at the next major turning point. Ideally, reviews should be regular (but not routine) and not conducted in an atmosphere of upheaval and haste. Where necessary they should be a prelude to deliberate and carefully considered changes of plan, accompanied by adequate preparation and consultation. Yet these kinds of reviews appear to be the exception rather than the rule. Where a review is statutorily required it tends not to result in change unless it happens to coincide with some form of crisis; even though it is often accepted that matters are far from satisfactory or worsening.[29] Alternatives may not be readily apparent however and, in any case, staff working under pressure will be reluctant to precipitate more work before it becomes absolutely necessary. There is a danger that reviews may become a rubber stamp for confirming present arrangements.

As we have already intimated, some confusion exists about the nature and process of review. In some instances a review may take the place of assessment; for example, when there has been no formal assessment at intake. Case conferences are usually called to deal with critical situations, but they may turn into a review and the re-planning of a child's care or treatment. Some people see staff discussion of cases with supervisors as part of an on-going process of review.

Despite these difficulties of interpretation we consider that regular reviews should be conducted for all children in substitute care, ideally when matters have *not* reached a point of crisis. However, this cannot always be avoided and it may, therefore, be useful to distinguish between regular and special reviews. The latter could take a variety of forms depending upon the circumstances. We feel that it is the creation of an effective system of regular reviews, however, which should receive priority. Its value is at least threefold. It provides a means by which continuity in planning may be achieved. Carefully conducted, it ensures that children do not languish where they are for want of reconsideration. It also offers a way of monitoring the actual implementation of national and local policies and adds further information to the estimation of overall needs. It is difficult to set out ideal review procedures without being impractical or unhelpfully pedantic. Nevertheless, there are several major questions which call for special attention.

How far should reviews be mandatory?

There is, of course, now a requirement that each child in care should be reviewed at six-monthly intervals. In the case of those who are boarded out an initial review must be conducted within three months of placement. The third schedule to the Children Act, 1975, enables the Secretary of State to make regulations about:

1. the manner in which cases are to be reviewed;
2. the considerations to which local authorities are to have regard in reviewing cases; and
3. the time when a child's case is first to be reviewed and the frequency of subsequent reviews;

but action has yet to be taken although we understand that regulations are being drafted. We would wish to offer several suggestions about their scope.

We recommend that the initial mandatory three-monthly review of boarded-out children should be extended to all children in care. A distinction might usefully be made between regular and major reviews since not all reviews are likely to be of the same importance. Major reviews would be less frequent and perhaps coincide with the new time limits that we have suggested earlier or with those introduced by the 1975 Act. Consideration should also be given to extending the mandatory review system to children in forms of substitute care other than those provided by local social services or social work departments; for example, where children are living in their own homes but subject to supervision orders or accommodated in long-stay educational establishments or hospitals.[30]

Reviews of private foster children in particular require clarification. Research suggests that they are vulnerable to multiple moves and unsatisfactory standards of care. It also demonstrates that private foster parents, the children and the natural parents receive little attention from social workers.[31] Consequently, private foster children are subject to many of the disadvantages of separation from parents yet receive few of the safeguards due to children in care. However, local authorities do have a responsibility to oversee their well-being. The Children Act, 1975 (under section 95(3)) empowers the Secretary of State to make regulations concerning the timing of visits from social workers to these placements. These are not yet available.

We recommend that children in private foster homes be reviewed on the same time scale as children in care. Although local authorities lack the financial powers to aid private foster parents, the review system should be beneficial in two directions. First, the need to gather information for the reviews should promote closer contact between social workers and foster homes. Second, regular reviews should alert social services departments to impending breakdowns in private fosterings. Social workers could then attempt to work with the foster parents, children and natural parents either to preserve and improve the placements or to find a satisfactory alternative. Some unnecessary moves might thereby be avoided and higher standards promoted.

Lastly, guidance about all reviews should include, or be accompanied by, clear indications of *who* should be involved, *what* should be reviewed and *how* decisions arising from the review are to be implemented and checked. We turn to these issues next.

Who should be involved in reviews?

The DHSS circular on the programme for implementing the 1975 Children Act[32] has made a valuable start in providing guidance on this matter. It says:

> . . . discussions of a child's future should always include parents except where this is obviously inappropriate. Foster parents, residential staff, teachers and other people directly involved in the child's life should also be included in discussions. The welfare principle requires that so far as practicable, the wishes and feelings of the child should be ascertained when a decision is made. It is therefore essential that a child's social worker should be able to communicate with the child and those around him or her who are likely to know what the child feels. A child who is mature enough to understand the implications of such a review could be invited to be present at least during part of the discussion and review, but only in very exceptional circumstances should even a teenager be expected to carry the burden of decision about his or her future.[33]

In our experience present practice falls short of these guidelines. Their incorporation (or the incorporation of the spirit behind them) in subsequent regulations would go a long way to ensuring improvements. Where there are no parents (or where substantial differences of view are likely to arise) some of us see a case for the attendance of an independent 'child's spokesman', perhaps along the lines of the 'separate representation' of section 64 of the 1975 Act.

What should be reviewed?

A review should assess the 'success' of a child's placement as it progresses. Yet one cannot help wondering what yardsticks are used in arriving at such judgements. It seems to be relatively rare for a statement to be written into the record about the purposes of admission or the objectives of a placement. Likewise there are references on review forms to 'treatment plans' but comparatively little emphasis seems to be laid on the actual work that has been accomplished in carrying out such plans from one stage to the next. It is almost as though the review consisted of comments made on the sideline by an observer rather than a report by staff intimately involved in influencing a child's progress. This may occur especially where there are rapid changes of staff, each of whom is less than fully committed to the judgements of a predecessor. But for whatever reason, without a recorded starting point, a prior statement of expectations and an account of what subsequently happened, there is no real basis for review.

We have to look back in order to make judgements about the present. Having formed a view from this perspective, however, it has to be set alongside considerations of the future. The single biggest difficulty here is the identification and evaluation of possible alternatives. One particularly valuable, but unpublished, report on 'Positive Planning for Children' stresses that 'the idea of looking at alternatives is a crucial process which is totally ignored when placements are being reviewed. Instead, there appears to be a . . . commitment of resources to making a placement work and failure is not to be considered or recognised even when it should be apparent'.[34] But for a review (or assessment) group to be able to consider alternatives it has to possess good information about their availability and quality, as well as the capacity to think outside the standard range of provisions: especially to know about the changing circumstances of the child's family. This is not easy or inexpensive in terms of time or commitment. Nevertheless, that is the minimal price which has to be paid in order to forge a review system which *really* serves the best interests of the child rather than one which exists to place a routine seal of approval on the arrangements of the moment.

None of what we have said so far should be interpreted as a desire to see children moved more frequently. When it *is* necessary, it is usually better done early than in the eye of the storm. More often the task of reviews is to see how the existing placement might be improved; for example, with respect to developments in the child's health or education. As the 1975 Act is gradually implemented there will also be an increased need to examine a child's legal status and the changing rights of his parents. How far and when should the social worker encourage adoption or custodianship? When should 'rights and duties' be sought? Should there be an application to the court for the discharge of a care order? Some of these issues are discussed in the next section of this chapter but we can illustrate the kinds of legal issues which should arise at reviews by reference to two pieces of recent research.

A study by Lambert and Rowe of the assumption of parental rights pointed out the wide variations in practice between authorities and noted that although six-monthly reviews on all children in care were mandatory it depended very much on 'the practice and ideology of each individual authority' whether or not the assumption of parental rights was considered.[35] Moreover, it was observed that in some larger authorities variations also appeared to exist between different areas.

In another study of foster home care carried out by Shaw and his colleagues, it was shown that little discussion took place between social workers and foster parents about the possibility of adoption; despite the fact that the department concerned would have welcomed applications in about half the study cases. Moreover, about half of those foster parents in turn said that they would be likely to apply.[36] There was some potential disagreement about *which* children might be adopted but as Shaw says, 'one sad corner is occupied by children whom foster parents would like to adopt and whom social workers would be glad to see adopted but where there is no discussion and social workers assume foster parents to be uninterested'.[37] Reviews which focus on such questions with the parties concerned would dispel such assumptions.

By contrast, one can understand the apprehension about the conflicts to be confronted when reviews reveal marked differences of viewpoint; thorough reviews may well disturb matters and rekindle antagonisms. We would not wish to gloss over these problems but do suggest that regular reviews which from the start include all the interested people will reduce the likelihood that smouldering differences are pushed out of sight only to flare up later but unexpectedly.

How should any change of plan arising from a review be implemented?

The recently published guide to foster care practice[38] points out that 'to ensure that the plan formulated at the review is executed, additional decisions will need to be made concerning the action required, the methods to be adopted and the individual responsible for action'. Unless these things are decided, 'plans tend to remain written hopes on case records'. We share these views. A review must allocate tasks if work is to be done and must set time limits for their fulfilment and reporting back. Unfortunately, the six-monthly interval may be too long for these purposes and simpler means of monitoring progress and making decisions in the meantime need to be available, probably through the oversight of senior staff. Especial vigilance will be needed on their part where high rates of staff turnover prevail if the decisions emerging from the review process are to be implemented.

So far we have discussed a number of the many dimensions of the review process. We have not looked at how informal day-to-day reviews of progress and events are integrated into the more formal procedures; nor have we considered how *overall* local or national performance in child care is monitored. Though important, we are not in a position to examine the first of these additional perspectives: however, we do discuss the second question in a later chapter.

Discharge

> *You're not under their care any more, they don't have to look after you, and they're not paid to look after you, you are completely left on your own.*

Discharge from substitute care is the last of the four major decisions around which the discussion in this chapter has been organised. Although in most years nearly as many children pass out of public care as enter, the point of departure has attracted comparatively little attention. Yet, in many ways, it is the most important stage; certainly for the individual child and, more generally, because some resources are thereby released for reallocation.

Since 1972 the number of children leaving care in England and Wales has been less than the number of those received into care; with a widening gap each year. In the five years between 1972 and 1976 there has also been a noticeable increase, from 12 to 16 per cent, in the proportion of all discharges accounted for by 'attaining the ages of 18 or 19'. At the same time, the return of children below this age to the care of parents, relatives or friends has fallen, as a proportion of all discharges, from 77 to 71 per cent. The relative importance of leaving care because of adoption has remained unchanged (3 per cent). This includes those children who were specifically admitted for the purpose of adoption placement: few other children in care are adopted. The position of 'discharged care orders' (5 per cent) as a reason for going out of care has also stayed unchanged.[39]

At present, only minimal information is available about the composition of the groups of children who leave care, and there is hardly any indication of the detailed circumstances in which it occurs or how children fare thereafter. We should know more than we do about these matters. In particular, the role of the local authority *after* discharge from care might be more carefully considered. When children over compulsory school age are discharged from care, having been received under section 1 of the Children Act, 1948, the authority has a duty to provide 'after care' unless they decide that it is unnecessary. What actually happens and how are the relevant decisions made? Similarly, how often and when do authorities exercise their discretionary power to supplement the earnings of young people under 21 who have been in care?

Care resumed by the parents or parent

If the child has been 'voluntarily' admitted to care then the parents have only to ask for his return, although the requirement that they give twenty-eight days' notice once the child has been in care for six months or more has recently come into force.[40] This new provision should direct more attention to the discharge decision. Local authorities will have to decide whether to waive the month's notice in order to speed the return of the child or let the period of notice run its full course to enable preparations to be made.

Many children in care *do* return to the care of their parents, often after a comparatively short period away. It is hard to know how far this happens without major efforts on the part of social workers or how much more rehabilitation could be achieved (or achieved more quickly) given regular contacts with parents and the mobilisation of help and support. Much of what we have said about prevention could be repeated in this context. What might enable parents to keep their children in the face of adversity is likely to be similar to what is needed to help them resume their care: adequate housing;

sufficient income; day care facilities and so on. There are certainly circumstances in which the mode of discharge blends into preventive measures to avoid further admissions to care. A recent project in New York showed that intensive family case work, accompanied where appropriate by day care, home help, educational and community services, can forestall admission and hasten the rehabilitation of children in care.[41]

As in the case of reception, therefore, we must ask how many children remain in care when, with help and encouragement, their parents or relatives could assume their care. It is important, however, to note just how many children who are formally recorded as being in care on a voluntary basis are actually boarded out with relatives. In 1975 the proportion stood at nearly 9 per cent: in Scotland the proportion is probably higher but firm figures are not available.[42] When one considers that 70 per cent of these children were *already* living with these relatives when received into care, it may amount to little more than a means of helping such families financially; a not inconsiderable transfer payment through boarding-out allowances of some £1.6 million in 1975 in England and Wales.[43] It may well be that special child allowances provided through the national insurance system could achieve this equally well and without stigma.

This is an appropriate point to recapitulate that altogether 22 per cent of children in care in England and Wales in 1976 were actually living with a parent, guardian or relative: 17 950 who had been committed on care order and 4360 voluntary admissions – a total of 22 310.[44] How many of these children should or could be discharged from care is a question of considerable importance, but one which is hard to answer on the basis of present information. Nor is it easy to determine whether being 'in care' ensures more help for child and family than not being in care but regarded as 'needing support'.

The retention in care of children who are boarded out with relatives may be more than a financial device. Many of these relatives are grandparents and reception into care offers background support against the day when they die or become infirm. Although case work help may be required where the placement results from complex family problems, it is necessary to ask whether this could not be provided without the child actually having to be in care.

These observations bring us to the second way in which children may be returned to their parents before reaching the age of 18: that is, by the discharge of a care order. A juvenile court has the power to do this upon the application of a local authority, the child or the parents or guardian on his behalf. In 1976 in England and Wales 2919 orders were so discharged (about 5 per cent of those outstanding) but we do not know the sex or ages of the children concerned or the source of the initiative.[45] We do know that 8 per cent of applications under section 21(1) of the Children and Young Persons Act, 1969, were rejected in 1973.[46] In none of the authorities we visited had children themselves been known to lodge an application; indeed few social workers seemed to be aware of this right. However, as matters stand at the moment it is hard to see how an application from a child separated from his parents could easily be made.

It is more important that authorities consider the desirability of seeking the discharge of an order when children's progress is being reviewed. We must also express our concern that both older children and their parents should be aware of their rights in this matter. It is interesting to see that although the 1975 legislation (section 64) makes provision for the separate representation of the child in both opposed and unopposed applications for a revocation, only the latter provision has so far been implemented. This rather assumes an automatic coincidence of the views of the authority (opposing the parents) about the interests of the child and the interests of the child as he, or an independent person, might see them. One of the most difficult decisions that the staff of local authorities are called upon to make in marginal situations is precisely whether or not to oppose a parental application.

In order to decide whether they should themselves apply for the discharge of an order, a local authority must know enough about the parents' circumstances to be able to convince a court of law that it would be in the child's best interests to return to them. Where parents have been 'lost', or where there has been little contact, the possibility of applying for discharge may go by default.

In general we wish to stress the importance of these various discharge decisions. Local authorities should not always wait upon parental initiatives. Discharge from care should be regarded as one of a range of care options. That will be more easily achieved if the kinds of assessment and review procedures which we have suggested become more common and if long-term plans are made.

One note of caution must be added before we leave this matter. Although all parents and children need to be clear about their rights in relation to care procedures, these should be pointed out at the beginning of the transactions involved in taking children into care. A great deal of harm could be done if enthusiastic social workers, at arbitrary points in time, inform parents and children of their rights, and stimulate requests to have care orders discharged when in fact this may be detrimental to the child. The situation is quite similar to that in which a new and energetic social worker suddenly begins to arrange visits between a child and his long-lost parents, believing that this will inevitably be to the child's advantage.

It needs to be recognised that there are parents who, while guilty about having their children in care and theoretically keen to be reunited with them, cannot in fact manage a harmonious family life. Re-admission to care then follows the child's return. Quite often the bonds that the child has made with substitute parents are not evaluated adequately, nor are the child's feelings sufficiently considered. Once broken, substitute care arrangements may be impossible to restore when a child re-enters care later. It is then very difficult indeed to find yet a further adequate placement, and the chances that it will go well are diminished. Regular reviews should have as an aim the assessment of the positive aspects of the child's current placement and its contribution to his future welfare, as well as the consideration of his early return home. Only in this way can we prevent an increase in the numbers of 'yo-yo' children.[47] It may be preferable for children to be in care and to have the ties with substitute parents strengthened than to be returned to a family which is disrupted by violence and the personality disorder of a parent. Some parents may need to be helped (or allowed) to relinquish their children although this is a hard option for social workers and others to face.

Discharge through adoption

The DHSS statistics show that between 1500 and 1700 children in England and Wales are discharged from care each year because they are adopted.[48] These figures need careful interpretation. In the first place, a majority of these children are infants taken into care solely with a view to arranging their adoption. Relatively few (the actual number and ages are unknown) are children who come into care for other reasons and are then subsequently placed for adoption or adopted by their foster parents. There are also marked differences between authorities. Of the 116 authorities in England and Wales, 26 do not act as adoption agencies. A good many others have little more than a token adoption service, while about a third place twenty-five or more children for adoption each year. Some authorities encourage adoption by foster parents if natural parents are not in touch; in others, it is virtually unknown for a child in care to be adopted. These differences are almost certainly due to varying social work attitudes rather than differences in the children or in their circumstances. Unfortunately, the authorities' annual statistical returns have proved to be inaccurate in relation to adoption and thus of limited use in assessing their overall adoption work.

The Children Act, 1975, will, when fully implemented, require each authority to ensure the provision of a comprehensive adoption service in its area in conjunction with the available voluntary societies. Although the overall effect of the Act will be to reduce the number of adoptions by providing the alternative of custodianship for relatives and by discouraging adoption of legitimate children by their step-parents, the Act will make it somewhat easier for long-term foster parents to adopt the children in their care. Since November 1976, foster parents who have cared for a child for five years or more and who apply for adoption are secure in the knowledge that the child cannot be removed from their care before the hearing, except by leave of the court. This does not, of course, mean that their application will succeed, but it has important implications for the selection of foster parents and for the review of foster children. It should help to achieve more explicit planning for children in long-term care. Adoption has seldom been considered as one of the possible futures for the child in protracted care. Many social workers seem distrustful of its finality, some doubt their own capacity to achieve it and are particularly cautious because of the risks of 'failure'. Of all the options indeed, adoption seems most often to be measured against a yardstick of near perfection. By contrast, the risk of failure in foster care is more readily accepted.

Transfer

The statistical category 'discharge from care' currently includes a number of situations in which a child is transferred to another administrative system. In particular, there are those whose care is taken over by another 'authority'; those who are removed to borstal; those who go to remand centres or prison on unruly certificates and some who emigrate. There may be as many as 1000 children a year falling into these combined categories. It is impossible to judge how far such decisions are appropriate, well-considered or in the child's best interest. Particular concern has recently been expressed about the unruly certificates issued by courts in respect of children in care (section 23(3) of the 1969 Act). The Home Office evidence to the Expenditure Committee made clear that in their view local authorities sought such certificates primarily because of staffing difficulties.[49]

Attaining the age of 18 or 19

We have already suggested that the possibility of a flexible maximum age for being in care might be considered. Indeed, some children are already discharged from care when they become 'self-supporting' prior to their eighteenth birthday. However, many children only leave care upon reaching that age. Where exactly do they go? How many stay with their foster parents? How many return to one or both parents, to brothers or to sisters? How many have already begun to live independently in the community? Do, or should, the local authorities maintain contact? We have hardly begun to pose the questions, let alone discover any answers.

It might be noted that an increasing number of children are staying in care until their nineteenth birthday: presumably because care orders made after the age of 16 have increased and these remain in force until that age. In 1971, 123 young people went out of care at 19, rising to a peak of 870 in 1975 and declining somewhat in the following year.[50] Whether or not these trends are favourable or unfavourable is far from clear.

Ideally, this final point of discharge should not represent a major transition for the child. Even so, a review should be undertaken at that time. From the collected evidence which these reviews ought to provide we would learn how many young people are unemployed; how many are already parents themselves; how many are receiving higher or further education; and how many have residual handicaps of one kind or another. Such information would offer one means of monitoring the overall performance of the child care services:

given, of course, that similar information is collected at earlier stages of the child's stay in care.

Death

A small number of children die in care and, statistically, this is recorded as a discharge. These deaths deserve rather more attention than the 150 cases in 1975 and 132 in 1976 would suggest.[51] Because precise information about the ages and sex of children in care is not available, it is difficult to apply national death rates to this particular population. However, a rough estimate of the likely number of deaths amongst children in care suggests that typical figures are higher than might be expected. Once the new system of DHSS child care statistics comes into operation it will be easy to check on this, and possibly incorporate it into a set of indicators of service quality. Of course, it may be that children coming into care (the abused or neglected especially) are more at risk of dying because of their background. Yet, at the same time, it can be argued that if children survive long enough to come into care their life expectation should be normal, unless they are grossly handicapped mentally or physically. Even in these cases being in care should ensure a particularly high standard of medical supervision and safety which would offset some of these special risks. It also needs to be noted that the proportion of young children under two coming into care is falling and it is amongst them that high rates of mortality are most likely.

Our discussion of discharge (and reception) decisions may convey the impression that we consider that care systems should be self-contained, with neat boundaries at the points of entry and exit. This is not our intention. Indeed, later on we argue for a much extended range of 'intermediate' forms of care which will inevitably reduce the sharp division between being in care and not being in care.

Conclusion

We are aware that the recommendations and suggestions contained in this chapter represent enormous claims upon scarce resources. But these are such important decisions, both for the child's well-being and for future levels of expenditure, that they must be well-informed. We are quite convinced that decisions taken without due care or allowed to evolve by neglect constitute acts of irresponsibility to the children and waste public resources.

It needs to be recognised that different kinds of decisions are needed for different categories of children. For example, the decisions facing social workers and local authorities in the case of infants and toddlers under two differ substantially from those in the case of older adolescents committed to care as a result of delinquency. In the first group removal from parent figures to whom the child has become attached must be viewed as an extremely serious step and plans must be made as a matter of urgency. That does not mean that assessment should be short-circuited, but it does mean that those involved have to act without delay. In the case of adolescents, many of whom are capable of providing their own inner continuity and of participating actively in plans for their future, residential placement for assessment is not a step to be avoided at all costs and continuity of care is not at such a premium.

These are examples; but awareness of the significance of the ages and histories of children is crucial, as is an appreciation of the actual circumstances of their parents. Young couples facing early marriage breakdown; parents under stress because of physical or psychiatric illness; parents locked in marital conflict; parents confronted by poverty and poor housing all create different contexts for key decisions.

Of necessity we have been obliged to generalise in this chapter. That should not detract from the importance we attach to the need for *differentiation* in the pattern of responses to the needs of the child in care. By the same token, we do not wish our suggestions for a greater degree of *systematisation* in the key decisions to deny the need for skilful, knowledgeable and sensitive staff to exercise professional discretion. Both are required.

Part III

The Future

7

New Categories: New Resources, New Solutions

When I grow up, if I have kids I'm going to really fight to make sure they have a better life than I have.

There is a complicated variety of services for separated children. So much so that some would deny that a set of children's services with any unifying features actually exists; especially since the disappearance of the former children's departments. Yet the difficulties in discerning the precise boundaries of the 'child care system' may well be a mark of progress. We take this view because we believe that the problems which give rise to the long-term separation of children are usually complex. In turn, they require complicated solutions, many of which can only be found in a combination of responses from different individuals and organisations. Indeed, we are tempted to conclude that one of the impediments to better services is undue simplification. This appears in many guises, but especially in the kinds of categories commonly employed in this field. Social and administrative categories are, of course, necessary, and we have already argued for improved forms of classification. But when these categories are few in number, and when they are conceived as mutually exclusive, we are in danger of thinking too narrowly and too rigidly. This is liable to obscure the actual needs of children and their families and to lead to an inflexible use of available resources.

By identifying and avoiding some of the oversimplified polarities in child care policies a way may be found to improve the quality and relevance of services. We have noted the following as some of the conventional polarities; others could be added.

parental care	:	substitute care
needs	:	resources
residential care	:	community care
theory	:	practice
education	:	care
in care	:	not in care

Parental care: substitute care

Although the principle of 'shared care' now seems to be widely accepted, progress in practical terms is still slow. There is a long tradition in this country that *either* the state assumes responsibility for the care of specially dependent people *or* that families (usually the mothers) are left to manage as best they can.[1] Intervention and the provision of tangible help tend to wait upon the development of a crisis. The very notion of admission or committal to care implies a legal and physical transfer of responsibility but also carries a symbolic significance. We have developed a variety of services to advise mothers about the care of their children; to give case work support and to help families financially. The process of daily care, with its emotional and physical dimensions, has been only reluctantly shared. Day care, in particular, has been underdeveloped and home helps, where provided, have concentrated on housework not child care. Only by designating services as educational or medical (for example, nursery education rather than day care) do we seem to have been able to overcome the unwillingness to share care.

'Shared care' might mean a number of things. It may mean encouraging mutual help between families; it may mean day care or partial residential care, either regularly or at points of crisis. It may mean that certain caring tasks are shared with others. Evaluative studies are needed to assess the value of different kinds of auxiliary care and to establish the necessary ingredients of success. Alongside this there is a need for a comprehensive review of what is being done and, then, what might be done.

There may be families who cannot accept sharing the care of their children: and it is possible that those who are in the greatest need of help are the most reluctant to seek or accept it. The National Children's Bureau study *Playgroups for Children in High Need*, for example, indicated some of the difficulties in reaching the children and families in greatest need.[2] Other studies have also shown that those in most need are not always able or willing to seek relevant services.[3] It may be that families are self-conscious about their poverty and poor housing or fearful that asking for help will be seen as an admission of failure. In these circumstances help may only be sought in the most extreme situations which call for drastic solutions. Some families may find it very difficult to accept 'shared care' if, by so doing, they see their competence or worth placed in question. There may also be differences between mothers and fathers in their readiness to agree to some sharing arrangement.

It is important also to remind ourselves that it is the child who experiences shared care. How does he or she perceive it at different ages and in light of different prior experiences? Is it reassuring or bewildering?

Like so many apparently simple concepts 'shared care' is more complicated and diverse than it at first appears. None the less, we think that a rigid division between parental care and substitute care prevents the discovery of imaginative and effective ways of providing optimal care for children. The present patterns of local authority expenditure give some indication of the extent to which new balances could be struck.

Making a rough estimate of the total local authority personal social services budget spent on children and their families, about 62 per cent goes on residential care; 16 per cent on day care; 8 per cent on boarding out and 1 per cent on preventive and supportive services. Approximately another 8 per cent is spent on field social worker salaries and expenses and the remaining 5 per cent on administration. What stands out is the dominant position of residential forms of care. The expenditure on day care is almost wholly devoted to day nurseries.[4]

'Shared care' may provide the link between prevention, substitute care and rehabilitation. We believe that it is the actual tasks of daily caring which need to be shared more than they are. That is not an argument for casual discontinuity in caring, nor does it discount other forms of help in cash and kind. But it does focus upon a key issue which, although sensitive, may offer a valuable way forward both in preventing children having to be admitted to substitute care in the first place and in creating new opportunities for working with parents if substitute care becomes necessary. This brings us to a related polarity: that between needs and resources.

Needs: resources

It is easily assumed that needs (or people with needs) stand on one side of the equation and the available resources (or resourceful people) on the other. The children and parents with whom we have been concerned in this report are usually seen as forming part of the need element. Children and their parents are a little-used resource in the child care services and we have made recommendations in earlier chapters for ensuring their involvement in planning and for stimulating self-directed groups which can influence the pattern of provision. There are other examples of what we have in mind.

Parents who have faced great difficulties in bringing up their children may be able to play a valuable part in counselling (or consoling) others who are going through similar experiences. For example, mothers of newly-born handicapped children may be helped to accept and overcome feelings of anger and rejection by parents who know and understand the feelings at first hand. Furthermore, if we are to learn from past experience then ways need to be found of tapping the experience of children and parents who have faced being brought up in care. All can, and do, contribute something to the pool of direct experience. The National Children's Bureau publication *Who Cares?* is an encouraging example of what might be done in this way. As we have noted it provides a first-hand commentary on the problems of being in care from a group of children who have shared that experience.[5]

Much of what we know about stigma, social skills and personal esteem in our society indicates the profound importance of gifts and giving.[6] Self-confidence and status are related to giving; stigma and self-depreciation from constant receiving. A comfortable balance is achieved by most people through processes of reciprocal exchange. Being 'in care', or being the parents of a child 'in care', is liable to cast people into semi-permanent positions of disadvantage in these respects when, in any case, they are, or feel themselves to be, relatively disadvantaged in the first place. If their talents, skills and resources, however modest, can be recognised and used then not only might there be marginally more resources but there might also be better services. Having one's resources recognised, valued and used is, in itself, a common need. The 'new careers' projects and the DHSS-funded 'alternatives to residential care' project are examples of what we have in mind, but the principle has wider applications.

In short, we should not too quickly reach conclusio
has needs and who has resources. We might take,
example of proper uncertainty, the case of private chi
Are they regarded as a community resource or as a liabi
emphasise the needs they create and leave unmet the con ... ons
they make to day care? And then there are the elderly. Do we pay enough attention to the demographic change which is adding many more old people to our population? What might their contributions be to child care: as honorary grandparents for instance? How far could *their* needs be converted into extra resources for the harassed and hard-pressed mother or residential home staff?

Residential care: community care

Community care has been regarded as the preferable alternative to residential care, although the term is sometimes used without making clear what is meant. Community-based residential care avoids these polarised options.

By community-based residential care we mean making available reasonably small units which offer their facilities in a variety of ways to meet the needs of children and their families as they arise in reasonably local areas. Such centres would be part of the preventive *and* more permanent care resources; provide short-term back-up and respite for families facing great stress or foster homes under pressure. Some may offer opportunities for day or residential assessment. We recognise that there will always be children with rare handicaps and emotionally damaged children who will benefit by moving out of their own localities into highly specialised residential units: but they are a minority.

We appreciate that in recommending community-based residential care we do no more than reflect now widely accepted principles and this was clear from our evidence. Nevertheless, it is as well to rehearse the major advantages of community-based residential care since much remains to be done in converting principles into practice.

1. Most important of all, many children will benefit from a system of residential care which emphasises their continuing links with home and school and which is geared to meeting their common needs as children as well as their special needs as disturbed or handicapped people. Local residential care enables links with

familiar places to be maintained. Parents are better able to visit.

2. Community-based units are in a good position to offer a flexible service. It is unwise to plan all residential care on the principle that parents should accept total responsibility for their children or none at all. As we have already said, some parents can and wish to 'share care'. Those with mentally or physically handicapped children desperately need holiday breaks which are at present difficult to obtain. Residential units which are sited close to the families and schools which they serve and which are allotted the task of providing supplementary care as well as substitute care would be in a position to negotiate with parents about the timing and extent of care and would be able to offer it in a flexible and predictable manner. Our earlier discussions of time-bounded admissions to care and 'contracts' illustrate how firm arrangements might be facilitated. Parents who know that they can obtain further short-term relief at a future time are likely to be more willing and able to share care.
3. Community-based residential care offers a better prospect for the smooth return of the child or young person to his or her family and neighbourhood. It may also supplement the continuing support that is likely to be required afterwards.
4. Many of the staff in charge of residential homes who spoke to the working party suggested that their most permanent members of staff were non-resident. They were generally married women living in the immediate vicinity who often worked on a part-time basis. Community-based residential units may be able to draw upon a pool of other local people to help in various capacities and with different jobs. We are inclined to conclude from our evidence that non-resident staff who have a personal link with the neighbourhood are more likely than young unattached staff to enter into a long-term commitment to residential work. But as we pointed out in Chapter 3, much more remains to be learned about patterns of mobility, their costs and their benefits.

In a somewhat different vein the various 'intermediate treatment' projects which have been developed in the last five years or so offer a way in which older children in trouble might be helped and controlled within the community rather than in residential settings. Intermediate treatment is a requirement which may be added to a supervision order but it is, in most schemes, also used by other youngsters. While accepting the sentiment of a recent DHSS report that 'intermediate treatment is not likely to be adequate for the child whose difficulties of personality are severe or deeply rooted, whose home and family problems are intractable, or who has specific mental and physical handicap',[7] we suspect that more young people in trouble before the courts could be dealt with at least as well in intermediate treatment as residentially to their own benefit and at less expense.[8] This applies especially to the 8 to 14 year-olds.

The National Children's Bureau study of intermediate treatment defines it 'as a range or combination of programmes and provisions aimed at bridging the gap between the two extremes of compulsory removal of the young person from his family and community, and of leaving the young person in his environment without any controls or treatment provisions'.[9] This conception closely resembles our desire to avoid, wherever possible, a sharp and unhelpful demarcation between residential and community care. Of course, much of the impetus for the development of intermediate treatment has come from a concern about young offenders or those at risk of getting into trouble. It may be that this, in its turn, places an unduly restrictive interpretation upon the conception of intermediate provision. 'Intermediacy', as we see it, is about making connections between previously separate resources and moving aside established administrative boundaries. No doubt there is a danger of intermediate treatment itself becoming a new kind of fixed category in which the aims of flexibility and further development are lost. But if, from the start, the idea and practice are explored with a view to fresh applications, that can be avoided.

Although we do not know the potential demand for this variety of provision it is plain that many parts of the country remain without any such facilities at all. The Personal Social Services Council's report has pointed out that 'for too long the emphasis has been on fitting the child or young person into existing forms of provision'.[10] The idea of *intermediate* provision is at the heart of our desire to see less rigid lines drawn between residential and community care and to have resources used flexibly.

Theory: practice

Theory and practice are often treated as exclusive categories. Despite pleas for a better blend, the penetration of practice by well-grounded theory still seems to be a painfully slow process. The time lag is substantial and conventional wisdom is hard to dislodge. Evidence of this is the often-heard complaint that either no research exists about certain issues or that it remains in a highly speculative and hence unusable state.

Yet we actually know a good deal about the characteristics of good care in both residential and day facilities. It is unnecessary to feel our way forward in ignorance on all fronts. It is generally accepted that group living is difficult for young children to tolerate and that, for them, residential group care comes a poor second to foster care in meeting their emotional needs. There is also convincing evidence that it is better to place a child in a unit whose staff will remain committed to him than to keep moving him in search of an 'ideal' placement. Other work based upon comparative studies of institutions indicates that the structure and organisation of units are more important in influencing the quality of the care they provide than the characteristics of the children they admit.[11] We know that the language development of young children is most satisfactory when they are divided into small groups and when the staff who care for them directly are given considerable autonomy. The social structural features of an institution appear to have as important an impact on language development as do the personal qualities of the staff or their particular training.[12] It is also important that staff are aware of both their caring and educative functions in relation to the young children in their charge.

It is disturbing that, because of professional specialisations, theory in one field is not always linked to practice in another. Because problems look intractable from one professional perspective, it does not mean that nothing can be done. It is easy to dismiss the possible contribution of different disciplines or approaches simply because their knowledge base and practice skills are not fully appreciated.

We believe that there is a broad knowledge base from which a high quality care service can be created. The tasks are, first, those of dissemination and, second, those of providing the essence of reliable findings in a simple and easily applied form. The National Children's Bureau series of reviews on foster home and residential care research[13] is, in our view, a start, as is the DHSS guide to fostering practice.[14] But further distillation and vivid presentation are required. Training courses bear a big responsibility as do the professional bodies and employers. The media too could play an invaluable part in conveying well-grounded theory to a wide audience in a popular fashion.

Yet, even when the knowledge base is more generally appreciated its successful application demands sensitivity and commitment. It is quite possible to understand what needs to be done but be unable to accomplish it. Knowing, feeling and doing cannot be separated out in good practice.

Education: care

We have already expressed our conviction that at the pre-school stage the present administrative division between care facilities and education is artificial and unhelpful. Others, too, have made the case for combining educational and caring provision for this age group.[15] On the continent pedagogy is a recognised area of knowledge and skill, combining what we tend to refer to as child care with education. Yet the distinction between these two fields is firmly maintained in the United Kingdom, for example in various DES publications.[16]

In boarding and day schools too there is a natural preoccupation with education that at times seems to deny the other roles that teachers do and might play and the range of contributions that schools could make to the pool of community resources available for helping the children and families with whom we are concerned. We have already explained some of our ideas in the chapter on prevention.

It is a cause for concern that members of the various caring professions are often divided in their views about how best to help children at risk or in substitute care. This certainly seems to be true of teachers and social workers. Common core training may overcome some of the difficulties; and schemes whereby teachers in training spend time attached to a social worker and social workers spend time in double-harness with a teacher could contribute greatly to increasing the knowledge and skills of both professions.

As we said in the chapter on prevention, a falling birth-rate offers a particular opportunity to use school buildings in more imaginative ways. With services such as heating, plumbing and lighting already installed it would take little adaptation and furnishing to prepare rooms for extended day care in the evenings and at weekends. In this setting teachers and social workers could work together with members of the local community. But such changes depend upon the blurring of boundaries between the domains of education and social work in relation to their resources.

The problem of 'rootless' children is frequently stressed, as is the importance of providing children with continuity and a sense of belonging. In the school, where by law the child has to be for long periods, we have a ready-made place to which to 'belong'. It does not change much materially; it stands from year to year with recognisable and fairly predictable routines as well as familiar peer groups. A useful guideline might be evolved if we agreed that children who are likely to experience short- and long-term changes of home base should have this offset by *no* change in school. They should always live within travelling distance of the same school.

The implication of this recommendation might be pursued further in the case of the education of handicapped children. The Association of Education Committees, the Society of Education Officers and the National Council for Special Education all impressed upon us the need to educate children with single major handicaps within the ordinary school system and to provide more day special education units for children too disturbed or handicapped to be accommodated within ordinary classrooms.

In short, we would wish to see fewer distinctions made between education (and its resources) and care services. Some of the best care can assume an educational form; and some of the best education and efficient learning can be attained in what is narrowly regarded as a 'care' setting.

In care : not in care

One of the sharpest divisions is that between the child who is in care and the child who is not. It is readily acknowledged that the latter category contains children who are 'at risk' as well as others who are separated from their parents for long periods. Yet the fact that they are not in the care of a public body places them in a different position from the child who is in care. They are likely to receive different kinds and amounts of service. For example, the child at risk of non-accidental injury may command much attention; once admitted to care, however, contact with the family and close concern about the child may decline. Conversely, children in private foster homes or in mental subnormality hospitals who are not formally in care may receive little visiting or attention from the statutory social services unless they are admitted to care.

Children in care are likely to be perceived differently from those who are not in care, even though their circumstances be similar. Likewise, the perceptions and self-images of both parents and children tend to change when, in this respect, the child's status changes. As a working party we have also concentrated primarily upon children in care. This is because they are a recognisable group at risk of discontinuities and broken relationships. Additionally, more information is available about them.

Even when children in care live with their parents or relatives they are regarded by authorities as more like other children in care rather than like other children living at home with their parents. There are good reasons for this but the situation is inevitably ambiguous. The footnotes to the DHSS *Statistics of Children in Care* exemplify the point. They indicate that 'in arriving at these figures [the total number of children in care upon which various percentages are calculated] the number of children in lodgings, residential employment or in the *care* of a local authority and allowed to be in the *charge* of a parent, guardian, relative or friend has been deducted from the total number in care' (our italics).[17] This subtracted category, it must be noted, accounts for 20 per cent of the total number of children in care.

On the other hand, there are examples of experimental schemes in various parts of the country where local authorities and voluntary agencies have recruited and employed foster parents to look after children who are not actually in care: for instance, in cases where the parents of handicapped children need temporary respite. In other places and at other times some of these children might have been received into care.

Earlier we suggested that an additional category of short-term reception into care under section 1 of the 1948 Children Act might be helpful. There may be other circumstances where an appropriate service can be provided without recourse to formal admission. This may avoid some of the stigma likely to be associated with the status of being 'in care'. Rather than giving a service and assuming considerable parental responsibilities (or acting *in loco parentis*), the state might provide only the service. That would not imply an abdication of responsibility but it would impose a different kind of responsibility: one which focused upon working with parents, giving help and support to those caring for the children or overseeing their general well-being as, ideally, in child protection provisions. This is also what the best hospitals and schools do. In these cases there is less stigma for parents and children; and the service is also free.

We do not suggest that these kinds of loose arrangements would be appropriate in all or even a majority of cases, but in some they may offer a less drastic solution than reception into care. Moreover, they might be grouped together with day care, even though children are away from their parents for some weeks, and more easily be seen as a preventive provision.

Assessing resources

We have been at pains to reassess the use of some of the traditionally separate groups of resources available to help the child who is at risk of separation or who has to live away from his or her parents for long periods. Yet together with this reconsideration there needs to be some way of knowing just what resources *are* available at any particular time. No standard procedures exist for reviewing child care resources locally, although at the regional level the planning committees have made a useful start.

The need for a continuously up-dated local audit of resources becomes especially urgent when community-based care is expanded in preference to traditional residential facilities.[18] Preventive and supportive services, intermediate treatment and foster care depend heavily upon people rather than buildings with people in them, and so they are fluid and difficult to count. Their fluidity is, of course, their strength and there is usually no case for imposing rigid controls upon them. But we do need to monitor changes in their availability so that coherent plans can be made for meeting the needs of different groups of children within the community context and adapting to the needs of individual children as they change with time. Not least, it is quite crucial to know if community resources are lacking or disappearing; for example, as a result of urban renewal or an increasingly mobile population. What differences will changes in the levels of unemployment make; the closing of a factory; the building of several new estates; or improved opportunities for the employment of women? A shift towards community-based social work makes it essential to keep the repercussions of such changes under close review.

There is a case for a number of experimental schemes in which child-orientated community workers are attached to specific neighbourhoods with the job of locating and assessing those local resources which might helpfully augment other child care facilities. Sonia Jackson, for example, points out that the *major* form of day care in this country is private child-minding. 'Registered child-minders alone', she tells us, 'care officially for 87 000 children, more than all the local authority private and factory day nurseries put together.'[19] She might have added that this figure is only slightly less than the total number of children 'in care'. Any adequate programme of community day care must know more about these resources, their strengths and weaknesses: a kind of 'who's who' in child-minding, as well as a 'who might be who' with help (toys, advice, books) and generous support. Without some idea of the scale of day care resources it is hard to plan sensibly for substitute care provision. The two are interrelated.

Conclusion

The major theme of this chapter has been the reconsideration of the ways in which the problems and remedies associated with the need for substitute care are perceived. We do not foresee that new categories or new images alone will lead to improvement; but in some cases they may well help by achieving a fresh and more accurate assessment of what needs to be done and what might be done. In particular, we have concentrated upon the problems of evolving helpful categories.

Our present classifications often fall short of practical relevance on at least three counts. First, they are often based upon administrative categories rather than the child's circumstances. Second, they are often mutually exclusive and hence polarise our thinking around unduly simplified alternatives. Third, some derive from outdated administrative or legal requirements. In short, we argue for a review of the categories currently in use and for the development of new classifications to facilitate the integration of theory with practice and to reflect accurately the needs of children and the resources available.

8

Some Questions to End With

I keep asking how we are supposed to live a normal life . . . and no one gives me an answer.

It is customary for a report of this kind to end with a rather general plea for more research. We would like to depart slightly from this practice by posing some specific questions which, in our view, deserve attention. These questions might be tackled in various ways: by the collection of biographical information about individual children and families using the methods of literary research; sociological and psychological research studies; or by experimental medical, social work or educational projects.

It is not appropriate to advocate particular methods since the choice is governed by the question to be answered. We do, however, see particular advantage in locally-based research work. Local projects tend to be economical in their use of resources and can be sufficiently close to children and care-givers to obtain access to the qualitative information on attitudes, expectations and perceptions that is so important in this field. Relevant research and imaginative experiments can directly influence the practices of sponsoring agencies and help to boost staff morale. Also, they frequently provide lessons and prompt questions and ideas that may be used in the development of child care policy at national level.

At the same time, we must emphasise that the value of small-scale studies depends upon the availability of regular and reliable national, regional and local data about the circumstances of the children with whom we are concerned and about the resources which are available. The new unit returns to the DHSS should enable considerable improvements to be made. Smaller-scale and experimental work is no substitute for the collection and dissemination of this kind of information, although both are needed.

We have already pointed out several areas of work with children and families which could be strengthened by research. We have also discussed the need for innovative experiments which demonstrate new ways of providing support for families and their individual members. We now raise some further questions which we hope will be taken up by research workers and practitioners in the child care field.

How far can the existing stock of child care resources be advantageously rearranged?

At several points we have suggested that child care resources tend to be inflexible and difficult to put to new uses because of an overwhelming historical commitment to the bricks and mortar of residential care. We have tended to assume that only marginal changes in the use of existing resources are possible and that, because of the prevailing economic climate, it will be difficult to obtain additional resources to commit to much-needed community care projects. But how correct is the assumption about the inflexibility of resources? As a start two questions might be posed for research and experiment.

How much residential care is needed?

The question is crucial but complicated. It is complicated because it contains both normative and practical elements, and because it cannot be answered without reference to the availability, actual or potential, of alternatives. Equally important, answers will depend in part upon the variety and quality of the residential care itself. A number of observations might provide interesting and helpful points of departure in a search for answers.

Despite the growing costliness of residential care it remains extensive. How far do costs have to rise before a radical and extensive change is demanded? If, as a society, we are willing to shoulder these high costs what are the even higher costs which they are presumed to avoid? Are these presumptions correct?

In a similar vein it is important to consider *whose* interests (or what interests) are being served by certain kinds of residential care for certain children. Are they those of the family; of the administrative 'system'; of the staff; of the child; or of wider groupings within society? How far and when do these various interests conflict or coalesce?

In the past certain kinds of institutions fulfilling a particular function have been withdrawn from the stock of resources available to the health and personal social services. For example, residential institutions for epileptics were abolished in some authorities during and after the Second World War and, more recently, some authorities have ceased to provide residential nursery provision. Little is known about the impact of such marked changes of policy although the recent tendency to discharge large numbers of long-stay psychiatric patients from hospital has been accompanied by disturbing accounts of the neglect that they have subsequently suffered within the community. Historical case study research into the impact of the withdrawal of certain residential services is needed in order to begin to assess the capacity of families and neighbourhoods to 'reabsorb' adults and children who were previously set apart by circumstance or handicap. Information might thus be gained about the costs of community care to the individual and his family and about the additional burdens (if any) imposed upon community health, education and social services by individuals who have been discharged from residential care.

It might also be illuminating to look in detail at the child care practices of minority groups who appear to make little use of public substitute care services, and hence residential care. In one of the large metropolitan district authorities we visited we were told that no Jewish child was in care and yet the Jewish population numbered some 50000. And in other authorities there were indications that comparatively few Asian children were in care. It would be valuable to discover whether these communities experience child care problems that are different in kind from those experienced by the majority of the population or whether they respond differently to the same child care problems because they do not consider public care as a way out of their difficulties. Do groups who are under-represented in the population of separated children actually not encounter such intense problems, or do they have access to alternative systems within the community which may be preferable and from which we could learn? Or do their problems emerge in a different form and place to be counted in quite different sets of statistics?

Answers to such questions might begin to be supplied if, for example, an experimental project were established in which professional care-givers and ordinary members of the community co-operated to plan alternative methods of care, control and help for children who have come to be regarded as sufficiently difficult, handicapped or vulnerable to require residential care. A limited area of a local authority (perhaps a set of neighbourhoods served by one area team) might be chosen as a suitable location for such a scheme. Local authority social services workers, voluntary agencies, self help groups, families and neighbours would then be invited to work together to deal with child care problems within that area for a period without resort to residential care. A project of this kind would aim to demonstrate the range of options that actually exists for managing child care problems in informal or in organised ways within the community. It would also help to pinpoint those children for whom community care is not 'good enough' in providing the security, stimulation or intensive care they require, and who therefore need good residential care.

'Good residential care', however, begs the question that we have posed. Under what circumstances *is* residential care 'better' than community care, or vice versa? And for how long? How are comparisons to be made? Research into such questions is well known to pose very difficult methodological problems. For example, for ethical reasons children cannot be randomly allocated to resources and grave difficulties arise in trying to match groups of children or groups of resources. An appreciation of the difficulties, however, should not excuse us from moving forward with comparative studies as far as the constraints allow.

The question of just how much residential care is required is one important aspect of the size and arrangement of child care resources. There are other related questions which we hope will be considered by research workers and practitioners in this field. We discuss one of them briefly below.

Can residential units be converted successfully into community-based multi-purpose centres for families and children?

In an earlier chapter we suggested the advantages of a system of community-based residential units which serve small, well-defined neighbourhoods and which offer a variety of services to local families and children.

During our deliberations we were able to meet the head of a children's home in London who for several years has offered day care and short-term respite care as well as permanent residential care to children and parents from the surrounding community. She spoke frankly to us about the difficulties that this policy has generated. There were obvious administrative problems and more fundamental dilemmas about the extent to which services should prop up obviously disintegrating families.

We acknowledge the gravity of these problems but we would nevertheless welcome the development of 'mixed' residential centres of this kind as demonstration projects. Their obvious advantage lies in the flexible mixture of day care and residential care which they are able to provide so that parents are not forced to make premature decisions to seek permanent residential care. They would also appear to offer an obvious focus for health care and welfare rights counselling for vulnerable families and to offer substantial benefits to children in permanent residential care by enhancing the participation of the community in the life of the unit. Such community-based centres can also provide opportunities for education and training in pedagogy – that is, child care and the education of young children – for social workers and teachers as well as mothers and fathers.

Do clients and professionals hold different views about the purposes and effectiveness of child care services?

The view of the child care services which is held by their workers and which is reflected in reports such as this is likely to differ from the view which the client holds.[1] We imply that statutory provision is at the centre of the child care system and that voluntary agencies and informal care systems are satellites which operate somewhere on the periphery. Moreover, we imply that the services can be understood as forming a recognisable network of provision, despite divided responsibilities and poor communications we know exist.

But how do these services appear to the recipients? Our essentially harmonious picture may be unrecognisable to parents and children who receive a range of unconnected services from a series of apparently unrelated helpers or who see statutory services as a mere adjunct to the mutual aid networks and informal care systems that provide a central source of support.

We need to understand how parents and children interpret their experiences of professional help if we are to provide assistance and care that they consider appropriate to their needs. Our understanding has already been increased by such work as Bayley's[2] study of the families of more than fifty grown-up mentally-handicapped children in Sheffield. He established that the central preoccupation and means of survival for these families was the maintenance and management of the daily routine which centred on the care of the handicapped child. The help which they judged to be most important was that which was sufficiently permanent, regular and reliable to be incorporated into this routine. Significantly, families tended to receive this kind of help from their own members and relatives rather than from professional workers. The intervention of the social services department was seen as significant when it resulted in permanent day care for the handicapped person but otherwise it tended to be too short-lived, too infrequent and too unrelated to the practical problems of daily living to 'make any difference' to the families concerned.

Studies of this kind need to be repeated with families experiencing different kinds of stress in order to discover whether the timing, duration and location of social service help is regarded as appropriate by families who are struggling to cope with chronic problems. It may be that while social workers see their clients' problems as comprising a succession of crises, the clients themselves see these problems as continuous and repetitive and are preoccupied with managing the daily grind of life under stress. If so, important questions need to be asked about the level and direction of family services. Should the current emphasis on crisis intervention be augmented by a more comprehensive (and in some ways less ambitious) system of routine practical support? And what are the limits of such support, especially where families face internal problems of great severity?

Together with this the different ways the same help is experienced by individual members of families also needs to be explored. As we suggested earlier, services which are well adapted to the needs of mothers (or fathers) may be less well designed to help their children, and vice versa.

How are child care services allocated?

It is tempting to assume that important decisions about receiving children into care, discharging them from care, providing day care services and so forth, are based upon rational and predictable criteria and that one can expect a reasonable degree of uniformity in the ways in which services are provided in different parts of the country.

Authoritative studies on the distribution of child care resources, however, have for a long time demonstrated the tenuous relationship between measurements of need and levels of actual provision.[3] Evidence from the authorities we visited also suggest that patterns of service provision can vary considerably between the area teams of a single social services department. For example, rates for reception into care are sometimes highly variable, and the differences cannot always be explained by contrasting local conditions.

We believe that there is a need to examine such variations at local level by looking in depth at the decisions which underlie the distribution of resources. Hall's study[4] has demonstrated the important role played by receptionists in filtering clients to social workers. More needs to be known about the roles of other advisers encountered by the client along the path to social services departments and other statutory agencies, about the routines used by the professional workers in matching clients and services, and about the parts played by management in directing practice by drawing up guidelines and policy statements for workers.

Finally, there is interesting work yet to be done on the fate of families whose applications for the reception of their children into care are refused. One might compare their responses and subsequent development with those of families in similar circumstances whose children are admitted to care.

What happens when children are discharged from care?

The responsibilities of a local authority or of a voluntary child care agency are discharged when a child in care reaches the age of 18 or 19, although limited powers exist to provide a degree of support beyond this age. The quality of care a child receives could be expected to be reflected in the quality of life upon leaving care, but very little information has actually been collected about the subsequent careers of children leaving foster homes or residential units at the age of 18.

Two very different pieces of research are called for in the examination of this question. First, we need some broad statistical data comparing the development of young adults who have been in care with a group of contemporaries who have not. We would wish to find out more, for example, about comparative rates of delinquency, levels of income and employment, and ages of marriage and divorce. The National Child Development Study has generated comparative information about a younger age group of children and one hopes that this comparative work will continue into the early adult life of the cohort.[5]

To complement this quantitative work, it would be necessary to gather biographical data from individual children leaving care. We need to know how children themselves see the impact of care upon their own future lives as workers, spouses and parents. We also need to know how far children retain links with their life in care. Do they regard the foster home or children's home as a refuge to which they can return or do they deliberately sever their links with the substitute care-givers as soon as they attain independence? Are there differences between voluntary and statutory services in this respect?

How is good substitute care to be realised?

Sadly, substitute child care services tend to be evaluated on the basis of their failures. Rates of breakdown for residential and foster home placements offer an obvious indicator of the outcomes of care but we know less about those arrangements which are successful, sometimes against the apparent odds. A useful and morale-boosting piece of research might look at such satisfactory arrangements and investigate the procedures that were used to match child with care-giver, to involve the parents in planning, to supply information to the care-giver about the family's background and so forth. Excellent work *is* being carried out in some foster homes and in some residential homes and it would be a great advance if any common features could be identified as a guide to improved practice. We know, with increasing confidence, *what* constitutes good child care, particularly for the younger age groups. The link still to be found in many instances is *how* these constituents are to be realised for separated children of different kinds.

Appendix A

Background Information to the Working Party

Methods of work

The working party began its task early in 1975. It met on seventeen occasions and also devoted a residential weekend to its deliberations. Subgroups were formed to consider particular issues as well as to visit local authorities and voluntary organisations. Work progressed partly by discussions within the working party; by the preparation of individual notes and papers; later, by considering and reviewing the various evidence which we received. We were not able to undertake research of our own, nor could we embark upon a comprehensive examination of the relevant literature. However, our secretary did provide a series of valuable information papers which aided our deliberations. Although we have paid close attention to the evidence that we received, the report does not summarise it: rather the evidence was used to inform and guide our thinking.

The evidence was gathered in the following ways:

1. By visiting seven local authorities in England, Wales and Scotland where we talked to staff who planned and provided child care services within education, social services and social work departments. We were able to visit a large hospital for mentally subnormal children and on several occasions talked to practitioners from the regional health authorities. In one authority we talked to a group of foster parents.
2. By inviting written evidence from local authority associations, voluntary child care agencies, professional associations, interest groups and pressure groups.
3. By visiting branches of Dr Barnardo's and the National Children's Home.

4. By talking to children and parents. We were grateful to parents who wrote to us after seeing items about the working party in the press. But we would especially like to thank the parents from London and Nottingham who came to the Bureau to meet us and the young people from the *Who Cares?* working group who talked to us and made available to us transcripts of their own discussions.
5. By holding a number of seminars on special topics. We are grateful to those who joined us for these meetings.

Organisations and groups who provided evidence

Association of County Councils
Association of Education Committees
British Association of Social Workers
Campaign for the Mentally Handicapped
Church of England Children's Society
Community Schools Staff Association
Convention of Scottish Local Authorities
Dartington Social Research Unit
General Nursing Council for Scotland
General Nursing Council of England and Wales
Gingerbread
Guild of Service
Invalid Children's Aid Association
Joint Council for the Education of Mentally Handicapped Children
Mind
National Association of Certified Nursery Nurses
National Association for the Welfare of Children in Hospital
National Council of Civil Liberties
National Society for Mentally Handicapped Children
Parents without Partners
Queen's Nursing Institute
Royal National Institute for the Blind
Royal National Institute for the Deaf
Rudolf Steiner Schools
Society of Education Officers
Spastics Society

Appendix B

Possible Classifications of Children in Need of Long-term or Recurrent Substitute Care and of their Circumstances

Age

The age of children is a factor of the utmost importance and any system of classification must incorporate this dimension. Obviously there are a number of different groupings. We suggest the following:

1. *Newborn babies and infants under a year.* This group would include certain illegitimate babies; babies whose mothers have deserted them; have died; or who are hospitalised or imprisoned for long periods; babies at risk of non-accidental injury or neglect. Here, problems of parental assessment arise, especially in terms of determining the probable duration of substitute care and the consistency with which parents can see a plan through. There are also the special child care needs of infants to be taken into account, wherever they may receive care outside their families and however long the care may be required.
2. *Children aged between 1 and 4 years.* Once on their feet children are less likely automatically to accompany their parents into hospital, live with relatives in a crisis or go with them when they move to temporary lodgings. Mothers are more likely, when separating from husbands, to leave these young children rather than babies behind. At these ages children are at the height of

their attachment-seeking stage, most susceptible to discontinuity of care and, if requiring long-term placements, most susceptible also to deprivations of bonding. Moreover, the capacity to form new, long-lasting attachments declines after about the age of 3 years, so that permanent substitute care must, if possible, be arranged before that age. Children in this and the younger age group are still relatively easy to look after, since they do not usually display serious behavioural or educational difficulties to adequate care-takers. Wetting, soiling, eating problems and interrupted sleep are the main difficulties.

3. *Children aged between 5 and 10 years.* Children in this broad age band can be very disturbed, depending on their life experiences. They do not form new attachments easily. They do not forget their former attachment figures. They may still operate with pre-logical (animistic) thinking and tend to misperceive the reasons for their own predicament. They are still very dependent on the adults who look after them for information and explanations. They may be much more difficult to look after than younger children and they require more highly skilled substitute parents and also more investment of physical resources as well as of time in maintaining relationships between their families and their substitute parents. Unless looked after by people who provide adequate role models and who are also personally committed to the child and have an 'investment' in his future, children of this age will be deprived of some essential ingredients of normal childhood.
4. *Children of 11 and upwards.* By this age children have acquired their basic personality traits. They have entered a stage of rational thinking and are by no means as dependent and vulnerable as younger children. They can be expected to participate actively in decisions about their own futures, a responsibility that should not be imposed upon children during their earlier stages of development. Their needs are different from the needs of younger children. They often present a difficult challenge to their substitute parents: problems of adolescence are likely to be accentuated and hard for adults to accommodate.

Finer age graduations might be constructed: the importance of age differences at points of major decision cannot be overemphasised. In considering children's futures the obvious fact of growing up must be recognised.

Medical and educational factors

The factor of age relates to developmental considerations. There are others which might be termed medical and educational. A number of groups defined in these terms might also usefully be identified:

1. *Basically healthy children requiring care because of family bereavements, breakdown or pathology.* This is probably the largest group. One important requirement is to *know*, with reasonable confidence, whether a child is or is not basically healthy and without impairments. That can only be established by regular and comprehensive medical examination and treatment as well as a comprehensive psychological examination and treatment where required.
2. *Children with severe physical handicaps.* This is a smaller group but one which needs separate consideration at all ages. There are probably two valuable and main subdivisions. First, there are children who are separated from their parents for *other* reasons but who are also handicapped. Second, there are those whose handicaps require periods of separation from parents; for example, for the treatment of congenital malformations such as spina bifida. In these cases parents usually provide continuity and expect to resume care as soon as possible.
3. *Children with severe mental handicaps, with or without associated physical handicaps.* Few will need to be separated from parents for purposes of treatment; many more will need substitute care when handicap is combined with family disruption or rejection. High grade defectives should be able to receive similar kinds of substitute care as normally intelligent children and even severely handicapped physically healthy children can be accommodated in small children's homes provided there are adequate medical and educational support services.
4. *Children with special educational needs requiring residential schooling.* Again there are those who are separated because of their education needs and others for whom the separation is determined largely by family and social circumstances. The former group includes children in rural areas where low population density does not support the full range of special day school provisions catering for the blind, deaf and those suffering from specific education retardation or psychiatric disorder. It should

be noted that children in this category are over 5 years old except for deaf and blind children whose education is usually started earlier even when this has to be on a residential basis. Within this latter group children may be at special risk of inadequate care.

Circumstances of reception into care

Another useful basis for classification may be found in the circumstances in which children come into care, certainly for initial planning decisions. We suggest some subdivisions below.

1. *Children admitted to care with a view to adoption.* There is a small number of cases where adoption is the acknowledged reason for admission. The category may grow in size as the provisions of the 1975 Children Act are implemented.
2. *Collapse of previous substitute care arrangements.* This would include cases where private fostering can no longer be continued, for example. Children will often already have experienced dislocation and sometimes a variety of *ad hoc* arrangements for their care. It may be helpful to consider separately those children who have been living with relations who are no longer able to care for them, such as elderly grandparents.
3. *Breakdown of family.* Occasionally caused by a parental death, but increasingly the result of divorce or separation in which the single-handed parent is unable to care for the child. 'Inability', of course, begs many questions about other support services both of day care and income maintenance.
4. *Compulsory separation.* Where placement away from the family results from care or criminal proceedings in the juvenile court or, in Scotland, appearance before a children's hearing or the Sheriff. It is helpful to distinguish between the main categories of care proceedings – neglect, ill-treatment, non-attendance at school – and offenders. There is also the rising number of admissions to care as a result of matrimonial proceedings.

Although these suggestions focus upon the circumstances of admission to various forms of substitute care, there may be a parallel set of categories to be developed when changes of substitute care are contemplated or changes in legal status occur (for example, the assumption of parental rights).

Parental circumstances

A classification of the circumstances of the child's parents may also be helpful in practice although most often there is a considerable overlap between the groups listed below, a crisis arising when more than one disadvantage exists simultaneously.

1. *'Normal' parents in temporary situations of stress or incapacity.* Perhaps optimal intervention is to remedy the source of stress whilst providing the minimum of substitute care that will enable the family to cope. It may be useful to draw a further distinction between two- and one-parent families.
2. *Parents with chronic handicap.* Where one or both parents suffers from physical or psychiatric handicap or both.
3. *Unstable parental relationships.* Changing parent figures, separations and reunions often associated with high levels of mobility and with family disharmony.
4. *Personality disordered parent(s).* Intense marital disharmony, domestic violence, excessive drinking, overt sexual perversion and hostility to children.

We offer the above categories as a checklist of the important considerations in the evaluation of children, parents and their circumstances. Throughout the body of the report we have argued for more practical groupings and for the dismantling of large and unhelpful administrative categories in order that the needs of children may be considered in a more specific and relevant fashion. Yet such description is not a once-and-for-all process. As time passes and conditions alter, reformulations are needed in the light of up-to-date information.

We have not considered the classification of resources in this appendix, although that too is much needed. A start has been made in studies such as Moss's survey of residential provision[1] and Holman's essay on foster parents.[2] But much more needs to be done.

Appendix C

Some Statistics about Separated Children

Introduction

Arriving at an estimate of the total population of separated children using the different official statistical sources is a difficult and perplexing undertaking. The form of the statistics is liable to differ between England and Wales, Scotland and Northern Ireland. Major legislative changes, such as the 1968 Social Work (Scotland) Act and the 1969 Children and Young Persons Act make it hazardous to draw reliable comparisons between the years before and the years afterwards. There is considerable risk of double-counting because, for example, many children live in accommodation not directly under local authority control or which is used by one department although provided by another. Moreover, the dates in the year on which the local education authorities, social service departments and health authorities submit their returns often differ. Some make twice-yearly returns. There may be as much as two years' difference in the speed with which the statistics of the various organisations are published: hence, comprehensive figures are always related to the last year in which the most laggardly bodies produce their material. There is also a penumbra of provisions in the private sector which is almost certainly under-represented in the returns.

On top of all these difficulties, the working party was often reminded that they should treat various official statistics with caution, since interpretations and degrees of accuracy varied from authority to authority and within an authority at different times. In short, we can make no more than informed guesses in many instances. Even these, it must be remembered, refer to a population at one point in time. More children *throughout* a year are likely to have experienced the substitute provision in question. We have little idea how large this more realistic total might be.

Children living in 'non-private' accommodation

Information is given in Table A.1 (pp. 164–5) about the number of children, below the age of 15, accommodated in non-private establishments. A breakdown of the population of children by age and by type of accommodation is also available. It is important to bear in mind that these were children resident on census night. They may have been temporary or more permanent residents.

Some trends in the statistics of children in care of local authorities

Table A.2 (pp. 166–7) shows some trends in the statistics of children in the care of local authorities in England and Wales in 1956, 1966 and 1976.

TABLE A.1 *Children living in 'non-private' accommodation: information from the 1966 Sample Census and the 1971 Census, England and Wales*

Total population of children enumerated in non-private establishments by age

	Number of children	
Age	1966	1971
0–4	39 370	36 050
5–9	30 390	32 930
10–14	52 930	80 975
Total	**122 690**	**149 955**

Children accommodated in psychiatric hospitals

	Number of children	
Age	1966	1971
0–4	630	705
5–9	2 430	2 170
10–14	3 610	3 505
Total	**6 670**	**6 380**

Children accommodated in all other hospitals

	Number of children	
Age	1966	1971
0–4	19 130	20 960
5–9	5 190	4 970
10–14	4 810	3 765
Total	**29 130**	**29 695**

TABLE A.1 *continued*

Children accommodated in homes for the disabled

	Number of children	
Age	1966	1971
0–4	280	45
5–9	110	65
10–14	80	100
Total	**470**	**210**

Children accommodated in places of detention

	Number of children	
Age	1966	1971
0–4	20	35
5–9	20	35
10–14	3950	3175
Total	**3990**	**3245**

Children accommodated in children's homes and educational establishments

	Number of children	
Age	1966	1971
0–4	7500	5205
5–9	9940	10050
10–14	12440	12200
Total	**29880**	**27455**

SOURCE Housing Tables (part I), Census Reports.

TABLE A.2 *Some trends in the statistics of children in care of local authorities in England and Wales*

1. Proportion of children received into local authority care under the age of 5 years during the preceding year
2. Proportion of children in local authority care under the age of 5 years at 31 March
3. Proportion of children received into local authority care over school-leaving age in the preceding year*
4. Proportion of children in local authority care over school-leaving age at 31 March
5. Proportion of boys in local authority care at 31 March
6. Proportion of all children admitted to local authority care in the preceding year who were committed by the courts
7. Proportion of all children in care at 31 March who were committed by the courts
8. Proportion of all children admitted to care during the preceding year who were committed by the courts as offenders
9. Proportion of all children admitted to care during the preceding year who were committed by the courts under care proceedings
10. Proportion of all committed children in care at 31 March who were allowed to be in the care of a parent, relative or friend
11. Proportion of all children in care on 31 March who were boarded out
12. Proportion of all children in care on 31 March who were boarded out with a relative
13. Proportion of all children in care on 31 March who were actually living with a parent, guardian, relative or friend
14. Proportion of all children in care on 31 March who were accommodated in residential homes†
15. Children accommodated in residential nurseries on 31 March as a proportion of all children in care under 5 years
16. Proportion of children discharged during the preceding year who had reached the ages of 18 or 19

SOURCE Compiled from *Children in Care of Local Authorities in England and Wales*, 1956, Cmnd. 3204; 1976, HC 506.

* The school-leaving age was raised from 15 to 16 as from the start of the new academic year 1972. Thus 1973 was the first full year of the new requirement. Before then it was plain that 'children received into care over school-leaving age' meant the 15, 16 and 17 year olds. The statistics for the year ending 31 March 1973 continued with the same designation so that one might assume that half of that year's intake were only the 16 and 17 year olds. One would expect to see a reduction in the numbers. In 1974 for the first time the statistics noted the age groups of children coming into care in the preceding year as at 31 March 1974. This will mean that some 15 year olds are still included. The variation in specifying ages at reception since 1974 may have the general effect of slightly exaggerating the number of older children coming into care (items 1 and 3).

TABLE A.2 *continued*

1956		1966		1976	
%	No.	%	No.	%	No.
55	21 200	55	30 000	36	18 800
18	11 200	22	15 300	12	12 400
2	900	4	2 100	4	2 300
20	12 500	21	14 600	20	20 200
55	34 600	55	38 000	61	61 000
8	3 100	9	4 700	25	12 900
30	18 700	32	22 400	51	51 600
na	na	3	1 400	11	5 600
na	na	6	3 300	14	7 200
na	na	20	4 400	35	18 000
43	27 100	46	31 800	33	33 100
9	5 800	7	5 100	4	4 400
na	na	14	9 500	22	22 300
46	28 500	39	27 000	41	40 900
40	4 400	20	3 000	15	1 900
10	3 800	8	4 300	16	8 300

† It is difficult to arrive at a satisfactory definition of residential care: these figures included special schools for the handicapped but exclude children in 'hostels'. To obtain a 'corrected' figure for 1956 and 1966, the number of children in approved schools should be included (after the 1969 Children and Young Persons Act they were counted as 'in care'). For 1966 this raised the number in residential care to 36 600 and the proportion to 46 per cent.

OBSERVATIONS

1. Noteworthy 'relative' *and* 'absolute' changes: items 1, 6, 7, 8, 9, 10, 13, 15 and 16.
2. Noteworthy 'relative' changes: items 2, 5 and 11.
3. Noteworthy 'absolute' changes: items 3, 4 and 14.

Notes and References

Preface

1. R. Dinnage and M. K. Pringle, *Foster Home Care – Facts and Fallacies* (Longman, 1967); Dinnage and Pringle, *Residential Child Care – Facts and Fallacies* (Longman, 1967).
2. H. Prosser, *Perspectives on Foster Care* (NFER, 1978); Prosser, *Perspectives on Residential Care* (NFER, 1976).
3. J. Cooper, *Patterns of Family Placement* (National Children's Bureau, 1978).
4. J. Parfit (ed.), *The Community's Children* (Longman, 1967).
5. R. Page and G. Clark, *Who Cares? Young People in Care Speak Out* (National Children's Bureau, 1977).

Chapter 2

1. Sources for Table 2.1 are *Children in Care of Local Authorities in England and Wales* (1956) Cmnd. 9881; (1966) Cmnd. 3204; and (1976) HC 506. Also Home Office, *Reports of the Work of the Children's Department* (1961–3) HC 155; and (1964–6) HC 603. For Scotland see *Children in Care of Local Authorities in Scotland* (1957) Cmnd. 461; *Child Care* (1966) Cmnd. 3241; and *Scottish Social Work Statistics* (1974).
2. See, for further discussion on the Scottish system, P. Parsloe, *Juvenile Justice* (Routledge and Kegan Paul, 1978) and J. Spencer *et al.*, *Face to Face with Children* (MacDonald, 1976).
3. Sources for Tables 2.2, 2.3, 2.4 and 2.5 are as for Table 2.1 and in addition Home Office, *Seventh Report of the Work of the Children's Department* (1955), *Statistics Relating to Approved Schools, Remand Homes and Attendance Centres in England and Wales for the Year 1966*, HC 541.
4. See the annual statistical returns, *Children in Care of Local Authorities.* The pattern of numbers in registered foster homes is as follows: 1962 – 7297; 1966 – 10 600; 1970 – 10 811; 1973 – 11 180; 1976 – 8707.

5. See for example, R. Holman, *Trading in Children* (Routledge and Kegan Paul, 1973).
6. DHSS, *Mentally Handicapped Children in Residential Care* (Harvie Report) (1974).
7. DHSS communication.
8. See *Children in Care of Local Authorities* for respective years for the data in Table 2.6.
9. OPCS, *1971 Census of Great Britain: Housing Tables – Non-Private Households*.
10. P. Moss, 'Residential Care of Children', in J. Tizard, *et al.* (eds), *Varieties of Residential Experience* (Routledge and Kegan Paul, 1975).
11. For a more detailed commentary see, for example, *Leedings Child Care Manual* (Butterworth, 1976 edn).

Chapter 3

1. DHSS and DES, *Fit for the Future: Report of the Committee on Child Health Services* (Court), Cmnd. 6684, 1976.
2. Ministry of Housing and Local Government, *Report of the Committee on the Staffing of Local Government* (1967) pp. 48–50, Tables 3.20 and 3.21. See also *Report of the Work of the Children's Department*, 1964–6, HC 603 and 1967–9, HC 140. Although the trend was upward it must be noted that part of this was accounted for by the inclusion of those qualifying for the Declaration of Recognition and Experience introduced as from 1965. It is interesting to see that about 10 per cent of staff initially meet the requirement, which varied from nine to fourteen years prior experience.
3. See for example, OPCS, the *Introductory Report of the General Household Survey* (1973). This shows that in 1971 in Great Britain 51 per cent of households with professional heads had moved in the last five years compared with a national average of 35 per cent. About 20 per cent of the 'professional households' had moved more than once during the same period.
4. DHSS, 'Local Authority Social Services Departments: Social Service Staff, 1973', 1974 S/F74/1, unpublished.
5. DHSS, *Manpower and Training for the Social Services* (1976).
6. Department of Employment, *Report of the Inquiry into the Work and Pay of Probation Officers and Social Workers*, Cmnd. 5076 (1972). See Appendix II, especially Table 3C, p. 81.
7. *Manpower and Training*, p.1.
8. E. M. Goldberg, R. W. Warburton, D. J. Fruin and B. M. McGuinness, *Towards Accountability in Social Work* (1976) unpublished preliminary report, p.11.
9. Calculated from figures provided in the Chartered Institute of Public Finance and Accountancy, *Local Health and Social Services Statistics*, 1973–4 (1975) col. 210. Returns are provided for about 85 per cent of local authorities.

10. See for example, A. S. Hall, *The Point of Entry* (Allen and Unwin, 1974).
11. See note 9.
12. *Manpower and Training*, Chapter 2.
13. Derived from Home Office, *Criminal Statistics, England and Wales* Cmnd. 4398 (1969) (see especially pp. 197–8 and tables I(d) and (e), 'Proceedings – Magistrates' Courts'); and DHSS, *Children in Care of Local Authorities in England and Wales (March 1976)*, HC 506 (1977).
14. Calculated from *Criminal Statistics*.
15. See *Children in Care of Local Authorities*.
16. *Eleventh Report from the Expenditure Committee, Session 1974–5, The Children and Young Persons Act, 1969, Vol 1*, HC 534-i, see paras. 101–3. 'The heads of approved schools could, but rarely did, refuse to accept children. During the reorganisation they have taken a much greater authority to themselves in this field.'
17. K. Judge, *Rationing Social Services* (Heinemann, 1978) p. 8.
18. *Public Expenditure to 1979–80*, Cmnd. 6393 (1976) para. 2, p. 94.
19. *The Government's Expenditure Plans*, Cmnd. 6721-i (1977) p. 14.
20. Judge, *Rationing Social Services*, Table 7, p. 93.
21. R. Klein (ed.), *Inflation and Priorities* (Centre for Studies in Social Policy, 1975).
22. See for example, K. Judge, 'Economic Analysis and Productive Efficiency in the Personal Social Services: the Differential Use of Manpower', *International Journal of Social Economics*, III, 2 (1976) p. 89.
23. DHSS, *Children in Care of Local Authorities in England and Wales*, Cmnd. 3063 for 1965 and HC 506 for 1976.
24. DHSS, *Priorities for Health and Personal Social Services in England: A Consultative Document*, 1976, and *Priorities for Health and Social Services: The Way Forward*, 1977. See also *A Joint Framework for Social Policies*, (report by the Central Policy Review Staff, 1975).
25. See *Criminal Statistics*.
26. *First Report from the Select Committee on Violence in the Family: Violence to Children, Vol. 1, Report*, Session 1976–7, HC 329-i (1977) p. xv.
27. *Public Expenditure to 1979–80*.

Chapter 4

1. DHSS, *Manpower and Training*, (1976) para. 9.11, p. 64.
2. See for example, J. A. Schofield, 'The Economic Return to Preventive Social Work', *International Journal of Social Economics*, III, 3 (1976).
3. *The Report of the Committee on Local Authority and Allied Personal Social Services* (Seebohm), Cmnd. 3703 (1968) Chapter XIV.
4. See for examples, DHSS and DES, *Low Cost Day Provision for Under-Fives*, 1976. Also J. Tizard, *et al.*, *All our Children* (Temple-Smith/New Society, 1976).

5. DHSS and DES, *Low Cost Day Provision for Under-Fives*; B. Plowden, 'Low Cost Day Care Facilities, and the Part Which is Being and Can Be Played by Voluntary Organisations', p. 17. See also DHSS circular LASSL (76)5, 'Co-ordination of Local Authority Services for Children under Five'.
6. M. Bone, *Pre-school Children and the Need for Day Care* (OPCS, 1977) p. 13.
7. Bone, ibid., Chapter 4.
8. Estimated from DHSS, *Children in Care of Local Authorities in England and Wales, March 1976*, HC 506 (1977).
9. *Concern* (Autumn 1975) p. 18.
10. Central Policy Review Staff, *Services for Young Children with Working Mothers* (1978); TUC, *Under Fives* (1977).
11. DHSS and DES, *Low Cost Day Provision for Under-Fives*, p. 2.
12. Bone, *Pre-school Children and the Need for Day Care*, p. 8.
13. See for instance the National Educational Research and Development Trust's *Childminder's Charter*.
14. See DHSS, *Health and Personal Social Services Statistics for England*. See also A. Hunt, *The Home Help Service in England and Wales* (Government Social Survey, 1970).
15. H. R. and E. B. Schaffer, *Child Care and the Family* (Bell, 1968) p. 80.
16. See for example, M. J. Power *et al.*, 'Neighbourhood, School and Juveniles before the Courts', *British Journal of Criminology*, XII, 2 (April 1972).
17. DHSS, *Prevention and Health: Everybody's Business* (1976).
18. *Fit for the Future: The Report of the Committee on the Child Health Services*, Cmnd. 6684 (1976).
19. DHSS, *Report of the Committee of Inquiry into the Provision and Co-ordination of Services to the Family of John George Auckland* (1975). See also the general comments on the Health Visiting Service, pp. 90–1.
20. See *Fit for the Future: The Report of the Committee on the Child Health Services*, pp. 74–5 and 88–91.
21. It is interesting to note the especial problems in securing the attendance at clinics of young children placed with daily minders. B. Mayall and P. Petrie, *Minder, Mother and Child* (University of London Institute of Education, 1977) report that in their small study 'eight children (28 per cent) had not been taken in the last twelve months, excluding any whose mothers reckoned her GP offered a comparable service. Six of these eight children were not seen at the minders' by the health visitor either. In fact, most of the children who did go to the clinic were taken by their mothers, who usually took time off work for this: in some cases this was classed by their employer as part of annual leave' (p. 60).
22. DHSS, *Children in Care of Local Authorities in England and Wales*.
23. Drawn together in, for example, M. Kellmer Pringle, *The Needs of Children* (Hutchinson, 1975).
24. DHSS, *Family in Society: Preparation for Parenthood* (1974). See also

First Report from the Select Committee on Violence in the Family, vol. 1, HC 329-i, pp. xix–xx.

25. See the parallel arguments in the Seebohm Report, Chapter XV.

Chapter 5

1. The Children Act, 1975, makes provision, for example, for the separate representation of children in care and related proceedings before the juvenile courts (section 64).
2. *Report of the Care of Children Committee* (Curtis), Cmnd. 6922 (1946).
3. Justice, *Parental Rights and Duties and Custody Suits* (Godfrey Committee) (Stevens, 1975) pp. 5–6.
4. See for example, J. Shaw, *In loco parentis* (to be published) who writes, 'A classical education is supposed to be particularly good for training scholars to think precisely yet Latin terms are most usually inserted into English discourse just when the subject is getting dangerously ambiguous and confused. The case of the phrase "in loco parentis" is no exception and, despite its quasi-legal tone is deceptive. It does not refer to a set of clearly defined rights and duties which parents have and may, on occasion, transfer to some other responsible adult such that that person is equipped to take charge of their charge' (p. 1).
5. See M. Rutter, *Maternal Deprivation Reassessed* (Penguin, 1972). J. Bowlby, *Attachment and Loss: Vol. 1: Attachment* (Penguin, 1971). H. R. Schaffer, *The Growth of Sociability* (Penguin, 1971).
6. See J. Robertson, 'Young Children in Brief Separations: A Fresh Look', *Psychoanalytic Study of the Child*, XXVI (1971) 264.
7. B. Tizard, O. Cooperman, A. Joseph and J. Tizard, 'Environmental Effects on Language Development: A Study of Young Children in Residential Nurseries', *Child Development*, XLIII (1972) 337.
8. G. R. Patterson, R. A. Littman and W. Bricker, 'Assertive Behaviour in Children: A Step Towards a Theory of Aggression', *Monograph of the Society for Research in Child Development*, XXXII, 5 (1976).
9. See J. Newson and E. Newson, *Seven Year Olds in the Home Environment* (Allen and Unwin, 1976). A. Bandura and R. H. Walters, *Social Learning and Personality Development* (Holt, Rinehart and Winston, 1963).
10. See for an excellent general discussion of this theme P. Marris, *Loss and Change* (Routledge and Kegan Paul, 1974). He speaks of the essential incoherence of social change: 'the viability of conventional understanding rests on the refusal to make connections. But the latent contradictions may become open and unmanageable, as the consequences of *actions* play themselves out' (our italics), p. 125. See also S. Jenkins and E. Norman, *Filial Deprivation and Foster Care* (Columbia University Press, 1972).
11. R. Holman, 'The Place of Fostering in Social Work', *British Journal of Social Work*, V, 1 (1975) 3–29. He identifies two forms of fostering: exclusive and inclusive. The exclusive 'attempts to contain the child

within the foster family while excluding other connections' (p. 8).

12. Section 59 of the 1975 Children Act amends section 12 of the 1948 Act in order to introduce the 'welfare principle', with respect to children in care. It includes the obligation to ascertain the wishes and feelings of the child as far as possible and to give due consideration to them. This requirement covers all children in care irrespective of their legal status.
13. DHSS, LAC(76) 5, '. . . only in very exceptional circumstances should even a teenager be expected to carry the burden of decision about his or her future' (p. 3).
14. For example, R. Thorpe, 'Mum and Mrs. So-and-So', *Social Work Today*, IV 22 (1975).
15. DHSS, *Mentally Handicapped Children in Residential Care*, p. 7.
16. *Judicial Statistics, England and Wales*, Cmnd. 6634 (1976), Table G.6.
17. 'All remarriages' refers to all marriages in which one or other partner was previously married. See CSO, *Social Trends* (1977), Table 2.10, p. 54.
18. DHSS, LAC (76) 15.
19. DHSS, *Children in Care*, and Scottish Education Department, Social Work Services Group, *Scottish Social Work Statistics* (1975).
20. DHSS, *Manpower and Training*, p. 155 and *Scottish Social Work Statistics.*
21. DHSS Development Group, B. Kahan, 'Decisions and Resources', (unpublished) p. 15.
22. See CCETSW, *Residential Work is Part of Social Work* (1973). Also DHSS, *Manpower and Training.*
23. The Committee's terms of reference are as follows: 'to consider recommendation 74 of the Report of the Committee on Nursing (Briggs Committee) in particular to enquire into the nursing and care of the mentally handicapped in the light of developing policies, to examine the roles and aims of nurses and residential care staff required by the Health and Personal Social Services for the care of mentally handicapped adults and children; the interrelationship between them and other Health and Personal Social Services staff; how existing staff can best fulfil these roles and aims; in the interest of making the best use of available skill and experience the possibilities of the career movement of staff from one sector or category to another; the implications for recruitment and training; and to make recommendations'.
24. See for example, M. Oswin, *The Empty Hours* (Allen Lane, 1971).
25. See, for example, S. Millham, R. Bullock, P. Cherrett, *After Grace – Teeth* (Human Context Books, 1975). Also R. D. King, N. V. Raynes and J. Tizard. *Patterns of Residential Care* (Routledge and Kegan Paul, 1971).
26. DHSS, *Foster Care: A Guide to Practice* (1976).
27. DHSS, *Children in Care.*
28. Ibid.
29. See, for example, R. Holman 'The Place of Fostering in Social Work'.

30. For example in Kent, by the NCH and Barnardo's.
31. See D. Norbury, 'Summary of Findings of "Custodianship Project" in the South West'. Unpublished but available from the Association of British Adoption and Fostering Agencies.
32. M. Shaw, *et al.*, *Children Between Families* (University of Leicester School of Social Work, 1975). See in shortened form in *Adoption and Fostering*, 84 (1976). Also 'You Don't Think of Them as Foster Children . . .', *Conversations with Long-term Foster Parents* by the same authors, unpublished, 1976.
33. Shaw, *Children Between Families.*
34. Social Services Research and Intelligence Unit, Portsmouth Polytechnic and Hampshire CC, *The Portsmouth Fostering Study* (1974).
35. See, for example, R. A. Parker, *Decision in Child Care* (Allen and Unwin, 1966).
36. For a general review of most relevant studies in the field of foster care see R. Dinnage and M. Kellmer Pringle, *Foster Home Care: Facts and Fallacies* (Longman, for the National Children's Bureau, 1967); and H. Prosser, *Perspectives on Foster Care* (National Foundation for Educational Research, 1978).
37. See *General Household Survey* (1973).
38. Ibid.
39. R. Klein and P. Hall, *Caring for Quality in the Caring Services* (CSSP and Bedford Square Press, 1974) p. 46.

Chapter 6

1. See particularly J. Packman, *Child Care: Needs and Numbers* (Allen and Unwin, 1968).
2. C. Loewenstein, 'An Intake Team in Action in a Social Services Department', *British Journal of Social Work*, IV, 2 (1974) 133.
3. J. Rowe and L. Lambert, *Children Who Wait* (Association of British Adoption Agencies, 1973).
4. See DHSS, Local Authority Circulars (75)21, *Children Act: Main Provisions and Arrangements for Implementation* and (76)15, *Children Act: Programme for Implementation in 1976/7.*
5. Packman, *Child Care: Needs and Numbers.*
6. P. Moss, 'Residential Care of Children: a General View', in J. Tizard *et al.*, *Varieties of Residential Experience* (Routledge and Kegan Paul, 1975).
7. T. Asuni, 'Maladjustment and Delinquency', *Journal of Child Psychology and Psychiatry*, IV, 3–4 (1963) 219–28.
8. M. Rutter, J. Tizard and K. Whitmore (eds), *Education, Health and Behaviour* (Longman, 1970).
9. This division is usefully employed in S.W. Children's Regional Planning Committee and S.W. Social Services Research Group, *Observation and Assessment* (1976).
10. See MIND, *Assessment of Children and their Families* (1975).

11. DHSS, *Children in Care in England and Wales, March, 1976*, HC 506 (1977) Table 1.
12. See S.W. Children's Regional Planning Committee, *Observation and Assessment*. For corroborative evidence see also, Hampshire County Council and Portsmouth Polytechnic Social Services Research and Intelligence Unit, *First Year at Fairfield Lodge* (1976).
13. *Observation and Assessment*, Table 1.8, p. 14.
14. Ibid., Table 11.18, p. 37.
15. Ibid., pp. 12 and 22.
16. Wessex Children's Regional Planning Committee, *A Study of Placement Recommendations Made in Residential and Non-Residential Assessments of Children Who Have Been Received into Care* (1976).
17. This, of course, is in part a reflection of the rising numbers of juvenile delinquents; caution is needed, however, in interpreting these trends. 'Persons under 17 found guilty of indictable offences' is a rising figure: non-indictable offences are fairly steady, whilst motoring offences have shown a sharp decline.
18. See *Eleventh Report from the Expenditure Committee*, session 1974–5, vol. 1, p. xxv.
19. Expenditure Committee, Social Services and Employment (Subcommittee), *Minutes of Evidence*, Session 1974–5, Children and Young Persons Act, 1969, HC 84-i (1974) p. 119.
20. S.W. Children's Regional Planning Committee, *Observation and Assessment*, p. 52.
21. See B. Davies *et al.*, 'The "Silting Up" of Unadjustable Resources and Planning of Personal Social Services', *Policy and Politics*, I, 4 (June 1973) 341–55.
22. MIND, *Assessment of Children and their Families*, pp. 17–20.
23. See *Eleventh Report from the Expenditure Committee*, Children and Young Persons Act, 1969, vol. 1, HC 534-i (1975) para 71, p. xxvi, 'One way of easing the shortage of assessment centre places is to provide assessment on a daily basis. The Royal College of Psychiatrists told us that in London and Liverpool at least, about half the assessments their members undertook were conducted on an out-patient basis. The DHSS is encouraging the use of assessment centres on a daily basis.'
24. Ibid., p. 14.
25. For example, by the Dartington Social Research Unit.
26. See, for example, E. Mapstone, 'Children in Care', *Concern*, no. 3 (1969) 23–8.
27. M. Shaw and K. Lebens, *Regional Planning for Children Who Wait* (University of Leicester School of Social Work, 1977).
28. See for example. Hampshire County Council and Portsmouth Polytechnic Social Services Research and Intelligence Unit, *First Year at Fairfield Lodge* (1976).
29. A point made strongly in an unpublished report by Newcastle Social Services Department, 'Positive Planning for Children in Care' (1976). An abbreviated version appears in *Social Work Today* (12 Oct 1976).

30. See DHSS, *Mentally Handicapped Children in Residential Care* (Harvie Report) (1974).
31. R. Holman, *Trading in Children* (Routledge and Kegan Paul, 1973).
32. DHSS, LAC (76) 15.
33. Ibid., Annex A, p. 3.
34. Newcastle Social Services Department, 'Positive Planning for Children', p. 2.
35. L. Lambert and J. Rowe, 'Children in Care and the Assumption of Parental Rights by Local Authorities', *Child Adoption*, no. 78 (1974) 13–23.
36. M. Shaw, K. Lebens and A. Cosh, *Children Between Families* (University of Leicester School of Social Work, 1975).
37. Ibid., Summary, p. 10 (unnumbered pages).
38. DHSS, *Foster Care: A Guide to Practice* (1976) para. 339, p. 142.
39. See DHSS, *Children in Care, 1976*, Table 4, p. 6.
40. DHSS, LAC(76)15. Took effect 26 Nov 1976.
41. M. A. Jones, 'Reducing Foster Care Through Services to Families', *Children Today* (Nov/Dec 1976).
42. See DHSS, *Children in Care, 1975*, Table I, footnote.
43. Calculated on an average cost of boarded-out children of £7 p.w. (*Children in Care, 1975*, Table III).
44. DHSS, *Children in Care, 1976.*
45. Ibid.
46. See Home Office, *Criminal Statistics, England and Wales, 1973.* Cmnd. 5677 (1974) p. 216, subtable to Table V(a).
47. See NSPCC, *Yo-Yo Children: A Study of 23 Violent Matrimonial Cases*, no date.
48. DHSS, *Children in Care, 1976* and earlier.
49. See Expenditure Committee, *Minutes of Evidence*, Home Office, HC 286-ii (1974) especially p. 95 (Mrs P. D. White).
50. DHSS, *Children in Care, 1976.*
51. Ibid.

Chapter 7

1. For a good general discussion see R. Moroney, *The Family and the State*, (Longman, 1976) pp. 117–25.
2. E. Ferri with R. Niblett, *Disadvantaged Families and Playgroups* (NFER, 1977).
3. See P. Wedge and H. Prosser, *Born to Fail?* (Arrow Books, 1973) or H. Land, *Large Families in London* (Bell, 1969).
4. See DHSS, *Health and Personal Social Services Statistics for England* (1974).
5. R. Page and G. A. Clark (eds), *Who Cares?* (National Children's Bureau, 1977).
6. R. M. Titmuss, *The Gift Relationship* (Allen and Unwin, 1970).

7. DHSS, *Intermediate Treatment Project: Development Group Report* (1973) p. 15.
8. For various accounts and other commentaries see DHSS, *Intermediate Treatment* (1972); A. Leissner, T. Powley and D. Evans, *Intermediate Treatment: An Action Research Report* (National Children's Bureau, 1977); and Personal Social Services Council, *A Future for Intermediate Treatment* (1977).
9. Leissner, *et al.*, *Intermediate Treatment Project: An Action Research Report*, p. 16.
10. Personal Social Services Council, *A Future for Intermediate Treatment*, p. 41.
11. See J. Tizard, I. Sinclair and R. V. Clarke (eds), *Varieties of Residential Experience* (Routledge and Kegan Paul, 1975).
12. B. Tizard, O. Cooperman, A. Joseph and J. Tizard, 'Environmental Effects in Language Development: a Study of Children in Long-stay Residential Nurseries', *Child Development*, XLIII (1972) 337–59.
13. For example R. Dinnage and M. Kellmer Pringle, *Foster Home Care – Facts and Fallacies* (Longman, 1967); H. Prosser, *Perspectives on Foster Care* (NFER, 1978); R. Dinnage and M. Kellmer Pringle, *Residential Child Care – Facts and Fallacies*; and H. Prosser, *Perspectives on Residential Child Care* (NFER, 1976).
14. DHSS, *Foster Care: A Guide to Practice*. See also M. Kellmer Pringle and S. Naidoo, *Early Child Care in Britain* (Gordon and Breach, 1975).
15. Pringle and Naidoo, ibid.
16. For example in DHSS–DES, 'Nursery Education: Current Provision and Policy', *Low Cost Day Provision for Under-Fives* (1976) 13–16.
17. DHSS, *Children in Care of Local Authorities in England and Wales* (1976) HC 506, p. f14.
18. See A. Glampson, T. Scott and D. N. Thomas, *A Guide to the Assessment of Community Needs and Resources* (National Institute for Social Work, 1975).
19. S. Jackson, 'A New Policy for Childminders', *Social Work Today*, VIII, 13 (January 1978) 19–20.

Chapter 8

1. See for accounts of the views of children in care, *Who Cares?* (National Children's Bureau).
2. M. Bayley, *Mental Handicap and Community Care* (Routledge and Kegan Paul, 1973).
3. J. Packman, *Child Care Needs and Numbers* (Allen and Unwin, 1968), and B. Davies, *Variations in Children's Services among British Urban Authorities* (Bell, 1972).
4. A. Hall, *The Point of Entry*.
5. For example, E. Mapstone, 'Children in Care', *Concern*, no. 3 (Nov 1969); J. Essen, L. Lambert and J. Head, 'School Attainment of

Children Who Have Been in Care', *Child: Care, Health and Development,* II, 6 (1976) 339–51; and L. Lambert, J. Essen and J. Head, 'Variations in Behaviour Ratings of Children Who Have Been in Care', *Journal of Child Psychology and Psychiatry* XVIII, 4 (1977) 335–46.

Appendix B

1. P. Moss, 'Residential Care of Children: a General View', J. Tizard (ed.), *Varieties of Residential Experience* (Routledge and Kegan Paul, 1975).
2. R. Holman, 'The Place of Fostering in Social Work'.

Consolidated Bibliography

Books and pamphlets

A. Bandura and R. H. Walters, *Social Learning and Personality Development* (Holt, Rinehart and Winston, 1963).

M. Bayley, *Mental Handicap and Community Care* (Routledge and Kegan Paul, 1973).

J. Bowlby, *Attachment and Loss: Vol. 1 Attachment* (Penguin, 1971).

Central Council for Education and Training in Social Work, *Residential Work is Part of Social Work* (1973).

Chartered Institute of Public Finance and Accountancy, *Local Health and Social Service Statistics* (Annual Reports).

B. Davies, *Variations in Children's Services among British Urban Authorities* (Bell, 1972).

R. Dinnage and M. Kellmer Pringle, *Foster Home Care: Facts and Fallacies* (Longman, 1967).

R. Dinnage and M. Kellmer Pringle, *Residential Child Care: Facts and Fallacies* (Longman, 1967).

E. Ferri *et al.*, *Playgroups for Children in High Need* (National Children's Bureau, 1977).

A. Glampson *et al.*, *A Guide to the Assessment of Community Needs and Resources* (National Institute for Social Work, 1975).

A. S. Hall, *The Point of Entry* (Allen and Unwin, 1974).

Hampshire County Council and Portsmouth Polytechnic Social Services Research and Intelligence Unit, *First Year at Fairfield Lodge* (1976).

R. Holman, *Trading in Children* (Routledge and Kegan Paul, 1973).

S. Jenkins and E. Norman, *Filial Deprivation and Foster Care* (Columbia University Press, 1972).

K. Judge, *Rationing Social Services* (Heinemann, 1978).

Justice, *Parental Rights and Duties Custody Suits* (Stevens, 1975).

R. D. King *et al.*, *Patterns of Residential Care* (Routledge and Kegan Paul, 1971).

R. Klein (ed.), *Inflation and Priorities* (Centre for Studies in Social Policy, 1975).

R. Klein and P. Hall, *Caring for Quality in the Caring Services* (CSSP and Bedford Square Press, 1974).
H. Land, *Large Families in London* (Bell, 1969).
A. E. Leeding, *Leeding's Child Care Manual* (Butterworth, 1976).
A. Leissner *et al.*, *Intermediate Treatment: An Action Research Report* (National Children's Bureau, 1977).
P. Marris, *Loss and Change* (Routledge and Kegan Paul, 1974).
B. Mayall and P. Petrie, *Minder, Mother and Child* (University of London, Institute of Education, 1977).
S. Millham *et al.*, *After Grace – Teeth* (Human Context Books, 1975).
MIND, *Assessment of Children and their Families* (1975).
R. Moroney, *The Family and the State* (Longman, 1976).
National Educational Research and Development Trust, *Child-Minders' Charter* (1978).
National Society for the Prevention of Cruelty to Children, *Yo-Yo Children: A Study of Twenty-Three Violent Matrimonial Cases* (no date).
Newcastle Social Services Department, *Positive Planning for Children in Care* (unpublished, 1976).
J. and E. Newson, *Seven Year-Olds in the Home Environment* (Allen and Unwin, 1976).
M. Oswin, *The Empty Hours* (Allen Lane, 1971).
J. Packman, *Child Care: Needs and Numbers* (Allen and Unwin, 1968).
R. Page and G. A. Clark (eds), *Who Cares?* (National Children's Bureau, 1977).
R. A. Parker, *Decision in Child Care* (Allen and Unwin, 1966).
P. Parsloe, *Juvenile Justice* (Routledge and Kegan Paul, 1978).
Personal Social Services Council, *A Future for Intermediate Treatment* (1977).
M. Kellmer Pringle, *The Needs of Children* (Hutchinson, 1975).
M. Kellmer Pringle and S. Naidoo, *Early Child Care in Britain* (Gordon and Breach, 1975).
H. Prosser, *Perspectives on Foster Care* (NFER, 1978).
H. Prosser, *Perspectives on Residential Child Care* (NFER, 1976).
J. Rowe and L. Lambert, *Children Who Wait* (Association of British Adoption Agencies, 1973).
M. Rutter, *Maternal Deprivation Reassessed* (Penguin, 1972).
M. Rutter *et al.* (eds), *Education, Health and Behaviour* (Longman, 1970).
H. R. Schaffer, *The Growth of Sociability* (Penguin, 1971).
H. R. and E. B. Schaffer, *Child Care and the Family* (Bell, 1968).
M. Shaw and K. Lebens, *Regional Planning for Children Who Wait* (University of Leicester School of Social Work, 1977).
M. Shaw *et al.*, *Children between Families* (University of Leicester School of Social Work, 1975).
South West Regional Planning Committee and South West Social Services Research Group, *Observation and Assessment* (1976).
J. Spencer *et al.*, *Face to Face with Children* (MacDonald, 1976).
R. M. Titmuss, *The Gift Relationship* (Allen and Unwin, 1970).
J. Tizard *et al.*, *Varieties of Residential Experience* (Routledge and Kegan Paul, 1975).

J. Tizard *et al.*, *All our Children* (Temple Smith/New Society, 1976).
Trades Union Congress, *Under Fives* (1977).
P. Wedge and H. Prosser, *Born to Fail?* (Arrow Books, 1973).
Wessex Regional Children's Planning Committee, *A Study of Placement Recommendations made in Residential and None-Residential Assessments of Children who have been Received into Care* (1976).

Government publications

Home Office

Children in Care of Local Authorities in England and Wales.
Reports of the Work of the Children's Department.
Statistics Relating to Approved Schools, Remand Homes and Attendance Centres in England and Wales.
Criminal Statistics, England and Wales – Annual Reports.
Judicial Statistics, England and Wales – Annual Reports.
Home Office/Department of Education and Science/Ministry of Health and Ministry of Housing and Local Government, *Report of the Committee on Local Authority and Allied Personal Social Services* (Seebohm) Cmnd. 3703 (1968).

Department of Health and Social Security

Health and Personal Social Services Statistics for England – Annual Reports.
Children in Care of Local Authorities in England and Wales.
Local Authority Social Services Departments, *Social Service Staff – Annual Statistics.*
Intermediate Treatment (1972).
Intermediate Treatment Project: Development Group Report (1973).
Mentally Handicapped Children in Residential Care (Harvie Report) (1974).
Family in Society: Preparation for Parenthood (1974).
Report of the Committee of Inquiry into the Provision and Co-ordination of Services to the Family of John George Auckland (1975).
Circular LAC (75) 21. *Children Act: Main Provisions and Arrangements for Implementation.*
Circular LAC (76) 15. *Children Act: Programme for Implementation in 1976/7.*
Foster Care: A Guide to Practice (1976).
Prevention and Health: Everybody's Business (1976).
Priorities for Health and Personal Social Services in England: A Consultative Document (1976).
Manpower and Training for the Social Services (1976).
Priorities for Health and Social Services: The Way Forward (1977).

Department of Health and Social Security/Department of Education and Science, *Fit for the Future: Report of the Committee on Child Health Services* (Court), Cmnd. 6684 (1976).
DHSS/DES, *Low Cost Day Provision for Under-Fives* (1976).

Office of Population Censuses and Surveys

1966 Sample Census of Great Britain: Housing Tables – Non-Private Households.
1971 Census of Great Britain: Housing Tables – Non-Private Households.
Reports of the General Household Survey.
Social Trends.
M. Bone, *Pre-school Children and the Need for Day Care* (1977).

Other Government publications

Department of Employment, *Report of the Inquiry into the Work and Pay of Probation Officers and Social Workers* (Butterworth) Cmnd. 5076 (1972).
Ministry of Housing and Local Government, *Report of the Committee on the Staffing of Local Government* (Mallaby) (1967).
Central Policy Review Staff, *A Joint Framework for Social Policies* (1975).
Central Policy Review Staff, *Services for Young Children with Working Mothers* (1978).
Government Social Survey, A. Hunt, *The Home Help Service in England and Wales* (1970).
Eleventh Report from the Expenditure Committee, Children and Young Persons Act, 1969, Session 1974–5, HC 534 (1975).
First Report from the Select Committee on Violence in the Family: Session 1976–7, Violence to Children, HC 329 (1977).
The Government's Expenditure Plans, Cmnd. 6721 (1977).
Public Expenditure to 1979–80, Cmnd. 6393 (1976).
Report of the Care of Children Committee, Cmnd. 6922 (1946).
Scottish Home Department, *Children in the Care of Local Authorities in Scotland.*
Scottish Education Department, *Child Care* (separately published extract from *Education in Scotland* – Annual Reports).
Scottish Education Department, *Scottish Social Work Statistics.*

Articles

T. Asuni, 'Maladjustment and Delinquency', *Journal of Child Psychology and Psychiatry*, IV, 3–4 (1963).
B. Davies *et al.*, 'The "Silting-up" of Unadjustable Resources and Planning of Personal Social Services', *Policy and Politics*, I, 4 (1973).

J. Essen *et al.*, 'School Attainment of Children who have been in Care', *Child: Care, Health and Development*, II, 6 (1976).

R. Holman, 'The Place of Fostering in Social Work', *British Journal of Social Work*, V, i (1975).

S. Jackson, 'A New Policy for Childminders', *Social Work Today*, VIII, 13 (Jan 1978).

M. A. Jones, 'Reducing Foster Care Through Services to Families', *Children Today*, (Nov/Dec 1976).

K. Judge, 'Economic Analysis and Productive Efficiency in the Personal Social Services: the Differential Use of Manpower', *International Journal of Social Economics*, III, 2 (1976).

L. Lambert and J. Rowe, 'Children in Care and the Assumption of Parental Rights by Local Authorities', *Child Adoption*, no. 78 (1974).

L. Lambert *et al.*, 'Variations in Behaviour Ratings of Children Who Have Been in Care', *Journal of Child Psychology and Psychiatry*, XVIII, 4 (1977).

C. Loewenstein, 'An Intake Team in Action in a Social Services Department', *British Journal of Social Work*, IV, 2 (1974).

E. Mapstone, 'Children in Care', *Concern*, no. 3 (Nov 1969).

G. R. Patterson *et al.*, 'Assertive Behaviour in Children: A Step Towards a Theory of Aggression', *Monograph of the Society for Research in Child Development*, XXXII, 5 (1967).

M. J. Power *et al.*, 'Neighbourhood, School and Juveniles before the Courts', *British Journal of Criminology*, XII, 2 (1972).

M. K. Pringle, 'Whither Residential Child Care?', *Concern*, no. 26 (1978).

J. Robertson, 'Young Children in Brief Separations: A Fresh Look', *Psychoanalytic Study of the Child*, XXVI (1971).

J. A. Schofield, 'The Economic Return to Preventive Social Work', *International Journal of Social Economics*, III, 3 (1976).

R. Thorpe, 'Mum and Mrs So-and-So', *Social Work Today*, IV, 22 (1975).

B. Tizard *et al.*, 'Environmental Effects on Language Development: A Study of Children in Long-stay Residential Nurseries', *Child Development*, XLIII (1972).

Unpublished reports

E. M. Goldberg, *Towards Accountability in Social Work*.

B. Kahan, *Decisions and Resources*.

D. Norbury, *Summary of 'Custodian Project' in the South West* (ABAFA).

Index

Making Ways

The visual artists' guide to surviving and thriving◄

edited by
►David Butler◄

Second edition
revised by
►Susan Jones◄

►ISBN 0 907730 07 8 2nd edition◄
►ISBN 0 907730 04 3 1st edition◄

►Acknowledgements◄

Thanks to:
►**Carole Pemberton, Anne Francis, Shelley Partridge** and **Sandy Lynan** of the ILEA Careers Service; **David Cheetham, Yvonne Parkin, Rod Bugg** and **Simon Roodhouse** of Newcastle Polytechnic; **Andy Christian** and **Alyson Brien** for their help in establishing what this book should cover.

►**Douglas Fisher** for assistance with the article on insurance.

►**E.W. Padwick** for compiling the index.

►Cartoons◄

►**Natalie d'Arbeloff**

►**Damon Burnard**

►Printed◄

Mayfair Printers, Print House, William Street, Sunderland SR1 1UL
☎ 091 567 9326

►Designed & produced by◄

Richard Padwick with **David Butler** and **Susan Jones**

►Financial Support◄

The first edition received an interest-free loan from **Northern Arts** and a guarantee against loss from the **Arts Council of Great Britain**

►Artic Producers Publishing Co Ltd◄

PO Box 23, 20 Villiers Street, Sunderland SR4 6DG ☎ 091 567 3589

Contents

Introduction

Introduction

Carole Pemberton

This book is for those of you who are involved in activities encompassed by the broad and blurred definition of fine arts – painters, sculptors, photographers, printmakers, film and video makers; and those artists and craftspeople who see their future in terms of one-off or small-scale production work. All of you are people who are concerned to be constantly producing new work in response to personal change and development, rather than in response to consumer demand or expected profit. Such ideologies place you in a vulnerable position in a capitalist society, a vulnerability recognised in the National Advisory Body on Higher Education's definition of fine art courses as *'unprotected'*. In putting together this book, the collective authors are concerned that artists should be enabled to gain some protection against those who under-value, under-use, under-price and under-estimate the contribution made by the visual arts.

To survive is *'to continue to live after the end or cessation of some thing or condition'*, according to the Oxford English Dictionary, and that is what this book aims to help you do: to continue to live as a professional artist after the security of education and the termly grant have been removed. To use the term *professional* immediately raises the issue of what it means when applied to the visual artist. A definition that links professionalism with the provision of a livelihood, would preclude most practising artists in the UK; the linking of profession to the provision of a service for which there is a demand, would be to over-vaunt the public response to much of the work you may do. It seems that a definition based purely on extrinsic factors: money, recognition, regular showings and critical acclaim won't do, because it denies the importance of personal intent and commitment. If you bridle at the thought that your efforts would be dismissed as *hobbyist* by the Inland Revenue because they've failed to provide a taxable profit, then it's an indicator that you invest your work with a value unrelated to monetary return and regard yourself as a professional.

Self-regard is one indication of professionalism, but to leave it at that would be to allow the Shavian definition of an artist to stand unchallenged:

> *The true artist will let his wife starve, his children go barefoot, his mother drudge for his living at seventy, sooner than work at anything but his art.*[1]

This image of the ego-centred creator, oblivious to the needs of others and prepared to starve for his art may be romantic in the abstract, but I have yet

to meet an artist for whom it was a career objective. Indeed applied to any other profession than art it would be regarded as an indication of failure. This book is based on the belief that along with personal conviction, there are aspects of living as an artist that need to be considered by anyone thinking of making that commitment in order that the individual can take some control of how his or her working life develops. Immediately I need to add that it is not a 'How to win in the art system' handbook as though there were formulae that could be universally applied. Rather we hope it will be a manual that you can use to work out your own personal plan. That is why the first chapter is entitled 'Looking at Yourself', because until you have thought through what being an artist means for you, reading the rest of the book will be a worthy activity, but lacking in vitality. 'Looking at Yourself' is a base from which to direct yourself to those chapters that relate to your specific interests, and from which to devise your own support system.

A support system is what every artist needs. In Shaw's definition the sacrificial mother constituted the support system, for art college leavers it is often the bar job taken to earn money while things are sorted out after graduating. Nothing wrong in that, except when two years on the artist/bar person has become the bar person who once went to art college. The movement from the first to the second position can be almost imperceptible, and only brought to consciousness when an old college friend is met, or you are asked if you still paint, photograph, sculpt.... To

hang on to a sense of self when you are ostensibly being defined as the shop assistant or warehouse worker relies on having a conscious support plan. Having looked at the careers of a large number of artists over the five years after leaving college, the most commonly used pattern for those who continue with their work, seems to be:

Stage One

Art Work (non-earning) with some Non-Art Work (earning)

Stage Two

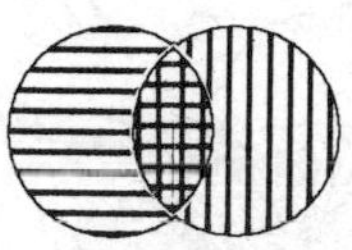

Non-Art Work (earning) with some Art Work (some earning)

Stage Three

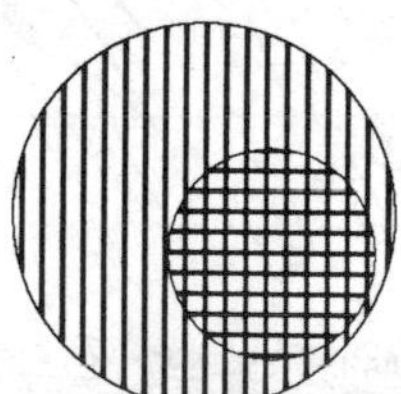

Art-Related Work (earning) with Art Work (earning)

Stage Four

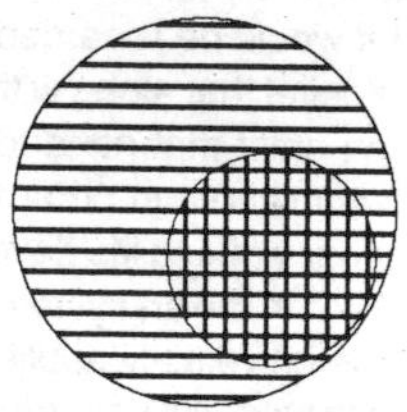

Art Work (earning) with some Art-Related Work (earning)

Stage Five

Art Work (earning)

What seems to differentiate those who carry on with their art from those who don't, is that the *stickers* don't make a separation between the continuance of their art and the support system needed to ensure it: a difference seen in these comments from two fine art graduates:

> It is hard, and I'm very poor, but being able to carry on doing my own work makes my life richer than any monetary system could offer

> Having to exist in a series of second rate part-time jobs... is becoming extremely dispiriting.

In the first quote the speaker's self-image is related to being an artist, in the second the self-image has become tied in with the unskilled work activity leading to a questioning of the viability of continuing with art. I am not suggesting that artists should be prepared to starve for their beliefs, but that, if personal needs are honestly recognised an appropriate support system can be sought. It could be, that the second speaker could have valued their work more highly if they had obtained a post graduate vocational training that could then have acted as a support. It's *different strokes for different folks*, and the task of college leavers is to recognise the *strokes* they need if they are to continue their art work with satisfaction.

It should be apparent by now that it's not a book on how to make a large income from the visual arts, and if that's your prime goal you need read no further. But, if you're wanting assistance to withstand the vicissitudes of committing yourself to the visual arts, and are willing to participate in the process of devising strategies that are right for you, then we believe this book will give you an informed starting point.

Looking at Yourself

Looking at Yourself

►Carole Pemberton◄

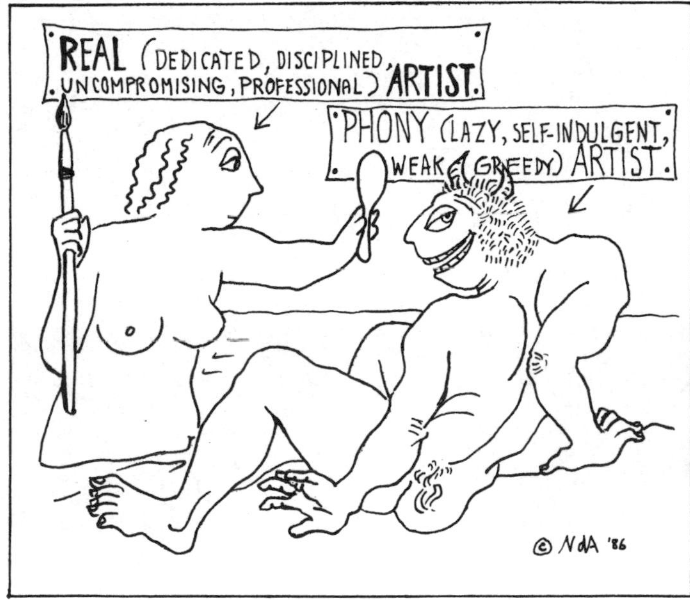

In the Introduction I suggested that to get value for money from this book, you need to spend some time looking at yourself, so that you can decide on what support system you need to achieve your ends. In writing this, I am immediately aware that self-analysis is not an activity with which people are generally comfortable, so that if you are going to continue reading this section, I've got to convince you of what's in it for you. If you were sitting in my office, at this point you would probably have arrived with a list of pragmatic questions: how can I find out about studies in ..., who'll pay for me to do a travelling scholarship to..., who does a course in..., which RAA gives most money to ... . All reasonable questions in themselves, but often totally unconnected to any sense of the individual and their personal strengths, weaknesses, commitments, fears. With time, you may decide to open up, to let me know in what way you are different from the ten other course members who also want to study overseas, and we may eventually

discover that it's not such a good idea for you to spend considerable amounts of time and money on applications right now when there are other more accessible ways of your carrying on with your work. I won't be able to help you make that decision, however, unless you take the risk of thinking through your motivations. The problem was stated clearly by that ursine philosopher Winnie the Pooh:

> Here is Edward Bear. coming downstairs now, bump, bump, on the back of his head behind Christopher Robin. It is, as far as he knows, the only way of coming downstairs, but sometimes he feels there really is another way, if only he could stop bumping for a moment and think of it.

What you are being asked to do here is to take some time out to stop bumping along whatever path you are following to consider where is that path leading, why and how did you choose it in the first place, and could there be others around you haven't even noticed that would be more direct, or more enjoyable to travel along. To take time out to think through the path you want to follow as an artist, and the system you will need to carry with you, moves you from the position of being a passive to an active participant.

If so far you've been a passive participant you may recognise yourself in these statements:

> Things will be OK when... *'I get a good degree'* ... *'The Royal College offers me a place'* ... *'Someone discovers me'* ... *'I get a grant'* ... *'I'm offered a show in a West End Gallery'* ... *'A studio turns up'*

Each of these statements assumes that either by just waiting, or by luck things will happen for you. They may. More likely they will not. Luck tends to happen when you've created the conditions in which the opportunity can arise. To live in expectation of something happening is a condition described by Hopson and Scally[1] as 'pin-ball living', that is where like pin-balls we have no life of our own, but are set in motion by someone else, and bounce from place to place with no clear directions – sometimes hitting big scores, but as likely to go down the hole, and stay there until someone sets us off again. The opposite to pin-ball living is a philosophy which sees you as a force behind what happens to you, controlling *as far as you are able* possible outcomes. To do this implies:

- ▶ Using your own feelings to recognise discrepancies between how things are and how you'd like them to be
- ▶ Specifying desired outcomes and the action/steps needed to achieve them
- ▶ Acting to implement goals

A useful example of this approach can be seen in the article by Paul Donnelly and Geoff Staden, who from a position of actively desiring sponsorship for AIR, recognise their feelings of unease at sponsorship offers from multi-nationals dealing in arms, and subsequently initiate a campaign to make visitors to a major exhibition at the Tate aware of the incongruity of the relationship: a protest that leads to a public debate at the gallery. In the process they have not only clarified their own views on the acceptability of sponsorship, they have also empowered others to take a stand.

◁see **Sponsorship** & **Ethics**▷

To act from a sense of personal power, as Donnelly and Staden did requires that you have thought through:

▷**1** *Life Skills Teaching*, B. Hopson & M. Scally. McGraw Hill, 1981

▶ What is important to you
▶ What you would like to happen
▶ What beliefs you hold that would support you through
▶ What information you need
▶ What skills you have and what additional skills you need to acquire

The process can be encapsulated in the phrase *'if you don't know where you're going you'll end up somewhere else'.* [(2)]

Living out the life of a frustrated artist is a common and at times comforting stance – there are so many others sharing the same ground, there are so many very real economic, structural and bureaucratic obstacles to survival. But to take on the role of victim who has to accept the ways things are, means you will be ill-prepared even to notice chance when it does appear. Carlos Casteneda wrote of using opportunity in these words:

> All of us... have a cubic centimetre of chance that pops up in front of our eyes from time to time. The difference between the average man and the warrior is that the warrior is aware of this and one of his tasks is to be alert and deliberately waiting so that when his cubic centimetre pops up, he has the speed, the prowess to pick it up.

It's the ... the ... RUBICUBE!

To recognise your cubic centimetre of chance, requires that you are prepared to assess yourself in two ways:

▶ What have you learnt about yourself as an artist up to now?
▶ What do you want to achieve as an artist in the future?

▶What have you learnt about yourself as an Artist?◀

Considering this question is important because it is a means of recognising the skills you have, the interests you hold and the values they embody.

▶Exercise◀

Think of a number of occasions when you have experienced a sense of enjoyment and achievement from art activities in which you have been involved eg:

▶ Organising a mural painting event for children during a summer vacation
▶ Seeing a piece of your work in a gallery
▶ Mastering a particular technical skill
▶ Organising a campaign for greater council support for the arts in your home town

The list is not prescriptive, let your mind wander as far back and as widely as you like, in order to identify occasions on which involvement in art has proved satisfying for you.

Having identified these occasions, consider each of your *satisfiers* and ask yourself:

▶ Why it was satisfying for you.
▶ What does it tell you about the way in which you work best, your values and needs. Are there any patterns?

▷**2** *If you don't know where you're going you'll end up somewhere else*, D. Cambell. Argus 1974

In asking these questions you will be clarifying a view of yourself as an artist. For example:

► Is recognition through sales important to you, or irrelevant?
► Do you see your art as a social tool?
► Do you want your work to occupy public space, or to be owned by private individuals?
► Do you get more enjoyment out of work being permanent or ephemeral?
► Do you value critical attention or is your art an activity that need only to meet your own critical standards?
► Do you need an audience?
► Is involvement in administration and organisation of exhibitions, degree shows or group studies as satisfying as doing your own work?
► Is it important that issues related to gender, politics, race or sexuality be reflected in your work?
► Do you need academic *success* in order to feel validated?

The satisfiers that you have identified for yourself will reflect the concept that you hold of yourself, and this differs for each of us.

►Goal Setting◄

The second stage of planning how you need to use the rest of this book is to decide what it is you want to attain. Goal setting is a means by which we state how we would like to be. It is a way of rechecking our present interests, values and needs to see if we want to carry them forward, of highlighting skills we may need to acquire and risks we would need to be prepared to take. It is also a direct means of confronting how large or small a part we want art to play in our future.

►Goal Setting Exercise◄

One way of identifying possible goals is to allow ourselves the luxury of fantasising. Imagine there are no constraints in terms of time, money or commitment, and then construct for yourself:

►A Fantasy Day◄

Write down (or close your eyes and think) what would be a perfect day. Where would you be, what would you do, who would you be with, what would be the major achievement of the day? How large or small a part would work play in it?

►Fantasy Artist◄

Now close in on you as an artist during that day. Are you there at all? If you are, what are you doing, and does it seem to be a major or minor part of your life? Is the art for yourself? are you working with others? are you working to commission or for an exhibition? Try and get a sense of what it would feel like to be that artist.

Using fantasy to set goals can be a very powerful and direct way of acknowledging what we would like to experience. In using it with an illustrator who was seriously considering giving up her work for a *safe* career, it became clear that once she allowed herself the luxury of doing work for herself she could begin to value herself as an illustrator again: for

in her fantasy far from seeing a business woman, she saw an old lady surrounded by her own art work that she was showing to her family. Similarly in working with a photographer who had spent unhappy years as a salesman, his fantasy of being in Papua New Guinea looking at the proofs of a travel book he was producing, gave him the courage to give up work and enrol in the Enterprise Allowance Scheme. One year on, he had not reached Papua yet, but was the photographer for the local tourist department.

The purpose of declaring our fantasies is also to expose the conflicts that may be inherent in them, and to recognise the self limitations or external restrictions that may exist. A fantasy of regular London showings implies a willingness to self-promote, the ability to develop a network of useful professional contacts, and an acceptance of being within reach of London. All of these may be in conflict with your assessment of your personal skills, your enjoyment of rural seclusion, and the greater importance that domestic responsibilities have in your life at the moment. Recognising the conflicts can allow us to rewrite the goals in a form that has meaning, allows for their achievement and incorporates longer-term

planning. A more appropriate statement could then become *'Right now I need to give time to the family, but in three years time I will.... and in the meantime I can'*. This rewriting of the goal still maintains its practicality and avoids the syndrome described by Alan Bennett as *'I could have been a judge but I never had the Latin'*.

▶Transferable Skills◀

It is axiomatic that artists have transferable skills – the limitations of the fine art market mean that practically no artist pursues a linear career pattern which utilises solely those particular skills acquired at college. A survey of fine artists from Brighton Polytechnic(3) found that over a five-year period 80% had worked in art-related areas: jobs which required creative abilities, but were indirectly linked to the official course curriculum. Painters had become knitwear designers, film-makers, model makers and set designers; sculptors were now arts administrators, architectural stonemasons and restoration workers; and printmakers had become community artists and art therapists. Each one had gone through a process of identifying their particular skills and looking to see how they could be matched to the needs of the market. This drawing out process is often slow and painful, and accounts for the apparently high unemployment and under-employment of art graduates in the first years after college. Unfortunately, art courses sometimes fail to acknowledge the hidden curriculum skills that are imparted over three years: self-discipline, time management, critical thinking, self-reliance, inventiveness, problem solving, working with others, living on a shoestring – abilities which are vital to surviving as an artist but can be equally applied elsewhere.

▶Skills Exercise◀

Acknowledging skills is a means of acquiring greater confidence in achieving a goal, and of also opening up new possibilites.

List all the skills which you have acquired over the course of your art education - these could be technical, creative and personal. Stick at it - British diffidence often makes this a difficult task. Refer to the exercise on satisfying experience, or ask a close friend what skills s/he would say you had. Skills which were recognised by graduates from one art course included:

> I feel capable to make new connections and take new views of life around me. I also feel more able to make decisions for myself and feel independent in my thoughts.
>
> As one who had difficulties in previous social communication, exercising my freedom of expression gave me an identity, social position and confidence in relation to my success.
>
> The fine art course has the ability to provide students with an education which not only allows them to research a subject fully, but also gives them an attitude of self discipline and self reliance, which assists them in life no matter what they choose to do.

Such apparently untangible skills are rarely spoken of yet surviving as an artist can call upon them as directly as upon more creative abilities. The exercise may also highlight for you personal skills which you feel you are lacking.

▷**3** *Survey of the Post College Experiences of Brighton Polytechnic Fine Art Graduates 1978-82*. Brighton Polytechnic Careers Service, 1985

►Technical Skills◄

Recognising technical skills acquired in college can suggest related work that could be used to support your art activity, or conversely the exercise may have made you aware of deficiencies in your technical skills. When graduates from one course were asked to list things which they wished they had known or experienced before leaving, the desire for greater technical competence was a major complaint. It meant, for example, that a photography major was unable to find work as a photographer's assistant because of very limited experience in film developing. Easy at this point to bad-mouth the college, but a more positive response would be to learn more about film development within a part-time City & Guilds course *(see Chapter on Training for further discussion on this issue).*

The alleged non-vocationalism of Fine Art courses can cause considerable anxiety as to how graduates can compete in an increasingly specialised job market. It is true that major organisations delineate roles, but it is equally true that in smaller organisations a variety of skills can be called for. You can be sure that if a national museum advertises in *The Guardian* for a graphic designer, it is only graphic designers who will be considered; but when a local museum advertises for a designer they will often expect a 2D designer, restoration worker, publicity officer, exhibition assistant and display designer rolled into one. In this situation the fine artist

can come into their own. You can benefit also from the general ignorance of small employers. Very often little distinction is drawn between art and design disciplines, and you could be offered graphics work even though you last saw Letraset on your foundation course. Having watched the transformation of fine artists across disciplines, I have become convinced that confidence and *chuzpah* are prime survival skills.

Linked in with the issue of recognising, transferring and acquiring skills is the need to value the self. In the present educational climate, it is easy to be hooked into believing that a Fine Art degree is a valueless commodity. It is irrefutable that a painter faces a chiller wind than a Business Studies graduate when leaving college, and the difficulties of finding a personally appropriate survival route are not under-estimated in this book, but it is also important to recognise that we can exaggerate problems through projecting our anxieties onto the *art system.* When facing hostilities we have the same choice as other animals: stand our ground, fight or flight. Standing ground, or assertiveness, will be covered in the next section, but fight and flight can easily become muddled. Each year when working in an art college I received letters from recent graduates who were angered by my enquiring as to what they were now doing. Their anger normally took the form of berating the art college, or decrying the art world and stating their decision to have no part of it. Fair enough if that's an honest statement, but often what I read into the anger was disappointment that nothing happened at the degree show, or that a much-desired MA place wasn't forthcoming, and a lack of knowledge or confidence as to how to get started. Projecting our anxieties onto people and things is a means by which we delude ourselves we are fighting when in reality we are fleeing. The artist who withdraws, when their fantasy self would like to belong, is failing to recognise and value themselves.

►Assertiveness and the Artist◄

Several contributors to this book make mention of the need to be assertive, and so in this final section of 'Looking at Yourself', I want to define what assertiveness is and suggest how it can help artists to survive.

Assertiveness is behaviour by an individual which is guided by such strongly held beliefs as:

- ► I have the right to be treated with respect as an equal by others (with regard to my sex, age, ethnic origins, work activity, etc).
- ► I have the right to deal with situations directly without making myself dependent on others' approval.
- ► I have the right to ask for as much information as I need in order to make a decision.
- ► I have the right to ask for what I want.
- ► I have the right to change my mind.
- ► I have the right to say *No* without feeling guilty.
- ► I have the right to say what I feel and think without having to justify or apologise for it.

You may find it difficult to accept some of these *rights.* If you do, they probably highlight aspects of your behaviour with which you are uncomfortable. For example, if you don't accept yourself as an equal when dealing with funding bodies, commissions or gallery owners, it will have an

obvious effect on how you behave with them – you may be reduced to feeling like a child who has to accept whatever is meted out, or you may have an overwhelming desire to hit out at them before they *put one over on you*. If saying no is a problem, then you will probably find you overload yourself: agreeing to take part in activities for which you have no real enthusiasm or time, because of not wanting to hurt others, or appear unpleasant. Being unassertive could also mean your career is being directed by the will of others and not yourself – the craftsperson who becomes tied into producing work which is no longer enjoyable because of the pressure of retailers is an obvious example of this. If you found it easy to accept all the rights listed, then ask yourself if you give the same rights to others. If you feel you are entitled to be treated with respect as an artist but wouldn't accord the same respect to the janitor who helps put up your exhibition, or the tutor who offers criticism, then you are operating aggressively not assertively. We can only claim those *rights* that we are prepared to give others.

Assertion is based on the premise that *I'm OK – You're OK,* [(4)] that is I am equal, but no more or less equal than anyone else. When we are not being assertive we are moving from one of three other positions:

►Passivity: *I'm not OK – You're OK*◄

When we are passive we feel we are dependent on others to decide what's best for us. Waiting to be *discovered* and relying on fate are common passive fantasies. Passivity allows us to see ourselves as victims of unfairness without having to consider how we colluded in the outcome. *I never said anything, but they should have known,* is an example of how when we are passive we endow both ourselves with importance, and others with greater abilities than they possibly have. If you want someone to know something you have to tell them. Passivity is strongly linked with a desire to be liked and to avoid conflict, yet ironically the passive response can cause resentment and a lack of respect from others. It is a behaviour model much rewarded in the socialisation of women, but it is by no means exclusive to them. When we choose to be passive we hold onto our feelings and thoughts, so building up tensions which either eventually blow out – usually in a safe situation or with an inappropriate context (the *kick the cat* or *row over the washing up* syndrome) or we internalise the tensions as psychosomatic conditions.

►Aggression: *I'm OK - You're not OK*◄

When we are aggressive we are feeling no more confident than the passive respondent, but we choose a different strategy, one based on the premise *get them before they get you.* Whilst using aggression can seem very powerful, it can leave us afterwards feeling we've lost control, looked stupid and wondering how to make amends. It leaves the recipients of aggression feeling angry and hurt, and if used habitually they will develop their own defence mechanisms: contact will be minimised, letters will replace face-to-face communication, they may look for ways of sabotaging our activities, or plot how to 'drop' us in it. Since assertion and aggression are often confused it is important to be clear as to the difference. When we are aggressive we view situations in win or lose terms and there will be no room to compromise, we have an investment in the other person feeling bad, and we will not be prepared to hear what they are saying.

▷**4** *I'm OK – You're OK,* Thomas Harris. Pan Books. Popular book on transactional analysis theory that relates closely to assertiveness, and helps us understand why we are not assertive. Eric Berne's writings on transactional analysis *Games People Play* and *What do you say after you say hello* are also useful.

►Manipulation: *I'm OK - You're not OK*◄

Manipulation is indirect aggression in that we try to get our own way without getting found out. Manipulation often starts from an apparent position of *You're OK*, in that flattery and *friendship* may be used to persuade us to comply with the manipulator's wishes, but if thwarted the iron fist in the velvet glove will be revealed. Manipulation is another means by which we hope to avoid conflict, and in our society it is much rewarded as *political* behaviour and as an acceptable female ploy. When uncovered however it leads to the same feelings of resentment and defensiveness as aggression engenders.

►Assertion◄

Assertion differs from the three behaviours outlined above in that:

► It starts from a position of mutual respect.
► It believes that open direct communication is preferable to games.
► It doesn't automatically see situations in win or lose terms, but allows that compromise can be acceptable.
► It separates out the issue from the person. As an assertive person I can lose on a particular issue but still respect myself as an individual if I've done my best
► It accepts responsibility for its own actions and doesn't expect others to make the world right for them

In discussing assertion it is important to recognise that there is nothing inherently wrong in any of the non-assertive behaviours, and each has its place, but it is when we use them inappropriately and feel discomfort as a result, that we need to consider whether an assertive response would be more satisfying and effective.

►Recognition Exercise◄

Consider these situations and your actual (or imagined) responses to them, using the behaviour models of: Assertion · Aggression · Manipulation · Passivity.

► You arrive at a gallery as arranged to be told the owner is busy and can't see you.
► A piece of work is dismissed as *unexciting* in a tutorial.
► A meeting is being held to decide on exhibition space, and the space you had mentally stored for yourself is taken by a vociferous group member.
► When you receive your cheque for works sold at a craft gallery it is considerably less than you had expected, as publicity costs have been deducted from the fee.
► Your application for funding from your local arts association is rejected with no explanation.
► The tax inspector looks at your accounts and suggests it's *just a little hobby.*
► Having sent a press-release to your local newspaper, the reporter visits the show, only to report its tabloid sensational aspects.

You may find you have one preferred mode of behaving, or there may be some situations in which you are happily assertive, and others where it is difficult for you. Factors linked to perceived status, authority and the degree of intimacy in the relationship can control the extent to which we can allow ourselves to be assertive.

►Becoming More Assertive◄

Since, behavioural psychologists suggest, we learnt in our first years of life how to be passive, aggressive and manipulative, we can learn also how to be assertive.

The basic assertive skills are these:

►Define your goal◄

Many times we fail to obtain a satisfactory outcome because we didn't take time to think through what we wanted. For example, if I as a sculptor am unhappy at the way in which a piece of work has been placed on site I have a number of ways of expressing my dissatisfaction:

► I moan to my friends but do nothing (passive).
► I complain to the commissioners and ask them to do something about it (still passive because I'm leaving control of any outcome with them – the *something* that transpires relies entirely on their commitment, interest and integrity; none of which may be present).
► I write a letter telling the commissioners how incompetent they are and saying I'll never work with them again (aggressive – you've let off steam, have a temporary sense of satisfaction, but then, what have you achieved?)
► I get a friend who knows one of the commissioners to express some concern at the siting of the piece (passive and manipulative).
► I'm on site at the time of installation to take charge of the process, so the problem doesn't arise (assertive).
► I contact the commissioners as soon as I'm aware of the problem, express my concern, make suggestions as to what could be done, and ask to speak with them about the issue (assertive).

The second to last solution is the most direct way of dealing with the issue, because it assumes that as an artist I am responsible for my work and the way in which it is seen by my audience. However, assuming it is not possible for me to have taken responsibility for the installation, the last solution is equally assertive because I have expressed my anxiety without loading blame, and have stated my needs through making suggestions as to how the situation could be rectified.

►Acknowledge◄

If we are going to be assertive, rather than aggressive then we have to be prepared to listen to the other person's point of view. This needn't change our original goal, in fact it may reinforce it, but if we don't give the other person clues that we are listening they will see us as being aggressive, and may move into that position also. In the case of the sculptor, asking the commissioner to respond to the suggestions gives him the opportunity to offer information that may alter the sculptor's perspective and make her willing to move toward a workable compromise, ie one that works for both

Rembrandt, *Self-portrait*, etching, 1634. Rembrandthuis, Amsterdam

parties rather than an act of submission by the sculptor.

If however, having offered suggestions, the sculptor feels she is being stonewalled, she may want to use additional skills.

▶Broken Record◀

Broken record is a term coined by Anne Dickson[5] to describe the necessity to repeat our viewpoint or need, in order that it is heard. When an initial request is refused, people often withdraw because they feel they've done their bit and failed. Frequently, however, the request hasn't even been heard, perhaps because the non-listener's mind is tied up with other concerns, they have little investment in the issue, or to hear would be to involve them in extra work. Repeating the request several times may be necessary before it is taken seriously. Equally, repeating the request is a means of reminding us that we are here to discuss X when the listener may be anxious to divert us into Y or Z as quickly as possible.

Let's analyse what's gone on between the sculptor and commissioner so far:

> **Sculptor** I'm ringing because I've just seen the way in which my piece of work has been placed on site and I'm concerned at its safety. (Assertive – issue is the safety of the sculpture not the failure of the installers).

▷**5** *A Woman in Your Own Right*, Anne Dickson. Quartet Books, 1981

Commissioner Oh I'm glad you've rung, there's some more paperwork I need from you before we can settle your fee (refusal to listen and attempt to hook).
Sculptor Thanks for mentioning it I'll sort it out tonight (Acknowledgement) but I'm really ringing because the piece is in danger of collapsing and I need to discuss with you how it can be stabilized (broken record).
Commissioner Well all my workmen are busy right now, so there's nothing can be done for a while. But don't worry it looked fine to me when I saw it. Very attractive I thought. (Double hook).
Sculptor I'm pleased you like it (acknowledgement), but I won't allow it to stay as it is. It needs to be more tethered to the ground, and I'd like to see you as soon as possible to discuss how it can be done (broken record).
Commissioner I'm up to my eyes in it right now dearie. I've far more important things than your sculpture to think about (Commissioner - uses put down, an indication he is moving into his aggressor).
Sculptor I know you're busy (acknowledgement and refusal to respond to the put down hook), but when can I see you? (broken record).

If the commissioner continues to block then the sculptor may choose to:

►Switch Gear◄

In the type of interaction outlined above the complainant often backs off, from a feeling of embarrassment at being a nuisance. If the issue is important to you, however, it is important that you pursue it, as otherwise you will be left with a feeling of failure that will knock your self-esteem. Manuel Smith,[3] suggests that every opposer only has so many *Nos* in their repertoire and it is the assertors' task to have one more *Yes* in theirs. Just carrying on repeating your case, may, however become fruitless if the opposer has a large investment in not moving. Authority figures are often over-endowed with a sense of their superiority and rectitude, that makes it impossible for them to listen to the rational content of what is being said to them. Eric Berne describes this as the *'Critical Parent ego state'*, which means that they may be willing to be pleasant to you if you act as a compliant child, and punitive toward you if you show signs of resistance; but they may find it difficult to respond to you as one adult to another adult (I'm OK – You're OK).

Once it is clear that the commissioner cannot engage his adult to recognise the danger of an unstable sculpture, then the sculptor has to bring in a new strategy. This means switching gears to identify a person who could effect a solution.

To return to the dialogue:

Sculptor I know you're busy, but when can I see you?
Commissioner I'm not committing myself to a time to discuss one small bit of metal which I've got major policy meetings to prepare for (use of Critical Parent in put down).
Sculptor So you're saying you're not concerned that a considerable weight of metal could collapse and cause injury? (refusal to respond to put down. Use of questioning to elicit his position).
Commissioner I'm concerned, but I judge it is unlikely, so it's not a priority.
Sculptor Well to me it is a priority as my reputation is tied in with the work (assertive - owning of responsibility). As you have told me you're not willing to do anything now I'm going to contact. . . . . (Switch of gears).
Commissioner You do that, but they won't say any different to me.
Sculptor Well, I'll keep going till I find someone who will take this seriously.

Pursuing an issue in this way can be mentally exhausting but the pay-off to our sense of self when we do respect our own opinion is enormous, and creates a cycle of confidence that gives us courage to take on greater

▷**6** *When I say no I feel guilty*, Manuel Smith. Bantam, 1975

challenges. Had the sculptor backed down s/he would have reinforced a belief that s/he had no right to interfere or to challenge 'experts' and would have reduced the likelihood of taking on any similar situation that arose in the future, and if the sculpture did collapse s/he would have been left with the guilt of *if only....* This way, even if s/he fails to find someone willing to listen, s/he will know that s/he has done her best and not failed him/her sense of self as an artist.

►Summary◄

In this chapter I have argued that in order to get the most from the rest of this book you need to spend some time considering your abilities, interests and values in order that you can identify goals that you wish to achieve, and can thereby design a support system that will help you towards them.

I have also suggested that assertiveness skills have a place in that support system in helping you to respect yourself, your opinions and your needs.

Or as Charles Kettering once said *'No one every stumbled across anything sitting down'* – so now it's over to you.◄

►Information◄

►Further Reading◄

►*Life Skills Teaching*, Barry Hopson & Mike Scally. Lifeskill Associates, 1981

►*Artworkers – a report on the employment and further study patterns of UK art and design graduates shortly after graduation,* Bill Farrington, Linda Johnston & Anne Webb. Association of Graduate Careers Advisory Services, 1988

►*I'm OK – You're OK,* Thomas Harris. Pan Books. Popular book on Transactional Analysis Theory that relates closely to assertiveness, and helps us understand why we are not assertive. Eric Berne's writings on Transactional Analysis *Games People Play* and *What Do You Say After You Say Hello* are also useful

►*When I Say No I Feel Guilty*, Manuel Smith. Bantam, 1975

►*Build Your Own Rainbow: A Workbook for Career and Life Management*, Barry Hopson & Mike Scally. Lifeskills Associates, 1984

►*Don't Say Yes When You Want To Say No* H Fensterheim & VL Baer. Futura Publications, 1977

►*The Assertive Woman*, S Phelps & N Austin. Ardington Books, 1975

►*Student Guide to Living, Studying and Job Hunting,* Abbey National. Longman

▲
Stained glass window by **Sasha Ward** at Lansdowne Hospital, Cardiff. This commission was organised by South East Wales Arts with support of the Welsh Arts Council.

Exhibiting ▼

Why Exhibit?◄

On Home Ground◄

Alternatives◄

Public Spaces◄

Public Galleries◄

Private Spaces◄

Open Exhibitions◄

Exhibitor's Checklist◄

Touring Exhibitions◄

Moving Work◄

Commission & VAT◄

Why Exhibit?

►Richard Padwick◄

Why do artists want to exhibit? Welsh artist, Phil Nichol[1], gives four reasons:

►**To show your work to the public** – to exhibit is surely the reason behind working, without its exhibition the art work can have no meaning or context. The exhibition turns an introverted activity into an extrovert one.

►**To see your work** – the exhibition provides a rare opportunity for the artist to see a bulk of his/her work, altogether, in good light, in neutral surroundings, and away from the cluttered and personal space of a studio. The exhibition gives the artist the time-out and the facilities for a studied reassessment of the work.

►**To get known as an artist** – an important function of an exhibition is for the artist to introduce himself/herself to fellow artists, critics, exhibition organisers and art administrators as well as the public. The better known you are as an artist, the more likely opportunities are to come your way.

►**To sell your work** – sales are obviously important or essential to cover the costs of preparing the exhibition and to bring in some kind of income for your work as an artist.

Very few galleries exist primarily for the benefit of the artist. They may provide an 'opportunity' or a 'platform' for contemporary artists to exhibit their work in public but it rarely goes much further than that. The principle responsibility of the *public* gallery is to provide a service for its community as a whole, ie the rate-payers who provide the funds. The *private/commercial* gallery exists at best to make a profit or at worst to survive financially. Each gallery has its own set of reasons for staging exhibitions and these rarely perfectly match the requirements artists have in an exhibition. Each venue has its own constraints, be it the physical space, the availability of finances and staff, the requirements of the owner, who may be the local authority, an independent trust or an individual. These constraints determine the nature of the exhibitions presented and the relationship between the gallery and the exhibiting artists.

The *library* exhibition space can, and I am now talking in generalised terms, offer a very large audience, but it is not a specialised one. You may regard this feature as an advantage or a disadvantage. The private/commercial gallery will do its best to sell work – a mutual benefit to the artist

▷**1** 'The Reason for Showing', Phil Nichol, *Artists Newsletter*, September 1984

and the gallery. But you may not regard your work as a 'commercial product', nor be happy with the often 'exclusive' nature of some commercial galleries nor want your work to be owned by the 'upper middle class'. The municipal gallery must satisfy more of your requirements but it is unlikely to put much effort into selling your work.

►Exhibiting and Selling◄

How good are galleries at selling work? A survey carried out by John Kaser[2] in 1986 showed that theatre foyers, village halls and art and craft fairs were, on the whole equally as effective as galleries in selling work, and they proved to be better than public galleries outside London. What this survey couldn't show was how effective each type of venue was at selling different styles of work. Did the sales, for example, at village halls consist of a particular type, size and price of work?

The survey went on to show that a male full-time painter typically earns an annual income of £5000 from selling 25 works at around £200 each, whilst a woman typically earns £1400 (10 works at £140). Sales for part-time painters (there were more part-time than full-time painters) are considerably less, typically £875 for men and £700 for women. The figures for sculptors and printmakers were slightly better.

If this is depressing, then another survey[3], also carried out in 1986, is even more so. It shows that an artist holding a solo or two-person exhibition in a *public* gallery typically loses nearly £400. This is worked out at by balancing the income from sales and fees from the exhibition against the artist's costs of preparing for it. And these figures exclude the costs of materials and time involved in making the work in the first place. If these were included the resulting loss would be many times larger.

The clear conclusion from all this is that unless you produce work specifically in response to consumer demand or expected profit, you are very unlikely to make exhibiting a profitable activity. You are far more likely to lose substantially – exhibiting is unlikely to be your main means of financial support. There are, of course, other reasons for exhibiting, as Phil Nichol points out.

►Waiting List◄

The Directory of Exhibition Spaces lists some 2000 exhibition venues throughout the UK. The 1981 national census found 40,000 people who describe their main occupation as 'artist'. Assuming the 2000 spaces each hold on average ten exhibitions each year every artist would be able to exhibit once every two years. In fact the situation is far worse than this because many municipal galleries show only a few exhibitions of work by living artists, and library spaces show only a few visual art exhibitions in their programmes. This rate also assumes that every artist has an equal opportunity to exhibit but in fact the better known you are (or the more fashionable your work is) the more opportunities are offered you. There are far more artists looking for exhibitions than there are exhibition opportunities available. As a result, all spaces operate some kind of selection process to decide who is to be the lucky person. In a library the selection is usually based on the 'first-come-first-served' basis. The private

▷**2** 'Marketing Art' John Kaser, *Artists Newsletter*, October 1986
▷**3** 'Sales of Contemporary Art in Public Galleries', Richard Padwick, *Artists Newsletter*, November 1986

gallery/commercial gallery will base its selection on an assessment of how well the work is likely to sell to its clients. The major public galleries may formulate their programmes on the basis of invitation only and won't accept applications to exhibit. They may only show artists of international reputation.

> Even the youngest and lowliest arts administrator in the smallest gallery selects art and artists. The artist tries to be selected since he/she hopes that from selection further opportunities will come. The arts administrator in the public sector is the fisherman. Once caught the fish is transferred to a larger pond where other fishers fish. These fishers are the dealers that can transfer the artist (fish) to the tank where the big fish swim. The artist just keeps swimming, trying to lure an angler (strange role reversal). (Eric Moody[4]

Having your work rejected from galleries is always disheartening, whatever the reason.

►Private Enterprise◄

Fed up with being turned-down, dissatisfied with the constraints imposed on you by the galleries, feel you are being manipulated? Then there is always the possibility of taking matters into your own hands. Many artists, no longer content with the traditional gallery structure, are now organising their own exhibition spaces or exhibition opportunity, both as individuals and as groups. They are creating their own galleries, permanent or temporary; they are organising touring exhibitions and exploiting the potential of alternative venues like pubs or empty shops. Such ventures are full of their own problems, constraints and compromises but the artist is always much more in control of their work and the way it is promoted and presented. The first section on exhibiting looks at artists taking the initiative and organising their own spaces and exhibitions.

►Information◄

►Further Reading◄

►'The Reason for Showing', Phil Nichol. *Artists Newsletter*, September 1984

►'Support for the Avant-garde in the Visual Arts in the 1980s', Eric Moody. *Journal of Arts Policy and Management*, August 1984

►'A suspected heart condition in the garden', Eric Moody. *Artists Newsletter*, January 1986. On the politics of selection

►*Directory of Exhibition Spaces*, ed Susan Jones. Artic Producers Artists Newsletter Publications 1989

►*Economic Situation of Visual Artists*, Nich Pearson & Andrew Brighton. Calouste Gulbenkian Foundation, 1979. Not published but copies lodged with arts councils and regional arts associations

►'Loss-Making', Richard Padwick. *Artists Newsletter*, October 1986. Survey on the financial viability of artists exhibiting in public galleries

►'At Grass Roots', Tony Warner. *Artists Newsletter*, October 1986. Economic survey of artists in Norwich

▷4 'Support for the Avant-garde in the Visual Arts in the 1980s', Eric Moody, *Journal of Arts Policy and Management*, August 1984

▲
Catalyst, a performance/multi-media group of eight dancers, performance artists, photographer, lighting designer, musical director and stage and costume designer. *'Some of the work is well structured and set within a conventional gallery or theatre space; at other times they work spontaneously and take their work out onto the streets of Edinburgh or occasionally into the Scottish Highlands'*. (Peter Hill).

▶'Marketing Art', John Kaser. *Artists Newsletter*, October 1986, April, May, June 1987
▶'Benefactors or Beneficiaries', Richard Padwick. *Artists Newsletter*, June 1985. On the relationship between artists and public galleries
▶'Sales of Contemporary Art in Public Galleries', Richard Padwick. *Artists Newsletter*, November 1986. Survey on how good public galleries are at selling art
▶'Jeux Sans Frontieres or Liaisons Dangereux', David Briers. *Artists Newsletter*, November 1985. On artists' exchanges through twin-town schemes
▶'A Twin-Town Arrangement', Benjamin Eastwood. *Artists Newsletter*, April 1985. Exhibiting abroad through the twin-town scheme
▶'Payments to Artists for Public Access to Their Work', Roland Miller. *Artists Newsletter*, Part 1 December 1984; Part 2 March 1985
▶'Editorial', *Artists Newsletter*, July 1986. On discussions about the future of exhibiting fees
▶'Looking at Your Exhibition', David Briers. *Artists Newsletter*, January 1984. An idiosyncratic glossary for artists exhibiting in public galleries
▶'Payments to Artists', Sheila Hayward. *Artists Newsletter*, February 1989
▶*EPR – Exhibition Payment Right, Artists' Consultative Meetings 1987/88*, report by Roland Miller for the National Artists Association. Includes Arts Council and regional arts association papers and recommendations
▶'Contact Gallery', Tony Warner. *Artists Newsletter*, February 1987

On Home Ground

compiled by
►Richard Padwick◄

►Studio Exhibitions◄

Some artists choose to run the occasional home or studio exhibition. In one case, for example, an artist has held an exhibition in his home once every two years over the last several years, advertising this widely as well as inviting all past purchasers of his work, and has successfully sold a substantial part of his past two years' work on each occasion. The whole house is turned into an exhibition space for two weeks, during which time he and his wife work flat out to run the exhibition and to act as hosts. Important to the success of the exhibition is, no doubt, the very 'personal' nature of an exhibition involving the artist's home, and the regularity of contact maintained with all former buyers through this. (Nich Pearson)[(1)]

'Throughout 1985 I have had solo exhibitions in public galleries throughout England lasting a total of 46 weeks. Total sales at these amounted to just nine prints (total £400) – all but one of which were sold at previews where I was present.'[(2)] When artist Alan Stones decided to open his studio for a week he sold 2 paintings, 3 drawings and 33 prints and received a commission for a print edition worth £1000. *'Since the Open Studio Week, and as a direct result of it, there have been further sales of prints and a substantial painting commission.'* The total income received from holding the open week was £9,500 against an expenditure (publicity, refreshments, insurance, catalogue, of £500).

In another case, a number of artists working together, mounted small exhibitions in turn in each other's homes. On each occasion the main audience would be the friends and acquaintances specific to that house. Such a way of exhibiting utilises, in a sense, the 'Tupperware Party' model the occasion and experience benefiting from the informality and intimacy of an event being in someone's home, and from the ties of friendship between that person and a circle of friends. (Nich Pearson)[(3)]

Members of the public may be hesitant about visiting the artist in his/her studio, perhaps feeling a certain obligation to buy. On the other hand those that do visit will have done so not only because they may be prepared to make a purchase, but also because they wish to meet the artist personally and possibly to discuss his/her or even their own work or problems! A first-time buyer (the unforeseen visitor) may become, or may already be a committed admirer of the artist's work, and can become a valuable supporter in future years. (Philip Wright)[(4)]

▷**1** 'Alternatives', Nich Pearson, *Directory of Exhibition Spaces*, first edition, ed. Neil Hanson & Susan Jones. Artic Producers, 1983
▷**2** Alan Stones, report on his open studio week
▷**3** *Directory of Exhibition Spaces*
▷**4** 'The Artist, The Work and the Public', Philip Wright, *Directory of Exhibition Spaces*

►Artist's Gallery◄

◄
Off-Centre Gallery, a room in printmaker Peter Ford's house in Bedminster, Bristol. The gallery is used to display his own work but also exhibits the work of other artists, particularly those whose work has a social or political content. The aim is to keep prices accessible and a proportion of the profits is given to War Resister's International, Survival International and the International Association of Art.

Throughout Britain, but particularly in the more attractive rural areas, artists set up permanent galleries in or adjacent to their own homes or studios. Providing one's own gallery is, in the fullest sense, an alternative to working through or relying upon the existing public and private galleries.

At the simplest level, such 'galleries' are no more than a display area within a studio, or a room in the artist's house kept clear of normal domestic uses. But many are 'proper' galleries in their own right, with clear signs, frontages, lighting, information, etc.

The advantage of artists running their own galleries are threefold: first, they have a permanent exhibition of their own work, organised and developed according to their own priorities. Potential buyers can be brought back to a full and professional display; second, however successful the artist may or may not be in obtaining exhibitions or placing works in other galleries, they always have their own base and exhibition to work from; third, there is no commission to pay. All monies earned, less costs, are income for the artist. (Nich Pearson)(5)

►**Note:** If you hold an exhibition in your studio or home you should take out public liability insurance (*see Insurance*)◄

The economic base of a gallery run by an individual artist, is in fact, quite unlike that of a normal private gallery. In a conventional private gallery the gallery's income is not the money received from work sold, but, rather the commission taken on sales, minus all the costs associated with the building.

With an artist-run gallery all sales income accrues to the artist. There is no commission because he/she is both gallery and artist... The artist, maintaining a gallery can be part of the overall and total activity of being an artist. He/she does not earn a living from the gallery; the living is earned from making and selling works of art, the maintaining of the gallery being part of this. (Nich Pearson)(6)

▷see Working at Home◁

But artists should remember that exhibiting at or working from home may cause many complications, eg with tenancy agreements or mortgage, planning laws, rates, disruption to family, neighbours or fellow occupiers. (Philip Wright)(7)

▷**5** *Directory of Exhibition Spaces*
▷**6** *Directory of Exhibition Spaces*
▷**7** *Directory of Exhibition Spaces*

►Group Studio Open Exhibitions◄

Many artists' studio groups either organise open days, weekends or weeks or have their own permanent exhibition space. These are very different in concept. The purpose behind open studios is to invite the public into the artists' working environment – giving an insight into each artists' individual working processes. The atmosphere of a studio is often more conducive to generating dialogue between members of the public and artist than the anonymity created by an exhibition space. On the other hand group studios, for the very reason that several artists are involved, avoid the over-personal and perhaps intimidating atmosphere of intruding into the 'private domain' of an individual artist's house or studio.

> Holding exhibitions and open-days is an important part of the Society's role. Besides the obvious objectives of providing space, contacts and encouragement, the Society was founded with the aim of providing a focus for practising artists in Leeds. The open day, organised eight months after the artists moved in, was seen as a means of publicising the studios, as a practice for later exhibitions and as a way of strengthening links with grant-aiding bodies and between the artists themselves.
>
> Signs were placed at the entrance of the site and artists took turns to direct visitors to the building itself. Publicity was in the form of posters and invitations distributed by artists and sent out together with a regular mailing by a local gallery. Among those contacted were the local authority, the RAA, ACGB, local colleges, other studio groups and the press. Press releases sent well in advance brought prior notices in local newspapers and *Artists Newsletter*. A loose-leafed catalogue was produced with a page for each artist's information and photograph. The format enables artists to send out their own sheets as applications for exhibitions and other sheets can be added as new artists join.
>
> Some days before, the artists collaborated in cleaning and white-washing the building. On the day, explanations, statements and places to sit were much in evidence but it would have been helpful to see more prices by the works. In five hours from 3pm to 8pm, 200 people visited the studios including those from the RAA, the press and staff from one local and one London gallery. (Leeds Arts Space Society)[8]

►Exhibiting in Group Studios◄

Several artists' groups have provided an exhibition space as part of their communal facilities. The spaces are used primarily to show the work of the artists in the group, to provide a clean display space removed from the clutter and dirt of their studios. The cost of the space (rent, rates, etc) is usually shared amongst the artists in the group who then have the right to make use of it. The costs of mounting, publicising and invigilating the exhibitions are the responsibility of the exhibiting artist.

►Studio Group Exhibition Spaces◄

One way of spreading the cost of having an exhibition space is to let it out to other artists or artists' groups who pay all the necessary costs, the studio group providing only the space.

One of the first artists' groups with showing-space available to artists outside the group was the Waterloo Studios in London.

▷**8** 'Leeds Arts Space Society', *Artists Newsletter*, November 1984

◀
Nicola Russell and **Elaine Callen**, of the Artists Collective of Northern Ireland, distributing posters in Belfast for an open day at the Queen Street Studios.

> Originally the whole space was designated as studios but one large open area provided such an excellent exhibition space that it was decided to use it as a gallery.... As with the studios, finance was a major problem and there is no full-time administration.... At one stage the group considered employing an administrator but apart from the economic impossibility, it was also felt that the gallery would be more lively if run by an artists' group, who selected work for the programme.... The overall philosophy for the programme is to provide a venue for young artists whose work would otherwise be unlikely to be seen.
>
> Obviously, none of the studio artists want to be side-tracked into organising the gallery at the expense of their own work and, in order to keep administration to a minimum, slide applications for exhibitions have been invited from groups of artists rather than individuals. Applicants are asked to outline their reasons for wanting to show together and to describe how they intend to use the space. The selected artists are entirely responsible for providing their own posters, invitations and advertising, for transport, for invigilation during the show and for electricity expenses. The average costs per show has been £200-£350.
>
> An aspect of the gallery which is being reconsidered is that of exhibiting exclusively little known artists. Attendance at shows has been poor. Several of the committee now feel that there would be an advantage in showing some better known artists (perhaps twice a year) which would expand the potential audience for other shows. (Steve Alley)[9]

Waterloo Studios eventually closed down. It had been faced with a massive rates demand backdated several years. If the studio group had known that rates would have had to be paid, it is likely that the gallery would never have been included or that exhibiting artists would also have been charged a hire fee to cover the rates and other overheads. Some studio groups now do this so that, although the artists are instrumental in providing the exhibition space, they are not saddled with the costs.

◁see **Private Spaces**▷

▶Artists' Group Run Galleries◀

Some studio groups take the exhibition space one-step further creating to all intents and purposes a traditional gallery. The only difference, and

▷**9** 'Waterloo Studios & Gallery', Steve Alley, *Artists Newsletter*, November 1981

perhaps it is a fundamental one, is that the control of policy and programming lies with the artists. Manchester Artists Studio Association is an example of an artists' studio group which runs a gallery (the Castlefield Gallery) in the traditional sense. It is physically separate from the studios and is not seen as a facility in which studio artists can exhibit as of right. It was set up to show contemporary art in a city, which at the time had poor provision.

> The first step towards starting the gallery was to find suitable premises.... The next step was to convince various funding bodies of our sincerity and actually raise enough money to equip the gallery, pay overheads and plan the exhibitions.
>
> It was never the intention of the artists that the gallery should be completely artist run. The bursts of enthusiasm that happen when a group of like-minded people get together can't be expected to last and it was understood right from the beginning that the project would be a full-time job for someone. If you are divided between painting and 'gallery sitting' one is bound to win over!
>
> The artists make all the decisions regarding the exhibition policy/programme.... As members of the studio leave and others take their place, so the exhibition programme and policy may change. At present the foremost motive in choosing exhibitions is to bring high-quality new work to Manchester and to spotlight exciting work made within the region. If showing 'big-names' helps place the gallery firmly in the public eye, then that is so much the better for everyone, but that is not why we show artists such as Hoyland or Caro. (Sheila Seal)[10]

The Collective Gallery, which is run by the Artist's Collective in Edinburgh. *'The aim of the gallery is to provide a platform to younger or less established artists operating outside the existing structures. All exhibitors must be members of the Collective which is an artist run organisation emphasising membership participation and decision-making.'*
▼

▷**10** 'Castlefield Gallery', Sheila Seal, *Artists Newsletter*, November 1984

►Art Weeks◄

In 1976, as part of the Cambridge Festival, the Festival Association arranged for six artist-craftspeople to open their studios to the public for at least one or two specified days. The openings of the various studios were staggered, so that at least something was available on any one of eight days – during the 15 day Festival. The exhibitions were combined with a display in the central library, and a booklet was produced about the participants. The event appears to have been successful: one participant reports that over 120 people signed his visitors book over a two-day period (ie something more than that number actually came.)

Now, that event, of course, was organised by an overall Festival Association. It benefited from the audiences attracted to the whole festival and from the publicity for the festival as a whole. But the experience points to possibilities for artists and craftspeople in organising such events themselves. The combined opening of different studios makes it a bigger event – and the group can share costs to produce more significant publicity. (Nich Pearson)[11]

◁see **Publicity**▷

Several similar events have now been organised by artists. The first was the Oxfordshire Visual Arts Week which now runs as an annual event. Others have been held in Birmingham, Leicester and Manchester.

Oxfordshire Visual Arts Week could happen anywhere in any location. It is run for artists by artists – it is an attempt to draw the attention of the public to the way artists work – to introduce artists to their public and the public to them – and to raise issues for discussion. The Arts Weeks make no attempt to select either the artist/craftsperson or the type of work they do. They include anyone and everyone who designates themselves as artists; they go someway towards breaking the barriers and mystification that surrounds the visual arts in this country, and perhaps they provide a balance to the selection and rejection process that is usually involved with the showing of artist's work to the public.

It is surely healthy that art should occasionally be offered to the public without it first having gone through, what is necessarily a subjective selection process by those who may be equipped to judge it, and equally healthy that the public should be able occasionally to form their own opinions as to which work they choose to look at. An event such as Arts Week provides the means for doing this. (Sarah Eckersley)[12]

The Oxfordshire Arts Week is quite a large event. Over 200 artists and craftspeople throughout Oxfordshire, both in urban and rural areas, participate. It costs over £7,500 to organise, the major costs being the employment of a free-lance administrator and printing for publicity. Participating artists are charged £10 raising £2000, the remainder being found in grant aid from ACGB, the regional arts association, the tourist board, the city and county councils, commercial sponsorship and advertising in the publicity. An indication of the value to the artists is that most involved in the first also participated in subsequent ones. 360 works were sold in the first week and 36% of the artists made useful contacts as a result of participating.

►In 1988, the budget was £15,000 and over 600 artists took place. A total of 50,000 visits were made to studios, events and exhibitions and £60,450 was made in sales and commissions◄

▷**11** *Directory of Exhibition Spaces*
▷**12** 'Oxfordshire Visual Arts Week', Sarah Eckersley, *Artists Newsletter*, November 1984

►
Cover for a catalogue introducing an open day at the Queen Street Studios in Belfast. The studios are run by the Artists' Collective of Northern Ireland.

►Information◄

►Further Reading◄

►'Castlefield Gallery', Sheila Seal. *Artists Newsletter,* November 1984
►*Directory of Exhibition Spaces*, first edition, ed Neil Hanson & Susan Jones. Artic Producers, 1983
►*Art Galleries and Exhibition Spaces in Wales*, Nich Pearson. Welsh Arts Council, 1989
►'Oxfordshire Visual Arts Week', Sarah Eckersley. *Artists Newsletter*, November 1984
►'Leeds Art Space Society', *Artists Newsletter*, May 1983
►'Making More Ways', Susan Jones. *Artists Newsletter*, November 1988

▲Left
A green field gallery – **Denys Short** uses a two-acre field at Dinas Cross to exhibit his sculpture annually and a nearby barn is used for drawings, paintings and models.

▲Right
Denys Short, *Bird Table No 4*, stained wood, 12ft high. An exhibit in his outdoor exhibition.

Alternatives

compiled by
Richard Padwick

The Vacant Shop

High street shops, particularly the medium and larger stores and supermarkets, can attract hundreds of thousands of customers each year. This is largely because of what they are and what they do, but it is also because of where they are. Simply being in a city or town centre, on a main street, and with all the other main shops and facilities means that they are where everybody comes.

From time to time, shops close or move: centrally located shop spaces stand empty. If permission and agreement can be obtained, these can offer an ideal siting for an 'alternative' exhibition.

In the summer of 1980, 15 final year students at Cardiff College of Art organised and held an exhibition called 'Not Just Another Art Show' in an empty former supermarket in Cardiff's High Street. The exhibiting space was significantly larger than anything normally available in Cardiff's 'regular' art galleries – venues which, anyway, would not normally consider a major show from such a young and inexperienced group.

They successfully obtained some sponsorship for the exhibition, as well as help 'in kind' – such as the loan of industrial cleaning machinery for preparing the exhibition area.

During the ten days that the exhibition was open, over 11,000 people came. It was Festival time in Cardiff, and the exhibition was open for 12 hours a day. The organisers of the exhibition have written *'The type of surroundings and atmosphere of most art exhibitions have a tendency to limit their audience and discourage a large sector of the community. Many art centres and Arts Council exhibitions, because of their situation and 'aura' cater for the initiated exhibition-goer as opposed to the general public. Exhibiting in a disused supermarket in the High Street was a positive attempt to combat the atmosphere of the mystery, unapproachability and elitism that is stifling contemporary art.'*

Preparation, however, took eight months. Finding premises was very difficult. Large cities usually have vacant shops – but persuading the owners or agents to let you use the space can prove difficult. And then, even if you can get the space rent free, there will be bills to pay. The costs of lighting a large space are high. Further, the former users of a vacant shop won't necessarily leave their premises in the best condition....

Then there is publicity and invitations. The exhibitors were keen to get a wide coverage for their unusual intitiative. Many people were invited to the show, and letters were sent to major art magazines and critics. The latter did not come, and further follow-up letters were written, with similar effects. The exhibitors wanted, and obtained sponsorship. Each exhibitor wrote several letters in search of sponsorship. About one in three of those approached replied. Several gave small amounts of money, but fortunately

an aluminium firm gave generously. But all this involved seeing people, trying to persuade and interest them, and often finding that interest and sympathy were all that people would or could give.

Two and a half years after the event, I asked one of the exhibitors if he would do it again. He said probably not. The show had been successful, and much had been learned. The work and time put in had paid off. However, a great deal of work and time had been expended before a definite place and time had been secured, and he felt it had been important that in 1980, all the exhibitors had been students. They had had the time; they had all been working in the same place; they had had the backing of a college; and they had had, in a sense, 'nothing to lose'. He felt that there had been a lot of risk combining and maintaining the enthusiasms and commitments of the group during the long process when there had been no definite sense of whether or how the time and effort would pay off in the end.

Groups formed for a specific occasion or event are always more difficult to maintain and work with than groups that have an existing function and life. An existing group will find it easier to attempt what the Cardiff group achieved, than will an ad hoc group formed solely for the purpose... (Nich Pearson)[1]

◄▲

Exhibitions of work by members of the Tyneside Artist Contact Group running concurrently in a cafe, pub and shopping arcade. The group is not studio-based but members meet fortnightly to exchange information, resources, opinions, to seek commissions, and to promote their work. (Photo: Keith Pattison)

▷**1** 'Alternatives', Nich Pearson, *Directory of Exhibition Spaces*, first edition, ed. Neil Hanson & Susan Jones. Artic Producers 1983

►Pubs, Hotels and Restaurants◄

While a vacant high street supermarket offers prime site and opportunity, pubs, hotels and restaurants offer more regular and normal possibilities for different kinds of display – from the small to the fairly ambitious. There are pubs, hotels and restaurants throughout Britain, where, because of the existing interests or contacts of the proprietor or publican, a specific point is made of having regular and changing displays and exhibitions.

However, outside the small number where an interest in art has already been shown, there are many more where the space is suitable, and with a little careful persuasion and enthusiasm on the part of an artist, work could be exhibited. Many hotels would benefit greatly from having works of art around the walls; and, meanwhile, far too many pubs, hotels and restaurants rely on prints and reproductions that have little connection with the particularity of the building, town or region, and reflect in no way the wealth and variety of skills and achievements of the artists working in their locality.

Of course, all pubs, hotels and restaurants are different and so the ways work can be hung and shown will be different. A large hotel may have foyers and meeting areas that are ideal for some kind of larger exhibition; medium sized restaurants (with, perhaps, variable and lowish lighting) may be suitable for only three or four carefully placed and strong works; while in some pubs one would want to ensure that the works displayed were away from a late Saturday night drunken crush. The exact possibilities have to be assessed and defined for each case. (Nich Pearson)[2]

►Windows◄

Another venue worth considering although it is usually overlooked by most artists is the window display. A well-positioned display in the centre of a town has more people seeing it in a day than most galleries have in six-months, and you rarely have to pay for it. If you aren't too sensitive about the 'prestige' angle, this is worth investigating, especially for displays of small works. (Nick Clements)[3]

They are not spaces that can embrace the generalised function of an exhibition. Rather, in a narrower sense, they are useful for advertising. The point of a high street window display is to encourage and excite the passing stranger to think of doing something or going somewhere. If a portrait artist places two or three selected works in a window (along with information about the artist, what they do, and where they are), it is to encourage people to visit and commission work. Or if an artist is having a full exhibition somewhere, the window display will serve as an advertisement for that. Or an artist may be running an 'open' studio – and wish to use the window display to advertise that and encourage more people to visit, see more work, and so forth. Whatever the case, there must be a purpose to a window display, and a purpose which goes beyond the immediate experience of the works on display. (Nich Pearson)[4]

►Persuasion◄

Of course, the owner of a business, an office, as also a pub, restaurant or hotel, will need careful persuading by the artist or artists seeking a show. The owner may well be very cautious; will want to know what they are getting; that it will be well presented; that it will not offend and that while it may attract, interest and even 'impress' visitors or customers, it will not interfere with their business and activities. Most people do not read

▷**2** *Directory of Exhibition Spaces*

▷**3** 'Actions will always speak louder than words', Nick Clements, *Directory of Exhibition Spaces*

▷**4** *Directory of Exhibition Spaces*

exhibition reviews; so the only media image of art they will gain results from the occasional 'freak' story – the 'bricks', the soiled underwear, and the obscure joke. There is bound to be a little suspicion until the artist has made clear who they are, what they do, and the kind of exhibition or display they are proposing.

With a business, office, restaurant, hotel, or pub or similar institution, the artist is not simply asking for a favour; they are also offering something – and for nothing. The artist wants space and access to an audience, but the business is receiving the interest, publicity and attraction of an exhibition. They will benefit from that.

Hotels, pubs and restaurants like and need good publicity. Newspapers, TV, and radio, thrive on stories of the unusual and the personal. Exhibitions in unusual situations always make good copy for local (and, often enough, regional) newspapers.

In terms of 'benefits' therefore, an exhibition in such a setting is a collaboration between the parties; both can and should benefit from working together; and neither should be seen as being the one 'doing a favour' for the other. So with that confidence, the artist seeking to persuade somebody of the advantages and worthwhileness of hosting an exhibition should be working from a position of strength and equality.

This does not mean that they will necessarily get what they want; but it makes it more likely. (Nich Pearson)[(5)]

The image you project counts for so much, if you have a cohesive and attractive image, they may be interested but if you have no clear idea of what form the show will take, insurmountable obstacles will be put in your way. Persistence and polite business behaviour are therefore essentials. (Nick Clements)[(6)]

►Information◄

►Further Reading◄

►*Directory of Exhibition Spaces*, first edition, ed Neil Hanson & Susan Jones. Artic Producers, 1983

►'Witness', *Artists Newsletter*, November 1987

►'Making More Ways', Susan Jones. *Artists Newsletter*, November 1988

►'14 Days', Staden et al. *Artists Newsletter*, February 1987. Covers the Lewisham visual arts festival

►*Organising Your Own Exhibition – A Guide for Artists*, Debbie Duffin. ACME Housing Association, 1987

▷**5** *Directory of Exhibition Spaces*

▷**6** *Directory of Exhibition Spaces*

Public Spaces

compiled by
▶Richard Padwick◀

The term 'public' in regard to art galleries and exhibition spaces refers to their funding from public money (out of rates or taxes). Public galleries are provided as a public service and are thus non-commercial. They may attempt to sell work but that is not their main function as it is with private and commercial galleries. The term covers an extremely wide and diverse range of organisations from schools and libraries to the major city or county museum services and the national galleries.

Within this definition, however, two types of public exhibition venues are clearly discernable:

▶Art Gallery◀

'An art gallery is more than a hanging space; it should be a used and living space.'[1] Its primary purpose or one of the primary purposes of the host organisation is the presentation of visual art. Temporary exhibitions of contemporary art may be the organisation's sole function or it may be part of a much wider museum service, or part of a range of art media presented by an arts centre. The gallery has specialist staff and budget. It attracts a public because of the programme of exhibitions it presents.

▶Exhibition Space◀

An exhibition space *'is essentially a receiving area; shows initiated elsewhere are placed in the space. The venue initiates none of its own shows; it has no creative exhibition-making staff.'*[2] *It has a small or non-existent budget for exhibitions, but exhibitions are regarded as part (however small) of the organisation's function, and are regularly held (however few a year).*

> An exhibition space is frequently housed in a building whose purpose is essentially something other than for the presentation of visual arts. It may be a school hall, theatre foyer or library. It may be a purpose-built space, with good lighting and display facilities or a make-shift arrangement formed by temporary screens with general lighting. A feature of most exhibition spaces is that the exhibition is usually seen, not as a primary purpose of a visit to the building but as a bi-product of some other purpose – changing a book at the library, attending an evening class in a school, or going to the theatre to see a play. (Richard Padwick)[3]
>
> The exhibition will enhance the 'feel' of the place as 'cultural' (cultured) centres. Rarely, however, can or will the exhibition programme be

▷**1** *Art Galleries and Exhibition Spaces in Wales*, Nich Pearson, Welsh Arts Council, 1981
▷**2** *Contemporary Art Exhibitions in the East Midlands*, Richard Padwick. East Midlands Arts, 1983
▷**3** *Contemporary Art Exhibitions in the East Midlands*

maintained in terms of and with an active, on-going, creative relationship with a regular and involved exhibition audience. (Nich Pearson)[4]

Exhibition spaces should not be regarded as second class galleries with small, poor display facilities, inadequate lighting, unskilled staff and minimal budget, but seen as a quite different and distinct species. If this is the case then the principles behind initiating exhibitions for non-gallery venues may also need to be quite different and distinct from those destined for galleries. This applies throughout the exhibition origination process: the selection of the work, the way it is presented, its contextual information, its promotion and publicity, and its accompanying activities.

In order to do this the nature of the venue must be understood, not in the first place by its physical qualities, but how it operates as a public building and the nature and concerns of the public who use it.

The exhibition space should be understood in terms of the useful role it can play within its natural and proper limitation rather than as a surrogate to or replacement for a professionally staffed and funded gallery. (Richard Padwick)[5]

►Libraries◄

Many libraries have exhibition spaces or facilities. Library services regard exhibitions as an important aspect of their work but *'exhibition presentation forms only a very small part of the work of any one library'.*[6] As such, few resources, staffing time or expertise and finances are specifically allocated to exhibition activities. Some library services do run traditional galleries, particularly where there is no separate museum service in the borough or county, but in the main, exhibition facilities in libraries are used for a wide variety of displays not just visual arts.

What you do not get (if you exhibit in a library) is to be part of an exhibition programme wholly devoted to the visual arts, as you would in an arts centre.... So you may find your one-person exhibition preceded, or accompanied, by an exhibition prepared by the area health authority, or 'Fungi, Friend or Foe?' or a display by the local Wargaming Society....

A non-exclusive policy towards exhibitions seems to apply nationwide in public libraries, but it's about the only thing that does. The exhibition spaces themselves vary from the purpose-built galleries to pin-board in a tiny pre-fabricated structure in a village street. Every possible variation of exhibition 'rooms', 'areas', foyers, walls, screens, noticeboards and pegboards exist in between.

Given each particular set of circumstances, however, you will be unlikely to disagree with how your works are hung, because you will, more than likely, have to hang them yourself.

And that's not all you'll have to do yourself. If you feel a catalogue (or even price list), a poster, or mailed invitation cards to be necessary, you will very likely have to arrange and pay for such luxuries yourself.

And that's not all you may have to pay for. You may be asked to pay a fee for the privilege. (David Briers)[7]

With smaller, and less adequate display facilities, no catalogue, no smart posters, less opportunity of reviews, no prestige gallery name to include on your CV, less chance of a sale, greater security risk, probably no insurance cover, and frequently more work involved in hanging the work, why should an artist bother with non-gallery venues? (Richard Padwick)[8]

You are likely to encounter a much less rigorous selection procedure or length of pre-booked programme than at public galleries. (David Briers)[9]

▷**4** *Art Galleries and Exhibition Spaces in Wales*

▷**5** *Contemporary Art Exhibitions in the East Midlands*

▷**6** Leicestershire Libraries and Information Service, *Contemporary Art Exhibitions in the East Midlands*

▷**7** 'Exhibiting in Public Libraries - Second Class Art Galleries', David Briers, *Artists Newsletter*, October 1984

▷**8** *Contemporary Art Exhibitions in the East Midlands*

▷**9** 'Exhibiting in Public Libraries'

> They are often programmed on a first-come-first-served basis and libraries do try to accommodate all requests to exhibit, with minimal amount of bureaucratic procedure. (Richard Padwick)[10]

> The artist/craftsperson is able to test their abilities in informal, sympathetic surroundings, gaining experience in showing work. The public exposure to criticism can be a daunting experience and the library exhibition is a useful way of gaining confidence in offering one's work to the public. (Northampton Libraries)[11]

> Many library services recognise that a programme dominated by local work can become monotonous without the occasional injection of work drawn from a wider source. The minimal time available to library staff and their lack of exhibition skills, however, inhibits active programming. They rely on artists or groups contacting them. (Richard Padwick)[12]

Artist Bob Evans describes a tour of his work to six libraries in Nottinghamshire.

> The batch of work, mostly watercolours, was moved from branch to branch by the inter-library van – no breakages, and I was able to get to most of the libraries to hang or display the work at each changeover. The paintings were always carefully stored in the head librarian's office, and any delays in setting up settled by telephone amicably. The venues varied from

▶ **Tony Ashton**, *It started with the Unions in 1933*, 36"x38" – one of the two paintings which 'offended' at Sydenham Library.

▷**10** *Contemporary Art Exhibitions in the East Midlands*
▷**11** *Contemporary Art Exhibitions in the East Midlands*
▷**12** *Contemporary Art Exhibitions in the East Midlands*

modern well-lit brick and glass boxes to the 1950 s concrete and Critall. The newer buildings had runs of pockmarked white notice boards and various screens – quite adequate – the oldest meant propping the paintings on top of the bookcases above head height and against dark olive and dead red painted concrete walls! The librarians' reactions ranged from slightly baffled to downright enthusiastic – all were as helpful as possible. None were permitted to handle any money on my behalf although the works were for sale. This rule resulted in no sales from half a dozen enquiries. Delay is fatal in such circumstances. Publicity only occurred if generated by the artist. Some branches pursue a more rigorous policy of exhibitions than others. So the upshot? A little local fame? I hope so. No money – common enough. No feedback. I suppose, I hope, that I provided some sort of service. (Bob Evans)[13]

Most library services are organised in three tiers. The exact pattern, however, varies considerably with different library services. Branch Librarians are responsible for booking spaces within a particular library. Branches are grouped into districts headed by a district librarian (or a designated member of staff) who may well organise mini-exhibition tours within their district. And there may well be someone at county or borough level who is responsible for overseeing exhibition tours throughout the council. But because they have no specialist staff and limited transport they will usually only be interested in small shows which can be easily handled and transported.

The relevant regional arts association may well respond favourably to a grant application to package a body of work specifically to tour libraries in the region.

►Schools◄

Exhibition activity in schools varies far more, if that's possible, than it does in libraries, as there is no overall education authority policy on exhibitions. Whether it takes place or not, where and how, depends on the nature of the buildings, the school's community, the enthusiasm of the principal and staff. Exhibition spaces are rarely provided for in the design of new schools, a few screens may exist but as a rule display provision is achieved by an active member of staff scrounging space and materials. Occasionally parent/ teachers associations may take up the idea to raise funds. The community college type school may regard exhibitions as part of its community activities and can allocate some of its funds towards developing and programming the space. Otherwise there are no funds at all. No teacher is time-tabled for exhibition work.

Despite these handicaps some schools run quite active programmes. Schools are not always 'closed' to the public – many are open for adult evening classes, some larger ones revert to public community and leisure/ sports facilities in the evenings and weekends. (Richard Padwick)[14]

The schools active in exhibition presentation can usually be spotted through exhibition listings in local papers and regional arts associations' diaries.

Exhibitions in schools can have two functions: to act essentially as a 'visual aid' relevant to the art and design curriculum, or to be of general cultural benefit to the school's wider community. If the first is the purpose, the exhibition space is usually contained within the the art and design department, if the latter in the school foyer, corridors or other more accessible places.

One advantage to school and artist alike in school is the contact between artist and students. Art teachers on the whole, who often feel very

'My aims in showing in public places were to show to a large audience who would not normally see contemporary art; to show figurative and abstract work together, as well as formal, spiritual, political and system painting; and to inspire others to be creative. There was, of course, the more down to earth reason – Lewisham does not have a public gallery.

There were a few sales; most being from Deptford Library which had a beautifully lit print room upstairs, where I was able to hold a private view to which the Mayor of Lewisham came.

One hiccup in the otherwise smooth running of these twelve shows was at Sydenham Library, where one member of the public created such a disturbance about two of my paintings that they were taken down. The staff had never dealt with this sort of problem before and were under great pressure of work, so I did not create a fuss. I just replaced the paintings with some others and I considered just as strong, and informed the staff that any complaints should be made to me personally. No more were made.

Although it has been tremendously hard work shifting paintings about every month for a year and has involved a lot of administrative work; and it isn't ideal showing on boards – with paintings messily wired to them for security reasons – the advantages of showing a huge audience and widening public awareness of the visual arts far outweighs the disadvantages. I recommend it to anyone who is more interested in showing than selling.

In retrospect, I should have applied for a large grant from Greater London Arts much earlier as I see now they are encouraging artists to show in public spaces. In addition I should have made more use of the council publicity department.' Tony Ashton – 'Twelve by Twelve', *Artists Newsletter*, November 1896

▷**13** 'Exhibiting in Public Libraries', David Briers quoting Bob Evans
▷**14** *Contemporary Art Exhibitions in the East Midlands*

isolated from contemporary art activity in their area, welcome this contact. But the problem, as ever, is that there are no funds – they don't even have enough to supply sufficient art materials for their students. However a package consisting of an exhibition and a lecture and/or workshop, project, 'artists-in-school' placement, the production of work on site – may well generate sufficient enthusiasm to attract parent/teachers association money, support from the local education authority's arts adviser and a grant from the regional arts association.

A few schools in some areas have clubbed together informally to set up a small touring network for exhibitions. An exhibition taken in by one school will be passed on to others, the work usually being transported by the art teacher in his/her own time. The local education authority arts adviser may well encourage and assist exhibition tours throughout the county.

Experience has shown that when exhibitions are held regularly in a clearly defined space, there is considerably less risk of accidental or wilful damage than there is to an occasional or ad-hoc display. But insurance for exhibitions in schools is a problem because most authorities do not insure schools or content because it is cheaper simply to replace and repair. This is hardly satisfactory for artists because there is no legal obligation for the local education authority to pay out for lost or damaged work which has been loaned to schools. It is advisable to check whether the school (or library for that matter) can handle the insurance or whether you have to – most won't be able to.

►Theatres and Arts Centres◄

Many theatres, some alternative cinemas, dance studios and arts centres which concentrate on the performing arts, whilst not having a gallery as such, run exhibition programmes.

> To put it a little unfairly, the placing of exhibitions in theatres is becoming a little like the placing of magazines in a dentist's waiting room. We expect them to be there, we browse through them, but we do not really read them. We glance at whatever is there, while waiting for the main business. (Nich Pearson)[15]

There is a tendency for theatres to treat visual arts as an inferior art-form. They like exhibitions because they add life and variety to the building – constantly changing decoration. Exhibitions are rarely integrated into the theatre's overall programme publicity and when they are, only with the briefest details. However, theatre exhibitions can be used to advantage. You can use the theatre mailing list – they will often insert your printed information into their publicity shots. You have access to a press and publicity officer who will have established good contacts with the local press and media – they will get you press coverage. This is, after all, as much in the theatre's interest as it is yours. You can organise promotional openings – theatres are licensed, often have catering facilities, and they are always trying to find ways to ensure the facilities are being used throughout the day and not just during performances. Sales can usually be handled through the box office.

Like libraries and schools most theatres don't go out looking for artists to exhibit – you must get in touch with them – the house manager, or the publicity officer, is the person usually responsible for taking bookings.

▷15 *Art Galleries and Exhibition Spaces in Wales*

◄
Installation by **David Shepherd** at Cefn Saeson Comprehensive School in Neath. This continually changing installation was organised as part of West Wales Arts Association's 'Sculpture Loan Scheme' which enables sculptors to take their work to schools and to give accompanying talks and workshops.

►Information◄

►Further Reading◄

►*Directory of Exhibition Spaces*, ed Susan Jones. Artic Producers, Artists Newsletter Publications, 1989

►*Art Galleries and Exhibition Spaces in Wales*, Nich Pearson. Welsh Arts Council, 1989

►'Exhibiting in Public Libraries – Second Class Art Galleries?', David Briers. *Artists Newsletter*, October 1984

►'Twelve by Twelve', Tony Ashton. *Artists Newsletter*, November 1986. An artist's experience of touring his exhibition round libraries in Lewisham

►'Bigos: artists of Polish origin' Stefan Szczelkun. *Artists Newsletter*, May 1987. Explores the decision-making processes and problems of a group of artists working on a didactic exhibition

►*EPR – Exhibition Payment Right, Artists' Consultative Meetings 1987/88*, report by Roland Miller for the National Artists Association. Includes Arts Council and regional arts association papers and recommendations

Public Galleries

compiled by
Richard Padwick

Local Authority Galleries

Local authorities are not required by central government to provide public museums and galleries, as they are with public lending libraries. Most local authorities do but the quality and the level of the provision varies considerably. Some county councils provide exhibition spaces as an integral part of the county library service. City, district and borough councils provide museums and galleries as they see fit. There are no national guidelines or recommendations. Many of the older galleries were founded upon the bequests of Victorian collectors. More recently galleries have been incorporated as a facility within arts centres. Funding also varies greatly from the major city museum services to the small, largely unstaffed exhibition spaces.

> The word 'Municipal' you might think, carries with it a dull unhelpful undertow of bureaucracy and parochialism. It is a far cry, perhaps from municipal galleries' opposite number, the independents, with all their bouncy vitality that independence conjours up. The two types have different responsibilities and priorities, however, and in general terms are not really comparable. Municipal galleries, financed through the rates, provide a public service and are publicly accountable...
>
> The thrust of the municipal gallery's service has always been as much towards looking after, displaying, interpreting and building up a permanent collection as towards running a temporary exhibitions programme. (James Hamilton)(1)

> The longer established municipal galleries are collection based, and therefore pictures or objects, and buildings, rather than artists, are the chief initial concern.... They have a duty to integrate the art of the day with the art of the past represented in their collections. Moreover they, as institutions functioning as part of the community, have a duty to sustain the artistic life of their community by involving themselves in the work of their artists. (Mike Tooby)(2)

> The Castle (Nottingham) acknowledges its responsibility to bring to the public's attention the wealth of talent in its own region. Wherever possible, group shows include the work of local artists and sculptors and are incorporated into large touring exhibitions which will travel outside the region. The aim is to create a dialogue between local artists and the administrators to produce a better service to the community. (Michaela Butter)(3)

▷**1** 'Municipal Galleries', James Hamilton, *Directory of Exhibition Spaces*, ed. Neil Hanson & Susan Jones. Artic Producers 1983

▷**2** 'Mappin Art Gallery', Mike Tooby, *Artists Newsletter,* December 1984

▷**3** The Castle Museum', Michaela Butter, *Artists Newsletter*, January 1985

> A danger on the part of artists is that they tend to assume that the nature of support a municipal gallery can provide is equated with support provided by other galleries, such as commercial galleries. It is not the job of Mappin Art Gallery to court an interested audience with a view to selling work....Nor is the job of Mappin Art Gallery to concentrate on a restricted art world reputation through advertising campaigns. More important aspects of provision such as catalogues must serve a long-term function beyond the life of the exhibition, and are outside the budgets of most municipal galleries....
>
> The municipal gallery can provide support for living artists in totally different spheres: in purchasing works of art, promotion through local working contacts such as school and adult education, residencies in local institutions, schemes involving collaboration with local groups, and utilising established collections and facilities. (Mike Tooby)[4]

> Several municipal galleries will not handle sales directly but like the Mappin, will make a price list available but direct purchasers to the artist(s). Many a sale has been lost this way. (Brian Lewis)[5]

> Although the museum has responsibility to present a balanced programme of exhibitions to reflect the various facets of the museum collection, in reality there is an emphasis on fine art shows – of some 15 shows a year at least 11 will be on fine art or photography. These are a 'mixture of 'home-grown' shows, touring exhibitions from ACGB and other galleries or exhibitions from individuals....
>
> One advantage the Castle has is that it has been cleared for high level security/value shows about artists of international reputation, bringing high quality work out from London and into the region.
>
> Besides these types of shows, it is felt the best way for the Castle to present contemporary work is in group shows often using a theme to link the work together. This gives the audience a point of reference and often means that 'difficult' work can be presented in such a way as to encourage the audience to look at the work sympathetically. (Michaela Butter)[6]

Municipal galleries have responsibilities far wider than just with contemporary fine art. They also have responsibility to the art of the past, to applied arts and crafts. They increasingly favour thematic exhibitions (often in the form of touring shows). They want to provide the opportunity for their audiences to see art of 'international' reputation as well as supporting the art in their region. As a result of all these responsibilities competing for limited showing space, few solo exhibitions of young or less established artists are possible unless the gallery, like the Castle Museum, Nottingham, runs a specific programme and has a designated exhibition space for regional artists.

►The Independent Gallery◄

Really a misnomer, the so-called 'independent 'gallery is one run by an independent trust or limited company usually with charitable status, but which is almost always, almost entirely dependent upon public funding from art councils, regional arts associations and/or local authorities.

The independent gallery is able to exercise a freedom which would be impossible for the municipal or commercial gallery. Once removed from a direct responsibility to the payers of rates and taxes, it is also once removed from any direct accountability to them. Supported by the public purse it does not have to depend upon sales to survive.

▷**4** 'Mappin Art Gallery'
▷**5** 'The Tale of Two Exhibitions', Brian Lewis, *Artists Newsletter*
▷**6** 'The Castle Museum'

▲
Exhibiting on the roof. *Aerial Crown* by **Vera Simons** on the roof of Edinburgh's National Gallery of Scotland.

This freedom offers the artist many advantages over other types of gallery, but it also has its problems. The independent gallery does not have to worry about a permanent collection, it does not have to attempt to offer everything to everyone. It can concentrate on a specialist area within the visual arts. In the main they were established to specialise in contemporary art and craft and to show a large proportion of solo and small mixed exhibitions – just what most most artists are looking for. Inevitably there is much competition to exhibit in independent galleries. They can present much more adventurous programmes, with the freedom to show 'avant garde', experimental or 'difficult' art. They tend to be far more sympathetic to artists' presentational needs than other galleries and are more likely to offer catalogues, posters, previews, etc.

And yet many, including artists, would argue that this comparative freedom has been abused by the independent gallery, they have grown soft, failing to establish any real policy and without the discipline required to translate policy into programme. Because they don't have to sell, they make very little effort to do so, so no income for the artist. Because they tend to be artist rather than public orientated they have, as a rule, failed to attract more than small specialist audiences. They have made few attempts to deal with the public in terms of getting them in in the first place (publicity tends to be geared for the art world, not the public as a whole) or to cater for them once they do come in – little thought has been given about how to put over contemporary work to a non-specialist audience. Nor is their specialist nature any guarantee that they deal with artists reasonably. Very many do, but a disturbing number don't.

►Information◄

►Further Reading◄

►*Directory of Exhibition Spaces*, second edition, ed Susan Jones. Artic Producers, Artists Newsletter Publications, 1989

►*Art Galleries and Exhibition Spaces in Wales*, Nich Pearson. Welsh Arts Council, 1989

►'Arts Centre Gallery – Aberystwyth Arts Centre', Alan Hewson. *Artists Newsletter*, September, 1984

►'Mappin Art Gallery', Mike Tooby. *Artists Newsletter*, December 1984

►'The Castle Museum', Michaela Butter. *Artists Newsletter*, January 1985

►'Crusading Darkroom', James Frank. *Artists Newsletter*, August 1985. The Cambridge Darkroom Gallery

►'Putting Art in its Place', Richard Padwick. *Artists Newsletter*, October 1985. Report on ACGB· 'Glory in the Garden' policy of supporting selected municipal galleries

►'Making the most of it', Margaret Ochocki. *Artists Newsletter*, August 1985. Involving the public in exhibitions

The Scottish Arts Council's travelling gallery which takes exhibitions to places which don't have galleries.
▼

Private Spaces

compiled by
►Richard Padwick◄

►Private Galleries◄

The exhibition in a public gallery is about not only the individual pieces but about the way all the pieces work together as a group in a given space. *'Works may be for sale, but that is usually not the the first reason they are there. From the artist's point of view the sale may be important; but this is not necessarily the (public) gallery's view.'* (Nich Pearson)[1]

Private galleries, on the other hand, not being publicly subsidised have to sell work in order to survive. Their interest in, and needs from, an exhibition will be very different from those of the public gallery – they need to introduce an individual client to an individual piece of work to secure a sale.

> Private galleries are sometimes reproached with making profits at the expense of artists whose work they exhibit and sell.... On the other hand, private galleries are under no obligation to bankrupt themselves by attempting, or being obliged to promote an artist's work which they cannot hope to sell.' (Philip Wright)[2]

> There are, in fact, very few art galleries in the commercial/private sector in Britain... for whom the selling of original contemporary works of art is a money making concern. (Nich Pearson)[3]

> Almost all private galleries are obliged to subsidise exhibitions of contemporary artists' work by making profits from dealing in works by dead artists or from selling artist's materials or frames, or from paying artificially low or otherwise subsidised wages. (Philip Wright)[4]

Private galleries act either as shops, displaying and selling art, or as artists' agents promoting a few very carefully selected artists and their work. As 'shops' they seek work usually on a 'sale or return' basis. As work is sold it is replaced by other items. Such an operation may or may not include the occasional small mixed or solo exhibitions.

Some private galleries will have a much clearer programming and physical distinction between shop and temporary exhibitions. The exhibitions may be used either to highlight a particular artist whose work is always held in stock or it may be to introduce new artists who have had no connection with the shop side of the business. In the latter instance the exhibitions may run much like those in public galleries although with a much greater emphasis on selling.

▷**1** *Art Galleries and Exhibition Spaces in Wales*, Nich Pearson. Welsh Arts Council, 1981

▷**2** 'The Artist, the Work and the Public', Philip Wright, *Directory of Exhibition Spaces*, ed. Neil Hanson & Susan Jones. Artic Producers, 1983

▷**3** *Art Galleries and Exhibition Spaces in Wales*

▷**4** *Directory of Exhibition Spaces*

As 'artists' agents private galleries establish a small 'stable' of artists. In contrast to public galleries showing a wide variety of work, style and media, the 'artists agent' gallery usually deals in a narrow range establishing a small but dedicated and specialist clientele. As agents they will usually carry a stock of work by each artist, organise a solo exhibition for each artist at least every other year, and seek exhibitions in other galleries and countries. They may also undertake to arrange lecturing, commissions and other 'engagements' on behalf of the artist. In return the gallery may expect an exclusive contract with the artist, having sole right to deal in the artists work.

►Galleries for Hire◄

READ THIS! if you have ambition

Large Art Gallery to be opened shortly in thickly populated Essex area on main road (10 miles London). Offers unique opportunity to the Amateur and Semi-professional artist.

Have your pictures hung at the moderate weekly fee of 5/- per picture. Usual commission on sales effected. No obligations.

If you feel that your work is of a reasonable standard write *at once* for full details enclosing s.a.e. or 4d. stamp to:—

RAYMOND F. BRETT,

40 Arragon Road, East Ham, E.6.

No personal callers please.

◄ From *The Artists Magazine*

Galleries for Hire... these so called galleries are ripping artists off hand over fist in my opinion.... The establishments I am thinking of not only charge the artist to use the space, they also make them pay for the publicity, insurance and private view and in some cases make them invigilate on top of that and charge commission on sales. What a rip-off! No self-respecting professional artist should go anywhere near these people.... (Sally Morgan)[5]

Galleries for hire may be an anathema to some artists, but they are not doing anything illegal – in fact, their operation is quite in line with conventional business practice. You rent a studio space, so why not an exhibition space, or hire a church hall to put on an exhibition during the Edinburgh Festival, why not rent a showing space in more conventional circumstances?

There appear to be three main categories of galleries available for hire. Firstly there are the privately owned galleries which hope to make a profit from hiring the space....

▷**5** 'Letters', Sally Morgan, *Artists Newsletter*, October 1984

►
The Hanover Galleries, in Liverpool, can be rented by artists.

'We charge a commission of 20%, with a minimum charge of £15 per week. The gallery covers insurance provided the exhibition is not left unattended, the artist is responsible for installing, invigilating and removing the exhibition.' (Municipal Gallery)

'The Hanover Gallery (Liverpool) is privately funded but not self-financing. For a rental of £40 a week for each gallery and commission of 12%, we provide: a full-time receptionist, a comprehensive alarm system giving full surveillance, insurance cover up to £35,000, sixty adjustable spot-lights, a total wall run of 166 feet, catalogues, posters, press releases and advertisements, private view, invitations.... (Susan Prescott, Hanover Galleries). In 1990, the charge is £40 a week for gallery/ commission is 15%.

Some private galleries offer 'continually changing exhibitions', or permanent collective exhibitions with new work replacing old as it is sold. It is quite common in such circumstances to charge artists a weekly 'hanging fee' per item.

Quite a few libraries, arts centres, community centres, colleges, municipal galleries – spaces run by or funded by local government charge artists to exhibit.

The decision by an institution to charge a fee for use of an exhibition space is usually in line with the charges it makes for hiring rooms for meetings. Often such policies are out of date and not in line with current professional practice, and geared towards the world of the amateur art society.

And lastly, there is a 'new wave' of independently owned showing spaces which have to charge rental in order to continue to exist, but which have not been established simply in order to make money....

Many of these are set up and run by young professional artists as a direct response to a situation in which the numbers of fine art graduates leaving polytechnics each year outstrips showing possibilities in public galleries. (David Briers)[6]

Personally I have never found hire galleries a 'rip-off'. Wherever I decide that I want to exhibit, I, like any intelligent consumer, look around, compare prices and eventually choose a gallery with a good location, friendly management and terms I can afford. (Rick Gibson)[7]

Hire galleries offer the artist(s) greater control of the selection and hanging of the work...

▷**6** 'Galleries For Hire', David Briers, *Artists Newsletter*, May 1985
▷**7** 'Letters', Rick Gibson, *Artists Newsletter*, May 1985

The nature of 'Women's Work' and the fact that the artists wanted to select their own work helped to determine which gallery to show in. They decided to hire the Showroom. Hire galleries are sometimes able to show work which would be too difficult for a municipal gallery. They are open to

experimentation – they have given us the chance to publicly play with innnovative ideas. ('Speak, Look, Listen, Learn' symposium)[8]

I have been renting galleries for over five years because they are the only places which allow me to charge the public an admission fee to view my sculptures. (Rick Gibson)[9]

►Information◄

►Further Reading◄

►Private Galleries:

►*Directory of Exhibition Spaces*, first edition, ed Neil Hanson & Susan Jones. Artic Producers, 1983

►*Directory of Exhibition Spaces*, second edition, ed Susan Jones. Artic Producers, Artists Newsletter Publications, 1989

►*Organising Your Own Exhibition – A Guide for Artists*. Debbie Duffin, ACME Housing Association, 1987

►*Running a Workshop – Basic business for craftspeople*. Crafts Council 1986. A useful section on exhibiting

►'Making it Pay – Gallery Opening' by Gordon Gapper. *Artist's & Illustrator's*, No 18 March 1988. A private gallery owner describes the background to setting up his gallery

►Hire Galleries:

►'Galleries for Hire', David Briers. *Artists Newsletter*, May 1985, and subsequent 'Letters to the Editor'

►'Covering Costs', Rick Gibson. *Artists Newsletter*, October 1985. Artist describes beneficial use of hire galleries

▷**8** Report on 'Speak, Look, Listen, Learn' symposium, Susan Jones, *Artists Newsletter*, January 1985

▷**9** 'Letters', Rick Gibson, *Artists Newsletter*

Open Exhibitions

compiled by
Richard Padwick

The term 'open exhibition' refers to exhibitions which have an open-submission rather than open-entry. Artists are invited to put their work up for selection for inclusion in the show. The term also normally applies to those annual or biennial 'survey' exhibitions which have no theme but are seen as survey exhibitions, showing a 'representative' sample of contemporary art. Open-submission is also a method used by galleries looking for contemporary work to put together an exhibition on a particular theme or subject matter.

Open exhibitions are a controversial topic. They generate more letters from artists to art magazines than any other topic. The following extracts from letters to *Artists Newsletter* indicate some of the issues open exhibitions raise:

Submission or Hanging Fees

As an ex-student attempting to survive on £25.75 a week, I find it impossible to indulge in something like the Tolly Cobbold at £7.50 along with £12 delivery service.[1]

It would be outrageous, in my view, if any part of it (the handling fee) was used to fund the exhibition and rejected artists' fees involuntarily subsidised the showing of professional rivals.[2]

The submission fee incurred by artists not selected for exhibition is only a contribution towards costs. In the case of the 1985 Royal Society of Painters in Watercolours Open Exhibition submission fees raised £4779 against a total expenditure of £10,201 (made up of £12,055 administrative and running costs and £6,336 printing, advertising and PR).[3]

Selection

Not a single artist's work from Scotland was accepted. Apparently this was also the case for Northern Ireland.... I cannot believe that every entry from Scotland & N. Ireland was so bad, so dull, so unimaginative or whatever to be unacceptable.[4]

A quota system is one in which the judges are asked to choose a number of artists from each region. The number of 'allocations' per region could be in proportion to the number of entries sent from that region. I have found little support, nationally, for selection by quota.... Such a system

▷ **1** Stephen Wager, Letters, *Artists Newsletter*, April 1985
▷ **2** 'Dubious Openings', Richard Rush, *Artists Newsletter*, December 1985
▷ **3** Michael Spender, Letters, *Artists Newsletter*, January 1986
▷ **4** Mary Louise Coulouris, Letters, *Artists Newsletter*, July 1984

encourages parochial attitudes and ultimately does not serve those who the quota seeks to 'protect'.[(5)]

The unfairness, if any exists, is not so much in whose work is selected or from which part of the country they may happen to come (although there may of course be justifiable reasons here for suspicion), but in conveniently keeping artists ignorant at the submission stage of approximately how many works will be selected.[(6)]

►Treatment of Artists and Their Work◄

I submitted a piece for the Young Blood exhibition at the Barbican and heard nothing about whether or not it had been accepted.... It was eventually found broken.

Collection times for the Camden Open were the weekdays of June 20/21. I received my rejection note in the late morning of June 20. It said *'no storage space is available for work not collected on time. Uncollected work will*

▷**5** Mike Collier, Letters, *Artists Newsletter*, August 1984
▷**6** Andrew Ryder, Letters, *Artists Newsletter*, September 1984

> *therefore be disposed of'*. When contacted they revealed that we weren't to take the threat too seriously for it was meant to cajole artists into collecting their work. *'You know what artists are like.'*[7]

> I heat-sealed the 0.5mm thick polythene so I can prove that it had not been removed. I maintain that no picture especially watercolours can be given fair assessment by the panel of judges through a thick translucent plastic film.[8]

> Damage is not necessarily a result of negligence but often artists not fulfilling the requirement of submission and placing projections on the back of frames, thereby damaging other frames or glass.[9]

> If we entrust expensive frames (let alone the art work) to the care of a gallery and pay a high handling fee as well as delivering them ourselves we are surely entitled to claim for the damage caused by careless handling by the organisers?[10]

> We are not prepared to accept such liability for the simple reason that our exhibition budget does not include insurance of all the works. In the event of a major calamity we would be unable to meet the necessary repayments but... we have been known to be generous in cases of minor damage to pictures.[11]

Most galleries will only insure work actually exhibited. Work in store and whilst being handled for selection as well as rejected work is rarely insured – and this is the time when most damage occurs. It is essential to read the conditions of entry (in effect the contract between the submitting artist and the gallery) to find out what the gallery's responsibilities are and what they are not. Also watch out for conditions in which organisers assume limited reproduction rights in works submitted or selected. Artists, however, should always insist that the minimal acceptable standard of practice is for the gallery to insure the work whilst it is on exhibition and should withdraw support from galleries that do not. The conditions of one open exhibition stated that the organisers accepted no responsibility for insuring the work but when questioned about this said that work would be insured whilst on exhibition but that they did not want to publicise the fact because of the danger of fraudulent claims by artists!

Whilst much is wrong with the way artists and their work are treated by open exhibitions (a clear need here for a code of practice), but for for those that are selected, they can bring several benefits. It is not always the big names who get selected (there is usually an attempt to keep the authorship of the work anonymous during the selection procedure). Relatively unknown artists are often selected and win prizes. Open exhibitions generally receive much media attention, although often get bad reviews. They are well visited by the public and others in the trade. Many solo, thematic, group exhibitions are selected from the work of artists included in open exhibitions.

> Open, competitive shows are in many ways demeaning. Like talent shows they may be taken less seriously by the organisers than by the participants. Why do we put in for them? Because there aren't too many alternatives.[12]

▷**7** 'Dubious Openings', Richard Rush, *Artists Newsletter*, December 1985
▷**8** Sam Ackers, Letters, *Artists Newsletter*, May 1985
▷**9** Michael Spender, Letters, *Artists Newsletter*, January 1986
▷**10** D. Hutchins, Letters, *Artists Newsletter*, May 1985
▷**11** Michael Spender, Letters, *Artists Newsletter*, January 1986
▷**12** 'Dubious Openings', Richard Rush, *Artists Newsletter*, December 1985

►Information◄

►Further Reading◄

►'Dubious Openings', Richard Rush. *Artists Newsletter*, December 1985, and subsequent 'Letters to the Editor' January, February & March 1986

►'A Tale of Two Exhibitions', Brian Lewis. *Artists Newsletter*, January 1985. Comparing two open exhibitions

►'Draw Back the Curtain', Peter Ford. *Artists Newsletter*, October 1986. A report on biennales in Eastern Europe

►'International Exhibition Opportunities', Peter Ford. *Artists Newsletter*, June 1988. Listing of exhibition opportunities worldwide

►'Open Exhibitions – Positive Effects', Cally le Poer Trench. *Artists Newsletter*, March 1986

◄ Work by **Tom Mallon** in the 1985 'Sculpture in the Open Air', an annual open exhibition organised by the Corridor Gallery at the Lurgan College of Further Education, Craigavon.

The Exhibitor's Checklist

►Richard Padwick◄

►First published in *The Directory of Exhibition Spaces* first edition 1983◄

►Applying for an Exhibition◄

►In Advance◄

►Have good slides and/or black and white photographs of recent work which are clearly marked with the way up, title and medium of work, date, size and your name and address. Send a check list of the slides or photographs supplied when you submit them. Use plastic pages rather than boxes when sending slides.

►Prepare a good, typed, curriculum vitae or biography giving only relevant details and make several photocopies.

►When applying to a gallery or exhibition space, find out which are the right ones for your work (consult the *Directory of Exhibition Spaces*). Many galleries have specialist programmes or only show well-established artists and craftspeople with thematic exhibitions, etc. Before applying to galleries in your region, make yourself known by visiting them in advance or by asking to be put on their mailing list. For first exhibitors, try local and regional galleries first. Find out the name of the Visual Arts Organiser or Director to whom you should address your application.

►Approaching the Gallery◄

►Find out how shows are selected; many galleries have selection committees, others invite artists rather than welcome submissions yet others have gallery artists only, etc.

►Many galleries select initially from slides so make sure yours are good, and accurately represent your work. Once you have submitted slides, don't expect a speedy reply, most galleries don't acknowledge applications. Telephone if an unreasonably long time has lapsed (thus the advantage of knowing the name of the person you sent the slides to).

►Don't load up a van and arrive unannounced at any gallery, few organisers would be able to look at the work without a prior arrangement. Print galleries may, however, accept folios to view, as may galleries dealing with photography.

►Private galleries respond more favourably to introductions by fellow artists or other gallery directors. They may be more interested in seeing a carefully selected portfolio than slides.

►If the Gallery Says No◄

►Exhibitor's Checklist◄

You may be refused an exhibition for many reasons:
►They may not like your work
►Your work may not fit into their programme
►They may be fully booked for a year or eighteen months

Consider the sheer volume of applications a gallery can receive before getting too downhearted.

►Private galleries will not only have to be convinced that the work is good but that it will sell to their clientele and that it is well constructed and will last in good condition.

►If the Gallery is Interested◄

►The gallery organiser will probably want to see your work in the flesh before making a final decision either at your studio or at the gallery.
►If the gallery agrees to show your work and you want to show there, discuss the practical details as soon as possible. The seemingly minor details are those which, ultimately, can cause problems and bad feelings: thus all discussions are better written down and agreed.

►Exhibition Contracts◄

◁see **Contracts**▷

►Artists, quite naturally, want to get the best possible results from holding an exhibition and the gallery will, necessarily, have one eye firmly fixed on costs and the annual budget. For the artist, the exhibition is the focus of his or her concerns at that time; for the gallery, it will be one in a continuous programme of exhibitions. An exhibition, therefore, must be seen as a co-operative venture to the benefit of both. An exhibition organiser should not make the artist feel beholden to the gallery for its generosity, nor should an artist play 'prima donna'! When the relationship between artist and gallery sours, it is normally because there have been misunderstandings, rather than deliberate attempts on either side to obstruct. The best way to avoid confusion is to discuss all details well in advance and to ensure that an agreement is written down. The most effective way of establishing the arrangement is to use a contract. Some contracts, however, may be biased towards the gallery and additional points may need to be discussed and mutually agreed. A formal contract is not always essential, but a letter from the gallery, stating the terms for the exhibition as a result of discussion, ensures a good working relationship.

►Practicalities◄

► What space is allocated to your exhibition; are there show cases, plinths or other display materials for you to use? What kind and how many lights are there, what hanging system does the gallery use?
►The selection method for the work to be exhibited varies – some galleries will leave it to you, some will want to choose it all themselves, some will choose in consultation. The exhibition organiser may also want to have some control, similar to that of magazine editor, as they are responsible for

the programme and must justify to the public and press. Selection should be mutually agreed as intransigence on either side is undesirable.

►Who will transport your work, who will pay for transport, who is responsible for transit insurance? Who packs the work for transporting? Make a checklist of the work sent. Use a delivery note.

►If your work needs framing, who will provide or pay for the frames? Will someone help you to hang the exhibition? Are there restrictions on fixing to walls or floor? Will you be able to hang the exhibition at the weekend or evenings (many galleries cannot handle this arrangement)?

►Who is responsible for insurance cover, both in transit, on exhibition and in store?

►Sales/Publicity◄

◁see **Commission & VAT**▷

► What commission does the gallery charge, does it include VAT? Establish whether the commission is deducted from or added to your sale price. Never state that 'prices are negotiable', no one will negotiate! Say whether the prices are inclusive or exclusive of frames. As many galleries are not geared up to selling work, make sure the price list is readily available and that your name and address can be given to prospective buyers if the gallery will not handle sales for you.

►Will there be a poster – how many will be printed/distributed, who will design the poster (do you have to supply a photograph)? Will the gallery discuss the poster with you before it is printed? Will they send you a proof of the design for approval?

►Will there be a poster – how many will be printed/distributed, who will design the poster (do you have to supply a photograph)? Will the gallery discuss the poster with you before it is printed? Will they send you a proof of the design for approval? How many copies will they give you?

◁see **Publicity**▷

►Will there be a catalogue? As printing is expensive, many galleries use a combined invitation card, leaflet with biographical note, artist's statement. Can you write a good statement? What is the deadline for information/photographs for inclusion? How many catalogues will you get? you? How many cards will they let you have for your own use?

►There should always be a press release which gives sufficient information for newspapers and periodicals to cover the exhibition briefly. A differently 'angled' release should go to the local and regional press rather than to the art press, all of whom have different deadlines so find out when they are. Will the gallery organiser write the press information or will you have to?

►If the press do visit the show, they will probably only want to photograph it with a pretty girl draped around it – be warned! Don't expect any national coverage but send the information to all the national critics nevertheless. Contact your RAA for a good press list if you have to devise your own.

►Will the gallery have a private view, will you have to provide the wine or beer? Will there be a separate press view?

►Gallery Events◄

► As many galleries have a programme of lectures, seminars, or workshops with their exhibition programme, check whether you have to give a talk or slide show. Have you got enough good slides, can you talk to the general public, colleges and schools without too much problem?

►Do you want to suggest a complementary workshop to run with the exhibition?

►Costs◄

Mounting any exhibition is an expensive business for both gallery and artist. Artists holding an exhibition in public galleries should be eligible for Exhibition Payment Right. This is intended not to help artists or galleries to cover some of the exhibition costs but to recompense artists for allowing public access to their work. It operates in England and Wales but not in Scotland and only in very selected galleries in Northern Ireland. The scheme offers an artist about £200 for a solo and £100 for a two-person exhibition, though the scheme varies from region to region. The participating galleries (and not every gallery does participate) pay the fee directly to the exhibitors – the galleries seeking a percentage of the fee from the appropriate regional arts association. Check with the gallery whether, and how much, you will receive under this scheme and when it will be paid. If the gallery does not operate the scheme, ask why not and persuade them that they should!

►Information◄

►Further Reading◄

►'Organising exhibitions for non-exhibition organisers', Richard Padwick, *Artists Newsletter*, December 1983

►*Organising Exhibitions – a manual outlining the methods used to organise temporary exhibitions of works of art,* Francis Pugh. ACGB 1978

►*Arts Review Yearbook*, Arts Review. Annual publication, lists municipal, independent and commercial galleries throughout the UK

►*Directory of Exhibition Spaces*, ed Susan Jones. Artic Producers, Artists Newsletter Publications, 1989. Comprehensive list of exhibition spaces and galleries in UK and Ireland. Written with artists looking for exhibition opportunities in mind. Also articles on applying for exhibitions and Exhibition Payment Right

►*Organising Your Own Exhibition – A Guide for Artists*, Debbie Duffin. ACME Housing Association, 1987

►*Running a Workshop – Basic business for craftspeople.* Crafts Council 1986. Useful section on exhibiting

►*The Artists' Directory*, Heather Waddell & Richard Layzell. Art Guide Publications, A&C Black

►*Independent Photography Directory*, Mike Hallett. Artic Producers, Artist Newsletter Publications, 1989

Touring Exhibitions

▶Richard Padwick◀

▶Edited from article first published in *Artists Newsletter*, December 1983◀

▶Organising a touring exhibition◀

The normal way for artists to secure an exhibition is to send details, CV, and slides of work to those galleries which accept applications. The larger, more established (more subsidised) galleries, as a general rule, rarely welcome applications but rather invite artists to exhibit. Of the many galleries that do accept applications, most have small to tiny budgets and will be receivers rather than originators of exhibitions. In other words, they have insufficient resources (money, staff, expertise) to be little more than a space which takes in exhibitions conceived and put together elsewhere, either in the form of a ready-made exhibition or as individual artists mounting their own work. There is a need and indeed a 'market' for a greater variety of exhibitions and for moderately-sized and priced touring exhibitions for smaller venues. A demand artists and artists' groups can satisfy.

▶Being Realistic◀

Organising a touring exhibition is a major undertaking and can be very costly in time and money, and unless you are prepared for this, do not be over ambitious. It is possible to organise modest-sized exhibitions with limited funds, but on the other hand, ambitious projects may be more likely to attract grant aid. It is essential at the outset to decide carefully on the size of the exhibition. The larger the exhibition the more expensive it will be to produce and insure, and the smaller the number of gallery exhibition spaces will be capable of fitting it in! An exhibition which requires 150 foot of wall space is, in fact, quite a large exhibition and the percentage of galleries capable of hanging it is quite small. There are, however, a large number of venues with between 75-120 linear feet of wall/hanging space. There are also a large number of spaces in libraries, theatres and schools with around 50 linear feet.

▶Thinking Ahead◀

Most galleries are booked up 12-18 months ahead and the smaller exhibitions spaces frequently 6-12 months ahead. It may well take six

months from the conception of the idea to obtain sufficient firm bookings. That amounts to a total of between 18 months and two years of preparation before the first showing.

►Budgeting◄

The Projected Income and Expenditure list below indicates the headings to be considered when setting out to organise a touring exhibition. Many of the costs may not be relevant to your particular project – other costs may be absorbed through your contacts, such as typing, access to a free photocopier, etc. Other expenses, the most likely are those marked with an asterisk, will depend upon negotiations and the 'general rules' of the gallery – they may either take on all the costs or share them with the artist(s).

►Projected Income and Expenditure◄

EXPENDITURE

Selling the Exhibition to Galleries

- ►Information sheet:
  - Typing ______
  - Photocopying ______
- ►Introduction Letter:
  - Typing ______
  - Photocopying ______
- ►Slides/Photographs
  - Photographer's Fee ______
  - Materials ______
- ►Envelopes/Postage ______
- ►Follow Up Telephone Calls ______
- ►Preparation of Additional Follow Up Material:
  - Photographs/Slides ______
  - Photocopying ______
  - Postage/Stationery ______
- ►Travel to Galleries ______

General Administration

- ►General communication with galleries to finalise all arrangements:
  - Telephone ______
  - Photocopying ______
  - Postage/Stationery ______

Preparing the Exhibition

- ►Framing ______
- ►Plinths ______
- ►Showcases ______
- ►Labels ______
- ►Crates/Packaging ______
- ►Graphic Display ______
- ►Installation Materials ______

Printing/Publicity

- ►Photography for Catalogue/Poster/Press-photos ______
- ►*Poster:
  - Design ______
  - Setting/Printing ______
  - *Overprinting ______
  - Distribution to Galleries ______
  - *Mailing ______
- ►*Catalogue:
  - Design ______
  - Setting/Printing ______
  - Distribution to Galleries ______
- ►*Invitation Cards:
  - Design ______
  - Setting/Printing ______
  - *Overprinting ______
  - Distribution to Galleries ______
- ►*Press Release:
  - Photocopying ______
  - *Mailing ______
- ►*Information Leaflets/Price List:
  - Design ______
  - Setting/Printing ______
  - Distribution to Galleries ______
- ►*Advertisements ______

Opening

- ►*Preview expenses ______

Tour Arrangements

- ►*Insurance (transit, display, storage) ______
- ►*Transport Costs ______
- ►*Accommodation ______
- ►Repairs, refurbishing work and stands ______

SUB TOTAL ______

Add Contingency at 5 or 10% ______

TOTAL EXPENDITURE ______

INCOME

- ►Hire Fees at £ per venue ______
- ►Estimated income from catalogue sales ______
- ►Lecture/Workshop Fees ______
- ►Commercial Sponsorship ______
- ►Exhibition Payment Right Fee ______

TOTAL INCOME ______

SHORTFALL *(grants to be applied for)* £______

* Items most likely to depend upon negotiations with the receiving venues

►Funding◄

◁see Funding Bodies▷

Existing budget headings for exhibition subsidy (particularly for touring exhibitions) tend to be aimed at galleries and art centres. There is no specific national system for supporting touring exhibitions organised by artists or artists' groups, but such ventures can be grant aided by the English RAAs and the Welsh and Scottish Arts Councils, and the Arts Council of Northern Ireland.

It is important to discuss your project at an early stage with the officer in the relevant funding organisation to find out exactly what the possibilities are in your area and what is a realistic amount to apply for. Whether you are an individual or an artists' group, it is very unlikely that you would be offered a grant to cover the total cost of the project. You will be expected to include in your budgets any income which is likely to be made by the exhibition (such as hire fees) and assistance from other sources. Raising sponsorship from business or industry is more viable if you are an established artists' group, but even then requires much effort and promotional gulle. Nevertheless it is often possible to raise some sponsorship, often from the most unlikely sources. The response from the funding bodies may be that you will have to find a gallery which will either organise the exhibition on your behalf or at least accept responsibility for it – it will depend on the scale and total cost of your proposal.

Whilst it is not customary for artists to charge hire fees for exhibitions, there is no reason why they should not for a professionally organised touring exhibition where posters, invitation cards and a ready-packaged exhibition are provided.

►Selling your exhibition to galleries◄

The *Directory of Exhibition Spaces* lists over 2000 organisations showing temporary exhibitions. It is, therefore, essential to draw up a short list of galleries to whom to send details. It is pointless to waste time and money sending to galleries which are too small, don't take touring exhibitions, don't show the medium in which you work or have a programming policy which is incompatible with your work.

The initial information you send to the 'short-listed' galleries should be concise and give a clear description of the work, the purpose of the exhibition and details of what the gallery will be expected to pay and be responsible for. You will need to send a small package consisting of: introduction letter, information sheet, curriculum vitae (for a group exhibition, send a brief resumé of each artist's exhibitions rather than a full CV for each) and a few slides/photographs of work (slides in a plastic sheet not a box!). All information should be typed. Keep a check list of the galleries to which you have sent information.

►Information about the Exhibition◄

The information should include:

- ►Brief description of the work and the rationale behind the exhibition.
- ►Number and size of the proposed exhibits.
- ►The linear hanging feet (the total horizontal length of wall space)

required by the exhibition or the square footage if works are floor based.
▶**Availability** – give the dates the exhibition is available.
▶**Transport** – who will be responsible for transporting the exhibition and what kind/size of transportation is required.
▶**Packaging** – how the works are packaged for transportation.
▶**Insurance** – who is responsible for insurance.
▶**Announcement/Invitation cards** – will they be available within the hire fee, if so how many and who is responsible for overprinting venue details.
▶**Catalogues/Information leaflets** – will catalogues/information sheets be available.
▶**Other requirements/limitations** – are there any other requirements (projectors, show cases, plinths) that the gallery should supply or any limitations on showing the work (lighting, humidity, security control).
▶**Extra activities** – are you offering any extra exhibition activities (talks, workshops, etc). It is very unlikely that you will be able to get all this information firmly established at this stage, but give as much as you can and clearly describe the information as 'provisional'.

▶Information about the Work◀

At this stage you will probably not be able to afford to send a complete photographic documentation of work. In any case, by sending out the information sheet 12-18 months in advance of the first showing date, it is likely that you will have very little work completed that will be included in the exhibition. If this is so, make it clear that the slides are examples of the artist's work not of the actual exhibits.

▶Following up◀

Few galleries will acknowledge receipt of the information package so if you feel happier knowing whether it has arrived, enclose a stamped addressed envelope with it for the gallery to use for their reply. Better still, a week or two after you sent the information, telephone the gallery to check. By phoning in this way you can also insure the quick return of slides from uninterested galleries, so that they can be circulated to other galleries lower on your short list.

▶Fixing the Tour◀

Some galleries will confirm quickly, others only give provisional dates such as 'in the autumn' or April/May. Now follows the tedious task of shuffling round dates and venues to arrive at a sensible transport route, with adequate time between each showing for transport and installation but without 'gaps' requiring storage. Whilst most galleries are sympathetic to these problems, inflexibility in their programming may make it difficult to arrange a totally smooth and consecutive tour. Some galleries will be forced to drop out and you may have to find alternatives.

Any telephone conversation in which an arrangement is made should

be followed up in writing – it keeps records straight and prevents misunderstanding.

►Taking Stock – Sohcdule◄

A useful procedure at this stage is to re-budget the exhibition in light of the result of negotiations with the hiring galleries and the more up-to-date information on costs.

Touring exhibitions involve many deadlines and as overall organiser, you will have to keep on top of all of them. Keeping a single schedule sheet is a good reference to what you have to do and when.

►Touring Exhibition – Deadlines Schedule◄

Photography
Completed ______
Poster
Copy ready ______
Artwork to printer ______
Delivery date ______
Invitation Card
Copy ready ______
Artwork to printer ______
Delivery date ______
Catalogue
Copy ready ______
Artwork to printer ______
Delivery date ______
First Venue
Posters/invitation cards needed by ______
Press releases sent out ______
Exhibition to be delivered on ______
Preview/opening date ______
Closing date ______
Workshop/lecture dates ______
Collection for transport to next venue ______
Second Venue
Posters/invitation cards needed by ______
(and so on)

►Insurance◄

There are essentially two ways of arranging insurance cover for a touring exhibition. The most secure way is to arrange a single cover for the complete tour. This ensures that the exhibition is covered at all times during the tour. You will, however, have to pay the premium! An alternative is for each gallery to cover the exhibition whilst in its care. Although this is the method used by most smaller galleries organising touring exhibitions, there are a number of problems and dangers in it. The first is that there should be no gaps in insurance cover between one gallery and the next. Galleries must, therefore, accept responsibility not only when the work is on show, but also when it is in store or in transit (either whilst collecting it from the previous venue or forwarding it to the next). Each gallery should therefore confirm, in writing, that the exhibition (works, showcases, plinths, other display material) is insured against all risks (fire, theft, loss, accidental and malicious damage) and 'nail to nail' (covering transit, handling, as well as showing and storage risks).

An additional problem with this method is that it is frequently difficult to assess where any damage occurred and therefore which gallery's insurance company is liable. If you are installing and dismantling the show at each venue, you should inspect the state of each piece of work each time it moves and keep a record of the damage. If, however, you can't follow the exhibition round, each gallery must be relied upon to check the work both as it is unpacked and repacked. It will be necessary to supply a checklist upon which any damage can be marked.

Small exhibitions going to smaller (non-art) venues such as libraries, schools, etc should always be insured for the complete tour by the organisers as few of these venues have their own provision for exhibition insurance.

◁see **Insurance**▷

The gallery or your insurance broker will initially require:

- ►the total value of the exhibition work, the stands, the display material
- ►the number of works
- ►the maximum value of any work (ie the value of the most expensive piece)
- ►the dates and venues for each showing
- ►how the work will be transported
- ►whether the exhibition is under constant surveillance during open hours and on an alarm system at night.

You must keep a fully itemised list of each exhibit and its value which will be needed by the insurance company if any claim is made.

►Information◄

►Further Reading◄

►*Organising Exhibitions – a manual outlining the methods used to organise temporary exhibitions of works of art,* Francis Pugh. Arts Council, 1978

►'Twelve by Twelve', Tony Ashton. *Artists Newsletter*, November 1986. An artist's experience of touring his exhibition round libraries in Lewisham

►'Exhibition Diary: Organising an Exhibition', Mel Noble, *Artists Newsletter*, August 1984. Report on an artist organising a touring exhibition of his work

►*Running a Workshop Basic business for craftspeople*, Crafts Council, 1985

►*Organising Your Own Exhibition – A Guide for Artists*, Debbie Duffin. Acme Housing Association, 1987

►*Directory of Exhibition Spaces*, second edition, ed Susan Jones. Artic Producers, Artists Newsletter Publications, 1989

Moving Work

compiled by

▶Richard Padwick◀

▶First published in *Artists Newsletter*, December 1983◀

▶Packing◀

The method of packing work for transport depends upon four factors: who is transporting the work and how, the value of the work, the nature of the venue, the nature of the work.

▶For Skilled Transport◀

If you are undertaking your own transport or relying on the gallery's (skilled) transport, then packing and crating can be considerably less substantial than if the work is handled by a national carrier. Framed, two-dimensional works can be cheaply wrapped in blankets or corrugated paper and a few works are easily transported tied securely face to face/back to back. The Arts Council of Great Britain recommends(1) that framed work up to 40″x50″ can be safely transported in this way. Corrugated paper, however, wears out with regular handling and fresh wrapping should be used at regular intervals in a long tour. Works framed in glass should always be protected by applying a grid of masking tape to the surface. This helps to prevent breakage and minimise damage to the work if breakage does occur. Perspex should not be taped.

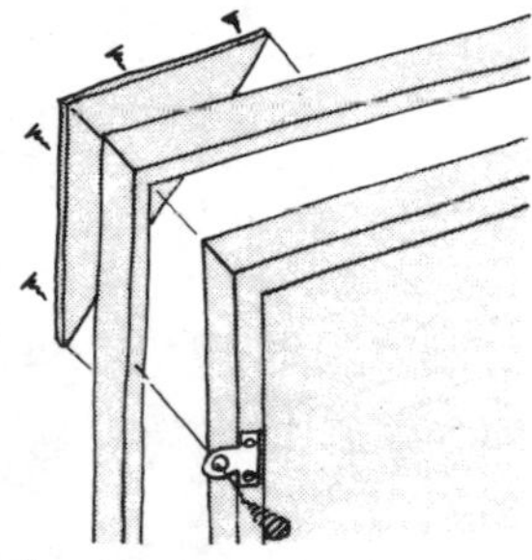

▲ Simple surrounding frame with polythene to protect the front surface of the painting

For larger paintings (glazed and unglazed), the Arts Council recommends the construction of a surrounding frame, protecting the edges of the painting and keeping dust and damp out with an outer wrapping of polythene sheet. The advantage of this method is that the painting itself is never handled directly.

However, the cost is prohibitive for most artists and artists groups who usually transport work by wrapping it in polythene sheeting with cardboard corners stapled into the back of the frame. It is worth noting, however, the Arts Council's warning that polythene should never come into direct contact with the painted surface as it encourages condensation, can stick to the paint, and attracts dust through static electricity. If you do use this method, an inner layer of tissue or clean paper (preferably acid-free) should be inserted to separate paint from polythene.

There is no standard or easy way of packing three-dimensional work because every piece presents a different problem. When using skilled transport for small objects however, one of the best methods is to use tri-wall cardboard boxes which are, in effect, a triple layer of corrugated

▷1 *Handling and Packing Works of Art*, Francis Pugh. Arts Council of Great Briatin, 1978

cardboard. These can be custom-made to whatever size you want. The material is light and absorbs most shocks and is fairly resistant to penetration by sharp points. The one disadvantage is that it must be protected from water or damp which quickly diminishes its strength.

A variety of fillings can be used to absorb shock – wood-wool, chip foam, polystyrene pellets and shredded paper. For touring, wood-wool, chip-foam and polystyrene are best. Shredded and crumpled paper disintegrates after a few handlings and will often need to be replaced or topped up on tour.

Very fragile and small objects should be double-packed – each item in its own small container and a number of these packed together in a larger tri-wall box. For larger three-dimensional objects, bubble-pack – a polythene sheet with a grid of air pockets – is a useful material.

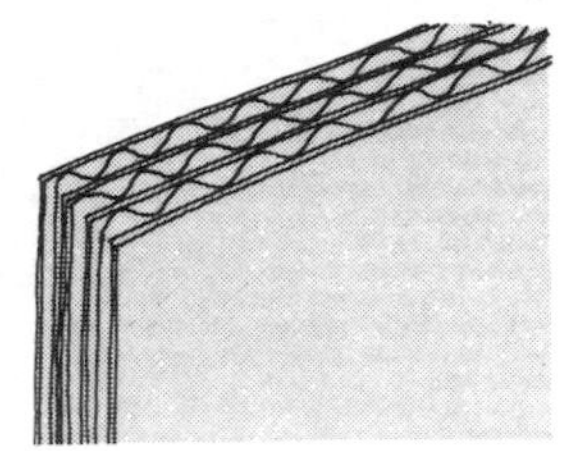

▲
Triwall – treble thickness corrugated cardboard – makes very strong but light boxes for three-dimensional work

►For General Carriers◄

If you are using a general carrier (not a specialist art transporter), you can't afford to take short cuts. Solid crates are essential if work is to survive and insurance companies are unlikely to pay out if work is damaged through inadequate packaging. It is more economical to send small framed works in purpose-built crates by national carriers than it would be to use specialised transport. Two kinds of case recommended by the Arts Council are shown in the accompanying diagrams.

Bear in mind that it is far better to use several medium-sized (easily carried) crates, than to pile everything into one crate which would need a forklift to move it! Smaller crates are also easier to store in galleries as most have a limited amount of storage space.

One final point on which method to use: it can be cheaper when transporting both large paintings or sculpture to hire your own transport or use the gallery's own than it is to construct sufficiently robust crates for a national carrier.

However the work is packed, it is important to label very clearly which work goes where in each crate. Hanging fittings should always be removed and packed separately.

Note: A specialist carrier, either a gallery's own transport or a fine art carrier, may well want to pack the work themselves and may not accept responsibility for any damage to work they have not packed.

▲
Slotted crate for small glazed works

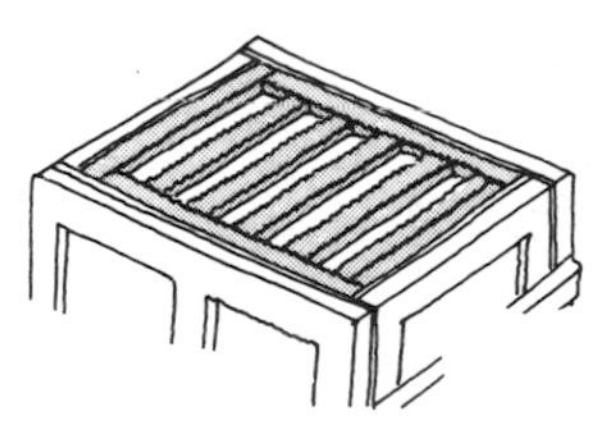

▲
Frames packed 'solid' in foam sheets

►Transporting Work◄

Many of the larger galleries either have their own transport or regularly use a reliable carrier, but an equal number will require you to organise the transport. You can either undertake the work yourself or employ a commercial carrier.

►Doing the Transport Yourself◄

Doing it yourself usually works out much cheaper, but not always. The daily hire of a van, the mileage charge, petrol and insurance may prove more expensive than employing a firm. But in calculating which is cheaper, add the cost of your travel to hang or attend the opening if this is separate from transporting the work, as well as the extra packing costs.

►Using a Carrier◄

If you have to employ a carrier don't just pick one out of yellow pages, get recommendations from galleries or artists in your region. There are now a number of small, or one-person businesses (often run by artists) specialising in art transport, who are cheaper than the larger firms and who are more sympathetic to the particular requirements of handling art work.

►If I choose to instruct a carrier, what do I do?◄

►List your works, noting media, size and, if heavy, the estimated weight.
►Contact at least three companies and ask for a quotation, giving the size of the largest work, the delivery and collection addresses, telephone numbers and value if you wish to insure the works. (Most companies do not insure unless specifically instructed to).
►Ask for two types of quotation, a part-load quotation (when the piece is collected or delivered as part of a day's work with other items) and a special delivery quotation solely for your work. The former can only be done when you allow the carrier to collect and deliver at any time on a stated day: the latter is when you are working to specific times.
►Ask them for insurance, on All Risks basis. Be wary of a company that says it does not insure fine art. It can mean it has been deleted from their cover because of high claims or that they just haven't bothered to establish a suitable cover.
►Check to see exacly what is included. Will they pack the works? Will they unpack the works on delivery? Are their vans equipped with blankets and webbing?
►Make sure the company is aware of complicated addresses. Which floor do they have to go to? Is the lift large enough to take the works?
►Establish who is paying the delivery charges and advise the carrier. (There is nothing more embarrassing than a driver trying to collect charges from your client when you are supposed to pay...). If the charges are over, say £100, ask the company how they calculate them; you may be able to keep the cost down by doing part of the work yourself. (Rees Martin)[2]

►International Transport◄

I strongly advise against international transport on a DIY basis. It can be worthwhile if the works can be carried by hand, but the complexities of foreign customs formalities can make the entry into the country a nightmare. Frankly, the procedures are not made to accommodate artists transporting their own work.

International transport presents a new set of problems. When taking goods through borders, each customs point must be given particular information in a certain way. Do not believe that the concept of free trade within the EEC exists; the differing customs, taxes, duties and laws make a nonsense of this ideal. (Rees Martin)[3]

It is possible to travel with work which is of little value – display copies of prints, which can then come under the umbrella of duty free allowance or be of no commercial value at all, unsigned prints. Many artists travel abroad with their own work as gifts. (Silvie Turner)[4]

Even though work may not necessarily be sold abroad, foreign customs laws will nearly always require the correct documentation to be presented before works are allowed to enter the country concerned. It is vital to be aware of the customs and VAT regulations of each and every country the work will pass through. (David Binding)[5]

▷**2** 'Transporting Your Work', Rees Martin, *Artists Newsletter*, July 1985
▷**3** 'Transporting Your Work'
▷**4** 'Exporting Work for Exhibition and Sale', Silvie Turner, ed Susan Jones, *Artists Newsletter*
▷**5** 'Exporting Work for Exhibition and Sale'

As a rule, customs assume that all goods including artwork passing from one country to another do so for the purpose of commerce and will treat them in this way requiring from you any import duty or VAT fees **unless** you

have the correct paper work to show differently. If you have neither the cash in hand nor the paper work, the customs can and do impound your work. Even with the right paper work the customs will want to be sure that someone, somewhere, will guarantee to meet all duties and VAT charges, just in case. The best bet is to get the gallery exhibiting your work abroad to handle all the arrangements. If this is not possible and you are not exporting it directly for sale, your 'passport' is an ATA Carnet which is for temporary importation of goods, free of customs duties and taxes. It is available to individuals and companies who need not be continually engaged in the exportation or importation of goods. The Carnet can be issued under three categories:

▶Commercial Samples (eg a printmaker taking samples of print editions abroad to raise orders)
▶Professional Equipment (eg for video, film, sound equipment used to fulfil an overseas engagement)
▶Exhibition/Trade Fairs (eg for a non-selling exhibition)

The catch is that the Carnet, available only from certain offices of the Chamber of Commerce, costs £71. In addition you will either have to deposit a cash equivalent of the total duties and taxes chargeable or give a bank guarantee for the same amount. If the work is sold or not reimported within the one-year time-span of a Carnet the deposit/guarantee is forfeit. Clearly, the lower the valuation you put on your work, or declare on your Carnet, the less you will have to put up in the way of a guarantee. The ATA Carnet can be used for a large number of countries, and is explained in an introductory leaflet available from Chambers of Commerce and in the Customs leaflet code number R2-11.

▶Information◀

▶Further Reading◀

▶Exporting:

▶'Selling Abroad', Phil Rogers. First published *Creft-Craft* quarterly newsletter; reprinted *Artists Newsletter*, October 1985
▶'A Tale of Two Cities – ATA Carnets Explained', Steve Chettle. *Artists Newsletter*, December 1983
▶R2-11 leaflet on ATA Carnets. HM Customs and Excise
▶'Exporting: Laurie Short, Potter', Andy Christian. *Artists Newsletter*, July 1984. A potter's experience on selling in Europe

▶Transport and Packing:

▶*Handling and Packing Works of Art*, Francis Pugh. Arts Council, 1978
▶'Transporting Your Work', Rees Martin. *Artists Newsletter*, July 1985
▶'Framing for Exhibitions', Roy Willingham. *Artists Newsletter*, February 1984
▶'Organising exhibitions for non-exhibition organisers', Richard Padwick. *Artists Newsletter*, December 1983
▶'A short guide to conservation mounting and framing works of art on paper for display', Jane McAusland. *Artists Newsletter*, August 1984

Commission & VAT

►Richard Padwick◄

Most galleries whether private or public will charge a commission for selling work. This is normally worked out as a percentage, but beware – what is it a percentage of? Usually the commission is a percentage of the retail price, but it can also be a percentage added on to the artist's price. Very different figures result. For example a 33⅓% commission of the retail price is equivalent to a 50% mark up on the price the artist wants from the sale (eg a painting selling for £150 with a gallery commission of 33⅓% off the retail price makes £50 for the gallery and £100 for the artist (that is the same as a 50% mark-up). Check which system is being used.

VAT further complicates how the retail price is established. This is another issue over which there is much confusion.

VAT is chargeable in the following circumstances:

►The Gallery is registered for VAT, the Artist is not:

►Gallery acts as an agent selling work on behalf of the artist (ie the gallery does not own the work at any stage – as in most temporary exhibitions). The gallery should only add VAT on the commission it charges the artist. No VAT is charged to the purchaser.

Retail Price	£500
Gallery Commission (40% of £500)	200
VAT on Commission (15% of £200)	30
Gallery charges Artist	230
Artist receives	270

The gallery accounts to the Customs and Excise for £30 VAT on its commission.

►The registered gallery buys a work from an unregistered artist and then resells it. The gallery charges VAT on the full retail price:

Retail Price inc VAT	£575
VAT on Retail Price (15% of £500)	75
Retail Price exc VAT	500
Gallery Commission (40% of £500)	200
Artist's Price	300

►Both Gallery and Artist are registered:

►The gallery acts as an agent selling work on behalf of a registered artist. The artist (or the gallery on the artists behalf) charges VAT on the full retail price. The gallery adds VAT on the commission it charges the artist for acting as a selling agent.

Retail price inc VAT	575
VAT on retail price (15% of £500)	75
Retail price exc VAT	500
Gallery commission (40% of 500)	200
VAT on commission (15% of £200)	30
Gallery charges artist	230
Artist receives	345

The artist receives £575 less the gallery commission and the VAT on the commission, ie £345. Out of this the artist has to account to the Customs and Excise for the VAT on the retail price, ie £75, and makes a net income of £270.

►The gallery buys a work from a registered artist and resells it.

Retail Price inc VAT	£575
VAT on Retail Price (15% of £500)	75
Retail price exc VAT	500
Gallery commission (40% of £500)	200
Gallery buys for	300
VAT on artist's price (15% of £300)	39.13
Artist's Price	260.87

The Gallery accounts to Customs and Excise for VAT on the full retail price (15% of £500 = £75). The artist accounts for VAT on the price he/she sells the work to the gallery (15% of £260.87 = £39.13).

►VAT Registration◄

You are legally required to register for VAT if your business turnover (ie all receipts received in a financial year without deduction of expenses) exceeds £23,600 in any one year (1989) or £8,000 in any quarter.

Most artists never reach the level of turnover and therefore VAT registration is not applicable. It is possible, however, to register with a turnover less than £23,600. There are advantages and disadvantages, but on balance for most artists, it is best not to voluntarily register.

►Information◄

►Further Reading◄

►Artlaw 'Contracts, VAT and Insurance', Roslyn Innocent, *Directory of Exhibition Spaces*, first edition ed Neil Hanson & Susan Jones. Artic Producers, 1983

►*Collected Artlaw Articles,* Henry Lydiate, ed Jenny Boswell. Artlaw Services, 1981

►'VAT and Artists' Groups', Robert Schon, 'Artlaw Supplement No 3', *Artists Newsletter,* February 1983

Public Art

Residencies◄

Commissions◄

Art Agencies◄

Residencies

▶Daniel Dahl◀

▶What are Residencies For?◀

▶to increase understanding and appreciation of art amongst the public via a direct contact with artists and their work?
▶to increase the status of the individual artist (and the arts organiser)?
▶to create greater understanding and appreciation of the role of the artist in society?
▶to provide artists with an income that is an alternative to grants, teaching or selling work?
▶to increase public access to art and demystify its processes?
▶to create a greater degree of interchange between artists and public in order to create long-term 'working relationships?'
▶to promote one style or form of art over another?
▶to help democratise culture because residencies increase both contact and accountability?
▶to benefit the public, in the sense of an increased realisation of what contribution art can make to their lives and to society as a whole?
▶to promote the pursuit of 'excellence'?
▶to stimulate further funding for the visual arts?
▶to fund artists in a justifiable way because residencies have a quantifiable benefit to the public?

or to put the questions another way:
▶why might residencies be important for art?
▶why should art matter to people?
▶why should people matter to art?

▶Their Purpose◀

Although residencies and placements have been going on now in one form or another for well over 20 years, and there's a fair amount of information around on *how* they should be run, there's less about *why* they should be run. This might not matter except that inadequately conceived schemes are often a source of great suffering for artists and a matter of disappointment for the public. An understanding of *why* is necessary before decisions about *how* can be adequately answered.

Put simply, residencies are a way of improving relationships between art and public by generating direct contact between artists and the public. The intention is to create learning experiences through which people will gain insight and an increased understanding of the arts. For artists this can be interesting because it means having direct contact with the audience. For the public, getting to know something about an individual artist and how he or she works can result in being more able to understand other art and artists. For art, this means a wider and better informed audience.

Residencies provide a platform for an active relationship with art and an opportunity for people to become participants rather than passive receivers.

▶Different Types of Residencies◀

Different types of residencies involve different types of relationships. On one hand there are residencies which are exclusively about the artist and the artist's activity. On the other, there are those which are exclusively concerned with people and people's activity. The difference is the degree to which the 'clients' – the people whom the project serves – are considered as an active element in it.

These poles provide a range of possibilities and most residencies will be somewhere in between.

▶Artist-centred residencies◀

There are essentially two types of artist-centred residency:

Transferred-Studio: possibly one of the most common types of residency is where an artist transfers his or her studio to a new site, be it a gallery, library, arts centre, factory, community venue, hospital, school etc. The artist's work and processes go on more or less as they did before and public involvement may be minimal. It may only require the artist to give a few lectures (in a university situation for example). Or it may involve considerable contact with a public as with the National Gallery's annual artist in residence programme. This variation of the transferred-studio could be described as a 'peep-hole' based residency because at regular times the public is allowed to look in and ask questions. It can mean a regular and demanding commitment for the artist.

Commission: In some ways, this isn't a true residency in that the intention is more the production of an artwork for a specific site than an interchange with the public. However, like any residency, the commission-based residency could involve the public's participation. Indeed, some artists believe the public has to be involved in some way if a commission to make work for a public site is to be accepted by the public.

▶People-centred residencies◀

Community artist type: In this situation artists put themselves at the disposal of the community, acting as facilitators or 'animateurs' assisting in the creation of work that is seen more as the community's than the artist's. Such a residency might be based in a housing estate or school to create a work in the immediate environment or to improve recreational or community facilities.

Other site-related residencies, however, may place less emphasis on working with the people connected with the site. These are:

▶Why do a residency?◀

Do you recognise your motivation amongst this list of possibles?

▶Do you see it as a way of being *paid* to be an artist; a means of providing yourself with *time* and *money* to work for a sustained period of time.

▶It's important to your work as an artist: you have recognised that particular situations/groups of people are vital as part of the process of making artwork, that they are not only a necessary *subject* for your work but that their *reaction* and response are also vital.

▶Do you wish to become a participant in the workings of society/community/industry as an *active element* in their processes. You consider your insights and experiences as an artist will make a unique contribution to such sitations, although the end product may not necessarily be what is normally regarded as art objects.

▶Perhaps you are fed up with working in the studio isolated from people and need more contact than you can get through exhibiting in galleries. You'd like more feedback as you work and you are someone who *enjoys* contact with people.

▶You prefer to put yourself at the service of the community, to be the means by which *they* rather than *you* express themselves.

▶You are interested in creating artworks for public situations and you recognise that this entails the involvement of the people and the communities concerned.

These are only some of the reasons why artists wish to do a residency or placement. You might want to identify with one or a combination of some of them. Recognising just why it is that you want to work in this way will help to identify the right situation for you. Earning the money is the bonus, but matching your needs to the situation in which you are placed will inevitably be more successful for everyone concerned. A mismatch may result in trauma for you and possibly alienation from the people you have to work with.

Response Requirement type: This term is used to describe a situation where the artist is expected to respond directly to the situation in which s/he has been placed. This will vary from being asked to incorporate the processes, materials and skills available within the site (for instance, making sculpture from a factory's metal off-cuts), to building a residency around a site's physical characteristics such as using trees, planting techniques or other landscaping skills in a forestry residency.

Consultation type: This type was pioneered in the early 1960s by the Artists Placement Group who identified a difference between object-based and time-based artistic activity. They defined the 'incidental person' approach in which an artist, by being attached to large, often governmental institutions, can make a creative contribution by perceiving new possibilities and making connections across conventional demarcations. More recently, other residencies and placements have drawn on this feature, albeit in a less 'pure' form. The artist's creative work, therefore, consists of suggesting courses of action for a situation rather than making art objects.

Interchange type: lies somewhere between the artist-centred and people-centred poles. Relying on a balance between the interests of the artist and public, those of the people, this type of residency, could include elements from almost every other type – a commission, perhaps, or a programme involving people's activity as well as the artist's. In it, *learning* is the main emphasis. People use the situation to build up a relationship with the artist and the artists work – through the way the project relates to their lives, their work place, or their activity. For instance, it may involve an artist making a sculpture in response to a work place or community situation. Or it may create the opportunity for people to make their own artwork alongside the artist.

Although residency projects can take all sorts of forms, and each artist makes a 'unique' project, the basic elements consist of the artist, the artist's work, and the activity of the people involved. If the artist's work, however this is perceived, is not a presence in the residency, the benefits will inevitably be limited.

An artist in education residency could be based on any of the residency types but it is important that the artist does not take on the responsibility of a teacher, as they will be perceived by all concerned as a teacher, not as an artist and the full value of the situation will not be realised.

Although categorising residencies in this way may seem unnecessarily academic, an understanding of the possible differences not only gives the artist freedom of choice, but also determines the quality of the experience gained. The way an artist's interests and motivations are matched to the nature and demands of the site is crucial if the aims of the residency are to be achieved. The key to success lies in identifying the

Transferred studio
'Peep-hole'
Response requirement
Community Artist type
Interchange
Commission
Consultant type

ARTIST-BASED ⟵⟶ SITE OR PEOPLE BASED

residency or placement that is appropriate for you. This will mainly apply if you are contemplating taking on a residency which has been organised by others, though analysing just what your aims are will be useful when setting up a residency on your own. Making the right decisions will mean thinking about the sort of artist you are, and what you want out of a residency.

Artists Health Warning! There is always a possibility that the organisers themselves might not be too clear about the aims of their own residencies or placements!

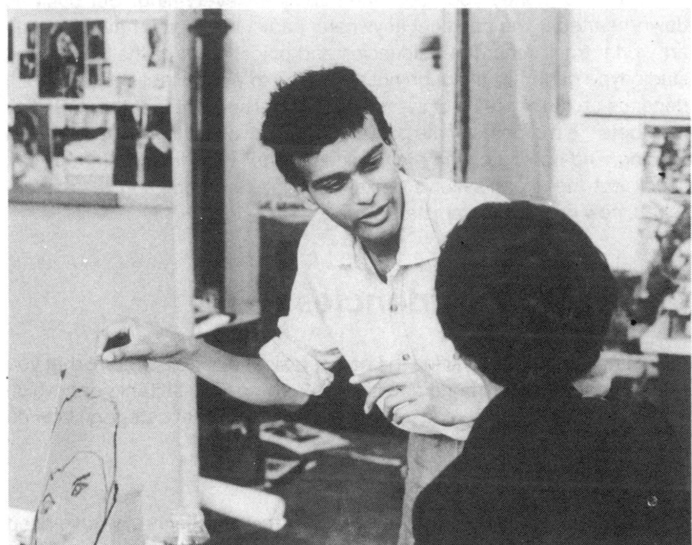

Alarí de Souza at Daneford Secondary Boys' School, Bethnal Green.

►Choosing◄

If the residency or placement has reasonably specific requirements – to work with a particular set of people say, or a specific type of location – then there are advantages in showing that your art practice is relevant. On the face of it, your work as a flower painter would not seem appropriate for an industrial residency, unless you can make a carefully-reasoned case. If you've had little to do with the public, it will be hard to be convincing as a candiate for a residency in a school, hospital or other community setting.

Although it is possible to persuade the interviewer that you are the right artist for the job even though your work practice seems inappropriate, of far greater importance is the question of whether the residency or placement is right for you and your practice. It's unlikely that you'll be able to learn very quickly how to deal with people whilst developing the residency itself.

You must, therefore, look critically at yourself and your practice. Would this residency or placement make a mutually beneficial match? Although the prospect of being able to work as an artist might seem to override everything else, is it *really* a good idea to let yourself in for a period of what might become hell? Will that benefit your work in the long-run? If you feel that it's your duty as an artist to take an uncompromising stand over artistic standards rather than to create accessible work, and that the serious artist cannot afford to be prescribed by the 'ignorance' of the public, you definitely should not apply for interchange residencies. The more interchange is involved, the more the situation will demand a response from your work.

You will achieve far more in a situation which is a creative balance between your interests and those of the project's audience and participants.

►Being Chosen◄

If you are particularly interested in the commission type residency or placement, then look for the advertisements, but make sure it is really your type of work they have in mind. Write or telephone and ask for more details if the brief isn't clear.

If it's the money you need, then apply for everything. But don't be down-hearted if you don't get anywhere, particularly if you haven't got an art world 'track record'. Residencies and placements of the transferred studio type generally although not always go to well-established artists. It depends on the make up of the selection panel and whether there are 'lay members', ie members of the public who'll be involved in the proejct when running, and how much they'll be guided by the 'experts'. When applying, check out the organisation's declared policy on appointing less-established, new or unknown artists.

►Finding Residencies◄

Assuming you have identified the sort of residency or placement that you would like to do, it's either a question of applying for a suitable one which is being advertised *or* setting up your own. In the former category, how do you find out about those on offer?

►Where to find them◄

If they are thought to be of 'national' appeal, they are generally advertised in the art press, in *Art Monthly, Artists Newsletter*, and the *Guardian's* Creative and Media section. They may, however, just be advertised locally or regionally if the organisers only want applications from their area.

◁see **Art Agencies**▷
◁see **Funding Bodies**▷

Also contact the regional arts associations who not only organise residencies and placements, but may also fund schemes run by others. Northern Arts, for instance, helps to fund the Artists' Agency. In some cases, local authorities set up residencies and placements as also do artist-run bodies. Although schools and colleges host residencies and placements, as do hospitals, they will usually be organised by education authorities on their own or via RAAs or arts organisations. The Whitechapel Art Gallery is an example of a gallery running schools' placements as part of a community programme, whilst the Ikon Gallery in Birmingham runs short placements as part of its exhibition programme.

►Useful preparation◄

One method of preparing for a placement is to find opportunities to work in relevant situations as part of your own (unpaid) programme of work. This could involve:

►arranging to go into a factory to work, perhaps through a friend or other contact.
►getting permission to go into a particular location either to draw, or to work with children or patients. Being on a site in this way will stimulate comment and be valuable experience in learning how to develop relationships with a public unfamiliar with art.

►Research, research◄

Above all, find out as much as possible about the residency or placement for which you are applying. Although the brief may give a clear idea of its aims, too many residencies and placements are advertised without resolving the conflict of aims. You need to find out as much background as possible.

►The Interview◄

►Questions to expect◄

Don't assume all interviewers are acquainted with art. Prepare to give clear, simple explanations of your work; about your ideas for the residency or placement and what you hope to achieve in it; about how you will fit in, both as an individual and as an artist; about possible *strategies;* such as how you plan to operate, how you will introduce yourself, etc (*see 'techniques'*).

►Questions to ask◄

►although it might be difficult, you must find out what the organisers expect to be achieved with this residency or placement, especially if the brief is unclear

►ask about the fee, how it will be paid: what it covers, eg removal expenses, materials, rent

►is the studio secure and are the contents insured? What about access and the possibilities of displaying work?

►are there specific expectations? ie do they want you to produce a mural or other piece of work?

►must the residency be undertaken in one continuous block or can you take a holiday or go back to your own studio to 'take stock'?

►what happens if things go disastrously wrong? What sort of back-up is there? Even one person to discuss problems with is better than being expected to cope single-handed.

►check that the ownership and *rights* of any work produced rests with you, unless there is a clearly stated commission element, or the host is being offered 'first refusal'

►Artists' Health Warning!◄

Acting professionally includes knowing when to withdraw!

Although artists need the money and the chance to work without interruption as an artist, can you really face the possibility of, say, a year's trauma, caught between conflicting interests? Will this benefit your work? Listen to the warning bells in your head if there is vagueness, ignorance or disagreement amongst those interviewing you.

►Organising Your Own◄

Some artists organising their own residencies and placements will do so as a natural extension of their own practice: the concerns of their work lead logically to 'placing' it in a real world situation.

Others want to set up situations as a means of 'employment', finding a way for artists to work as artists.

There are, therefore, two alternative approaches:

►look at the artist and work, then find the residency or placement to suit or

►look at the residency or placement, then find the artist to suit.

►Finding Sites◄

Although it is possible to to start 'cold', by approaching a site, it's obviously

better if some groundwork is done first. Once a relationship has been offered, developing it into a residency or placement becomes much easier.

Artists can get together to canvass for residencies and placements by contacting selected sites, persuading them to host a project. A simple, well produced leaflet would be a good idea. (Groups need not be studio-based. There are many examples of groups formed specifically to create work for artists).

Ideas for sites:

▶hospitals, health centres, homes, institutions
▶galleries, museums, libraries
▶prisons, probation hostels, community service units
▶schools, colleges, nurseries, universities
▶commerce & business: offices, institutions, shopping centres
▶industry, not just factories but service industries, farming, etc
▶government: local & national departments: police, armed forces
▶trades unions
▶communities: housing estates, community projects
▶outdoor situations, eg lakes, forests etc

In fact, there is no site that doesn't offer some artist somewhere a potential residency or placement!

▶Negotiating◀

Although easiest if a relationship already exists with the site, a 'cold' approach can be successful if properly handled. The latter approach will involve being prepared for:

▶unfamiliarity with art, especially contemporary art practice: it's no good being contemptuous of people who think painting is all portraiture, for instance. It still comes as a surprise to some artists that the 'uninitiated' regard Picasso or Moore as 'modern', unintelligible, and rubbish. The job here is one of education!
▶the assumption amongst people that the artist will profit financially from the residency or placement
▶that it's a sort of 'commission' situation, ie production-based: it will be necessary to explain that its the *artist* who's being financed, not the work.
▶the need for adequate facilities. People often have the vaguest ideas about how artists actually work, in terms of work space, display space and what types of access are needed. Although the artist needs access to their public, s/he also requires privacy when necessary (You must define 'access' and 'interaction' otherwise you'll find that people think you are going to 'perform', or give demonstrations.)
▶expectations about the artist's 'allegiances' eg. that they represent management, rather than workers.
▶dealing with unacceptable or inappropriate responsibilities.

Don't sweep the problems under the carpet for the sake of short-term gain, you'll only suffer later. For instance, the host should understand that an artist's work will not always be celebratory: it can be critical and penetrating.

Show them the sort of work you do, and the sort of artist you are. (Be patient!)

Be ready to explain what residencies and placements are, how they

◀
Dianne Murphy did a two and a half month residency at Bodedern Comprehensive School in North Wales, a post funded by North Wales Arts Association. *'Before I began, I was advised that I was in the position of being a cheap extra teacher for the school. In my case, this has proved not to be so – if anything, I was nagged to keep on with my work. Because I worked with relatively-mature A level students, it proved easy to spread the basic skills of etching by using a 'chain reaction' method. I explained the process to one student, so that when the next had their idea ready, the first can be asked to show him/her how to proceed.'*

can function: documentation from others is useful to show. Explain that residencies can take many forms.

Find out about restrictions that might affect an artist's freedom of movement. The Official Secrets Act, for instance, governs all work carried out in a factory dealing with armaments.

▶A Clear Agreement◀

You must end up with a clear agreement in writing: put down as much as possible on paper through exchanging letters. You will need this firstly to ensure that the site really has agreed to host the residency or placement, and that they agree with you on its aims and nature.

The next problem is *funding*. Remember to explain to the host that obtaining this can be a lengthy process, possibly taking as long as a year!

▶Funding: The Crunch◀

This is the tricky bit: possible sources of money include:

▶the host, who may be persuaded to stump up cash as well as hosting the residency or placement. Some are more willing to give money if they get an artwork at the end.

◁see **Financial Support**▷

▶arts bodies – regional arts associations have budgets for projects including residencies and placements. (But see warning on page 99!)

►sponsorship or donation, usually from large companies
►charities, including those formed to help specific sites, eg hospitals, education. Look out for local charities, often very old and sometimes very rich! These and others are often looking for ways to give money away. NB: it will help considerably if you are connected with an artists' group which has charitable status.
►local government – might be willing to help, particularly on community-based projects through funds, for instance, designated for inner city areas.
►Trades Unions – they should even if they don't, particularly if the residency or placement involves their members
►local education authorities – check whether yours has a scheme for putting artists in schools

►How Much Will You Need?◄

►the minimum going rate for an artist is £60 a day or £9000+ a year (1989)
►also add in a budget for material and equipment (if specially required), publicity, documentation, accommodation, transport, overheads and other expenses.

►Fund-Raising Campaign◄

Ideally, get the site to join forces with you in launching a fund-raising campaign, especially if the project will be viewed as a 'worthy cause' for instance, a placement in a hospital. Producing a leaflet describing the project can be useful – and then the host can either pay for the printing of it, or produce it 'in house'.

Since it is unlikely that you will attract the complete amount from one source, you will probably have to find joint funding. Here, the problems can begin afresh. Having negotiated the nature and objectives of the residency or placement with the site, you can find that bringing in other parties will mean, quite understandably, that they want to have their say in the project. Every funding body has its own policies and parameters and any conflicts of interest need to be resolved in the planning stages.

You may find it best to create a Steering Committee comprising representatives from each party involved. This can be an essential means of resolving differing expectations and identifying and agreeing common ground. This committee could remain throughout the residency or placement and provide an important form of support.

The most likely source for the amount of funding needed is the regional arts associations in England. In Wales, residencies are funded through the Welsh regional arts associations and in Scotland, they are handled by the Scottish Arts Council.

▷see **Funding Bodies**◁

►Artists' Health Warning!◄

Consider the implications of working within RAA guidelines! Problems arise because those who agree to fund residency and placement schemes invariably want to have a say in the choice of artist. Their view is that in making decisions about public funding, they must be publicly accountable.

If your scheme is to be funded by them, the usual stipulation is that the post must be advertised and the artist chosen by their panel. (This rule also applies to other artist-initiated projects.) There are instances where the need for funding has meant that the RAA has 'taken over' the scheme, and, despite the groundwork done by an artist or group of artists, the residency once advertised has been given to another applicant.

Approach your RAA with your eyes open, and be ready to accept the consequences! One way of reducing their influence is to have as many other sources of finance behind you as possible and thus be less reliant on the RAA's support. Another possibility may be for you to apply for money to carry out a special project under 'awards to artist'. Unfortunately, awards under this category usually fall far short of the sum needed to finance a residency or placement of any length.

There is still a reluctance from the RAAs to finance artists' initiatives and perhaps this is to do with 'defining' art practice; what art is, or should be, and who is recognised as an artist. Since the artist-generated schemes generally arise from how they practice as artists, the residency or placement is self-defined.

The relationship between public funders and artist-initiated projects is linked with the debate on who controls culture in society and how accountable the controllers are. Artists, by initiating their own projects and determining their life style and income, can help to change the system, if they choose to.

►Contracts and Conditions◄

►Fees and Tax◄

Most residencies and placements offer around £9000 for a year's work. This can mean more in real terms if the venue provides free accommodation and a budget for materials and transport.

And this is a fee, not a wage. All sorts of rather quaint words are used to describe it: bursary, fellowship, stipend, for instance, but the fact remains that it's a fee. (If a wage is being offered, the specification will make this very clear.) A fee makes you a contractor – you are being contracted to provide certain services, to be artist in residence. The difference is one of tax: with a wage you are liable to pay tax under PAYE, because you are being employed: with a fee you will pay tax on a self-employed basis under Schedule D, negotiating your tax after allowing all expenses. So a £9000 a year fee is worth more than £9000 a year as a wage, unless you have to cover your expenses from it. If the site is a long way from your base, these expenses may have to include the cost of accommodation, in addition to the costs of your normal home and studio costs (unless you give both these up, or sub-let).

◁see **Employment & Tax**▷

One major advantage of being fee-paid, is that you will be able to set *all* these expenses against tax, not just those relating to the residency or placement. You will be taxed as an artist for the whole year (or two, if it falls in two tax periods.)

Being fee-paid also means that you won't be covered for National Insurance Contributions, unless you make them yourself as a self-employed person. Thus, no sick-pay or maternity allowance. (As a contractor, you could in theory be sued if you were ill and could not complete the residency or placement). And what happens if you have an

◁see **Benefit**▷

accident?

It is sensible to agree with the host exactly how and when the fee will be paid. In instalments? In advance?

You should check whether the host is guaranteeing to buy work resulting from the residency or whether they only expect 'first refusal'.

►Points to look out for◄

First of all, you should have something in writing. Do not rely on the perfectly amicable meetings where everyone got on splendidly and was in full agreement. Put down what you understand as having been agreed and send as a letter of confirmation. This will serve as a form of contract, since by accepting it, those offering the contract can be said to have agreed its contents. If they disagreed, they would have to write back setting out their understanding of the agreement.

In simple terms, the contract means that you are 'selling' the use of your services as an artist and that they are agreeing to purchase those services. Here, we must define what the services are and what an agreement needs to cover.

►the fee, what it covers and when it's paid
►the brief agreed for the residency or placement: its aims and objectives
►any specific requirements of the residency or placement, eg a commission or other specified piece of art work, any teaching, or lectures, etc.

►the ownership of the work produced in the residency or placement. Unless specified, ownership (and rights) will remain with the artist. There may be a 'first refusal' arrangement, where the artist will offer to give first choice of purchase to the host, or organising body.

◁see **Copyright**▷

►attendance: are you expected to be there five days a week for 52 weeks? Must your working hours coincide with the workforce's? Can you take a holiday? Can you mount an exhibition scheduled in before the residency or placement started?
►what happens if things go wrong, if the relationship between artist and site completely breaks down? Is there some form of arbitration, or back-up?
►can you get out of the contract if necessary? Can they? How?
►who takes responsibility in the event of sickness or injury, either to you or to anyone else? (Your 20-foot metal sculpture falls on the Managing Director's husband and she sues you.)
►facilities: arrangements for the provision of working space and display space (if different). Access: can you work at the weekend, or in the evenings? Are the services suitable for your needs – light, water, etc?
►is living accommodation provided, and on what terms?
►is there an obligation to mount an exhibition relating to the residency or placement?

◁see **Looking at Yourself**▷

Raising these questions can be misconstrued as being just awkward and 'rocking the boat'. Lurking behind this is an attitude that implies you are really lucky to be offered this opportunity. *'Since we are doing you such a favour in letting you work as an artist, how dare you be so ungrateful as to question our generosity'.* In other words, *' we don't really see this residency or placement as a proper job of work being done by a real professional'.* Further more, the underlying message is that there are plenty of other artists out there who would be only too glad to have the opportunity being

▲
Residencies formed part of Yorkshire Sculpture Park's 1986 summer programme linked to their exhibition *Bretton Menagerie*. During June **Sophie Ryder** was in residence making a flock of sheep from steel rod and wire to coincide with the lambing season. She also ran public workshops.

offered you! Thus, you must decide how to act professionally in order to be treated professionally by those with whom you want to have dealings.

►Techniques◄

Every artist is skilled in the techniques and methods necessary to produce their art. But residencies and placements call for other techniques and methods. Some of the strategies that might be adopted are listed here.

►Preparation◄

Presumably, in your application and subsequent interview you will have thought about and put forward some idea of how to approach the residency or placement. Once selected, you can afford to spend more time on laying the foundations for a successful residency.

If you can, get permission to visit the site in advance to talk to people there. This may seem obvious, but for a surprising number of artists their first day is also their first visit. Experience of the site gained before you start is invaluable in planning out your approach. Also, you can check that physical arrangements (workspace, access and so on) are adequate.

◁see **Publicity**▷

The next stage is concerned with starting the residency or placement, including how people are informed about you and the reasons you are there. But preparation could include getting this process underway before you arrive – talks to the workforce, or an interview with the press. Does the site have any form of in-house communication – a bulletin, or journal? It will be useful to have something published in it and to arrange the publicity to coincide with when you start.

►Starting: The First Contact◄

Touched on have been the questions of how to present yourself and how to put over the purpose of the residency or placement. It is essential to get this information across as soon as possible, especially if it's a residency of less than six months.

Consider the advantages of introducing yourself through your best representative – your work – by holding an exhibition. Put it where it's most accessible, or even move it around if the site's large. Be on hand to talk to those coming to look at it, to answer questions. You could arrange a meeting or get-together to introduce it. You can distribute a leaflet or handout about yourself and your work in the form of a bulletin. This could be produced regularly throughout the project. On a large site, a letter describing the project and asking for help or advice, and publicising the introductory display of your work might elicit a response from the people with whom you want to become closely involved. Perhaps you could include a questionnaire which would make people aware of their participatory role. Their response could not only highlight problems at an early stage, but also give you ideas or inspiration!

What do you say in these letters, leaflets or bulletins? Obviously something about your work as an artist; certainly about the residency or placement itself. Maybe you can involve other parties – the organisers, the company etc.

To dispel myths about artists, you may need to explain in detail the employment status and income-earning ability of artists in general and of the placement in particular. In which case, spell out what you'll get: your expenses, who is providing funding and so on. Explain that artists, on the whole, don't live on the proceeds of selling work.

Say how you want people to be involved and ask for suggestions. Any form of early feed-back, whether through returned questionnaires or questions at a meeting can be invaluable in forming a firm basis for the project. Misunderstandings over your role and status can over a period of time, develop into enormous problems.

There are also advantages in establishing working relationships with other artists in the area as soon as possible. Although some may be hostile, suspicious, and frankly envious, meeting them, asking their advice, making use of their local knowledge shows you not only acknowledge their presence and value their opinion, but also that they are an important source of support for your project.

These artists have to survive in the area: they may have spent years building up a relationship with the community, the local authority, the arts associations and businesses there. They will be reassured to find you plan to enhance their long-term position, rather than be a hit-and-run artist who breezes in, causes a furore, and then breezes out, never to return, leaving local artists to pick up the pieces. Local artists may, after all, have been the pressure group through which your residency or placement was established!

►Operating the Residency or Placement◄

Making initial contact with the people involved has been mentioned, but how do you continue with this? How do you deal with their curiosity and, hopefully, enthusiasm?

►although this sounds obvious, they won't be able to give you their full

attention when they're working. So use the lunch or tea breaks instead. (One artist had lunch *twice* in a day so he could be sure he had a chance to speak to everyone)

▶regular displays or exhibitions about the work and its progress

▶regular 'bulletins', or handouts

▶open studio – some artists are perfectly happy to have a constant flow of visitors as they work whilst others need a time to concentrate and a time to talk. Establish early on which arrangement you want and publicise it. The studio could be open at break times, at the end of work, or after work.

It may prove important to work the same hours as the workforce. Strolling in at 10.30am after people have already been at work for two and a half hours may not impress!

You may like to establish regular meetings with a 'consultative' or contact group, whether made up from representatives from the site, or of the committee that selected you, or both. Such meetings could prove crucial if things go wrong and if your relationship with the people on site shows signs of breaking down. The last thing you need in this situation is to be left isolated. Someone with whom to talk problems through and someone who can help resolve them could save the residency or placement.

◁see **Publicity**▷

Maintain your relations with the local press: they will be only too pleased to publish interesting material. What's best: a 'scandal' story about your project as a result of an enraged rate-player, or informative features explaining the value and purpose of the residency or placement?

You may find that the stimuli from the site are overwhelming, and that you need to get away and have time to 'process' the material. This presents a problem in that you might appear to be an 'absentee artist' (and there have been plenty of them!) But if you feel it is vital, discuss it with your committee or contact group, and negotiate a mutually beneficial arrangement. Residencies and placements in which the artist is 'on call'

◀ Many residencies are linked with commissions and the Provident Financial Group commissioned *Foundation Stones* from **Gordon Young** as a result of his artist in industry placement there in 1985. The sculpture is of two 7′ high figures carved in Mansfield stone which *'Present the relationship between Provident agent and customer'*. It took nine months to carve and was funded by Yorkshire Arts. The illustration shows pages from *Provident Log*, one of a series of Gordon Young's working notebooks for his sculpture.

every day for three months don't take this problem into account. There are so many instances of artists realising how they might have done better if they had only had a break and time to reflect. Consider the advantages of, say, providing a three-month residency into three blocks with breathing space in between, even if you are paid only for the time you spend on site?

►Concluding the Residency or Placement◄

Even if it isn't expected, it is advantageous to put on an exhibition of the work done during the placement. It gives people the opportunity to fully understand what you have been doing and see how their contributions were used.

Although the site of the residency or placement would seem the logical place for this, there is a tendency for placement organisers to put exhibitions in galleries – places that the people on site may not go to. And last but not least, please sit down and write a report, even if the organisers/funders don't ask for one! They *should*, because how else can the success or failure of residencies and placements, be evaluated and the situation be improved on? If possible, get your report published so other artists can read it and benefit from your experience.

►
Andy Goldsworthy making an ice-arch on Hampstead Heath – a 'residency' arranged by the Artangel Trust.

►Information◄

►Contacts◄

►*See list of Public Art Agencies and Funding Bodies*

►Further Reading◄

►*What the hell do we want an artist here for?* Sue Hercombe. Calouste Gulbenkian Foundation, 98 Portland Place, London W1N 4ET

►*Art Within Reach*, ed Peter Townsend. Thames & Hudson with *Art Monthly*

►'Codes of Practice', Rosemary Christmas and Daniel Dahl. *Artists Newsletter*, February, March & May 1986. Set of collected articles looking at codes of practice

►*Call Yourselves Artists*, Mike Ormsby. The Pioneers, 1984

►'Art in Hospitals', Roger Hewson. *Artists Newsletter*, September 1984

►*Art at Work*, Sue Hercombe. Artists' Agency, 1984. Catalogue of Artists' Agency placements

►*Manchester Hospitals' Arts Projects*, Peter Coles. Calouste Gulbenkian Foundation

►'Residencies', a set of eight articles from past *Artists Newsletters* covering residencies for visual artists in a variety of settings

►'Not Just Icing', Julia Hagedon. *Crafts* No 88, September/October 1987

►'Letting Loose the Half-Wild Dogs' by Bill Laws. *Crafts* No 93, July/August 1988

►'Payments to Artists', Sheila Hayward. *Artists Newsletter*, February 1989

►*Code of Practice for Independent Photography*, Vince Wade. Artic Producers, Artists Newsletter Publications 1989. Although specifically for photography, the book is useful for the general principles discussed

Commissions

▶Peter Fink◀

▲

Malcolm Glover initiated a commission with the Welsh Development Agency photographing the Lleyn Peninsula in North Wales. The agreed fee was £5000, a touring exhibition was arranged and a selection of the work was used in a Welsh Development Agency calendar.

A public art project offers you a unique opportunity to shape a new social role for yourself and your work. This new role centres on both the social and creative demands of such projects, as well as on active leadership by you as the artist.

In these circumstances, you need to have not only the will to take your work out of the confines of your studio and the gallery system, but more crucially you will need to have the relevant skills to deal with the existing social and economic systems on their own terms, without sacrificing your artistic integrity in the process. The practical evidence of artist-initiated

projects in the USA, Holland, Sweden and to a small extent, in the UK, shows the tremendous potential which you could explore and develop in partnership with others, be it local government, development agencies, industrial concerns, community groups and so on.

Whilst these types of projects and commissions are ultimately only realisable with the involvement and energies of others, it is nevertheless essential that you, as an arti[illegible] have a clear-cut ability to, among other things, act as the project's pr[illegible]ipal developer, negotiator, finance director, construction supervisor and publicity agent. Only a convincing leadership by you in these areas will give the project the necessary aesthetic and philosophical coherence over the considerable length of time it will take from the initial idea to its full realisation.

The analysis of some completed projects shows that the biggest difficulty facing you when trying to get your project off the ground is not as commonly assumed a financial one, but one which centres on the immense credibility gap that exists in our country between contemporary art and the general public. Consequently, your first hurdle is most likely to be the closing of this gap through patient lobbying and education, on the one hand, and through the establishment of the project publicly in partnership with those willing to support you and your ideas. The main practicalities of your project, such as fundraising and planning permission, can only be tackled once your proposal is backed by a solid organisational structure.

►Winning a commission◄

During the last seven years an increasing number of commissions have been advertised in art magazines and newspapers as either *open competitions* or *open submissions for limited competitions*. In the first case you are expected to produce a full competition submission without receiving any fee. In the second you are expected initially to submit only documentation of your work (usually in slide form), on the basis of which a small number of artists are invited and paid to develop their ideas. These are later judged in a limited competition by a jury. In some situations such limited competitions are not even advertised and you may be invited to participate directly by the client or the selection jury. In such cases, the actual shortlist of invited artists is usually compiled from an RAA, Crafts Council or gallery index or a survey show. This form of shortlist compilation is becoming more and more frequent as it is seen by many clients as an efficient way of finding a suitable artist for small to medium-size commissions.

The critics of the competition system claim that considerable time and effort extended by artists in unsuccessful submissions is difficult to justify in the end, and yet there is still a continuing demand for competitions by various organisations and clients to counter this criticism.

When entering a competition it is useful to ask yourself:

►How can I present my ideas and work to the client or selection panel as on the one hand unique and on the other right for the given brief?

►How can I make my presentation visually and conceptually as effective as possible?

►How can I communicate my professional competence to the client/selection panel?

Finally, when taking part in a competition it is good to realise that the selectors face an enormous task when assessing a large number of submissions, so help them to see beyond the presented image towards the core idea of your proposal by carefully-chosen captions and descriptions.

►Direct Commission◄

Treasures of Tutankhamen – Statuette of the King upon a Leopard

In most negotiating situations or interviews the first impression you make is probably the most important. These first meetings are crucial for the establishment of the initial confidence between you and the client. A successful first meeting helps to create an atmosphere of constructive engagement which automatically optimises your chances. To help to make this first meeting successful, you should make sure that you have done the necessary preparation before you go, such as making sure you know

enough about the person or organisation you are dealing with. You should run through your presentation and also check again where and when your meeting is to take place.

If you are meeting the client in your studio make sure that you have organised a clean and quiet place to make your presentation without undue interruptions. These preliminary meetings are by no means a one-way business – equally as important, they give you the opportunity to assess the client and thus to help you to decide if and how much you want the job. When you feel doubtful about the proposed commission or client you should not be afraid to reject the offer as this might in the long run, save you a lot of trouble. However, it is advisable to give yourself some time after the first meeting to think your position through, as a better strategy than a blunt refusal might perhaps be to try to renegotiate the client's original concepts and expectations.

►Commissioning Process◄

When you are involved with undertaking a commission or trying to get one, it is important that you are able to see your work at all times against the logistics of the whole commissioning process, taking into your perspective both the social as well as practical implications of your work. Many artists, perhaps as a result of insufficient art college training, tend to think that their only responsibility is to do their bit in the studio and that such matters as consultation with the community who will receive the work, planning permission, maintenance and so on are matters which concern someone else. As a result, some commissions run into various troubles later or are even dramatically rejected at the planning permission stage or through consistent vandalism after their unveiling.

The main stages of any commissioning process are the design/idea and the contractual/realisation stage.

►Design/idea stage◄

After you have either received from or put together with a client, a brief for a commission you are ready to engage in the crucial stage of winning or securing for yourself a contract for its realisation. A workable brief should usually answer the following points:

- ►Who are you dealing with?
- ►What does the client expect?
- ►Where is the commission to be located?
- ►Has the commission got a theme, subject etc?
- ►What are the social circumstances related to the proposed commission?
- ►What is the proposed budget of the commission and expected timetable for its realisation?
- ►What are the specific limitations of the commission?
- ►Where and from whom can you obtain additional information if needed?
- ►How much time have you to sort out the details of your submission, what form should it take, what sort of fee should you receive, where and when must you deliver your submission?

▲Left
Ana Maria Pacheco, working on *Requiem* in Portland stone, steel, slate and bronze. This work was commissioned for the Stoke Garden Festival with grant aid from the Henry Moore Foundation. (Photo: Peter Goodliffe)

▲Right
Peter Fink, *Red Wave*, welded aluminium, 10m high x 9m x 6.5m. The piece was commissioned by Kingston upon Hull City Council with financial assistance from Lincolnshire and Humberside Arts and the Arts Council of Great Britain, and sponsorship from British Alcan Aluminium, Angle Ring Company and International Paint Protective Coatings.

►When and by whom is the commission awarded?

►Who is the final owner of the submission material and its copyright?

As in the next stage of the commissioning process *(see Contracts below)* you should obtain a clear-cut, legally binding agreement on most of the above areas.

Having thought about the answers to these questions it is prudent to form in one's mind as clear a picture of what is actually possible to create within the given brief and then start working in your normal manner on exploring relevant ideas.

With the initial investigative idea stage completed, you should decide on the format of your presentation as it is important to make it as effective as possible whilst putting in the right amount of time and effort. The basis of any good presentation is the realisation that the proposal should clearly communicate your ideas, rather than being over-elaborate and flashy.

►Contractual, Realisation Stage◄

Having secured or been offered a commission it is essential that this stage of your involvement is fully supported by a legally binding document before you start working or spending any money.

The main function of such a legal agreement is the protection of the interests of everyone involved, the delineation of everyone's mutual

obligations as well as the making of clear cut provisions in areas which could be a source of difficulties at a later stage, such as the cancellation of the commission due to unforseen circumstances or the destruction of the commission by fire in your studio or during transit.

In the case of most small commissions and in the design idea stages, such contractual agreements take a form of letters of intent signed by both parties, whilst in the case of a complex architectural commission the agreement will turn out to be a hefty legal document. Consequently, it is advisable that a solicitor should draw up the final version of any such agreement and that you take independent legal advice before you sign on the dotted line.

Most contractual agreements need to deal with the following areas:

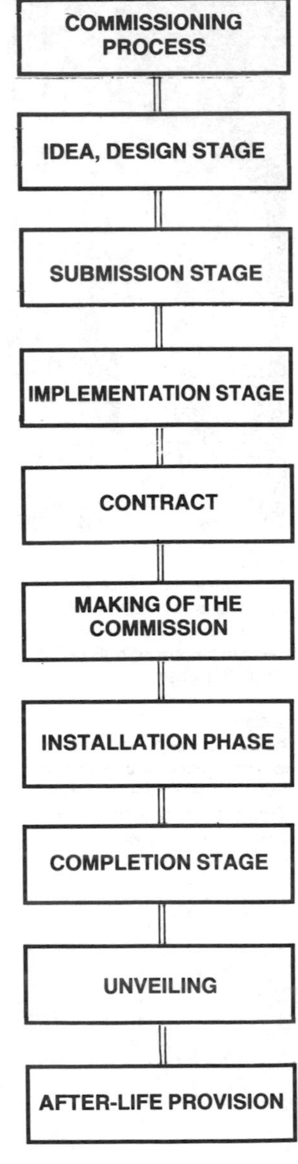

►The identification of the involved parties◄

►*You – your tax and VAT status during the commission.*

►*The commissioner's name and address.*

In some cases this might prove difficult, for example, in a case where the RAA is providing incentive funding, the local authority the site but no funds and an industrial concern the remainder of the funds as sponsorship. The agreement in such a case must clear this matter up, by for example, establishing a new entity such as a trust to act as a commissioner.

►*Agent – name and address.*

This clause should also specify on whose behalf the agent is working.

►The description of the commission◄

►*Title.*

►*Medium, materials, method of fabrication.*

►*Subject matter.*

This section might also include:

►*a clause guaranteeing fidelity of the commission to the accepted proposal and a clause preventing further editions of the original.*

►*a clause specifying a need for a mutual consent to any changes.*

►Financial aspects◄

This clause should include:

►*if inclusive or exclusive of VAT.*

►*if this figure covers the cost of delivery of the work to site, installation cost and the cost of the related ancillary works such as flood lighting.*

►*a timetable of stages of payment and the definition of these stages –*

for example: you might be paid 50% of the budget on the date you start working, 25% when the complete work is seen and approved by the commissioner as finished in your studio, 20% when it is installed and 5% might be held by the commissioner for one year against hidden defects.

►*the specification of any other payments due to you such as incidental expenses during installation.*

►Insurance◄

This clause must establish who is responsible for obtaining the necessary insurance cover and to what level of indemnity to avoid under-insurance.

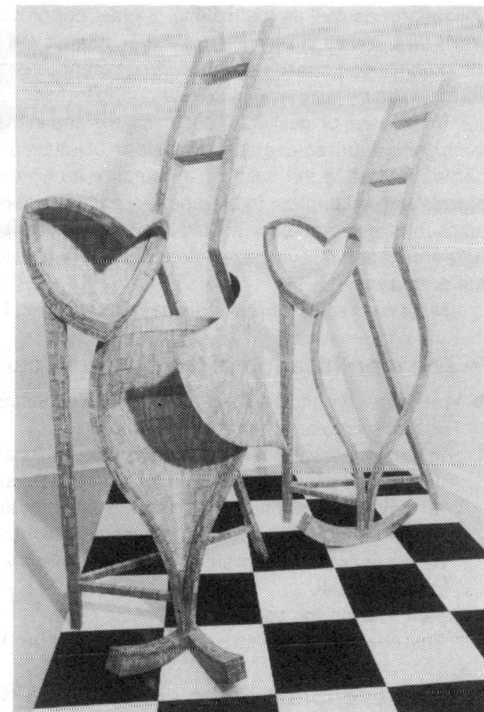

▲Left
Decorative environmental work by **Partnership** on the exterior of the Cornerhouse, Manchester to celebrate the opening night of *Evita*. (Photo: S. Halligan)

▲Right
Martin Cronin, *The Night Hunter*, laminated paper and card, 6ft high, commissioned for the Cirencester Workshops touring exhibition 'A Dozen Views on Paper'.

The usual insurance cover consists of:

►*all risk insurance while the commission is being made –*
protecting you, for example, in a situation when you have already spent most of the materials budget and had a fire in the studio in which you lost all the purchased material.

►*your personal accident insurance.*

►*public liability insurance –*
during the installation phase this insurance is absolutely essential but is also available during other stages. (As a result, the level of indemnity might vary, as for example, during installation you should have a higher level of indemnity than during the period when you are working in your studio).

►Timetable◄

This clause needs to specify:

►*the date when you can start working.*

►*the date when the commission should be ready for inspection, delivery and installation.*

►*the date for the completion arrangements.*

The precise identification of all these dates is related to other possible clauses which, for example:

►*protect your interests in a situation where you finished on time but the commissioner has not made the site available, did not obtain planning permission....and you as a result might be incurring expenses such as storage costs.*

►*protect the commissioner's interests in a situation where money is lost as a result of your late delivery and which deal with the subsequent penalties you would incur in these circumstances.*

►Responsibilities of the involved parties◄

►*a guarantee by you to exercise diligence and skill in the execution and installation of the work.*
►*the need for further guarantees, for example, from fabricators and material suppliers.*
►*an indemnity clause protecting the commissioner from any loss or damage from your negligence or wilful acts of omission.*
►*the establishing of the responsibility for obtaining the planning permission where necessary –*

The clarification of the need for planning permission and the actual planning process is in practice often one of the most difficult hurdles your work will have to get over. Consequently great care should be taken when dealing with this process.

► *the establishing of the responsibility for the provision for access to site and of the responsibility for its readiness for installation.*
► *the establishing of the responsibility for the ancillary works.*
► *the establishing of the responsibility for an increase in cost due to circumstances beyond your control.*

►Termination of the agreement◄

This section should include clauses:
► *determining the ownership of the partly or fully finished commission in cases where the agreement is terminated by you, for example, due to illness, or by the commissioner for whatever reason.*

►Completion arrangements◄

This section should determine:
► *the formal acceptance of the work.*
► *the effective transfer of responsibility from you onto the commissioner for the finished commission in areas such as insurance.*
► *an acknowledgement clause specifying that the commissioner will at all times acknowledge you as the creator, as well as specifying the wording on the plaque.*
► *the determination of the period during which you are responsible for any possible hidden defects.*

►After life provisions◄

This section needs to specify mainly the maintenance provisions:
► *who is responsible for the maintenance?*

In some cases, you as an artist can contract this responsibility from the commissioner for a specified yearly fee.

► *who is responsible for producing a maintenance manual?*

This manual must contain all the relevant technical data such as type of material used, method of fabrication, etc as well as a timetable and procedures to be used in maintaining the work.

►Copyright and moral rights section◄

Whilst the copyright clauses are directly related to the protection of your legitimate extended economic rights, moral rights are concerned with the

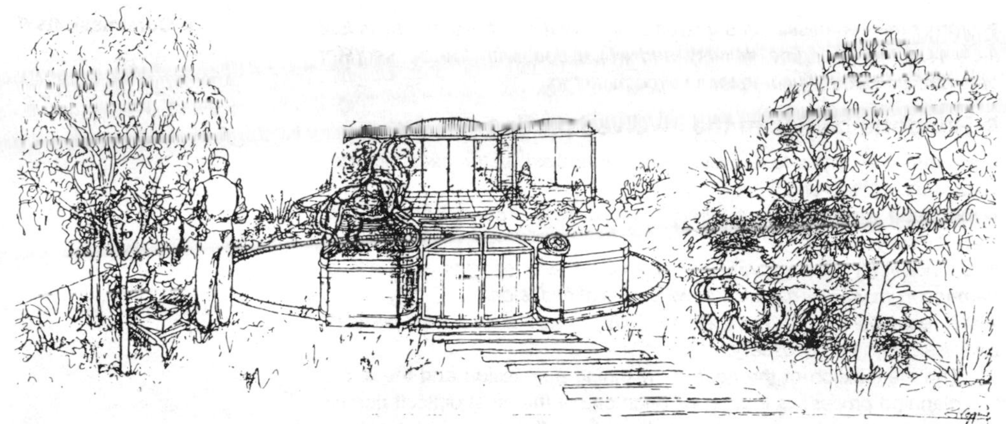

▲
Siobhan Coppinger, *The Gardener and the Truant Lion*. Plans for a commission in ferro-cement and bronze. The completed work was subsequently installed at the Chelsea Flower Show and the Stoke on Trent Garden Festival before being permanently sited at Stoke Mandeville Station.

protection of the integrity of the finished work as well as of your personal integrity as the maker. The clauses dealing with the area of moral rights should cover such issues as the protection against acts of distortion, mutilation or modification of the finished commission. Such a clause in practice is also linked to one giving you the right of the first option to repair any kind of damage in order that the work can continue legitimately to be taken as created by you. Similarly, with for example permanently sited outdoor sculpture, you may wish to stipulate that you should be consulted if a need arises to consider changing the original siting for whatever reason.

►Concluding clauses◄

This section usually involves clauses dealing with:

►*Proper law – specifying, for example, that the contractual agreement is governed by the law of England and Wales and may be changed only by a further mutual agreement signed by everyone involved.*

►*Arbitration – specifying that the settling of any disputes related to the contractual agreement shall be done in accordance with the Arbitration Act.*

◁see **Copyright**▷

► *Signatures and addresses of involved parties.*

►Consultation◄

The very issue of consultation is often seen by some artists as a trendy and empty procedure devised by bureaucrats to justify the expenditure of funds on bland, populist type art works. Consequently some artists tend to feel that the whole issue is best left to *community arts* and that even the broader social issues surrounding *public art* should not be a part of their immediate concerns when thinking about and working on a commission.

However it is this very attitude towards working in the public sphere which I feel is frequently the strongest contributing factor to why so many commissions are indeed bland and non-communicative, as the private world of the artist does not create any sense of resonance in the surrounding public domain. Yet it is precisely the often overlooked area of consultation in its many varied forms that offers you a potentially exciting

strategy of how to start creating this necessary resonance in the public domain.

By choosing an appropriate method of research and of consultation you should be able not only to gather together some initial information about a particular place and its people, but also to start developing ways of incorporating this understanding into your work, thus making it site-specific in more than only the architectural sense.

►Planning Permission◄

Under the current legislation, most types of permanently-sited public works of art will require planning permission before they can be installed. Consequently, in the first instance you will need to check with the planning authority if your work requires such a permission or if it falls under the small number of exceptions which do not. These include murals which are not painted for reasons of advertising or direction giving. Secondly, if the need for permission is established, you or the commissioner will be required to fill in an application for either outline or full planning permission. Such an application is lodged on a standard form to the local authority, which has the jurisdiction over the proposed site. In the case of a full planning application you will be required to support the information on the form with a complete set of visual and technical documentation of the proposed work.

▲
James Peet, *Portobello Market*. One of a series of posters commissioned by London Underground.

If you only intend to test the reaction of the authority to an idea, you should only apply for outline planning permission. This, if granted, means that the authority in principle has no objection to a proposal being further considered for a specific location. However, before proceeding with the actual installation or work on site, you will need full planning permission, which can only be granted for a specific project.

Once an application is lodged, the authority must consider the matter and give you a decision within eight weeks, unless an extension of time is agreed. In practice, this stage is usually preceded by an informal meeting with the planning officer, which should give you the opportunity to discuss the finer points of detail of your commission as well as any possible impact a particular planning policy of the authority may have on your project.

To help ensure that the commission is looked at in as objective and informed a manner as possible during the committee stage, you should ensure that:

- ►The proposal is well represented visually and that its technical details are well explained.
- ► Your professional background and your past work is well documented.
- ► Any public, ACGB, RAA support for your commission is well known to the members of the committee.
- ► The planning officer is well acquainted with the details of your proposal before the actual meeting.

However, it needs to be pointed out at this stage that the experience of artists with the planning process is a rather mixed one so far.

Although many commissions do proceed smoothly, a high number, mainly in more 'provincial' localities, do not. This unfortunately results in

▲
Magdalena Jetelova, *Place* 1985-6, Oak, 25′ x 15′ x 15′. Forest of Dean Sculpture Project, commissioned by Arnolfini Gallery, Bristol and the Forestry Commission with support from the Henry Moore Foundation.

some commissions not being realised at all, whilst others are seriously delayed by up to several years. Whilst the actual refusal to grant planning permission is expressed in terms of the planning law, in reality it is clear that in most cases the overriding factor in the decision is the desire of councillors to block a potential controversial project. This commonly found instinct in politicians is also in this instance, heavily fuelled by their own aesthetic prejudices, and the best advice is to become aware of and efficient in using the existing DOE policy statements on aesthetics. The main relevant passages are to be found in the DOE circular 22/80 (para 19) and in the Development Control Policy Note 10 *Design.* What becomes clear after reading these documents is that aesthetics should be recognised as an extremely subjective matter by councillors and that the purpose and intention of the Planning Acts is not to give the elected representatives the power to start censoring the public's access to the enjoyment of contemporary art.

▶Brickman◀
Leeds City Council decided in November 1988 not to grant planning permission for Antony Gormley's proposal for a 120ft high **Brickman** to be sited at the Holbeck Triangle in Leeds. The £650,000 project had already raised a considerable amount of the budget and the sculpture had been the subject of a Channel 4 'Signals' programme.

Should you find yourself, together with the commissioner, faced with a final refusal, do not panic, as you have a right of appeal to the Secretary of State within six months from the date of refusal. The Secretary of State then looks fully into the project, hears you and the planning authority and may or may not hold a public enquiry. After completing the investigation s/he takes the decision and the announced result is final. Whilst there are a number of examples of artists appealing successfully, it needs to be pointed out that the actual process can be a time, energy and expense-consuming business.

▶Information◀

▶Contacts◀

▶*Arts & Architecture Ltd.*, c/o Peter Rawstorne, 'Dunsdale', Forest Row, E. Sussex RH18 5BD ☎ 034 282 2748. Holds a database of members and also publishes the *Art & Architecture Register*
▶*Art Workers Guild*, 6 Queen Square, London WC1N 3AR ☎ 01 837 3474
▶*Applied Arts Showroom*, 109 Highbury Hill, Highbury, London N5 1TA ☎ 01 354 3073
▶*Association of British Blacksmiths*, c/o Alan Dawson, Dawson Architectural Engineering Ltd., Joseph Noble Road, Lillyhall, Workington CA14 4JX ☎ 0900 68368
▶*(see also Public Art Agencies)*

▶Slide Indexes:
▶*Crafts Council Index*, 12 Waterloo Place, London SW1Y 4AU ☎ 01 930 4811
▶*Welsh Arts Council*, Holst House, Museum Place, Cardiff CF1 3NX ☎ 0222 394711. Computerised database linked to slides
▶*Women Artists Slide Library*, Fulham Palace, Bishops Avenue, London SW6 6EA ☎ 01 731 7618
▶*African & Asian Visual Artists Archive*, The Coach House Small Business Centre, 2 Upper York Street, St Paul's, Bristol BS2 8QN ☎ 0272 244492
▶Also indices are held at most regional arts associations *(see Funding Bodies)*
▶Indices are kept by some of the public art agencies *(see Public Art Agencies)*

▶Further Reading◀

▶*Crafts Commissioning Scheme*. Scottish Development Agency
▶'Private Decoration or Public Good – The % for Art', Roland Miller. *Artists Newsletter*, August 1986
▶'1% in Alaska,' Richard Padwick. *Artists Newsletter*, March 1986
▶'The % for Art – Enter Mickey Mouse', Roland Miller. *Artists Newsletter*, November 1986
▶'Public Art in Los Angeles' – 1½% Plan', Peter Hill. *Artists Newsletter*, March 1987
▶*Art within Reach*, ed Peter Townsend. Thames & Hudson with *Art Monthly*, 1984
▶*Open Air Sculpture in Britain*, WJ Strachan. Tate Gallery, London, 1984
▶*Building Failures – Diagnosis and Avoidance*, W Ransom. Spon
▶'Working with Architects, Part One & Two', Tim Ostler and Steve Field. *Artists Newsletter*, October 1984, February 1985
▶*Mural Manual*, ed Carol Kenna & Steve Lobb. Artic Producers and Greenwich Mural Workshop, 1986
▶'Oxford Sculpture Commissions – How it Began', Peter Fink. *Artists Newsletter*, June 1984
▶'Dire Straits – outside the gallery', Henry Lydiate, Artlaw. *Art Monthly* No 95, April 1986
▶'Monumental manoeuvres in the dark', Henry Lydiate, Artlaw. *Art Monthly* No 86, May 1985. Moral rights and commissions

►'Tomorrow is a Long Time', Henry Lydiate, Artlaw. *Art Monthly* No 83, February 1985. Moral rights and commissions

►'Art in Churches', Tony Warner. *Artists Newsletter*, November 1987

►*Art for Architecture*, ed Deanna Petherbridge, HMSO 1987. Subtitled 'a handbook for commissioning' the book covers art in architecture with examples from here and abroad

►*Running a Workshop – Basic business for craftspeople.* Crafts Council, 1985. Section on 'Selling' contains detailed information on working to commission

►*New Milestones – Sculpture, Community and the Land* by Joanna Morland. Common Ground 1988.

►'A Cautionary Tale or a Lesson for Artists', Maggie Humphry. *Artists Newsletter*, May 1987

►'Glasgow – the Garden Festival', Alice Bain. *Artists Newsletter*, October 1988

►*Arts and the changing city: An Agenda for Urban Regeneration*, British American Arts Association 1989. The latest thinking on urban regeneration looking at examples in the USA and UK as a report from the symposium in Glasgow in 1988.

►'Arts and the Changing City', *Artists Newsletter*, May 1989. Responses to the presentations at this symposium

►'Private Commissions and the Law, Part 1, Henry Lydiate. *Art Monthly* No 120 1988

►'Private Commissions and the Law, Part 2, Henry Lydiate. *Art Monthly* No 122 1988/89

►'Art and Urban Renewal – A World Problem', Brian Sedgemore. *Art Monthly* No 126 1989

►'The Possibility and Problematic of Permanence', Deanna Petherbridge. *Art Monthly* No 118 1988

►'Commissioning for the Locality', Malcolm Miles. *Artists Newsletter*, June 1989

►*Art for Public Places*, Malcolm Miles. Winchester School of Art Press, 1989

Robert Kennedy's commissioned carving for Cardiff. *'The 30ft long and 5ft high wall took four months to complete. It includes a Viking longboat, a galleon and a modern ship carved in Bathstone by me, as well as 25 fish and other sea creatures cast from clay into concrete and fixed to the wall. The sea creatures were the product of workshops with school children aged eight to ten. In addition, the wall was built during the summer holidays, involving kids aged eleven to sixteen'.* (Photo: Huw Gwilliam)
▼

►*Architects Journal* (weekly), 9 Queen Anne's Gate, London SW1H 9BT ☎ 01 222 4333

►*Building Design* (weekly), Morgan-Grampian House, Calderwook Street, Woolwich, London SE18 6QH. Issued free to registered architects, on subscription to others.

►*RIBA Journal* (monthly), 66 Portland Place, London W1. The organ of the Royal Institute of British / :hitects

►*Architectural Review* (mc. ıly), 9 Queen Anne's Gate, London SW1H 9BT, ☎ 01 222 4333

►*a&A Newsletter* (quarterly), 5 East Arbour Street, London E1 0PU ☎ 01 790 6237. Free to members of 'Art & Architecture'

►*Artists Newsletter* (monthly) for regular coverage on commissions, offered and completed plus practical information, addresses, etc

►*Art Monthly* contains articles, conference reports and practical information on public art

►*Crafts* magazine (bi-monthly), contains regular coverage of craft commissions as well as practical articles

Public Art Agencies

►Revised by Susan Jones from an article by Annie Wheeler in *Artists Newsletter*, October 1986.

►
Peter Randall Page working on *Scales and Horizons* at Leicester Royal Infirmary. The piece was commissioned by the infirmary with assistance from the Arts Council and East Midlands Arts.

The Artists' Agency, based in Sunderland, *'seeks to bring artists working in all fields into contact with businesses, public services and the community by means of placements and commissions... Our aim is to create new forms of support... through employment, commissions and sales as well as offering artists the chance to extend their work through new environments.'* The aim of the Public Art Development Trust is *'to promote opportunities for younger artists, help realise the potential for art to enhance the environment and at the same time, stimulate public awareness of this capacity for art to contribute positively to our surroundings.'*

The Artists' Agency and the Public Art Development Trust are typical of a new breed of arts administrators who are all loosely described as 'artists' agents'. But this term suggests a parallel operation to actors' or musicians' agents who promote the artists for whom they act. Many of the agencies working in the public art field have a very different policy. Most agencies are a kind of double or triple agent, with a brief to benefit both artist and client (who may be architect, local authority, private patron, developer, business or industry, educational or health authority) as well as their own organisation. In this sense they are not strictly artists' agents at all but 'initiating brokers', setting up schemes, raising funds and seeking both suitable venues and artists. They do not act on behalf of artists, having a concern for the different and often conflicting interests of all the participants in the project. This 'honest' brokering is essential if the projects are to be successful for all concerned.

As more attention is focused on public art projects, commissions and residencies, on finding the new sources of private funding to supplement the dwindling resources of the arts councils and regional arts associations as well as bridging the gaps between the studio-closeted artist and the rest of the public, artists' agents are both initiators and enablers. The agent will help to set up placements and/or commissions and sales, act as a liaising mediator between artist and client from the conception through to completion of a project, provide an advisory and consultancy service and often shoulder most if not all of the financial, legal and administrative responsibilities that are involved.

▶Commissions◀

There's no doubt that the work being done by artists' agents is succeeding in finding a great deal of new opportunities and sources of funding for artists. In the five years during the early '80s that Isabel Vasseur was Commissions Officer with Eastern Arts, £200,000 worth of work was purchased or commissioned. Only half this sum came through grants. A conservative estimate for expenditure on public art in 1986/87 indicates around £30 million that year going to projects. The Public Art Commissions Agency's Birmingham Conference Centre programme has a starting budget of £800,000 plus £250,000 to be raised from sponsorship. Public Arts in Yorkshire is well-resourced by grants from the regional arts association, from local authorities and from the Gulbenkian Foundation and plans both short and long-term projects ranging from pavement art competitions and temporary celebratory work to a two-year artist's residency in Doncaster's planning department. Funding for projects is drawn from a wide range of sources. The public art agencies have campaigned hard for the establishment of a nationally-agreed per cent for

▲Left
Paul Amey, artist in residence at the Nuffield Orthopaedic Centre, Oxford, with his painted cardboard relief, *Montague-Burrows Ward*, of one of the children's wards. The residency was organised by the City Gallery Arts Trust in association with Southern Artlink.

▲Right
Krzysztof Wodiczko, detail of projection on the Duke of York column in the Mall, London – an event arranged by the Artangel Trust with the ICA. (Photo: Harry Chambers).

art programme here. This would ensure that an agreed percentage of the costs of a new building were spent on the commission or purchase of art works and would release to the visual arts very large sums of money from construction budgets.

►Placements◄

As well as growth in the number and scope of commissioned projects, the number of placements for art in industry, art in hospital and art in schools and other community schemes multiply throughout the country. The agencies 'sell' the ways in which artists and community can work together for mutual benefit.

One of the longest running artists' agents – the Artist Placement Group – was formed in the 1960s and laid many of the philosophical and practical foundations for the subsequent widescale development of placements and agencies. APG aimed for the placement of individuals in association with service organisations of all kinds, during which time the artist should have the status of an autonomous professional whose work has a fundamental role in the social, economical and conceptual structure of the community of which he/she is a part. Placements organised in public organisations and industries included those at British Rail, the Department of Health and Environment, ICI, Post Office, National Bus Company and Esso Petroleum Company. The motivation was not to decorate or enhance environments, or find new employment for artists, but grew from the belief that the artist had very special skills and a way of seeing and thinking that could lead to far-reaching dialogue with organisations and *'address the critical problem*

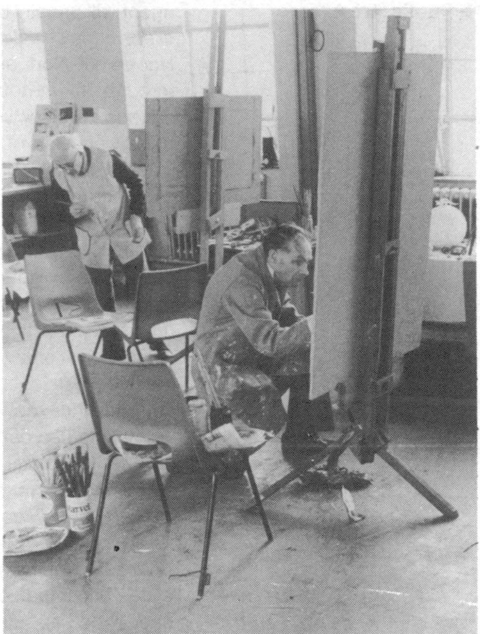

of the restructuring of our institutions (national, industrial, judicial, local, and in communications and education) with quite a new democratic inventiveness.' While most artists' agents operating today see their role in less ambitious terms, most still stress the aspect of their work that involves stimulating a greater awareness and understanding of the role art and artists can play in society and the environment.

'Placements mean that artists spend a concentrated period of time – anything from three weeks upwards – with either an organisation or a group of people, thus learning to understand and respond to the new environment as well as doing their own work on site. They can also encourage others to develop their creative skills ... and to encourage a more general appreciation of the arts,' says Lucy Milton of the Artists' Agency. Echoing some of APG's ideas she says that, *'Most importantly, the artists will attempt to produce work which changes people's perceptions about themselves and their organisations, which can lead to profound changes, both structural and personal.'*

Many placements result in commissions and sales of the artists' work. Vivien Lovell, Director of the Public Art Commissions Agency, links public art projects to residencies in a setting in the locality to ensure that the work is made in context and in consultation with the public.

▲Left
Kevin Atherton, *Upon Reflection*, 1985. A life-size bronze with over life-size reflection at the Philip Noel-Baker Peace Garden, Elthorne Park, Islington, London. The commission was arranged through the Public Art Development Trust.

▲Right
A workshop run by **Simon Granger**, artist in residence at Aycliffe Hospital, a long-stay hospital for the mentally-handicapped in Co. Durham. The residency was arranged by Artists' Agency. (Photo: Keith Pattison)

►Selection◄

Consultancy is usually part of the package offered by an artists' agent, a service for which they'll generally charge the client a fee as part of the overall budget. The client may approach the agent with an idea, or the agent may have the idea (perhaps responding to a suggestion from an artist) and then go out and sell it. Once a project has been confirmed, the

agent will usually be active in the selection process. *'We'll usually point a client in the direction of certain artists we think would be suitable'* says Les Hooper of Northern Arts, an arts association which handles public art through an in-house, but free-lance, agent. For many agencies, the method of selecting artists and makers for commissions or purchases usually consists of competition between a short list of invited artists. Clients view slides of work by regional and national artists to draw this up.

Alternatively the projects are advertised as an open competition. Public Arts offers all its commissions and residencies through open competition although this inevitably increases the costs and extends the timescales for getting projects off the ground. For a large commission this process, plus the final production of the work, its installation and the necessary raising of funds can take in excess of three years. To reduce some of this time factor (a problem noted by many agents), competitions are used less for selection, and increasing use is made of artists' registers and slide indexes. Agents have developed their own slide indexes, as well as making use of those held by regional arts associations. Some agents also make a practice of visiting studios and workshops, sometimes taking clients with them, and may do the rounds of exhibitions and art schools hunting out new artists for their files.

◁see **Publicity**▷

It is critical, therefore, for artists to make sure they are well represented on artists' registers and slide indexes – these usually require a selection of slides accompanied by a CV and statement about the work. Information should be kept up to date, and agents will also often require an idea of prices of work. Where selection interviews take place – such as for a placement – the agent will probably play a key role in interviewing and advising the client as to which artist would be most suitable, particularly if the client hasn't any previous experience in working with artists.

►Consultation◄

Agents will usually act as consultants on site suitability for commissioned work, and most encourage clients to involve the artist at the very earliest stage of a project. The degree of consultation needed will vary from client to client and on the number of parties involved. Local authorities might want to consult tenants of a local estate; maquettes or mural proposals may be exhibited in local libraries or displayed in another public site so that comments can be collected prior to decision-making. The process can be lengthy and may involve many committee meetings.

Most agents will also give general advice to artists in negotiations with a client, with drawing up contracts and in coping with any problems that may arise. Alistair Warman, formerly Art in Public Places Officer with the Arts Council, points out: *'One works very differently with a public body as opposed to a private company. A public body could mean all sorts of departments within a local or regional authority – a planning department, or leisure and amenity committee, art and libraries, or architects department – or an educational authority, an area health authority, forestry commission or so on. But with all of these, the project usually has to run the gauntlet of more than one committee, and is subject to political pressures and personnel changes. It can take months, even years before the artist is actually brought in.'*

►Differences◄

Each of the public art agencies has a different policy and emphasis, structure, funding sources and staffing, although all of them have increased the range of clients and artists they deal with. Several regional arts associations and arts councils undertake agency work. Sometimes this is handled by the visual arts officer or, where the workload has become significant, they have appointed a special commissions or public art co-ordinator as a new member of staff, or funded a free-lance person to work on their behalf. Others have helped establish and fund independent organisations to specialise in this field.

►Supporting Artists?◄

Most public art agencies claim to be supportive of artists' initiatives but in practice very few find it easy or possible to respond whole-heartedly to artists' proposals – the outstanding exception being the Artangel Trust based in London. In most situations, artists are involved only after others have thought up the idea.

Although no Code of Practice to set minimum conditions and fees yet exists for residencies and commissions, there is a greater emphasis on the exchange of information through workshops, conferences and through publications. It is nevertheless the case, however, that many residencies and commissions, even those which are supported by the regional arts associations are inadequately funded and thought out.

What has also not been fully resolved is how to handle the complexity of partnerships involved in public art – artist and community, artist and funders, funders and developers, education and public art – and the communications necessary.

And, equally important, what say should the public have about the artwork which will be placed in their environment? Should artists confirm or challenge expectations, record experiences or make personal interpretations of them?

►The Agencies◄

►This listing includes art agencies which are working primarily in the field of public commissions and residencies and receive funds from public bodies. It excludes those which are primarily commercial concerns and also organisers of residencies and commissions who are RAA or arts council-based *(see Funding)*

►**ART IN PARTNERSHIP SCOTLAND,** 5 Northumberland Street, Edinburgh EG3 6LL ☎ 031 556 0004. Contact: Robert Breen. Deals with art in public places and commissions. It aims to provide opportunities for artists living and working in Scotland, but artists from England and abroad are involved in many of the commissions. Artists and craftspeople can make use of the service by joining the slide index, which is *'a valuable reference and first filter for potential clients and ourselves.'*

►**THE ARTANGEL TRUST,** 133 Oxford Street, London W1R 1TD ☎ 01 434 2887. Contact: Roger Took. Supports work which is temporary and non-gallery based, and particularly supports those artists who through their work wish to address particular political or social issues. Artists and curators wishing to submit proposals to Artangel should first send for written guidelines.

►**ARTISTS' AGENCY,** 1st & 2nd Floor, 16 Norfolk Street, Sunderland SR1 ☎ 091 510 9318. Director: Lucy Milton. It aims to create new forms of

►
Ali Allen, mural at West Gate, Wakefield next door to the Royal Opera House. The mural was arranged through Public Arts with funding shared between Yorkshire Arts and Wakefield Metropolitan District Council. The mural is painted on marine plywood and supported on a steel and wood framework.

employment and support for artists as well as a chance to extend their work through new environments.

►**CITY GALLERY ARTS TRUST,** The Great Barn, Parklands, Great Linford, Milton Keynes ☎ 052 526 617. Director: David Wright. Organises exhibitions and sites works in public places, initiates and manages commissions, organises residency schemes and acts in an advisory and consultancy capacity.

►**NEW MILESTONES PROJECT (COMMON GROUND),** The London Ecology Centre, 45 Shelton Street, London WC2H 9HJ ☎ 01 379 3109. Contact: Sue Clifford, Angela King. Aims to *'encourage a new generation of town, village and countryside sculptures by involving artists and craftspeople with local communities in celebration of their locality'*.

►**PARTNERSHIP – The Environmental Art Organisation,** Providence Mill, Second Floor, Alexandra Street, Hyde, Cheshire SK14 1DX ☎ 061 367 8640. Contact: Terry Eaton. Partnership is an environmental art team which encourages, designs and makes works of art for public places. It also acts as agency consultants in the commissioning process, advises on

publicity and sources of funds. The slide index is being extended to enable more artists to have the opportunity to work on public art projects.

►**PUBLIC ARTS,** Room 210, County Hall, Wakefield WF1 2QW ☎ 0924 367111 ex 4791. Contact: Graham Roberts. Proposes more substantial public roles for artists: as '*magicians*' who demonstrate the mysteries of the human condition; as catalysts for social and economic dynamics; and as environmentalists. The emphasis is on public funding rather than private sponsorship.

►**PUBLIC ART DEVELOPMENT TRUST,** 5th Floor, 1 Oxendon Street, London SW1Y 4AT ☎ 01 976 1132. Director: Lesley Greene; Assistant Director: Michaela Crimmin. The first of the public art agencies to be established, it encourages works of art in public places by initiating and organising commissions in collaboration with public and private bodies, developers, architects and individuals. PADT has built up its own unselected index of artists and craftspeople.

►**PUBLIC ART COMMISSIONS AGENCY,** Suite 22, Guildhall Buildings, Navigation Street, Birmingham B2 4BT ☎ 021 643 4407. Director: Vivien Lovell. Launched in 1987 as an independent body, the agency initiates and organises large-scale public art projects involving public and private funding. These include commissions and artists' residencies. A computerised index of artists has been established, linked to the slide index.

►**WELSH SCULPTURE TRUST,** 2 John Street, Cardiff CF1 5AE ☎ 0222 489543. Director: Tamara Krikorian. Sees itself in a catalytical role, creating the climate for sculpture in Wales. It organises commissions, educational programmes, artist-in-residence schemes, foreign exchanges and touring exhibitions.

▶Information◀

▶Bibliography◀

See Residencies and Commissions

Using Skills

Part-Time Teaching◄

Studio Teaching◄

Sessional Work◄

Community Action◄

Part-time Teaching

►Cameron Scott◄

For artists/designers, part-time teaching is a very handy supplement to any other income, and for it, you do not normally require a teaching certificate. It is relatively well paid (see rates at end of chapter), and does not usually require too much preparation or marking (teaching history of art and design being an exception). It usually only provides 36 weeks work a year, and most establishments will only employ you for twelve or less hours a week. It can be slightly risky, in that you are normally working to a week's notice, with no guarantee of more work the following year. However, as a member of staff, you may be allowed the use of college facilities for your own work.

You will hopefully be employed for complete days, which leaves the rest of your week free. Unfortunately, it is not unknown to be offered two hours Monday, four hours Tuesday, and so forth. This, including travelling time, can drastically shorten the time left to do your own work. You must try to find your own balance.

Ideally, teaching at the highest level is what you are after, but these posts are not that common. There are, however, a great range and variety of teaching jobs available. Two important points:

- ►Most jobs go to those who go out to find them.
- ►It is your work being seen which normally gets you your first job.

►Finding teaching posts◄

Posts are advertised in the *Times Educational,* and *Higher Educational Supplements* the Tuesday *Guardian,* local daily, evening or weekly papers. Do apply, but make sure you have a good application, and expect a large number of applications. Advertised positions are the tip of the iceberg, the majority of jobs are waiting for you to ask for them.

They occur in BA Hons, BTEC Higher Diplomas, B Eds, BTEC National Diplomas in all areas of specialisation, General Art and Design, Foundation, Pre-Foundation, Regional and College Diplomas, GCSE, YTS, Training Agency Programmes, Hairdressing and Beauty, part-time day and evening classes. They mostly take place in colleges of Further Education, Schools of Art, Polytechnics, Colleges of Higher Education, Universities and Technical Colleges.

There are still other possible areas. Day and evening classes for the general public covering every conceivable art area, are found in colleges of further education, arts centres, community centres or schools. Other classes exist in prisons, borstals, youth clubs, W.I.s, community centres, hospitals, mental institutions, armed forces and galleries, these in addition to weekend and holiday courses. For supply teaching in schools, you will have to be teacher-trained. On the lowest pay scale is demonstrator/technician which, if you are encouraged to use your aesthetic judgement as well as your technical skills, is a good entry into teaching.

Having listed the types of courses and establishments, now to find them. Look at a map of your area, with a bus or train timetable (unless you have your own transport), and work out to where you can realistically travel. Then you need to consult the publications listed in the bibliography below to pinpoint the courses.

Damon Burnard

▶How to gain an Interview◀

This should be done by a combination of the formal and informal approaches. Start with the curriculum vitae and letter of application, then follow this up with more direct methods.

The purpose of a CV is to gain you an interview, so take care over it. Whereas you can send the same one with all applications, the letter of application needs to be slanted to the job you are applying for. Don't let it repeat the CV, use it to bring out other qualities which can't be listed. Looking for a job teaching drawing/illustration to graphic students, show that you are aware of the restrictions, but excited by the creative aspects; applying to teach general drawing on a Foundation course, show a willingness to work with students in all areas of specialisation. Make it short and succinct, we don't want to hear your theories of teaching.

◁see **Publicity**▷

Interviews for part-timers are normally held towards the end of the summer term, so mail your CV and letter of application during May. Don't wait for the adverts, get them out (second class, to save a bit of money). If you are still at college, see if you can send them out through the college. Formally, your application should be sent to the Principal, who gives it to the Head of Department, who photocopies it for any interested section. Applications are pieces of paper, and pieces of paper are lost in all establishments, so mail it to the Head of Department. For complete saturation, you need to mail one to each section who might possibly

employ you. If you can find out the name of the head of section, all the better. People prefer letters addressed to them by name, it makes them think their names are well known outside college. Play on their ego. In your mailing, include art advisors, they often run classes, in-service training, etc.

Keep a note of to whom you've sent information, and when. If you've heard nothing in a month, telephone the head of section, to whom you've applied (checking with the college telephonist for the name of the head of section). This helps you pinpoint them in the future. Remind them of your application, check on developments, and keep the conversation going. Don't take no for an answer, don't be put off. The purpose of the phone call is to gain an interview. The British are easily embarrassed, so make use of that, browbeat the person until you gain satisfaction. Go on long enough, and they'll agree to something, just to get you off the phone.

If you are told there are no jobs, ask if your folder can be looked through, for future reference. If again no, ask if you can look round the department. From my own experience, it's difficult to refuse such a request. When you turn up, have your folder with you and, with an innocent face, say you misunderstood the telephone conversation, and usually someone will look through your folder. In other words, use any lever you can think of, to get yourself into that college. You are supposed to be a creative person, so be creative.

Always ask when the college will next be looking for part-timers, and if given a date, make sure you follow it up. When courses start in September, there are often panics through increased student numbers, etc so ring around again. If the college puts on exhibitions, ask to be put on the mailing list, and always turn up for private views. Be persistent.

►The Interview◄

It's an art department, we are not looking for grey anonymity, nor scruffs. Artists are supposed to be individuals, so be one, but a neat and presentable one. Don't smoke unless invited to.

Have your work well organised. I've been presented with a brown paper bag, out of which tumbled a dozen slides. That just lost the job. Have a good folder, and well-mounted/presented work. If you are bringing slides, telephone beforehand, and ask for a projector to be set up, and arrive in plenty of time to get yourself organised before the interview. Read all the college publicity, so you know what they offer. Even telephone before, pretending to be a potential student, and obtain details of the courses. Having done your homework on the college, make sure you drop it into the conversation, eg *'I believe you run a two-year fashion course with a marketing option'*.

You are trying to impress, so impress. But not with heavy art language. Teachers are communicators, keep your answers succinct and to the point, don't ramble. Have questions prepared to ask your interviewer, eg *'What happens to your students after the course?' 'How much time do students have for drawing each week?'*

If you are offered a job, accept (unless you've plenty other work), and worry about problems afterwards. Most colleges can re-arrange times, but ask about that the day you start. That way they haven't time to find someone else (it's your future, so look after number one), but be terribly

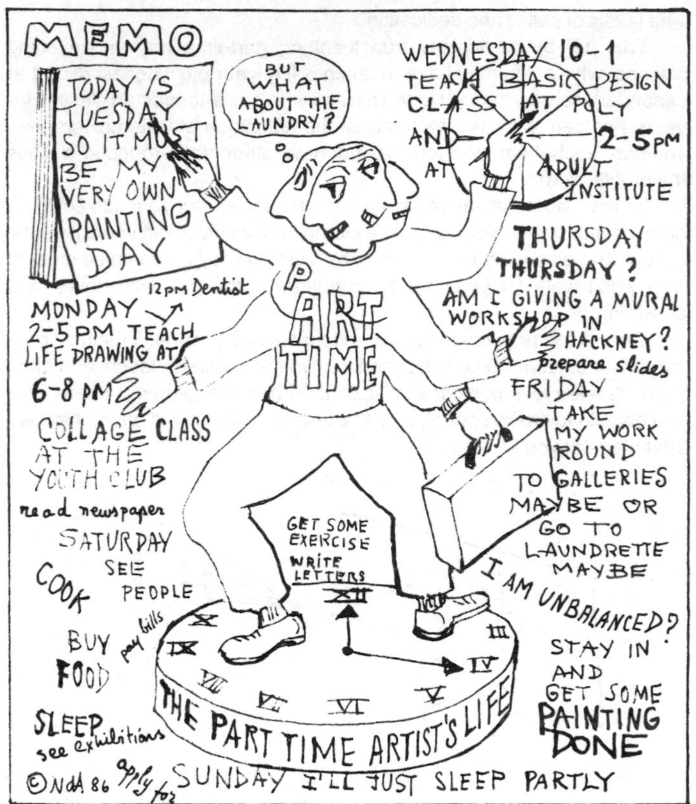

apologetic. Accept, even if it's low level work, it's another line on your CV. Accept, it may lead to other, better work. Accept, it pays your bills.

◁see **Publicity**▷

►Other Possibilities◄

If you have something particular to offer, perhaps a one-off lecture or a particular technical demonstration, which is out of the normal order of things, circulate this information. Not as part of your letter of application, but by a separate mailing. Funding in colleges, for special lectures, is often separate to the part-time budget, so a department, which may not be able to offer part-time teaching, may be able to offer you the odd lecture.

►Starting◄

If you have gained a part-time teaching position, it's probably because you were one of the better students when you were at college, and it's very easy to think all students will be much like you – want to work and willing to work. I'm afraid it doesn't always work out that way. Remember back to your own training, remember the lazy ones, the poor ones, the ones thrown off the course. Things haven't changed. You will have to deal with all types

and levels of ability and dedication.

This will be particularly true teaching part-time day and evening classes, where you may have to teach a fifty-year old who last did art at secondary school, through to the person who has attended art classes for years and can teach you more about the technique of watercolours than you can teach them; and you may not have other staff around to discuss the problems with.

It takes more than an ability and an enthusiasm for your subject to be able to teach it well. You have to be willing to work hard with your students, accept that all you try will not work, be frustrated by the talented student who won't work for you, and be annoyed by the pair who never stop gossiping.

One of the problems you will encounter is discipline. Whether to be friendly or strict. It's nice to be liked, but you are there to teach, and often it's necessary to impose strict discipline to achieve results, sometimes it can be akin to crowd control; and students at all levels will attempt to take advantage of you.

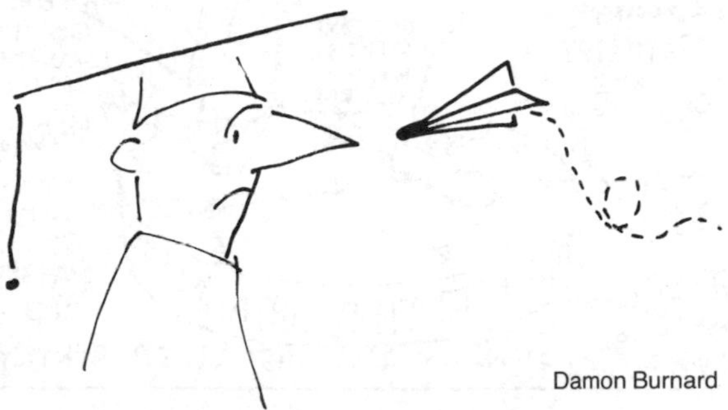

Damon Burnard

There is also stage fright when facing a group for the first time, and having to make yourself understood. You will have to be able to adjust your teaching to the level you are teaching, which can be difficult, when you are teaching more than one level. There is also the problem of continuity, resulting from only seeing a group once a week, and not being able to keep contact with what else the students have been doing.

However, when you pin the group's work on the wall for the crit, and you can see that the students have learned from you, and are willing and able to talk about their work, then teaching is great. I wish that always happened, but it doesn't, so be prepared for elation, but possibly also disillusionment.

Part-time rates of pay per hour as of May 1989:

- ►Grade 5 (below foundation) £10.59
- ►Grade 4 (foundation level) + A level £14.43
- ►Grade 3/9 (BA Hons, Higher BTEC) £16.92

►Information◄

►Contacts◄

►*Workers Educational Association*, Temple House, 9 Upper Berkeley Street, London W1H 8BY

►Further Reading◄

►*Design Courses in Great Britain.* Design Council, 28 Haymarket, London SW1Y 4SU

►*CNAA Handbook of Art and Design Courses in England and Wales.* Association of Art Institutions, Imperial Chambers, 24 Widemarsh Street, Hereford HR4 9EP

►*Directory of First Degree and DipHE courses.* CNAA Publications, 344-345 Gray's Inn Road, London WC1X 8BP. Within the three books above are listed all the art and design courses in England, Wales and Scotland

►*Education Authorities Handbook.* It's quite expensive, so use the copy in the library. This lists all education establishments, from secondary schools to universities, as well as all local education authorities. An excellent reference book for finding educational establishments in your area

►*Teachers' Pay and Superannuation.* Free from DES, Information Division, Elizabeth House, York Road, London SE1 7PH

►*Teaching Craft, Design and Technology.* Free from DES, Information Division, Elizabeth House, York Road, London SE1 7PH. Gives information on courses available

►*Teaching in Schools and Colleges in the UK.* AGCAS information booklet available from university and polytechnic careers services

►*Graduate Teacher Training Registry.* 3 Crawford Place, London W1H 2BN. Clearing house scheme for graduates who want to teach in primary/middle sector; clearing house open from the September prior to year of entry

►*I Can't Wait for Wednesday – the Crafts in Adult Education*, Cherry Ann Knott, Crafts Council 1987

Studio Teaching

▶Oliver Bevan◀

If you want to teach but there are no jobs, why not teach in your own studio? With the sculptor Lauretta Rose, I decided to do exactly that in order to subsidise a large and none too cheap space. We made a fair number of mistakes at the outset despite much careful preparation and advice taking. We did eventually hit upon a good formula which has solved most of the problems which were:

- ▶How to attract people and more specifically the right people for the kind of teaching that you wish to do.
- ▶How to accommodate those who can only come at weekends and evenings, and those who can only come during weekdays.
- ▶How to compete with adult education which appears to be offering the same kind of thing.

We wasted a fair amount of money advertising in many sectors of the art and general press. What we were offering could not be communicated effectively and I would suggest that unless your studio has stunning views of the Splurge Estuary or you are running the only course in the country on papermaking from discarded thatch or something equally easily communicable, you will also be wasting your money. The only exception is probably a regular slot in *The Artist* magazine. My occasional ads have had occasional results.

Our first objective was to get some activity in the studio and this we did by approaching various Friends of the Gallery type of organisations offering to run workshops specifically for their members, putting details in their mailing in return for a donation to their funds. An art history course, a local heritage group or art society may equally wish to adopt your project if you can plan something that appeals to them. The principle is to graft your operation on to an existing structure whose members are known to have an interest in visual arts. The workshops were often topical, relating to an exhibition they were currently mounting at the gallery. A good response to this can be expected because it is assumed correctly that your class has been vetted, and that you are therefore recommended by the organisation. This manoeuvre does what no end of advertising can possibly achieve, that is to get you through the credibility barrier, after which your vital mailing list will start to expand. We also established an evening class and a weekday class on a tiny scale so that those who wanted to build on the workshop experience could immediately follow it up. These classes have

▲
Louise Sheridan guest artist at the Cowcross Studios Workshop. (Photo: Oliver Bevan)

always been unprogrammed so that students can go at their own speed and with half a dozen, this is entirely manageable. We added weekend workshops advertised through our mailing list and within a year, the studio was paying its way on an average of two days teaching a week. Later refinements have included a regular life class, a summer school with visiting lecturers, tutorials and folder preparation for interviews.

If you can be as open about your own work as possible and if you can continue with it during class hours when things are quiet the students will benefit from the atelier atmosphere and support you when you exhibit. This levelling makes for a creative community.

How much you charge depends on what you are offering and your costs. I prefer to supply consumable materials and charge £20 per person per day. Setting up inevitably involves outlay in the form of easels, stationery, materials and if possible a plan chest, but luckily teaching is traditionally paid for in advance.

From the beginning it is important to make the mailing shots as visual as possible. If you have a postcard of your work send it out to each person who enquires about your classes. Draft your course description very carefully and spell out that no previous experience is necessary. Make contact with the secretaries of the fine art and foundation departments at your nearest art school. They get many enquiries from would-be students who need coaching before applying.

Teaching in your studio needs plenty of energy, organising skills, verbal skills, typing skills, patience and intuition, but it is a great deal more satisfying than being caught up in the internal worry machine that art schools have become in this era of applied philistinism. It can also be more profitable.

►**Note:** If you use your studio to run classes or workshops you should take out public liability insurance (*see Insurance*)◄

Sessional Work

►Lee Corner◄

Extra-mural teaching, running classes with the WEA, working on projects with Shape/Art Link, involvement with any educational activity not linked to a recognised course is 'sessional work'.

►All This and Undervalued Too◄

Visual art sessions, arranged by Northern Shape, at a hospital for people with mental disability. (Photo: Keith Pattison)
▼

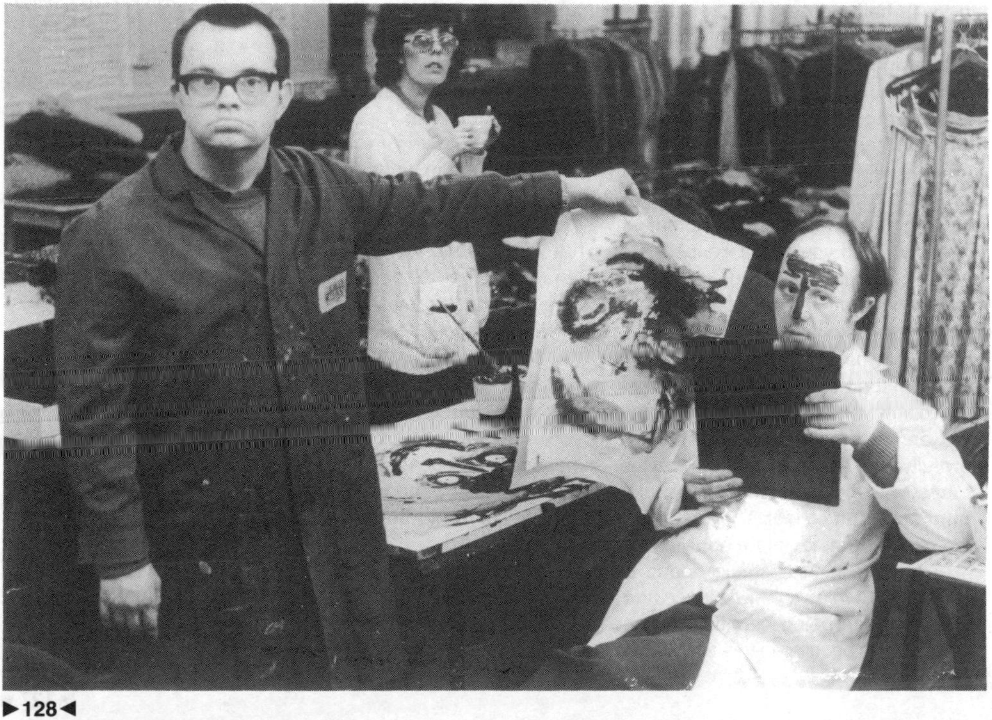

A number of reasons are given for the growth in sessional work opportunities over the past five years. Some put it down to the demise of teaching opportunities for visual artists - the traditional 'earner' allowing

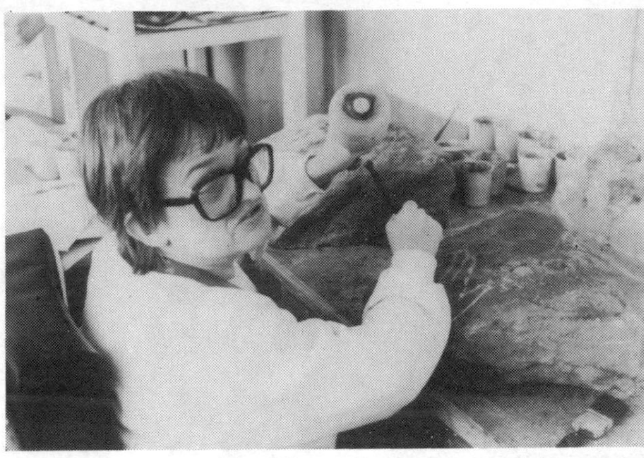

▲Left
Fish and Stars, by **Pam** made during a sculpture project run by **Alain Ayers** at the Grocott Centre, Stoke on Trent

▲Right
Stone carving during **Alain Ayers** sculpture workshop

time to pursue private studio practice; some suggest changes in the nature of arts funding resulting in fewer direct grants and bursaries to artists and more demands for public interface to prove arts organisations' commitment to accessibility; others might cite a growing political awareness and a desire amongst artists to join the struggle for cultural democracy through collective or collaborative creativity.

Whatever the reasons, the issues relating to sessional work and to sessional arts workers, have become fashionable. This is not however, to diminish the importance of these issues. The problem with fashions though is that once they have been identified, an agonising period of analysis seems inevitably to follow – *'what is the exact definition of....'; 'why does it defy definition'; 'what is the historical perspective';* we feel the need to understand, label and pigeon-hole before we can go any further.

All this is by way of an excuse for tackling the issue of sessional work from the broadest possible base, and risking dissension over the looseness of the terminology.

Whether the work takes place with the youth service, the regional arts association, community groups, or local colleges, the pit falls are potentially enormous. Unless the worker has a clear understanding of the work to be undertaken – both in planning and execution – and a negotiated contract, at the very least they could be asking for trouble.

At worst, sessional art workers have no entitlement to employment protection rights and no job security. They are vulnerable, open to exploitation, and undervalued. The work they do can result from someone else's administrative accountability (*'But we've got to have something in the rural areas'*); a needy public relations exercise for the factory; or free publicity for the host organisation. Above all they will probably be someone's way of expressing an accessibility policy.

At best, being a sessional arts worker can create new challenges; facilitate opportunities to explore new methods of working; bring freedom from isolation. It can allow the development of personal skills and the possibility of engaging with others in the movement toward a cultural democracy. It can create the opportunity for contact with isolated communities – people with mental disabilities, those in prison, elderly people. Above all, sessional arts workers are paid as artists – not teachers, not therapists, but artists.

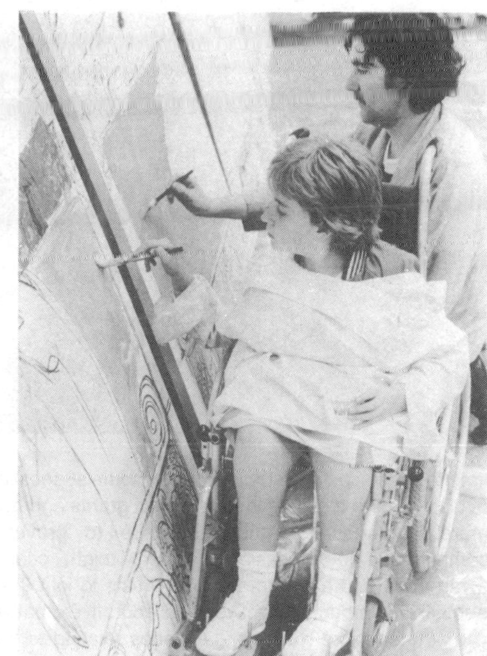

▲Right
As part of a collaboration between Northern SHAPE and the Sanderson Centre in Newcastle-upon-Tyne, painter **Stephen Marshall** and sculptor **Chris Humphries** were employed to make a large mural at the Sanderson Centre. Much of the work was undertaken through workshops organised by Northern SHAPE with physically handicapped children from the Community Physiotherapy Summer Playscheme in Pendower Hall Special School in Newcastle. The 40ft by 6ft mural incorporates two and three dimensional imagery using ceramics and paint. (Photo: Keith Pattison).

▲Left
Art Link project at Magnolia House Day Centre in Birmingham (Photo: Dee Keeling)

'I was waiting for the bus after the first session in the hospital and I suddenly thought 'God I'm an artist' *and for the last two years I'd just been unemployed or on the dole and suddenly I was getting money for being an artist. It gave me self-respect.'* (Bryn Jayes)

Many of the problems which apply to sessional arts workers are a result not only of the spasmodic nature of the work, but also the range of employment/employers. There is little, if any, coming together of the users of such workers or, indeed, of the workers themselves. A global picture cannot be attempted without a prohibitive amount of time and finance, but perhaps some of the issues can be explored by a closer examination of one particular aspect of sessional work: that which takes place in 'less usual venues'.

►Shape/Art Link Services◄

A network of sixteen Shape/Art Link services covers most of the UK and, although there is no statistical evidence, it might be reasonable to assume that they constitute a major body of 'users' of sessional arts workers.

Set up in the years since 1976, most of these autonomous organisations encourage the provision of creative activities for a wide range of people in the community and particularly in relation to those with special needs. Much of this work takes place in institutional settings such as hospitals, homes and day centres for those who are elderly, mentally or physically disabled, mentally ill, on probation or in prison. The work often involves artists with specific skills such as painters, clay workers and puppeteers who undertake weekly sessions of participatory activity with

groups in such settings.

The encouragement of personal creativity which results from a belief that everyone has a creative potential, is a prime factor in much of this work. The aim is often to facilitate such creative and artistic activity with a view to redressing the imbalances of power, influence and decision-making, which tend to be present in many establishments. The arts are thus contributing to more developed self-awareness and self-confidence amongst individuals, and the establishment of a voice for those who are generally disenfranchised.

The organisations which constitute the Shape/Art Link network are very different, having developed in response to the needs of their own regions, and it would be misleading to make broad generalisations. But it is reasonable to assume that opportunities for sessional arts workers do exist in these organisations, and artists should bear this in mind when considering sessional work.

▶Therapy?◀

There are often misunderstandings about the nature of work with people with special needs, and one of these is due directly to the looseness with which the word 'therapy' is bandied about.

Most people involved with this area of work would reject the notion of providing therapy for clear reasons: art therapy is a professional specialisation, and though the art therapist may have initially pursued a fine art training s/he has chosen to pursue a career as a therapist; attained appropriate academic qualifications; found full-time or part-time employment in an institution; become part of a treatment team; and is concerned with *'the totality of the patient - the history, family, immediate problems, goals of treatment, etc.'*[(1)]

While there may be overlaps in the practice of art therapists and sessional arts workers the distinctions will probably lie in the perceived goals, the approach and the relationship which is developed.

▶What Opportunities?◀

Having touched on the broader issues relating to work with the people with special needs some mention might be made of the sort of opportunities available to sessional workers. Art Link, set up in 1977 and operating across the West Midlands, for example, has about a hundred artists on the 'register' and works with them in a number of ways. For example, they undertake:

- ▶Weekly sessional work, as mentioned above
- ▶Courses in the introduction of creative activities to staff working in institutional settings
- ▶Celebratory events combining more than one art form and a multi-media approach
- ▶Skill sharing events with other artists

Variations of these basic approaches will be found in many other organisations and such flexibility should appeal to many sessional workers.

▷**1** *The Healing Role of the Arts – Conference Report.* 1983

►Approaches◄

Throughout the areas available to sessional workers there is an enormous, and somewhat unexplored, potential for artists to initiate their own projects. Such initiatives might range from an artist noticing the local elderly persons' home, going in for a chat, coming away with an idea for a project, and contacting the local Art Link, or Shape, or even RAA, to put forward the idea.

It is important to note that most arts organisations positively welcome such approaches from artists, as they are always looking for ways of developing work and new initiatives are crucial to such development. While, in the case of some RAAs particularly, the red-tape and paperwork might appear off-putting, it must be remembered that these organisations have a specific brief based on the accessibility of the arts and an idea from a potential sessional worker will, generally, be listened to.

As mentioned above, it is not helpful to make generalisations about Shape/Art Link services and the best advice is for the artist to make contact with the local Co-ordinator to discover the lay of that particular land, but it really should be reasonable to assume that that approach will be welcomed.

Alternatively, a number of artists might group together, advertise their skills and undertake sessional contracts suited to particular skills but co-ordinated through the group. While the latter might be the ideal (a group of artists controlling their own work pattern, needs and direction), it remains the case that most sessional arts workers are isolated individuals. Calls have been made to the users of the sessional workers to come together to discuss improved support mechanisms, information exchange, contracts and payments. Calls have been made to the workers themselves to come together for the same reasons. Such forums could help to clarify many of the issues concerning workers and users; issues of professionalism, leadership, control, ownership and status.

►Feedback◄

◁see **One Studio Group**▷

Until these debates take place it is important to emphasise a particularly positive aspect of sessional arts workers. The nature of the relationship between the worker and the group is frequently supposed to be one-way, *you* feed *them*. Experience would forcefully prove the contrary. The relationship is two-way at the very least. Artists find that their own practice, ideas, methods and perceptions are equally influenced by the group and this cannot be denied. This may be temporary and technical, *'Seeing the success of the members of the group using the monoprint method, I have for the present postponed my work concerned with etching to produce a selection of images by this process'*, Les Hickinbottom. Or to do with changed perceptions, *'I was already tackling the problems of making work which is accountable beyond the inward criteria of the studio or gallery but the naivity in which the patients approach their painting has refreshed my attitude to my own work. Whether this shows in my pictures as much as I would like, I do not know, but it is important for me,'* Bryn Jayes.

On the face of it there is no reason why any arts project should work successfully in an institution, whether that institution be a hospital, prison, probation centre, or whatever.

The participants in that project come together in a strange environment to share in an activity that while being the project's raison d'etre has very different definitions and associations for all involved. For the artists it is a total activity evolving out of time spent at college and further years spent developing the private studio practice necessary to secure a firm basis for their continued involvement in that activity. For the other participants it is so often an activity that carries with it dim recollections of childhood and of being at school. An activity that as they get older they feel less and less qualified to take part in or even to voice an opinion on.

But these arts projects are successful and each time success is different and unique to that particular project and group of people. Why? I don't think I know. But in the project at St Matthews we found ourselves in a position to strip the Art out of art and recognise that we were not making 'works of art'. What we were making instead were evidences of shared activity where the stamping of humaneness and individuality on inert materials was more important than gilt frames and pedestals.

For me there has been the opportunity to learn from the easy, inventive responses people make when faced with new materials and processes, and my present work is as it is because I have been privileged to see those responses.

For the other participants their success is that in a setting that is inherently anonymous they have found a means of expression, a voice, that is both individual and collective. (David Patten)

▶Shape Organisations◀

▶Shape East

c/o Eastern Arts, Cherry Hinton Hall, Cherry Hinton Road, Cambridge CB1 4DW ☎ 0223 215355

▶Southern Artlink

Unit 1, St John Fisher School, Sandy Lane West, Blackbird Leys, Oxford OX4 5LD ☎ 0865 714652

▶North West Shape

The Green Prefab, Back of Shawgrove School, Cavendish Road, West Didsbury, Manchester M20 8JR ☎ 061 434 8666

▶Artlink (West Midlands)

17a Hanover Street, Newcastle-under-Lyme, Staffordshire ST5 1HD ☎ 0782 614170

▶Artlink South

Hornpipe Community Arts Centre, 143 Kingstone Road, Portsmouth, Hampshire PO2 7EB ☎ 0705 826392

▶Northern Shape

Whinney House, Durham Road, Low Fell, Gateshead, Tyne & Wear ☎ 091 487 8892

▶Artlink Lincolnshire and Humberside

Central Library, Albion Street, Hull HU1 3FF ☎ 0482 224040

▶East Midlands Shape

27a Belvoir Street, Leicester LE1 6SL ☎ 0533 52933

▶**Arts for Disabled People In Wales**
Channel View, Jim Driscoll Way, The Marl, Grangetown, Cardiff CF1 7NF ☎ 0222 377885

▶**Scottish Council on Disability**
Princes House, 5 Shandwick Place, Edinburgh EH2 4RG ☎ 031 229 8632

▶**Artlink Edinburgh and Lothian**
4 Forth Street, Edinburgh EH1 3LH ☎ 031 556 6350

▶**Artability (South East)**
St James Centre, Quarry Road, Tunbridge Wells, Kent TN1 2EY ☎ 0892 515478

▶**Shape Bucks**
c/o Buckinghamshire Arts Association, 55 High Street, Aylesbury, Bucks HP20 1SA ☎ 0296 434704

▶**Artshare South West**
c/o South West Arts, Bradninch Place, Gandy Street, Exeter EX4 3HA ☎ 0392 218923

▶**Shape Up North**
191 Bellevue Road, Leeds LS3 1HG ☎ 0532 431005

▶Information◀

▶Contacts◀

▶*Directory of Social Change*, Radius Works, Back Lane, London NW3 1HL ☎ 01 435 8171. Runs a range of courses for voluntary and art groups

▶*Commission for Racial Equality*, Elliot House, 10-12 Allington Street, London SW1E 5EH ☎ 01 828 7022

▶*National Council for Voluntary Organisations*, 26 Bedford Square, London WC1B 3HU ☎ 01 636 4066. Provides training for community organisations and has information on sources of help and funding

▶*Research Training Initiatives*, 18-20 Dean Street, Newcastle upon Tyne N1 1PG ☎ 091 261 6581. Provides training and consultancy exclusively for voluntary and public sector organisations and a national training programme in management skills. Also publishes the *Funding Digest (see Funding)*

▶*Arts for Health*, Manchester Polytechnic, Manchester M15 6HA ☎ 061 236 8916. Gives advice and information on funding on health care arts

▶*British Health Care Arts Centre*, Duncan of Jordanstone College of Art, Perth Road, Dundee DD1 4HT ☎ 0382 23261. Founded 1989 to provide consultancy and advice which will improve the total environment in health care buildings and to establish a research base

▶*Hospice Arts*, The Forbes Trust, Forbes House, 9 Artillery Lane, London E1 7LP ☎ 01 377 8484

▶Further Reading◀

▶*Call Yourselves Artists?* Mike Ormsby. The Pioneers 1984. A report on work by the Pioneers Art Group in South Wales

▶'Art and Special Needs', Paul Drake. *Artists Newsletter*, November 1985

▶'The Tyranny of Don't Touch', Kirsten Hearn. Ibid

▶'Art in Hospitals', Barbara Taylor. *Artists Newsletter*, February 1988

▶*Art and Health Care*, Linda Moss, DHSS 1989. Intended for artists and organisations, aimed at the way the arts work in hospitals

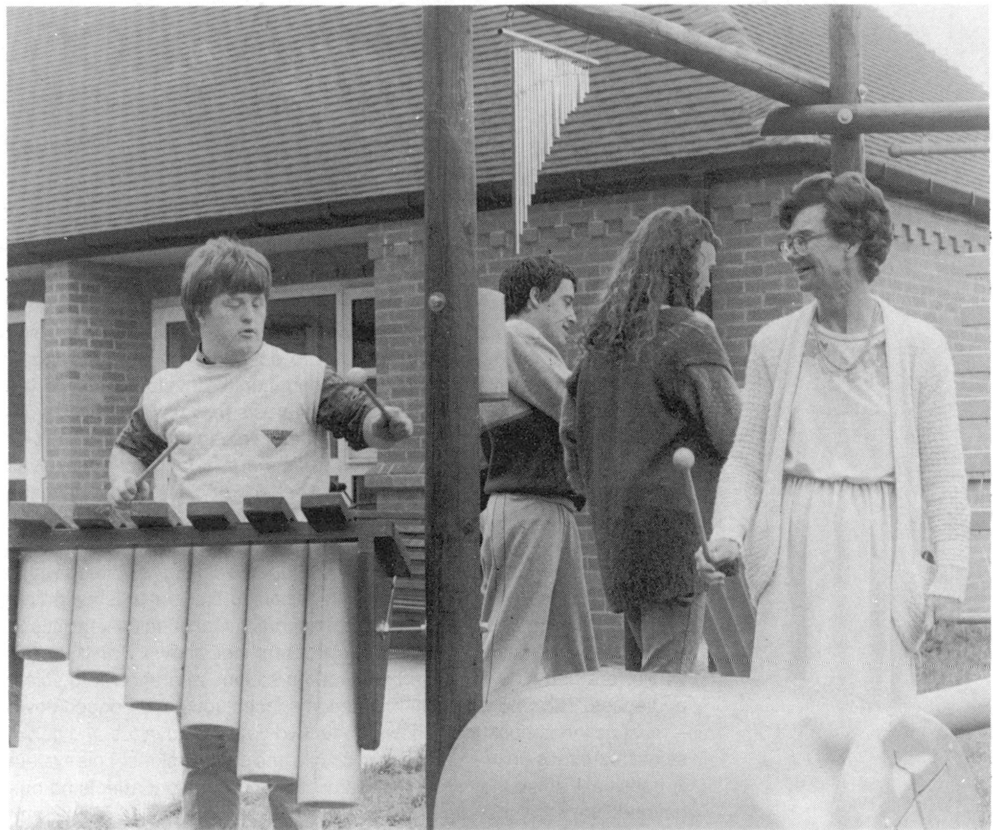

▲
Tony Dale, running a sound workshop (Photo: Dave West)

▶*Art and Touch Education for Visually Handicapped People.* Leicester University, 1988. Transcripts from a conference and workshops on work with visually impaired people

▶'Hands On', Linda Moss. *Artists Newsletter*, January 1989. The Arts Council's role in supporting disabled arts access

▶'Disability Arts: The Real Missing Culture'. *Feminist Arts News*, No 10 1989. An issue devoted to the disability arts movement

Community Action

►Nick Clements◄

Definition of 'Community':

► All those people you could be influencing if only you tried
► Everyone from children up to old age pensioners

Throughout all artistic endeavour in the community the recurring theme is one of hard work, lots of pre-planning and a great deal of activity which doesn't at first seem to have anything to do with art – the lobbying of councillors, the active participation in community development and the seeking of funding for projects. Individual artists may well find such work beyond their capabilities, however that doesn't mean that we shouldn't do anything about it. Throughout Britain, artists are organising themselves into co-operatives and groups, which are better equipped to undertake the communal administration needed to secure the sort of actions outlined below.

Over the years, the art world has developed a style and attitude which I can only describe as 'passive'. Art colleges are turning out artists with little or no chance of gaining full-time art employment. Galleries do very little to encourage any real new influx of spectators for their shows. Artists, on the whole, are happy to continue their work in studios and show it to select audiences. The whole system has become incestuous and bogged down – most galleries book their shows about two years in advance and only a select few ever gain the 'prestigious' shows and commissions. This system is passive – artists have few political views and our work affects no one beyond very restricted barriers. It is altogether a stagnant and unimaginative world.

There are, however, a growing number of young artists who are fed up with this exclusive system and want to change it for something which offers them more of a chance. Part of a new system would be to form groups and become involved in community action. Not just because there seems to be more money there, but out of a conviction that such work is valid and can bring about change. It isn't a simple option and it is not one which will bear fruit immediately – but it is the only real chance we have.

Active art would encourage people to join with artists in the production of artwork. It should, if it is successful, involve the community in a deeper understanding of the way in which the arts can be used.

▲
Cefn Glas Residential School, Bridgend. Set up by Mid-Glamorgan Education Authority and South-East Wales Arts Association. This was a two week mural painting project involving two artists from the Pioneers working with children of all ages who were educationally subnormal. The mural was designed and painted by the children in their kitchen area.

►The Alternative Service Structure◄

One aim of all artists should be to gain a wide audience, but to do this, they have to be involved in a wider range of activities:

►Artists need to overcome a deep-rooted distrust and disinterest in their activities.
►They need to gain people's confidence and show that the arts are relevant to today's society.
►They need always to perform as professionals, otherwise they won't be treated as such, and more importantly, won't be paid as such.

If artists can achieve all this they may become accepted as part of the 'alternative' or 'caring' service structure. At base level this includes community centres, health centres and leisure centres – play-schemes, day nurseries, Scouts, Guides, the martial arts and aerobics. On a wider and more advanced level this can include all the social services and town and country planning.

Within this alternative service structure artists cannot act in a vacuum, they must work with other community activists. It is no good artists just producing a mural without any community involvement, as has too often been the case in the past. Any initiatives must have the backing of the other community services and should be aimed at giving everyone involved benefit or enjoyment. These initiatives can take the form of exhibitions of art work, murals, environmental improvement schemes, play-schemes, workshops or consultative work.

►Exhibitions of Art Work◄

Why do artists scramble for shows in established art galleries? Because they're well-lit, well designed show places or because of the prestige built into them? More people see a display in a high street window in a day than go to a gallery in a year, and if we are really want to make our art accessible, these are the sort of venues we should be approaching. Artists must start showing what they do in 'public' – that is the only way that they will ever get more publicity, more acclaim and ultimately more money. To make their work public they must take their art out into shop windows, community centres, pubs, social clubs and many other spaces which will take it. As these spaces are frequently very amenable and keen to exhibit work, it is well worth trying.

You should be able to get a list of local community centres with exhibition spaces from your regional arts associations – if they don't have one ask why not because they certainly ought to. For such shows there is never enough money to cover even minimal publicity. The way the Pioneers (artists' group) normally raise cash for publicity is to approach several venues and then get together a tour for the show. This means that you can approach every venue for a contribution to the overall costs and the RAA as well. You can produce a poster which will cover all the venues but don't go over the top, A3 is big enough and two colours is quite sufficient. The venues will not necessarily attract massive crowds, but if they are any good they will have regular visitors who will attend anyway. Try to arrange a workshop through the centre as, apart from its own value, it may attract other funds. Always provide a comments book if you can't supervise the space. These are great fun and a constant source of wonderful quotes about your art.

◁see **Publicity**▷

Exhibiting in these types of venue means thinking creatively and imaginatively. Too often artists make no concessions to the venue, they treat them as if they were galleries and are disappointed by the end product. Artists must adapt to their circumstances – we won't always be able to exhibit in prestigious venues so make the most of the other ones. The one important point is to make sure you know exactly who is responsible for what, and how much help you can expect.

►Play-schemes and Workshops◄

Play-schemes and workshops are the most common form of community work which artists participate in, and they also provide the main source of income available to young artists at present. Unfortunately, because art colleges don't teach artists how to work on play-schemes or run workshops, the first experiences of some artists in such jobs are abysmal. This is not only due to lack of experience but because play-schemes are frequently badly-organised and not orientated towards visual arts activities; often the children are only interested in sport. However, well-organised community-based play-schemes can provide stimulating experiences and are useful stepping-stones to other and more exciting work. Playschemes and similar workshops are also invariably poorly paid, involve long hours and are short-term job options.

Most play-schemes are organised by the local leisure and amenities

▲
A Public Sculpture Workshop at Bretton Hall, Yorkshire. Two artists **Sophie Ryder** and **Christopher Campbell** worked with visitors to the park on an animal trail for Bretton Menagerie.

department of your local authority. They are either based at adventure playgrounds or community centres. The experience gained at each can be very different, and it is up to you to go into the centres and find out if they are sympathetic to your ideas. There is, for instance, a long history of theatre companies going into such centres and doing tours of a single show. Similarly artists can perform their particular skills in the centres and gain both inspiration and acclaim.

In 1982 the Pioneers set up a touring community workshop, called the Pioneers Travelling Arts Circus. We toured the Rhondda Valley, visiting over fourteen different sites in just under a month. The centres we visited were pubs, community centres, working men's clubs, an old disused theatre and open spaces. We produced exterior and interior murals, workshops using cardboard, small processions and performances, a large football match and did lots of drinking. The only reason the tour went ahead was that we planned it well in advance, and were adaptable enough to cater for the people's needs rather than sticking to our own ideals and rigid standards.

We raised all the money ourselves. We involved the local RAA, the Workers Education Authority and other sources of money were also tapped through local contacts. This involved a great deal of work, all of which was non-art, but great fun. Personally, I enjoy this type of work; it's exciting and you get to meet a variety of people. In the end, eight artists were employed over the month on an average wage of £60 per week. Having done this sort of thing for over five years we are now able to pay our artists between £200 and £250 a week.

Such work only occurs during school holidays and is a short-term solution to income earning. The people involved in the alternative service structures which I have mentioned are social workers, care workers and

the like. They are all trying to find new ideas and new stimulation for their clients. Art can often be this and much more. Following the Pioneers tour we have been invited back to many centres and have continued a working relationship to the benefit of all concerned.

For example, in 1983 we were invited to visit Hendrefadog Community Centre, a large graffiti-covered building in a remote highly-depressed area. At the centre we produced a 150 foot mural with about 40 children and the Centre's workers over a four-week period. In 1985 we were again involved there in the production of a large concrete octopus and snake in their new garden area, again over a four-week period. This work came about because we had kept in contact. Even now, the relationship which we had built up with the local community still flourishes.

►Campaign Involvement◄

Another short-term involvement in community action in which artists can participate is campaign work. The Pioneers, artists and community workers are mainly based in areas of high social need, and in an attempt to do something positive about this, the alternative service structure is constantly involved in campaigns. Whether these be housing, rent or general work campaigns they can all benefit from artistic input. This includes designing posters, taking photographs and making videos. We have the skills and the tools and we should be using these to change society today. Historically, artists have been involved in similar work and have been used by popular social movements, so why shouldn't today's artists continue this practice?

Although this sort of work normally arises out of the friends you know or by common contacts, you should be paid for the work. It's essential that your skills are used in a professional manner and that you're not expected to produce large amounts of work for little or no recompense.

►Community Residencies◄

◁see **Residencies**▷

Over the years, I have been involved in many long-term residencies most of which were set up by the artists and the community together. Our policy was to set up discussions and once the project was planned the RAA, local authorities and other funding bodies were approached. Initial contact often leads to longer-term involvement and in 1985 three artists worked in a local primary school on an exterior board mural to be sited in the local community. The mural was used as a backing for an adventurous re-development of wasteground which includes planting and seating areas. The artists, pupils and teaching staff involved found the experience to be stimulating and productive. Having started this work we returned to the school in the winter of 1985 and ran a competition for the pupils to design our new letterhead. The contact will be continued this year with a large exterior wall mural in the school grounds, negotiated by the artists and the staff.

The initial mural at the school was part of the Nova Street Project which was jointly funded by the Cardiff City Council, the Prince of Wales Committee and South Glamorgan Council. The subsequent work there has been funded by South East Wales Arts Association and the city

council. As with everything else, you need to work hard to find the funds, but as we have made a firm commitment to continue working in the school, it has been easier. All funding bodies seem to want to encourage a long-term relationship between artists and communities.

Surely artists should try to set up direct involvement in their community, and if, as seems likely, the ACGB and the RAAs are doing less 'instigative' work, we as artists, are going to have to start doing it ourselves. Artists have to accept that the rest of society is not very aware of what art is or what it can achieve. It seems to me that the only way that mainstream society will accept artists is if they are prepared to bring their art out into the open – into such places as schools, community centres and pubs.

►Community Commitment◄

If artists are to play a role in the long-term development of community advancement they have to be aware of what they are capable of doing and how wide their influence can be. They can get involved in all kinds of activities of community benefit – ranging from changing the school curriculum to involvement in the construction of play structures and environments and artistic input into the new building developments.

In South Glamorgan, the county council have introduced a recommendation that at least ½-1% of the cost of new public buildings be spent on the arts. Such policies have been in practice for some years in parts of America and Canada, and artists should campaign for percent for art to be common practice in all county, city and borough councils. In South Glamorgan the council was persuaded by individual artists who in their meetings with councillors talked about how they thought they could be helped. Eventually, the council set up an Art Sub-Committee which took the decision.

We have now a very active role to play in the council, but there is no easy route to successful involvement. Our work can only be achieved with the assistance of councillors who are keen, and the only way to find them, is to meet them socially and then to go to meetings and badger them. I feel that the arts bodies should help artists to affect decision-making by putting

Work in progress on the 112 sq ft ceramic relief for Clapham Park School for the Partially Sighted. The relief was designed and made by a group of a dozen or so students from the Clapham School with Crispin House Adult Training Centre for the Mentally Handicapped and Morpeth School. It was made during a four day workshop at Unit Seven Studios in Camberwell, organised by Priya Commander and Carol Farrow. Members of the Studios have been involved in various community workshops over the last two years. To extend their links with the community and especially with Crispin House, who they had particularly enjoyed working with, they organised this workshop to bring Crispin House together with other groups, the aim being to work together to a specific end, each being sensitive to the abilities and disabilities on other members of the group. Greater London Arts gave partial funding and the project began in June 1985, staffed by members and friends of Unit Seven.

▼

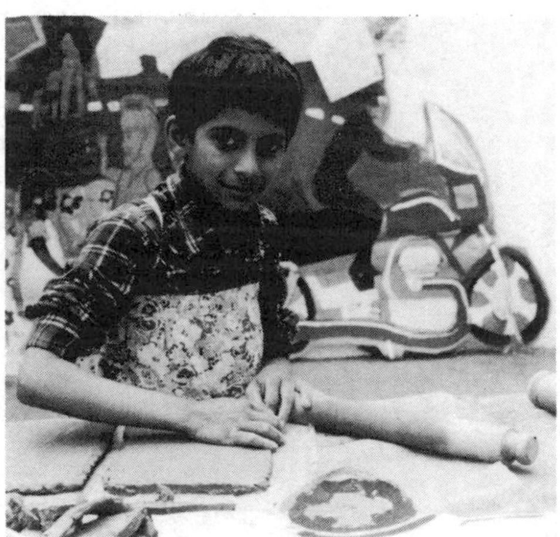

pressure on councillors. It is only by working together that we can bring visual arts to the fore.

Long-term commitment to the community by artists means the building of bridges and common experiences. Nowadays, in South Glamorgan it is common practice for the council planning department to contact artists in the planning stages for new buildings or projects, and artists are used to taking part. Integrated public art projects must include artists in the planning stages. Art shouldn't be an afterthought to cover a blank space.

Such work develops out of a mutual trust built up over years of common experience. The artist is just like any other craftsperson or specialist, and they will only receive the amount of acclaim and respect they deserve through hard work over a long time. It is possible for artists to influence the everyday lives of a great many people if we can affect their attitudes and work with them to change their environment.

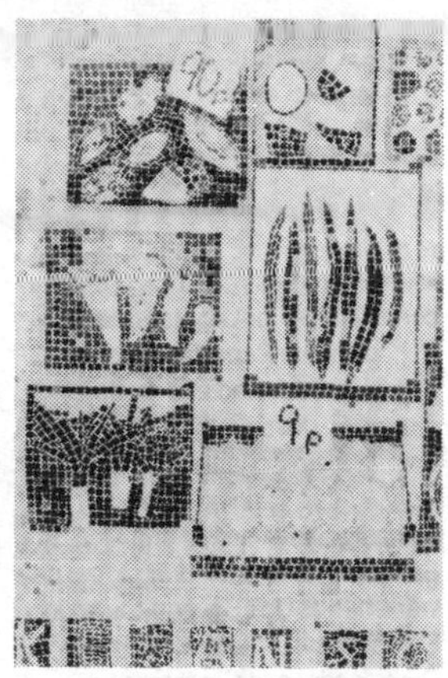

▲
Children of Pakeman Primary School, Islington, working with **Patsy Hans,** used the theme of fruit and vegetable displays in local shops for the mosaic they made for Kinloch Park in London. Every child in the school was involved in the project, which was initiated by parents together with the school, and funded by Islington Council under the Ward Improvement Scheme. Patsy Hans will now be working with the school on a mural project of the playground.

►Information◄

►Contacts◄

►*See Sessional Work*

►Further Reading◄

►*The Mural Kit.* Directory of Social Change. Detailed advice on how to paint murals in the classroom, community or street corner. Mural slide packs from DSC: *An introduction to mural painting; Different types of mural painting; Community and ethnic murals; Murals by artists; Personalising the environment; Driftwood sculptures*

►*Mural Manual*, ed Carol Kenna and Steve Lobb. Artic Producers and Greenwich Mural Workshop, 1986. Detailed advice on organising and painting murals

►*Call Yourselves Artists?* Mike Ormsby. The Pioneers, 1984. A report on work undertaken by the Pioneers Art Group in South Wales

►'Action will always speak louder than Words', Nick Clements, *Directory of Exhibition Spaces*, first edition, Artic Producers 1983

►'Art and Special Needs', Paul Drake. *Artists Newsletter*, November 1985

►'Artists Initiatives', Richard Padwick. *Artists Newsletter*, August 1987

►'Making More Ways', Susan Jones. *Artists Newsletter*, November 1988

►'Local Councils & the Arts', Roland Miller. *Artists Newsletter*, June 1989

►'Councils & Culture', Roland Miller. *Artists Newsletter*, August 1989

►*Code of Practice for Independent Photography*, Vince Wade. Artic Producers, Artists Newsletter Publications, 1989

Promotion

Publicity◀

Photographing Work◀

Publicity

▶Susan Jones◀

Publicity and, in the broader sense, 'marketing' is the central problem for the visual arts. If the desired number of people can't be brought to the work and if, once there, the work isn't communicated, there is little future for the visual arts than as an academic pursuit or as a hobby. (Nich Pearson)[1]

▶What it is and what it's for◀

In other art forms, promotion and publicity are integral to doing the work. It's no use being an excellent singer if no one knows your specialisation and availability. For visual artists though, promotion and publicity are barely dealt with on college courses. They are skills which are picked up (or not) as and when needed. The problem with this way of tackling it is that promotion and publicity tend to be what you do after you've completed the art work, often at the very last minute. Much time and energy is wasted sending the wrong information to the wrong people and then feeling disappointed when there's no response. In this section, I'll be showing that promotion involves the things you already do, like sending out a CV, and that publicity can be cost effective and produce results. Rather than a step-by-step guide, I'll be showing how some artists have tackled specific projects and their results.

▶What is promotion?◀

In a nutshell, promotion is making sure what you have to offer – services, products – is brought to the attention of the people who might want them. This involves working out who those people are and considering how you can best attract their attention to what you are offering.

To take an example. You are holding an exhibition. Who do you especially want to visit it? If you want to attract local business people, bankers or other professionals because your paintings have, in the past, sold to such people and you'd like not only to sell some more but also to get some commissions, then presenting your exhibition to that audience is different from presenting it to art critics and gallery directors.

Business people regularly receive promotional material – people trying to sell them computers, cars, office furniture, services, special offers, etc. Your information will inevitably be compared with this as it falls on to the

▷1 'Alternatives', Nich Pearson, *Directory of Exhibition Spaces*, first edition ed. Neil Hanson & Susan Jones. Artic Producers 1983.

business person's desk.

Look at it from another angle. Promotion is part of any application you make – be it to a gallery or for a residency or commission. What will ensure that the gallery or agency will take your application seriously and that your art work is viewed in the best possible circumstances?

►What is publicity?◄

Publicity is the nuts and bolts of promotion. Thinking of it in the broadest sense, it is the leg work of promotion. Who'd have thought of a CV as a piece of publicity – boring old date of birth and college qualifications typed on a sheet! But it is. It is the one piece of information that details what you are, what you do and what you want to do and, presented in a creative way, it's a piece of publicity that all artists can use more effectively.

Is publicity expensive? Can I afford to do it? In the business world, you must invest to get returns. When business is quiet, firms embark on a marketing campaign to get new orders. Although there's no hard-and-fast rule about the percentage of an overall budget you should spend on publicity, making comparisons between what you want to achieve – in sales, commissions, press coverage, other opportunities – and what you need to spend to get there is useful.

Unfortunately, the visual arts world has always tended to treat publicity as an optional extra. When grants get cut, so does the range and scope of publicity. In one sense it's an obvious choice, because for a visual arts 'business' there's very little income anyway, so publicity won't improve it! This is short-sighted, because there's a far greater interest in visual arts than most people realise. And in other forms, like opera, a minority interest has become highly popular in a relatively short time because of good promotion and publicity campaigns.

If you believe in the value of what you do, then use each opportunity you have to present yourself and your work in the best possible way. In the long-term, the more people who become sympathetic and involved in visual arts, the better it will be for you and for all artists.

►Ask yourself why?◄

Because it's the 'done thing' to put out publicity and because of other pressures such as limited time and money, it's easy to fall into the trap of rushing to do the next poster and invitation card for an exhibition without asking yourself 'why?'.

> Moreover, the common mistake of artists and groups organising their own exhibitions is to try to do what the established galleries already do – that is concentrate energy and resources on posters and private view cards. Posters in particular are a questionable device for attracting people to most 'ordinary' exhibitions while at the same time they can be expensive to produce and difficult to distribute. (Nich Pearson)[2]

All publicity should follow the AIDA rule. It should **attract** (so it will at least get noticed), it should **inform** (so that the target audience will know who, what, where, when), it should create **desire** (ie it should be persuasive) and it should induce **action** (tell the audience what they have to do – attend an exhibition, open day or whatever).

▷**2** *Directory of Exhibition Spaces* first edition.

►Exhibition Preview Cards◄

What are they for? How can you improve them? They tend to fall into the following types: full-colour illustration A5/A6 cards with biography/preview information on the back, single-colour (usually black on white) A5/A6, or ⅓ A4 cards with simple text and occasionally an image.

None are generally very informative and they seem seem to be aimed at the art world's 'in crowd'. (Some don't even bother to caption the work illustrated so the recipient has no idea of size, medium, whether it is part of a series, or which way up it should be, etc.) Make your preview card **interesting**, make it stand out from the rest so that recipients are informed both about the artist and what is being exhibited. Your invitation card is an item known as 'direct mail'.

Direct mail is the sending of promotional literature (mainly through the post) to specified addresses. Theatre, music, film and literature make great use of direct mail; visual arts and crafts less so, perhaps because those arts activities haven't got a 'box-office' through which to experience the benefit.

Direct mail has two main aims: advertising and selling. The former is straightforward and the latter covers not only selling actual pieces of work but also encouraging more people to look at and participate in the visual arts and crafts by increasing visual awareness and, in the long-term, the 'market' for work produced.

Thus, the invitation card, going to a specialist art list, is an item of direct mail so use it carefully. Make sure that it follows the AIDA rule which has been explained above.

If the gallery you are showing in is hard to find, include a map (showing where the parking is) or at least explain that the gallery is '100 yards from the central library' or include bus routes, train/tube stations or whatever.

If you are putting the card into someone else's mailing list – check what envelope size they use so your card fits without folding. Use paper or card economically, go for standard 'A' sizes and remember that fancy trimming and folding cost extra.

Photographs for printing must be good-quality black and white and they are better printed on coated or art card or paper. A bad black and white photograph with thumb prints or dust spots will not miraculously turn into a good printed image. Full-colour printing requires a non-absorbent card or paper and bear in mind that 35mm slides are not ideal for blowing up to A5, as inaccuracies in colour balance and focus will be magnified.

When deciding what sort of illustrations to use, ask yourself whether they are likely to attract the people you want to come to the exhibition – the architect who says he likes your work, the gallery director interested to show it next year, the art teachers bringing school groups, etc. Look at your illustrations objectively. If your work doesn't reproduce well, then a studio shot is definitely more appealing.

Printing on the reverse side doesn't double the cost, so don't waste the reverse side – there's space for the map, an illustration of the work, a picture of the gallery, the 'source material' for the work, etc, etc – all things which may tempt your audience to come.

Don't forget also, that your preview card can be a postcard in the real sense, with space for the recipient's name and address, thus saving envelope costs and time 'stuffing' them.

CASTLEFIELD GALLERY
Open Tuesday – Saturday 10.30 – 5.00
Sunday 12.00 – 4.30 Admission Free

5 Campfield Avenue Arcade, Corner of Liverpool Road and Deansgate, Manchester M3 4FN.
Phone 061 832 8034

FABIAN PEAKE
NEW PAINTINGS:
New York Thoughts
10 JANUARY – 15 FEBRUARY 1986

PRIVATE VIEW:
THURSDAY 9 JANUARY 6.00 – 8.00 pm

Fabian Peake was born in Sussex in 1942. He studied at Chelsea School of Art and the Royal College of Art between 1958 and 1966. His work has been exhibited extensively in group shows, most notably the 1972 John Moores Exhibition in Liverpool, the 1983 Tolly Cobbold Exhibition and the 1983 Royal Academy Summer Exhibition. In 1983 he was awarded a Greater London Arts Association Bursary. He had a one man exhibition at the Woodlands Gallery, Blackheath in 1983 and at the Vortex Gallery, London in 1984. A visit to New York in 1985 inspired him and had a profound effect on his paintings. Early in 1986, his work will be included in a group exhibition at the Vortex Galleries. Fabian Peake has lectured in numerous art schools in England, including Wolverhampton Polytechnic, Canterbury College of Art and Manchester Polytechnic, where he is currently a Senior Lecturer in the Painting School. His work is represented in public and private collections in England, Europe and America. Fabian lives and works in London.

Fabian Peake
"EARLY IN THE MORNIN'!" 1985
Oil on Canvas 75" × 67"

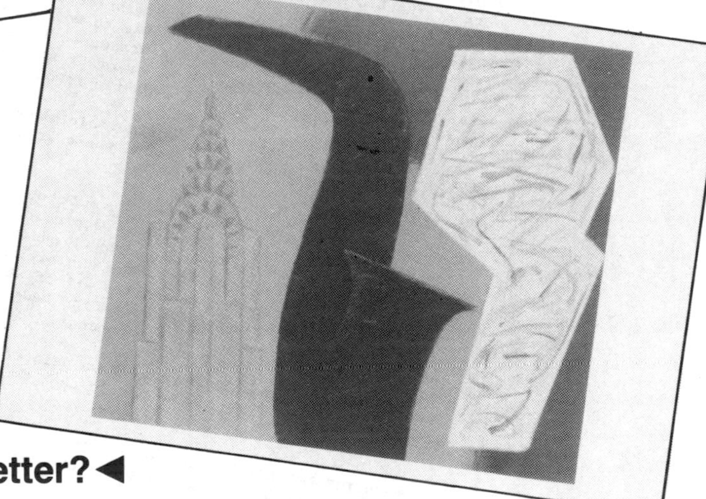

◄
An A6 preview card with a colour illustration on the front and information on the back. Printing more of these than are needed as preview cards would enable them to be sent out as an interesting CV.

►Leaflet or Letter?◄

Along with their preview cards, most galleries send out an A4 leaflet giving information on the artist, their work and may include a CV, the artist's statement and an illustration. The leaflets tend to be rather dreary items – lengthy CV and difficult-to-understand artist's statement, so why not think of an alternative. Look at the direct mail technique of sending a letter with the preview card and you might get a bigger response than you thought. Here's five ways you might start off the letter:

- ►Ask a question that demands a positive answer
- ►Tell the reader they should read the letter
- ►Tell them why you have written to them
- ►Tell them something flattering
- ►Present them with an original proposition

And remember, a letter is a personal communication; people expect to receive them and like getting them. A letter enables you to comment, expand or make more human the rest of the information you are

Spirit of St Louis!

October 5, 1982

PRESS RELEASE

Susan Jones - Drawings & Fredrick Nelson - Paintings

The Bode Gallery in Jarrow is the first in the North East to host an exhibition arising out of the artists' exchange programme between St Louis, USA and the United Kingdom. The Exchange Programme began in 1981, when sculptor Bill FitzGibbons came from St Louis and exhibited work at the LYC Museum and Art Gallery in Cumbria.

In the depths of the St Louis winter in February, Susan Jones, an artist from Sunderland, journeyed to St Louis to work in a studio to produce new work for exhibition, and to give a series of lectures on English art. The visit was a huge success and the Mayor of St Louis presented her with 'the key to the City' - a replica of the famous St Louis Arch.

Fredrick Nelson, an artist of considerable standing in St Louis now divides his time between London and St Louis where is now is preparing for several major exhibitions.

The exhibition at the Bede Gallery from October 13 - November 12 brings together Susan Jones' fine delicate watercolour drawings - several of which were completed in St Louis - and Fredrick Nelson's strong, exciting abstract paintings and collages. The exhibition goes a long way to contrast the differences between the art of St Louis and that currently happening in England and visitors to the Bede Gallery will be able to see the fruits of this cultural exchange.

The next artist from St Louis will be painter and printmaker Michael Rubin who will be visiting Newcastle upon Tyne in June 1983.

FURTHER INFORMATION ON THE EXHIBITION AND THE ARTISTS IS AVAILABLE FROM SUSAN JONES, SIMPSON STREET STUDIOS, OLD SIMPSON STREET SCHOOL, SUNDERLAND TELEPHONE 0783 673589.

Black and white photographs enclosed

Notes for Editors

The Artists' Exchange Programme is supported by the Arts and Humanities Commission, the Neighborhood Arts Council and Central West End Savings and Loan, all of St Louis. Susan Jones' travel grant to St Louis was awarded by Northern Arts.

▶

Press release compiled by the artists aimed at attracting local press and media. Emphasising the 'local interest' and accompanied by two photographs (one of Susan Jones in her studio with drawings in the background, the other of one of Fredrick Nelson's constructed paintings), it elicited an immediate response from three local newspapers and a local radio station who all covered it without trivialising the work. A different press release was used for the national art press.

presenting. If you want to use a letter to 'sell' your exhibition:

►Start with specific objectives
►Aim the letter at your 'target' audience (architects, interior designers or art teachers and school children)
►Translate the benefit of going to the exhibition into personal advantages for them (they can get a discount if they buy something, will be stimulated by a talk, free wine or whatever)
►Ask yourself whom you are writing to and write with that person in mind
►State all the benefits
►Tell the recipients what you want them to do – go to the exhibition, buy some work, come to a talk, bring a school group along, etc
►Repeat the opening times, make them feel welcome

►Poster◄

Who looks at posters? This depends on where you site them. If concentrating on local coverage leg it round and find the best sites; the central library will usually take posters to distribute to all branch libraries; put them in other galleries, museums and arts centres; don't forget art schools, adult education centres and community centres; try hotels, conference centres, theatres, film clubs, performing arts venues, graphic, photography and art supply shops, framers and other likely shops. This homework will be useful next time so keep a list of all the poster sites!

In short, posters reach hundreds and thousands of people: leaflets and private view cards only reach the people you send or give them to; advertisements only the people who read that newspaper or periodical. A well-established press and publicity officer for a major regional theatre, when asked what was the most effective local publicity method said *'fly posting or regional TV advertising'*.

If you are putting your poster up in these public places remember that most sites can't take posters bigger than A3, so don't print A2 ones unless your are sure there are enough places to put them. A2 horizontal format takes up an enormous amount of poster board space in a busy library. Another problem is that attractive posters get stolen.

For public sites, your poster must have public appeal in terms of text and image. Don't use 'art jargon' like 'recent work', 'works on paper', 'abstract paintings' – all the sort of phrases which put off all but the 'in crowd'.

Look at posters which are selling other products – theatre, music, folk, jazz, film programmes, circuses, opera – see how they use text and image to entice an audience in (they have to as their budget is dependent on box-office income rather than in visual arts where there is no direct relationship between income and the number of exhibition visitors). Imagine that you are actually telling the readers of the poster to come to the exhibition because:

►They will enjoy looking at the work
►There's free coffee in the gallery
►It's open in the evenings for people who are at work all day
►There's a talk/demonstration on Monday afternoon
►All the work is for sale at prices they can afford

►The artist will be in the gallery, doing some painting/drawing during gallery opening hours
►The 500th visitor gets a free signed etching
►They shouldn't to miss the show as it's only on for seven days.

►Compiling a Curriculum Vitae◄

A curriculum vitae is a document which describes your background, qualifications and experience and how you can be contacted. It is something every artist needs in some form or other. The basic format for a CV, extracted from an article by Alan Mitchell in *Artists Newsletter*, is outlined below. Other examples of using and abbreviating CV information are also illustrated.

►Standard CV◄

A curriculum vitae is simply a personal, detailed information list showing what you have done to date. Stating the obvious, leaving out the bad things, accentuating the good things. The reason a standard format for CV presentation has evolved is solely to enable recipients of it to obtain 'pre-interview' information at a glance without wading through lengthy written explanations.

This is the information it should contain and why:

►**Name** – Full name
►**Address** – Full address including postcode
►**Telephone number** – Give a day number and an evening number. If you don't have a phone give a friend's or relative's who can contact you quickly and state just that. By giving no number you may fall at the first fence
►**Date of birth** – State clearly in numbers, then give age separately. This may seem crazy, but don't argue, just do it
►**Place of birth**
►**Nationality**
►**College/Education** – Showing all dates, results and awards
►**Other professional qualifications**
►**Current employment** – Be honest. If unemployed be frank
►**Previous employment or work experience** – Chronologically since leaving college including any part-time work that may be relevant
►**Experience** – this section will emphasise or playdown various aspects of your experience according to what sort of application you are making
►**Exhibitions** – Here's your chance. The longer the better.
►**Awards** – Well, some people get them
►**Residencies and Commissions**
►**Referees** – Give two names, addresses and telephone numbers. Standard references or testimonials which you may already have are looked on as wallpaper.

You should bear in mind that your CV is a personal statement. It is in no way, shape or form an establishment document. There is nothing official about it. Information given will not be leaked to GCHQ.

Everyone, regardless of who they are, what they have or have not

Himalayan Trek. Linocut by Katie Clemson. 21½"x 10".

Katie Clemson

Katie Clemson was born in Temora, N.S.W., Australia in 1950. She completed her B.A.(Hons.) in Fine Art at the Central School of Art and Design, London, U.K. in 1977.

She has made the linocut her print speciality and has lectured in printmaking departments throughout the U.K. and in Sydney, Towoomba and Perth in Australia.

Katie was a printmaking tutor at Eton School in 1979, and printmaking specialist at St. Pauls Girls School, London, 1979-81. In 1984 she was the Artist-in-Residence at Tresillian Community Centre, Perth, W.A.

Since 1978 Katie has had 8 one-person shows in England, U.S.A. and Australia.

Her linocuts, paintings and paperworks have been purchased for collections in the U.K., Italy, U.S.A., Canada and Australia.

walkerprint London 01 580 7031 New York (212) 475 5451

◄ A short CV with an illustration of the artist's work on the reverse, printed up as an A6 postcard.

done, has the information and ability to prepare their own CV. The CV is not a job to be done in a rush when you eventually find something to apply for. It is something to be written up and perfected now, before you ever make your first application.

The point is once it's done and photocopied, it will stand you in good stead. But don't send the same one to every type of opportunity. A CV must be adapted and updated all the time if it is to be the basis of every application you make.

►Blencarn Open Day◄

It is valuable here to look at the way in which some artists have compiled and used publicity, beginning with open studios.

Painter Alan Stones, who lives in a village of only 30 houses five miles from the nearest A road, 10 miles from Penrith in Cumbria, held an open studio week in June 1985. The intention of the week was to attract visitors and to sell work – Alan Stones derives his income from sales and commissions of work rather than supplementing this with teaching or other part-time work.

In terms of publicity, he designed a four-page A5 brochure, printing 4000. One thousand went to a mailing list devised by him – he used the

about the artist . . .

1947 Born in Manchester
1967-71 Studied at St Martin's School of Art, London
1971- Worked as a self-employed artist in Thetford, Norfolk, and since 1982 in Blencarn, Penrith, Cumbria

Recent Exhibitions:
1979 & 81 2nd & 3rd Tolly Cobbold / Eastern Arts National Exhibitions
1982 Six East Anglian Artists — Kettles Yard, Cambridge
1983-84 Artist in Industry — Mappin Art Gallery, Sheffield and touring
1984 Wetheriggs, Clifton Dykes, Penrith, Cumbria. One-man exhibition
1985 Abbot Hall, Kendal, Cumbria. One-man exhibition
1985 Oldham Art Gallery. One-man exhibition
1985 Doncaster Museum and Art Gallery. One-man exhibition
1985 Royal Academy Summer Exhibition.

Awards and Grants:
1976&78 Eastern Arts Association
1979 Eastern Arts Association Major Award
1982 Artist in School with Samuel Whitbread Upper School
Bedfordshire Education Authority/Eastern Arts Association
1982&85 Northern Arts
1983 Artist in Industry Fellowship with Cooplands Bakery
Yorkshire Arts Association
1984 Gulbenkian Foundation Printmakers Award

Collections:
Bedfordshire Education Authority, Sheffield City Art Galleries, Northern Arts, Derbyshire Museum Service, Carlisle Museum and Art Gallery, Haworth Art Gallery Accrington, Dromcroon Wigan Education Art Centre, Bolton Museum and Art Gallery, Preston Polytechnic, Sealink, Cooplands (Doncaster) Ltd., Rothschild (New York), Gulbenkian Foundation.

Forthcoming Exhibitions:
July 16 - Aug. 10 1985 Lady Lodge Arts Centre, Peterborough and touring to
The Fermoy Centre Kings Lynn, The Wells Centre Norfolk,
The Minories Colchester,
The Harris Museum and Art Gallery Preston
Aug. 16 - Sept. 27 1985 Dove Cottage, Grasmere
May 1986 onwards Carlisle Museum and Art Gallery and touring to Ayr,
Hawick, Orkney, Bradford, Blackburn and London

▲
Alan Stones' A5 brochure giving the open studio dates, illustrations and information about the artist and the work and a map.

▶Post Office◀
Unfortunately, the post office has now withdrawn their free mailing offer.

Post Office's £125 free mailing offer for this mail shot. He also sent 3000 to the Tourist Information Centres in the area. Accompanying his press release were up to six black and white and colour photographs (he printed up 200 photographs specially for this). Advertisements were bought in two art magazines and two regional newspapers. In addition, 50 posters were circulated locally.

As a result of the press releases, journalists visited the studio and articles were published in the *Cumberland News, Cumberland and Westmorland Herald, Cumbria Life, Cumbria Gazette* and *Lake District Life*. Each used the black and white photographs he supplied, supplemented with photographs taken by them. This approach to the local press, and getting a five minute spot on Border TV, brought in nearly 200 visitors to the studio who bought eight prints. The leafets at the Tourist Information Centres brought in 80 visitors who bought a painting, three drawings and nine prints.

By using a visitors book, Alan found out how people heard about the open week and, for the future, ascertained which publicity methods were the most cost-effective. A press release to *Farmers Weekly* resulted, ten months later, in a two-page full-colour feature on the artist and his work. Note that no sales and few visitors resulted from advertisements in *Arts Review* and *Artists Newsletter*.

Analysing the results of the promotion – which cost a total of £643 – shows that most visitors and sales came from the free publicity brought about from press releases to the local and regional press. Income from sales and commissions was around £10,000 with 700 visitors and more still turning up a year later. Not only did he sell prints, paintings and drawings, but he also got three commissions worth £4700 for new work, enough to keep him going for around eight months.

A useful comparison can be drawn between this event and a touring exhibition which contained fifteen months of the artist's work and which in

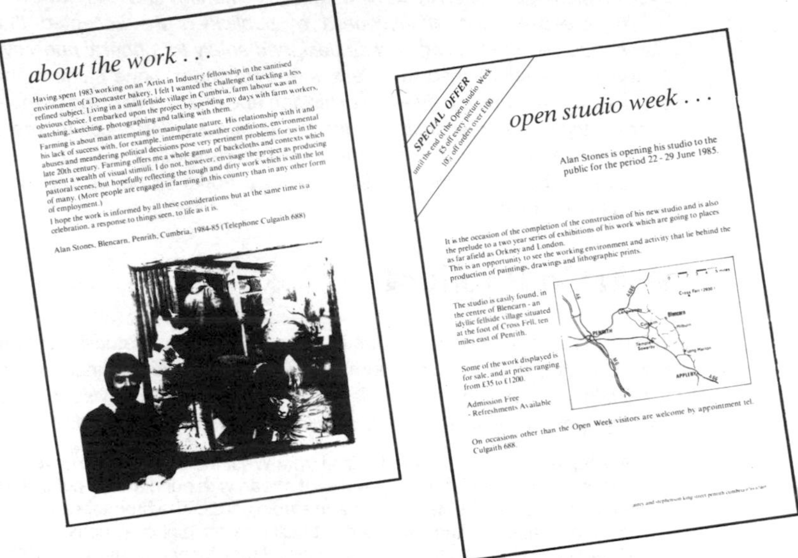

about the work . . .

Having spent 1983 working on an 'Artist in Industry' fellowship in the sanitised environment of a Doncaster bakery, I felt I wanted the challenge of tackling a less refined subject. Living in a small fellside village in Cumbria, farm labour was an obvious choice. I embarked upon the project by spending my days with farm workers, watching, sketching, photographing and talking with them.

Farming is about man attempting to manipulate nature. His relationship with it and his lack of success with, for example, intemperate weather conditions, environmental abuses and meandering political decisions pose very pertinent problems for us in the late 20th century. Farming offers me a whole gamut of backcloths and contexts which present a wealth of visual stimuli. I do not, however, envisage the project as producing pastoral scenes, but hopefully reflecting the tough and dirty work which is still the lot of many. (More people are engaged in farming in this country than in any other form of employment.)

I hope the work is informed by all these considerations but at the same time is a celebration, a response to things seen, to life as it is.

Alan Stones, Blencarn, Penrith, Cumbria, 1984-85 (Telephone Culgaith 688)

SPECIAL OFFER
until the end of the Open Studio Week
£5 off every picture
10% off orders over £100

open studio week . . .

Alan Stones is opening his studio to the public for the period 22 - 29 June 1985.

It is the occasion of the completion of the construction of his new studio and is also the prelude to a two year series of exhibitions of his work which are going to places as far afield as Orkney and London.
This is an opportunity to see the working environment and activity that lie behind the production of paintings, drawings and lithographic prints.

The studio is easily found, in the centre of Blencarn - an idyllic fellside village situated at the foot of Cross Fell, ten miles east of Penrith.

Some of the work displayed is for sale, and at prices ranging from £35 to £1200.

Admission Free
- Refreshments Available

On occasions other than the Open Week visitors are welcome by appointment tel. Culgaith 688.

46 weeks of touring achieved only nine print sales, a net income of £400. Alan Stones doesn't think that exhibitions are a waste of time, but says they need more back up. With this year's touring exhibition, he'll be spending a day with each showing so that the public can meet the artist and he hopes this will encourage them to buy work.

►Leicester Art Space◄

Open studio days/weeks are being used by an increasing number of artists – individually or in groups – to promote themselves and their work to the community. Leicester Art Space Project (Knighton Lane Group) held their first open studios in 1983. The publicity was budgeted at £515, which included £100 for 500 posters and £340 for 2000 twelve-page illustrated brochures of the artists' work.

> Given unlimited funds, we might have contemplated producing more than one type of brochure variously suitable for approaches to business, industry, galleries and the general public. Since this was clearly financially impossible, our brochure set out to attract a wide range of audience. Whilst statements were kept deliberately unpretentious.... we realised in retrospect that they probably contained specialist turn of phrases which we hadn't recognised as such. Before devising publicity designed to attract business sponsors, we'll have to do some market research on our style of presentation. (Adrian Lewis)[3]

Brochures, press releases and posters went out to around 600 individuals and organisations, including commercial and municipal galleries and art schools. *'The list was compiled from the* Artists Directory *and* New Exhibitions of Contemporary Art *(London's gallery guide) and from art magazines and East Midlands Arts' press list. We put the list into a word processor for future use.'* In terms of paid advertisements, the group spent

▷**3** 'Leicester Arts Space', *Artists Newsletter*, August 1983

£108 on display space in *Artists Newsletter, Art Monthly* and *Arts Review*.

'In assessing the effectiveness of publicity... we accepted that distribution beyond the region was designed solely for general publicity'. Although they telephoned the press with a reminder, none came to the press view: *'perhaps the five-day exhibition and the lack of some human-interest angle were responsible... the ten to fourteen day notice for press and gallery administrators was rather short in retrospect.'*

Over 300 came to the preview and three works on paper were sold during the exhibition.

►Art in Public◄

In November 1984, artists in Birmingham held an open studio event to coincide with the *British Art Show* at Ikon Gallery and the Birmingham City Art Gallery. They felt that *'while there was a focus on visual art in Birmingham, locally-based artists should be as visible as possible.'*

> We applied for and received funding from West Midlands Arts to cover publicity and administration ... we went ahead with our planned publicity in the form of broadsheets, posters and studio cards. The broadsheets included maps locating each studio, black and white photographs, statements, studio addresses and opening times for each artist. Over 1000, along with the posters, were distributed with Ikon Gallery's mailing for the *British Art Show*. The rest went to galleries, Tourist Information and Birmingham Central Library. (Caroline Russell & Alison Saint)[4]

Earlier, in 1983, the Oxfordshire Visual Art Week had been established around the Oxford artists' groups. Two hundred and twenty eight studios and exhibitions became part of the Art Week which is now a regular event, with major sponsorship.

> Sponsorship by its nature is a two-way arrangement... the English Tourist Board were keen to publicise Art Week as much as possible and suggested some sort of launching event to attract the public's attention; part of their grant was to be spent on this. Much persuasion was needed to convince some of the artists who in principle disliked the idea of a publicity stunt in case it descended into a vulgar jamboree. In fact, the event turned out to be a bizarre performance of charm, originality, surrealism and integrity. On the opening day of Art Week, on a central open space in Oxford, a large crane was hired and a man in full evening dress complete with top hat was suspended on a strong piece of elastic. At the appropriate press of a strawberry button on an iced cake, he shot out of a box to dangle 60foot in the air. This was accompanied by a string trio also in evening dress – it was then 11.30am – sitting on gilt chairs playing silent music. Silent music because of the crane's engine roar! Balloons were distributed with the Art Week logo and many people arrived in strange clothes. (Sarah Eckersley)[5]

►Exhibitions in Galleries◄

Promoting an art exhibition is, in essence, like promoting almost anything else. The big mistake is in assuming that there is a special art way of doing it. It involves only common sense, realism and careful thought. People will not come unless you ask them, there are always a limited number of ways to ask them and the 'asking' has to be exciting and communicative, one must never assume that people know things they probably do not know. Most people know a little about many things and a lot about few things. That

▷4 'Artists in Public', Caroline Russell & Alison Saint, *Artists Newsletter*, January 1985
▷5 'Oxfordshire Visual Arts Week', Sarah Eckersley, *Artists Newsletter*, November 1984

◄
Stephen Taylor Woodrow, *The Living Paintings* 1986. This performance at the Laing Gallery, Newcastle-upon-Tyne was organised by Projects UK as part of *'New Work, Newcastle '86',* a festival of performance. Tyne Tees Television were interested in presenting what they saw as 'difficult' work and picked upon **Stephen Taylor Woodrow** as a means of doing this. Woodrow got a lot of TV coverage nationally including a piece on *Blue Peter,* where presenter Peter Duncan became a 'living painting'. (Photo: Steve Collins)

> is why good communication has to start with serious consideration of what has to be said, and to whom and how. (Nich Pearson)[6]

Embroiderer Kathryn Salomon organised an exhibition in 1985 called *Art in Jewish Ritual* which was shown at the Manor House Centre for Judaism in London. The exhibition included silverware, stained glass, embroidery, bookbinding, calligraphy and graphics and was seen by nearly 3000 people in two weeks.

> I started planning the exhibition a year in advance. A public relations person gave me a calendar of when to approach different types of magazine. A well-planned publicity campaign was essential because we couldn't afford to advertise. Press releases were sent to glossy magazines about six months in advance. Later the monthlies, colour supplements, the weekly and daily newspaper, local and national radio and TV were approached. The Embroiderers' Guild held an international festival of embroidery four

▷**6** *Directory of Exhibition Spaces* first edition.

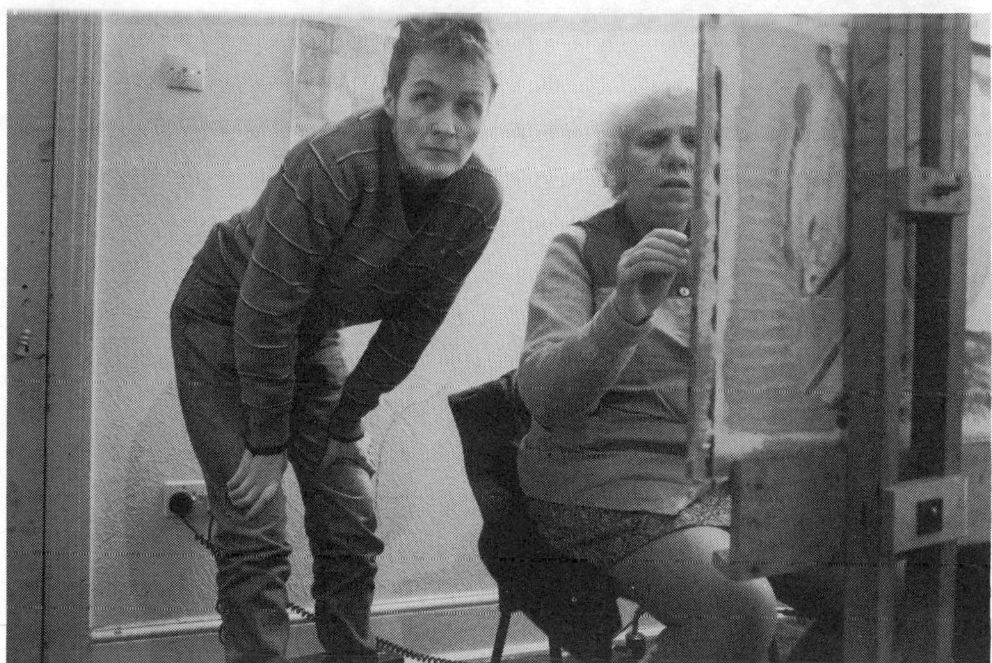

▲
Suzanne Montgomery at Cherry Knowle Hospital 1984, working on a residency organised by the Artists' Agency and co-funded by Northern Arts, Sunderland Health Authority and the WRVS. Publicity sent to Tyne Tees Television to stimulate interest for a short piece on '*The Works*', a regional arts programme, eventually led to a documentary that was networked nationally. **Suzanne Montgomery** continued to work at Cherry Knowle through Sunderland Education Department. (Photo: Keith Pattison)

> months before the exhibition so I sent them handouts and a poster. Thousands of handouts were produced and sent to local educational and community organisations, art schools, libraries and everyone we could think of. Because there was far too much work for one person, we formed a committee. They followed up the press releases with telephone calls and helped with the mailing. (Kathryn Soloman)[7]

In January 1984, Mel Noble's touring exhibition of paintings, prints and drawings – *Spurn Point* – opened at the first of a seven-venue tour organised by the artist. In order to find interested galleries, in January 1983 he: *'Assembled three sets of ring folders with CVs, list of proposed exhibits, ten slides and a large SAE. Kept a fourth set in case of loss or non-return. I used these sets to send to seven galleries and got five positive replies. As a result, the first exhibition was booked for January 1984.'* [8]

In terms of the time-scale for the publicity for the tour, by November 1983: *'The publicity graphics was done and taken to the printers. 5000 poster/pamphlets, 500 catalogues, 500 CVs and 500 poster blanks. These were all delivered by the end of November.'*[8]

▶On the Receiving End◀

More people look at TV and listen to the radio than read newspapers or magazines. Radio and TV are the most powerful of the media and perform a key role in establishing the tenor of our lives. All the more surprising then, that they are not accorded a place of greater importance when it comes to the discussion of publicity for art and artists. The paucity of art coverage on

▷**7** 'Organising an exhibition with no previous experience', Kathryn Soloman, *Artists Newsletter*, July 1985
▷**8** 'Organising an Exhibition, Mel Noble, *Artists Newsletter*, August 1984

the national networks makes the attempt to achieve a little for oneself seems hardly worth trying – like sending in slides for a solo exhibition at the Tate or Hayward galleries. (David Briers)[9]

As well as the BBC, about 15 independent, regionally-based TV companies make or buy the programmes shown on ITV and the amount of interest shown in the arts varies considerably. Television South West, for instance, has a Visual Arts Consultant and, as well as producing films about contemporary artists, it set up the TSWA touring open exhibition with a series of linked TV programmes.

At Tyne Tees Television, researcher Derek Smith works in the Arts Department and receives *'mountains of publicity'* covering all art forms. Tyne Tees' late night arts programme *The Works*, of which there are 20 programmes a year each of between 40-60 minutes, has a visual arts/crafts coverage of roughly 25%. For this programme, they work up to three months in advance, although the 'What's On' listings of events and exhibitions have only to be a month in advance. Some of *The Works*' documentary films are used independently – one on painter Suzanne Montgomery and her placement at a psychiatric hospital was 'networked' and seen probably by three million people. Covering 'difficult' as well as traditional visual arts, one programme looked in depth at a performance art festival in Newcastle with extracts from performances by Bow Gamelan, Stephen Taylor Woodrow (hanging from the gallery walls all day) and Silvia Ziranek.

Asked what attracted him to follow up a press release, Derek Smith said anything which suggested a theme, an angle or hinted at an interesting process. Paintings are extremely hard to show on TV, hence all the panning in and out of the frame, zooming in on a details etc so that the viewer isn't presented for too long with a 'still' image.

Here's a check list for artists to consider when trying to get TV coverage:

►Try to pick out a theme or angle for your press release without cheapening the work.

►Send at least two photographs – they don't have to be large (but not colour slides) with the release. Derek Smith always tries to return the photographs sent him.

►If you must send a CV, don't make it the main part of the information – put it in small print instead. Try for an interesting and concise artist's statement, no more than two paragraphs.

►Ring up and see whether they want any more information after a few days. It is essential for you to give a daytime telephone number for them to be able to contact you if they do decide to cover your exhibition or event.

►If you're a group publicising an exhibition, remember that that alone isn't a 'selling' item to the TV researcher, there must be something positive to catch their attention.

►Groups should definitely elect a spokesperson to be the telephone and press contact, preferably someone with a flair for it or at least some experience.

▷**9** 'Publicity 3 – Radio & TV', David Briers, *Artists Newsletter*, August 1984

►Gallery Views◄

Also on the receiving end of large quantities of publicty and promotional material are the people who run galleries and organise exhibition programmes. I asked two of them – Antonia Payne of Ikon Gallery in Birmingham and Anna Pepperall, then at Darlington Arts Centre, for their feelings on the matter.

Both galleries show up to 20 exhibitions a year. Darlington has a gallery plus a foyer and corridor space to use. The number of applications to exhibit – including offers to take touring exhibitions from other galleries – is large: up to 300 for Darlington and 200 at Ikon. Most applications come by post – slides and information sent by artists from their region and also from other parts of the country, usually on a speculative basis.

Anna Pepperall wanted applications to exhibit to be more informative – to give an indication of what the artist's intentions were with their work, how previous exhibitions had been received and whether they were interested in giving talks, doing workshops or other events in their educucation programme.

Whilst she preferred to have type-written information – its easier to read and means fewer pieces of paper to deal with – Antonia Payne has no objection to hand-written applications, providing the information is succinct. Standard CVs are the least informative – better to have a shorter version or just list recent and current exhibitions. Antonia Payne suggested that if you haven't had other exhibitions, send good visual material with a covering letter and dispense with the CV altogether.

On the subject of the visual material, Anna Pepperall bemoaned the senders of packages of slides of old work with the offer to 'send new work if you're interested'. For Ikon the purpose of the slides is to get the gallery to see the work – either at the studio or in an exhibition. Twelve slides of your best work are preferrable to 40 showing the full range. Labelling slides is essential and don't forget to include the size of the piece as 35mm slides can be very misleading.

Galleries often need to hold on to slides for quite a while – they are often trying to link artists' work or match work to themes. If you need your slides back quickly,then say so and send a return envelope for them when you write in.

Both organisers prefer to see actual work than slides and made this suggestion. When you've got an exhibition up, send a copy of the poster/ invitation card/catalogue plus your slides and personal covering letter to the galleries you want to show in. Invite the organisers to view your work in an ideal situation – well-hung, well-lit and uncluttered by studio debris. This is preferable to sending slides and information after the show's closed. Don't rely on the fact that galleries get your poster as a matter of course, they receive hundreds of pieces of publicity every week and your application needs the 'personal' touch to ensure it stands out.

►The Glossies◄

Glossy magazines... are those general periodicals which you find in dentists' waiting rooms, hairdressers and office foyers and which you see people reading on trains. The big bonus of publicity in such magazines... is the enormity of the audience. The weeklies sell over a million copies and

even the most expensive monthlies shift over 100,00 copies. Get a picture with a caption in *House and Gardens* and you will be amazed at the number of people you meet who have seen it. (David Briers)[10]

Artist Judith Richardson-Dawes had her first solo exhibition in October 1985 at the Forum Gallery, a small gallery in Hadleigh, Suffolk. Ten months before the exhibition opened she decided to use the exhibition – the result of two years work – as a means of creating more opportunities for her work. *'One's natural instinct is to concentrate on doing the work, heave a sigh of relief when its finished, attend to the practicalities of having an exhibition and only then to consider whom to tell about the event'.*[11]

As the result of reading David Briers' article on art coverage in glossy magazines, she decided to try the methods he outlined and drew up a list of 31 publications to send her 'publicity pack' to.

A personal press release – this was an extended version of the one used by the gallery – was essential, one which made the most of past achievements. *'This was no time for modesty'*, thus the press release used paragraphs like:

> Judith Richardson-Dawes inhabits an earthly paradise. Her paintings reflect her world, where objects have a character of their own. They are, however, essential components in a world constructed of luminous colours. Cups and saucers rejoice at being cups and saucers. Teapots exude the essence of teapot.
>
> Both people and objects are wholly modern and real and possess the timeless quality of older images. A delivery van becomes a latter-day haywain, a beer label an illuminated manuscript. And like her Morris men, Judith claims inspiration from the English folk tradition, taking titles for several of her pictures from early song. In August 1983, she was one of the 151 artists selected by BBC Woman's Hour and *Radio Times* for their 'Summertime Exhibition at the Tate Gallery.' (Judith Richardson Dawes)[12]

The press pack, therefore, consisted of the press release, a 4" x6" black and white photograph of a picture from the exhibition, two 35mm colour slides, a covering letter and a stamped addressed envelope. Slides and photographs were clearly labelled and the information on them repeated in the letter.

The press release was written so that it could be used either verbatim or snippets of it used for photo captions or for 'what's on' listings. The SAE ensures that you can ring the magazine if you don't hear and also that you get your material back so you can use it again for another magazine on your list.

The budget for the publicity pack was as follows:

postage	£13
black and white photographs	£35
slides	£7
photocopying	£6
Total	**£61**

The evaluation of the campaign shows that of 31 magazines, seven either used the photograph or slides or made contact with the artist. *Out of Town* published the black and white photograph in their listings under 'Highlight of the Month', *Art and Design* listed the exhibition in 'Roundup', *House and Garden* put a colour slide in the 'Gallery Guide' as did the World of Interiors in their 'Exhibition Diary'. *Vogue* kept the black and white photograph

West Country artists

NEWSMAKERS

ROKER CAN-CAN

IF THE CAP FITS

NO WORRIES, NO WRINKLES!

SOAPY SILKS

SUPER SKATE

OLIVER AND PINK

Forecast

BILLBOARD

DUET FOR THREE

HAT STAND

NUCLEAR REACTION

SOUNDS OF THE SITAR

STOKED UP

▲ 'Glossy' arts coverage.

▷**11** 'How I got into the glossies', Judith Richardson-Dawes, *Artists Newsletter*, June 1986

▷**12** 'How I got into the glossies'

saying they would use it but didn't in the end, *Good Housekeeping's* 'Country Living' filed the artist's work as a possible future illustrator. Correspondence with *Cosmopolitan* on doing a feature for their food and cookery section still continues.

> In number terms, the failure rate was high, but in terms of feedback, prestige and confidence-building, just the colour photograph in *House and Garden* made the exercise worthwhile. Better still, I sold a painting on the strength of that mention. (Judith Richardson Dawes)[13]

GOOD NEWS!
LATEST AND GREATEST FROM ALL AT GH
CLASSY CANVAS CARRIERS
HOUSING THE HOMELESS
FRIENDS OF THE ZOO

▲
Root Bag's coverage in *Good Housekeeping*

Other examples of the power of reaching such large readerships are becoming more common. Root Bags in Newcastle on Tyne wanted to establish their mail order business for bags and decided to invest in an A4 folded, two-colour leaflet. Using a comprehensive mailing list of newspapers and magazines, Romy Meagher took the unusual step of ringing them all before she sent out the leaflet, as well as afterwards. *Good Housekeeping's* 'Good News', however, contacted her straight away and a news item with a line illustration of one of the bags resulted in as *'much work as we could cope with'*. Three months later, orders were still coming in.

By choosing examples which indicate how artists have learned, often by trial and error, the best methods of using publicity for their projects, my intention has been to show that every situation needs individual attention. Here is a final check list of points to consider when you start the publicity and promotion for a visual arts event:

- ▶Plan well in advance and certainly no less than two months beforehand
- ▶Decide which is your 'target' audience and direct the majority of your publicity at it
- ▶Decide on your budget and examine each piece of publicity for cost effectiveness
- ▶Don't underestimate the value of free publicity – that which comes from sending press releases to local, regional and national press and media. Accompany releases with good-quality black and white photographs.

◁see **Photographing Work**▷

▶Information◀

▶Contacts◀

▶Contact your RAA for information and advice on marketing

▶Further Reading◀

▶*Survive, the Illustrators Survival Kit.* Association of Illustrators 1988
▶*Running a Workshop – Basic business for craftspeople.* Crafts Council 1985
▶*Royal Mail Inland Compendium.* GPO
▶*The Art of Survival – Some Ideas on Selling for Artists*, Tony Parkin
▶*TMA Marketing Manual Volumes 1-4*, Glyn V Robbins and Peter Verwey. John Offord Publications
▶'Making an Application', Amanda Hare. *Crafts* November/December 1982
▶'Do You Sincerely Want to be Poor?', Alan Mitchell. *Artists Newsletter*, April 1984

▷**13** 'How I got into the glossies' *Artists Newsletter*, June 1986

▶'Publicity 1 – What's it For?', Helen Petrie. *Artists Newsletter*, April 1984
▶'Publicity 2 – Reaching the Audience', Susan Jones. *Artists Newsletter*, May 1984
▶'Publicity 3 – Types of Publicity', Susan Jones. *Artists Newsletter*, June 1984
▶'Publicity 4 – Radio & TV', David Briers. *Artists Newsletter*, August 1984
▶'Publicity 5 – Dear Artists Newsletter'. *Artists Newsletter*, October 1984
▶'Publicity 6 – The Glossies', David Briers. *Artists Newsletter*, January 1985
▶'How I got into the Glossies', Judith Richardson Dawes. *Artists Newsletter*, June 1986
▶*Working For Yourself in the Arts and Crafts*, Sarah Hosking. Kogan Page 1989
▶*Press Mailing & Contacts List,* Arts Council. Published annually and based on their own lists, excludes crafts
▶*How to Promote Your Own Business – A Guide to Low-Budget Publicity*, Jim Dudley, Kogan Page
▶'The Bottom Line', Susan Tyler. *Crafts* No 92 May/June 1988
▶'The Bottom Line', Susan Tyler. *Crafts* No 93 July/August 1988
▶'The Bottom Line', Susan Tyler. *Crafts* No 94 September/October 1988
▶*A Basic PR Guide*, Directory of Social Change
▶*The Marketing Handbook*, Rosalind Druce & Stephen Carter. National Extension College 1989. Not specifically for the arts but provides basic guide to developing a marketing mentality
▶'Who will Review?', David Hughes. *Artists Newsletter*, March 1989. Coverage of non-London shows in the national press

Photographing Artwork

▶Peter White◀

This is an examination of some of the special problems encountered in photographing artworks – paintings, sculpture, ceramics, etc.

In the sections on photographing your own work some basic knowledge of photography is assumed. Photographing works of art can be one of the most difficult of tasks because of the high quality of the photograph as a photograph comes second to how accurately it shows the object.

To achieve consistent results requires some understanding of the technical aspects of photography such as exposure measurement, depth of field and colour temperature. If you want to take pictures of your work but don't already know an F-Stop from an ISO you should refer to one of the many excellent general photographic instruction books by such authors as John Hedgecoe or Michael Langford. Evening classes in photography can also be a good source of basic knowledge.

◁see **Training**▷

▶Using Professionals◀

The easiest way of getting photographs of artwork is to get somebody else to do it for you. Unfortunately, unless you have friends who are both skilled and generous with their time and effort this will mean spending money, possibly quite large amounts of money.

If you have to employ a professional photographer, how much it will cost and how easy it will be to find someone capable of doing the work will depend on where you live, or how mobile your work is. There are many firms and individuals who describe themselves as 'Fine Art Photographers'. Most of them are based in London or other larger cities and they specialise in high-quality work for catalogues, book illustrations or reproductions. Most will do very good work but at a price which will range from high to very high. The services provided by 'fine art' photographers are not aimed at the needs of working artists who usually want large quantities of 35mm slides. The ubiquitous 'High Street' photographer may also not be able to supply the combination of quality and cost that artists require. Photographing, for example, a 10 foot wide shiny oil painting requires equipment and skills which a photographer whose normal business is portraits and weddings may not possess.

But there are a few professional photographers who can offer the kind of service that artists and craftspeople require and the way to find them initially is to ask other artists. If that doesn't work try looking at the classified ad columns in magazines like *Artists Newsletter, Arts Review, Crafts Magazine,* etc.

If you've found a photographer and he or she doesn't come with recommendation of another artist, one guide to how professional they are is how they respond to the question *'How much will it cost?'* – professional photographers tend to lose sleep worrying about how much to charge and they should be able to give you a straight answer to the question. But how much should you expect to pay? As an example, three slides from each of ten paintings taken to the photographer's studio should cost £35 at the very least and if the photographer is coming to you then it should cost at least £55. Some photographers will ask for much more but anyone asking much less is earning their living in some other way. Another question you could try asking is *'What sort of lighting do you use?'* If the answer is something like *'I prefer natural daylight'* it is unlikely that the photographer has much of the sort of experience you need. Daylight is very inconsistent and unpredictable and professional photographers have to produce consistent and predictable results without waiting all day for the sun to come out. The correct answer is either *'tungsten'* or *'flash'*.

A very important point is to find your photographer in good time and to have the photographs taken at least a month before you actually need them. This will give time to re-do anything that doesn't 'come out' (and however good the photographer is, it sometimes happens) as well as giving enough time to look at contact sheets and order prints, etc. Once you've located and booked your photographer the next task is to make the most of them and not let yourself in for more cost than necessary. To this end, if the photographer is coming to your studio you will need to make sure that they have enough space to work – if you're photographing large paintings provide, if you can, a space which is at least one and a half by three times the width of the largest work so that the photographer can get far enough back from the work and, something that is sometimes forgotten, allow for the positioning of lights on either side. Other things to ensure are that there are at least two power points within reach; that there is not strong sunlight entering the room; and, possibly most important, that you have a good idea of what you want and that the work is ready to be photographed.

To reduce costs it may also be possible to get together with other artists so that you can book your photographer for a larger quantity of work and negotiate some form of bulk discount.

It is likely, especially if the photographer is coming to you, that you will be charged an hourly rate. How much work that can be done in a hour will depend on the type of objects being photographed, the working speed of the photographer and how much you can help things along. As a rough guide, large paintings can be photographed at about three to five an hour, small paintings at about ten an hour (if the paintings are all the same size it should be possible to photograph them at a rate of twenty to thirty an hour). How long it takes to photograph 3D objects is very difficult to forecast. There are photographers who will take all day to photograph one piece, but for straightforward work it should be possible to do three to five an hour.

►Prints or Transparencies◄

When booking the photographer you should discuss the type and quality of photographs you require: transparencies (35mm, 6x6cm, 5x4ins), colour prints or black & white prints. The type of photographs you require depends upon what you intend to use them for. If you are sending publicity to newspapers or magazines then you need black and white glossy prints (or for colour magazines colour transparencies or prints). Slide indexes obviously require 35mm slides whereas a work for a poster or catalogue may require large format transparencies. A publicity pack to be taken to prospective clients for commission might best use large colour prints. Decide what your needs are and discuss with the photographer the cost of taking prints (black & white and colour) and transparencies at the same session.

◁see **Publicity**▷

Always make sure that you have large enough quantities done and if you want, for example, five 35mm slides from each piece of your work the photographer should be able to produce five original slides, rather than taking one and subsequently copying it. However, if you are having 6x6cm or 5x4ins transparencies made, remember that you can have 35mm copies made from these. It defeats the purpose of high-quality medium or large format transparencies if they are made by copying from a smaller format. There is an inevitable loss of quality.

►Quality◄

After all this, what sort of results should you expect from a professional photographer? To some extent this will depend on what you pay, but one thing which you are unlikely to get at almost any price is a completely accurate facsimile of your work. The colours in colour photographs are made from the combination of three dyes corresponding to the three primary colours – red, yellow and blue. If these primary dyes could reproduce any colour paint, manufacturers would presumably use them instead of the vast range of natural and artificial pigments that they do use. Colour photography in general seems to be quite good at reds but not so good at blues and greens; light greens, for example, will sometimes turn to grey in slides and print processes sometimes seem incapable of reproducing commonly-used blues such as cobalt and cerulean. Accurate tonal reproduction is also difficult to achieve, especially where the range is wide. If your work contains very dark and very light areas within the same piece, photographs will have to be something of a compromise. This is least true of black & white prints, where contrast is easily controlled and most true of colour prints, especially prints from slides where the process is inherently contrasty.

Your photographer is not responsible for all these deficiencies, because s/he can only work with the materials available. What you can expect is that the photographs give a reasonable impression of what your work is like, that they are in focus, not too light or too dark, that they show the work without any unwanted background and that they are produced in a reasonable amount of time.

Finally, remember that the photographer cannot claim the copyright of any photographs taken of your work. You own the copyright of the work itself (unless the work is a print or object produced in quantity where you have been commissioned by someone else); you own the copyright of the photographs because you are commissioning the photographer.

◁see **Copyright**▷

►Flat Artwork◄

The easiest way to deal with the problems involved in photographing paintings is probably to look at the faults most often seen in the slides of artists' work and to examine how these faults can be overcome. There are four main areas where things can go wrong:

►**Lighting:** The colour of light used can give a false impression of the colours in the work; lighting can be uneven; there can be reflections from shiny paint surfaces.
►**Exposure:** Slides can be either too light or too dark.
►**Framing:** The image of the painting can be too small or too large within the frame of the slide, it can be crooked or not central.
►**Background:** The background, a brick wall for example. can distract attention from painting.

►Exposure◄

All photographic exposure meters assume that they are always looking at an 'average' subject and that an average subject is one that reflects 18% of the light that falls on it. This means that whatever you point it at, the exposure you get will give a picture which, if you mix up all the lights and darks, will have a tonal quality similar to brown wrapping paper. In the same way, if you point your camera at a predominantly black painting the exposure meter will try to make it average in tone and will give you a photograph of a middle-grey painting; point it at a white painting and it will also give you a picture of a grey painting.

For this reason, unless your paintings are all tonally average, an automatic camera, which works out and sets the exposure for you, is not very useful for photographing artwork. What you need is a manual camera (or an automatic camera which can be set manually), which allows you to measure and set the exposure with its own through-the-lens meter (or with a separate hand-held meter).

◄
Taking an incident light reading using a Weston meter fitted with an invercone.

What we need to measure is the light **falling** on the painting (the incident light) and not the light **reflected** by it. This can be done with a hand-held exposure meter with an incident light attachment or 'invercone'. With a through-the-lens meter, or with a hand-held meter not capable of measuring incident light, you need to measure the light reflected from a *tonally average surface.* Place a sheet of brown wrapping paper or a special Kodak 'Grey Card' which refelcts 18% of light. Alternatively, you can take a reading from a sheet of white paper and then give two and a half stops **more** exposure.

Once you've measured the light by one of the above methods and set the exposure it should be the same for every picture taken in the same lighting set-up. However, it is wise to bracket exposures. This means taking pictures at the exposure that you've calculated and also at a half or one stop either side to allow for any slight errors. In practice, however, you can usually limit this bracketing to under-exposing light and middle-toned paintings by a half or one stop and over-exposing dark paintings by a half or one stop. For example, photographing a very dark painting you work out that the exposure should be half a second at f8, so you take one at that setting and one at a half or one stop over-exposure depending on how dark the painting is.

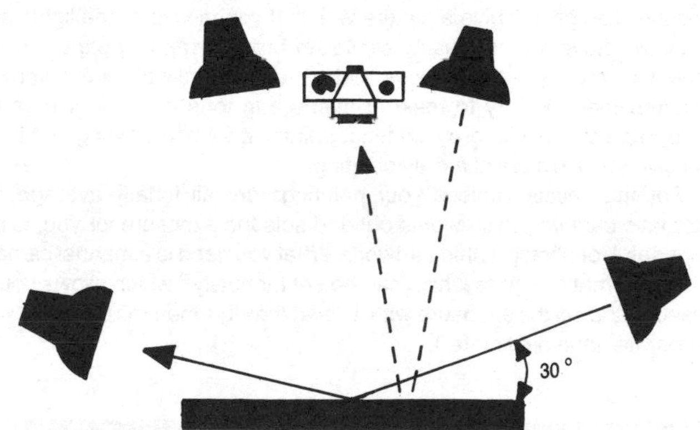

▶ With the lamps at 30° (A) to the painting reflections miss the camera. At more acute angles (B) reflections go straight to camera lens.

Reflections from shiny paint surfaces will decrease as you decrease the angle between the lamps and the surface of the painting (see diagram). With pictures in a long landscape format it is sometimes difficult to get the lights far enough away and at the right angle; in this case placing the painting vertically will effectively give you more room on either side for placing lights. If your paintings are particularly shiny and reflections are a serious problem a polarising filter will help.

When using tungsten lights it is important to make sure that the normal light in the room isn't too bright to affect the colour. To check this, take a light reading with your exposure meter with the tungsten lights off – it should be at least three stops less bright than when you turn the lights on.

Finally, one light source that should always be avoided is a flash gun, especially one mounted on the camera. There are two reasons for this: firstly,flash guns give a very uneven light so that your pictures will probably come out lighter in the middle than at the edges and secondly, the flash will reflect in any shiny areas on the painting.

▶Framing and Focus◀

Framing and focusing, together with picking the right background, are the least technical aspects of photographing artwork and yet it is here that the do-it-yourselfer often makes the most obvious blunders – and blunders that can be overcome simply by **looking** harder.

In a slide, a painting should look rectangular (assuming that it is of course). It should almost fill the picture area and be centrally placed. To do this effectively you must use a **single-lens-reflex** camera (an SLR) because it shows you almost exactly what will appear in the picture. With other types of camera, the viewfinder shows an area slightly different to that seen by the taking lens so that accurate framing is almost impossible. Another piece of essential equipment is a tripod; it is possible to focus on a painting and get it square in the viewfinder while holding the camera but the concentration and co-ordination of the eye, brain and body required to do this more than once or twice a day will leave you in a state of nervous, squinting exhaustion. Moreover, most of the time you will be using fairly low shutter speeds so that hand-holding the camera will give you blurred pictures because of camera shake.

Squaring up the camera to the painting is fairly simple. Hang the picture to be photographed on a wall, or set it up on an easel so that it is vertical, and stand the camera, on its tripod, right in front of the middle of it. Then, raise or lower the tripod to get the camera lens pointing at the centre of the painting. If you now move back at right angles to the painting until you can get it all into the viewfinder it should look square; if not, move the camera on the tripod head until it does. Look very carefully around the edge of the viewfinder and double check that everything looks straight. If you regularly need photographs of small works (up to about A3 size) you should consider investing in a copy stand.

Next, check the focus: if your paintings contain areas of flat colour which make focusing difficult either stick a piece of masking tape on the surface so that you can see it through the split-image or microprism in the viewfinder (remember to remove it before taking the picture) or, if the surface of the painting is delicate, get someone to hold a strip of paper against it.

▶Background◀

Although photographs of paintings *in situ* can be useful, especially with large works where a white painted studio wall and a bit of floor will give an idea of the size, most medium- and small-size paintings look best in photographs which show them with no background at all. In slides this means a black background and there are only two effective ways of doing this. Firstly, if the work is not mounted or framed, surround the work with black velvet (made of cotton rather than the man-made fibre kind) as this will photograph as completely black. Black paper tends to photograph as grey or green but is better than nothing. If the work to be photographed is framed or mounted, or you can't afford a big enough piece of black velvet, the next best alternative is to use black tape to mask out the background on the slide. There are special photographic tapes made for this purpose but ordinary black PVC electrical insulating tape does the job just as well.

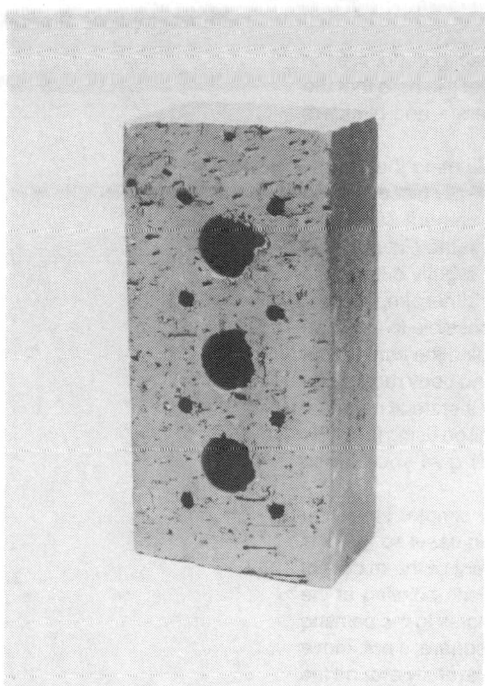

▲Left
Taken with one lamp overhead and reflector to the right. Plain backgrounds concentrate attention on the object but can look bland.

▲Right
A graduated background, made by casting a shadow behind the object – gives a more atmospheric effect.

►3D Objects◄

There is one big difference between photographing paintings and photographing 3D objects. With paintings we are trying to make as accurate a copy as possible – it seems that there is usually only one way that you can look at a painting. With 3D work we want to show it at its best, to manipulate lighting and the angle from which we view the object so that we see it most effectively.

The range of objects that artists and craftspeople produce and the photographic possibilities available are both so vast that all we can do here is to suggest a few of the possibilities and examine ways round some of the more common problems. Fortunately, the main problems and possibilities in photographing 3D work can be dealt with under two simple headings: backgrounds and lighting. Of course there are many other things to be considered, but if you get these two right you are more than half way to success.

►Backgrounds◄

For small three-dimensional work the most useful background is without doubt a plain one. It may be that photographing your work in some real life situation, with a view of the studio behind it or outside in the garden for example, will give a clue to the scale of the piece. Unfortunately, it will also almost always distract from the piece itself and, worse still, will very often just look scruffy. With very large work it may not be possible to get a plain background big enough, or the object may be too large to move, so that you

are stuck with the environment the piece inhabits as a background. Often this seems not to be too much of a problem because of the environmental nature of many large objects.

For 'plain' backgrounds there are several options. The simplest is a large piece of paper running from horizontal foreground to vertical background giving a 'seamless' effect. Or, we can use two pieces of paper, one laid flat and one vertical to produce an 'horizon' line; these two pieces of paper can be either of the same or of different colours. If you do use a background with an 'horizon' line in it always keep it horizontal in the photograph. The background can also be altered by lighting; for example, on a seamless paper background a shadow can be thrown behind the object being photographed to create a continuous graduated tone from light to dark.

►Lighting◄

As with photographing paintings, it is possible to take good photographs by natural daylight. However, whereas direct sunlight can be very good for photographing paintings it does give strong shadows and sharp contrasts on three-dimensional objects, so the best results are obtained on slightly overcast days or by working indoors with reflected or diffused light.

For consistent results it is best to use artificial light. If you are building a collection of slides of your work over a period of time, changes in the photographic quality between one slide and the next can distract attention from the work itself and the easiest way of ensuring consistency is to work out some form of simple lighting set-up which suits the kind of work that you do and to use it every time you need photographs. This is fairly easy for small and medium-sized work and, using *ad hoc* materials and a little ingenuity, should not cost more than about £40. As mentioned in the section on photographing 2D work the most useful lights for photographing

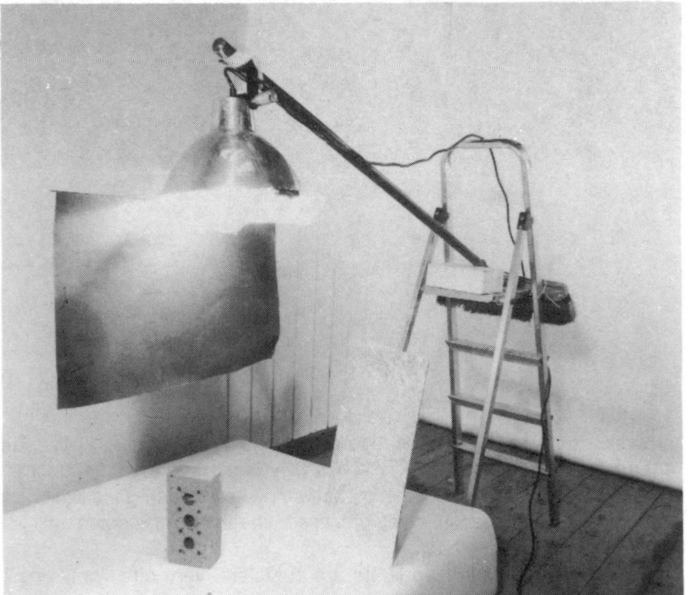

◄
The sort of improvised arrangement that can produce very good results. A boom arm, made here by supporting a broom on a set of steps, holds a lamp above the object being photographed. Glass fibre mesh clipped to the reflector diffuses the light, a sheet of paper also clipped to the reflector casts a shadow for a graduated background and a reflector, made from crumpled aluminium foil stretched over a piece of board, reflects light back into the shadows.

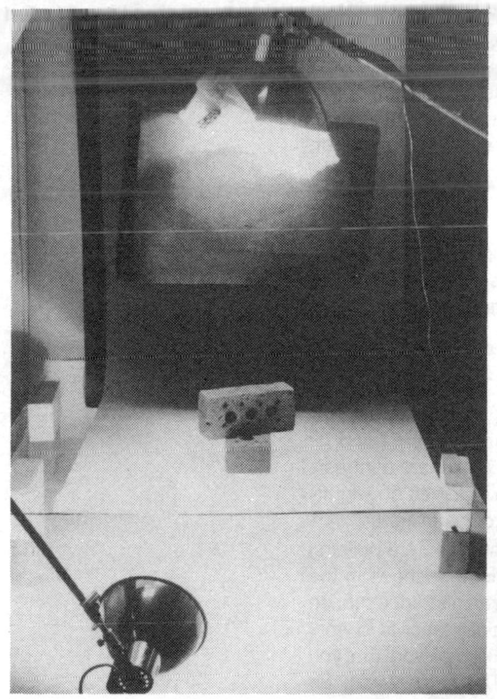

▲Left
Shadows cast underneath more complex objects can cause problems but these can be reduced or eliminated by lighting from below. Here a sheet of glass is supported on bricks, tracing paper runs from foreground to background to provide a seemless effect and one lamp is pointed up from below while another is used overhead. Black paper has also been used here to darken the background.

▶
Object taken with the set up described above.

▲Right
If you are photographing outside a relatively wide lens aperature can help to keep a potentially disctracting background out of focus.

artwork are tungsten lamps made especially for photography. The alternatives are 'studio' flash, which is very expensive (over £400 for the cheapest useful set-up), or ordinary battery powered flash-guns, which are very difficult to use because you can't see what the light is doing until you actually get the picture back.

For most purposes two lights are sufficient, very often only one is needed *(details, suppliers and approximate prices are given in the section*

▲Left
Angle of view will suggest scale. Looking down on an object implies that it is small.

▲Right
A low viewpoint suggests large scale.

on equipment below). The quality of photographs depends on the quality of light and there are several ways in which the light you use can be controlled to give the kind of results required.

On their own, most light sources (including the sun) give a very harsh and contrasty light; so, one of the first things that you must consider is whether you want to **diffuse** the light. With tungsten lights the easiest way of doing this is to place some form of diffusion material in front of the lamp. Because tungsten lamps get very hot the diffusion material has to be heat-resistant; there are special plastic materials available, or you can use glass fibre matting from hardware or car accessory shops. Heat-resistant diffusion material can be bulldog-clipped onto the lamp reflector. For an even softer light the diffuser must be larger and placed at a distance from the lamps. Again there are special materials available but tracing paper or thin cotton sheeting attached to a frame will work just as well.

Another way in which lighting **contrast** can be reduced is by using reflectors to reflect light back into the shadows. The simplest reflector is either white paper or card. You can also make a very efficient reflector by scrunching up a large sheet of aluminium kitchen foil and then unscrunching and stretching it over a thick card or board. Some of the most annoying shadows are those cast underneath the object being photographed and the only effective way to deal with them is to use a translucent base (Perspex for example) and light it from below.

►Other Considerations◄

Whatever the background and lighting set-up you will find that successful photography of 3D objects depends, no matter how much 'proper'

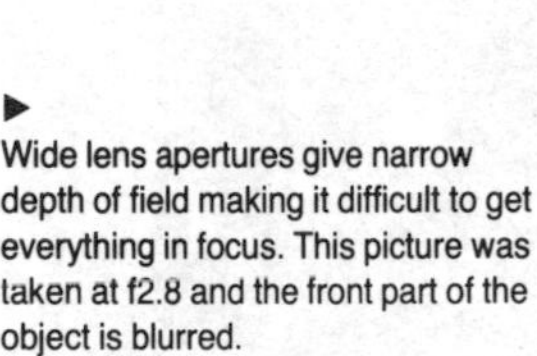

►
Wide lens apertures give narrow depth of field making it difficult to get everything in focus. This picture was taken at f2.8 and the front part of the object is blurred.

equipment you have to access to, on a large amount of improvisation. Such things as masking tape, blue tack, bricks, odd bits of wood and anything else that comes to hand can be used to get the object being photographed, the lights and background all into the right position. When you are photographing your work remember that the best professional photographers don't necessarily expect always to get things right first time; for example, getting the exposure right, especially in slides, is always difficult and most professional photographers will 'bracket' exposures as a matter of course. Be prepared to experiment and to do things more than once.

►Equipment and Materials◄

The equipment needed to photograph works of art is fairly simple. Obviously the minimum needed is a camera, to this can be added a tripod as the next most important, then a separate exposure meter, then lights, and so on in diminishing order of importance. Let's look in detail at the necessary and useful equipment.

►Camera◄

You must use a single lens reflex camera (a SLR) because you get what you see *(see framing and focus above)*. Almost any SLR will do the job. A second-hand Practika costing £30 can produce pictures as good as a new Nikon F3 costing £700. If you are only using it to photograph your work (maybe three or four films a month?), you don't need a sophisticated camera designed for heavy professional use. The only other essential is that your camera has a manual setting; some of the cheaper cameras available are only automatic.

Apart from showing you what you're actually going to get the other advantage of SLRs is that you can use different lenses on them. For most purposes the standard lens (normally 50mm) is sufficient, but for 3D work you may get better results with a zoom lens with a range of either 70 – 200mm, or 35 – 70mm or a 'short' telephoto of 100 or 135mm. If your work

◄ 'Stopping down', in this case to f22, brings much more of the object into focus.

is small always check when buying a lens that it will focus close enough. If you can't focus close enough with the standard lens, the best solution is to use a macro lens, but as these are expensive (£150+), the most practical alternative is a set of close-up-lenses (£20) which screw into the front of the standard lens.

►Tripod◄

Almost any tripod is better than none at all. Prices range from £20 up to about £120. Some of the more expensive tripods, such as the Kennet Benbo or some of the Manfrotto range, incorporate or can be fitted with a 'lateral arm' so that the camera can be pointed at the floor which makes photographing smaller works on paper and overhead views of 3D work easier. When you use a camera on a tripod also use a cable release to fire the shutter.

►Lights◄

Tungsten lights are the cheapest, most adaptable and easiest to use form of photographic lighting. The cheapest available tungsten lights are Photax Interfit and the minimum required for photographing small paintings and 3D work would be:

►Two ES Lampholders at £10	£20
►Two 11″ Reflectors at £5	£10
►Two clip-on frames at £3.50	£7
►Two P2/1 lamps at £6	£12
►Total	**£49**

An improvement on this basic list would be to replace the clip-on frames with stands (£13 each). For large paintings you will have to use stands and two more lampholders and reflectors. For 3D work, a boom arm (£22) will make placing a light above the work easier.

There are two types of bulbs that can be used with these lights: photofloods and photolamps. You should use photolamps (500w P2/1) which last an average 100 hours and provide a light which gives correct colour when used with tungsten film. The slightly cheaper photofloods

(either 275w P1/1 or 500w (P1/2) have an average life of only four hours and give a light which is slightly too blue.

Photax equipment is cheap and not very robust, but it does work and the better alternatives by firms such as R.R. Beard and Hedler will cost about five times as much.

►Exposure Meter◄

A separate exposure meter isn't essential (unless you're using a very old camera which doesn't have through-the-lens-metering) but it does make things much easier. For photographing paintings and for taking slides of anything the best way to set the exposure on the camera is from an incident light reading – measuring the light falling on the subject rather than that reflected by it. One of the better light meters is the Weston Euro-Master at about £90; the cheapest is the Leningrad at £11.

►Filters◄

If you use daylight type slide film in daylight, or tungsten film in tungsten light you should not need any filters except a polarising filter to reduce reflections. If using daylight film in tungsten light, use an 8OA filter (blue) and for tungsten film in daylight, an 85B (orange). For tungsten film with photofloods an 81A (pink) will stop your pictures being too blue.

►Film◄

For slides, use either Kodak Kodachrome or any E6 process film such as Ektachrome, Fujichrome, etc. It is wise to avoid any process-paid films other than Kodachrome for one simple reason: at some point you may need copies of your slides and almost all slide copying services use Kodak Duplicating film which is designed for copying Kodachrome and E6 process slide films. Some other process-paid films, Agfa or Boots for example, sometimes give copies with a very marked colour change.

It is often said that some films are better at reproducing certain colours or that a particular film gives results which are 'too blue' or 'too pink'. However, colour films of the same make and type can differ from batch to batch in the accuracy of their colour reproduction and other factors such as the quality of the processing and how long (and at what temperature) the film has been stored can have such an effect that in practice it is fair to say that there is little difference between the well-known makes. If you are going to need a reasonable quantity of slides in the course of a year it's a good idea to buy several films at once and to store them in the fridge. The best films for slides are the 'Professional' ones such Kodak Ektachrome EPY (50 ISO Tungsten) or EPN (100 ISO Daylight) but these films must be stored in the fridge (and when buying them make sure they come out of a fridge).

Prints can be made from slides but they are expensive. If you need a large number of prints use a negative film. Again, you will get best colour quality from a 'professional' film such as Kodak Vericolor 111. Negative films only come in daylight type, so if you're using tungsten lights use an 80A filter.

For black and white prints use a medium speed (125 ISO) film such as Ilford FP4. Fast films such as HP5 and slow films like Pan F both tend to be too contrasty for photographing artwork.

►Suppliers◄

The well-known chain stores that sell photographic equipment as well as hi-fi and televisions should be avoided because they are often not the cheapest place to buy equipment and usually have a staff who appear to have had all of ten minutes training. The few remaining small photographic retailers should also be avoided because, though they may offer good advice, they tend to be expensive. The best place to buy is from one of the big specialist retailers and you will find details of these in *Amateur Photographer* (choose one of the weeks when it hasn't got a sexist cover). If you're buying equipment looking through *Amateur Photographer* is the easiest way of finding out what is available and how much it should cost.

An alternative to buying (or borrowing) equipment is to hire it. This is obviously only practical if you live near a city or large town that has a hire firm in it. But hiring can be surprisingly cheap and could be a way of getting medium or large format photographs of your work without enormous expense.

►Glossary◄

►Aperture: Size of the lens opening through which light passes. All lenses are marked with basically the same set of numbers (although there are differences in where the sequence starts and finishes – as shown by the ( ) below:

(1.2, 1.4, 1.8 or 2), 2.8, 4, 5.6, 8, 11, 16, 22, (32, 64, etc)

These are known as f-numbers or f-stops. Each number represents half and double the amount light admitted by the numbers on either side of it. For example f8 lets through half as much light as f5.6 and twice as much as f11 (smaller f-number equals more light).

►Colour Temperature: The colour of the light. Cloudy daylight tends to be blue or 'cool', candlelight is more orange or 'warm'. Colour temperature is measured in degrees Kelvin (°K). Mid-day daylight is about 5500°K and domestic bulbs are about 2900°K.

►Depth of Field: The amount of the picture that is in focus. Depth of field increases at smaller apertures (ie the larger f-numbers)

►Exposure: The amount of light allowed to reach the film. Exposure is set on the camera by a combination of *Film Speed* and *Lens Aperture.* Over-exposure results in slides which are too light, *under*-exposure in slides which are too dark.

►Film Speed: Film speed indicates how sensitive to light the film is. Recently, the system used to designate film speed has changed from ASA and DIN to ISO, but the numbers remain the same. What used to be called a 400ASA/27DIN film is now an ISO 400/27° film. The higher the number the faster the film, ie more sensitive to light.

►Focal Length: The focal length of a lens indicates its *angle of view*. Focal length is measured in millimetres and the smaller the number the wider the angle of view. For a 35mm (film size) camera 50mm or 55mm is the focal length of the standard lens. Less than 50mm means a *wide angle* lens and more than 50mm means a *telephoto* lens.

►**Format:** Size of the slide or negative a camera takes. The most common formats are 35mm, 6x6cm, 5"x7" and 8"x10".

►**Incident Light:** Light falling on the subject, rather than reflected by it. Incident light readings are usually the most reliable way of working out the exposure, especially when taking slides.

►**ISO:** *See Film Speed*

►**Macro:** A macro lens is one which will produce a same size image on the film. For example, the image on 35mm measures 1"x1½" so a macro lens for 35mm should be able to focus down onto objects as small as 1"x1½".

►**Shutter Speed:** The shutter speed controls the length of time light is allowed to reach the film.

►**SLR:** Single Lens Reflex. Cameras in which the viewfinder sees through the lens that takes the picture.

►**Stop:** *See Aperture*

►**Transparency:** A positive (as opposed to a negative) picture on film. 35mm transparencies are usually called 'slides'.

►**TTL:** Through the Lens. Usually refers to the light meter in SRL cameras which measure the light through the lens.

►**Tungsten:** Light source used in photography which has a *colour temperature* of 3200°K. Some film is balanced to give correct colour in this light.

►Information◄

►Further Reading◄

►*Photographer's Studio Manual*, Michael Freeman. Collins, 1981
►*Basic Photography*, Michael Langford. Focal Press
►*Starting Photography*, Michael Langford. Ebury Press
►*Darkroom Handbook.* Ibid
►*Advanced Photography*, Michael Langford. Focal Press
►*Workbook of Darkroom Techniques*, John Hedgcoe. Mitchell Beazley
►*Pocket Guide to Practical Photography.* Ibid
►'Getting Your Work Photographed', Sally Jo Poer Trench. *Artists Newsletter*, March 1986

Studio

Home or Away◀

Working at Home◀

Finding a Studio◀

One Studio Group◀

Home or Away?

►**David Briers**◄

As artists more often than not employ themselves, and are not provided with a place to work by an employer, they must find their own workplace or 'studio'. There are as many different sorts of studio as there are different sorts of artists. Some artists like to work near a telephone and a set of box files. Others like to work amidst a clutter reminiscent of Francis Bacon's famous midden of used paint tubes. Some like Spartan bareness, while

others prefer carpet and kettle. One artist's hell-hole is another's seventh heaven, and for many artists, the wrong studio is acceptable as long as it is in the right place, be it Newlyn, Soho New York, or Wapping. The modern proliferation of media and attitudes has meant that north light and a proper taboret next to your easel are no longer the indispensible prerequisites of every artist's studio, and like the work that they do, the nature of an artist's studio establishes itself at a point balanced between the correlates of personal temperament, professional ambition, and sheer unmitigated material practicalities. Indeed, at first (or even later), you may not be able to afford 'a studio' at all.

Young artists, suddenly stepping outside the environment of full-time art education, quite commonly find themselves on the horns of a dilemma. On the one hand, they are sharing cramped and unseemly rented accommodation, or even the unfixed abode of a squat, or may be forced, minus a grant, to return for a while to the parental nest - none of these being a good place to start work. The opportunity may be present to rent a self-contained studio elsewhere, but it is impossible to afford it.

On the other hand, an artist whose work has developed since entering the world of home-ownership, and who has found it easily possible to arrange a suitable working space at home, may be reluctant to consider the possibility that the very proximity of their activity as an artist to the kitchen or television set may be at the root of the problems with which they have become bogged down.

►A Real Artist!◄

Alongside the practical restraints which affect the decision of whether to work at home or in an outside studio may lurk the influences of professional expectations and peer group pressures. As collective group studios and studio-based artists' associations get off the ground and flourish in our big cities, usually where there are polytechnic fine art degree courses, the securing of one of these studios seems sometimes to have been undertaken by the art college graduate as if it were the 'done thing'. Sometimes, indeed, the ambience of these hurriedly secured studios is a continuation of the art college environment. If there is one maxim which those leaving college need to keep reminding themselves, it might be: you don't *have* to do anything. It may take a while - years - to find out what work environment suits you best, and it may not necessarily be what everyone else seems to be chasing. Having a *real studio* does not make you a *real artist.* As Brian Clarke said, *'A lot of people seem concerned with getting a studio before they know what they want to do with it when they've got it. It's almost a prerequisite of being an artist'.*

If you don't have a studio, it doesn't mean you can't be an artist. The chicken and egg sequence of the studio producing the artwork is not necessarily the one-way sequence generally supposed. Joseph Beuys is supposed to have said that his best drawings were done on his mother's kitchen table, and certainly R.B. Kitaj and John Hoyland started off making paintings in their front rooms, and Morris Louis' best known canvases were painted in his basement.

►
Valerie Pragnell at work in her studio

►Artists and Studios◄

Artist A (all of these anonymous alphabetical artists are real people) is obliged to live at home with his parents for the time being, in their semi-detached house. He uses a small bedroom as a studio. There are size and storage problems, though no greater than those presented by many rented studios, and they have not prevented him from recently having a one-person exhibition in a well-known gallery. **Artist B** does not live with his parents, but his studio is in their vacant garage. The lighting is bad and space cramped, but it doesn't cost him anything, he can be as messy as he likes, and having produced the work instead of worrying about getting a better studio, he is now showing at a Cork Street gallery, which may enable him to get a better studio.

◁see **Working at Home**▷

But a lot of artists work where they live by preference rather than as a necessity. **Artist C** shares a rented ground-floor flat which is large enough to use one of its rooms as a studio without bothering the other tenants or her landlord. The room is quiet and overlooks the garden. It is sympathetic to her work and working methods in a way that most outside studios would not be. **Artist D** is a busy artist and illustrator, whose 'studio' is a specially made bench at one end of the not very large living room of his flat. This is where he works by preference, it is all he needs; a large rented studio would be an unwarranted extravagance.

As more people, and therefore more artists, become owner occupiers, and enter into the infinitely protracted usury called a mortgage, so more artists build their studio, literally or otherwise, into the fabric of their house. **Artists E & F** each live in terraced houses with three floors. **E** uses the entire ground floor as his studio, with all domestic life going on above, whereas **F** works on the top floor of the house, which is easier to keep out of bounds to his two children at busy times, as no-one has to pass through it. With less space available, **Artist G** has converted his attic into a studio for small-scale printmaking.

Other artists who work at home do not separate their work as artists so distinctly from their domestic life. **Artists H & I** are married, and have converted a rural schoolhouse into a living and working space. They work

together in its large central area, a combined studio and living room, which is overlooked by the kitchen and bedroom. They cannot escape from their work, which is all over the house anyway (nor can they escape from their two small children and cat), but this is a conscious decision on their part.

Practical considerations beyond those of being able to afford it, do of course sometimes dictate that certain types of work as an artist cannot take place in a house or flat. For example, a sculptor working in heavy stones or steel needs a concrete floor and lifting gear, a printmaker with one or more large presses cannot put them in the attic, and some new media such as holography require very stringent conditions indeed. Lasers in the living room is not a good idea.

However, there is no clear dividing line between *home* and *outside* studio, and a garden studio or end-of-garden garage used as a sculpture workshop, can seem as separate from the house as a studio rented five miles away. **Artist J** uses a separate outbuilding of his rural home as a studio - he can forget it's there if he wants, but it's next door if he has to work late. Having carefully considered the long-term financial and legal ramifications, **Artist K** vacated her rented studio and took out a second mortgage on the small house next door to her own when it came up for sale, and uses it as her studio.

The dividing line between having a studio in your home or a home in your studio is also a blurred one, particularly since the formation of the ACME Housing Association. The proverbial *artist's garret* was, after all, a studio in which the artist also slept and starved, and there are not a few artists who are still occasionally obliged to sleep in their studio, having found a studio easier to get than a home. **Artist L** vacated his rented group studio recently, sold his house, and moved into a small disused warehouse in an urban development area, suitable for living as well as working. With the aid of local authority grants, he has renovated the premises as a fine sculpture studio (the lifting gear and concrete floors were already there) with living accommodation above.

Quite a few artists, particularly in rural and coastal tourism areas live, work, and seasonally exhibit and sell their work from one premises (financial assistance of various sorts is often available from local authorities and tourist boards for such ventures). In the city too, artists' studios sometimes have double identities. **Artist M** (for Matts Gallery) periodically turns his studio into a public gallery, exhibiting the work of other artists. **Artists N & O** rent the top floor space above a haberdashery wholesalers and a secondhand bookshop. They never intended to be open to the public, but a sign encourages the clients of the bookshop to go up to their studio for a look, and they have made sales that way.

Artist P's studio is a self-contained operation which includes selling the work. After working in a small studio at his flat for a number of years, **P** considered joining the local artists' studio association, but instead opted for a more expensive studio on his own in a city-centre Victorian building alongside wholesalers and designers. Adjacent to the working area are smaller rooms for storage, and a tiny office with a telephone. Having slowly built up a local clientele for his work over a number of years, **P** realised that he was in a position – if he so chose – to 'leave out the middleman'. Now, he invites friends and potential clients to an opening at his studio every few months, and always sells enough work and gains enough commissions to buy time to complete a further body of work.

►Group Studios◄

◁see **One Studio Group**▷

Renting a studio unit at cost within a disused warehouse, school or factory run by an association or collective of artists is certainly cheaper, but also has its pros and cons apart from financial considerations. You cannot, usually, locate such a studio space and move straight in. There is likely to be a lengthy waiting list, and there may also be a selection procedure, and even some form of interview. If you are involved in actually setting up a group of studios you may have to contribute a great deal of your own unpaid time, energy and materials to making good a studio space which would not otherwise exist. The building itself is likely to have been secured as a low-cost group tenancy on a short-term basis, either because it or the area it is in are due for eventual demolition or re-development. You will have no real security of tenure, and may only be granted a licence to work there by the association, revocable on a monthly or even weekly basis. Some artists find it difficult to work with the spectre of possible eviction hanging over their heads, however unlikely it might be actually to be put into practice. And it can be distressing to have to move out of a splendid and sound Victorian building in which you have made your working space and become part of a community of artists, and to see it pulled down and bulldozed flat overnight, or foreclosed, vacated and facelifted as part of a gentrified marina.

◁see **Finding a Studio**▷

Some of the studio spaces in such complexes are magnificently solidly built, but often large areas are sub-divided by chip-board partitions with no sound-proofing whatsoever. Privacy is only summarily maintained, and a continual commentary to your work by Simon Bates from the transistor radio with its battery running out next door can soon pall. Indeed, the very aspects of such a community of art practice which are attractive to some artists, may alienate others. You may, for example, like the idea of working next door to a potter, rather than another painter, or you may not. You may also find that the other studios are predominatly occupied by artists in their mid-twenties, fresh out of college, and you may prefer to share the company of more experienced artists. Or vice versa.

And remember that you will have to take some part, however small, in the management of the studios, be it as an unpaid administrator, contributor to members' meetings, or just being on the rota to clean the lavatory once a week. If you want to shut the door to your studio and pretend the rest of the world - and particularly other artists - doesn't exist, don't join a studio organisation. Also, if the hours you work best are the late ones, to find yourself the lone artist working late in a dark, draughty ex-warehouse can be unnerving, to say the least.

There are compensations to working in group studios, of course, not least that of feeling part of an evident artistic community – of having something immediately adjacent to measure up to, in terms of practice as well as end result. In practical terms, group studios tend to have a higher profile than individual studios. They are places that local arts administrators know about, and they may drop in on you when visiting someone else, just to keep up with what you're doing. Some group studios seek to build towards providing greater professional security for the artist, while others are exploring alternative ways of working from a studio. Some of these groups seek and secure exhibitions as a group, and some even have their own gallery. Shared equipment or tools, however, is a facility more often spoken of than put into practice.

▶Arts Centres◀

There are not many arts centres which have artists' studios as part of their overall activities, but there are some, and they are becoming commoner (one even offers studio space with living accommodation). They are attractive propositions, but again with as many cons as pros. Other artists might be noisy, but a theatre group or percussion ensemble next door is even more disruptive. You may be involved in one way or another with the art centre's other activities – as a teacher in public workshops, perhaps, or just serving behind the bar to make ends meet – and working in such surroundings may provide you with invigorating social contacts. Or you may suffer continually from unwarranted intrusions upon your time, or conversely, alone in your studio with all that activity going on around you, you could end up feeling even more isolated than you would working on your own at home.

Damon Burnard

▶Living with Work◀

Beyond the unavoidable constraints of physical, financial and legal limitations, another major factor determing whether you work at home or elsewhere will be whether you live with someone else, particularly if 'someone else' comprises or includes a baby or small children. Here again, although the set of circumstances presented by having children is impossible just to ignore, the ways of fitting it into the jigsaw of your activities as an artist are manifold, and dependent entirely on what works best for you. (For example, **Artists Q & R**, who have a small baby, both rent studios outside their home, but separately, in different parts of town, and take it in turns to child-mind at home, whereas **Artists H & I**, already mentioned above, built their whole life-style around living, working, and bringing up small children in the same place).

◁see **Working at Home**▷

Such decisions are commonly seen to relate to privacy and self-discipline. Total privacy is, of course, impossible, even at home, and a studio elsewhere may paradoxically offer more privacy. Anyone who has worked at home for any length of time will tell you of the innumerable interruptions from those trying to sell you insurance, double-glazing, stone-cladding, and assorted forms of religious belief. It is necessary to devise and deploy a fearless technique to dispense rapidly with such interruptions, though these are of no use with friends and relatives who tend to think of what you are doing as a hobby. But sometimes such interruptions can provide useful excuses not to get down to work, just as a television set in the next room can become like opium, and you may find yourself, against your better judgement, watching Australian soap operas in the middle of the afternoon instead of facing up to a problematic canvas.

A biologist would call this a displacement activity, and in a group of studios it might manifest itself in the form of habitually going to the pub at lunchtime and staying till closing time. Despite the aid to self-discipline provided by going to a studio to work, the various efforts involved are no different whether at home or away, and the act of actually starting to work may, in fact, be more difficult in a freezing cold outside studio (many group studios, badly insulated and unheated, are almost seasonal workplaces). Embarking upon an elaborate studio building or renovation scheme, if you are not careful to build into its time-scale the alternative means to carry on work as an artist, can also end up as a prolonged and elaborate excuse never quite to get round to making art again.

►Ethics at Work◄

Because of the way most of us have been brought up, working at home can easily produce feelings of guilt, and self-accusations of laziness from which even the most industrious and prolific artists (perhaps those most of all) have admitted suffering. It is easy to work longer than is good for you at home, and proper breaks and a bit of exercise should be built into your work pattern. There is no need to become a health freak (heaven forbid), though conscious attention to such things is needed to avoid slipping into a vicious spiral of seediness and negative introversion without realising it, and therein lie the seeds of agoraphobia.

Unfortunately the dictum persists that good art can only come out of mortifying working conditions. The catalogue for a group studio exhibition a few years ago included the following statement *'...by definition an artist who is willing to rent and maintain a studio which is all too often physically uncomfortable, cannot but take his work seriously and expect to be taken seriously'*. The implicit supposition that more suitable conditions would produce work which is *not serious* is just one of the nonsenses which might divert the inexperienced artist from devising (and re-devising, according to changing needs) a set of working conditions which work for them.

Being able to decide where, how and when you work is one of the privileges (and there are few enough) accorded to a self-employed person. Do not waste it.

Working at Home

►Adrian Barr-Smith◄

►First published in the *Artists Studio Handbook*◄

Many artists would like to maintain a studio but cannot, usually for economic reasons. They have no alternative but to work at home. In the majority of such cases, problems may arise for one or more of the following reasons:

►Illegality◄

►Owner-Occupiers◄

An owner/occupier with a mortgage is usually bound by a term of the mortgage deed to use the premises only as a residential dwelling. If the mortgagees (building society, bank, local authority, etc) discover that the artist is working at home, they may either terminate the mortgage facility or, more commonly, require the mortgagor to cease working there.

►Tenants◄

A tenant is similarly placed if his/her lease/tenancy agreement contains a clause (most do!) requiring him/her to use the premises only for residential purposes. If the landlord discovers a breach of this clause, s/he may either terminate the lease/tenancy agreement or, more usually, require the tenant to cease working there.

A tenant who enjoys protection under the Rent Acts, loses that protection if s/he is 'carrying on a business' (ie any trade or professional activity) at home.

►Answer◄

A solution to the problems of both owner/occupier and tenant is to insist, if confronted, that their artistic activity is merely a 'hobby' interest, ie just like a 'Sunday' painter.

An alternative solution, which is preferable, may not be appropriate in all cases. A simple letter can be written to the mortgagees or landlord explaining that the artist intends to work from home in the forseeable future due to extenuating circumstances, etc. Many building societies are happy to accept this state of affairs, provided certain safeguard measures are taken.

Artists who are wary of informing mortgagees or landlord that they work at home, should take care to restrict the use of any business letterhead showing their home address.

►Building and Public Liability Insurance◄

►Owner-Occupiers◄

An owner/occupier with a mortgage usually pays insurance premiums on the policy which the mortgagees take out against the structure collapsing, or against death or injury caused to members of the public at the premises. Such a policy will, like the mortgage deed, prohibit any use of the premises other than residential. If the insurers discover that the artist is working at home, they may cancel the policy or worse – because of this 'non-disclosure' – they will avoid liability in the event of any claim.

►Tenants◄

A tenant with a lease will often pay premiums on a building insurance policy taken out by the landlords. If the tenant is an artist, by working at home s/he runs the same risk as the owner/occupier. *(see above)*

►Answer◄

As under Illegality. For preference, notify the insurers. Provided the risks are not increased, eg by the use of volatile chemicals, this should not materially affect the premiums.

►Contents Insurance◄

Any artist working at home may have a policy covering household contents. All insurance policies require disclosure of every 'material fact'. Whether or not the contents policy is intended to cover work, equipment, etc, the insurers should be informed of any artistic activity or storage of work on the premises.

►Planning regulations◄

A building in a residential area can be used for any activities 'incidental to the enjoyment of the dwelling house as such'. The artist working at home should always argue that his/her artistic activity is a 'hobby', ie merely incidental to his/her residence at the premises.

Planning permission is required where an artist:

- ►intensifies his/her operation, eg by employing assistants or actively selling work at home.
- ►changes the use to light industrial purposes
- ►alters the external appearance of the house (but not by painting it)
- ►improves/alters the construction, eg by building a shed or an extension (unless the size of the building is **not** increased by 1/10th or 50 cubic metres)
- ►constructs a driveway

In these circumstances the Planning Officer at the Local Authority will give a preliminary view as to whether permission is required and as to the chances of succeeding with a formal application.

Breach of the regulations by doing the above without permission is not

a criminal offence. Officers will allow time for compliance with the regulations. If dissatisfied they will serve an Enforcement Notice which compels the artist to comply within a reasonable period (usually 28 days). An aggrieved artist should appeal against the Notice.

Unless there is excessive traffic or noise, planning problems will probably arise due to overzealous officials or poor relations with neighbours.

►Rates◄

Premises are divided into three categories for rating purposes: domestic, commercial, mixed domestic-commercial. Where an artist works at home, the premises might technically be reclassified by the Valuation Officer as 'mixed'. The consequence of this would be higher rates, and loss of entitlement to pay by instalments and to claim rate rebates. However, where the artistic activity is confined to an identifiable space (eg studio in a converted garage) the artist is able to pay higher rates only on the non-domestic space.

►Tax◄

◁see **Employment & Tax**▷

The self-employed artist usually deducts a proportion of his/her household expenses, appropriate to his/her artistic activity, when calculating income tax liability.

Capital Gains Tax (CGT) complications can arise when an owner/occupier sells his/her house. Any profit on the sale of an artist's home is usually exempt from CGT where it is his/her principal private residence. But the Inland Revenue may not exempt part of the profit if the artist has been claiming income tax deduction in respect of that proportion.

For example, Leonardo buys a house for £36,000. He paints at home and claims 25% of his household overheads – including the mortgage repayments – as deductable business expenses. After five years, he sells the house for £60,000 – net profit £24,000. If Leonardo had not painted at home, that profit would be exempt under the normal rules. But his tax inspector will probably insist that Leonardo pays CGT on 25% of the profit, ie £6,000.

The rationale for this is simply that the part of the dwelling which is claimed as a business expense cannot also have been used for residential purposes.

►Social Security◄

◁see **Benefit**▷

An artist 'signing on' as unemployed is entitled to supplementary benefit in respect of his accommodation needs and living expenses. The Department of Social Security (DSS) will usually pay the claimant's rent if a tenant, or mortgage interest payments if an owner/occupier. But where the artist works at home, the DSS will not pay the proportion of the cost attributable to the workspace.

►Neighbours◄

Artists who work at home will frequently encounter problems if they do not enjoy a friendly relationship with their neighbours. This can be achieved by paying conscious attention to:

- ►Noise (particularly late-night)
- ►Traffic (general coming and going)
- ►Parking (obstructing driveways)
- ►Refuse and rubbish
- ►External appearance of the property

Neighbours who create trouble are usually motivated, not by malevolence, but by fear that the value of their property, or their enjoyment of it, is threatened.

Finding a Studio

▶ **Adrian Barr-Smith** ▶

▶ First published in *The Artists Studio Handbook* ◀

▶ Assess needs ◀

The first task is for the artist to decide what s/he requires. S/he who correctly assesses his/her individual needs at the outset will avoid wasting time viewing unsuitable premises.

When determining their needs, artists should consider the following:

▶ Is *living accommodation* also required?
▶ Will space be *self-contained* or shared?
▶ What *geographical location*?
▶ What *size*? (in square feet)
▶ Daylight or artificial *light*?
▶ *Ease of access* (eg bulky objects)
▶ *Right of access* (limited or 24hrs)
▶ *Facilities*
(i) power supply (ii) heating (iii) water supply (iv) WC/washing facilities
▶ *Special requirements* (eg soundproofing)
▶ *Security risk* (eg valuable equipment)
▶ How many *artists involved,* who will handle lease, group accounts, etc?

◁see **One Studio Group**▷

▶ What can I afford? ◀

Before setting out to look for a building suitable to requirements, it is advisable for an artist to make an objective assessment of his/her means. Taking on a studio can involve a heavy 'capital' (ie one-off) commitment, as well as the burden of the 'revenue' (ie running) costs.

An artist who cannot afford the expense is well advised not to waste time looking for a bargain offer. Dream studios (ie inexpensive ones) no longer exist, if they ever did!

An artist who can afford the commitment (eg thanks to teaching job) should consider whether s/he could borrow money and buy a freehold/long leasehold space.

▲ **Manchester Artists Studios Association** studios

►How do I search?◄

Searching is the hardest and most soul-destroying task of all. Artists should avoid being persuaded to spend time viewing unsuitable or over-expensive buildings. The following are suggested methods, in order of probable effectiveness:

►*Approach* a helpful organisation (Acme, SPACE, WASPS, local RAA or Arts Council, AADW)
►*Talk* to other artists, lecturers, friends (circulate a handout)
►*Advertise* (on notice boards, in *Artists Newsletter*, etc)
►*Cycle* round streets (armed with notebook, camera)
►*Drive/bus* round streets (you'll see more than by tube, but less than on two wheels)
►*Walk* (you'll cover a smaller area)
►*Visit* SUITABLE estate agents, ie who handle suitable property, not luxury penthouses (specify requirements, ask to be sent particulars of potential spaces)
►*Telephone/write* to SUITABLE estate agents (specify as above)
►*Write* to local authority (estates department) (specify as above – some larger authorities publish lists of available properties)
►*Write* to landlords of other artists' studios
►*Scan* advertisements in local papers

Lined writing paper doesn't look business-like

No name and address of recipient – no record on carbon paper for future reference

15 Bolingbroke House
Main Road
Mudcaster

Address of well-known squat

No telephone number – could be a handicap

16 July 1981

No name – ensures letter will bounce around the office for several days

Dear Sir,

Indicates unfamiliarity with conventions of business letter writing

Irrelevant to this request

Handwriting difficult to read

I have just completed a BA degree course in sculpture at Mudcaster Polytechnic, and am now looking for a studio, ~~probably~~ to share with other artists from my college.

Scruffy, indecisive

Who, how many?

We are very interested in renting a suitable large building from the Council. Could you please let me know if you have anything available?

Landlord is unlikely to put him/herself out on information given

What would be suitable?
– where?
– how much?
– how big?

Yours sincerely,

Jonathan Brown

JONATHAN BROWN B.A.

Pretentious and unnecessary

▲
An example of how not to compose a letter to prospective landlords

►Where do I look?◄

The most obvious possibilities may be in the run-down inner-city locality, for example.

►*above shops* in the High Street
►tops of *warehouses*
►*disused* shops, factories, churches, warehouses, schools
►areas blighted by *redevelopment* proposals (ask the local authority planning department, the tell-tale sign is boarded-up buildings)
►*locations* keen to attract occupants – industrial estates, enterprise zones, etc.

Once an artist has found a building s/he must assess, as objectively as possible, whether the space is suitable for his/her stated requirements.

Well-typed letter, keep carbon on file

Use 'best' address available amongst group members

Telephone helpful

Writing to a person means they have to make sure something is done about the letter

Involve local personalities if possible

Emphasise LOCAL angle

'Letrset' letterheading looks professional and inspires confidence – artists group already formed

Full name, title and address of person being written to

Reference number looks good

Heading helps clarify subject immediately

Makes recipient feel its up to him/her

Set out basic requirements clearly

Attempts to get officials interested and involved

Sending large SAE is gesture of goodwill and efficiency

BOLINGBROKE ARTISTS LTD

c/o Suzanne Williams (Sec)
20 Albert Square
Mudcaster

(0732) 61228

A.L.Jobsworth Esq.,
Borough Valuation Officer
Mudcaster Town Hall
High Street
Mudcaster

BAS/SW

16 July 1981

Dear Mr Jobsworth,

Studio Accommodation- Bolingbroke Artists Ltd.

Councillor Wilson has suggested that I contact you , on behalf of Bolingbroke Artists Ltd., as he hopes you may be able to help us.

B.A.Ltd. is a group of local artists, and we are currently searching for premises in the Borough, suitable for conversion into artists' studios. Our requirements are as follows:

1000-2000 sq.ft.
Minimum ceiling height 7'
Availability 2 yrs or more
Natural light desirable, but artificial light acceptable

We are willing to pay rent compatible with current commercial rates (at the lower end of the scale), but are particularly interested in low-cost accommodation awaiting re-development. We are willing, and able, to carry out basic repairs and conversion work.

Please let me know if you require any further information from me at this stage. I could attend for interview, if so required, at any time.

Yours sincerely,
Suzanne Williams
Suzanne Williams
Secretary, Bolingbroke Artists Ltd.

P.S. I am enclosing an invitation to the private view of a small exhibition of work by B.A.Ltd. members in Mudcaster Library; you might be interested to see the work we are doing.

(enclosures: invitation
stamped addressed envelope)

▲
An example of how to compose a letter to prospective landlords

►How do I trace the owner?◄

If the space has been located through the landlord/agent, etc, no problem. An artist who spots an unoccupied building should be able to trace the owner by one of the following means?

- ►Estate agent's board on building
- ►Neighbours
- ►Shop/pub on corner of street
- ►Local authority planning department (if development is proposed, they may own the building)
- ►Local rates office (if they are unwilling to reveal name and address of owner, they will forward a letter addressed to the occupier)

A Scottish artist once suggested that a surefire way to contact the owner of unoccupied premises was to move in straightaway. Unfortunately, many landlords are reluctant to come to an agreement with a squatter in these circumstances and may, instead, eject him.

►What will the space cost?◄

An intending tenant must estimate as accurately as possible what will be the capital and revenue costs of the space

►Capital Costs◄

These 'one-off' expenses may include:

►alterations/repairs to roof, floor, walls (must comply with local building regulations and have approval of District Surveyor)
►installation of fire-doors/fire-proofing/means of escape (must have approval of local Fire Officer)
►installation of power supply, re-wiring, etc.
►installation of water supply, plumbing, wastepipe, drains, etc (responsibility of Borough Engineer)
►purchasing fixtures from landlord/outgoing tenant
►miscellaneous DIY supplies and restoration jobs
►survey or legal fees

▲
Cardiff Sculpture Workshop

These can be crippling expenses and must be met before the space becomes workable. Artists should be wary of committing such money in establishing a studio with a short life-expectancy. Most local authorities will under-estimate the period of time available for occupation. But grants towards the conversion/establishment costs will not be available from the arts councils or regional arts associations unless the occupancy is likely to continue for a reasonable length of time.

►Revenue Costs◄

These 'ongoing' expenses may include:

►rent
►general rates
►water rates and sewerage charges
►building insurance premiums (get a quotation)
►third party insurance premiums (to cover members of the public – this includes your friends – who fall down your stairs!)
►contents insurance premiums (equipment, work, etc)
►service charges (caretaker, rubbish collection, etc)
►minor repairs
►heat and light
►telephone
►transport from home to studio and back

►Negotiations with landlord◄

Having added up the potential capital and revenue expenses, the prospective tenant should not proceed further unless he can afford to make a better-than-derisory offer. Negotiating methods vary from landlord to landlord. The following rules of thumb should serve as a guide:

►Never offer the asking price, it's usually inflated
►If the building is unoccupied the landlord may accept a very low offer (he's getting nothing from an empty building and probably paying rates)

►Don't make a derisory offer without good reason (this may prove counter-productive and abort the negotiations before they start)
►Glamorise the offer, especially if it's low (when making a proposal, particularly to a local authority, explain who you are, what you want to do in the space, and point out how your occupancy can benefit the landlord – caretaking role, prevention of vandalism/squatting, preservation of fabric, cultural benefit to the community, etc)
►Rents are expressed in square feet per year, eg 'Studio 20 x 13 ft: £2 per sq ft' means that the total rent is £520 per annum or £10 per week.
►Rent-free periods can often be arranged where a tenant has to carry out repairs before occupying the space. A typical example:
Pablo agrees with Sylvester, his landlord, that he will have a rent-free period of 3 months provided he carries out, at his own expense, an agreed schedule of repairs. Pablo pays the first quarter's rent in advance in December and moves into occupation. He carries out the repairs by March and invites Sylvester to inspect the work. Sylvester is happy with the work and the rent-free period operates from April to June, whereupon the next quarter's rent falls due.
►All written or verbal negotiations should be conducted on a 'without prejudice' or, more commonly, *'subject to contract'* basis. These words, which should appear at the top of all offer letters, etc, indicate that the agreement will be later recorded in a formal contract and either party can withdraw from the negotiations at any time before that final moment.
►An artist should be aware of weakening his/her security by accepting a lease which requires him/her to use the premises other than for the purposes which s/he intends to use them, eg if the lease specifies 'use: storage', the artist is not legally entitled to use the space for working or living.

►Formalities◄

It is important that any agreement made between landlord and tenant is recorded in writing before any money is handed over or irrevocable commitment undertaken. The written record may be as simple as an exchange of letters, or as complicated as a lease with 50 clauses. The documents are normally drawn up by the landlord's solicitor/agent. In all such cases, artists should seek legal advice from a solicitor.

The formal arrangement made is usually one of 4 types:

►'Legalised' Squat◄

Where the artist's presence is tolerated by the owners, who can revoke their tacit permission at any time.

This arrangement tends to be attractive at the outset because it is easy. It is not a worthwhile proposition in the long term because it is precarious and insecure (artists have no right to have the services – gas, electricity – connected).

►Licence◄

Written or verbal agreement for occupation by artist ('licensee') which is not a tenancy – usually because the artist shares the space and does not have exclusive possession. Upon termination the licensee is entitled to be

given specified notice, eg if paying weekly, one week's notice.

Studio licences *(see specimen, page 198)* are increasingly common because the rights of the artist occupier are limited and the arrangement is attractive to property owners.

►Tenancy◄

Written or verbal agreement for occupation by artist ('tenant') usually weekly or monthly. Upon termination the tenant is entitled to be given specified notice.

If it is a 'studio' tenancy lasting over six months, the Landlord and Tenant Act 1954 (Part II) ensures that it continues automatically after expiry, unless terminated by notice given by the landlord. In such circumstances the tenant should immediately give counter-notice that s/he is unwilling to give up the tenancy. If s/he had a tenancy exceeding twelve months, the tenant can only by removed if:

- ►the tenant has breached his/her obligations ('covenants')
- ►s/he has persistently delayed paying rent
- ►the landlord offers reasonable alternative accommodation
- ►the landlord intends to demolish or renovate the building
- ►the landlord intends to occupy the premises for business or residential purposes.

Many tenancies and leases are granted only on condition that the tenant waives his rights under this Act. The Act, which covers 'business' (ie non-residential) premises, applies unless specifically excluded with the sanction of the County Court.

►Lease◄

Contract between landlord ('lessor') and tenant ('lessee') which must be written and contains all the covenants binding each side. If a lease (or tenancy) is for a term of several years, the tenant is under an implied obligation to carry out timely repairs. A lease terminates upon expiry of the fixed term (eg one year, seven years) unless continued automatically by the Landlord and Tenant Act as above.

In all four instances, the occupant(s) cannot be evicted from the premises, even after expiry of proper notice, without a Court order.

▲
Looking for a new studio, I decided to think big and contact indusrialists who owned old Victorian mills in the North West. After discreet investigation and a lot of footwork, I found out the names of several firms. After three telephone calls, I got through to an owner sympathetic to my plight - I explained I was a young artist needing a place to work. He arranged a meeting between the mill manager and I, and in return for doing some drawings of sections of the mill and producing some designs for fabric prints, I was offered 20,000 feet of mill to use.

There are dozens of old mills lying vacant or partially-occupied in and around Manchester which would make ideal studio space. My advice, when addressing business people, is to show them that it could be in their interest for you to use part of their premises. If you have enough cheek and spirit, it can be achieved. Though desperate for a studio, I never dreamed I'd get one as big as a football pitch!'
Kane Cunningham

►Checklist◄

Most documents whether leases, tenancy agreements or licences will contain terms dealing with the following points:

- ►Name and address of *landlord*
- ►Name and address of *tenant* (all names if more than one artist)
- ►Date of *commencement* of agreement
- ►*Rent,* paid weekly/monthly, etc (artists are advised to pay by bankers order where possible)
- ►Is *surety* required to guarantee payment of rent?
- ►Whether rent will be *'reviewed',* ie increased (if so, how often?)
- ►Is a *deposit* required? If so, what will it be credited against, eg unpaid rent, damage, etc?
- ►*Building insurance premium,* usually paid by tenant

▶*Rates,* payable by the 'occupier' and usually paid by tenant
▶Is *service charge* payable? If so what services are offered, eg caretaker, heating, etc?
▶*Interior repairs and decoration* – landlord usually responsible
▶*Exterior decoration* – tenant often responsible
▶Purpose for which premises may be *used* (ie studio)
▶*Duration* of agreement, ie length of occupancy
▶*Option to renew* or extend agreement (on what terms?)
▶*Option to terminate* agreement before expiry
▶Whether agreement can be *'assigned'* (and studio handed over) to another artist with/without landlord's consent
▶Whether *subletting* allowed – of whole/part of premises
▶*Legal fees* – usually paid by tenant
▶*References required* (usually previous landlord, bank, accountant, solicitor, etc)
▶*Date of agreement*
▶*Signatures* of both parties

Use this as a checklist to ensure that all points have been discussed with the landlord, before the lawyers are called in.

▶Doing it with other artists◀

◁see **One Studio Group**▷

Many artists are involved in sharing studio space with others, usually in order to reduce costs. There are other benefits. For example, when searching for space or carrying out conversion work the tasks can be divided up amongst the group. The presence of other artists can lend stability; it means that the ability to pay the bills is not dependent solely upon the cash-flow of one individual.

Whenever artists collaborate together for this purpose they should be careful to decide the following points and to record their decisions in an appropriate fashion, eg minutes of a meeting

▶Who are *members* of the group?
▶What the *aims* of the group are
▶Which members will undertake the following responsibilities:
(i) Chair – spokesperson (ii) Secretary – convening meetings, writing letters (iii) Treasurer – finances
▶To keep a separate *bank account* for group business
▶What the rights and obligations of members are to each other, eg in the event of the group becoming insolvent
▶Whether a formal constitution is required
▶Whether any tenancy/lease should be in the name of the group, or of one or more individual members.

Groups can be established quite informally, as above. If a more formal structure is necessary, members can legally constitute themselves as an unincorporated association, co-operative, housing association, company limited by guarantee, or trust. Any of the latter three groupings can apply for registration as a charity, provided their aims and objects are charitable and for the public benefit. Several benefits are enjoyed by charities, including mandatory 50% rate relief. Artists are warned, however, that their group will not be considered 'charitable' merely because it is non-profit-making.

►
Licence reproduced by kind permission of ACME Housing Association

It is impossible to give general advice as to which formal structure is preferable; the answer will depend on the group's circumstances. In the majority of cases, artists are well advised to seek legal help *before* they make any commitment to each other or to a third party, eg landlord.

►Specimen Licence Agreement◄

An agreement for a licence made this
day of One Thousand Nine Hundred and
Between
of
(hereinafter called 'The Licensor') of the one part and
of
(hereinafter called 'The Licensee') of the other part.

WHEREBY IT IS AGREED AS FOLLOWS:

1. The Licensor agrees to let the Licensee occupy and the Licensee agrees to occupy the property situated at and being

with the land held therewith (hereinafter called 'the Premises) for the term of one week from the day of 9 and thereafter from week to week until determined by either party giving to the other not less than four weeks notice to determine the licence created at the licence fee of £ per week payable in advance on the Monday of each week.

2. THE LICENSEE HEREBY AGREES with the LICENSOR as follows:

a. To pay the licence fee at the times and in the manner aforesaid.

b. To pay all rates taxes duties assessments impositions and outgoings which are now or which may at any time hereafter be assessed charged or imposed upon the premises or on the owner or occupier in respect thereof.

c. To use the premises in a licensee-like manner.

d. To keep in repair the structure and exterior of the premises (including the drains gutters and external pipes).

e. To keep in repair and proper working order the installations in the premises for the supply of water gas and electricity and for sanitary convenience.

f. To keep in good and complete repair order and condition (damage by accidental fire only accepted) the interior of the premises and the painting papering and decorating thereof and the fixtures and appliances therein.

g. Not to use or permit to be used the premises for any purpose other than that of artists studio and living accommodation.

h. Not to do or permit to be done upon the premises any act or thing which may be a nuisance damage or annoyance to the licensor or the licensees or occupiers of any of the adjoining premises.

i. Not to part with the possession of assign charge or let the premises or any part thereof.

j. That the licensor or any person authorised by the licensor in writing may at reasonable times of the day on giving 24 hours notice in writing to the occupier enter the premises for the purpose of viewing their condition and the state of their repair.

k. At the expiration or sooner determination of the licence to deliver up to

the licensor in such order condition and state as shall be consistent with the due performance of the obligations of the licensee herein contained.
l. That there is no rehousing liability at the expiration or sooner determination of the licence.

3. PROVIDED that if the licence fee or any part thereof shall be in arrears for fourteen days after the same shall have become due or in the event of the breach of any of the agreements on the part of the Licensee herein contained the Licensor may re-enter upon the premises and immediately thereupon the tenancy shall absolutely determine but without prejudice to the other rights and remedies of the Licensor.

4. I am aware that the Licensor is allowed to use the premises under an agreement with the superior landlord and that if the superior landlord demands that the premises be handed back to the superior landlord with vacant possession, then the Licensor must do as it is told. For this reason I appreciate that the Licensor can only grant me a revocable licence such as I am now getting instead of a tenancy; and that as a licensee I am not protected by the Rent Acts. Unlike a tenant I shall not be entitled to security of tenure under the Rent Acts.

5. I hereby agree the terms and conditions herein set out relating to the premises, and acknowledge receipt of a copy of the terms and conditions.

SIGNED:

The Licensee of the Premises

COUNTERSIGNED:

An Officer authorised to sign
on behalf of the Licensor

DATED...............

▶Scottish Differences◀

▶Charles MacLean◀

▶First published in *The Artists Studio Handbook*◀

Broadly speaking, all the foregoing guidelines apply in Scotland, but the following distinctions should be borne in mind:

▶Most property transactions in Scotland are conducted by solicitors rather than estate agents and in many towns there are *'Solicitors Property Centres'* where solicitors advertise the properties available for sale and a limited number of properties to let. These centres are a useful addition to the other ways of finding studio space.

▶The English concept of 'Long Leases' is alien to Scots Law, property being owned absolutely (ie freehold) or leased on a continuing, short term or renewable, basis.

▶The contract to purchase or lease property in Scotland is constituted by the exchange of letters (ie offer and acceptance, called *'missives'*) before the title deed or lease is drawn up. The term 'subject to contract' is never used in this context: the missives are the contract and become binding once both parties have agreed all the particulars. Likewise the term 'without prejudice' is redundant: it is implied in the negotiations.

▶The leasing of commercial property (a studio alone would probably come into this category) is entirely contractual in Scotland, unaffected by statutory requirements or protection such as the Landlord and Tenant Act

1954. This means that care has to be taken to make sure that all forseeable contingencies have been agreed upon at the missives stage: resort to statute cannot be made if a dispute arises.

▶Licenses to occupy property, while being recognised by the Law of Scotland, are rarely used.

▶Glossary of Terms & Phrases◀

▶**'agent':** (in this context) usually a surveyor or estate agent acting on instructions, and receiving commission, from the property owner

▶**agreement:** legally binding arrangement between A and B (and C and D etc.); A makes an offer, B accepts the offer and communicates his acceptance to A; (except for sale of land) needn't, but should, be in writing

▶**business:** (as in 'business premises' or 'business tenancy') any commercial, professional, vocational or related activity (includes non-profit-making)

▶**charity:** a body registered with the Charity Commission

▶**clause:** a term of a written agreement, lease, etc

▶**company:** a body registered with the Registrar of Companies ('Companies House'); two-part constitution consists of Memorandum and Articles of Association; liability of members is limited by shares (profit-making) or by guarantee (non-profit-making)

▶**constitution:** formal legal skeleton around which a body is constructed; binding on each member; must be in writing

▶**contract:** an agreement (the two words are virtually synonymous)

▶**co-operative:** a group working collectively, largely for mutual benefit; usually registered as a 'Friendly Society'; usually not registered as a charity – even if non-profit-making

▶**covenant:** an obligation contained in a lease which the convenantor promises to undertake, eg not to use the premises for illegal or immoral purposes

▶**'deal':** an agreement

▶**deed:** a formal document signed and 'made' under seal, usually in front of witnesses (most leases are concluded in this way)

▶**fixtures and fittings:** items attached to the structure, more or less permanently, which therefore pass from one occupier to the next (often with financial compensation) eg shelving

▶**freehold:** owner of *freehold* owns that property outright whilst a *leasehold* owner owns the property for the duration of the lease, whereupon it reverts to the *freehold* owner

▶**'land':** (in this context) includes buildings thereon

▶**landlord:** freehold or leasehold owner of property who lets it to a tenant

▶**lease:** written contract whereby lessor gives right to occupy to lessee in exchange for rent and sundry other covenants

▶**licence:** verbal or written agreement whereby licensor gives very limited right to occupy to licensee in exchange for licence fee

►**offer:** *offer* and *acceptance* are essential features of any agreement/contract; any preliminary move (eg distributing particulars of available properties), is called an 'invitation to treat', ie invitation to make an offer

►**premium:** key-money sometimes demanded by landlords from prospective tenants of long leases; normally negotiable

►**possession:** someone occupying premises lawfully is said to be 'in possession', although needn't be freehold or leasehold owner

►**sale:** agreement/contract by which vendor transfers ownership to purchaser in exchange for the purchase price

►**security of tenure:** protection given to tenants against landlords seeking to evict tenants and recover possession of premises

►**squat:** unlawful occupation of premises; squatter is never 'in possession' of premises

►**stamp duty:** fee payable by purchaser to the Inland Revenue on all commercial transactions relating to land

►**'subject to contract':** magic words, legal shorthand for *subject to* (a formal) *contract* (being drawn up in due course which will supersede the earlier verbal/written agreement)

►**tenancy:** verbal or written agreement between landlord and tenant(s)

►**term:** (a) one of the clauses/provisions of an agreement/contract (b) (as in 'a term of 7 years') length of time/duration of, eg lease

►**title:** legal ownership

►**trust:** a body consisting of trustees who own property, to be used for the benefit of others, ie beneficiaries

►**unincorporated association:** a body, which has not been formally incorporates, eg regional arts association; may, but need not, have a constitution

►**vendor:** the seller

►**'without prejudice':** more magic words meaning 'off the record'; legal shorthand for *without prejudice* (to my right to argue something completely different on a more formal occasion)

One Studio Group

▶Daniel Dahl◀

A history of the Barbican Arts Group 1970-1989.

When we first took space in an old building just north of the Barbican, City of London, in 1970, none of us had any intention of working together as a studio group. Far from it – we just wanted to establish a working situation and get on with being artists.

I suppose this must be a typical reaction – artists do not want to waste the very limited time at their disposal on what they see as 'un-artistic' activities involving bureaucracy and paper-work. The history of BAG is maybe the history of the realisation that our freedom to be able to have space at work as artists depended on making sure this freedom would not be restricted or curtailed by bad, eg inefficient organisation.

▷See **Trading Status**◁

However, we soon realised that the college leaver who had signed the agreement was neither involved in the building nor running it effectively. So we had the choice – take on the building (and the debts) or find somewhere else!

There was a feeling we needed to be something, legally constituted, but what? No one had a particularly clear idea: limited company? We found, and paid, a solicitor to advise us. The simplest, and cheapest answer was to form what amounted to a 'club' – an unincorporated association. (Some regional arts associations are still 'unincorporated associations'). In 1972 a document – based on standard legal formula – was drawn up and 'Barbican Arts Group' formed. This 'constitution' set out the aims and defined who was a member, what their rights were, and who the organising committee should be and how and when they were elected. And it has done us reasonable service ever since! The landlord registered four signatories – individuals who were willing and able to be responsible for the rent – trustees. For some reason these tended to be 'respectable' outsiders, eg people with jobs.

Practical, painful experience led to supplementing these legal forms with our own internal 'rules'. Don't leave the door open – someone lost an expensive saw. Keep food inside an airtight container – we were overrun with mice. No dogs – freshly painted surfaces ruined by its tail, the studio a health hazard from bones. Each new member gets a copy. It looks very obvious but it works.

What one might call a 'tradition' or continuity of practice becomes important. New situations call for new procedures, but there doesn't seem any point in re-inventing the wheel every time the same sort of problem presents itself. It doesn't seem sensible to ignore practices which have been born out of experience and hard work. All that is required is knowledge of such practices, and a respect for the work and thinking that went into their formulation.

The committee began to develop its role. From the beginning it had

been responsible for organisation, particularly in relation to finance. But what happens when an impossible individual falls out with his space sharer? And nobody wants to swap? As it acted to deal with this matter, the committee became more than just three individuals. It had been entrusted by the group to represent and embody its interests. When we said we had done our best but could find no solution, the artist accepted that what we were saying represented the opinion of the whole group, and left, voluntarily. He wasn't thrown out – maybe it comes to the same thing, but we have never told anyone to leave. People have come to realise that their position within the group is untenable, and have gone. Of course, the group, acting through its committee, has the power to throw members out – it must have. But the process of realisation about a situation becomes a painful but necessary element of group existence.

And the dreaded rules? It's amazing how glad we are of them when they there are to function as the neutral element in disputes. We can ignore the rules, or vote to override them, but when it comes to the crunch, they act as enabling guidelines. It has proved important to consider and amend them before a crisis blows up, and to see them as embodying the spirit of group practice rather than 'the letter of the law'. In the end, though, it is always for the group to decide.

►Finance◄

One of the first things we had to come to terms with was finance. Were we charging ourselves enough to meet our bills? Were we charging too much? From ignorance of finance, and a declaration that as artists we were 'innumerate', we – through necessity – developed a system that anyone (well, almost anyone) can operate. This certainly didn't happen overnight! It was, like the rules, the result of bad experiences and wasted time.

Another necessary development arose from the realisation that the treasurer couldn't do everything. So we developed a finance group to act as a back-up for the treasurer, principally as book-keepers. This served as an on-going check on our finances. It was also a 'training ground', allowing for the sharing of knowledge and enabling self-styled 'innumerate artists' to find that they are perfectly capable after all.

We paid our rent quarterly in advance but charged ourselves monthly, so we had a cash-flow problem. And we needed to indemnify the trustees against loss, eg see that they didn't have to pay if we all skidaddled. So our deposits were born – an amount to be paid by every member which also served as a hedge against bad debts. Rather than limit new entrants to the well-off, we decided to charge a small lump sum on entry, then collect the rest at so much a month over and above the usual charge until an agreed maximum was reached. This was returnable and of course banked in a separate account. However, a proportion of it had to be left in the number one account to cover these payments in advance.

All this, and a proper accounting system was achieved after both trauma and then practical advice from a member's accountant. We learnt to keep the books, and to implement a workable budget, eg work out what our costs were over a year, divide that into months then share it out amongst each studio, but we never could puzzle out how to produce a balance at the end of the year, a statement of accounts. Just finding out what was in the bank didn't tell us anything – after all, we might be owed

money by members, or have paid the rent in advance, but not yet have collected it, etc. Another member put us in touch with his accountant who became our auditor. This didn't cost us much – it's done out of friendship really – but only because we did all our book-keeping properly.

And what did we do when someone's debt got too much? The committee could throw anyone out for owing one week's rent, but we weren't in existence for that, we were there to help each other function as artists, so we carried debts wherever we could. But the committee has the job of keeping a check and seeking assurance from debtors that the money is on the way. These initial committee warnings later became a standard 'first warning letter' which made it clear that if arrangements weren't made, the matter would have to be taken to the full group. And since it wasn't that clever to throw out someone owing rent and have to cover the loss, we then evolved a system whereby the debtor was, after due warning, suspended for six months and their studio sublet so the debt didn't go on building up. If debtors paid off the rent they could then reapply for their studios.

►Letting◄

I suppose the greatest source of tension and worry, after finance, was letting and sub-letting. At first, it was all fairly haphazard. The 'Rules' stated that the Committee was empowered to select. This was soon amended so that the person who might be sharing had a vote too. Then various problems occurred. Two members of the committee each told separate applicants that they had been successful. Or things were left too late and we all had to find the lost month's rent. Or you might come across someone wandering about the building who had apparently been told they were in – and nobody had been consulted. Gradually procedures evolved, procedures that guaranteed the rights of members and the rights of applicants. Members must know a studio is vacant. They must be informed about the deadline for applications. There must be a form for outsiders to fill in so their application could be kept on file.

Along with this had grown the realisation of just how much we depended on each other – any chain is only as strong as its weakest link. For instance, it was no good taking on people who hadn't the slightest intention of doing their share of the work, or who had no collective sensibility. And, of course, we all wanted worthwhile, interesting artists who would make good use of the space. So applicants' slides and statements were available enabling everyone the opportunity to see them and comment if they wished. And members expected to be informed when selection interviews were going to take place. As many people as possible went along to selections – perhaps half the group at least.

At one time we followed the unwritten principle of a balanced membership – a balance between men and women, between old and young, between painter, sculptors, ceramicists, and other sorts of artists. Later this became written in as a policy statement on equal opportunities.

At one point we had enormous problems over internal applications. This had always been difficult. One person who had hardly used his studio or contributed much to the group left after a better studio space went to someone else – but only after a terrible row with added paranoia and much reference to the rules (a sure sign that suspicion reigns). And that's what was happening on this occasion. Two existing members had applied for a

space. Unfortunately the committee had only short-listed outside applicants. A heavy 'let's-argue- about-interpreting-the-rules' meeting was called. After a complex, but ordered debate, it was confirmed that no-one had a right to a studio, but members had a right to first refusal. At the interviews, the group selected the outsiders. The two members were very slighted and subsequently left the group. This is all very painful – but who wants to remain part of a group that doesn't want you and won't support you?

All of this strains relationships and takes up precious time and energy but whenever the group has sat down together, used its rules, hammered out an understanding and resolved a potentially destructive situation it has emerged each time stronger and more confident as a body.

►Security of Tenure◄

Our tenancy had never been particularly secure. We had always known we were what one of our advisors calls 'caretaker-tenants'. This meant the landlord was happy to let us use the building for a so-called 'low' rent (though really the market price for a building in its condition); the landlord did the absolute minimum repairs (if any), didn't have to pay empty property rates (then double) and knew there was someone keeping an eye on the building, all pending developing the building at the first opportunity into an office block.

◁see **Finding a Studio**▷

Around 1975 we thought we'd had it. The landlord had got rid of the occupants of adjacent buildings and had given us notice. We looked at alternative accommodation. Then they couldn't get planning permission for what they wanted so we were OK for a while again. Not only that, but we were able to take over a further six spaces, making fifteen in all. (These 500 sq ft spaces were mostly shared by two artists). Not everyone wanted to expand. *'Small was beautiful'*. A referendum decided in favour. On balance, a larger group did mean more work – but also more people to do it!

Then, in 1983 we heard that our building was going to be sold. By this time we had met another of these indispensable professionals, a property consultant, who was interested in art, did some painting himself, and eventually became a trustee of our charity. He said why not buy a building. We said don't be crazy, we're only artists. At that time the GLC was making capital grants towards the purchase of buildings. We all subscribed an extra £5 a month to provide campaign expenses. In the end, we didn't make it (the government took away the GLC's right to make such grants) but other groups did succeed. It was an interesting example of how artists lack confidence and undervalue their potential.

►Charitable Status◄

Keeping the cost of studio space as low as possible was always a problem. Ours were comparatively low charges. But, as one member said, only one part of the cost is money. The other 'cost' must be seen in terms of the work one has to contribute. (Which makes it very hard when a member does very little). For many years we had been aware that we could reduce our costs if we became a charity (and therefore pay half rates). After eight years of trying to do it ourselves we hadn't succeeded, even after advice

So the structure of the group is now headed by Barbican Arts Group Trust, which holds the lease and pays the rates; Barbican Arts Group Studios, the association of artists who administer the studio provision for the Trust; and the 'Art Works Project', the promotion of 'public interchange' section, with its Art Works SPACE.

from Artlaw. It wasn't until we met and attracted the voluntary help of a tax lawyer that the Charity Commission agreed to the formation of our charitable trust, which was finally registered in 1984.

Although the initial motive had been cost-reduction, our attempts to attract funds to buy our own building had made us aware that grants and donations were more likely to go to a body that could be seen to function *'for the public benefit'*. And some of us were seeking a better relationship with the public, a relationship that could go beyond the buyer/seller one. We therefore developed the 'Art Works Project' as a means of acting collectively in relation to what happened to our work once it had been made. To start with, we agreed to pay extra (only £2.50 a month) and take over a ground floor studio as an exhibition space. (Artists from Canada who had visited the building in the '70s had been at a loss to know why we hadn't created such an 'off-the-street' gallery space). Around this time, we finally achieved charitable status and thus rates relief. The group agreed to continue paying the same rent, and devote the rates saved to a budget to finance the Art Works Project. Along with the exhibition programme in the Art Works SPACE, we developed an education programme, and tried to initiate various 'outreach' projects to include residencies and a work-in-hospitals scheme. Apart from anything else, we hoped the project could generate paid work for its artists.

The project could only really justify its existence if it could be its own means of attracting funding for its operation – an administrator's salary, for instance. This did not happen and it was hard trying to do all the work necessary on a voluntary basis.

Barbican Arts Group never received funding to pay for administration. Maybe we were slow to take advantage of MSC and other employment schemes. In the end, though, we did everything for ourselves, and were probably the better for it.

We received the occasional small capital grant for things like heaters or rewiring. We dealt with necessary work by paying out of our rates relief money or, more commonly, by contributing effort via 'work-ins'. The group would decide we needed to plaster-board the basement ceilings (for instance). It set a weekend when everyone contributed five hours of their time, or paid a set cash equivalent.

►Art versus Administration◄

Years ago, a Finnish artist who did a lot of work for their artists' association warned me about not becoming too closely identified as an administrator and so lose respect as an artist. After a while it can become a trap. One invests effort and imagination in schemes to benefit artists. Then it becomes a matter of pride to see them succeed. It can mean you go to the studio and spend your time thinking about administration and not about art work.

The group survived. It provided many artists and craftspeople with workspace at low cost. It expanded its provision to include exhibition space and programmes *'to increase knowledge, appreciation and understanding'* of art. But it was always a struggle. Those who have given time and commitment know what a thankless task working for artists can be. An artist's first allegiance is to their work, even if it means exploiting those willing to be exploited. Worst of all, those who are willing to give up their time are probably despised for not being really 'serious' artists. One exploiter told me that the person who had spent a lot of time book-keeping, really preferred doing figures to doing art! The ultimate double-cross.

Another source of difficulty can be the differences between artists. Fine artists can look down on craftspeople, realists feel threatened by abstractionists, expressionists deride realism. It isn't artists who benefit from such divisiveness! Of course, BAG's mixed membership was a matter

of history – maybe if artists were starting from scratch they would form a group of like-minded artists from the outset. But surely what we have in common with each other more than with anyone else, is the wish to be able to make art?

Being a member of a democratic group is much harder work than being told what to do. Working collectively is cheaper but means no action without agreement. Agreeing means understanding the issues. This takes time. Often a few members spend hours discussing and formulating an initiative. They bring it to the group, only to find just how much 'catching-up' everyone else has to do conceptually. For instance, changing from having bi-annual open studio shows to a strategy involving regular individual shows in the Art Works SPACE took at least twelve months to be understood and gain acceptance.

Being part of a studio group has its drawbacks, but the advantages outweigh the disadvantages. A number of artists have more clout, more buying-power, than one – never mind the feeling of common purpose! Above all, it can mean being able to work as an artist. It wouldn't suit everyone. It suited me. I'd do it all again, given the chance.

►Postcript: 1989◄

Now a trustee but no longer a studio-member, I was recently taken to task for being too negative in this 'history'. It may have dwelt on the problems, but I hope the point of doing so was to show that difficulties can be overcome, that artists can work together to provide themselves with workspace – and a good deal more besides. All the efforts I described, all the struggles, were not in vain – they laid the foundation for a strong future.

►Information◄

►Contacts◄

►*Rural Development Commission* (formerly CoSIRA), 14 Castle Street, Salisbury SP1 3TP ☎ 0722 336255 and 11 Cowley Street, London SW1P 3NA ☎ 01 276 6969

►*National Artists Association*. Membership details from 17 Shakespeare Terrace, Sunderland SR2 7JG

►*Association of Artists and Designers in Wales (AADW),* Gaskell Buildings, Collingdon Road, Cardiff CF1 5ES ☎ 0222 407607

►*Association of Scottish Artists*, c/o John McCulloch, 4 Gardner Street, Dundee; Andy Stenhouse, Edinburgh Sculpture Workshop, Albion Business Centre, 78 Albion Road, Edinburgh EH7; John Clark, Glasgow Studios, 85 Hanson Street, Glasgow G31 2HF

►*Printmakers Council*, 31 Clerkenwell Close, London EC1 ☎ 01 250 1927

►*Workshop and Artists Studio Provision Scotland Ltd* (WASPS), 26 King Street, Glasgow G1 5QP ☎ 041 552 0564

►*SPACE*, 6&8 Rosebery Avenue, London EC1R 4TD ☎ 01 278 7795. Runs group studio buildings in London

►*Acme Housing Association*, 15 Robinson Road, Bethnal Green, London E2 9LX ☎ 01 981 6811. Provides living and studio space for artists in London and advice for groups setting up

►Arts councils, Crafts Council and RAAs *see Funding*. The visual arts officer of the appropriate arts council or regional arts association usually holds lists of group studios *see Funding Bodies*

►Further Reading◄

►*How to Obtain and Adapt Buildings for Community Use.* Community Development Section, Liverpool City Council
►'Funding art spaces', Daniel Dahl. *Artists Newsletter*, February 1987
►*The Artist's Studio Management Handbook.* Richard Seddon. Muller, 1983
►'Survey of Printworkshops', Silvie Turner. *Artists Newsletter*, April 1986
►*Survive – the Illustrators Survival Kit.* Association of Illustrators, 1988
►*Running a Workshop – Basic business for craftspeople.* Crafts Council, 1985
►'Artlaw Supplement No 3'. *Artists Newsletter*, February 1983. Deals with legal status of artists' groups, VAT and charitable status
►*Access to Local Government Information – Your Legal Rights and How to Get Them*, R Bailey. Local Government and Health Rights Project
►*Collected Artlaw Articles*, Henry Lydiate, ed Jenny Boswell. Artlaw Services, 1981
►'Wapping Blues', Henry Lydiate, 'Artlaw, *Art Monthly*, May 1983
►*Working for Yourself in the Arts and Crafts*, Sarah Hosking, Kogan Page 1989. See the section on 'Premises'
►*Caution: A Guide to Safe Practice in the Arts & Crafts*, Tim Challis & Gary Roberts. Sunderland Polytechnic 1984
►'Greenhaus Artists Group', Jennie Spiers. *Artists Newsletter*, October 1987
►'Artists Initiatives', Richard Padwick. *Artists Newsletter*, August 1987. Looks at the relationship between artists' groups and local authorities
►'Selling from the Studio', Oliver Bevan. *Artists Newsletter*, July 1989

Financial Support

Funding

▶David Butler◀

▶Introduction◀

Talk to artists about how they are funded and you will discover the oddest and most unexpected of sources. There are the traditional sources such as the arts councils and regional arts associations but, as direct public funding for the arts has become more restricted in terms of size and allocation and as artists have taken on new roles and gained more confidence, other sources of funding have been used. The government's war-cry is sponsorship – the privatisation of arts funding but this has always been a difficult area for the visual arts, particularly for individuals. There are alternatives to the traditional sources – for instance the EEC, local authorities, Department of Trade, Urban Programme, charitable trusts, regional development agencies, co-operative development agencies, tourist boards, British Council, foreign governments and so on.

◁see **Sponsorship**▷
◁see **Sponsorship & Ethics**▷

This chapter examines some of these options, starting with those that are specifically designed for the arts and then looking at other, more general sources.

▶What do you want money for?◀

This question may seem stupidly obvious. It is also vitally important. A potential funder is always going to be asking this question of you, both to assess the value of your project and to evaluate it against others. If the source has not traditionally funded the arts and is assessing your application against others that it, in its unsympathetic view, may see as more 'socially useful' or more 'economically viable' then *you* need to be more careful in asking yourself *'what do I need the money for?'*

Some sources of money have specific criteria which govern how they may be used – for research, marketing, equipment or training for example. Possibly such money is easier to raise since you do not have to persuade anyone to spend it – you just have to persuade them to spend it on you. With other funders you may be starting from scratch. You may be asking them to do something *new*. If *you* are also doing something new then they are going to feel doubly bewildered or suspicious. They will rely on you for some guidance and the keynotes for that will be clarity and confidence on your part. An unsure approach will only create alienation and the likely outcome of that will be a firm and long-lasting '*no*'.

Of course the result of a clear and confident application may also be '*no*' but if you are confident about what you are doing you should be able to see *why* you have been turned down. If you have not been told the reasons it is in your best interests to ask. This will leave you feeling that you can still approach other potential funders with your project or go back with another project on another occasion.

If it is clear to you and others what you want money for, you then have a sound basis for answering the following questions:

- ▶How much money do you need?
- ▶When do you need it?
- ▶What are you offering in return and to whom?

▶How much money do you need?◀

This may seem an obvious question but you need to be specific when asking for money. If you need to fund a project costing £1000 but are only asking for £500, you must show where the rest of the money's coming from. If you discover that your potential funder never gives more than £500 and then only for fees rather than for materials, then make sure your application is for £500 worth of fees and point out that the £500 for materials is being raised elsewhere.

▶When do you need the money?◀

This is as vital as how much you need and will determine whom you approach for money. If you have a deadline after which the project isn't viable, and as some funding is only available at certain times of the year, you must plan well in advance. Some funders will also only pay out against receipts or invoices, or give grants in instalments. You should, therefore, be clear about your cash flow requirements and be sure when you need each grant. You might be able to raise an overdraft on the prospect of getting a grant but as this costs you money, a figure should be included in the overall budget. If you work out a reasonably accurate cash flow projection for the project, this will determine the timetable for fundraising.

▶What are you offering in return?◀

Although you always have something to offer the funder – the satisfaction of helping your worthwhile project – it may be that they want something else, like publicity or political kudos. Find out what the funder expects or wants from you and then decide whether you are prepared or able to give it.

For instance, you may find funding by establishing yourself as a co-operative. But are you prepared to take decisions co-operatively, can you really organise your group that way? These latter questions are far more important than whether you get the money, because they affect what you do with it and how you feel about that. Projects can fail for a variety of reasons but if they fail because you have made false promises or have not thought the project through clearly, then the fault is plainly yours. Failure will inevitably affect future fundraising.

◁see **Co-operatives**▷

▶Track Record◀

A potential funder can also want to know about your 'track record' – what you have done so far. Although you may have never undertaken a project similar to the one you are proposing, your previous experience must have lead you to this point. Even if you don't have a CV full of exhibitions and

residencies, you do have some experience to support your application. Don't hide your light under a bushel, your experience is as worthy as anyone else's.

Of course, the most important collateral you have to support any fundraising is yourself. In 'Looking at Yourself', Carole Pemberton says *'If you don't accept yourself as an equal when dealing with funding bodies, commissioners, or gallery owners, it will have an obvious effect on how you behave with them.'*

◁see **Looking at Yourself**▷

The approach to a funder is another kind of promotion and the advice in the 'Publicity' section on how to organise information and ideas into letters, leaflets, CV and so on and using personal contact applies equally as well here.

◁see **Publicity**▷

Documenting all the work you do is vital. This might be photographs, videos, written reports, keeping a diary, recording other people's responses etc. It is useful to send some kind of a report to a funder on how a project went, whether they ask for it or not. This doesn't need to be extensive. In fact the more concise it is, the more likely it is to be read. The usefulness of this is that it shows that you have used their support effectively and it keeps you in their eye.

►Art Funding Sources◄

The direct government funding for visual arts which is accessible to individual artists is mainly channelled through the Arts Council of Great Britain which in turn allocates funds to the Welsh and Scottish Arts Councils. In Northern Ireland, arts funds are administered by the Arts Council of Northern Ireland. The Crafts Council funds the crafts in England, and in Wales through funding to the Welsh Arts Council. In Scotland, crafts come under the Scottish Development Agency and the Highland and Islands Development Board.

◁see **Funding Bodies**▷

►The crafts in Scotland may soon become the responsibility of the Scottish Arts Council. The SDA and the Highlands and Islands Development Board work in a way similar to the Rural Development Commission – see below◄

Although the Arts Council of Great Britain used to directly fund artists projects – for instance artist-in-schools – they have now devolved most of these functions to the regional arts associations in England.

The Arts Council, however, still offers grants to individuals through the Training Section. The Crafts Council deals directly with individuals through grants for setting up workshops, employing trainees, projects, bursaries, loans and advice. It seems to see its role, however, as promoting 'quality' rather than supporting makers.

◁see **Training**▷

There are twelve regional arts associations in England (and one Buckinghamshire Arts Association is a client of East Midlands Arts). As well as funding from the Arts Council and Crafts Council, they raise funds from the local authorities, sponsorship and the British Film Institute. There are three regional arts associations in Wales which operate schemes for artists. There are no regional arts associations in Scotland.

Local authorities also directly fund visual arts through arts development officers, who may have their own departments or be found in those dealing with libraries, recreation or leisure. A lot of local authority funding for the arts however, comes from other departments such as social services, so they are all dealt with later on.

►RAA Officers◄

Most regional arts associations have officers to deal with particular art

forms (visual arts, crafts, photography etc). These definitions, however, vary from association to association. In some, visual arts and crafts are linked with photography, in others photography is linked with film and video. In some associations, there is a specialist officer for each of visual arts, crafts and photography, in others one officer covers all three. Non-specific functions such as education and marketing may have separate officers and budgets or may be dealt with by each art form officer. This structure is further complicated because it is changing, and will change even more after 1990/91 with the recommendations from an Office of Arts & Libraries review. Some RAAs are getting rid of artform officers and/or artform budgets and will no longer have a visual arts officer or a craft budget. You may, therefore, have several people and artform budget headings to deal with.

What is essential, is to find out how your RAA works. It is fairly easy to discover the bureaucratic structure by asking for a copy of their annual report and any policy or advisory documents. These will explain who the officers are and how to contact them, as well as basic information on priorities, deadlines and schemes for artists. Every association's literature is different – some spell out very clearly the schemes and deadlines, others are more vague and less welcoming. If your work covers several art forms – a sculptor using video and performance for instance – you will need to discuss carefully with the officers to which budget heading an application should be addressed.

You may find some budget headings confusing – rather than an equipment grant or a bursary, some associations will consider your projects as a 'local opportunity' or a 'media' application. The 'invisible' bureaucracy can be time-consuming and it is demoralising to be passed from department to department. One way of minimising this is to do your research well and this includes talking to other artists in your area, although obviously artists have prejudices too.

►Other Support◄

There is a definite trend in the regional arts associations to offer a wide range of back-up and information services. These include slide indexes, marketing advice, reference facilities and 'survival' courses and information sheets. These services will only be developed and improved if artists make demands on them.

▷see **Co-operatives**◁

One photographer approached his RAA about advice with raising funds to market his work through postcard sales in department stores. He came away with £70 *'to buy an enlarger'*, but none the wiser about his project. Eventually, he found what he wanted at a local co-operative development agency. With their help, he carried out a feasibility study which showed that the project would not work in the way he envisaged. This didn't dispirit him because it lead to other possibilities. What was dispiriting though, was the fact that his RAA's information was of little use. When they realised he wanted to work in a co-operative setting, why didn't they direct him to the relevant agency?

This example accentuates the need for all regional arts associations to develop information services which encompass details of funds and support from a wider range of sources and which are responsive to new working patterns.

►Other Funding Sources◄

►Local Government◄

Getting money from local government is to some extent an illogical process. It may not even be clear what channels you should go through and which tier of the local government structure you should be approaching. Certainly, many organisations in London which tried and failed to raise money from a borough council simply went to their county authority instead. There's no guarantee that failure at one level of local government precludes success at another level. And very often the fact that you may have come from one level of local government to another under quite different political control could mean that consideration of your application is influenced by the fact that your application has been turned down by an authority of the opposite political colour. (Ken Livingstone)[1]

Facts and figures can be vital in getting government funding, particularly new funding. Government surveys are prime sources of information, being readily available and having official backing. The main one is the Census. Effective use of census data persuaded Brighton Council to apply for Urban Aid funding. Urban Aid funds projects in areas of urban deprivation and Brighton Council, not considering itself such an area, had never submitted an application. A charity for the single homeless used census data to demonstrate that areas of Brighton suffered in the same way as other areas in receipt of Urban Aid. They persuaded the council to support the application and received funding. Easy enough for a charity for the homeless? Yes – but many arts projects also receive Urban Aid, EEC funding, social services money, etc. Bureaucracy depends on statistics for planning strategy, so use whatever information is available – it proves your project is not 'oddball'! (See *Doing Research*, Directory of Social Change)

Illogical or otherwise, all councils provide arts funding of some kind. Your first problem is identifying who administers it. You may discover an actual 'arts budget' which, when you look further, proves to be useless for you because it's for the museums service to operate their permanent collection. It could prove that social services, recreation and amenities, housing, education, parks, planning, borough architects, engineers and refuse are the departments to try, depending on your project. Or the council may operate a grants sub-committee for all independent applications. Some councils fund semi-autonomous local arts councils or associations, which in turn give out grants to projects.

All council departments have, or can make, budgets for supporting work that may not seem to be directly related to their function. This is for a number of reasons. One is purely administrative – somebody has to look after something. It may seem obvious to a council to allocate mural painting to planning because they are responsible for the walls on which it happens. Another vital reason is that council departments are responsible to the public via the elected members. Public relations is therefore in their interest and art can be a good promotional activity. For the right project, you can use this to your advantage. Alternatively, it can be an integral part of a department's function – eg artist in schools for education, community arts for social services.

As all councils operate differently, you will need to do your research in your area. If you are sure about what you want, don't worry too much about approaching the wrong person: their experience can help you get to the right person. As their job is to respond to public demands, don't be fobbed off. Press your case not only with council officers but also with the elected members – the councillors.

How do you go about this? First, find out the names of councillors and council officers by ringing the council and asking for a list. The information on councillors usually contains not only names and home addresses, but also which Ward they represent and which committees they sit on.

But in order to raise money effectively from local government, you'll need to be clear about which council controls which services in your area.

Since the abolition of the six metropolitan councils and the Greater London Council in 1989, England and Wales have only one tier of local government in the metropolitan areas of Merseyside, Tyne & Wear, Greater Manchester, East and South Yorkshire, West Midlands and Greater London. These are the London Borough Councils and the

▷1 *Raising Money From Government.* Directory of Social Change.

Metropolitan Borough Councils.

Elsewhere in England and Wales, there are two main tiers: the upper tier is the county council, the lower tier the district, city and borough councils. The county council's remit is to support broader-based services such as education and social services and the district council is responsible for those aspects which involve the general well-being of the local district. These two tiers may be supplemented by a third tier of small local councils. In England, these are the parish or town councils and in Wales there are community councils. Scotland's two tiers of local government are divided into an upper tier of regional councils and a lower one of district councils. Although it all sounds very complicated, whatever the name, each operates in a similar way with similar powers.

You can see now the force of Ken Livingstone's statement. The various levels of local government often divide up responsibility for the arts very oddly. Partly it depends upon their statutory structure, partly upon personal interest of officers or councillors, thus you will need to do your own local research.

For instance, you may find your district council is responsible for leisure and sees art as part of that... so you might get support from them for a residency.. but you want to make contact with schools and find the art adviser works for the county council.. but the district council doesn't want to involve the county council so advises direct contact through teachers... but the RAA won't give support unless you involve the art adviser...

So, funding the arts is a political issue and the artist becomes a political lobbyist. Lobbying is simply talking to council officers and members and persuading them to give you support. Councillors expect this to happen so don't be worried about doing it. But find out who is on the right committee, who is favourable to the arts, who is politically powerful, who is your local councillor. Very often, what it takes to stimulate a 'philistine' council is one voice supporting the arts – one person who stands up in committee and ensures your proposal is looked at and not just dealt with 'on the nod'. So cultivate your councillors and not just when you want something. Keep the dozen or so 'interested' ones informed about what you are doing. Invite them to openings, send them press releases and so on.

This also applies to council officers. Strictly speaking, members decide policy and officers implement it, but reality isn't like that. A strong officer will be very powerful. Members will rely upon them for specialist advice. So get them on your side. And feed them with ideas. Planning, for instance, may be very keen on some vague notion of 'public art' but have no fundamental knowledge of visual arts or inspired thinking to crystallise that. You are in a position to give it to them. Or social services will be looking for arts training or workshops but not have you on their list of resources. Let them know what you can do and what facilities you have.

Use officers as well to find out about the written and unwritten rules of council procedure. In the excellent book *Raising Money from Government* which looks at local authority funding from a grant-seeker's, a councillor's and a council official's viewpoint, Harriet Garland makes the following important point:

> Organisation X in Islington applied to the council to fund one salary for a house parent to work in an accommodation project. The salary was nearly £1000 lower than our own council workers get. If the project was to be successful, I felt that it was important that they should be able to pay a realistic salary in order to recruit a good worker and suggested

> that they applied for the money to cover this. They did and they got it with no trouble at all. It is very important, when you are planning your annual work load, to make sure that someone has enough time to research these sorts of facts and figures, whether it is a worker or a member of your management committee.(2)

This advice is for voluntary bodies – a studio group can be counted as a voluntary body. Voluntary organisations are often a good source of information about your local authority and there's usually a local forum for voluntary bodies, like the Council for Voluntary Services.

Harriet Garland advises people to *'spend as much time as you can getting to know how the council works'* but maybe it is easier to get to know someone who knows how the council works.

►Funding in Kind◄

Local authorities have, in some senses, far greater potential than other funders in that they control larger and more varied resources. Not only can they provide direct funding, they can also provide transport, labour, materials (wood from parks, scrap from refuse), printing and mailing facilities, buildings (possibly their most useful resource for artists?) and support for other funding applications.

When looking for studio space, the council is an important source of information about empty buildings. If they are concerned about buildings standing empty they could also be of help in persuading landlords to rent to you. If they actually *own* the building then they may offer it to you. And a cheap lease on a council building, if you can negotiate it, could prove to be a more secure form of long-term funding than any revenue grant. They can, at present, also give you discretionary rates relief.

▷see **Studios**◁

You need to be imaginative when approaching councils. As with other funders, you need to discover what they are interested in and, provided those interests are common with yours, make an approach accordingly. Having formed some relationship, make use of it in other ways. A council that is interested in public art may help to persuade the organisers of large, private building projects (eg a shopping precinct) to make use of local artists.

►Besides Money?◄

A lot of organisations are useful for reasons besides money. Organisations such as co-operative development agencies, initially are useful for advice and later may develop into funding sources. Or an area museums service, for instance, can be a good source of plinths, cases, boards, lights etc for exhibitions. A local voluntary group may be useful because you can put leaflets into their mailings for free. You have to search these kind of contacts out and be creative in using them. This is all part of seeking funding because it saves you money.

> Section 111 of the 1972 Local Government Act gives a local authority the power to do anything which is intended to facilitate the discharge of any of their statutory functions or is **conducive or incidental to this**, whether or not it involves the expenditure of money, the borrowing or lending of money, the purchase or disposal of property or rights, the provision of materials and supplies, the giving of advice, the secondment of staff, or whatever.(3)

So make use of those powers.

►Urban Development Corporations◄

Possibly the most far-reaching result of Thatcherism has been the transfer of powers from local authorities to central government, the 'privatisation' of local democracy by putting out services (like refuse collection) to outside contractors, and the transfer of powers to quangos – bodies whose members are selected but not elected.

The urban development corporations have the authority to take over the planning and urban programme allocations for the geographical areas they cover and, starting in London, have taken over vast areas of riverside urban 'decay' and developed them into marinas, tourist attractions, high-

▷3 *Raising Money from Government*

class accommodation and offices. In the process, they have dispossessed a great many artists of affordable studio space. At the same time they have put their own funding, and persuaded developers to put more, into the arts.

Urban Development Corporations have contributed to the placing of art and artists in a wide range of public sites. In Liverpool, the first Garden Festival was set up, and this incorporated an extensive sculpture programme. A social development award from the London Docklands Development Corporation enabled the Whitechapel Art Gallery to extend its artists in schools programme to the Docklands area. The Tyne & Wear Development Corporation contributes to local arts festivals as well as commissioning work from Freeform Arts Trust, including a major feasibility design survey for the Fishquay area of North Shields which will create public art and landscaping opportunities for artists. In Birmingham, the Public Art Commissions Agency is working with the UDC on commissions for gateways and artworks for a waterlinks scheme in the Birmingham Heartlands.

The interests of the UDCs are broad and they can provide funds both for projects and capital costs. They are a new element to the funding pattern and artists can play them against the regional arts associations and local authorities but....

►because they are government appointed, they are politically sensitive – deal with a UDC and your local authority may cut you out!
►they are market-lead, have no long-term strategy and deal primarily with development – buildings, roads, facilities etc
►their arts budgets and policies will be separate from their main role as developers and as such, be secondary to it
►they are undemocratic and therefore difficult to lobby. But it is easier to get straight answers from their staff

A UDC has a limited life and the government has no plans to increase the number of them. Once they have realised their objectives, they will be wound up, leaving everything they've set up in private hands. If you think that UDCs can help your projects, make your overtures quickly!

▷Urban Development Corporations◁
The first two UDCs, in Docklands and Merseyside, were set up in 1981, followed in 1987 with corporations in Trafford Park, Teesside, Tyne & Wear and the Black Country. Four 'mini-UDCs' were established in 1988 in Bristol, Manchester, Sheffield and Leeds. Part of the Merseyside and Docklands Corporations will be handed back to local authority planning control in 1990..

The first sculpture to be commissioned by Trafford Park Development Corporation was carved on site at the Ecology Park over a four-week period by sculptor **David Haigh** who used six tons of York stone to create *10 Stones*. This was the artist's first major public commission and he worked in conjunction with Partnership Art Ltd, a team of environmental artists who specialise in working with private developers, architects and the community. This is the first forerunner of several pieces for the development corporation, in a scheme organised in conjunction with landscape consultants Gillespies.

►Central Government◄

On the whole, central government is not a good funding source and it is certainly a difficult one to tap, and in any case, they may only be appropriate for groups. The Department of Education and Science project-funds local organisations through the Youth Service Unit. The Department of the Environment will fund inner city arts projects through Urban Programme. Both of these have to be approached via your local council. The Department of Trade and Industry funds business development and this can include arts projects, particularly via their Enterprise Initiative scheme. You can contact them via your local Enterprise Agency. Note that the DES and DoE funding will be linked to training, maybe even the creation of jobs, and the DTI funding is strictly linked to business development. This is very specific funding, but it can. and has been used by arts projects and artists.

►Enterprise Initiative◄
This scheme offers businesses access to information on marketing, design, manufacturing systems, business planning and financial and information systems. In Assisted or Urban Programme Areas there are grants available for capital and development initiatives.

►The European Community◄

The EC, like central government, is a funding source for groups rather than individuals. It is often approached via local councils and their Economic

Development Officers. Both the European Social Fund (ESF) and the Youth Initiatives Programme are tied in with training and employment. There is a Regional Development Fund which is operated in a similar way to the Rural Development Commission. None of these sources are arts-specific but the European Cultural Foundation is. This gives money to projects that involve three or more European countries, although they don't normally fund more than 50% of costs.

▶Rural Development Commission◀

Like the Department of Trade and Industry, the Rural Development Commission is intended to support business, although it has a particular interest in the crafts. The commission was formed in 1988 as an amalgamation of the Council for Small Industries in Rural Areas (CoSIRA) and the Development Commission. There are 28 rural development areas covering the North, the East coast, the Welsh borders and the West Country. The commission has 31 offices, each of which has business advisers and which operate a variety of services.

One of the RDC's objectives is to help small firms to become more successful and their business service provides not only business advice but skill training and some loan schemes. Although it expects the major part of funding a project to come from other sources, the RDC's loan fund is available to finance part of a project's costs, up to a maximum of £75,000. In some circumstances, in rural development areas only, grants are available towards the cost of converting unused buildings into workshops. In all areas, grants are available to cover 50% of the cost of taking a stand at a trade show or exhibition (up to £500), or towards the cost of hiring a consultant to plan a marketing strategy (up to £1000).

▶Further Education◀
A body like the Workers' Education Authority or a local college could be interested in funding workshops as part of an exhibition or residency. This is not because they want to put money into your project but because it fits in with what they are already doing. They are always worth contacting to see if there is a way of working together. The WEA is often interested in having arts representatives sit on its committee – so you can then influence policy.

▶Training Agency◀

The Training Agency, formerly MSC and the Training Commission, controls the Youth Training Scheme (YTS), Employment Training (ET) and the Enterprise Allowance Scheme (EAS). The most useful of these to an individual artist is the latter and this is dealt with separately. YTS and ET are schemes that allow organisations to take on trainees. For YTS, the employer makes a contribution to the trainees wages, and this is obviously cheaper than paying the full amount. You may have serious moral or political objections to using either of these schemes, but if you are serious about giving training and providing employment for more than a year, they could prove a useful support both for you and the trainee. Most people's experience of YTS and ET, however, is that they provide neither training nor employment but are merely a means of 'unregistering' the unemployed.

▷see **Enterprise Allowance Scheme**◁

▷Contact the Crafts Council to check on their trainee awards.◁

▶Charitable Trusts◀

These are charities which distribute money according to the guidelines outlined in their trust deeds and funds are administered by trustees. Some trusts have tightly defined objects which means that they can only distribute money to a limited range of activities, whilst others have much wider briefs.

Some trusts offer open schemes – for instance the Leverhulme Trust which provides study and research fellowships, the Calouste Gulbenkian Foundation who in 1989 solicited applications for 'large projects or events' and the Winston Churchill Memorial Trust which advertises annually for

▷see **Abroad**◁

applications for its travel awards open to everyone regardless of their educational or academic background.

Although dealing with a trust should be similar to dealing with any other funding body, it is often more complicated in that you need to be sure to make the right application to the right trust at the right time. Some trusts provide annual reports, guidelines or other helpful information for prospective applicants, whereas others might not even bother to acknowledge an application if it falls outside their terms of reference. It is, therefore, particularly important to check out which trusts are supporting the sort of project you are planning. Useful background information can be gained from the network of Charity Information Bureaux which compile and disseminate information on local and national grant-making trusts. In some areas, the local Council for Voluntary Services provides the same function.

Note, however, that charitable trusts can usually only distribute grants to other charitable organisations and if your group or organisation is not a charity, grants would need to be channelled through a regional arts association or another charitable body.

Julia Conibeer went straight on to the Government-backed Graduate Enterprise Programme once she had graduated from Camberwell School of Art in 1989. The course, which ran from July 10-September 29, involved two three-day and one fourteen-day residential blocks held at a college in Chelmsford. The course lectures, which ran from 9am to 8pm, covered a wide range of business practice including communication, law, marketing, promotion, business plans, bookkeeping, contracts and financial control. During the course, she received a £500 grant to undertake individual research into markets, customers and competition for her work, talking to shops, craft workshops and galleries. She also received Income Support whilst doing it and £10 week as the course forms part of the Employment Training schemes. She applied whilst still at college and attended two preliminary sessions before being offered one of the 40 places – open to graduates in all fields – available for her region. Over 400 people applied.

The course has given her confidence to set up a successful business and to promote herself '*as a businesswoman who is an artist*.' She has handled all the publicity and promotion for an exhibition at the Treske Shop in London and also plans to set up in a studio in South London in the near future. A bi-product of the course is a substantial set of reference books covering all aspects of running a business, back-up sheets for the residential courses plus information on grants and other incentives for small businesses. For further information contact: England – Cranfield School of Management ☎ 0234 751122, Scotland – Stirling University ☎ 0786 73171, Wales – St David's University College ☎ 0570 422351. Designers should contact LENTA, 4 Snow Hill, London EC1A 2DL ☎ 01 236 3000. Illustrated are porcelain landscape vessels.

▶Information◀

▶Contacts◀

▶*Directory of Social Change*, Radius Works, Back Lane, London NW3 1HL ☎ 01 435 8171. Send for their invaluable publications list

▶*British Tourist Authority and English Tourist Board*, Thames Tower, Black's Road, Hammersmith, London W6 9EL ☎ 01 846 9000

▶*Rural Development Commission* (formerly CoSIRA), 14 Castle Street, Salisbury SP1 3TP ☎ 0722 336255 and 11 Cowley Street, London SW1P 3NA ☎ 01 276 6969

▶*British Council*, Fine Art Department, 11 Portland Place, London W1N 4EJ ☎ 01 930 8466 ext 3043

►*BFI Production Division*, 29-35 Rathbone Street, London W1P 1AG ☎ 01 636 5587

►*Scottish Film Council*, Downhill, 74 Victoria Crescent, Glasgow G12 7GN ☎ 041 334 9314

►*Arts Development Association*, Vane Terrace, Darlington DL3 7AX ☎ 0325 465930. An amalgamation, in 1989, of the National Association of Arts Centres and the National Association of Local Arts Councils. Bi-monthly magazine *Local Arts UK* plus publications and events

►*Workers Education Authority* (WEA), check telephone directories for local offices

►*See also Enterprise Allowance Scheme contacts*

►Government◄

►*Minister for the Arts*, Office of Arts and Libraries, Great George Street, London SW1P 3AL ☎ 01 233 3073

►*Central Office of Information*, Hercules Road, London SE1 7DU ☎ 01 928 2345

►*Department of Education and Science*, Elizabeth House, York Road, London SE1 7PH

►*Department of the Environment*: Sport and Recreation Division, 6th Floor, Romney House, 43 Marsham Street, London SW1 3PY ☎ 01 276 3000 and Urban Programme, 2 Marsham Street, London SW1P 3EB ☎ 01 212 3434

►*Department of Trade and Industry*, 1-19 Victoria Street, London SW1H 0ET ☎ 01 215 5604

►*General Register Office, Scotland*, Ladywell House, Ladywell Road, Edinburgh EH12 7TF ☎ 031 334 0380

►*General Register Office, Northern Ireland*, Oxford House, 49-55 Chichester Street, Belfast BT1 4HL ☎ 0232 235211

►*EEC Directorate General for Information, Communication and Culture*. British office at 8 Storey Gate, London SW1P 3AT ☎ 01 222 8122

►Trusts◄

►*Carnegie UK Trust*, Comely Park House, Dunfermline, Fife KY12 7EJ ☎ 0383 21445

►*Leverhulme Trust*, Lintas House, New Fetter Lane, London EC4 ☎ 01 822 5252

►*Calouste Gulbenkian Foundation*, 98 Portland Place, London W1N 4ET ☎ 01 636 5313

►*Prince's Youth Business Trust*, 8th Floor, Melbury House, Melbury Terrace, London NW1 6LZ ☎ 01 262 1340

►Further Reading◄

►*The Wales Funding Handbook*, Clive Smithers. Wales Council for Voluntary Action 1988

►*CAFE (Creative Activity for Everyone)*, 23-5 Moss Street, Dublin 2, Ireland. Irish funding handbook published in 1989

►*Facts About the Arts 2*, John Myerscough. Policy Studies Institute, 1986

►*Cultural Trends*, a quarterly database of arts statistics. Policy Studies Institute

►*Directory of Grant Making Trusts.* Charities Aid Foundation

►*The Arts of Ethnic Minorities – Status and Funding.* Council for Racial Equality

►*Arts Address Book*, ed Peter Marcan. Peter Marcan Publications 1989, 31 Rowliff Road, High Wycombe, Bucks. A comprehensive national and international listing of arts organisations

►*Guide to Awards and Schemes*, Arts Council of Great Britain

►Crafts Council Publications: *Grants and Loans* – general leaflet on what's available and when to apply, *Setting Up Scheme, Advanced Training Scheme, Workshop Assistant Scheme, Grants or Guarantees Against Loss for Special Projects, Bursaries*

►*Schemes of Assistance in the Visual Arts.* Scottish Arts Council

►*Advice to Applicants for Grants.* Calouste Gulbenkian Foundation

►*Your guide to our employment, training and enterprise programmes.* Department of Employment and the Training Agency. A leaflet on government loans, grants and 'employment' schemes

►'An Innovatory Project – Grants from the EEC Social Fund', Susan Jones. *Artists Newsletter*, June 1985

►*Grants and Loans from the European Community.* EEC Directorate General for Information, Communication and Culture

►*Fund Raising Notes.* Directory of Social Change

►*The London Grants Guide*, ed Nicola Parker & John Stephen. Directory of Social Change, 1989

►*Raising Money from Trusts.* Ibid

►*Raising Money from Government.* Ibid

►*Raising Money from Industry.* Ibid

►*Industrial Sponsorship and Joint Promotions.* Ibid

►*A Guide to the Major Trusts.* Ibid

►*Arts Funding Guide 1989*. Ibid

►*Reading Guide to Marketing and Fundraising.* Arts Council, 1988

►*Directory of Enterprise Agencies.* Available from Business in the Community, 227a City Road, London EC1V 1LX and Scottish Business in the Community, Romano House, 43 Station Road, Corstorphine, Edinburgh EH12 7AF ☎ 031 334 9876. Listing the UK agencies which encourage new business

►*Finance for New Projects in the UK: A guide to government grants.* Peak Marwick, Mitchell.

►*Funding Digest*, published regularly by RTI with up-to-date information on new sources of money and sponsorship. Usually held by arts councils, regional arts associations and other information resources

►*Raising Money for Women*, Marion Bowman & Michael Norton. Bedford Square Press 1989

►*But is it legal? Fundraising and the Law*, Sally Cooper. Ibid

►*Opening the Town Hall Door: an introduction to Local Government*, Jane Hutt. Ibid

Enterprise Allowance

►Bill Laws◄

◄First printed in *Artists Newsletter* May 1989.►

Ten per cent of people currently on the government's Enterprise Allowance Scheme are artists and authors. Now nearly six years old, EAS could, perhaps, be put up for an informal award as arts patron of the decade.

There was a time when the weekly giro met many an artist's needs. (Who else was going to pay the rent, grocery and tobacco bills while one toiled to develop one's art.) The Arts Council of Great Britain's assistance to individual artists palled into insignificance when set alongside the paltry but sustainable contribution made by the Department of Health and Social Security over the years. But while the government happily tolerates income tax evasion (I'm sorry – tax avoidance) it shows no similar inclination towards the philosophy of welfare benefits as a safety net for the impoverished. Claimant artists may soon have to pass on their studios to someone more upwardly mobile and join the ranks of those sheltering beneath Westminster Bridge.

►Self-Reliance◄

EAS is a canny notion. Its protagonists claim it to be a cheap smoke-screen for concealing unemployment figures while the powers that be see in it the ideal system for weaning claimants off the state. As the then Employment Secretary Norman Fowler told celebrants at the EAS birthday party in 1988: *'The scheme has helped to replace dependency with self reliance.'* Whichever way you look at it, it works.

Four years ago I sat in a lecture room in the Droitwich job centre and prepared to become the master of my own destiny. With such a momentous future before me, I was actually worrying over more mundane issues: would they pay my travel expenses in cash (they wouldn't); might they balk at the idea of funding someone to write (they didn't).

There were 20 or so of us there, all itching to fill in our final forms and identify the date set to start up our own business. And all male. In 1985 only 16% of participants were women. By December 1988 the figure had risen to just over 32%.

Despite the patronising air of the officials, it was a relatively easy ride. Job Centres do not go in for the cattle market architecture of the dole office and the pen pushers aren't howling for humiliation like their brothers and

sisters at the Department of Social Security. If we had fallen for the Thatcher bribe of £40 a week for the next twelve months, no-one felt too bad about it.

A year later I returned to the unemployment office to re-establish my rights to a regular giro. After waiting one and a half hours amidst the familiar squalor and misery I gave up. I've never been back since. (Neither have I written my second book or a line of poetry. The urgent business of earning a living is a time-consuming priority.)

▶Eligibility◀

EAS gives former claimants £2000 spread over a year and eligibility rests more on the applicant's status than the nature of the business:

▶In their leaflet *Action for Jobs* (EAS T02), the Training Agency says that *'If you think raising £1000 may be a problem, please ask us as we may be able to refer you to sources of advice on how to raise the money'.*◀

▶The applicant must be in receipt of benefit, whether unemployment or income support.
▶They must register for unemployment for eight weeks (although people on invalidity benefit can apply, as can those who have spent time on rehabilitation or youth training schemes).
▶Other rules include the requirement to work at least 36 hours a week (checking procedures are hazy), being over 18 and under 65 and having access to £1000.

The business must not have started trading and is supposed to be able to stand on its own feet (ie not be dependent on sub-contracting work) and be *'suitable for public support.'* A print shop run by the National Front and a Welsh brothel for example both had their EAS funding withdrawn once the true nature of the business was revealed. Life painters may take note that businesses which threaten to bring the scheme into disrepute include those which *'involve nude modelling'.*

The list of cautious conditions is lengthy but reality, as it so often turns out, is different. In its early days, artists creatively concealed their occupations under the guise of graphic designer, visual aids consultant or three-dimensional engineer. Many of those I spoke to four years ago nervously refused to be quoted for fear of having their EAS withdrawn. They need not have worried. Artists and authors are now statistically listed in Department of Employment figures. By the end of last year, 10% of the businesses were arts based and the Department of Employment's press officer pointed me towards landscape artist Peter van Breda as their pet example.

▶In Practice◀

Van Breda ditched a career with the Sussex police to go on to EAS as a painter. It was a success. Twelve months after his allowance finished, he still rides round the countryside on a pushbike, sketching the landscapes which he reworks in acrylics and oils at his Brighton studio.

'I think it is tremendous; you need a basic income if you want to be an artist and the facility is there with EAS. I worried that being an artist might cause problems – one week you might have little or no work, another day you could be up till 3.00am – but no-one quibbled about the hours'.

►Financial Support◄

►You are entitled to a number of free advice sessions from the Small Firms Advisory Service after you have set up on EAS. The usefulness of this, however, depends on who you get. In Scotland and Wales, the advice comes from the Scottish and Welsh Development Agencies. The Welsh Development Agency has recently appointed three craft advisors specifically because of their understanding of craft practice.◄

He undertook an EAS book keeping course which gave him the basics in maintaining a double ledger system of debits and credits and for two years has done his own accounts. *'I had a problem over petrol since at the end of the EAS year I'd only recorded work journeys; the tax office told me I should have recorded all journeys and then negotiated with them over what proportion could count as business. The way round that is to talk to the tax people at the beginning of your year instead of the end.'*

►The Banks◄

Joining EAS supposedly involves collecting £1000 before you can pass 'Go'. Van Breda went to his local Lloyds Bank, taking along some of his work and the manager obligingly gave him an overdraft facility of £1000 and allowed him free banking for the year.

No budding EAS artist should expect to produce £1000 in used bank notes at the interview; the scheme merely requires the participant to have *'access to £1000 to invest in their new business.'*

The banks still seem to be wooing EAS custom and most will provide a secured overdraft facility (which need never be used) for the £1000. A spokesman for the National Westminster Bank, which reckons to have more EAS customers than any other bank, said they normally gave free banking as long as the business turnover was under £100,000 (be careful how you price your work!) They have also established a network of small business advisors in *'nearly every high street branch'* who provide a free service.

Peter James from Birmingham persuaded his bank to match a £500 exhibitions grant from West Midlands Arts for the qualifying £1000.

►Funding Cushion◄

►The Prince's Youth Business Trust gives grants of up to £1000 to people under 25 who are setting up in business. The Trust tends to fund individuals or partnerships. Low-interest loans of up to £5000 are also available. Applications are usually submitted through a Youth Enterprise Agency. Lucky recipients may be invited for a royal handshake!◄

James, who runs the Birmingham Photographic Heritage Project, was on the dole when he was trying to finish a dissertation in the History of Art and Design. He used EAS as *'a funding cushion'*. In common with many artists who have been signing on before, he found the £40 a week inadequate. For a start, he was told nothing about the national insurance exclusion clause. If you expect your profits (that is income less expenses) to be below £2500, the DSS will issue you a discretionary small earnings exemption certificate on form N127A) *'That, together with difficulty over housing benefit, made me worse off than when I was drawing dole.'* James was further restricted by the amount of outside work he could do; while artists often supplement their incomes with outside work, under the EAS you'are supposed to do no more than eight hours. (The solution here is to make your business description wide enough to encompass a wide source of earnings).

As James was coming to the end of his EAS, he was already facing a familiar dilemma: Is there life after EAS? *'I'm caught between two stools – I've almost enough sponsorship for an exhibition but it takes more than a year to get this up and running, to get in with the local arts constituency and agencies. I could either try staying self-employed which will be a struggle or go back on the dole.'*

►Second Year◄

Anyone who has done EAS before and is now signing on can apply for a second year's funding. To qualify they have to fulfill the usual conditions as well as having a year's gap between their previous EAS, have no fraud convictions during their EAS year, have no undischarged debts and not have lost their previous EAS through a breach of conditions.

Deborah Jones, a sculptor at Cardiff Sculpture Workshop is three quarters through her second year on EAS. *'One of the most marked differences second time round is that I had to wait three months before getting housing benefit. First time round they simply accepted my income as £40 a week but this time they wanted three months of accounts before they allowed it.'*

Jones, who does large scale woodcarvings, keeps her own accounts *'with some useful advice from Cardiff Citizens Advice Bureau.'* She found EAS staff more helpful back in 1985 than now and still finds EAS business

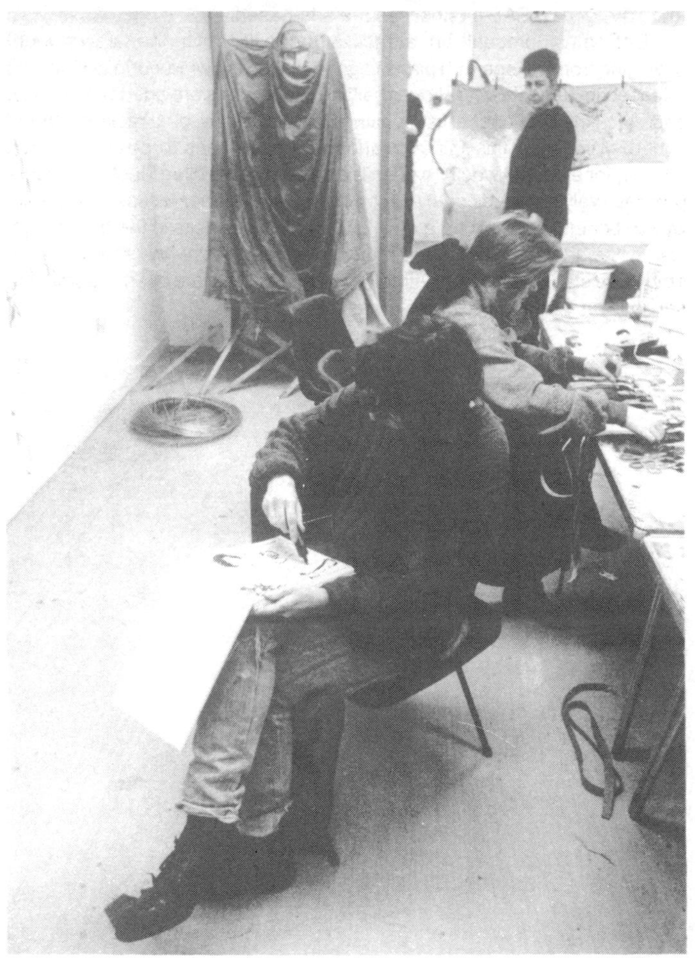

►Sally Sedgwick first went on EAS as an 'artist/teacher' and ran workshops, seminars and school projects, taught in adult education, for polytechnics and unemployed centres whilst at the same time researching a book on women artists in the 20th century. She found that EAS wasn't geared to her need to make and exhibit her own work and to generate the publicity necessary to establish her practice. When several prospective income sources fell through unexpectedly at the beginning of the educational year, her business encountered difficulties and she could not continue as self-employed without the EAS safety net. After a year, however, she reapplied and was accepted for EAS as a 'hand papermaker'. Illustrated is a women's workshop at the Laing Art Gallery, Newcastle upon Tyne. Photo: Liz Hadwin.◄

advice service of little direct relevance to the arts world. *'The EAS people are not there to give any value judgement on the success of your business venture; I think artists find this prohibitive.'*

Will she rejoin the dole queue at the end of her second term? Figures from the Department of Employment reveal that 74% of new businesses were still trading eighteen months after start up. No figures were available to show how many of the crashed businesses were arts-based. But overall, 65% were still trading after three years, an improvement on the old rule of thumb which put the small business failure rate at around two in three.

► More Places Available ◄

The number of people who have taken EAS has been rising steadily; 60,000 in 85/86, 106,305 in 87/88 and the government still likes the scheme. They have made 90,000 places available in the coming year and anticipate no waiting list for the aspiring small business person. It seems that 10% of new EAS businesses are arts-based.

► see **Employment Status** ◄

EAS must present an attractive proposition for the arts student emerging from college with plans to go it alone in the wide world and figures released in 1989 show that over half the participants are aged between 25 and 44. Any working artist looking for a change of direction should seriously consider this £2000 platform as the means to do it. A portrait painter, for example who has seen the safety-net of college lecturing hours progressively reduced could sign on during the summer recess, claim eight weeks benefit and start up a new EAS funded business in the autumn as, say, a fine arts consultant. And many potential clients who used to require employee status of their part-time workers are now more open to accepting services on a freelance basis.

►Information◄

►Contacts◄

►*Small Firms Service*. To contact your nearest, dial 100 and ask for Freefone Enterprise

►*Prince's Youth Business Trust*, 8th Floor, Melbury House, Melbury Terrace, London NW1 6LZ ☎ 01 262 1340. Provides finance for young people under 26 in the form of grants or loans

►*Instant Muscle Ltd*, 112 Burnham Lane, Slough SL1 6LZ ☎ 06286 63926. Provides business advisers to help young unemployed people to set up in business

►*Livewire UK Office*, 60 Grainger Street, Newcastle upon Tyne NE1 5JG ☎ 091 261 5584. Provides cash awards to support 16-25 year olds to create their own work

►Further Reading◄

►*See Funding*

►'The Enterprise Allowance Scheme', Brian Lewis. *Artists Newletter*, February 1985

►'Enterprise Allowance Scheme – A Means to an Active End', Nick Clements. *Artists Newsletter*, June 1984

►'A Baby Carrot', Marie Hillcoat. *Artists Newsletter*, June 1985

►'Payment to Artists', Sheila Hayward. *Artists Newsletter*, February 1989

Benefit

▶David Butler◀

Benefits, from Income Support to Enterprise Allowance, are paid to you on the basis that either you are not earning or you are earning very little. That also provides a very adequate description of the finances of most artists, which is why benefit is probably the largest state support for artists even though it is not recognised as such.

With the exception of Enterprise Allowance, when you apply for state benefit you are not applying as an artist. You cannot even register as unemployed as an artist (although an actor can do this when 'resting'). You are applying as someone who qualifies under the relevant rules and is therefore entitled to benefit. You may find though that being an artist confuses this – you are not available for work, you are working but not earning or, you have received a grant to buy materials etc. The only way to sort out such problems is to seek help from your local advice centre or Citizens Advice Bureau (go to the library or use the telephone directory to get addresses and telephone numbers). In this chapter are described the main benefits available and how they can be used. It doesn't, however, give any figures as these change and current figures can be found in leaflet NI 196 *Social Security Benefit Rates*.

Applying for benefit is governed mainly by necessity and partly by choice. That is no different from anything else you do, but two points are important to make. One is that benefit, including Enterprise Allowance, is neither a reliable nor a desirable method of arts funding. Reliance on benefit has been forced upon us by a chronic shortage both of state and private support for practising artists. The other is that benefit is not charity. You have a right to claim it, and you pay for that right through direct and indirect taxation and National Insurance Contributions. Being an artist does not deprive you of that right. If you are deprived of it, this is because of the meanness of a government which consistently deprives many citizens of their rights. As a committed artist you should not be standing in the dole queue at all. You should be able to practice your art in a community which values that practice and gives it the support it deserves.

▶Status◀

You can claim benefit whether you are employed, self-employed or unemployed. The basic criteria governing the type and amount of benefit

due to you are whether you are available for work, how many hours you work and how much you earn. The main distinction is between earning and not earning.

►Earning◄

Income can be from employment or self-employment or a mixture of both and includes money from Enterprise Allowance. You can claim the following benefits:

►Family Credit◄

This is a bit like a family railcard in that you have to have a child to make use of it, but the child doesn't need to be yours, though they have to live with you as a *'member of your household'*.

You can claim Family Credit as a single parent or as a couple, but if you are a couple it has to be a heterosexual relationship and the woman must claim. At least one person has to be working a minimum of 24 hours a week and this can be employed, self-employed or both. If you are self-employed, your income will either be assessed on a year's accounts prepared by a chartered or certified accountant, or on your gross receipts less expenses for the 26 weeks prior to your claim. You can claim Family Credit whilst on Enterprise Allowance. Students in full-time education qualify if they have a partner who works at least 24 hours a week but most of their grant income is taken into account.

What you receive is the maximum credit less a proportion of the difference between your earnings and a statutory figure called the *'applicable amount'*. You will receive that amount for 26 weeks whatever happens to your income. You then have to reapply and be reassessed. You can be asked to pay back any overpayments and, if your income drops, you can also apply for Income Support.

►Housing Benefit◄

You have to apply to the local council for Housing Benefit which is a means-tested support for the house or flat you are living in and is payable towards rent, rates or community charge (poll tax) but it doesn't cover mortgage interest repayments. You can claim it on top of Family Credit and Income Support. If you live and work in the same premises and run into problems, consult an advice centre.

►Other Benefits◄

Most other benefits are related to the kind of National Insurance Contributions you have made and these are different for employed and self-employed people.

►Benefit	Employed	Self-employed	Both
►Sickness benefit	Yes	Yes	Yes
►Statutory sickpay	Yes	No	Yes
►Invalidity benefit	Yes	No	Yes
►Statutory maternity pay	Yes	No	Yes
►Maternity allowance	Yes	Yes	Yes
►Retirement pension	Yes	Yes	Yes
►Widow's benefits	Yes	Yes	Yes
►Unemployment benefit	Yes	No	Yes

▶Not Earning◀

This includes people who are working less than 24 hours a week. You can claim:

▶Income Support◀

This is means-tested. It includes payments for yourself and family and accommodation costs like mortgage interest repayments not covered by Housing Benefit (see above). You can claim this while you are getting Family Credit or unemployment benefit or if you are working part-time or are unemployed.

▶Unemployment benefit◀

This is not means-tested. You qualify for it by having the right number of Class 1 National Insurance Contributions and being available for work. You receive a statutory amount and can claim other benefits on top of that. It only lasts for a year.

▶Housing Benefit◀

The same conditions apply as under 'Earning'.

▶Available for work◀

A prime requisite of being recognised as unemployed and therefore in receipt of benefit is that you are available for and actively seeking work. If you spend every waking hour in the studio then are you available for work? If you say that you will take any work offered and can be contacted to be offered work, then you could argue that you are *available for work*. But are you *actively seeking work?* If you are applying for jobs then yes, but could you argue that in pursuing your art work in the studio and trying to sell it you can also be actively seeking work?

One way of getting around this is, of course, to keep quiet about what you do. This puts you in a very difficult position with the Department of Social Security. Who could prosecute you for fraud. In practice, it may be difficult for them to do this, particularly if you are working at home. But if you are renting a studio, then you have made a commitment to work, and that can be checked on. (Artists' studios have been the subject of spot checks by DSS personnel in the past). The easiest way to claim benefit whilst continuing to work in the studio is to join the Enterprise Allowance Scheme.

►Information◄

►Further Reading◄

►*Collected Arlaw Articles*, ed Jenny Boswell. Artlaw Services, 1981
►*Welfare Benefits Advisory Service*, leaflets and information sources. Central Regional Council, Department of Social Work
►'Working on Supplementary Benefit', Henry Lydiate. *Art Monthly*, March 1985
►*Self-employed? – a guide to your National Insurance and Social Security benefits*, leaflet FB 30 from the DHS
►*Social Security Benefit Rates*, leaflet NI 196 from the DHS
►*Cash help while you're working*, leaflet FB4 from the DHS
►*Unemployed – A guide to benefits to make ends meet*, leaflet FB9 from the DHS
►*Which Benefit?*, leaflet FB2 from the DHS
►*A guide to Family Credit*, booklet NI 216 from the DHS
►*Statutory Sick Pay – check your rights*, booklet NI 244 from the DHS
►*A guide to Maternity Benefits*, booklet NI 17A from the DHS
►*Sickness Benefit*, booklet NI 16 from the DHS

Co-operatives

▶Susan Jones◀

▷see **Trading Status**◁

National statistics show that co-operatively-run businesses have a success rate comparable to that of conventional small businesses, although this to some extent reflects the extensive support structures available to co-ops through the co-operative development agencies. Also, it seems that whilst the high street banks have to write of between 40-60% of debts from new businesses over three years, the ICOF (Industrial Common Ownership Finance) loan scheme reckons on a write-off of only 10-15% for co-ops.

▶Resources◀

England has, as well as the national Co-operative Development Agency, a network of 100 co-operative development agencies. There are separate agencies for Scotland, Wales and Northern Ireland. Through these organisations, advice and support is available to prospective and established co-operatives.

The government plans, however, to abolish the national Co-operative Development Agency and, it seems, co-ops are no longer 'fashionable' in their eyes. The factors which generated the growth of co-ops in 1980 to 1986 have begun to disappear. Although unemployment is still high, it is falling and the local authorities, supporters of co-operative ventures, are now less influential through rate-capping and government restrictions on how they can use their money.

▶Structure◀

A co-operative differs from a normal business structure in that it is collectively owned and controlled by the people who work in it. Decision-making is not the responsibility of someone 'at the top' but shared by everyone in a co-operative. Although this can present enormous problems, if this power is used positively, decision-making is more effective and the members of a co-op learn and practice new skills and share in the successes and failures equally.

►Suitability◄

It could be argued that the ideology of a co-operative structure does not fit well into the traditional ideology of the visual arts, where the artist seeks to retain their individuality and therefore works in competition with other artists. In researching this article, it became clear that setting up as a co-operative was an exception for most groups of artists, and that several who'd intended to operate as co-ops or who had traded for some time in that way, had in the end opted for other ways.

Greenhaus Artists Group, a studio group in Newcastle upon Tyne, for example, although keen on a co-operative structure in the initial stages, discovered that several of the group were uncomfortable about registering and that the uncertainty was holding up the group's progress. They therefore opted to become, like most studio groups, an unincorporated association. A leaflet produced by Project North East, however, argues that

> There is a growing demand for artists working in all art forms who are prepared to work within a social context. The role of a community arts co-operative is to create self-supporting and viable jobs for local people by introducing them to art-related projects in which they can participate.(1)

It also points out that there are approximately 20 community arts groups in the UK which are constituted as co-operatives, although not all of these will be visual arts based. This compares with the national statistics of around 1000 co-ops overall. The Pioneers, a workers' co-operative formed in 1981, is an example of one which has not only survived but developed into a major visual arts project for Cardiff and Glamorgan.

> We were formed in 1981 as a loosely-knit bunch of ex-art students. We have now developed into a multi-thousand pound bunch of environmental improvement consultants. We are revenue funded by the Welsh Arts Council, received development funding from the Gulbenkian Foundation and have gained over £32,000 (1987) from projects undertaken in West, Mid and South Glamorgan(2)

►In 1989, the co-op has seven members, two of whom work part-time and they also employ a further two full-time and two part-time artists for project work. The annual turnover for 1989/90 will be around £150,000.◄

Artists in Middlesbrough grew up after a number of artists had come together in 1983 to use an old bank as studios. With the help of the Cleveland Co-operative Agency, they registered as a co-operative in order to *'provide low-cost studio space for local artists and to foster and promote the arts in Cleveland.'* In 1989, and now in a purpose-built studio after two short-life ones, AIM is part of the revitalisation of Middlesbrough. The studios are part of a group of community organisations including Age Concern, the Centre Against Unemployment and the Musicians Collective. They have 200 square metres of individual studio space plus an office and gallery with a regular exhibition programme.

►Funding◄

There are few sources of funding *specifically designated* for co-operatives, although the CDAs provide valuable help and business assistance through from the feasibility stage to registration and full operation. Under the terms

▷**1** *Setting up a Community Arts Co-operative,* Project North East, Newcastle upon Tyne

▷**2** Nick Clements, Letters, *Artists Newsletter*, January 1987

of the Inner Areas Act of 1070, agencies in the main urban centres can provide up to £1000 towards feasibility studies for businesses which seek to operate on co-operative lines. This is made possible through inner urban areas funding for which the agency can apply from the local authority.

The ten-month feasibility study for Dog and Dome Theatre Properties, featured in the last edition of this book, was assisted by a £1000 grant made available through Sunderland Common Ownership Enterprise Resource Centre.

> It wasn't just handed over though in one lump sum. We had to keep proper accounts and, on the strength of these, the grant was given out as we needed it. It could be used for any expenses related to the investigation of setting up a business – stationery, travel, co-operative registration fees and so on.[3]

In Grimsby, Public Arts Ltd, a co-op with three artists who undertake murals, sculpture projects and run workshops, obtained a £500 setting up grant from the Co-operative Development Agency in Hull. Dundee-based public arts group Site Specific obtained a £1000 grant from Dundee District Council offered through the Scottish Co-operative Development Company, a grant of £700 from the Tayside Regional Industrial Organisation plus an unsecured working overdraft from their bank. Funding for feasibility studies for proposed co-ops in Wales may be available through the Welsh Development Agency on the Welsh Office.

For co-operatives with some or all members under 25, grants may be available from the Princes Youth Business Trust or the Jubilee Trust, although indications are that visual arts groups have not always met with sympathetic or arts-aware assessors locally. When Dog and Dome applied, their application as a co-op was returned with the request for re-submission as a partnership. ICOM (the Industrial Common ownership Movement), however, maintains that co-ops are eligible for funding from this scheme.

Livewire UK, makes money available through a national competition for businesses run by people aged between 16 and 25 and these can include co-ops. In 1989, 4800 businesses entered and 400 received cash or other assistance. The overall winner, Colin Rafferty a furniture manufacturer from Hartlepool, won £3000.

▶Loans◀

There are around 20 locally-operated co-op loan funds which are backed by local authority funds, although loan funds are generally not available for co-ops in Wales, with the exception of West Glamorgan. Such schemes offer loans at a subsidised interest rate. Unsecured loans can be made available to co-ops who have been unable to borrow from a bank but whose business plan is acceptable to a committee of experienced people. It is likely, however, that this type of loan will start to dry up in the future and businesses will have to rely more on the banks.

There is also a national scheme generated by ICOM appropriately named ICOF, which also loans money at a subsidised interest rate.

▷**3** Helen Smith, 'Co-operatives' *Making Ways,* first edition.

Site Specific, a workers' co-operative, was registered in April 1989 by four graduates from the Duncan of Jordanstone College MA in Public Art course. All had experience of working on public art projects prior to the course and during the MA, there was an opportunity to make proposals for with hypothetical and real situations. The co-op members are all on the Enterprise Allowance Scheme, paying themselves £40 a week in order to build up their business in the first year. Already, they have two commission designs in hand for sites in Dundee. They also took part in an international symposium in Milokunst, Norway and their designs for a bridge in the town are under review by the town council there. Illustrated is *Creative man* by **Mark Jalland,** a linoleum construction and illustration.

►Enterprise Allowance Scheme◄

The Enterprise Allowance Scheme can be used as a stepping stone for co-operatives as well as individuals, although the condition is that at least half the members of a co-op must be accepted for EAS, up to a maximum of ten people. Each member must have £1000 to invest whether or not they are accepted on to EAS, although if the co-operative is also a limited company, only those receiving EAS need fulfil this requirement. Another stipulation for limited companies is that EAS members must hold at least 50% of voting shares.

►Marketing Co-ops◄

Marketing co-ops have been developed as a method of bringing together people who have products that will benefit from a joint marketing scheme. An example of this is Alice Ate, established in 1989 at Wrexham in Clwyd. It will provide marketing resources for up to eleven businesses who are based at the Wheatsheaf Workshops, a building converted under the auspices of the Wales Co-op Centre and housing other community-based activities. Over half of the arts and crafts businesses at Wheatsheaf are co-ops and most are recently set up. The common element between them is the need to market their work and with this, Alice Ate is already looking towards Europe with Wales Co-op Centre and European Social Fund aided training for Co-ordinator Mark Thomas who will look at exhibition opportunities for young people in Europe as well as the exporting possibilities post 1992.

At present, marketing co-ops have not been eligible for ICOF loans although Alice Ate hopes to see a change in this policy in the future.

►Financial Support◄

Public Art Limited in Grimsby was formed in 1987, but within eighteen months, had dissolved the co-op and become a partnership of three artists. Although assisted in the early stages with a grant from the CDA in Hull, they experienced difficulties when seeking funding as a co-operative. The Princes Youth Business Trust *'did not seem to appreciate the concept of co-operatives'* and the Jubilee Trust threw out their application once they realised that Public Art was a limited company. Added to this, was the realisation that if they folded as a co-op, all their assets – equipment, materials etc whether their own or bought through the co-op – would be transferred to another arts co-op. They have survived into 1989 with a one-year project grant from the Gulbenkian Foundation and the expectation of funding from Grimsby Borough Council. Illustrated is a low-relief play sculpture designed and created by children from Yarborough School in June 1989.

►The Future◄

Operating co-operatively can and has worked for some visual artists, but many co-ops don't get past the vulnerable stage – three years after setting up. Many survive only by exploitation of the workers, who must put in long hours for little reward, something which co-operatives were set up to avoid.

But the four artists who set up Site Specific in April 1989 are, for example, firmly committed to co-operative principles and see the structure as one which will provide them with the 'mutual support' they need to survive and thrive.

►Information◄

►Contacts◄

►*Industrial Common Ownership Movement*, Vassalli House, 20 Central Road, Leeds LS1 6DF ☎ 0532 461737

►*Co-operative Development Agency*, 21 Panton Street, Haymarket, London SW1 ☎ 01 838 2985 and Holyoake House, Hanover Street, Manchester M60 0AS ☎ 061 833 9379

►*Prince's Youth Business Trust*, 8th Floor, Melbury House, Melbury Terrace, London NW1 6LZ ☎ 01 262 1340

►*Livewire UK Office*, 60 Grainger Street, Newcastle upon Tyne NE1 5JG ☎ 091 261 5584

►*Co-operatives Research Unit*, Faculty of Technology, The Open University, Walton Hall, Milton Keynes MK7 6AA. Undertakes research and publishes directories and other books.

►*see also Trading Status* and *Funding*

►Further Reading◄

►*How to Register a Workers' Co-operative.* ICOM, 1989

►*The Pioneers Annual Report 1988.* Available free from 29 Coveny Street, Splott, Cardiff CF2 2NN

►'Making More Ways, Susan Jones. *Artists Newsletter*, November 1988. Includes information on Public Arts Ltd in an article on artists' initiatives

►*Surrey of Worker Co-operatives,* Phil Hobbs. Co-operatives Research Unit, 1989. By post £2

►*Finance for Worker Co-ops,* Chloe Munro. Co-operatives Research Unit, 1989. By post £5

►*Some Techniques for Collective Working,* John Martin. Co-operatives Research Unit, 1989. By post £6

►*Creating Successful Co-operative Business: A Summary Report,* Chris Cornforth et al. Co-operatives Research Unit, 1987. By post £2

►*See also Trading Status*

Sponsorship

Sarah Eckersley

The increasing use of business sponsorship as a method of supporting the arts is a sign of the political times that we are living in, and have to adapt to.

> Responding to a realistic appraisal of their lot, even artists are now acquiring managerial training in workshops funded by public agencies in the US. (Hans Haacke)[1]

Over the last few years the use of business sponsorship has been heavily promoted by the Arts Council of Great Britain together with the government. Sponsorship must be clearly distinguished from its counterpart, patronage, which always has been a traditional (albeit unreliable) method of support in one form or another for the arts. The term sponsorship used now can be crudely defined as a commercial transaction: certainly ABSA (the Association for Business Sponsorship of the Arts) puts the case for sponsorship by businesses in their own promotional leaflet *'Why Sponsor the Arts'* fairly bluntly: *'Business sponsorship of the arts as part of the company's public relations, marketing and advertising is growing in importance'* and *'Sponsorship can enhance a corporate image, increasing public awareness for both investors and consumers'.*[2] So it must be emphasised that sponsorship of the arts is as much a business deal as any other commercial move. The company/ business involved in sponsoring wants to see a return for their investment in terms of added publicity for the company, an improved promotional image for that company's product. *'...every bit of publicity my company receives through the medium of its arts sponsorship is valuable to us, enhancing our reputation...'.*[3]

A recent publication from the Adam Smith Institute, *The Art of the State*, contains a series of essays predictable in their rejection of public subsidy for the arts and based on arguments which do not stand up to close analysis. However the chapter entitled The Philosophy of the Business Sponsor by Clive Wright, formerly Manager of Public Affairs at Esso gives some idea of the needs of a large corporation in dealing with sponsorship and is useful for anyone preparing to approach such a corporation or business.

It is also important to realise that a company's priorities will always lie with their shareholders, employees, customers, etc. and that is the base from which they consider sponsorship; not from any altruistic feeling that art is a good thing and should be supported. Though of course there may

▷**1** Hans Haacke, *Art in America*, February 1984
▷**2** *WH Smith Sponsorship Manual*, Mary Allen. ABSA, 1983
▷**3** *WH Smith Sponsorship Manual*
▷**4** *WH Smith Sponsorship Manual*

be one or two individuals in the company who are personally committed to the arts, the sponsorship 'deal' will be looked at on the basis of what the company can get out of it.

The unfortunate truth that has to be recognised is that companies, firms and businesses will be unlikely to sponsor work that is in any way controversial, experimental or political.... *'I do not think too many companies want to be forming taste by financing avant-garde art.'* (Clive Wright The Philosophy of the Business Sponsor – Adam Smith Institute). Trades unions have, of course, sponsored more politically-inclined work and could possibly be encouraged to do more for the visual arts.

It is true that most companies seeking to improve their image and standing in their community would prefer to support the local children's home, the hospital, medical research, etc. – the arts come fairly low down on the list of popular appeals, and visual arts come much lower than music, dance or theatre. However some companies see the arts as having an upwardly mobile image appealing to an up-market section of society.

Equally, there are some companies whose own image is in need of improvement. It may be easier to get sponsorship from a company which manufactures armaments, tobacco, synthetic food products, fur coats, or whatever. The business ethics of the company, as an employer for example, are points which also need consideration. It isn't helpful to be too fastidious about the world of commerce but it is important to recognise the limits of your own integrity. It is better on the whole not to 'take the money and run'. It has been known that sponsors have felt themselves to have been exploited! If money is accepted from sponsors then all that goes with it must be accepted too.

Damon Burnard

▶Types of Sponsorship◀

The difference between donations towards a project and sponsorship for it can really be defined as a distinction in the tax system. It is generally understood that sponsorship can be a tax deductible expense for the company, since it involves items such as publicity, advertising,

promotional material, etc. Nevertheless donations can sometimes be written off as a tax deductible trading expense when the donation is in kind. Donations in kind range from providing raw materials to knocking 10%-30% off the cost of supplying goods. (It has been recently reported, however, that the discount can be assessed for the full amount of VAT which makes it less advantageous to the donor). More than one sculptor has financed their work through donations, but it would really only apply to a work that was for a specific public site. Donations in cash are usually only given to bona fide charities and this is true of most trust funds too.

There are increasing numbers of sponsorship agencies who are there to match sponsors to recipients, but these are more likely to take on major events and large budgets. *(Names and addresses of these arts sponorship consultancies are available from the Arts Council of Great Britain).* Such is the growth of sponsorship as a profitable industry that it has its own 'trade' magazine *Sponsorship News.* Making a sponsorship approach can take ages – months of research and preparation. You should therefore plan well in advance as most companies prepare their sponsorship budgets at least a year ahead.

Solentris - sculpture installation by **Chris Jennings** at Southampton General Hospital, 1986. Sponsorship for this work was raised by the artist. British Alcan Aluminium (Banbury) donated the aluminium for the triangles and Proctor Masts (Southampton) gave their services in fabricating the sides of the triangles. Other companies provided components either free or at cost.
▼

►Methods of Approach◄

There are very few successful approaches that an individual artist can make for sponsorship; unless perhaps, the end result was going to be a large exhibition of work in a prominent place. But there are smaller areas

of sponsorship to explore – a small printing firm might cut some of the costs of a catalogue in return for their name being on it; or the local TV rental company might provide facilities for showing a video in return for the display of a placard of acknowledgement. A community project very often attracts sponsorship – a mural for a hospital, involvement with school children, etc.

However there is no harm in presenting a well set out application for sponsorship for an individual project if the artist is prepared to invest time and money in doing this. The more aware people are of the needs of artists the better (especially in the commercial world).

In general then it is better to link with other artists and present a project which covers a wide range of work. This also has the added advantage in that work which could be considered controversial can be 'hidden' by the other work; (though sponsors might always want the details). The Oxfordshire Visual Artists' Week which is a non-selective event covering a wide range of work raises money from local sponsors simply on the basis of general support for the visual arts.

▶Projects◀

Sponsorship of an individual artist is rare. It is more readily available for a specific project or commission involving other agencies or for exhibitions, eg Shell recently sponsored a group of artists working on a community project during the Edinburgh Festival.

▶Finding Sponsors◀

It is generally true that it is better to look to local firms, or local branches of large companies for sponsorship. Most towns have associations or groups of businesses – The Rotary Club, Round Table, Chamber of Commerce. Approach the secretary of these organisations for lists of local companies. The public library should have a mass of reference books and directories on local and national companies (some titles listed below) to consult. Remember that all companies, however large or small, plan their budgets at least one year ahead of the following financial year. So be prepared to work to that schedule and preferably even in advance of it. Much sponsorship is allocated on the first come first served basis.

Select the companies whose products may have some connection with your project however tenuous. It may give you some link to build on.

'We are working on a 200 foot long mural for a local hospital, this is substantially supported by the local health authority and regional arts association, however we needed to raise some additional money. The mural is to be situated in a corridor leading to the children's ward so it seems an ideal project to attract commercial sponsors and 18 leading local companies, banks and building societies were asked for contributions. Out of the five replies, we received two donations of £25 and a £5 gift token – so much for the caring face of British Industry. This is the type of support which the Arts Council believes we should all be relying on, I'm sorry but I can't get much paint for £50 and a Christmas pack of deodorant.' (Nick Clements, 'Letters to the Editor', *Artists Newsletter*, January 1987)

▶How to approach◀

Nearly every company will require a written approach first. Keep this first letter short and succinct. Identify yourself and your project clearly: your audience: the benefits to the sponsorship company, and finally, the cost.

A two-page proposal with a covering letter should be quite enough as an introduction (if there are vast amounts of documents and statistics keep these for later).

▶The Letter◀

Some points for inclusion in the letter are:

▶It should be written on your (organisation's) stationery; this should include a list of those who are officially connected with the project – Treasurer, Secretary, etc.

▶It should be addressed to the correct person in the company. This can probably be found by a telephone call to the company simply asking for the name of the person to write to. National and international companies very often have a department to look after their sponsorship/charity work. Medium-size companies very often deal with such approaches through their marketing or publicity division (marketing manager or PRO); with

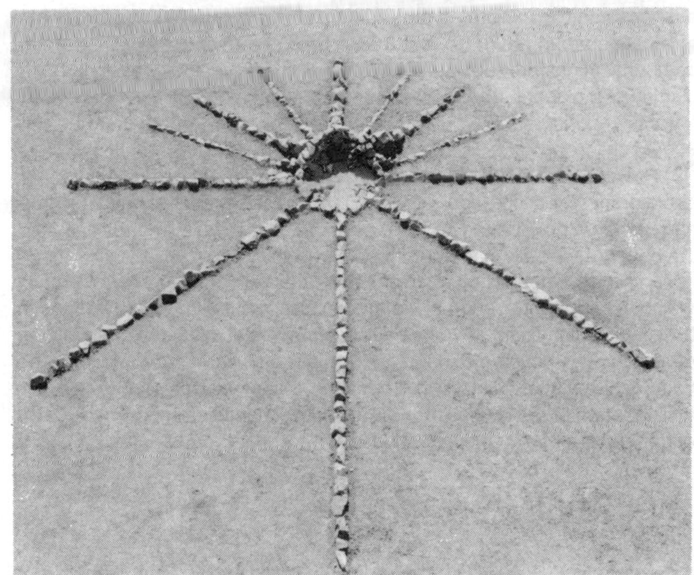

►
Lorna Green, *Rose Reflection*, stone, diam. 30′, height 2′6″ - a sculpture made at the Bishops Palace, St Davids, Dyfed, July - August 1986. *'In 1983 I had the opportunity to do some exploratory work in a brickworks in North Wales... after which I resolved to find a space which would give me the conditions I needed to develop my ideas. I approached Steetley Construction Materials Ltd at Moorside Quarry in Pott Shrigley, near to my home in Cheshire, who immediately offered a large space by a pond for an unlimited period using the materials in the vicinity that I could physically move myself. This is now my extension studio: the abundance of rock, stone aggregate, stone dust, the large area, the fluctuating levels of the pond, the changes in the season and weather all contribute to my thinking. After nearly two years there I feel I am discovering new thoughts and methods of working.'*

smaller companies, go directly to the owner/managing director.

►It should be as personal as possible (not familiar), and individually typed. It is better not to send word-processed or photocopied letters.

►It should be concise but should include:

►a brief paragraph describing the aims and objectives of the project (attach further details if appropriate).

►the time, the date and the place of the event.

►the overall budget (offer details). Indicate the other sponsorship being applied for, ie government (local or national funding), private, Arts Council, etc. Suggest the amount of contribution (money) you are looking for or, if appropriate, other forms of support.

►End the letter by suggesting that unless you hear, you will telephone for an appointment to discuss the proposal further, with either the addressee or the persons they might delegate.

►No thank you!◄

'To eliminate some of the 'No thank you's' think about what you have got to offer, what particular company might be expecting and how you can put the two together.' (Helen Petrie, ABSA Scotland)

Notes to the above: Don't send too much information. Think about the presentation, ie no badly or closely-typed pages with long single spaced paragraphs. Try to give numbers or headings to your points.

If you get a negative result there is nothing you can do. It is unwise to attempt to argue the case again. You could however politely ask why your application was turned down. But you'd probably only get the same standard answer *'...our funds do not permit...'* or *'...our commitments are already stretched to capacity....'*

◁see **Looking at Yourself**▷

However if you get a positive answer the next stage is to arrange a meeting.

►The Meeting◄

►Aim to engage their interest. Make your approach as an equal, which is what you are, (even though you are in the position of being a supplicant). Remember *'sponsorship is seen as a business transaction between two **equal** partners, both of whom are investing in the relationship'.*[6] Present

yourself well, though (sadly) you will have to dress to their conventions, not yours. Much depends on the 'tone' of this first meeting. Try to overcome any (natural) feelings of hostility towards the opulence and luxury of the surroundings – the warmth of the central heating, the depth of the carpet, the decor, etc. Try not to compare this with your miserable, unheated, leaking studio.

►Be knowledgeable about the company you are approaching. Find out before the meeting as much as you can about their products and show some interest in them. It is again possible to ask by phone for literature/brochures on the products to be sent to you.

►Ask some questions:

- ►How do they assess sponsorship proposals?
- ►What are their objectives and expectancies through sponsorship?
- ►What involvement does the company have in the visual arts?

►Listen, keep your wits sharp, and be prepared to modify your approach if it seems necessary. If they show ignorance, don't presume hostility. Many people hide their uncertainty and ignorance about contemporary art in facetiousness; you have to be patient with that attitude however irritating.

►If you are skilful at this sort of thing drop a few names of possible other interested parties! Nothing attracts **X** so much as to know that **Y** is interested in taking part, and that **Z** is very keen too. You may be able to develop a sense of competitiveness. Be careful here and don't overdo this – it can bounce back and trip you up.

►After the meeting follow up with a letter thanking them for their time and interest.

►Follow up◄

If any results are produced or offers of sponsorship made, you must confirm these with a letter of agreement reiterating the description of the project, time and dates. Describe the method and timing of the sponsorship money. Confirm the wording of the credit to be given to the sponsors on the publicity material or whatever. Make sure you have equal rights to see their press releases and publicity material concerning your project. Having achieved your sponsors, keep in close touch with them throughout the project. They may be willing to invest more money in publicity material.

►Finally◄

When the project is finished send a report to the sponsors giving, if possible, hard facts and figures, attendances, press coverage, public benefits, etc. By showing your professionalism you may be able to approach them again for collaboration on another project, in which you will have the benefit of previous experience. And if you have achieved a successful relationship with a commercial firm then you will have gained added respect for artists everywhere.

We hope for and look forward to the day when the arts in this country take their rightful place as a necessary part of the economic base, fulfilling their potential of producing earnings beyond their investments; and not as they are generally seen today by a philistine government and public as an irrelevant indulgence. When it is recognised that a strong culture can do much for the business community and in turn for the well-being of the country then perhaps we shall have the situation of sponsorship seeking the arts: that would be a true partnership of equals.

▶Information◀

▶Contacts◀

▶*The Arts Council of Great Britain*, Information Section, 105 Piccadilly, London W1V 0AU

▶*ABSA*, Nutmeg House, 60 Gainsford Street, Butlers Wharf, London SE1 2NY. They provide information for businesses to encourage them to sponsor the arts, and also administer the Government's Business Sponsorship Incentive Scheme whereby matching government monies are available for first-time sponsors

▶*ABSA Scotland*, Room 206, West Port House, 102 West Port, Edinburgh EH3 9HS ☎ 031 228 4262

▶*ABSA Northern Ireland*, 181A Stranmillis Road, Belfast BT9 5BU ☎ 0232 664736

▶*ABSA Wales*, 9 Museum Place, Cardiff CF1 3NX ☎ 0222 394711

▶*British Institute of Management*, Management House, Cottingham Road, Corby, Northamptonshire ☎ 0536 204222

▶*Confederation of British Industry (CBI)*, Centrepoint, 103 New Oxford Street, London WC1A 1DU ☎ 01 379 7400

▶*Institute of Directors*, 116 Pall Mall, London SW1 ☎ 01 839 1233

▶*Institute of Management Consultants*, 32-33 Hatton Garden, London EC1N 8DL ☎ 01 242 2140

▶*Institute of Personnel Management*, IPM House, 35 Camp Road, Wimbledon Common, London SW19 4UX ☎ 01 946 9100

▶*Co-operative Development Agency*, Broadmead House, 21 Panton Street, London SW1Y 4DR ☎ 01 839 2985 and Holyoake House, Hanover Street, Manchester M60 0AS ☎ 061 833 9379

▶*National Federation of Self-Employed and Small Businesses Ltd*, 32 St Anne's Road West, Lytham St Annes, Lancs FY8 1NY ☎ 0253 720911

▶*European Cultural Foundation*, 5 Jan Van Goyenkade, 1075 HN, Amsterdam

▶*Sponsorship Database*, 52 Poland Street, London W1Y 3DF ☎ 01 439 8957. Groups looking for reasonably large amounts of sponsorship can get their project listed free

▶Further Reading◀

▶*Grants from Europe*, Ann Davison. Bedford Square Press, 26 Bedford Square, London WC1 3HQ. Bi-annual publication

▶*Directory of Directories*. A guide to directories published in the British Isles

▶*Directory of Grant Making Trusts*, Charities Aid Foundation

▶*Directory of Grant-Making Trusts and Organisations for Scotland*, M Saunders

▶*Times 1000 – World's Top Companies*. Times Books. Address list included

▶*Key British Enterprises*, 2 vols. Britain's top 20,000 companies

▶*Raising Money from Trusts*, Directory of Social Change.

▶*Raising Money from Government*. Ibid

▶*Raising Money from Industry*. Ibid

▶*Industrial Sponsorship and Joint Promotions*. Ibid

▶*A Guide to Company Giving*. Ibid

▶*A Guide to the Major Trusts*. Ibid

►*Fund Raising Notes*. Ibid
►*Developing A Fund Raising Strategy*. Ibid
►*Writing An Application*. Ibid
►*Arts Funding Guide* 1989. Ibid
►*Funding Digest*, published regularly by RTI with up-to-date information on new sources of money and sponsorship. Usually held by arts councils, regional arts associations and other information resources
►*ABSA/WH Smiths Sponsorship Manual*, Mary Allen and Tom Stockil. ABSA 1987
►*Business in the Arts* ABSA. A leaflet on this scheme
►*Business Sponsorship Incentive Scheme* ABSA. A leaflet explaining how the scheme works
►*Business Sponsorship of the Arts: a tax guide*, Arthur Anderson & Co/ABSA. Aimed at sponsors but useful to those seeking sponsorship
►*Practical Sponsorship*, Stuart Turner. Kogan Page 1987
►'Making it Pay – Sponsorship', Harriet Lassalle. *Artist's & Illustrator's* No 9 June 1987. An artist's experiences with gaining sponsorship
►'Sponsorship', Tony Warner. *Artists Newsletter*, August 1988. Some ground rules for artists
►*Art Documentation Monthly*. Poly Products, Newcastle upon Tyne Polytechnic
►*Reading Guide to Marketing and Fundraising.* Arts Council, 1988. Bibliography of publications and documentation

Sponsorship & Ethics

►Geoff Staden◄
►Paul Donnelly◄

'Sponsorship' is the buzz word in patronage of the arts; it is the passport to survival for art institutions and a new financial incentive for artists. Industry and commerce are the pioneer areas for new sources of funding. Multinationals and big business are being encouraged to take up the short-fall left by declining government funds. Throughout the art world, competition is intensifying as art institutions, art workers and artists jostle to attract sponsorship from big business.

An increase in private patronage is part of the monetarist policies implemented by the Conservative government after their election in 1979. A signal to the art-world of this change was the appointment of former editor of the *Times*, Sir William Rees-Mogg, as Chairman of the Arts Council and Luke Rittner, former Director of the Association of Business Sponsorship of the Arts (ABSA), as his Secretary General. In 1988, Peter Palumbo took over as chairman.

Over the past decade the service, leisure and cultural industries have dramatically increased while manufacturing, the traditional mainstay of our economy, has steadily declined. This is now where the power and money lies and why big business and the Conservative Party are keen to privatise the arts. Sponsorship is a step towards this.

Two of the questions raised by this new partnership between industry and art are: will big business provide a sustained base for the level of culture to which we have become accustomed and what new pressures will this impose on the arts?

►Art Makes a Company Great◄

The head of Philip Morris Inc (who make Benson and Hedges, Marlboro cigarettes and beers), writes in a pamphlet on corporate sponsorship of the arts *'more people attend art galleries, museums... in a year than go to all the major professional sports combined. That's good box office; it's good business and it's good for business.'*

In the UK, the benefits of sponsorship are beginning to be appreciated as we follow the American example. IBM, Honeywell, United Technologies, are all leading the way in the sponsorship of art events. The Renoir show at the Hayward Gallery, sponsored by IBM, was the Arts Council's best attended exhibition with over 360,000 people visiting it.

But it is not just famous artists and established galleries who are benefiting from sponsorship. BP has sponsored artists to run workshops in educational programmes and open studio exhibitions. In an example of individual sponsorship, one artist has shown particular skills for self-promotion by securing not only £1300 from the Pirelli Tyre Company for materials, but also sponsorship from Shell for an artist-in-residence scheme, which was set up by the artist at the Natural History Museum.

For some time now, a number of companies have put their names and their money to 'open' art competitions and exhibitions which have become regular events in the arts calendar. For example there is the John Player Portrait Award at the National Portrait Gallery, Athena offers major awards and the Hunting Group runs an annual competition.

According to ABSA, funding from industry and commerce rose from about £600,000 in 1976, to £25 million in 1986. This increase is further stimulated by the introduction of the government's 'Business Sponsorship Incentive Scheme' which matches first-time sponsorship to a maximum of £25,000. Lord Gowrie, when launching the scheme, said that *'it is specifically to encourage more businesses to consider using arts sponsorship as a form of promotional activity paid for from their advertising budget, rather than as a form of charity'.*

But patrons have never funded the arts for altruistic reasons, they have always wanted something for their money. One incentive for businesses is tax relief. A company can persuade the Inland Revenue that sponsorship is a legitimate part of corporate promotion, like advertising, and a part of expenses which are deducted from profits before tax.

Robert Forsythe gives three reasons why his company, United Technologies, sponsors art events: *'Firstly: quite simply to get our name around'*, also *'if the corporation is seen to be associated with an active cultural life, it will become an attractive corporation to come and work for for the kind of people we want to get'*, and most importantly *'it gives us a very nice forum in which we can entertain and greet people who matter to us in our business'.*

United Technologies Corporation has sponsored a number of shows in the UK during the last few years. It sponsored the 'Hayward Sculpture Show' in 1983, enabling the organisers to provide free admission to the public. UTC was also responsible for bringing together from all over the world the sculptures of Anthony Caro for his 'birthday' exhibition at the Serpentine in 1984. With the help of UTC the show subsequently toured Britain and Europe. UTC's track record of sponsoring 'quality' shows led to the ultimate dream for the corporation: a sponsored show at the Louvre in Paris.

In return for this, the art world gets help with transportation, publicity, admission charges, equipment, etc. In this light, 'sponsorship' seems to be the answer to our problems.

►Art – Shaped by Corporate Promotion?◄

Of course the issue is more complicated than this, and there is a price to pay. One problem is the inherent conservatism of sponsorship.

Despite the fact that there are examples of what might be called

►
Paul Donnelly, *Don't Buy Racism – Preserved a Monument to the Destruction of a Racist Poster, Deptford '84*, acrylic on board, 6ft x 4ft, 1986

'innovative' sponsorship, it is generally the rule that a company will only sponsor art which has already attained respectablility. The exhibition must always promote the company but art is more than entertainment, decoration or 'corporate promotion'. The question is, what shape do patrons give to the exhibitions they sponsor? Do they put art into its social and political context or do they choose to represent art as a gilt-edged, luxury product? Museums and galleries have an educational function, they shape opinions and attitudes. What kinds of attitudes would sponsors like to promote or suppress? Would commercial sponsors be interested in someone whose artistic concerns centred on the peace movement? Would they sponsor artists dealing with racism? Would they be interested in sponsoring exhibitions by more experimental artists? The Tate Gallery, for example, was only able to secure sponsorship for the Francis Bacon retrospective show in 1985, when one of their trustees managed to persuade his own company to put up the money. Otherwise the exhibition by this internationally renowned artist might not have been possible.

There are companies with a more enlightened policy on sponsorship. BP involved themselves in AIR & SPACE, after the Arts Council of Great

Britain had withdrawn its grant. The gallery was set up to provide artists with their first London exhibition, an important role as many galleries are not prepared to take risks. At the time, Nancy Balfour, the Chairperson of AIR & SPACE, said that: *'Several business firms are interested in sponsoring exhibitions in the AIR Gallery and we expect that others will support our educational programme. Exhibitions will have to be designed to appeal to potential sponsors to some extent, but we are determined to maintain, as far as we can, artists who do not have commercial dealers and who have not had a major exhibition in London'.*

In 1985 the AIR Gallery invited SPACE artists to take part in the BP Arts Festival. Although BP has sponsored educational programmes at the AIR Gallery, they are a far from ideal choice.

BP and Shell are singled out by the Anti-Apartheid Movement as being major supporters of the South African Government. They are instrumental in assisting South Africa to maintain stockpiles of oil and supply one of the main users – the armed forces. BP and Shell were also loyal supporters of the racist regime in Rhodesia in the 1960s and '70s. Oil is the key factor in prolonging oppression and death in South Africa and Namibia.

It was because of BP's involvement in South Africa that some artists felt that they could not take part in the BP Arts Festival, while others withdrew work that had been selected when they found out more about the sponsor. The exhibition was hailed as a success in the AIR & SPACE newsletter. No mention was made of artists pulling out and an attempt to have this action and BP's South African interests printed in the newsletter, was given a cool reception and finally deferred. Sponsorship, however, has failed to keep the AIR Gallery open – it closed in March 1989.

The shift in emphasis from public to private funding at AIR & SPACE demonstrates that this can have a fundamentally detrimental effect by excluding artists who do not wish to support companies like BP. Other examples of intervention range from British Rail's censoring of an anti-nuclear mural at Aberdeen Railway Station to the international artist Hans Haacke being unable to exhibit at the Guggenheim because of the politics of his work. In 1985 the artist Peter Kennard had one of his photomontages *'Santiago Stadium 1974'* removed from an exhibition, and another large work covered with a blanket following discussions between mangement at the Barbican Arts Centre and a major British company who had hired facilities there to hold a conference with high-ranking Chilean officers.

Censorship of this kind can be expected but the insidious way sponsors select and shape exhibitions to suit their public image is more dangerous. Would John Player accept portraits of cancer victims for their National Portrait Award? It seems strange that a creative activity like art should be associated with a product which kills thousands of people a year in Britain alone. The John Player Award is especially directed at younger artists (age limit 40 years), because they want to associate their product with the positive aspects of youth and art.

►Money From The Mafia?◄

There are galleries who will not accept tobacco sponsorship yet draw money from even more harmful sources. In October 1984 the George Stubbs exhibition at the Tate Gallery opened to the press. This was also the start of a three-month picket outside the Tate organised by a group

called Artists Support Peace who were to draw attention to the sponsor of the exhibition, United Technologies Corporation. Multi-nationals make money in many ways; perhaps the organisers and participants of past exhibitions were not aware of how UTC makes its billion dollar profits, or perhaps they were.

It, in fact, makes its profits by the sale of military aircraft through Pratt & Whitney and Sikorsky, who are leading suppliers to third world countries. They also manufacture components for Cruise missiles, MX missiles and ICBMs. UTC is also one of the key corporations in the USA's Star Wars plans. It is also making profits through subsidiaries in South Africa and Namibia. As well as supporting racist governments, UTC has supported violent dictatorships around the world, often working hand-in-hand with the American military, many of whose officials end up in the upper echelons of the corporation.

Escalating defence spending is a burden for Western countries but in the third world, loans are set up so they can buy more arms: the interest payments alone are causing financial disaster. In these countries very little is left to be spent on the arts.

In June 1984 before the start of the Stubbs show, Artists Support Peace wrote a letter to Alan Bowness, then Director of the Tate. We gave him a profile on UTC and asked how he could justify using it as a sponsor. He replied that sponsorship was not something the Tate Gallery went in for lightly. If the sponsor was a tobacco company the Tate Gallery would not be interested *'but it is more difficult to take this attitude with great multi-national companies such as UTC who are involved in so many different fields'*. UTC does have many different subsidiaries but its main source of income is in the field of arms production. UTC's military hardware will kill more people that tobacco ever could; maybe if UTC carried a government health warning, Alan Bowness would think again.

After raising the issue of sponsorship at the Tate we then met with Luke Rittner at the Arts Council to discuss their policy on sponsorship of the arts. He said then that the ACGB has no guidelines for private sponsorship, that it was a *'dubious road to go down'*. He sees himself as *'a pragmatist'* and feels that more rules make life problematic and that guidelines would be unworkable. Unlike Alan Bowness, Luke Rittner could see no problem with the tobacco industry sponsoring art. He quoted the view of an American counterpart (who could not understand the British hesitancy about private sponsorship for the arts): *'I'd accept money from the Mafia as long as it was laundered'*. As for UTC and South Africa, he did not agree with apartheid but *'it was not the Arts Council's policy to interfere in companies' affairs'*. UTC is still on their books and they would be happy to use it again. We decided that our only course of action was to continue to expose sponsors like UTC and make it clear why they were sponsoring art.

The picket at the Tate Gallery continued every Sunday throughout the exhibition. We collected several thousand signatures for the petition and talked about the issue. Very few people would not sign the petition. Some of the people who did object took a fatalistic view and ignored the problem saying *'the art-world is corrupt and always will be'*.

Many objectors were of the opinion that art was above the critisms raised against UTC. They seemed to believe that they could make a distinction between art and the way UTC makes its money. Others seemed to think that the injection of a small percentage of tax-deductible profit into art mitigates the corporation's other activities. They did not accept that

UTC, with the eager approval of the Arts Council and government was merely using publicly-funded spaces for *'corporate promotion'*.

The arrival of Cruise missiles, the Sikorsky-Westland affair, the attempt to secure facilities at Imperial College for their Star Wars research programme, all demonstrate clearly that for a company like UTC, sponsorship of the arts is simply part of a wilder political and economic strategy. Notably, UTC decreased its UK sponsorship once it had secured the Westland deal.

A useful component of the sponsorship 'tool' is the private view. Through personal contact with MPs, the Civil Service and the City, who are all invited to lavish champagne openings, sponsors can facilitate the passage of favourable legislation and win government contracts. Prince Edward was amongst the VIPs at a Tate Gallery reception for the Oskar Kokoshka show sponsored by UTC.

Some argue that all money is dirty, even government money. The difference is that goverments are elected through democratic procedures and we have the power to change them. There is an absurd incongruity in a culture being sponsored by a corporation dealing in weapons.

The head of Philip Morris Inc put business sponsorship of the arts in perspective when he said, '*... let us be clear about one thing, our fundamental interest in the arts is self-interest*'.

►Artists Against Sponsorship◄

The signatures collected during the picket outside the Tate were presented to Alan Bowness. As we talked it seemed to us that he was more interested in UTC's sponsorship portfolio than finding out how it made money. We argued that the Tate Gallery had a responsibility to open up the debate on sponsorship. Several months later the Tate organised a debate called 'What Price Art Sponsorship'. Although this debate left much to be desired, the action against the sponsor succeeded in drawing public attention to the issue of funding.

Increased awareness of the problems of sponsorship is leading to a boycott of exhibitions by artists and public who refuse to support shows where they disapprove of the company concerned. A drop in attendances or applications to exhibitions as part of the protest against the use of an unacceptable sponsor would soon convince curators and gallery directors of the need to find alternative funding.

In the past few years, many artists have become politicised. For instance, a group of artists selected for the Whitechapel Open Exhibition of 1982 boycotted the show when they discovered that Barclays Bank was a sponsor. A discussion took place in which it was pointed out that the exhibition could no longer be considered open if artists disagreeing with apartheid felt they could no longer participate. The Whitechapel decided to drop Barclays from any future sponsorship of their open exhibition.

The Royal College of Art tried to raise money for its Printmaking Department by asking established artists and former students to donate prints for a fund-raising show at the Barbican. The sponsor of this show was UTC. Artists were not informed about UTC taking part or about its involvement in nuclear weapons or apartheid. After being informed by Artists Support Peace as to the true nature of the sponsor, some artists decided to donate the money from prints sold to the Campaign for Nuclear Disarmament.

►Barclays, IBM and now Mobil have announced withdrawal from South Africa in part due to anti-apartheid campaigns, but what of their other investments?

In an effort to stop the further use of BP as a sponsor for the AIR Gallery and SPACE Studios, the artists of Norfolk House (SPACE Studios), campaigned to get their organisation to boycott any sponsors linked with apartheid. To support this action they affiliated to the Anti-Apartheid Movement.

►Alternatives◄

Where does this leave the artist? For the majority of us, working in communities up and down the country, sponsorship from multi-nationals is not a realistic proposition. At best this type of funding is only a short-term solution to a long-term problem. Most artists are forced to raise money themselves, mostly by working part-time although this is increasingly difficult. The problem would be eased if artists ceased to work in isolation and began to share resources and work collectively.

Another possibility is 'Percent for Art', a scheme which will set aside a part of the money for new development and building work to be spent on the inclusion of art in those projects. The principal has been accepted by councils including Sheffield, Lewisham, Birmingham and Oxfordshire. If the scheme was taken up by parliament it would transform the position of art and artists in our society.

The artist would have a stonger economic base if there were stricter laws on copyright and re-sale. In France, artists get royalties every time their work is re-sold or appears in public (ie TV, magazines, etc), just as musicians, actors or writers do today, even in the UK. In France, when the artist dies, all the royalties continue to operate but go to a central fund used to buy art from living artists.

Something is wrong with our society when we spend £18 billion a year on 'defence' and 0.05% of that amount on the visual arts.

Art is not a luxury. Artists have as much to offer the community as, for example, teachers, bus drivers and nurses. Adopting this idea will require a radical change in thinking from both artists and public. This will come about if artists participate in the democratic process through groups like the National Artists Association, the Artists Union and Artists Support Peace. Artists must become aware of the mechanisms that manipulate their work. They can only affect these if they have political power.

►Guidelines◄

Sponsorship is here to stay. But there are ways to check on companies before accepting their money.

Ask to see copies of any material sponsors have published about themselves. A company's annual report or product catalogues will reveal a lot about them, and they are always keen to send these out in the hope of promoting investment. The company brochure will obviously show the company in good light and may gloss over the reality which lies behind the company's activities or may simply not give all information you need. For a more detailed picture of the sponsor you may have to dig deeper. This could mean one phone call to any of the agencies listed under 'information' chapter. One of these agencies: Ethical Investment Research and Information Service (EIRIS), will give a profile an a potential sponsor if it is

a company. EIRIS would be an ideal service for galleries to use. It also publishes a list of companies who are not involved in defence, alcohol, gambling or South Africa.

Beware of parent companies. An apparently innocuous sponsor may turn out to be a subsidary of a multi-national which may be far from acceptable. This was the case with Otis Elevators who ran an Artists Placement Scheme in Liverpool. We discovered that Otis was merely a subsidary of UTC and itself had branches in South Africa.

Beware also of hidden sponsorship. If you are entering open competitions, or exhibitions, or charity shows, check with the organisers if a sponsor is involved, who they are and what they do. If ever you decide to withdraw from a show, or not take part for ethical reasons, let the organisers know your reasons for doing so. Also try to let other artists, and the media, know.

▶Information◀

▶Contacts◀

▶*Anti-Apartheid Movement*, 13 Mandela Street, London NW1 0DW ☎ 01 387 7966

▶*Campaign Against the Arms Trade*, 11 Goodwin Street, London N4 3HQ ☎ 01 281 0297

▶*Campaign for Nuclear Disarmament*, Information Office, 22-24 Underwood Street, London N1 7JG ☎ 01 250 4010

▶*Companies House*, Department of Trade, 55-71 City Road, London EC1Y 1BD ☎ 01 253 9393

▶*Labour Research Department*, 78 Blackfriars Road, London SE1 ☎ 01 928 3649

▶*United Nations Information Service*, 20 Buckingham Gate, London SW1 ☎ 01 630 1981

▶*Friends of the Earth*, 26-28 Underwood Street, London N1 7JQ ☎ 01 490 1555

▶*Action on Smoking & Health* (ASH), 5-11 Mortimer Street, London W1N 7RH ☎ 01 637 9843

▶*Greenpeace*, 30-31 Islington Green, London N1 8XE ☎ 01 354 5100

▶*Artists Support Peace*, Space Studios, Norfolk House, Brookmill Road, London SE8 ☎ 01 692 4170

▶*British Society for Social Responsibilty & Science*, 25 Horsell Road, London N5 ☎ 01 607 9615

▶*Ethical Investment Research Information Service*, Unit 401, Bondway Business Centre, London SW8 1SQ ☎ 01 735 1351

▶*Choose Cruelty-Free* (British Union for the Abolition of Vivisection), 16A Crane Grove, Islington, London N7 8LB ☎ 01 700 4888

▶Further Reading◀

▶'Money from the Mafia', Geoff Staden and Paul Donnelly, *Artists Newsletter*, December 1984

▶*Socially Responsible Investment*, Sue Ward. Directory of Social Change, 1986

▶'Artists' Protest', *Artists Newsletter*, July 1987. Reports on artists' protests against Shell's sponsorship of a National Gallery exhibition

▶*Multinational Corporations & the Control of Culture*, Armand Mattelart. Harvester 1979

▶'The Art of Big Business', Brian Wallis. *Art in America*, June 1986

Abroad

Peter Hill

Why go abroad? If the lack of opportunities at home, and the steep competition for those scarce teaching posts and residencies were not enough, the visual and social stimulus of a new country and a different culture should persuade the adventurous to get on the road by whatever means possible.

If you are still a student, of if you have never taken up a post-graduate option, then most foreign countries offer an MA or its equivalent. Being accepted for such a course is only the beginning, as funds for living expenses, and often for fees, have then to be found. This is especially true in the United States where often two separate sources of income must be found, and possibly these will only cover the first year of a two-year course. Commonwealth scholarships are available for those wishing to study in another part of the commonwealth. Tasmania, for example, has a very strong MA course in Fine Art and actively advertises in the UK art press to recruit new students.

Artists and craftspeople under 35 can apply for five Commonwealth Foundation Fellowships offered annually. Worth up to £6000 each and tenable for nine months, the award covers air fares, accommodation and subsistence plus the cost of mounting an exhibition. One of the aims of the fellowships is to open up opportunities for younger artists to work with more established ones. Contact address at the end of the section.

The Scots are great travellers, and four students who left Glasgow Art School in recent years are good examples of this and ones which serve to show the range of opportunity open to graduates. Steven Campbell left for New York on a Fulbright Scholarship to study at the Pratt Institute; it was to have been a two-year course but by the end of the first year his paintings were selling for four-figure sums and the rest is history.

Leslie Finlayson and Anne Campbell were both accepted to do a post-graduate course at Cyprus School of Art, and both had to find their own funding. They applied to the Elizabeth Greenshield Foundation in Canada, to which all young artists and not just students can apply, and were both awarded one of the thirty or so awards that are made annually, worth approximately £4,000.

Mario Rossi, *The Archaeologist*, 1983. Rossi was awarded a British School in Rome Scholarship.

Mario Rossi left the sculpture department at Glasgow and went on to the Royal College of Art; from there he went to the British School in Rome, where he began to work as a painter. This is situated in one of Rome's main parks, the Villa Borghese, and its stately premises are divided between painters, sculptors and archaeologists. I paid the British School in Rome a brief visit and found that of the nine artists there most had arrived via one of the London MA courses. Any artist under 35 can, however, apply and one place is reserved for a graduate from Northern Ireland. Facilities there are excellent, the studios large, the living quarters comfortable with free meals in an oaken-halled dining room more akin to Oxbridge than Rome.

Many other countries, from Sweden to Spain, offer opportunities to graduates to continue practising their art, usually for one year. Rob Maclauren is an Edinburgh graduate who recently spent a year in Turkey on a Turkish government scholarship. He found materials expensive and hard to come by, and had a fairly low standard of living coupled with an unforgettable year. Most of these countries have foreign cultural centres or embassies from whom further details can be found.

▶The Wales/Philadelphia Visual Arts Exchange, a project co-ordinated by the British American Arts Association, is designed to promote contact between the visual arts communities of Wales and Philadelphia. Exchanges will be developed by and with artists and organisations in both places, until 1991 and the BAAA will act as a clearing house for ideas and opportunities.

The exchange grew out the experiences of two artists – **William Wilkins** from Wales and **Sydney Goodman** from Philadelphia, who had each benefited from residencies in the other's country. In 1988, a team of advisors from Wales helped to set up the format for exchanges and, as a result, **Sue Hunt** from the Pioneers worked on a mural project in Philadelphia; **Clive Hunt** exhibited at the Nexus Gallery as part of a residency; **Don Kaiser** from Philadephia, was artist in residence at the Glynn Vivian Gallery and also **Allan Edmunds** came to South Glamorgan Institute of Higher Education to research into computer graphics. These opportunities were followed by **Edwin Arocho** coming to work with the Pioneers, **James Dupree** being based in a studio at the National Museum of Wales and an exhibition of prints from Philadelphia shown at the Glynn Vivian Gallery in May 1989.

▶Travelling Hopefully◀

Most artists have long since graduated, yet the desire to travel abroad remains as strong. The opportunities are there if you are determined, if you have a thick skin, and if you use your initiative. Applying for opportunities abroad does not differ so much from those at home. If you can write a letter in the language of the country to which you wish to go, or can get a friend to help you, then obviously you stand a better chance than the person who writes to Greece, for example, in English. A badly-written letter in the language of the host country shows that you have at least tried, whereas one in perfect English may be incomprehensible to the person who receives it.

Either you know exactly where you want to go, and nowhere else will do, or you want to get abroad, just for the experience, and would gladly go anywhere. Whichever, the ground rules are roughly similar.

▶Amongst the first awards made from the Arts Council's International Initiatives Fund which covers all art forms, was £3000 to the Riverside Artists Group to enable 30 artists from Moscow to visit and show work at Riverside Studios in September 1989. 30 Riverside artists went to Moscow in 1988. Applications from groups and organisations (not individuals) can be made at any time. Details from Arts Council, 105 Piccadilly, London W1V 0AU.

If you know you want to go to Australia, Paris, New York, London, Berlin, or Amsterdam, then you are off to a good start because Art Guide Publications publishes fact-filled guides to all of these places and are always updating them. In them you will find information on commercial galleries, museums, studio complexes, cultural centres, prizes and awards, materials suppliers and art transporters. In addition each book includes a general guide to restaurants, street markets, hotels and transport systems. These guides can save you an enormous amount of time, both before and during your trip, and I cannot recommend them too highly. Through reading the *Paris Art Guide*, by Fiona Dunlop, I spent a memorable year in Paris at the Cité Internationale des Arts, which was described thus in the guide:

> 'An international artists' centre set in central Paris, founded in 1965, with the aim to house foreign artists (visual arts and music) for an average of one year in studio/flats. Other facilities include a concert hall, a large gallery, etching studios, etc. Three studios are reserved for qualified architects – application by November to Academie d'Architecture, 3 Place des Vosges, 4e. Rent is minimal – about 800F a month but demand greatly exceeds space, naturally enough. Certain studios are reserved by foreign organisations/art schools which select their own artists. Otherwise for applying on an individual basis submit photos of your work in November or April – the committee meets soon after'.

▲
Mary O'Connor with *Auden*, oil on canvas 48″x48″ (painting on right). Royal College of Art Studio, Cité Internationale des Arts 1984.

In fact, the majority of the hundreds of studios that make up the Cité des Arts are owned by either multi-nationals in America, east European governments, or the arts councils and foreign cultural centres of Canada, Australia, Italy, Germany, etc. Over thirty-five countries are likely to be represented at any one time, and the quality of work being produced varies enormously. To its shame Britain, and its regional arts associations, the Arts Council and the British Council do not have a single studio between them. Only the Royal College of Art has a studio there, plus a few individuals who made it under their own steam. By contrast Australia, for example, has studios in Tuscany, New York, London and Paris which gives their artists exactly the international outlook that British artists deserve.

Note: *'You can claim relief of tax if you spend at least thirty days during the year outside the UK and each of those days is spent travelling wholly and exclusively for business purposes or devoted substantially to business activities. You must supply your tax inspector with a list of days spent abroad and they will calculate the relief due under the Finance Act 1987 Section 27.* (Daphne Macara – Business Start-up Pack, Alliance of Small Firms & Self-employed People)

►Funding◄

Having been accepted for the Cité des Arts, I then had to find funding. My application to the British Council proved unsuccessful as did my later applications in search of funding for mounting exhibitions in Paris and for transporting my work back to the UK. I next applied to the Scottish Arts Council and was given a major award which covered all my costs in Paris and allowed for extensive travel. This may sound as if I struck it lucky after only two attempts, but at this time in my life I was applying for dozens of opportunities at home and abroad and receiving negative replies from all of them; half the battle is determination. Rejection after rejection can be quite crushing, especially if you spend half your dole cheque sending slides and CVs half-way around the world and are then faced with the artist's age-old dilemma – do I paint or do I eat?

◄
Silvia Ziranek seen here with *Diarama* went to Canada & USA with a British Council grant. (Photo: Steve Collins © Projects UK).
The British Council spends around £11.4 million a year on the arts, part of which goes on direct grants. The Visual Arts Department operates a grants to artists scheme to assist British artists to exhibit abroad in public or commercial galleries. Applications are considered four times a year. British Council offices abroad may also be able to award grants to British artists for conference participation, residencies or other arts events.

Had I been unsuccessful with my arts council application I would then have investigated the following, as I was determined that I was going to Paris:

►The possibilities of claiming social security from other EEC countries, asking such questions as: do I have to be a claimant before leaving my home country in order to qualify?
►The possibilities of finding part-time work in Paris. Do I need a work permit? What about National Insurance? One can earn a lot teaching English to foreign business-people, even if you don't speak a word of their language. Child-minding, cleaning, teaching art are all possibilities.
►Could the Department of Trade and Industry help?
►The local library: *(see Bibliography)*
►Using some of the information from the books below, I would have tried to raise money from local, national and multi-national industry. This involves writing hundreds of letters and is a bit like hitch-hiking: just as you think you are never going to get anywhere, and are about to give up, you meet with your first success. Nothing is wasted, for if at the end of the venture you end up with 250 rejection letters then you are now in the fortunate position of having 250 contact names in 250 organisations which will be of use in the future. File them away until that day comes, for your application is often looked on more favourably the second time your name comes up at a committee meeting. If any of the companies are local, then put the contact name on your mailing list for exhibition previews and you may find you have a sale next time you exhibit in your home town. Likewise, if you show in London then send preview cards to the contact names of the London companies.

►Connections◄

One of the advantages everybody finds from living abroad is meeting others from other countries. After a year in Paris I came away with friends

in Yugoslavia, New York, Germany, Australia and Canada; hopefully in the future I will be able to exchange studios with some of them. I know of others for whom a residency has lead to something quite different in another part of the world, often through chance encounters.

Kate Downie, an Aberdeen graduate who in recent years has had an artist's placement in industry, received a Greenshield scholarship, and spent a year at the Scottish Arts Council's Amsterdam studio. It was whilst in Amsterdam that she met a group of Europeans who lived in Tanzania and this eventually lead to her visiting Africa and experiencing a completely different way of life.

Lincoln Rowe, a Dundee graduate, spent almost a decade teaching art in the Merchant Navy, employed by the Marine Society. Towards the end of this period, he travelled frequently between Ascension Island and the Falklands; this led to a period on board a Royal Navy ship where he observed and recorded the Iran/Iraq war, and in turn led to him being invited to join an all-Forces climbing expedition to Nepal as official artist to the group. In the summer of 1986 he climbed in Peru with another team, and then went on to Everest in 1988.

Cardiff-based sculptor Tom Gilhespy was able to develop his life-long interest in the history of Soviet art through a working exchange with a Latvian Friendship Society. In 1988, he went to the USSR to work alongside a Soviet sculptor and also to participate in the Jurmala International Sculpture Symposium. A British Council scholarship also enabled him to travel to Moscow, Lenigrad and Yerevan to look at Soviet monumental sculpture.

For artists wishing to use travel to gain experience rather than to study, the Winston Churchill Travelling Fellowship provides opportunities annually. In 1989, from the 108 awards made from 500 applications, sculptor John Edwards was successful. His application combined two categories – *Projects in the Netherlands* and *Renewal* – and he was able to undertake a study of sculpture in public places in the Netherlands and Germany. Fellowships are open to anyone of any age, background and status and, in exchange for the award, applicants must show they can make effective use of their experiences when they return.

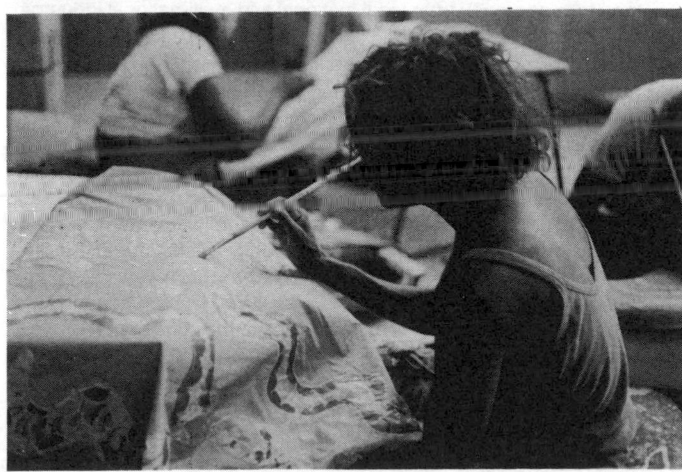

▶
Indulkana, batik, 1984. One of a series of workshops run by **Valerie Kirk** during a trip to Australia. She was involved in the 'Flying Art School' scheme

▶Information◀

▶Contacts◀

▶*The German Academic Exchange Service*, 2 Bloomsbury Square, London WC1

▶*Kennedy Memorial Trust*, 16 Great College Street, London SW1P 3RX ☎ 01 222 1151

▶*Art Information Center*, 280 Broadway, Suite 412, New York, NY 10007, USA

▶*Leverhulme Trust*, Lintas House, New Setter, London EC4

▶*Commonwealth Foundation Fellowships*, Education Division, Commonwealth Institute, Kensington High Street, London W8 6NQ ☎ 01 603 4535 ext 300

▶*Rome Scholarships*, British School at Rome, Tuke Building, Regents College, Inner Circle, Regents Park, London NW1 4NS

▶*Fulbright Award*, UK Educational Commission, 6 Porter Street, London W1M 2HR ☎ 01 486 7697

▶*Cité Internationale des Arts*, Mme Brunau, 18 rue de l'Hotel de Ville, Paris 4e, France

▶*Elizabeth Greenshields Foundation*, 1814 Sherbroke Street West, Montreal, Quebec, Canada H34 1E4

▶*Winston Churchill Memorial Trust*, 15 Queensgate Terrace, London SW7

▶*British American Arts Association*, 49 Wellington Street, London WC2 ☎ 01 379 7555. Acts as information exchange centre to aid professional artists to work in US; cannot help final-year students wanting postgraduate study in US; has good reference library

▶*US/UK Educational Commission*, 6 Porter Street, London WC1M 2HR ☎ 01 486 1098. Offers free leaflets on postgraduate art and design opportunities in UK and information on scholarships and methods of application

▶*Association of Commonwealth Universities*, 36 Gordon Square, London WC1H 0PF ☎ 01 387 8572. Offers a publication and information service (small reference library – appointment necessary to use facilities); can offer advice on awards, fellowships and scholarships

▶*Central Bureau for Educational Visits and Exchanges*, Seymour Mews House, Seymour Mews, London W1H 9PE ☎ 01 486 5101

▶*British Council*, 11 Portland Place, London W1N 4EJ ☎ 01 930 8406 ext 3043. Publishes annual directory of foreign goverment scholarships available for study overseas

▶*Charities Aid Foundation*, 48 Pembury Road, Tonbridge, Kent TN9 2JD

▶*Department of Education & Science*, International Relations Division, Elizabeth House, York Road, London SE1 7PH

▶*National Association of Arts Organisations*, 1007 D. Street NE, Washington DC20002. Publishes a bi-annual publication and a bi-monthly bulletin

▶*Commission of the European Communities*, 8 Storey Gate, London SW1P 3AT ☎ 01 222 8122. Has an information section open 2-5pm and has details of the network of European Information Centres

▲
Sebastian Boyesen seen here working on a large-scale polystyrene model for a stone carving commissioned by the Welsh Arts Council for Clwyd County Council. A travel grant from the Welsh Arts Council will enable him to spend six months at Carrara, carving a marble sculpture for the Welsh National Opera buildings in Cardiff.

► Further Reading ◄

► *Adventure and Discovery*. Central Bureau for Educational Visits and Exchanges. Lists thousands of study holidays throughout the world

► *Study and Employment Overseas*. AGCAS. Obtainable from university and polytechnic careers advisory services; gives addresses of embassies and relevant organisations for countries likely to interest UK citizens

► *American Universities and Colleges*. American Council on Education. Distributed by Walter de Gruyter Inc, 200 Saw Mill River Road, Hawthorne, NY 10532

► *Arts Address Book*. Peter Marcan Publications, 1989

► *Handbook on US Study for Foreign Nationals*. Institute of International Education, 809 UN Plaza, New York, NY 10017, USA

► *Higher Education in the European Community*. Commission of the European Communities, 1989

► *Specialised Study Options USA: A Guide to Short-Term Programs for Foreign Nationals*, ed Barbara Cahn Connotillo. Institute of International Education, 1984

► *Study Abroad – UNESCO*. HMSO bi-annually. Includes details of grants and awards

► *Summer Learning Options USA: a guide for foreign nationals*, ed Barbara Cahn Connotillo. Institute of International Education

► *The International Directory of Arts* (2 vols). Crosse Eschenheimer Strasse, D 600 00, Frankfurt am Main, West Germany. Lists museums, galleries, publishers, universities, booksellers all over the world

► *Directory of Grant Making Trusts*. Charities Aid Foundation, 1978. Useful if you are looking for funds to help study. In the main, amounts are small and criteria narrow

► *The Grants Register*. MacMillan Biennial publication. Listing all main sources of funding available for UK citizens to study overseas; those available to artists and designers are relatively few, but worth checking out

► *International Foundations Directory*. Europa, 1983

► *Artists Directory*, Art Guide Publications, A&C Black

► *New York Art Guide*, ed Deborah Jane Gardner. 1986/87. Ibid

► *Berlin Art Guide*, ed Irene Blumenfeld, 1988. Ibid

► *Australian Art Guide*, ed Roslyn Kean, 1989. Ibid

► *Amsterdam Arts Guide*, ed Christian Reinewald, 1988. Ibid

► *Madrid Arts Guide*, ed Claudia Oliveira Cezar, 1989. Ibid

► *Paris Art Guide*, ed Fiona Dunlop. Ibid

► 'Studios International', *Alba* No 10, Winter 1988. Looks at artist in residence schemes internationally

► *Grants from Europe*, Ann Davison. Bedford Square Press. Bi-annual publication

► *Arts Diary*, ed Giancarlo Politi. Lists artists, critics, galleries, museums, art magazines and cultural institutions world wide

► *Funding the Arts in Europe*, John Myerscough. Policy Studies Institute

Business

Employment Status and Tax

►Stewart Young◄

The definition of being employed or self-employed is in practice not always clear-cut. Many artists find themselves being employed, self-employed and even unemployed all at the same time, and others who thought they were self-employed are told by the tax office that they are only carrying on a hobby. What is the significance of these different types of status?

►Unemployed◄

Provided you have paid sufficient National Insurance Contributions and you are not undertaking any other paid work, you should be entitled to unemployment benefit and possibly income support. The tax position is that these benefits are taxable but in most cases will not actually be taxed because they will be covered by your personal allowance, which is the amount of income you can earn in a year without paying tax. If you are still unemployed the following April 5, the tax office will do a calculation to see if you are entitled to a tax refund. This arises because of the way the PAYE (Pay As You Earn) system works. An assumption is made that you will be in work for the whole tax year, and, if you are paid monthly, one-twelfth of your personal allowance is set against your pay each month. If you leave work half-way through the tax year then obviously you have only had half of your allowance. So the tax office waits until the end of the tax year to see if you can get another job, and then calculates your position.

►Example◄

Debbie, a single woman, worked as a teacher until October 5, 1989 when she was made redundant. During the six months from April 5, 1989 she earned £5,000 and paid £901.50 in tax. She then claimed taxable benefits of £975 in the period up to April 5, 1990. Her personal allowance for the year as a single woman was £2,785 and her tax position is as follows:

	£	tax
Earnings	5,000	901.25
Taxable benefits	975	
....	5,975	
Less personal allowance	2,785	
Taxable at 25%	3,190 =	797.50
Repayment due to Debbie		£103.75

Debbie will therefore receive a cheque from the Inland Revenue for £103.75.

For most artists, a period of unemployment occurs in between leaving employment and becoming self-employed.

The question arises as to how long you can continue to claim unemployment benefit, once you have started practising your art. The answer is determined by two conditions imposed on claimants.

- There is an earnings restriction of £2 per day.
- You must be available for work if a suitable vacancy arises.

So you can continue to claim, as long as you are prepared to take a job if it is offered to you or until your earnings exceed the limit of £2 per day.

►Employed◄

In the example above, Debbie worked as a teacher in a comprehensive school and there was no doubt about her tax status. She was an employee of the local education authority and was taxed under the PAYE system. She had a 'contract of service' with her employer who exerted a high degree of control over the terms and condition of her employment. For tax purposes, Debbie was therefore 'Employed' as opposed to being 'Self-Employed' and she fell to be taxed under Schedule E.

The tax schedules are simply a means of categorising an individual's income from all sources, and they range from Schedule A to Schedule F with some of the schedules being subdivided into cases.

The schedules we are interested in are Schedule D Case I or II, Schedule D Case VI and Schedule E.

Income falling under each Schedule is taxed in a different way and that is where the importance lies.

Let us return to Debbie. The vast majority of people in work are taxed, like Debbie, under the PAYE Scheme. Tax and national insurance contributions are deducted from their earnings at source and there is very little they can do about it. The amount of expenses which they can claim against their tax is restricted to those expenses incurred *'wholly exclusively and necessarily'* in the performance of their duties, a condition which is interpreted very narrowly by the courts.

►Self-Employed◄

The category most artists will fall into is being self-employed which comes under Schedule D Case I or II. The original distinction made in Victorian times between Cases I and II was between being in a trade or in a profession, a distinction which was important so that you knew whether to use the front door or the back. Today no practical distinction exists.

The key to being treated as self-employed is being able to convince the tax office that you are carrying out your trade or profession *'on a commercial basis with a view to the realisation of profits'*. If you can do that there are advantages to be had, mainly in the amount of expenses you can claim and also in what you can do if you make a loss. With regard to expenses, Debbie on Schedule E you will recall had to follow the *'wholly exclusively and necessarily'* rule but a self-employed person, because of the tax laws, only has to incur expenses *'wholly and exclusively'* for them to be allowed. This may not seem much of a distinction but it can make quite a considerable difference to your tax bill.

►Hobby◄

If you fail to convince the tax office that you are practising your art *'on a commercial basis with a view to the realisation of profits'* then the result will be that they will claim you are merely indulging in a hobby, and any profits you make will be taxed under Schedule D Case VI. The importance of this is not so much when you make a profit, as when you make a loss. Losses from a hobby can only be carried forward and set against any profits which may arise in the future. Losses from a trade or profession however could be carried forward, but could also be set-off against any other income you might have, thus resulting in a tax repayment. No wonder the tax office try to convince you that it is only a hobby!

►A Mixture◄

Frequently an artist will be self-employed but will also have part-time employment such as teaching. For tax purposes this income will be assessed under Schedule D Case I or II and Schedule E respectively but three important points should be noted.

►The earnings from teaching should not be included as income in the self-employed accounts, otherwise it may be taxed twice. Instead the net amount received, after deduction of tax and national insurance, should be shown as cash introduced into the business and should be entered separately on the Income Tax Return.

►I mentioned earlier that everyone is entitled to a personal allowance of tax-free income each year. It is your right as a tax payer to have this allowance allocated against whichever of your income you want, and it can even be split up. This will be achieved by adjusting your Notice of Coding, which is the instructions from the tax office to your employers telling them how much tax to deduct from your earnings under PAYE. Generally speaking, it is preferable to have your allowance set against your earnings from employment rather than self-employment because this defers payment of the tax. For example, if you are running an evening class at the local art college and expect to earn £500 in the year, write to your tax office and tell them to instruct the art college to give you £500 of allowance against that income. That way you should receive the income gross without tax deducted. It is far better to do it that way than to have to claim a refund at the end of the year, which can be very time-consuming.

►The Inland Revenue has recently been taking a hard line on course expenses received by a person with a mixture of employment and self-employment. As the expenses are not incurred *'exclusively'* for either tax Schedule *(See Self-Employed above)* the Revenue is attempting to deny any relief.

One final comment – going back to the example of Debbie claiming a tax repayment. If you leave your employment to become self-employed then don't wait until the end of the tax year before claiming a refund. You have your full personal allowance for the year to set against your earnings from employment which will usually result in a repayment. If you do this however you should remember that any self-employed earnings that year will then all be taxable, but the cash-flow advantages certainly make it worthwhile.

►The Preparation of Accounts◄

If you have decided to go self-employed, either on a full-time or part-time basis the first thing to consider on the financial side is the type of accounting records you will require. If this could be summarised in one rule it would be *keep it simple*. Book-keeping is just common sense and a methodical approach. Debits, credits and the mysteries of double-entry can safely be ignored. All that is needed is a record of your income and expenditure together with any supporting documentation. Even if you already have a personal bank account, open either a *separate business account* or a *second personal account* and try to use it for all your business transactions. Try and get a receipt for all of your expenses and issue copy invoices for your sales. Your bank statements provide a record of all your cheque transactions so all you need to do is to keep a note of cash received and spent. Sometimes, for convenience, you might meet a business expense using a cheque from your personal bank account or using cash from another source, eg a win on the horses. A record should be kept of such expenses as they can still be claimed for. Remember, you are basically going to have to pay tax on the difference between your income and your expenditure, and the lower this is (legitimately!), the less tax you will have to pay.

Not all expenditure however reduces your tax bill directly. Accountants like to distinguish between what they call 'Revenue' and 'Capital' expenditure. Revenue expenditure consists of the purchases of materials, eg clay, paint, film, day-to-day running expenses (heating and lighting in your studio, telephone calls, etc). These expenses are set against your income in full in the accounting period in which they are incurred. Capital expenditure on the other hand is expenditure on the purchase of assets for use in your business, eg a camera, an easel or a car. This type of expenditure is not claimed in full in the accounting period in which it is incurred, but the cost of the asset is spread out over its useful life as estimated by the Inland Revenue, and a proportion of the cost is given against your profits for each year in the period. It is done in such a way that more relief is given in earlier years than later, a system known as the reducing-balance basis. The deductions themselves are referred to as captial allowances.

►Example◄

Tony has been a photographer for several years. In the year ended December 31, 1988 he had income from commissions of £9,000 and incurred revenue expenditure of £4,000. He also bought a camera in the autumn sales for £300. His taxable profit for 1989/90 would be as follows:

	£
Income from commissions	9,000
Less revenue expenditure	4,000
Profit per accounts	5,000
Less capital allowance	75
Taxable Profit	**£4,925**

Capital Allowances on the camera have been claimed on 25% of the expenditure, leaving £225 unclaimed. In the next tax year 1990/91, Tony would be able to claim 25% of the unclaimed balance, or £56 leaving £169

►Tax Deductible Expenses◄

►Studio (rent, rates, insurance) OR proportion of domestic expenses
►Studio light and heat
►Repairs to studio and studio equipment
►Telephone OR proportion
►Cleaning or replacement of working clothes
►Materials
►Small tools and items of equipment (£50 maximum per item, above this items would be classed as capital costs – note this is a rule of thumb only)
►Framing expenses
►Commission paid to agents/galleries
►Exhibition charges and expenses
►Photography, publicity, advertising
►Newspapers, magazines, subscriptions
►Books (£50 rule of thumb)
►Printing and photocopying
►Postage and stationery
►Catalogues and admission to exhibitions
►Travelling expenses (UK) – from 'place to business' only
►Motor vehicle expenses OR proportion
►Foreign travel expenses
►Fees for assistants
►Bank charges and interest on bank loan-overdraft
►Accountancy and legal fees
►Depreciation
►Miscellaneous expenses

unclaimed. This process would continue until either all the expenditure was claimed or the camera was sold or scrapped.

Before leaving the subject of accounts, I want to highlight two areas which often cause problems:

►Use of House◄

Some artists are fortunate enough to have their own studio which may be rented or leased or perhaps shared with other artists. If that is the case, all the running expenses such as rent, heating, lighting, rates, etc, can be claimed in the accounts as revenue expenses. Frequently, however, many artists at least start off by using part of their house as a studio, either setting aside a room on a permanent basis or just working where they can whenever a room is free. In that case, they should be sure still to claim for a proportion of the running costs of the house, which could be said to be attributable to the business usage.

The exact proportion is a matter for negotiation with the tax office but they will accept any reasonable basis of apportionment. In the example above, let us suppose that Tony lives in a six-room house including a cellar and he uses one room as his photography studio and the cellar as a dark-room. He should claim in his accounts one-third of his expenditure on rates, water rates, insurance, repairs, heating and lighting.

►Motor Expenses◄

Many artists have a car or a motorbike which they use partly on business and partly privately. It is difficult trying to decide just how much should be claimed in the accounts as a business expense. One way would be to keep a note of all mileage incurred in the year distinguishing private from business and apportioning total motor expenses, including petrol, road tax, insurance and repairs, in that ratio. This is often inconvenient, however, and the best thing is to keep a record of all expenses and then estimate a percentage for business use. The basis of apportionment should be clearly shown in the accounts and you should be prepared to justify it to the tax office.

►How Your Tax is Calculated◄

In the example in the last section, Tony had been a photographer for several years and his accounts for the year ended December 31, 1988 formed the basis for his tax assessment for the tax year 1989/90, which is the year ending April 5, 1990. This basis of assessment is known as the PY (Previous Year) basis and is used for all self-employed people once they have been trading for a few years. The reason is to give you time to prepare accounts and have them agreed with the tax office before your tax becomes due for payment. When a person starts up in business, however, some fancy footwork is required to get them onto the PY basis. Without going into too much detail, if the year to December 31, 1987 had been Tony's first year of trading, and he had made a taxable profit of £1,200 then his tax assessments would have been as follows:

►**1986/87** – profits for the period January 1, 1987 to April 5, 1987: 3/12 x £1,200 = £300
►**1987/88** – profits for the first 12 months of trading: £1,200

▶**1988/89** – profits of the previous year, being the year ended December 31, 1987: £1,200
▶**1989/90** – as before, based on the accounts for the year ended December 31, 1988: £4925

Note that it takes Tony three years to get onto the PY basis, and most importantly, the tax assessments for each of those three years are based on the same set of accounts for the year of trading up to December 31, 1987. It is therefore vital to keep your profits down in the first year to as little as possible. If you can make a loss in your first year, then you will not have to pay any tax for the first three years of assessment.

Let me now look at these two possibilities in more detail:

▶Scenario 1 – You make a profit◀

Tony's tax assessment for 1989/90 was to be based on his profits of £4925 in the year to December 31, 1988. Suppose, as described above in 'A Mixture', Tony is single with a personal allowance of £2,785 for the year and two part-time lecturing posts at local colleges. So that no tax should be deducted from his earnings from these employments, he has instructed his tax office to apportion his personal allowance as follows:

To University	£1,500
To Polytechnic	£500
	£2,000
Balance available against profits from self-employment	£785
Total personal allowance	**£2,785**

His tax assessment for his self-employment will then look like this:

Profits as a photographer	£4,925
Less balance of allowances	785
Taxable profits	**£4,140**

Tony's income tax liability for the year will then be £4,140 at 25% = £1035.00. This will be payable in two equal instalments of £517.50 on January 1, 1990 and July 1, 1990. Tony is not liable for Class 4 national insurance contributions, about which more later.

▶Scenario 2 – you make a loss◀

Every cloud has a silver lining and whilst making a loss in your first year might not please your bank manager, it can be good news from a tax point of view. Firstly, as mentioned earlier, you will pay no tax for at least the first three years. Secondly, provided you have convinced the tax office you were certainly *trying* to make a profit, and are therefore being assessed under Schedule D Case I or II, there are three things you can do with the loss:

▶You can carry it forward against future profits, thereby reducing one of your future tax bills. This is *all* you can do with a loss under Schedule D Case VI if you are deemed to be only indulging in a hobby.
▶You can set it off against any other income you may have had in the year, which has suffered tax. This does not include bank and building society interest, the tax deducted from which cannot be recovered.

►In the first three years of trading you can carry the loss back to three years earlier and set it off against your income of that year. For example, a loss arising in 1989/90 could be relieved against income arising in 1986/87.

As a generalisation, in the first three years of trading it is more advantageous to carry a loss back rather than use it in the same year, if only because the Inland Revenue pays interest on tax repayments relating to fiscal years ending more than twelve months before the date of repayments. However, a word of warning – there is a complicated interaction between loss relief and personal allowance and if you want to be sure of getting the maximum relief possible, you should consult an accountant.

►Other Taxation◄

The above deals only with personal taxation which is what will directly affect most artists. Anyone who has established themselves as a limited company, partnership, association, charity or whatever, either to operate a business or for the purposes of a studio group or the like may become liable to such things as corporation tax, audited accounts, etc. If you are operating in this way you should seek professional advice both from an accountant and from other groups operating in a similar way to yourself.

►National Insurance◄

In addition to income tax, there is another liability which faces the aspiring artist, namely national insurance contributions. These come in four varieties, as follows:

►**Class 1** – These are deducted from earnings as an employee, which as previously stated are taxed under Schedule E. In addition to the employee's contribution there is also an employer's contribution which is a further payment by the employer on top of what has been deducted from your earnings. Class I contributions start as soon as your earnings from a particular employment reach a certain level. Employees often deliberately pay their workers below this level to avoid paying the contribution.

►**Class 2** – This is what used to be known as the 'stamp' because you kept a record of your contributions by buying special stamps sticking them on a card. Above a certain earnings level, all self-employed people have to pay Class 2 contributions which are at a flat rate each week. They can now be paid by direct debit if required.

►**Class 3** – These are voluntary contributions, again at a flat weekly rate, which can be paid by those not otherwise liable to pay contributions, in order to maintain their entitlement to benefit.

►**Class 4** – This is in the form of an additional tax on profits for self-employed people. It is calculated as a percentage of profits between a lower and upper limit.

It can be seen that the self-employed are liable to two types of contribution, Class 2 and Class 4. An important point concerns the small earnings exemption for Class 2 contributions. If your earnings are, or you anticipate that they will be, less than a certain level – known as the small earnings exemption – you can claim exemption from Class 2 contributions. Leaflet N1 27A from your local office of the DSS explains the procedure but you should be aware that by not paying, you may be affecting your entitlement to future benefits.

Class 4 contributions are calculated on the profits of your business above a certain threshold and are paid in two instalments at the same time as your income tax (normally on January 1 in the year of assessment, and July 1 following the year of assessment). A deduction equivalent to one half of your total Class 4 contribution is allowed against your profits for income tax purposes.

►VAT◄

This stands for Value Added Tax and is usually best avoided. However, if your taxable turnover exceeds £23,600 per annum, excluding grants, or £8,000 in any one quarter, then registration is compulsory. You will then be required to charge VAT on your output, and every three months you will have to add up the VAT you have charged, deduct from it VAT you have paid in running the business, and pay the difference to the VAT authorities. If on the other hand you have paid out more VAT than you have taken in, you will get a refund. VAT is a very complicated area and if you think you should be registered and particularly if you are involved in importing or exporting, you should seek professional advice.

►Conclusion◄

I have tried to explore some of the problems which a practising artist will come up against but I hope the complexities will not discourage anyone from starting up. My final advice would be that good accountants, for the help and support they can provide, are worth their weight in gold.

►Information◄

►Contacts◄

►*Small Firms Service.* To contact your nearest centre, dial 100 and ask for Freefone Enterprise

►*Industrial Development Board for Northern Ireland*, IDB House, 64 Chichester Street, Belfast BT1 4JX ☎ 0232 233 233

►*Scottish Development Agency* (deals with crafts in Scotland), Rosebery House, Haymarket Terrace, Edinburgh EH12 5EZ ☎ 031 337 9595

►*Welsh Development Agency,* Pearl House, Greyfriars Road, Cardiff CF1 3XX ☎ 0222 222 666

►*Mid-Wales Development*, Ladywell House, Newtown, Powys SY16 1JB ☎ 0685 626965

►*Rural Development Commission* (formerly CoSIRA), 14 Castle Street, Salisbury SP1 3TP ☎ 0722 336255 and 11 Cowley Street, London SW1P 3NA ☎ 01 276 6969 (and branches regionally)

►Further Reading◄

Available free from DSS:

►*National Insurance for self-employed people* (Form NI 41)

►*Class 4 NI Contributions* (Form NP 18)

►*Social Security benefit rates* (Form NI 196)

►*National Insurance contribution rates* (Form N208)
►*National Insurance for people with small earnings from self-employment* (Form NI 27A)
►*More than one job? Your Class 1 contributions* (Form NP28)
►*National Insurance for employees* (Form NI 40)

Available from Inland Revenue:
►*Starting in Business* (IR28) (this booklet contains form 41G which you need to complete and send to your local tax office when you become self-employed.

Available from H.M. Customs and Excise:
►*Should I be registered for VAT?* (Form 700)

►*Credo – Planning, Helping you succeed in business*, Midland Bank. An information pack for small businesses
►*Small Business Digest*, National Westminster Bank. A quarterly publication for small businesses
►*Croner's Reference Book for the Self-Employed and Small Business*, Croner Publications Ltd. Loose-leaf book that is updated monthly with new information on legislation, regulations affecting the self-employed
►*Directory of Enterprise Agencies,* available from Business in the Community, 227a City Road, London EC1V 1LX and Scottish Business in the Community, Romano House, 43 Station Road, Corstorphine, Edinburgh EH12 7AF ☎ 031 334 9876. Listing the agencies which exist throughout the UK to encourage new business.
►*How to Start and Run Your Own Business*, M Mogans. Graham and Trotman Ltd, 1982
►*New Enterprises, a start-up case book*, Sue Birley. Croom Helm, 1982
►*Self-Employment and Alternative Work*. AGCAS booklet available from polytechnic and university careers services
►*Self-Sufficiency 16-25*, Richard Bourne and Jessica Gould. Kogan Page
►*Starting Your Own Business*, Hodder/Consumers' Association, 1983. Strong on practical information and addresses of other organisations that may be able to help. Looks at various aspects of self-employment from mail order to market trading and franchising; available from Consumers' Association, 14 Buckingham Street, London WC2N 6DS
►*Tolley's Tax Guide*, ed A Homer & R Burrows, Tolley. Annual publication
►*Work for Yourself*, Clive Parsons & Angela Neustater. Pan Books, 1980. Coverage and case studies including art and design
►*Work for Yourself – a Guide for Young People*, Paddy Hall. National Extension College, 1983. Very good on assessing whether you would be suitable for self-employment as a workstyle and for working out ideas for making/selling/doing
►*Be Your Own Boss – Starter Kit*, DS Watkins et al. National Extension College
►*Be Your Own Boss – Growth Kit*, J Eversley et al. Ibid, 1983. Designed to follow the starter kit, examining areas for growth via new products and markets, exporting, product reform and new investment
►*How to Manage Your Money, If You Have Any*, T Lloyd. Community Accountancy Project, 1983. An accountancy book for community associations

►*Your Guide to Our Employment, Training & Enterprise Programmes*, Department of Employment and the Training Agency. Available from Job Centres, banks, libraries, advice centres, etc, listing all current government schemes, grants and loans

►*Be Your Own Boss* – a guide to the Enterprise Allowance Scheme

►'Artists on Enterprise Allowance', Bill Laws. *Artists Newsletter*, May 1989

►*Running a Workshop – Basic business for craftspeople*. Crafts Council, 1985

►*Accounting and Financial Management*. Directory of Social Change

►'Riding the D-Train, Parts I & II', Henry Lydiate. *Art Monthly*, September & October 1985

►*Collected Artlaw Articles*, Henry Lydiate, ed Jenny Boswell. Artlaw Services, 1981

►'Conversation Piece', Kate Russell. *Artists Newsletter*, February 1988. An artist's comments on moving from full-time employment to self-employment

►'Tax and the Visual Artist', Peter Haveland. *Artists Newsletter*, December 1987

Trading Status

► **Nick Sharp 1989** ◄

Deciding what legal form is best for your particular circumstances is not always simple. This will depend on for instance: tax, the costs of formation and on-going administrative costs, the risk of business failure and personal liability for debts incurred, public disclosure, the need to raise finance, employment of staff, ownership of property, the relationship you have with your trading partners and (one of the most important) whether the principal aim of your enterprise is to make profits, or not. There are few hard and fast rules; it is a good idea to talk to others who have had to ask similar questions in the past to see what solutions they have come up with. If you can, speak to a solicitor or accountant. So the following is intended to be only an outline of the various possible legal choices.

► Sole Trader ◄

If you are on your own, this is what you will automatically be. You will be responsible for paying any tax that is due on your business, and if your turnover (not your profits) exceeds the VAT threshold (in 1989, £23,600 in any year or £8,000 in any quarter) you will need to add VAT to your invoices and sales and complete quarterly VAT returns. You should advise your local Tax and DSS Offices what you do and where you are doing it from.

You will, as you would expect, be liable personally for any debts you incur in your business. Since there is no distinction between your personal assets and those that you use for your business, if you do incur debts in your business that cannot be repaid, your personal assets (eg your home) may have to be sold to satisfy creditors.

► Partnership ◄

Up to 20 people carrying on business 'with a view to profit' can be a partnership in legal terms. You can form a partnership without any written agreement, but because the Partnership Act 1890 implies agreement between you on certain issues *unless* you have agreed otherwise, to ensure that you don't have rules imposed on you which are inappropriate, you ought to have a clear written agreement on such matters as sharing of profits and losses, and provision of capital.

To the outside world, every partner can commit all the partners to *any* agreement and each partner is liable to the extent of his/her personal assets) for *all* the debts of the partnership business. For these reasons, partnerships are not very popular in the visual arts; used only where there is an established trust between the individuals concerned.

Each partner pays tax at his or her individual rates on any income from the partnership. There is no need to register a partnership with anyone and no formal accounts need be audited, or returns filed at Companies House.

►Unincorporated Association◄

Most artists groups tend to be these, as are other informal or formal groupings whose primary aim is not profit, eg members' clubs, theatre clubs, community and tenants associations, political parties and trades unions.

Unincorporated associations *can* exist without a formal constitution, but it is always wise to have one to ensure that everyone knows where they stand and the procedure for voting, decision-making etc. However, a constitution can be quite simple and the process of setting up an unincorporated association can be cheap and quick. You should have a Committee or Council of Management who will take responsibility for taking most decisions and for overseeing the group's finances.

Because an unincorporated association has no legal identity of its own, and in legal terms is only a collection of individuals, an unincorporated association cannot start legal action, borrow money or enter into contracts in its own name, and cannot hold property without appointing trustees (who will usually be members) to do so on its behalf. Officers of unincorporated associations can be personally liable for the debts of the group, as can individual members if they have signed a contract in their own name.

►Trusts◄

A trust is a legal structure where land, money or other property is held in the names of trustees for certain defined purposes, and is usually constituted by a formal trust deed drawn up by a solicitor. However for technical legal reasons, a trust will not be a suitable structure unless the body concerned is capable of being registered as a charity (see below). However, if this is so and the aim is to run a limited project or raise funds for a specific purpose, a trust can be the right vehicle.

Confusion arises with references to 'trustees' where, for instance, an art group holds the lease of the group's premises. This occurs because a group (not having its own separate legal identity) can only hold property in the name of up to four of its members, who (the law says) will automatically hold the property 'on trust for', or on behalf of, the rest of the group. This type of trust arises informally, without need for a written trust deed.

►Limited Companies◄

All companies are legal entities quite separate from their members, unlike all the above. Thus they can sue, hold property and enter into contracts in their own names. The owners will not be liable for their debts and liabilities but if the company needs to borrow money, the owners or directors are

often asked to give personal guarantees to the bank. Under recent legislation, directors can also be personally liable for debts incurred while the company is, or is near, insolvent.

There are two types of limited companies: those limited by *shares* (such as most commercial companies), and those limited by *guarantee* (usually charities or other non-profit distributing companies). Companies limited by shares are owned by their shareholders (a minimum of two) and run by Boards of Directors; whereas guarantee companies have *members* and are usually run by a Council or Committee of Management. The Directors or Council of Management are elected by the shareholders or members respectively. In either case, the liability of the members or shareholders to pay out of their own pockets if the company owes money is limited to a purely nominal account, usually £1.

At least two people are required to set up a company. Formation and running costs tend to be high, and annual returns have to be submitted to Companies House and accounts have to be audited and filed each year. The constitution, annual accounts and other documents that have to be filed at Companies House are all open to public inspection. A company structure is, however, suitable for any size of organization and a ready-made constitution is provided in the Companies Act 1985 which can be easily adapted to suit differing requirements.

▷see **Co-operatives**◁

Before opting to form a company, consider whether the added initial and running expenses are justified by the benefits of corporate status and limited liability. Always consider tax as well, since there are likely to be important tax considerations involved.

Companies pay tax at special corporation tax rates on their profits.

►Co-operatives◄

Groups of more than seven people can form a registered co-operative (or Industrial and Provident Society) under the Industrial and Provident Society Acts 1965-78. To form one you must be carrying on a business industry or trade and be 'a bona-fide co-operative society'. This means it should be established on sound co-operative principls, including open and voluntary membership, equal voting rights and the distribution of profits on the basis of participation, not (for instance) capital invested.

If you qualify, you can register a co-operative with the Registrar of Friendly Societies. Model rules are provided by ICOM and others. The current formation fee is slightly higher than for forming a company, but the formalities are less rigid. As with a limited company, individual members are not liable for the debts and liabilities of the IPS beyond a nominal amount (usually £1).

It is worth remembering that you do not need to form an Industrial and Provident Society registered co-operative if you want an organisation run on co-operative principles. Groups of less than seven people can form a co-op and register with the Registrar of Companies. Partnerships, unincorporated associations and limited companies can all be adapted to operate on co-operative lines.

►Charities◄

Registered charities are non profit-distributing bodies which fulfil the complex legal definition of 'charity'. This must always involve a sufficient

element of benefit to the public; in the view of the Charity Commissioners, this is often incompatible with benefiting the members, so most artists groups are excluded. However, if you think you may be eligible, talk to a solicitor or the NCVO, who offers an advice service to the voluntary sector.

Charities can exist in the form of unincorporated associations, trusts or companies limited by guarantee; the choice can be important if you are applying for registration.

Although substantial trading activity may stop a group obtaining charitable status, if the trading aspect is only secondary, a separate non-charitable body (eg a limited company) can be set up to conduct the trading, which will pay its profit to the charity, thus preserving charitable status.

The main benefits of charitable status are: reduced rates/poll tax, relief from income tax on profits and tax relief for donors. Under recent government proposals, charities will be subjected to increasing supervision and scrutiny.

►Information◄

►Contacts◄

►*Charity Commission*, St Albans House, 57-60 Haymarket, London SW1Y 4QX ☎ 01 210 3000

►*Companies Registration Offices* – England: 55 City Road, London EC1; Wales: Companies House, Crown Way, Maindy, Cardiff CF4 3UZ. Scotland: 102 George Street, Edinburgh EH2 3DJ. Northern Ireland: Department of Economic Development, 42/47 Chichester Street, Belfast BT1 4RJ

►*Co-operative Development Agency*, 21 Panton Street, Haymarket, London SW1 ☎ 01 839 2985 and Holyoake House, Hanover Street, Manchester M60 0AS ☎ 061 833 9379

►*Industrial Common Ownership Movement* (ICOM), Vassalli House, 20 Central Road, Leeds LS1 6DE ☎ 0532 461737. Largest and longest established of the national support organisations for workers co-operatives. Holds a booklist of useful reference books for co-operatives

►*National Council for Voluntary Organisations*, 26 Bedford Square, London WC1 ☎ 01 636 4066

►Further Reading◄

►Ring 100 and ask for Freephone Enterprise to get the information pack on setting up a small business

►*How to Register a Workers' Co-operative*, ICOM, 1989

►'Artists Groups Legal Status', 'Artlaw Supplement No 3'. *Artists Newsletter*, February, 1983

►*Setting Up*. Directory of Social Change. Part of the series of booklets *Fund Raising Notes*. Covers charity trading and the law

►*Guide to the Benefits of Charitable Status*, Michael Norton. Directory of Social Change, 1983

►*Charitable Status: A Practical Handbook*, Andrew Phillips & Keith Smith. Interchange Books, 1982

►*Penguin Guide to the Law*, J Pritchard. Penguin, 1982

►*Law for the Small Business: Daily Telegraph Guide*, Pat Clayton. Kogan Page, 1981

►*Starting a Voluntary Group*, Sally Capper. NCV0, 1987

Insurance

compiled by
▶David Butler◀

▶What is Insurance◀

Put simply, insurance is all about protecting yourself against risk. And let's face it, risk and uncertainty are part and parcel of life. Some people live and work dangerously, whilst others exercise extreme caution. Nevertheless, the fortuitous element cannot be avoided, whether its effects be good or bad. Quite naturally though, it is the 'bad' from which most people seek to shelter themselves. That shelter provides you with three things. Firstly it offers financial protection against future disasters, secondly it offers assistance with future certainties (eg pension schemes) and thirdly, because of these, it offers peace of mind. However, you have to pay for your peace of mind. Insurance costs money, and it is a cost that many of us try to economise on. But if your studio contents are stolen or go up in smoke, having an insurance policy will at least enable you to replace your tools and equipment.

▶Getting Advice◀

The combination of the need to insure and a shortage of finance make it imperative to get advice on insurance. There are two sources for advice and you should use both of them. The first is to talk to other artists or studio groups to see how they have solved the problem. They may have good advice on keeping down premiums or dealing with claims that you would prefer not to learn from experience. They ought also to be able to direct you to the second source, which is a good insurance broker.

Your insurance requirements will depend on your circumstances and the type of work you are engaged in. The cover you get will depend both on those requirements and on what you can afford. The types of policy and number of different companies is bewildering and it is here that a registered insurance broker comes in useful (preferably a broker with some experience of art insurance). The advice is free and it is also independent of the insurance companies but remember that it is only reliable if you supply the broker with all the information necessary and proper details of what you want. You may not be able to get or afford the cover you want but only a broker can tell you that. A broker can also assist with claims on your policy (and give advice on pensions and mortgages).

►Premises◄

Ideally, you should insure against fire, theft, lightning, leakage, water damage, flood or storm impact, earthquake or subsidence as well as riots or mallicious acts. If you can think of other likely risks, add them in.

You must ensure that you are covered not just for the restoration of damage (eg mending burst pipes) but also for rebuilding in the event of total destruction. The insurance should therefore cover:

- ►damage
- ►demolition of existing premises and site clearance
- ►the cost of rebuilding including architects' and surveyors' fees
- ►the cost of renting alternative temporary accommodation
- ►accidental damage to glass, pipes, cables, drains etc.

►Studio Insurance◄
Sunderland Artists Group, after several break-ins and insurance claims, was required by the insurance company to fit an alarm system. The local council gave a grant to cover 50% of the costs of installation.

Owners of property are responsible for their own insurance and artists who work from home and have a mortgage usually have cover through their building society for the fabric of the building. You should check, however, that this covers your precise needs and obtain additional cover if necessary.

If you work from home though and have a mortgage, it is unlikely that the building society policy will cover business use. If you breach your mortgage by working from home and an accident occurs which warrants an insurance claim, you may find yourself unable to claim. For instance, if a fire was caused when painting materials were set alight by a cigarette stub and the insurance company had not been told that such materials were stored there.

◁see **Working at Home**▷

If you lease a building, the terms of insurance of the fabric of the building are generally covered in the lease. If you rent studio space, check whether the lease has any exclusions on flammable materials because if it does, and you use them, the insurance will be nullified.

►Vehicles◄

Anybody who owns a car or van is compelled by law to carry insurance covering any damage, loss or injury suffered by others in the event of an accident. Most people will actually carry more insurance, covering them for damage to their vehicle by fire or theft or, comprehensively, for all damage to any vehicle they drive.

All this is very straightforward until you come to use the vehicle for business. You then have the same problems mentioned above in relation to property insurance. Your ordinary vehicle insurance may cover you for some business use but it is important to check your policy to find out. Make sure your broker knows the full use of your vehicle. This may increase the premium but if you fail to do it and have an accident while you are carrying out business (say transporting work to an exhibition) then, as with property insurance, you may find you have no or limited cover.

▶**Workshops & Demonstrations**◀

Whilst most artists are concerned about insuring their work during exhibitions and in transit, they are less likely to worry about themselves. When they are employed to run workshops or do public demonstrations or lectures during exhibitions in public galleries, most artists would presume that they are insured against injury and more or less dispiriting likelihoods, under the same cover as the full-time gallery staff. Many gallery staff would assume the same but in fact it is more than likely that the artist won't be insured at all.

Artist and museum gallery curator Sally Moss, decided to check up the exact position with her own employer's insurance company. This was the reply from Dyfed County Council regarding the insurable status of an artist or craftsperson giving a demonstration in her museum (or in any museum in the county, or in any of its public libraries, some of which have galleries).

'If the artist is a full-time employee, then the County Council's Public Liability Insurance operates.

If the artist is self-employed and is paid by the museum to give a demonstration, then they are performing a contract for the council and should *'have their own Public Liability Insurance'*, as they will not be covered by the council's own.

If the artist is not self-employed and is not a full-time employee of the museum and is paid by the museum to give a demonstration, they are still *'fulfilling a contract'* and should have their own Public Liability Insurance.

However, if they are *not* being paid (apart from expenses), and are volunteering their services, then they *would* be covered by the council's Third Party policy.'

Although this refers to the situation regarding one particular county council, it is likely that similar conditions apply in many of Britain's public galleries. (David Briers, *Artists Newsletter*, August 1987)

▷**1** 'Contracts, VAT & Insurance', Roslyn Innocent, *Directory of Exhibition Spaces*, first edition ed. Neil Hanson & Susan Jones. Artic Producers, 1983

▶People◀

People! Well there's you – life insurance, health insurance, pensions – and there's other people too. This is the area that most of us are probably most likely to ignore but there are two important areas to think about.

Firstly, if you are self-employed, what do you do when you are ill? You can get cover for personal accident and sickness that will pay you a regular weekly wage while you are ill. Try balancing the cost against loss of earnings! – but you will probably find it is only worthwhile if you have a reasonably high income. If you are paying Class 2 National Insurance contribution you can receive sickness benefit.

Secondly, regardless of the size of your business you have a potential legal liability to your customers and the public for injury, disease or property damage resulting from your trading activities. Claims for bodily injury, in particular, can prove expensive so adequate protection is essential. Cover is available not only for the actions of yourself or your employees but also for injury, loss or damage caused by any goods or articles you make, sell or supply. Additionally, if you employ anyone you are required by law to insure your liability to employees for injury or disease suffered by them in the course of their work for you. It is an important consideration when contracted for a public art project that you ensure that the commissioner has either taken out public liability insurance themselves or has taken the cost into account in the fee they are offering you.

Damon Burnard

▶Work and Work Materials◀

It is important to insure your work and work materials however small you consider their value.

It is worth insuring whatever their value because it will certainly cost less than replacement of damaged or lost work and materials. You can effect an 'all risks' policy which will cover you for all work and materials and specified valuables anywhere in the United Kingdom. It would be advisable to specify therefore certain valuable items of machinery or equipment you may have. (Roslyn Innocent)(1)

There is no point in over-insuring in that if you suffer loss the only possible

sum you can gain is the sum at risk, ie the 'real' value of the piece. Should you over insure then the only loser will be you, as you will be paying a higher premium than necessary.

Conversely, avoid under insuring. Most insurance policies contain an 'average' clause. The effect of an average clause on a claim can be quite dramatic, eg Fred insures his prints for £20,000. The prints are really worth £30,000. There is a fire in Fred's studio, £6,000 worth of damage is done to the prints. Fred will not receive £6,000 from his insurance company. He will only get £4,000. This is because Fred is under insured by ⅓. The insurance company 'averages' the sum at risk and the sum insured. Unless the sum insured is the same as the sum at risk a claimant will never receive full compensation for loss.

The above points about the perils of over and under insuring presume one very important factor. That is – it is possible to reach a 'real' value of a piece of art work. This is by no means always the case. If an artist has no 'track record' or cannot point to the sale of a comparable piece of work, then it can be virtually impossible to assess the damage or loss. This is true not only of 'junior' artists but also of more established figures who are beginning to work in an area that is new to them.

The most important point to remember as regards valuation is that **do not** assume that because you have fixed a value at the outset of an insurance agreement then that is the amount you will receive in the event of loss or damage. There are many ways of assessing a loss:

▶the cost of reparation – how much would it cost to repair?
▶the market value – how much would it sell for on the open market to a bona fide purchaser?
▶the artist's price – how much would the artist receive if the work were sold in the normal way? (ie deduct any commission payable)
▶the intrinsic value of the work – how much does the material cost and the cost of labour?
▶the income loss to the artist – how much does the loss mean in terms of the artist's annual profit, would there be any monies from reproduction?

The only safe presumption is that the insurance company will probably offer the least sum. (David Binding)[2]

▶Gallery Insurance◀

When a group of students organised their degree show in a London gallery, insurance was one of the problems they had to solve.

'The gallery did not provide any insurance and no-one seemed particularly bothered about it. However, about two weeks before the show I went around to investigate. Most companies required the gallery to be alarmed or to provide security until I discovered that Norwich Union have a special 'exhibition' insurance. I got a quote for 1-22 people – for up to £2,500 each with £1,000 as the most per single piece. This covered us for breakages in transit there and back, throughout the exhibition and for public liability. It worked out to be about £11 for £2,500 worth of cover or about £5 for £1,000. Everyone decided on their amounts and I arranged the cover. In the event, two glass pieces broke (one there, one back) and Norwich Union provided the £420 claimed with no problems'.
(Sally Penn-Smith, '8·8·8' *Artists Newsletter*, March 1989)

▶Exhibitions◀

When exhibiting work in a gallery, museum or other establishment you should be sure that your work is covered by insurance not only whilst it is hanging in the gallery but during transit to and from the gallery and your studio. It is likely that the gallery will have an insurance policy to cover damage and loss of work whilst it is hanging but you should check. It will probably be your responsibility to insure your work during transit to and from the gallery. There are several questions that you should ask when exhibiting your work and transporting it:

▶How much is the gallery insured for in respect of each piece of work?
▶How can you ensure that you will receive the full amount of the value of your work in the event of a claim?
▶How do you prove when the work was damaged, and therefore who is responsible for the damage?
▶If you employ carriers to deliver your work to the gallery what are the terms of their insurance cover?

A gallery may have insurance cover to the amount of £800 per piece of work. Let's assume your work is priced at £150 and £300. A piece priced at £300 is damaged and you consider you should receive the amount of restoration costs or full value of the work if restoration costs are estimated to exceed £300.

▷**2** 'Three Considerations', David Binding, Artlaw Supplement No 2, *Artists Newsletter*, September 1982

However, you may not have ever sold any work at £300 and indeed the only sales from the exhibition are of works priced at £150. How do you prove to the insurers that you should receive in excess of £150 which in their view is the market value bearing in mind that is the highest price you have ever sold at. This is a very difficult question to answer but one way to tackle it would be to try to persuade the insurers that the more highly priced work is different from the work sold at £150 and involved you in more expensive materials and more time. It will not be an easy task to convince the insurers so do not be surprised if you do not succeed.

Even assuming you manage to convince the insurers of the true value of your work the problems are not over. There remains the question of proving who is responsible for the damage. An insurance company will only pay out on a claim if they are convinced that their insured is responsible for the damage. If the damage to a piece of your work is only noticed once it has been hung in the gallery during the exhibition there are various times when the damage may have occurred as far as the insurers are concerned, eg:

- ►in your studio;
- ►whilst you were delivering it to the gallery, ie in transit;
- ►whilst hanging in the gallery.

(Roslyn Innocent)[3]

This is a particularly difficult problem with touring exhibitions. In a touring show A the artist may have given work to B the show organiser. B gives the work to C, a van driver, to deliver to D a gallery; D returns the work via E (yet another carrier) to F a friend of B (B being away on holiday.) B on his return gets the work back to A via G (yet another carrier.) The work is damaged. A notifies B who contacts C who in turn ... G swears blind that the work was OK when he returned it, and he has a signed receipt to say so! An example of a tricky, messy problem. (David Binding)[4]

◁see **Touring Exhibitions**▷

The only way to prove when the work was damaged is for you and the gallery director to gather as much evidence as possible from the gallery staff, people who attended the preview, anyone who has been interested in purchasing the work and the people who carried out the carriage of the work to the gallery from your studio as to their recollection of the state of the work when they saw it. If all the evidence points to the fact the work was damaged at the gallery or it is reasonable to assume in the absence of evidence to the contrary that the damage occurred in the gallery, the gallery's insurers must settle the claim.

If the gallery's insurers do agree to settle the claim for the full sale price of the work in the event of a total loss or if restoration costs are higher than the sale price you will not receive that full price. The reason for this is that an insurer will only pay out the amount of your actual loss. If the gallery takes 30% commission on all sales the insurer would deduct that from the sale price together with VAT on the commission if the gallery is registered for VAT. So you could end up receiving:

Sale Price		£300
Less 30% commission ...	£90	
Less 15% VAT	£13.50	£103.50
		£196.50

If the evidence proves that the damage or loss did not occur in the gallery then you would have either to claim under your own policy or if you employed carriers to deliver your work to the gallery under their policy. Again you would have to prove when and where the damage occurred.

In the case of a total loss of a piece of work it would, in theory at least, be worth claiming an additional sum for loss of copyright. If, for example, the piece lost or damaged beyond repair is a very reproducable work you will have lost the benefit of any money you could receive from reproduction. The amount to be claimed would obviously be difficult to establish and open

▷**3** *Directory of Exhibition Spaces* first edition

▷**4** 'Transit', David Binding, Artlaw Supplement No 2, *Artists Newsletter*, September 1982

to negotiation between you, the gallery and the insurer. To support this aspect of your claim you would need to show the insurer what the work was, by providing a slide or photograph. It would also be advisable to obtain the opinion of an expert in these matters.

In all cases of insurance and whether you consider it necessary to insure you should weigh up the cost of the premium for the insurance and the cost of losing your work, studio, materials etc. You may think that you cannot afford to insure but it is most unlikely that a loss will cost you more than paying for the insurance premium. Insurance premiums for all aspects of your work are tax deductible as a business expense. So do consider insurance. (Roslyn Innocent)[5]

►Paying Insurance◄

You can generally include the majority of business insurances in a combined policy that covers all various risks you need. This means you only have one renewal date and one premium to pay. It is possible to pay in instalments using insurance companies' own credit schemes. This will of course cost you additional interest but insurance companies tend not to ask for details of your credit record.

►Information◄

►Further Reading◄

►'The Artist and Insurance', 'Artlaw Supplement No 2'. *Artists Newsletter*, October 1982

►'Contracts, VAT and Insurance', Roslyn Innocent. *Directory of Exhibition Spaces*, first edition, ed Neil Hanson & Susan Jones, Artic Producers, 1983

►'Are you covered?', David Briers, *Artists Newsletter*, August 1987. Looks at the insurance and liability of artists running workshops in public galleries

►*Organising Your Own Exhibition – a Guide for Artists*, Debbie Duffin. ACME Housing Association, 1987. Contains a section on security and insurance

▷**5** *Directory of Exhibition Spaces* first edition

Contracts

Richard Padwick

Why Contracts?

A contract is an agreement between two or more people that a state of affairs exist and that each party to the agreement has certain obligations. Although it is not necessary for a contract to be in writing for it to be legally binding, it is strongly advisable. The fact that it is written will mean that at an early stage the parties will have a clear idea of what they have agreed. If later one or other can not remember a term, reference can be made to the written contract. It is difficult to prove the spoken word!

Contract of Sale

see **Copyright**

Without a contract of sale the buyer is able, whether the artist likes it or not, to alter, damage or destroy the work, to prevent access to it including to the artist, to re-sell it to anyone or any organisation. British law provides little protection over an artist's work once it has been sold, *except* that the copyright in the work remains the artist's unless this is specifically included in the contract of sale. The new moral rights provisions in the 1988 Copyright Law prevents a purchased work from being exhibited in public or published whilst being falsely assigned to a different artist or in an altered form whilst being assigned to the true artist. However, lack of any written clarification of the copyright or moral rights position often leads to misunderstandings by both parties.

At its simplest, a contract of sale is little more than a receipt describing what has been bought, for how much, from whom, by whom, where and when. Additionally, it should clarify the copyright position and could include clauses allowing the artist reasonable access to the work for purpose of photography or exhibition; giving the artist the first option to undertake or supervise repair of any damage; requiring the buyer to inform the artist if the work is resold or given away and to whom, and when and where it is to be included in an exhibition.

▶Contract of Sale◀

Basic Contract

▶Name/address/tel of Purchaser
▶Name/address/tel of Selling Agent if acting on behalf of the Artist
▶Name/address/tel of Artist

▶Title and description of Work
▶Price and how payment is to be made
▶The Artist retains copyright in the Work

Additional Protection Clauses

▶The Purchaser agrees to allow the Artist reasonable access to the Work for purpose of photography
▶The Purchaser agrees to lend the Work to Artist for purpose of public exhibition provided insurance and other defined conditions are met
▶The Purchaser agrees to inform the Artist if the Work is resold or is given away and to whom, and when and where it is lent for exhibitions
▶The Artist agrees to repair damage to the Work caused through faulty materials or workmanship (or if the Work is inherently of an unstable or fragile nature then this fact should be drawn to the attention of the Purchaser and any responsibility for repair disclaimed)
▶The Purchaser agrees not intentionally to alter, damage or destroy the Work
▶The Purchaser agrees to inform the Artist of loss or damage to the Work and gives the Artist reasonable opportunity to repair or supervise repairs to the Work

▶The Purchaser is permitted to reproduce or allow others to reproduce the work in exhibition or collection catalogues but is required to inform the artist of such reproductions. Reproduction for all other purposes must be referred to the copyright owner (normally the artist)
▶Both parties agree to inform each other of changes of address

▶Signed (Purchaser)
▶Signed (Artist or Agent)
▶Date

Other notes:

▶If the work is one of an edition the artist should agree not to increase the stated edition number
▶If the purchaser will not sign the contract, you should do so and give a copy to the purchaser

►Temporary Exhibition Contracts◄

►Basic Exhibition Contract for Alternative Venues◄

◁see **Exhibitor's Checklist**▷

This can be used when an artist seeks exhibitions in alternative venues such as pubs, clubs, leisure centres – places which are not in the business of presenting exhibitions and which will, in consequence, accept little or no responsibility for the work on their premises.

►Name/address/tel of the Venue
►Name/address/tel of the Artist

►Date of the exhibition and hours of opening
►Dates the Artist can install and dismantle the exhibition
►Agreed method of hanging
►Who is responsible for insurance?
►Does the Venue accept any responsibility for the safe keeping of the Work, if so, to what extent?
►Will the Venue handle sales on behalf of the Artist?
►Is any commission on sales to be taken by the Venue?
►List of Works with details and retail prices

►Signed (on behalf of the Venue)
►Signed (Artist)
►Date

►Temporary Exhibition Contract◄

This is intended for artists holding a temporary exhibition in a gallery or regular exhibition space

►Name/address/tel of Gallery
►Name/address/tel of Artist

►Title of the Exhibition
►If a two-person or a group show the names of the other artist(s) exhibiting
►Dates of Exhibition and hours of opening
►If a tour details of all the other venues

►List of Works (with retail price inclusive of Gallery commission and any relevant VAT)
►Gallery commission expressed as a percentage of the retail price
►Is the Gallery or Artist responsible for arranging and/or funding the following:

►Publicity (advertisements, posters, press releases)
►Photography of work for publicity and catalogue
►Catalogues
►Private view (printing of invite cards and mailing, wine, etc)
►Transportation of work (to and from the Gallery)
►Installation of exhibition and dismantling
►Insurance during transportation and whilst on display and during storage
►Framing, plinths, etc
►Invigilation
►Other (itemise)
►Will the Gallery refund you for undertaking any of these responsibilities? How much and when will you be paid?

►Will there be a public exhibition fee? How much and when will you be paid?
►When and how will you receive payment for sales of work?
►Will you be required to do any workshops, talks or demonstrations? If so when and for how long? Is there a fee, how much and when will it be paid?

Additional Protection Clauses

It should be made clear that:
►The Artist retains copyright in all the Work
►Outline the main provisions of Moral Rights under the 1988 Copyright Law
►The Gallery must immediately inform the Artist of any damage, loss or destruction of the Work and must not attempt any repair without the specific agreement of the Artist
►The Gallery can only use photographs of the Work for catalogue, poster, invite card or for publicity for the exhibition
►The Gallery should prevent the public photgraphing the work except for 'private study' purposes when a Copyright Agreement should be used
►The Gallery should make use of an agreed Contract of Sale
►The Gallery should consult the artist over the design of publicity and catalogue, and any written material describing the Artist and his/her Work

►Signed (on behalf of the Gallery)
►Signed (Artist)
►Date

►Sale or Return Agreement◄

For use when work is consigned to a gallery, shop or agent on a sale or return basis.

►Name/address/tel of Artist
►Name/address/tel of Gallery, Shop or Agent

►List of Work consigned to the Agent by the Artist detailing title, medium, size, (edition number), retail price, whether the Work is consigned ready-framed and whether the frame is included in the retail price, and whether the prices are inclusive or exclusive of VAT.
◁see Commission & VAT▷
►How, when, for how long and where the Agent will make the Work available for sale (ie can the Agent lend the Work to other agents or display it on other premises).
►How and when the Artist will be informed of and paid for sales.
►The Artist retains ownership until he/she has received payment in full for the Work.
►The Artist retains the copyright in the Work.
▷see Copyright◁
►Outline the basic provision of Moral Rights under the 1988 Copyright Law.
►The Agent to inform the Artist of the names and addresses of the purchasers and to use an agreed Contract of Sale.
►The Agent adequately to maintain the Work and have adequate insurance or agree to indemnify the Work against loss, damage or theft.
►The Agent to inform the Artist immediately of any loss or damage and not to effect any repairs without the agreement of the Artist.
►Limitation on the Agent's use of reproductions of the Work.

►Signed (on behalf of Agent)
►Signed (Artist)
►Date

►Gallery or Agent Contract◄

To be used where a gallery or agent acts on behalf of the artist arranging exhibitions, sales, commissions and/or lectures, etc.

►Name/address/tel of Agent/Gallery
►Name/address/tel of Artist

►Establish the extent of the Agent's responsibilities:
- ►Sell the Artist's Work (and use agreed Contract of Sale)
- ►Arrange commissions (and use an agreed Commission Contract) ◁see **Commissions**▷
- ►Arrange exhibitions of the Artist's Work in the Agent's own premises and/or elsewhere
- ►Arrange residencies, lectures and other opportunities for the Artist
- ►Arrange press and media coverage on the Artist and his/her Work
- ►Publish and market reproductions of the Artist's Work, or to license Reproduction Rights to others

►Whether any of the above rights are exclusive to the Agent or whether other arrangements can be made by the Artist with other agents and where the rights of each agent operate (ie worldwide, States, Europe, UK). Can the Artist arrange any of the above without going through the Agent?
►Does the Artist have a veto on any arrangements made by the Agent?
►Length of the agreement – is it for a one-off occasion, or is it a quarterly or yearly renewable agreement?
►Length of notice required by each party to terminate the agreement.
►How, when and on what basis the Agent is paid for his/her work.
►How, when and on what basis the Artist is paid for sales, commissions, and other work.

►Signed (on behalf of the Agent)
►Signed (Artist)
►Date

►Copyright Licence◄

◁see Copyright▷

For use when the copyright owner (normally the artist) permits a gallery, agent or publishing company to reduce a piece of his/her work.

► Name/address/tel of Gallery/Agent/Publisher
►Name/address/tel of Artist
►Details of the Work(s) to be reproduced (title, media, size, date)
►Form of reproduction (ie poster, postcard, calendar, book, greetings card, etc)
►Method of reproduction (ie four colour process lithography, duotone, etc)
►Size of reproduction
►Number of copies of the reproductions (ie the print run)
►Other details of the product in or on which the work is to be reproduced
►Whether the product is to be sold (if so how and at what price) or given as a gift (ie business Christmas cards)
►Does the agreement restrict the Artist from licensing reproduction rights in the Work to others?
►Is there an option for the Publisher to increase the print run or to reprint and under what terms?
►Does the agreement require the publisher to return the Work, the tranparencies, plate, negatives, etc after the agreed number of copies have been printed?

Attribution

►Will the reproduction clearly attribute the authorship and give details of the Work?
►Will the reproduction include the international copyright symbol © assigned to the copyright owner?

Integrity of Reproduction

►Will the Work be reproduced in full without cropping, the superimposition of text, image, symbol or other mark, or does the agreement permit this (in which case full details should be given)?
►Does the agreement give the Artist the right to view proofs and refuse permission to publish if in his/her view the quality of reproduction is of an unacceptable standard?

Payment

►Is the Artist paid royalties on sales (ie an agreed percentage of the wholesale or retail price)? If so what is the percentage?
►Or is the Artist paid an agreed lump sum?
►Or is the fee to be a combination of royalties and lump-sum?
►How and when payments are to be made?

►Signed (on behalf of the Publisher)
►Signed (Artist)
►Date

►Information◄

►Further Reading◄

►'Paper Promises part 2', Henry Lydiate, 'Artlaw'. *Art Monthly* No 99, September 1986. Exhibition contracts, contract of sale, agency contract, copyright licence

►*Collected Artlaw Articles*, ed Jenny Boswell. Artlaw Services 1981. Reprints from Artlaw articles in *Art Monthly*. Most contracts covered

►*Guide to the Law*, J Pritchard. Penguin 1982

►*Small Claims in the County Court*. Available from local county court: guide to procedures on how to sue and defend actions without a lawyer

►*Art Monthly*. Henry Lydiate writes a regular column on legal issues that face visual artists.

►'Contracts, VAT and Insurance', Roslyn Innocent. *Directory of Exhibition Spaces*, first edition ed Neil Hanson and Susan Jones. Artic Producers 1983

►*Draft Exhibition Contract*, National Artists Association 1987/88. This will be finalised during 1989/90 and made available to artists and galleries

►'A Cautionary Tale or a Lesson for Artists', Maggie Humphry. *Artists Newsletter*, May 1987

►*Art, Design & Craft – a manual for business success*, John Crowe & James Stokes. Edward Arnold 1988

Copyright & Moral Rights

► **Richard Padwick** ◄

On August 1, 1989 the new copyright law (the Copyright, Designs and Patents Act 1988) came into effect. It replaces the old law (1956), removing anomalies, making it more consistent, strengthening artists' rights, bringing UK legislation in line with the Berne Convention on moral rights (droite/moral), and making it easier to bring legal action against those who infringe copyright.

► Copyright ◄

The new copyright law only affects works produced after the change in law took place. Work produced before the change remains protected under the old 1956 law. It is important, therefore, that artists are aware of the provisions of both laws.

► What is copyright? ◄

Copyright is the legal right not to suffer any reproduction of an 'artistic work' without the express consent of the copyright owner – thus seeking to ensure that any economic benefits arising from reproductions etc are under the control of the copyright owner.

► What is protected? ◄

Both the old and new laws give copyright protection to work which passes three tests:

► It is must be produced by a citizen, domicile or resident (or in the case of companies, incorporated) in the UK or any country which is a signatory to the Berne Convention on copyright (most countries).

► The work must be original – it must not be physically copied from another original work. It must involve original skill and labour but not necessarily thought. In the case of a limited edition of prints, each print qualifies as original because it is not a copy from another print.

► The work must be of 'artistic merit'. Under the old law, paintings, sculpture, drawings, prints and photographs are assumed to have 'artistic merit' and are therefore automatically eligible for copyright protection. Other works (collage, montage, craftwork, artists' bookworks, body art, installations, laser and light works, mixed-media assemblages, performance art, video and holograms) under the old

law are only eligible for protection if they can demonstrate that they have 'artistic merit', ie the makers must have applied their skill and taste to its making with the intention to create a work which has aesthetic appeal. Such works are categorised as works of 'artistic craftsmanship'. After August 1, 1989, collages are elevated from works of 'artistic craftsmanship' to those that automatically qualify for protection. Holograms, as new technology, were not catered for under the old Act but are covered in the new law by the new definition of a photograph – *'a recording of light or other radiation on any medium on which an image is produced or from which an image may by any means be produced and which is not part of a (moving image) film'*. Under the old law, prints made by a photographic process were classified as 'photographs', and prints employing traditional methods such as woodcuts, lithographs, engravings, silkscreen, etchings, not using a photographic process, were classified as 'prints'. Under the new law, all prints however produced are classified as 'graphic works'.

►Copyright Byline◄

Provided all three of the above tests are passed, copyright protection is automatic – neither the old nor the new laws require the maker to publicly claim or register copyright ownership or endorse the work for it to be protected in this country. But endorsement is required for protection against copyright abuses abroad. Endorsement involves indelibly marking the work with '©', the artist's name and the date the work was created. Endorsement is a requirement for one of the new law's Moral Rights provisions (see below).

►Copyright Ownership◄

Both old and new laws make a distinction between works made by a freelance artist (contract for services) and those made in the course of employment (contract of service). If a work is made by someone as part of their employment (unless the contract of employment states otherwise) then under both the old and new laws the first copyright owner is the employer. The situation is more complicated in the case of works by freelance artists, the new law tidying up anomalies in the old:

Works made by a freelance artist before August 1, 1989

The first owner of copyright is the maker except for the following 'artistic works' when the first copyright owner is the commissioner:

- ►commissioned prints
- ►commissioned photographs
- ►commissioned portrait paintings and drawings

Note: the maker is the first copyright owner in any other artistic works or any sculpture and in any work of artistic craftsmanship whether commissioned or not.

The first copyright owner of an uncommissioned photograph is the person who owns the film or material on which the photographic image was first made – not necessarily the photographer.

Works made by freelance makers after August 1, 1989

The freelance maker is the first copyright owner of any artistic work (including photographs) irrespective of whether it has been commissioned or not. The freelance maker may be asked to transfer copyright to the commissioner, but this must be in writing signed by the maker.

►Length of Copyright◄

On works produced before August 1, 1989

Art work is protected for the maker's lifetime plus 50 years after death except for photographs and prints when length of copyright is determined from the date the work is published:

- ►Unpublished photographs and prints: copyright lasts forever
- ►Published photographs (including photographically made prints) whether they were published before or after the maker's death: copyright lasts 50 years from the end of the year of publication.
- ►Prints (ie not photographically made prints) published before the maker's death: copyright lasts for the maker's lifetime plus 50 years.
- ►Prints (ie not photographically made prints) published after the maker's death: copyright lasts 50 years from the end of the year of publication.

The meaning of 'publishing' as used here is issuing reproductions of a print or photograph to the public and not public exhibition of the original work. Putting a photographic print, for example, in a public exhibition does not qualify as publishing but reproducing the image in a catalogue, on exhibition posters or postcards does.

On works produced after August 1, 1989

The 1989 law tidies up these anomalies and copyright protection on all artistic works (including prints and photographs) lasts for the maker's lifetime plus fifty years from the end of the calendar year in which the maker dies. In other words, the length of copyright for prints and photographs no longer depends on whether and when they have been published.

►Infringements◄

Copyright protects artistic works from the following 'restricted acts' without the authorisation of the copyright owner:

Infringements before August 1, 1989

- ►reproducing the work in any material form
- ►publishing the work
- ►including the work in a TV broadcast

Infringements after August 1, 1989

- ►reproducing the work in any material form – now including the use of electronic means
- ►putting into circulation copies of a work not previously put into circulation, in the UK or elsewhere
- ►including the work in a TV broadcast (including cable television)

The new law acknowledges new technologies and the ability to store and display images on computers; 'publishing' is widened to 'circulating' and 'elsewhere' is used to include all countries, not just those who are signatories to the Berne Convention.

►Primary and Secondary Infringements◄

'Primary' infringers are those who either themselves commit the above restricted acts or who authorise others to do so; they are liable even though they may not know (or have reason to believe that they are infringing copyright). Secondary infringers are usually those who do not themselves

infringe but deal commercially with infringing copies or the means to make such copies.

►Permitted Copying◄

Copyright allows work to be copied for the following limited purposes:

Acts before August 1, 1989

►research or private study

►criticism or review provided it is accompanied by sufficient acknowledgement of the maker (and the photographer – both of whom may be copyright owners of the published photographic reproduction of a work)

►background use in TV and film (the work must be part of the background setting and incidental to the main matter of the programme, ie the camera should not show the work full-frame)

►judicial proceedings or reports of them

►Use within educational establishments so long as a duplicating process is not used and for examination purpose whether or not a duplicating process is used.

►Sculpture or works of 'artistic craftsmanship' if permanently sited in a public place or in premises open to the public may be painted, drawn, photographed, filmed or televisually broadcast (not by cable television) and any such reproductions may be published or televisually broadcast without the permission of the copyright owner and no acknowledgement is required. But a sculpture cannot be made of another sculpture sited in a public place.

►Artists who do not own copyright in their work can reproduce their original imagery in subsequent works so long as they do not repeat or imitate the main design of the original.

Acts after August 1, 1989

Much as before, except that reproductions may be used without copyright permission for the following additional purposes:

►Advertisement of work for sale – allowing galleries and artists' agents to reproduce works in catalogues, posters or on television, but only if the purpose is to advertise the original work for sale. However, museums and art galleries buying a work from an artist are not permitted to print and sell postcards of it without the copyright owner's permission.

►Copyrighted work, with the exception of photographs, can be used in reporting of current events, provided sufficient acknowledgement is given. Acknowledgement is not required in film or TV reporting. Photographs cannot be used without the copyright owner's permission.

►Artists are now permitted to use the copyright work of another artist provided it is incidental to the main image in the work.

►Reproduction is now allowed for statutory functions such as Royal Commissions.

Other changes include reproduction for educational purposes whether within educational establishments or not, so long as the copying is either done by the person giving or receiving instruction and that copying does not involve a reprographic process. Copying for examination questions is permitted however the copying is done. Reprographic process is defined

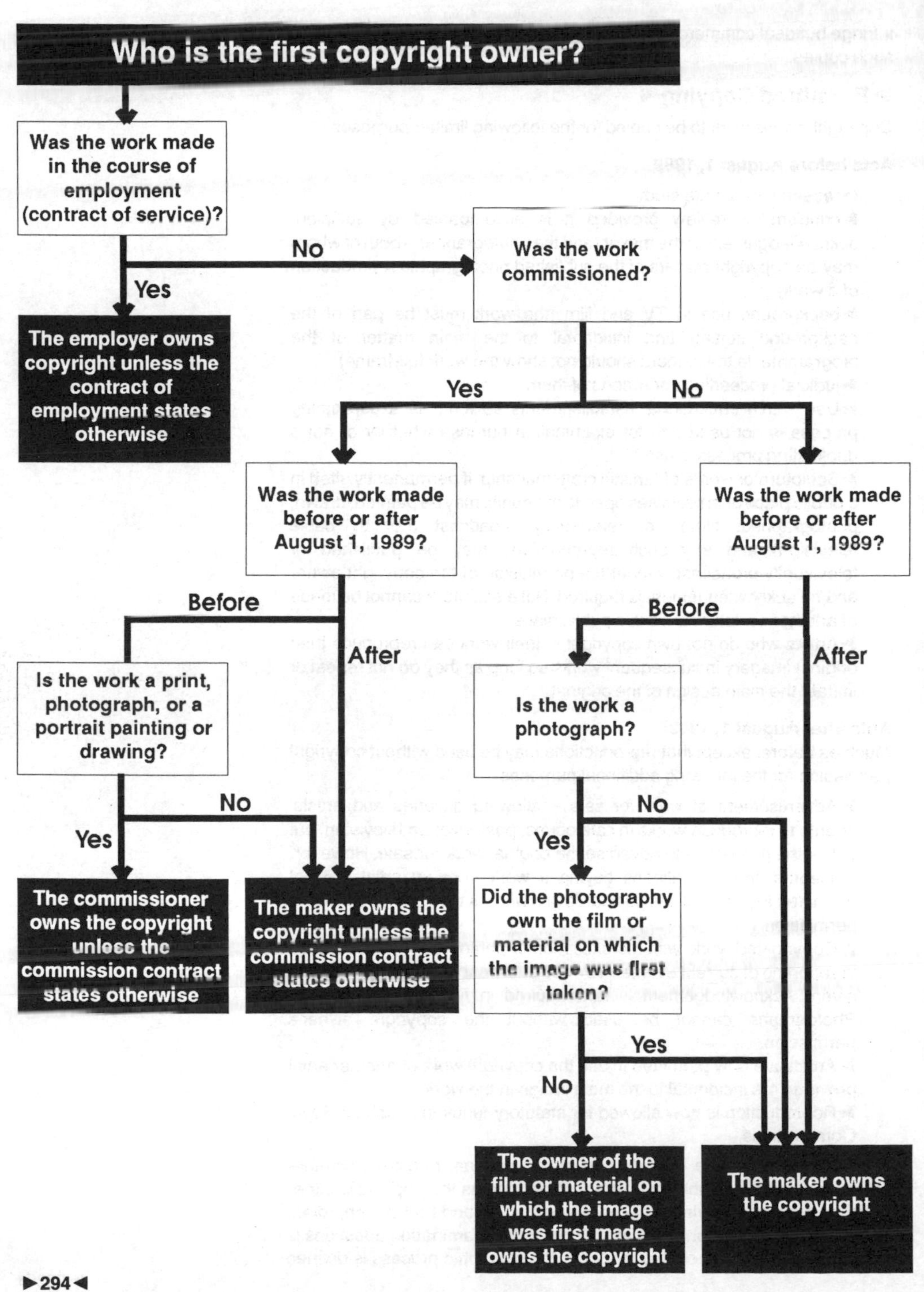

Who is the first copyright owner?
Was the work made in the course of employment (contract of service)?
Yes
No
The employer owns copyright unless the contract of employment states otherwise
Was the work commissioned?
Yes
No
Was the work made before or after August 1, 1989?
Was the work made before or after August 1, 1989?
Before
After
Is the work a print, photograph, or a portrait painting or drawing?
Yes
No
The commissioner owns the copyright unless the commission contract states otherwise
The maker owns the copyright unless the commission contract states otherwise
Before
After
Is the work a photograph?
Yes
No
Did the photography own the film or material on which the image was first taken?
Yes
No
The owner of the film or material on which the image was first made owns the copyright
The maker owns the copyright

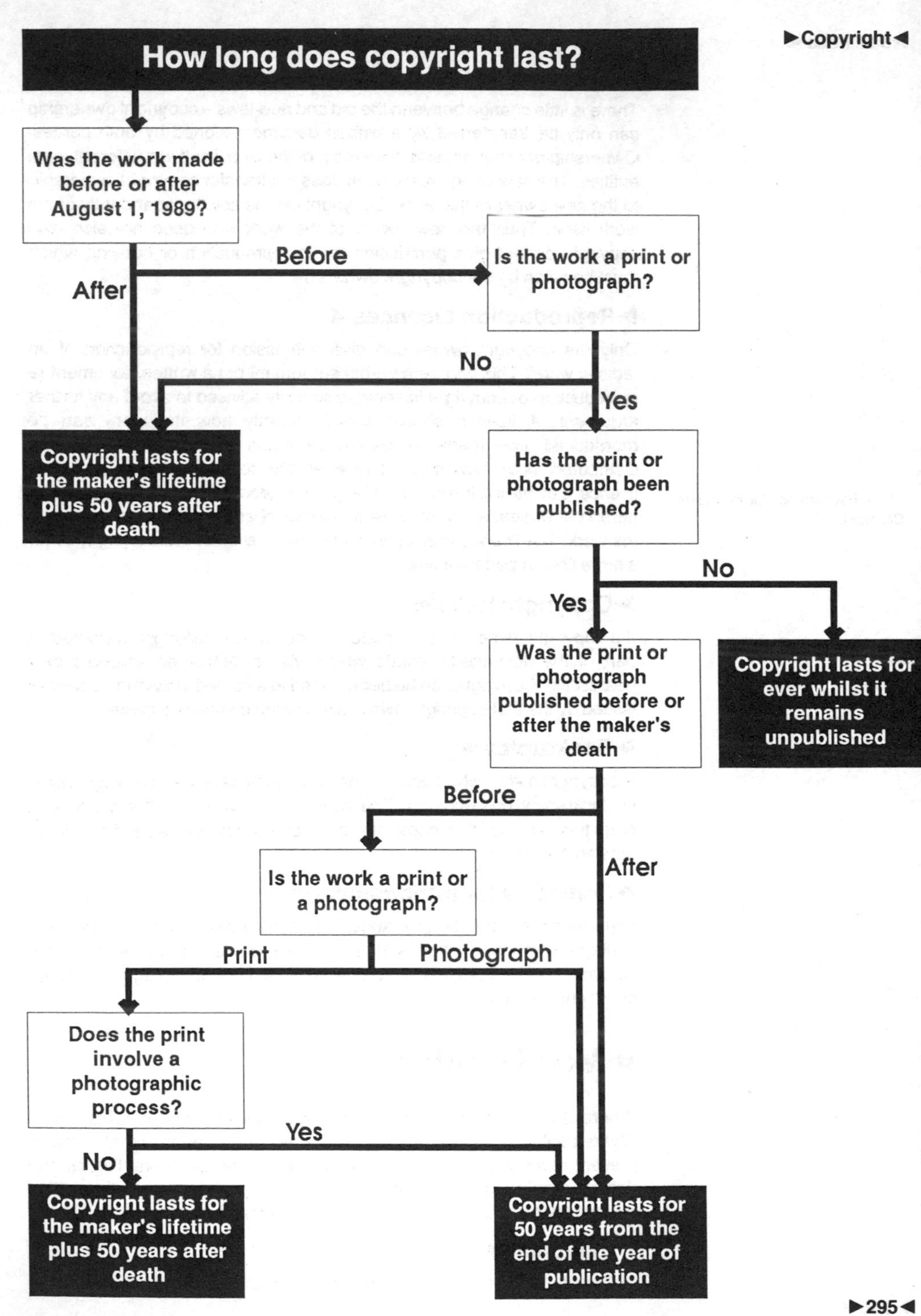
How long does copyright last?
Was the work made before or after August 1, 1989?
After
Before
Is the work a print or photograph?
No
Yes
Copyright lasts for the maker's lifetime plus 50 years after death
Has the print or photograph been published?
No
Yes
Was the print or photograph published before or after the maker's death
Copyright lasts for ever whilst it remains unpublished
Before
After
Is the work a print or a photograph?
Print
Photograph
Does the print involve a photographic process?
Yes
No
Copyright lasts for the maker's lifetime plus 50 years after death
Copyright lasts for 50 years from the end of the year of publication

as a process for making facsimile or multiple copies.

►Transferring Copyright Ownership◄

There is little change between the old and new laws – copyright ownership can only be transferred by a written document signed by both parties. Ownership of copyright and ownership of the work itself are different legal entities. The sale of an artistic work does not transfer copyright ownership to the new owner of the work. Copyright can be sold independently of the work itself. Thus the new owner of the work who does not also own copyright cannot give permission for its reproduction or copying which must be given by the copyright owners.

►Reproduction Licences◄

▷See Reproduction Licence under **Contracts**◁

Only the copyright owner can give permission for reproduction of an 'artistic work'. This can be a verbal agreement but a written document (a reproduction or copyright licence) is strongly advised to avoid any further argument. A licence should specify exactly how the work can be reproduced, how many copies can be made and where they can be distributed; how, how much and when the copyright owner is paid. A licence can be exclusive, ie selling the reproduction rights to only one person or organisation, or allow a number of organisations to reproduce the work. The licence may be valid for the duration of the copyright, or for a more limited period of time.

►Copyright Heirs◄

If a copyright owner dies intestate (without a will), copyright is treated as part of the deceased's estate which will be distributed amongst their nearest kin. Copyright can be bequeathed to a named individual. Licences issued by the first copyright owner are binding on the new owner.

►Bankruptcy◄

A copyright owner who becomes bankrupt may have their copyright taken in bankruptcy proceedings. The new owner, bank or other creditor, is permitted to use the copyright by reproducing the work to pay off outstanding debts.

►Remedies for Infringement◄

Infringements done before August 1, 1989 come under the old law, infringements done after August 1, 1989 come under the new law. Copyright owners can take the civil or criminal proceedings against alleged copyright infringers:

►Moral rights◄

Whereas copyright seeks to protect the maker's economic rights, Moral Rights deal with the maker's right to be recognised as the creator and to prevent derogatory treatment of work. There are four Moral Rights: the right of identification, the right to object to derogatory treatment, the right to prevent false attribution, and the right of privacy.

►Eligibility◄

All artistic works including works of artistic craftsmanship and of

architecture are protected so long as the work is original and it is of the author's own skill and labour though not necessarily thought. Copies or works which contain substantial elements of another original work are not protected by the law.

►The Right of Identification◄

The maker of an artistic work has the right to be identified as such whenever the work is published commercially, exhibited in public or a visual image of it is broadcast, included in a cable programme, or a film including a visual image of it is issued to the public. The identification must be clear and resonably prominent. This right is only valid if the maker asserts their right (see below) ie there is no infringement if the maker has not previously asserted their right.

►The Right to Object to Derogatory Treatment◄

The maker of an artistic work has the right not to have their work subjected to derogatory treatment whenever the work is published commercially or exhibited in public or a visual image of it is broadcast, including in a cable programme or in a film shown or issued to the public. 'Derogatory treatment' means any addition to, deletion from, alteration to, or adaption of the work which amounts to distortion or mutilation of the work or which is prejudicial to the honour or reputation of the maker. It remains to be seen how this last provision will be interpreted. Destruction of a work is not likely to constitute 'derogatory treatment'.

►False Attribution◄

A person has the right not to be attributed as the maker of a work they did not make. This right is infringed whenever it or a copy of it is publicly exhibited, issued to the public, or dealt with or possessed by someone knowing or with reason to believe that it is falsely attributed.

An artist also has the right to prevent anyone from dealing with a work or a copy of it which is attributed to the artist but which has been altered without the artist's permission.

This right exists without the need for the maker to assert their rights (see below).

►The Right of Privacy◄

The new law also gives the right to commissioners of private or domestic photographs not to have copies put on public display.

►Exceptions to Moral Rights◄

As with copyright there are a number of exclusions to the Moral Rights of Identification and Objection to Derogatory Treatment. The main ones being when:

- ►the work is computer-generated
- ►the work is produced by the artist as part of employment, ie when the first copyright owner is the employer.
- ►the work is made for the purpose of reporting current events
- ►the work is made for, or made available for, publication in a newspaper, magazine or similar periodical or encyclopaedia, dictionary, yearbook or other collective work of reference.
- ►the work is incidently included in a film/TV or artistic work.

►Assertion of Rights◄

For the right of identification to be valid the artist must assert this right; appropriate wording needs to be included in all copyright assignments and licences and the name of the artist put on all original work (or authorised copies) on the frame or mount.

►Length of Moral Rights

Moral Rights covering identification and derogatory treatment last for the same period as copyright and expire when copyright expires. Moral Rights covering false attribution last for the maker's lifetime plus 20 years.

►Transferral and Waiving of Moral Rights◄

Moral Rights cannot be transferred or assigned by the artist during their lifetime to anyone else. Thus the maker will still retain them even where both the original work and the copyright in that work have been disposed of. On death, Moral Rights pass to the person named as beneficiary of them in the will or if none,to the person to whom the copyright passes. The artist may waive (ie give up) any or all Moral Rights, conditionally or unconditionally, by a written and signed statement, for example in a contract, or more informally under the general law of contact. All artists should thus beware of giving away their rights unknowingly.

►Conclusions◄

►Keep your copyright, and only part with it if it is financially very worthwhile to do so.

►Always endorse your work on the back with the international copyright byline and assert your moral rights on all work ie '©' Artist's name, date of creation and 'All rights reserved'. Also assert your rights in all contracts and assignments of copyright.

►Detail your copyright and Moral Rights on all documents relating to the work such as contracts of sale, exhibition contracts, loan forms for exhibitions.

►Check before signing contracts, including open exhibition submission forms, that you are not unwittingly signing away any of your copyright or Moral Rights.

►Make a will stating who your heir is to be in respect of your copyright and Moral Rights

►Join the Design and Artists Copyright Society (DACS) who can act as your copyright policing and collecting agency.

▶Information◀

▶Contacts◀

▶*DACS (Design and Artists Copyright Society)*, St Mary's Clergy House, 2 Whitechapel Lane, London ☎ 01 247 1650
▶*British Copyright Council*, 29-33 Berners Street, London W1P 4AA
▶*Committee on Photographic Copyright*, c/o AFAEP, 10-12 Domingo Street, London EC1Y 0TA

▶Further Reading◀

▶*Artists Copyright Handbook*, Henry Lydiate, Artlaw Services, 1983. Available from DACS (*see above*)
▶*Photographer's Guide to the 1988 Copyright Act*, British Photographers Liaison Committee, 1989. They have also produced a useful double-sided sheet with a diagram outlining copyright for photography before and after the Act
▶*Art Monthly.* Henry Lydiate writes a regular column on legal issues that face visual artists.
▶*Guide to the Law*, J Pritchard. Penguin 1982
▶*Small Claims in the County Court.* Available from local county courts, a guide to procedures on how to sue and defend actions without a lawyer
▶*The ABC of Copyright*. UNESCO. HMSO 1981
▶'When I Paint My Masterpiece', Henry Lydiate, 'Artlaw'. *Art Monthly* No 80, October 1984
▶'Between Thought and Expression', Henry Lydiate, 'Artlaw'. *Art Monthly* No 87, June 1985
▶'Ignorantia Lex Non Fit Defensia', Henry Lydiate, 'Artlaw'. *Art Monthly* No 88, July/August 1985
▶*Collected Artlaw Articles*, Henry Lydiate ed Jenny Boswell. Artlaw Services, 1981. Out of print but invaluable if you can locate a copy
▶*Artlaw Supplement No 4*, Henry Lydiate, Mark Stephens & Kevin Garnett. *Artists Newsletter*, June 1983
▶'Copyright Law – the basic facts', Stephen B Cox . *Artists Newsletter* April 1988
▶'Droit Moral', Stephen B Cox . *Artists Newsletter*, October 1988
▶'Copyright & Moral Rights', Henry Lydiate 'Artlaw'. *Art Monthly* No 124 March 1989
▶'Copyright & Moral Rights', Henry Lydiate 'Artlaw'. *Art Monthly* No 125 April 1989
▶'Artlaw: Copyright & Moral Rights: New Legislation', Henry Lydiate. *Art Monthly* No 126, May 1989
▶'Artlaw: Copyright & Moral Rights: New Legislation', Henry Lydiate. *Art Monthly* No 128, July-Aug 1989
▶*A Printmaker's Handbook*, Silvie Turner. Estamp. Contains a three-page section on copyright and prints
▶*Copyright, Designs & Patents Act 1988*. HMSO

Studio Safety

Studio Safety

►Tim Challis◄
►Gary Roberts◄

During the course of our research into health and safety in the arts and crafts in 1983 and 1984, we were contacted by countless artists throughout the world with accounts of injuries and disabilities sustained through the course of their work. In many cases these were slight, but in some they involved serious injury, and in at least two cases involved death. There is no purpose in exaggerating, as some people have done, and pretending that art involves risks as shattering as industry can. Even so, the materials and processes of the arts and crafts are often the same as those used in industry, and involve the same hazards, albeit on a less dramatic scale.

The logical conclusion of this statement is simple; if the process you are using involves the same hazards as a similar one in industry, then it would be wise to adopt the same safety precautions. This is a conclusion supported by the law. Although many artists may not fully realise the fact, those earning a living from their work fall under the jurisdiction of the Health and Safety at Work Etc. Act 1974, and its associated legislation.

However, there are problems facing artists wishing to comply fully with the law. Art and craft processes can present their own peculiar demands, perhaps not always sympathetically answered by the guidelines of industry. In *Caution: A Guide to Safe Practice in the Arts and Crafts*[1] we, as individuals personally and practically familiar with the arts and crafts, translated the rules and regulations of industry into a form easily usable by the working artist. A synopsis of that work is reproduced here, but the onus is and must be on the individual to research subject areas more fully where necessary.

►The Law◄

The Health and Safety at Work Act 1974 is quite unequivocal in its application to everybody at a place of work, should they be employer, employee or member of the public. Part 1, section 3 of the Act demands that self-employed people, irrespective of whether they themselves employ others, must ensure their own safety as well as that of people around them. By the same token, the law applies amongst others to both self-employed artists and students in an art college.

Paradoxically, official provision for health and safety in the small workshop or studio is nevertheless almost non-existent. The Health and

▷1 *Caution: A Guide to Safe Practice in the Arts & Crafts*, Tim Challis & Gary Roberts. Sunderland Polytechnic, 1983

Safety Executive produces the occasional small leaflet aimed at such businesses, but otherwise expects people to consult the information provided for large industries. Even this advice is unlikely to be enforced. As well as the Executive's inability to carry out frequent inspections, they are not even aware of the existence of small workshops and studios.

Even so, this vacuum provides no excuse whatsoever. The full ramifications of safety legislation might only be felt by artists once an accident has occurred, and even though they have not been inspected it is still their legal duty to fulfil their various responsibilities under the regulations.

►Good Housekeeping◄

Good housekeeping is essential for a safe working environment. Generally, it is just a matter of common sense – the advantages of cleanliness and tidiness are fairly self-evident. Dirt and spills of chemicals or liquids should be vacuumed or wet-mopped, but never swept with a dry brush. Where dangerous dusts (such as silica) are concerned, it is important to use a commercial rather than domestic vacuum cleaner. Many domestic vacuum cleaners are incapable of filtering out hazardous, microscopic particles of dust, and simply spray them back into the breathing zone. The floor surface should be non-slip, preferably at one level, and free of obstructions. Smoking, eating or drinking must be forbidden in a dusty atmosphere – they can all increase the chance of ingesting hazardous chemicals or dust. People working with chemicals or materials at home, for instance, should avoid contaminating the living area, and must never use the kitchen as a workroom. Where chemicals must be disposed of, this should be done thoughtfully. It is illegal to pour toxic hazardous chemicals down a sink. If in doubt about a specific chemical, consult the Disposal of Poisonous Wastes Act 1972.

One rule of thumb should be remembered for all potentially dangerous processes. If a process is hazardous, **substitute** it with one that is less dangerous. If this is not possible then **isolate** the process completely, eg screening off and ventilating part of the studio to use as a resin room. Should even this be impracticable, then **protect** everybody in contact with the process with suitable protective clothing. Always remember – **substitute, isolate** or **protect.**

►Safety Consciousness◄

Prevention is always better than cure. Later, the potentially hazardous effects of various materials, should they be inhaled, ingested or brought into contact with the skin, will be described. To minimise the risk of this happening in the first place, the following general precautions should be observed.

►Inhalation◄

Adequate general ventilation as well as extraction equipment at localised work areas is vital to keep dust and fume problems to a minimum. Suitable face masks or respirators should be worn for any process likely to produce excessive dust or fumes. Wherever possible, confine dust-producing work

to extraction cubicles. Tools and workshops should be wet-mopped, not brushed, immediately after work is finished, and overalls and workclothes should be cleaned regularly.

Check the exact nature of materials being used before work commences. The ability of solvents to vapourise at very low temperatures is a particular cause for concern. The exact effect depends upon which particular solvent is encountered. However, in general, short-term exposure produces a narcotic effect, whilst liver and kidney damage and nervous disorders are common long-term hazards.

►Ingestion◄

Accidental ingestion of hazardous materials may occur through eating drinking or smoking in the work area. These should therefore be banned Hands should be thoroughly washed after contact with toxic substances.

►Skin Contact◄

Adequate protective clothing and goggles should be worn to protect against hot, corrosive or dermatitic materials. Some substances, such as phenol, benzene and carbon tetrachloride, are capable of penetrating the skin even without direct contact, thus entering the circulatory system and causing extensive damage. Obviously, adequate ventilation is essential in such circumstances.

Skin contact with solvents is particularly hazardous due to their ability, in varying degrees, to dissolve body fats and thereby become absorbed into the skin and circulatory system. This initially causes dermatitis, but eventually all parts of the body can be affected, especially the liver and kidneys. Adequate protective clothing should obviously be worn to prevent this. Uncovered cuts and abrasions on the skin facilitate and encourage contamination by toxic substances.

►Protective Clothing◄

►Face and Eye Protection◄

Work involving acids or solvents should never be carried out without goggles or a plastic face shield. Eyes must also be protected during grinding, chipping and drilling processes. Visible, infra-red and ultra-violet light are the main hazards to be guarded against during heat processes, such as welding or foundry work. During such operations, the face and eyes should be protected by a helmet and goggles, or hand-shield fitted with the correct filter lenses. If there is a risk of spatter of hot slag, a full head-helmet should always be worn.

The three main types of eye protection available are; spectacles with impact-resistant lenses and side shields, flexible or cushioned goggles and chipping- or eyecup-goggles.

►Hand Protection◄

The hands are the areas of skin most commonly exposed to hazards. It is therefore essential that they are adequately protected. Barrier cream should only be used in conjunction with gloves as it may not provide complete protection in its own right.

►Body Protection◄

Overall protection is especially necessary for work involving high temperatures. A flame-proof overall and leather apron should be worn for welding.

As foundry work involves the pouring of molten metal, the following protective clothing should be worn: spats or gaiters, high-impact visors, heat-resistant gloves and a leather or similar heat-resistant apron.

When working with toxic or corrosive chemicals, flame-resistant or cloth aprons should be worn over the body.

►Respirators◄

Respirators should not be considered a substitute for adequate ventilation. Any respirator has limited effectiveness over long periods, especially if it does not comfortably fit the face. Check for a proper fit by covering the air outlet and breathing in. You should not notice any air leaking around the nose or chin. Try the same exercise breathing out with the exhaust closed. The straps should not have to be tightened excessively to maintain a close fit. Respirators should be regularly checked and cleaned.

Respiratory devices fall into two main categories. Air-purifying respirators consist of two parts, the face mask and the filter which removes contaminants from the air being breathed. The correct filter must be selected for the particular hazardous material encountered. Change filters regularly. Air-supplying respirators should be used when more obviously harmful materials are encountered. An uncontaminated air supply is provided either from a self-contained breathing apparatus, a compressed gas cylinder or a compressor.

Inexpensive paper or cloth masks are not an effective protection against toxic materials and should only be worn as a barrier against non-toxic nuisance dusts.

►Lighting◄

Minimum requirements, as stated in paragraph 52 of the Standards for School Premises Regulations 1972, should be observed. Most colleges and professionals usually adhere to levels of lighting recommended in the 'Illuminated Engineering Society Code for Interior Lighting'.

Certain areas of the workshop may require different levels of lighting to others. For instance, forge and brazing hearth areas should have subdued lighting, but individual machines may require supplementary lighting above the general level. This must only be of a very low voltage, preferably 12 or 24 volts. Light intensity should increase according to the fineness and skill factor of the work. Whereas 200 lux may be adequate for rough sawing and coarse bench work, 500 lux may be required for fine detail work and around 1000 lux for very fine engraving or measuring work. Some examples of recommended lighting levels are: sheet metal work = 400 lux, painting and spraying = up to 500 lux, retouching and colour matching = at least 1000 lux.

Extreme changes of light intensity between different areas of the studio are dangerous and should be avoided.

If possible, always try to achieve recommended levels of light by natural means and only use artificial light as a supplement.

►Noise◄

Studio noise may cause potentially dangerous distractions of concentration. If machinery noise causes discomfort, wear ear muffs. If possible, work in short spells, taking frequent breaks.

Habitual exposure to excessive levels of noise may cause tiredness, nausea and eventually temporary or even permanent deafness.

►Ventilation◄

Adequate ventilation should be the first means of controlling air contaminated with toxic substances. This can be achieved by diluting the contaminant to a level below that hazardous to health (general ventilation), or removing the contaminant at the point of generation (local ventilation). General ventilation is less efficient than local ventilation and may even prevent fine dust from settling, thus prolonging its presence in the breathing zone. An individual working with a particular substance, such as a solvent, may be at risk from a harmful level of exposure even though the general level in a room is safe. In such situations, local exhaust is obviously an advantage.

The following points should be noted when using a local ventilation system:

- ►Enclose the source as effectively as possible.
- ►Capture the contaminant with moving air of adequate velocity.
- ►Keep contaminants out of the breathing zone by not working between the vapour source and the exhaust fan.
- ►Ensure exhausted air is replaced by clean air, i.e. adequate general ventilation.
- ►Discharge contaminated air in such a manner as to prevent it from re-entering the work place.

►Safety in Creative Processes◄

The following section deals with hazardous materials commonly encountered by artists and craftspeople involved in the various work areas of art and design. The more specific advice in this section should be taken in conjunction with the general advice given above.

►Machinery◄

Many of the general precautions concerning electrical machinery are again a matter of common sense. It is important to remember, however, that almost all machines are covered by one or more of the regulations in force, and that these must be adhered to for compliance with the Health and Safety at Work Act. Your local office of the Health and Safety Executive will be able to advise you of which regulations apply to which machine. To give one example, woodworking machinery must comply with the Woodworking Machinery Regulations 1974, which provide detailed requirements for the safeguarding of all woodworking machines, and for safe standards of ventilation, illumination and noise levels in areas in which such machines are operated.

Machines must be vibration-free, and securely fixed. The Health and Safety Executive recommends that a clear space of at least three feet should be kept on three sides of the machine. Machines of all types should, if possible, be stopped when not in use, and every machine should be fitted with its correct guard. Emphasis should be placed on ways of cutting out electricity supplies in an emergency. A main circuit breaker should be fitted in every room where electrical equipment is used, and each machine should be fitted with an isolating switch. Apparently minor precautions, such as ensuring correct fusing values and professional servicing, considerably reduce the risk of accidents to people and equipment.

►Power Tools◄

►Select the proper tool for the work in hand. Never try to force a tool to do one thing when it is specifically designed to do something else.
►Ensure that all tools are double-earthed or fully insulated. Extension leads should be avoided as they increase the risk of earthing faults.
►Ensure that all blades and bits are sharp, clean and regularly maintained.
►Remove adjusting keys and wrenches before turning on the tool.
►Never make adjustments to a tool while the power is switched on.
►Never leave a tool running unattended.
►Only use power tools when it is essential and where traffic is minimal.

►Highly Flammable Liquids and Sprays◄

Electrical equipment can usually present a potential source of ignition for flammable gases or liquids. In such circumstances, the use of explosion-protected apparatus will be necessary. The Electricity (Factories Act) Special Regulations 1908 and 1944 (which is the current legislation governing electrical safety at work) applies only to factories, mines and quarries. These regulations, however, are shortly to be revoked and replaced with the Electricity at Work Regulations under the Health and Safety at Work Act, which will apply to art and craft studios. The new regulations come into force on April 1, 1990.

There are three statutory classifications of flammability:

►Highly flammable; liquids with a flashpoint of 32°C (90°F) or below.
►Flammable; materials with a flashpoint above 32°C.
►Petroleum mixtures; those with a flashpoint of 23°C (73°F) or below are by definition highly flammable.

A flashpoint is a method of rating the relative flammability of liquids. The lowest temperature at which a liquid gives off a flammable vapour/air mixture which can be ignited by sparks or static electricity is known as its flashpoint. If a substance is cooled below its flashpoint the danger of ignition is much reduced.

Only use highly flammable liquids at a temperature lower than the liquid's flashpoint. Consider the liquid's properties and conditions of usage when assessing whether or not a dangerous concentration is likely to occur. For instance, a vapourised liquid used as a spray may still be ignited at low temperature by an ignition source of sufficient energy.

Cleanliness is the most effective precaution against fire or explosion where highly flammable liquids are concerned. Places where highly flammable deposits accumulate should be thoroughly cleaned at least

►VDUs◄

The dangers or otherwise of Visual Display Units (VDUs) have been a topic of considerable debate during the last few years, with claims that they cause miscarriages precipitating understandable concern. At the time of writing, it is looking increasingly likely that these fears are ungrounded, although computer technology is unquestionably leading to an increase in workload and therefore stress for many workers, often without proper provision for rests and safety precautions. Where artists or craftspeople are using VDUs, whether for writing, on-screen graphics or layout or typesetting, basic 'well-being' should be adhered to, even though (as the writers know) this can sometimes be difficult. Ensure that correct posture with upright back is maintained, and that a rest break of at least ten minutes in every hour is taken. Anti-glare screens help to prevent eye strain, and can be fixed either to the display unit or held by a clamp stand between the screen and the user. In general, colour screens (usually green on black) are easier to work with than monochromatic (white on black).

once a week. Use plastic, wood or phosphor-bronze scrapers, rather than metal, to remove nitro-cellulose residues. Spray booths can be cleaned more efficiently if preparatory coatings of sheet material or hardening liquid are applied to the booth surfaces before use and peeled off afterwards.

When spraying highly flammable materials, clear, dry filters should be used for each different material to eliminate the risk of spontaneous combustion of interacting residues.

►Ceramics◄

One of the chief hazards in a ceramics studio is the inhalation of silica dust from clay. Clay is composed of various mineral silicates. Of these, flint, quartz and calcinated sand (crystobalite) all have an equally high content of free crystalline silica. If inhaled in the form of dust, silica destroys the body's natural defences in the lungs, causing irreversible damage. The first sign of possible poisoning is increased breathlessness. Over a period of years, exposure can lead to silicosis, a form of pneumoconiosis which can prove fatal. Scrap clay presents a considerable dust hazard once dried. All scraps should therefore be deposited in covered containers.

Dust production may also be a problem when handling powdered glaze. Glazes contain silica and a flux or frit which usually contains lead. Lead compounds are highly soluble and can easily be dissolved into the bloodstream if inhaled in a powder or dust form. The permissible soluble lead content in a glaze is outlined in the Low Solubility Regulations. Any glaze which does not conform to these should obviously not be used. If unsure, contact your local Health and Safety Executive office for advice.

For preparing your own glaze use a low-solubility lead frit such as lead bisilicate and bear in mind when grinding down that the solubility of the lead frit increases as the fineness of the particle size decreases. Leadless frits are available. These substitute borax for lead. However, borax is also toxic in its raw state.

Colouring pigments which may be included in the glaze contain a multitude of chemicals many of which, such as cadmium and chromium, are hazardous in powdered form. Beware of toxic vapours which may be released when glazes are fired. Vapour-glazing techniques require special care. Kilns used for vapour-glazing techniques should be fitted with extraction equipment. Solvents present in decorating inks may present an inhalation hazard.

Accidental ingestion of toxic materials is a potential hazard associated with ceramic products designed for use as eating and drinking utensils. Leakage of lead, cadmium and other chemicals from incorrectly formulated or improperly fired glazes and colours may be caused by the action of organic acids present in food or drink. Acetic acid in vinegar, citric acid in fruits and acids in coffee are amongst those organic acids capable of producing such a reaction. Remembering forthcoming changes in UK product liability laws to bring them more into line with the United States, artists should be especially careful to guard against this possibility.

Incorrect formulation of glazes can occur quite easily. The use of lead frits does not guarantee a safe glaze. The relatively low temperatures involved in raku firing may affect the solubility of lead frits, and this process is therefore not recommended for food ware.

The ratio of glaze ingredients, thickness of application, duration and temperature of firing and the condition of the kiln atmosphere are all factors which affect the amount of lead extractable from the glaze. Therefore,

glazes should not be combined with other components without retesting the amount of soluble lead present. For example, a commercially produced, clear glaze may be perfectly safe until a colourant is added, which causes a massive increase in lead-release. Copper oxide is especially dangerous in this respect and as such its use should be avoided. It has in fact been abandoned in industry.

Skin contact with solvents present in decorative inks must be avoided. Prolonged skin contact with clay slips and glaze suspensions may cause dermatitis. Gloves should be worn when handling dermatitic materials. Barrier creams alone are not satisfactory, and should only be used in conjunction with gloves as an extra safeguard.

►Glasswork◄

Flint is the most hazardous source of dust in a glass studio as it has a high content of free crystalline silica (see references to silica in ceramics, above). Inhalation of toxic dusts can occur during batch mixing. Batch mixtures may contain lead oxide and a variety of sulphates and nitrates. The cutting, grinding or polishing of glass can present further dust hazards. A supply of water should be readily available to minimise dust production. Ensure that electrical motors and switches are completely protected where water is used.

Lead and other toxic substances are contained in stain pigments. These can become airborne if the stain is applied by an air-spray gun or if pigment is brushed or blown away from the glaze to achieve various contrasts before firing. Painted or stained glass produces noxious fumes when fired. An extraction hood should be fitted above any area where this is done. Lead fumes may be produced from solders, especially if they are overheated. The copper foil technique involves more solder than the lead came technique, and so involves more risk.

When etching with acid, a container full of sodium bicarbonate solution should be readily available for rapid immersion of any part of the body. It is useful to dye the acid a particular colour to ensure easy identification.

►Painting◄

Dry pigments are a dust hazard. A variety of hazardous chemicals may be present. Aerosol sprays can produce a mist of pigment dust and solvent, as can airbrushes and compressed air guns. Epoxy- and polyurethane-based paints are particularly hazardous.

Artists who indulge in the foolhardy but common practice of 'pointing' the paintbrush with the lips and tongue would do well to note the presence, albeit in comparatively small quantities, of such poisons as arsenic, cadmium and lead in widely-used art paints.

►Photography◄

A variety of photographic materials may prove hazardous over a prolonged period of inhalation. Adequate darkroom ventilation is therefore essential. The mixing of stock solutions poses the most serious hazard as the chemicals are in their concentrated form. Skin should be well-protected to prevent irritation or dermatitis; sometimes there may be a delayed reaction effect whereby this occurs some time after initial contact. Colour developers are more likely to cause skin irritation than black and white.

►Printing◄

►**Etching** – Concentrated acids release toxic fumes. The preparation of home-made grounds should not be attempted. Any contact of zinc with hydrochloric or sulphuric acid will produce highly toxic arsene gas.
►**Aquatinting** – Rosin dust is highly toxic. Spray lacquers used for aquatinting plates may produce highly concentrated solvent and propellent mist. Ammonium hydroxide vapour is a severe irritant.
►**Silkscreening** – The main hazard arises from the presence of solvents in inks, bases, thinners, retarders and silkscreen wash fluids. All possible ventilatory and good-housekeeping measures should be taken to avoid over-exposure to solvents released from such materials.
►**Lithography** – Some talcs (french chalk) or talc/resin mixtures contain asbestos, and should be avoided.
►**Photoprinting** – If the carbon arc is used as a light source, toxic fumes are produced. Dangerous amounts of these can be inhaled without noticeable initial discomfort. Carbon arcs should therefore be directly vented to the outside atmosphere.

Many printing processes involve chemicals which are dangerous when in contact with the skin. When etching, protective clothing should be worn to guard against burns from acid. It is especially important to wear goggles. In aquatinting, ammonium hydroxide liquid and vapour causes severe burns, and contact with rosin dust and spray should be avoided. All the silkscreen solvents mentioned above can be dermatitic to varying degrees. Avoid hand contact with process camera lamps, even when cold, as this could lead to shattering when they are in use. Exposure to mercury vapour lamps in printing-down tables can cause skin burns and conjunctivitis in the eyes. With lithography, desensitising etches, especially those which contain potassium dichromate, nitric acid and phosphoric acid, should be handled with extreme care. Lithographic crayons and tusche contain lamp black which is a mild irritant to the eyes and possibly skin and is a suspected carcinogen; avoid skin contact.

►Sculpture and Modelling◄

Fumes from forging and casting metals are toxic. All metal fumes, especially zinc oxide, can cause metal fume fever, the symptoms of which are similar to influenza. Oxy-acetylene and electric-arc welding create a variety of toxic by-products, the exact nature of which depend upon what is being welded. The welding of galvanised or coated metal is extremely risky in this respect. When soldering, care should be taken with tin, lead and silver solders, all of which release toxic fumes. Silver is especially dangerous when used with flouride fluxes. Silica (see ceramics) may be released as dust from sand used in the shell-moulding process. In this process it is also preferable to use a micro-crystalline moulding compound such as 'Gell-Flex' rather than vinamould resin binders which may release toxic vapours on decomposition. When finishing metals by grinding or abrading, take adequate precautions against airborne dust.

►**Plastics** – Many plastics release toxic fumes on combustion. Resin dust is toxic, as are the fumes from accelerator solutions and fumes and dusts from the various forms of catalysts. Only certain plastics are suitable for welding. Check beforehand on any likely fume release.

►**Stone** – Stone dust is potentially dangerous due to the presence of silica. Certain stones such as granite and quartz, have a higher silica content than others, such as limestone and marble.

►**Wood** – Respiratory ailments arise due to sustained exposure to wood dust. Certain dusts can produce a reaction after only a few hours, whilst some are carcinogenic. South American boxwood, beech and Western red cedar are a few of the most dangerous types of wood dusts. All measures should be taken to avoid inhalation.

As with other processes, the sculptor must take particular care to avoid skin contact whilst working. With metal, eye and body protection should always be worn to guard against heat and splashes when forging and casting. Infra-red and visible radiation created by welding causes burns, headaches, fatigue and eye damage if adequate protective clothing is not worn. When finishing metals, dust produced from grinding and abrading may cause dermatitic and eye problems. With plastics, dusts and fumes should be treated as potentially dermatitic. Wood dusts, as well as wood treatments and additives, are potentially dermatitic. Dust, oil, sap and extracts from many species of wood can cause skin irritation in prone individuals. Some woods are primary irritants capable of affecting anyone if proper protective clothing measures are not taken.

►Textile Crafts◄

Solvents present in textile dyes present a major inhalation hazard which should be guarded against. Dust from direct dyes is a suspected carcinogen. All steps should be taken to minimise dust problems created by spinning. Sustained exposure to cotton, flax and hemp dust can cause byssinosis (brown lung). Some animal fibres, such as wool, yarn or hair, can cause anthrax. Care should be taken against inhalation of materials associated with photoprinting textiles. Batik wax should only be heated in a double pan as it releases toxic acrolein fumes if overheated.

All skin contact with dyes should be avoided. All direct dyes, disperse dyes, fibre-reactive dyes and mordant dyes are highly dermatitic and possibly carcinogenic.

►First Aid◄

Whilst the philosophy of safety is prevention rather than cure, it is prudent and often a legal requirement for people to be properly prepared for accidents to occur. First aid cabinets are a must, and the contents should follow the guidelines of the First Aid Regulations 1981. Keen first aiders could join an organisation such as the National Register of First Aiders in London, or take special training courses for a small cost. In either case, it is important to study a recognised manual (such as that of the St. John's Ambulance Brigade), and try to learn the basics of treating an injured person – it could be yourself that benefits from such precautions one day!

►Feeling Good Working Well◄

The above all refers specifically to safety but remember your general health and well-being is as important to your work as anything else. Meeting deadlines, holding down part-time jobs, not being able to afford adequate studio space, all deny you the opportunity to organise your

working time as you would best like. But giving yourself some general rules about working conditions, even if you can not always keep them, is a good idea.

Try not to overcrowd the studio with people or things. That does not mean renting a huge studio on your own. A bit of thought about storage and allocation of working spaces can improve the use of your studio even if it does not make it perfect. Heat the studio to a comfortable temperature. This not only makes working pleasanter, it also avoids the risk of accidents. If the studio is a large and costly place to heat then try screening off part of it, particularly in winter, as a *warm area.* Be careful, when doing this, of fire risks from gas heaters. Keep a fire extinguisher around if possible, check it regularly and make sure that you know what it will and won't do (e.g. never use a water extinguisher on electrical fires, burning oil or solvents).

Do not allow your work to force you to eat irregularly or badly. Food like rest keeps you going. It is part of your creative energy. Do not let physical exertion destroy your creative energy. Be careful when lifting or carrying, working in a fixed or awkward position, straining your eyes, etc. Just

VAN GOGH SELF-PORTRAIT. *1888. Oil*
Fogg Art Museum, Cambridge (Wertheim Collection)

because the person in the next studio is a champion weight lifter doesn't mean that you have to heave your sculpture around yourself. Get help, it is better than a bad back.

Try not to work too long hours. Give yourself a maximum that you will work in any one day. Have a proper break at lunch and tea time. Stop for short rests, particularly if you are working a long day or feel over-tired. Have time off, you will feel better even if it is only a half-day holiday and remember even artists are entitled to take to their beds when ill. None of this need make you a nine-to-five weekends-off person. Arrange your time to suit yourself but not to punish yourself.

▶Information◀

▶Contacts◀

▶*British Safety Council*, 62-64 Chancellors Road, London W6 9RS ☎ 01 741 1231

▶*British Society for Social Responsibilities in Science*, 9 Portland Street, London W1

▶*Art Hazards Information Centre*, 5 Beekman Street, New York NY 10038, USA

▶*Royal Society for the Prevention of Accidents*, Cannon House, Priory Queensway, Birmingham ☎ 021 233 2461

▶Further Reading◀

▶Copies of regulations and booklets referred to in the text can be obtained from Her Majesty's Stationery Office (Books), Publications Department, PO Box 276, London SW8 5DT

▶*Caution: A Guide to Safe Practice in the Arts & Crafts*, Tim Challis & Gary Roberts. Sunderland Polytechnic 1984

▶*Artist Beware: The hazards and precautions in working with art and craft*, McCann. Watson-Gupthill, New York 1979

▶*Health and Safety in Printmaking – a manual for Printmakers*, Moses, Purdham, Bowhay and Hosein. Alberta Labour Occupational Hygiene Branch, Canada 1978

▶*Health Hazards in the Arts and Crafts,* BW Carnow. University of Illinois, School of Public Health

▶*Hazards Bulletin.* British Society for Social Responsibility in Science. Back copies from Trade Union Book Service, 265 Seven Sisters Road, London N4 ☎ 01 802 6145

▶*Health and Safety Executive Leaflet on Threshold Limit Value.* HMSO

▶*Art Hazards and Precautions:* A Handbook for Artists and Craftspeople, Michael McCann. Watson-Gupthill

▶'Hazards of Solvents', Sasa Marinkov, 'Print Supplement 3'. *Artists Newsletter,* August 1983

▶*Safety First*, James Tye & Tim Challis. JM Dent & Sons, 1988

▶'And meanwhile', Susan Jones, 'Print Supplement 2'. *Artists Newsletter*, June 1982

▶'Health and Safety...pregnant and nursing artists', Centre for Occupational Hazards. *Artists Newsletter*, April 1988

Training

Training

►Tom Smith◄

Two sculptors who had recently graduated were amongst a number of people who joined an European Social Fund training project making play-sculpture. As part of the project they were introduced for the first time to industrial fabrication techniques and planning to deadlines. They found that the methods suited their way of working. When the course finished they decided to go into partnership to design and make sculpture suitable for children which could be sited in public places. They spent some time preparing plans and on self-employment and typing courses which increased their range of necessary skills. With confidence acquired from training they eventually started 'trading' as sculptors.

In another case a craftsperson who was producing work of a reasonably high standard found he was having difficulty in dealing with potential customers and no success in the placement interviews he was attending. He was advised to attend a short course on interview technique where video was used. In the playback sessions he became aware of his aggressive manner and 'body language' mirrored on the monitor. By sensitive counselling and through infilling on to part of a drama course he was able to control his manner and to some extent this was reflected in his increased success.

◁see **Looking at Yourself**▷

By accident rather than design, all three had discovered the benefits of training but training needs need to be properly assessed and programmes planned.

►Why Further Training?◄

Interviewing artists, I was amazed by the range of skills they required in order to survive. Incredibly, very few had received any advice on essential survival skills whilst at college – even at the basic level of pricing their work or preparing a CV.

Though many recognised the need to acquire new skills there was some confusion as how to go about this. The most common assumption was that they 'could find out for themselves' and there was a reluctance to consider formal training. This is surprising because properly organised training can be the quickest, safest and most efficient method of learning skills.

Training is available in many forms from individually-tailored

programmes to joining a course at a local college. It should lead you step by step to the necessary level of competence, introduce you to methods of good practice, guide you in mastering difficult techniques and help you understand procedures including safe methods of carrying out dangerous tasks.

Though approaches may vary, most training should put you in touch with an instructor who has expertise and whom you can question. It provides a safety net, an advantage over learning from experience or trying to interpret complex information yourself.

►Identifying your Training Needs◄

Skill deficiencies common amongst artists are:

- ► Financial presentation and planning
- ► Administration and organising skills
- ► Communication skills from drafting CVs to negotiation
- ► Strategies for dealing with people
- ► Pricing, retailing and publicity skills
- ► Presentation of slides
- ► Skills in specialised technical processes

If you glance through this and like me think what a poor grasp you have of some of these then it is worth considering further training more carefully. Many artists and craftspeople spend far longer than is necessary trying to acquire these skills by other means.

Having decided on the need, you will want to identify for yourself the type and level of training. Firstly clarify exactly what you need - writing it down if necessary. Be prepared to be flexible as your plan might have to be amended after speaking to an adviser or to fit in with what is available.

If you are struggling as the treasurer of a studio association do you need to apply for a course in accountancy or is book-keeping sufficient? Similarly as a sculptor wanting to embed your work safely on an open site do you really need a full City and Guilds construction course in order to understand the basic principles of working with concrete? Is the object to gain a qualification or master the skill?

The training you seek will be specific to the problem you are trying to overcome but the skills learnt could be transferable to other purposes. There may be many training options available especially in common technical processes such as welding or where financial skills used in small business are concerned. Get advice on which option is best for you perhaps from a lecturer in the subject at a local college.

Joining a course can be a way of gaining access to an informal network by making contacts with engineering, building and business studies staff. Highly specialised training and advice can be expensive and it might be possible to identify cheaper or free alternatives by discussing it with someone who works in a broadly related field. I know of one instance where an artist interested in the patina of metals saved on a specialist short course when she received advice from a lecturer in metallurgy.

Most of us experience difficulty in recognising our need for training in communication, social and personal skills. We assume we can use the telephone effectively, handle people well, work collectively and where necessary, deal with officials. If not, we believe it will come with experience

and some people can handle these situations with flair. The majority of us however are not always very effective. We tend to be vague and imprecise, we do not record essential information accurately, we argue rather than negotiate and try to dominate rather than be assertive. In short our human failings contribute to our failure to survive as artists.

Training is available and can develop the ability to come across effectively. Courses are not always easy to identify though, and exist under titles including effective communication, wider opportunities, career counselling, assertiveness training and so on. To confuse matters they are also available from a wide range of sources. Make extensive enquiries in your area before deciding on the best course.

Communication training helps you develop verbal, listening and written skills and can be provided in a form similar to other skill training. It is slightly different with personal and social skills which are best developed through counselling, encouragement and other techniques, helping you to identify your strengths and weaknesses in various situations and drawing out potential from your own resources. Where this training is difficult to find or expensive (as it is through private agencies) it might be set up amongst a group on a do-it-yourself basis though it is wise to bring in a qualified specialist to organise sessions (see DIY courses).

When planning ask yourself the following questions:

► Can I learn the skill more effectively than acquiring it through experience?
► At what levels do I need to start and finish?
► What are the benefits and disadvantages of the different methods of training available?
► What are the comparative costs?

►Where to go for Information◄

Find out what is available before approaching providers and you will be in a position to make better informed choices.

A good starting point is your library where you will find a display of leaflets but finding the ones you want may be a chance process. Ask the librarian who should be able to give you further information.

Alternatively, local education offices will give you an idea of what is provided in further education colleges. If the training required is to do with business or related skills then call in at your local enterprise agency.

Some areas will have educational advice and guidance units. Ask at the education office. They can be invaluable helping you through the maze of options. They provide counselling, guidance in identifying your precise needs and help in planning the right course of action.

Other information can be obtained from college offices, the Rural Development Commission (formerly CoSIRA), The Co-operative Development Agency, local resource centres, extra mural departments, The National Extension College and branches of the WEA – see listings for details. Courses and training schemes will also be advertised in your local paper, national newspapers and *Artists Newsletter*.

Abraham Bosse: Printers workshop Etching 1642

►Providers and Methods of Training◄

Some training programmes may change from year to year – there is no guarantee they will run every year. Local and regional variations occur so don't assume that the same course will run at every college. It is essential that you have current and accurate information before committing yourself.

►Colleges◄

Overall these offer the widest range of provision. There are two categories; colleges of further education (sometimes called technical colleges, community colleges or tertiary colleges) dealing mainly with non-advanced work and colleges of higher education (including polytechnics). The grade of work is reflected in the fee structure, non-advanced courses are cheaper if you have to pay. Basic skills are covered very well by colleges of further education.

Colleges of further education have a wide range of facilities and offer full-time, part-time and short courses. Some operate on a September to July year, advertising part-time and short courses in the months prior to September but the growing trend is to offer these courses all year round. Colleges in rural areas, where travelling can be a problem, may offer forms of distance learning. In urban areas some operate through drop-in or community centres and use informal methods such as workshops and coures offered in modules or units are now common-place. By 1991 it is envisaged that many courses and units will carry the National Vocational Qualification kitemark (NVQ) giving them national recognition.

Most courses need minimum class numbers and classes can be cancelled if they fall short. Don't be pressed into joining if you are not sure as there is sometimes pressure to fill courses regardless of clients' real needs.

Full information may not be available in the prospectus, obtain

departmental and course leaflets as well. If you can't find what you want, or need advice contact the head of department. They may not offer the course you want but it might be possible to infill on to part of another course. If it is a large college it might be possible that different sections offer similar provision – ask at the office.

►WEA and Extra Mural Departments◄

These are associated with providing adult education in general subjects though in many areas they have the expertise to offer specialist training. In Manchester, for example, the University extra mural department runs an excellent career studies unit in association with the MSC offering assessment, aptitude and management counselling and guidance in a novel way.

►Other Providers◄

The Rural Development Agency offers short skill courses from pottery technology to thatching and business management both at its Salisbury headquarters and other locations. These are for people working in rural areas. Some Co-operative Development Agencies provide training seminars linked to setting up co-operatives. If you are into alternatives then the National Centre for Alternative Technology at Machynlleth, Powys, runs short residential courses. Some polytechnics and universities are now providing short courses related to arts management and finance. These include Newcastle Polytechnic, Liverpool University, Leicester Polytechnic and the City University, London.

At the other end of the scale, training consortiums have been established to sell commercial training packages – training has become big business. They operate PICKUP (Professional, Industrial and Commercial Updating) and other schemes which are expensive to buy. There is no reason however why applications for grants and sponsorship should not be made by a group on the basis of a proposed PICKUP scheme. *'Training tailored to meet your needs'* is their catch-phrase. Some photographic equipment companies run short courses on techniques related to their products.

The Crafts Council has run courses for degree students such as Creativity and Professionalism, a course on setting up and running a workshop and their officers will visit colleges when invited. Some regional arts associations run survival seminars, you should contact the visual arts or crafts officer about these and other services and advice they might offer.

►Distance Learning◄

This is becoming an increasingly popular method particularly in the field of updating skills. It is probably the most efficient way of organising training in highly specialised and some other skills, where those requiring training may be spread thinly across the country. The advantage of distance learning is flexibility and the opportunity to study at your own pace. It requires a great deal of self discipline and you rarely if ever come into contact with a tutor or other students.

Schemes can be very sophisticated and include audio–visual material, kits of practical work, carefully prepared written material and guided assignments. Some have telephone links with tutors and occasional seminars. Much innovative work has been done by the Open

University who provide excellent materials and a wide range of courses.

There are many other providers, and probably the most useful is *Open Tech* provided through a number of training packages and courses run by the National Extension College. Many colleges of further education in both urban and rural areas are now offering locally-based open and distance learning packages.

►Do-it-yourself◄

All learning processes are ultimately do-it-yourself and finding out for yourself is a form of training. Studio groups are well placed to organise their own training. You will need to decide on a programme but remember the purpose is to learn new and necessary skills and not reinforce what you already know.

You might bring in the WEA or other agencies for advice and help in finding specialist tutors. Your scheme could include bringing in speakers from RAAs, art galleries, the art adviser and other local authority officers who are unlikely to charge for their services. You would look to the groups for useful skills that could be shared but, as I have said, if you aim to extend communication, social or personal skills bring in a professional to lead and organise as tensions can develop. The group may develop training materials and expertise that are saleable.

►Sources of Finance for Training◄

Fees for training can be high and you need to take into account the cost of books, materials and equipment, travel and protective clothing; however, there are many forms of support.

If you are in receipt of supplementary benefit or family income supplement then most colleges allow you to attend many courses free of charge. If you do not receive either and there is obvious hardship some colleges may waive fees. The DSS will allow you to study for up to 21 hours per week without loss of benefit as long as you are available for work. There are more flexible arrangements for single parents.

You might qualify for a LEA award. There are two types, mandatory and discretionary. If you have received a grant for your degree course then you may only be eligible for another mandatory award on a recognised post-graduate course. Discretionary grants are small and cover course fees and a book allowance. Details on eligibility are obtained from your education authority.

If you are a part-time teacher then certain in-service training courses might be available. In some authorities you will need to be persistent to obtain a place, even checking DES and authority policy guidelines to secure your rights.

Certain charities make discretionary awards but these are often small (£50-£100) and you can make many applications without success.

Both the Arts Council and Crafts Council offer funds for 'training' projects and for further information, contact the respective training officers. Increasingly, the regional arts associations are also establishing funds for training purposes.

A studio group training scheme might be eligible for project funding from the regional arts association. Discuss your ideas with the visual arts or crafts officer. Funding may also be available from local authority and commercial sources. Again, discuss your ideas with the local enterprise agency and the further education adviser.

In Development Areas, there are opportunities for funding through the EEC Social Fund for projects which provide training for unemployed people. These need to be matched with other public funds, perhaps through Inner City Urban Aid. It is a long winded and paper-intensive programme but can work. Sunderland Artists Group has been funded for a three-year project to create employment opportunities both for the artists and others in the area by passing on art skills. In Bolton, training for artists and craftspeople has been possible by using a college's Social Fund budget. You can find out more about EEC Social Fund criteria and priority areas for funding from your town hall and civic centre.

▶Summary◀

Choose the form of training that best suits your temperament but remember it is better to learn with others than on your own. Don't be put off by the maze of options. If you do the groundwork and go to providers knowing the range on offer you will be able to make informed choices. Keep as close as possible to your assessment of need, though listen to advice, as you may have planned too narrowly or too widely. Beware of glossy brochures – make sure what is offered matches the quality of the advertising. Before signing up look at the facilities and speak to tutors and students.

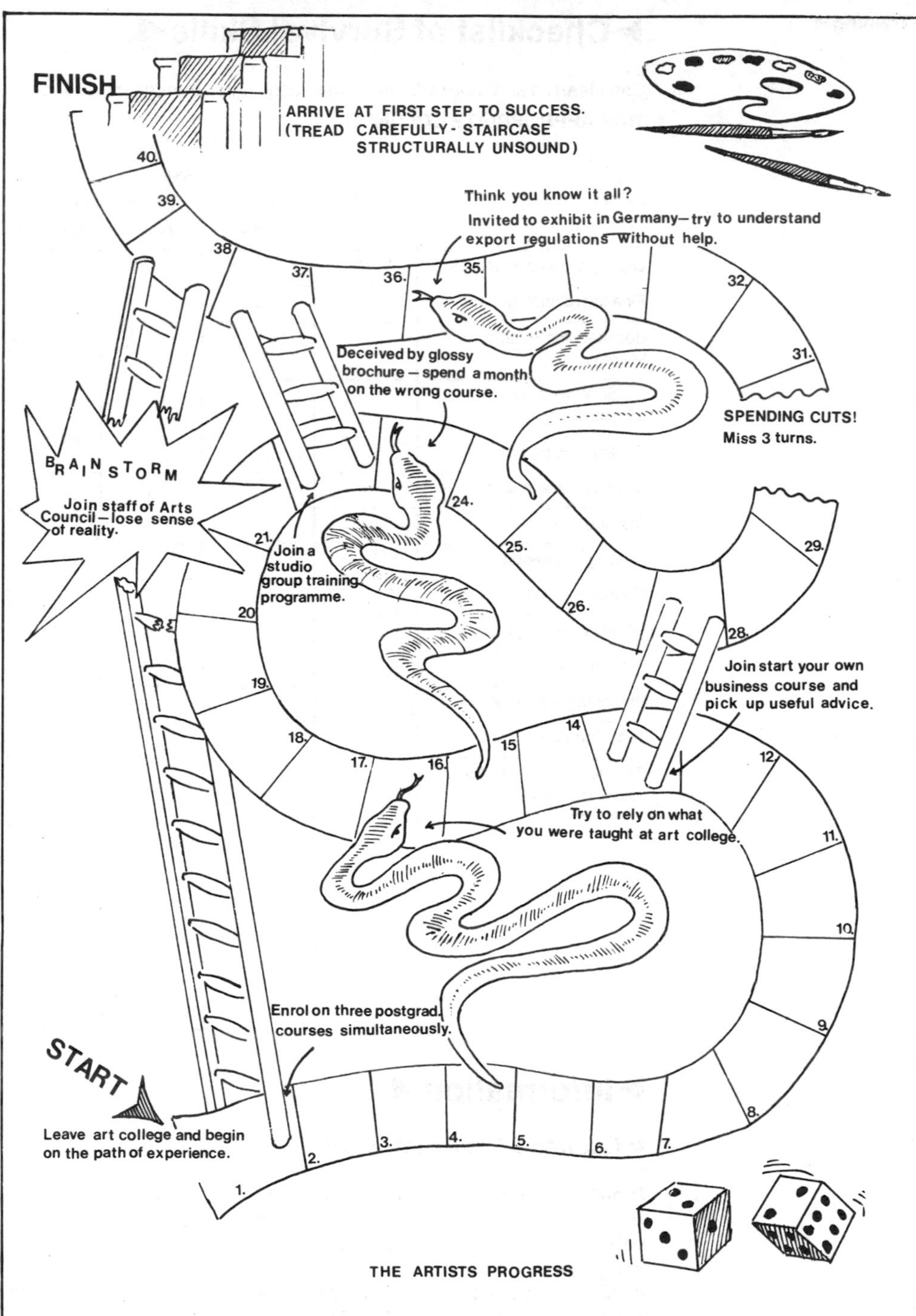

THE ARTISTS PROGRESS

►Checklist of Survival Skills◄

Can I **learn** a skill more effectively than acquiring it through experience?

TICK APPROPRIATE COLUMNS

SKILLS	SKILL LEVEL		SKILL IMPROVEMENT NEEDED	
	Good	Poor	Training	Experience
Organising time effectively				
Financial planning				
Bookkeeping/Record keeping				
Studio/Workshop administration				
Costing/pricing work				
Selling work/services				
Drafting CVs				
Dealing with people				
Negotiating skills				
Interview techniques				
Publicity skills				
Presentation of work				
Teaching skills				
Technical skills related to your work. List below				

►Information◄

►Common Abbreviations◄

►**Rural Development Commission** (formerly CoSIRA). Head Office, 141 Castle St., Salisbury, Wilts SR1 3TP ☎ 0722 336255. In Northern Ireland contact the Local Enterprise Development Unit, Lemont House, Purdy's Lane, Belfast BT8 4AR.

►**DES:** *Department of Education and Science.* Head Office, Elizabeth House, York Road, London SE1 7PH

►**ESF:** *European Social Fund*
►**TA:** *Training Agency*, formerly MSC, Manpower Services Commission
►**NAFE:** *Non-Advanced Further Education*
►**NIACE:** *National Institute of Adult Continuing Education*, 19b De Montfort St., Leicester LE1 7GE
►**AFE:** *Advanced Further Education*
►***WEA:*** *Workers Education Association*, District office address from local library

►Information◄

►Contacts◄

►*Training Unit, Arts Council of Great Britain*, 105 Piccadilly, London W1V 0AU ☎ 01 629 9495
►*Co-operative Development Agency*, Broadmead House, 21 Panton Street, London SW1Y 4DR
►*Crafts Council*, Grants and Services, 1 Oxenden Street, London SW1Y 4AU ☎ 01 930 4811
►*National Extension College*, 18 Brooklands Avenue, Cambridge CB2 2HN
►*Open University*, Guide to the Associate Student Programme, P0 Box 76, Milton Keynes MK7 6AN

►Further Reading◄

►*Second Chances: Annual Guide to Adult Education and Training Opportunities.* National Extension College. Comprehensive – easy to follow
►*Directory of Further Education.* Career Research and Advisory Centre – publishes through Hobson Ltd, Bateman Street, Cambridge CB2 1LZ. Comprehensive listings of colleges and courses
►*Directory of Independent Training and Tutorial Organisation.* Careers Consultants, 12/14 Hill Rise, Richmond, Surrey TW10 6VA
►*Directory of Opportunities for Graduates.* New Opportunities Press, Yeomans House, 76 St James Lane, London N10 3RD
►*Directory of Grant Making Trusts.* Charities Aid Foundation
►*The Grants Register*. MacMillans, Houndmills, Basingstoke, Hampshire RG21 2XS
►*Raising Money from Trusts.* Directory of Social Change
►*Opportunities for Expressive Arts Graduates.* Brighton Polytechnic Careers Counselling Unit
►*Your Guide to our Employment, Training and Enterprise Programmes.* Department of Employment & Training Agency
►*CREDO – Planning, Helping you to Succeed in Business.* Midland Bank, also available free from Enterprise Agencies
►*Paying for Training – a comprehensive guide to sources of finance for adult training*. The Planning Exchange, 1988

►Information◄

►Contacts◄

►Further Reading◄

Common Ground

Common Ground

▶Rosemary Christmas◀

▶Edited from the article 'Codes of Practice Parts 1 & 2', *Artists Newsletter*, February & March 1985◀

▶Codes of Practice◀

> There is no convincing evidence about the earnings of the visual artist, but the available statistics show that a majority live at a lower level than the national average & many near the level of poverty. Earnings from the sale of work constitute only a small part of their income, & this is supplemented, if possible, by teaching, by manual labour or by other work unrelated to their training. Unemployment and supplementary benefits are often drawn on.[1]

The evidence for this report was collected in 1975: things don't seem to have changed much in the last fifteen years, despite the activities of the Artists' Union, the National Artists Association and Artlaw and a general raising of the debate of the status of the visual arts and artists.

One of the ways of improving standards through the visual arts would be the adoption of a Code (or set of Codes) of Practice. Although the subject of debate in the area of photography, this is not a new idea when it comes to the visual arts. In 1977, the idea formed the basis of a correspondence between Conrad Atkinson (London Branch member, Artists' Union), via Hugh Jenkins (Member of Parliament) to Lord Donaldson (Minister for the Arts).[2]

The principle points raised by Atkinson were concerned with artists livelihood; - exhibition fees; a wage for artists; minimum standards for exhibitions; resale royalty rights; fellowships etc. to be for longer terms & more reasonable fees; more open discussion of grant applications; review of purchase policy of publicly funded galleries etc, exorbitant commissions and a national register of artists.

> What does seem to be an urgent priority is for visual artists as a whole to have the protection of a recognised Code of Practice to be adopted by all publicly funded galleries and by all Arts Associations in relation to bursaries & fellowships.[3]

It doesn't take much imagination to realise that this suggestion was not immediately seized and implemented by the government of the day, nor indeed was it pursued by the artists concerned.

▶What is a Code of Practice?◀

So, what is a Code of Practice? Basically it is a working agreement between two or more parties to ensure certain standards and rights, ie a set

▷**1** *Support for the Arts in England & Wales*, Lord Redcliffe-Maud. Calouste Gulbenkian Foundation, 1976

▷**2** *The Donaldson Correspondence,* Artists Union, 1979

▷**3** *The Donaldson Correspondence*

of rules about a method of working in the broadest sense. A 'CODE' is defined as a system or collection of rules and regulations and 'PRACTICE' is defined as habitual action or carrying on: method of legal procedure.[4] It can relate purely to legal principle, but mostly concerns both practical policy and philosophy, statutory and trade obligations, as well as good working methods.

Trade Unions and other representative professional bodies operate CP s in negotiation and co-operation with management organisations. Codes of Practice can also apply to specific jobs & industries. Most people will be aware that the energy supply industries recently adopted a code of practice which encompass the company's obligations to the supply of power; the consumers rights to supply in return for payment; and the company's method of requiring and extracting this payment from the consumer. There's also a code of practice in the back of every phone directory.

Other cultural workers have adopted similar methods of operating, eg the Writers Guild quota agreement with the BBC, Public Lending Right, the closed shop agreements operated by the Musicians Union and Equity, the most recent being the Workshop Declaration agreed between the Association of Cinematographic, Television and Allied Technicians (ACTT).

►Out in the Cold?◄

A visual artist in this country has no nationally agreed rights (in relation to the profession) and no democratically elected representative body although the National Artists' Association may eventually come to take on this role. The Arts Council of Great Britain (ACGB) and, to a lesser extent, the RAAs take a lot of persuading that visual artists have to be taken seriously, let alone accept they could be a force to be negotiated with in other than the most basic terms.

Aside from Exhibition Payment Right (EPR) there has been no nationally operated scheme for visual artists, and not enough inter-regional co-operation on this and other issues. Although the impetus for this scheme came from artists in the first place, it has largely fallen into disarray because of piecemeal operation and the lack of a national code of practice agreed by both the funders and the artists. Both the ACGB and the RAAs have always eschewed the idea of having 'representatives' on panels or committees. Not only do we not have the means to gain a 'representative' voice, but very few artists are actually involved in RAA panels and committees, let alone with the ACGB itself! This is a point that's been made before, but I make no excuses for repeating it – until visual artists' get more involved in the funding bodies nothing will change for their benefit!

◁see **Exhibition Checklist**▷

►Employment Status◄

The question of 'employment' status has come up time and again over the past few years. As pointed out previously, very few artists actually earn a living entirely from their own work. Individual artists may have a variety of employments – some may be self-employed and may or may not be fully supporting themselves from the sale of their own work; others may be employed, ie they may sell some of their own work but rely on another profession for their regular income (teaching, clerical, etc); others may be

▷**4** Oxford English Dictionary

involved in the grant aided sector, eg public projects such as murals, or residencies, school, hospital, etc placements. Lastly, there are those who consider themselves 'unemployed' who claim state benefit but continue with their own work.

Aside from temporary contracts (official war artists, etc), the state has never recognised how many artists it probably 'employs'. Apart from those directly employed in the education system and indirectly via grant-aided projects and schemes, there must be a large number who rely on the benefit system in part, if not totally, for their income. Yet there is no 'employment' status for visual artists, and no standard code of practice operated by either the Department of Social Security or the Inland Revenue in this area. Once again, the visual artist is dependent on the views of individual tax inspectors or social security officials for the treatment she/he receives. Direct negotiations with these departments by a representative body of artists could form the basis for a nationwide standard code of practice, and ensure equitable conditions for the taxation of and benefits for individuals. It could also go some way to making the state realise its role and responsibilities to the profession.

◁see **Residencies**▷

In the grant-aided/sponsored sector, short-term schemes such as residencies, fellowships and placements are becoming increasingly popular. In a similar manner to the EPR scheme, the operation of these is various and very much subject to the conditions imposed by sponsors, it is therefore likely to result in the same kind of muddled administration and less benefit all round than originally intended. There must be enough evidence around from both sponsors and artists as to the standard problems that arise from both the short and long-term schemes to form the basis of a code, to ensure in future that the artist is not exploited and the original benefits of each scheme are realised.

◁see **Sponsorship & Ethics**▷

Concerning private sponsorship, the issues of moral and ethical principles have recently been raised. There should be considerable discussion of the promotion and adoption of a code of ethical standards by the visual arts profession. There should be an increasing realisation that the public sector is under severe attack and there is reason to believe that many major exhibitions and schemes will be subject to the whim of private sponsorship. As has already been pointed out elsewhere, companies involved in missile production are sponsoring art events now (they'll be asking us to paint murals on their factories and silos next), but then we don't have an ethical code that says we won't get involved in this kind of thing. It's very difficult to refuse a placement when offered, even if you happen to find out that the sponsor is, say, involved in the manufacture and supply of arms to a fascist regime. It's very much up to the individual conscience what gets done, much as it always has been. Historically, the artist has accepted patronage from whatever source it could be found – the Borgias and their ilk are responsible for much 'great' art. The rich patron has always fixed the price of art. Again, I personally believe we have to make a stand somewhere on this issue, even if initially we are the losers. The matter of a strict code of ethics should be the subject of internal discussion within the profession.

◁see **Contracts**▷

► Horror Stories ►

To turn to another side of the private sector, some of the contracts put over on artists in the past by galleries and agents are horror stories in themselves. Historically, we have always been regarded as being grateful

for what we have got and not to ask for more, to take this kind of treatment and attitude and be happy to accept any crumbs offered. I heard one story concerning a particular artist – the gallery to whom he was contracted included in their agreement the point that the artist could not change his style of working without their consent, so that they did not stand the risk of losing a marketable and therefore highly profitable commodity; the artist's own finances were so inextricably bound up in this agreement (to have reneged on it would have cost him an arm, a leg and probably most of his body!), that he had no choice but continue painting in that style.

The case of standard contracts can also be illustrated from the public gallery side. In particular, an incident that came to my attention through a letter to *'The Guardian'* in 1981 from the artist Jack Smith, describing what had happened in an exhibition of social realist painting of the 1950s at Sheffield City Art Galleries. The gallery had written to the artist informing him of this. However, the artist did not consider his work social realist and objected to the inclusion of his work in this exhibition. An exchange of several letters followed in which the artist stated.

> 'I was never a social realist artist, nor had an interest in political concerns; I intensely dislike a small aspect of an artist's work being extracted from his life's work in order to prove someone's hypothetical idea; I disagree with ten-year period exhibitions which have nothing to do with the work.[5]

Despite his objections the gallery continued to insist on including his work, one of the primary reasons being that the two paintings were owned by the municipality concerned. I was actually prompted to write a letter to the newspaper in reply to this, deploring the presumption of the organisers of the show to know the content and context of an artist's work better than he does, and advocating the use of contracts of sale to avoid this kind of dilemma.

> It is up to the artist to take a professional, businesslike attitude to the exhibition and sale of their work and thereby make the establishment realise they cannot abuse artists' rights.... The artist must safeguard their interests (and the purchaser theirs) in that every work sold is covered by a written contract of sale, with clauses relating to 'use' of work; droite de suite; copyright; repair, etc with copies retained by both parties.[6]

I have heard of other cases where work has appeared in this kind of group exhibition (and the reverse when work is removed) without consulting the artist at all, so this artist should probably be grateful to have been informed that his work was going to be included!

▶Basic Operation◀

The whole area of exhibition and sale contracts should be part of the basic way an artist operates, and not seen as part of the 'alien' legal/business world. Both sides of the issue need tackling; the mechanics of a fair and watertight contract, and also changing the attitudes and assumptions of the purchaser that all rights concerning the work are forfeited by the artist once she/he accepts any money for it. Artlaw Services provided a national source of information on these kinds of problems and also promulgated standard forms of contract, but, worthy as these models were, they were not subject to comprehensive discussion with all the parties concerned. It should be borne in mind that all the previous models have been drawn up (the majority in isolation) by lawyers, galleries, agents and other non-practitioners. It's about time we did some drafting ourselves, but this is no

▷**5** 'Artist v Gallery', *Artists Union Journal*, January 1981

▷**6** 'Artist v Gallery'

reason to exclude the other parties as they have often done to us in the past. In fact, I would suggest that all sides are invited to discuss model contracts and their modus operandi, the involvement of representatives from across the board would at least ensure the beginning of a more harmonious relationship.

►Representative Group◄

However, our moral and political history as a profession has not helped the formation of a broad representative trade organisation and contentious political argument. The rise of radical politics involved in the community arts movement went some way to redressing the balance, but often the discussion and attitude of those concerned in art politics has nothing to do with the practicalities. They prefer to concentrate on arguments about political dogma, nitpicking about individual viewpoints and grievances, without being able to take a wider perspective. All the long words in the world will not make any difference unless backed by direct action.

However, the differences between right-wing self-employed of St. Ives (R) & left-wing unemployed of Leeds (L), examples of the opposing poles of the artistic community, can be reconciled if they are presented with an agreement or series of agreements that will cover both their sets of circumstances. This is not such a far fetched idea as it may initially seem – the medical profession of instance covers vastly differing areas of poulation, wealth, class, race, etc but manages from the top consultant to the humblest inner city general practitioner, to keep to the same code of medical ethics.

Likewise architects, a profession closer to ours, can, at the top of their profession be involved in multi-million pound/dollar contracts for vast industrial or housing complexes. At the other end, in community architecture, they may simply be giving advice to people on kitchen extensions or garages for little or no money at all. Both are required to keep to a set of rules.

►Universal Code◄

But back to R & L, the presentation of a code that could cover the situations encountered by these two sounds like fantasy, although if other professions can do it... But for one thing we don't have a professional representative body like the BMA, RIBA. Leaving that aside for the moment, what could possibly form the common ground between these two?

For a start, we can assume that they are both producing some kind of art work. R will be painting Cornish landscapes. L will be making abstract sculpture and conceptual pieces. So what do they have in common? The number of hours they work; how much each gets paid for the work they do; whether the materials they use are safe; whether the work is insured; the copyright of the work; the exhibition of the work; the sale of the work and the re-sale; the censorship of their work; the place they work in – rent, rates, light, heat, planning and other statutory regulations.

So they aren't as divided as they might appear at first. Whilst their ideologies and markets may be completely different, the problems at the base are very similar and may even be the same.

At present, however, they are as divided on the basic problems as they are ideologically, by their financial circumstances, but most importantly because neither of them have the backing of a national code of practice

►1989 & the future◄

Since this article was first published in *Artists Newsletter* in 1985, little appears to have changed from the point of view of artists organising themselves.

Some issues have attained a higher public profile. EPR and Percent for Art have been adopted and promoted by the Arts Council and the *Code of Practice for Independent Photography* was published in 1989. Public art, consultancy, freelance, research, cultural industries are all buzz words, but it's still administrators and not artists doing most of the talking. A whole new career structure is being built up round these words, but relativley few of the opportunities are for practitioners.

The market economy that now prevails, whilst trumpeting the freedom of the individual, only provides success for those who know how to manipulate the system. Our past record as professional practitioners does not augur well for the future place of the visual artist in the free market.

Two recent scenarios: polytechnics now have to attract and sell students; if they can undercut outside tenders for public art work by using unpaid student labour to line their coffers, who will protect the living standards of the outside professional artist? An artist's representative, speaking about the promotion and selling of work to business, was heard to say that the amount of time and effort an artist has to put into a piece of work should not be considered when fixing the price of that work. The price should be determined solely by what the market can stand.

Given that the arts as a whole seem to be in favour as part of the cultural and heritage industry, questions must be asked about the lack of professional training for visual artists, within and outside the college environment. Will we go into the 1990s in the same limping, selfish, isolationist divisions as we entered the 1980s?

How many know about, or have considered the implications of 1992? If we can't deal professionally with the 'art business' in our own country, how on earth will we cope with an open European market for the visual arts?

with a national organisation to operate it. For instance, R may be able to afford professional legal and accountancy help to overcome some of his problems. But then again, the help R gets may not necessarily completely understand what this dotty old landscape painter is on about when R says someone has copied one of his works (the landscape's everybody's isn't it?), or resold one for an enormous price, and his own tax bill has been reassessed on the basis of this sale. It may take many years and a lot of money to sort out this kind of problem, that's if the solicitor or accountant thinks it worth pursuing in the first place, which will probably not be the case unless R can produce a written or witnessed verbal contract. L will not be in a position to afford this kind of professional advice, but she probably won't fare much better at the local welfare rights office, when she complains that social security are harassing her about 'work'.

It doesn't take much imagination to realise what difference it could make in both cases if they had a code of practice for each situation to rely on. In the first case, R would be able to prove he had painted the original landscape (it would be registered as one of his works/the subject of an exhibition or sale contract) and sue for breach of copyright. If he had a sale contract covering resale royalty rights, he would be able to extract a percentage from the vendor, and prove to the taxman that his income would only be increased by that amount and not the wholesale price. In L's case, a ratified code of practice with DSS would have eliminated this problem, and L would be able to show this to the local office should they not already know of its existence. A comprehensive code of practice should encompass every aspect of artists' work and living as outlined above, without any conflict of philosophy or political ideology.

▶Representative Organisations◀

Visual artists in the UK are unique in that they belong to one of the few professions which is not represented by a professional organisation. Within the creative arts, actors, musicians and writers all have representative bodies protecting their interests, lobbying for change and acting as information clearing houses. In many other countries such as Japan, West Germany, Ireland, Scandanavia, Eastern Europe and Canada, there exist strong and representative national organisations of visual artists which have achieved solutions at economic, cultural and moral levels, which are comparable to many of the issues that artists in this country have been facing for many years.

It is almost axiomatic that, where there are strong artists' organisations – be they trade union, copyright collecting society, or professional association – there will also be recognised contractual agreements about conditions of work, remuneration, reproduction and royalty rights, pensions, tax status, and so on.

In the UK there exist many artists' associations acting as special interest or regional groupings, but inevitably, such fragmentation dissipates energy, duplicates effort and encourages factionalism and divisiveness. A national body uniting all professional artists and linking existing organisations could provide a strong focus for artists working towards the improvement of the professional status of visual artists within society and improving their economic position. These needs have become particularly urgent in the cultural and economic climate of the eighties. (Roland Miller)[(7)]

▷**7** Roland Miller, National Artists Association

►Representative Groups◄

►National Artists Association (NAA)
Membership c/o 17 Shakespeare Terrace, Sunderland SR2 7JG ☎ 091 565 4641. A representative organisation for artists in England, it holds regular meetings throughout the country, distributes a quarterly *Bulletin* and campaigns on artists' rights.

►Association of Artists & Designers in Wales (AADW)
Gaskell Buildings, Collingdon Road, Cardiff CF1 5ES ☎ 02212 407607. Representative group for artists in Wales, also organises group studio spaces.

►Artists Collective of Northern Ireland
22 Lombard Street, Belfast ☎ 0232 224429. Not really a representative organisation but the closest thing to it in Northern Ireland – runs group studio space.

►Association of Artists in Ireland
Liberty Hall, Dublin 1 ☎ Dublin 740529. Union for artists in Ireland.

►Independendent Film, Video and Photography Association (IFVPA)
79 Wardour Street, London W1V 3PH ☎ 01 439 0460. Originally set up by practising independent film and video makers it extended its membership to include photographers in 1986

►Association of Cinematograph, Television and Allied Technicians ACTT
111 Wardour Street, London W1V 4AY ☎ 01 437 8506. ACTT is a union for people working in film and television. It also has a section for photographers working in the independent sector

►Design and Artists Copyright Society (DACS)
2 Whitechapel Lane, London E1. Copyright policing and collecting organisation.

►Association of Scottish Arts (ASA)
c/o John McCulloch, 4 Gardner Street, Dundee ☎ 0382 22374; Andy Stenhouse, Edinburgh Sculpture Workshop, Albion Business Centre, 78 Albion Road, Edinburgh EH7; John Clark, Glasgow Sculpture Studios, 85 Hanson Street, Glasgow G31 2HF ☎ 041 551 0562. Founded in 1989 as a representative body for artists in Scotland.

Funding Bodies

Funding Bodies

►England◄

►Arts Council of Great Britain

Covers: England
105 Piccadilly, London W1V 0AU ☎ 01 629 9495
Sandy Nairne: Director Visual Arts; Barry Lane: Photography Officer; Rory Coonan: Visual Arts Officer (Patronage Schemes); Noelle Goldman: Visual Arts Officer (museums and galleries) Sarah Wason: Visual Arts Officer (publishing and special projects) Jeni Walwin: Performance Art Officer

►Wilding Review◄
A report, commissioned by the Office of Arts & Libraries and undertaken by Richard Wilding, covering the funding structures of the regional arts associations, the crafts council and the arts council was completed in October 1989. Recommendations from this are likely to affect the scope and number of these organisations in the future.◄

►Buckinghamshire Arts Association

This autonomous county-based arts association covers Buckinghamshire and is a client of East Midlands Arts
55 High Street, Aylesbury, Buckinghamshire HP20 1SA ☎ 0296 44704
Shaun Hennessy, Director: All visual art forms

►East Midlands Arts

Covers: Leicestershire, Northamptonshire, Nottinghamshire and part of Derbyshire except for the High Peak District
Mountfield House, Forest Road, Loughborough LE11 3HU ☎ 0509 218292
David Manley: Visual Arts/Photography/Performance Art; Carol Maund: Crafts

►Eastern Arts

Covers: Essex, Suffolk, Bedfordshire, Hertfordshire, Cambridgeshire, Norfolk
Cherry Hinton Hall, Cherry Hinton Road, Cambridge ☎ 0223 215355
Jane Heath: Visual Arts/Performance Art; Caroline Sier: Crafts; Liz Tagg: Visual Arts Development; Martin Ayres: Photography

►Greater London Arts

Covers: Greater London Area
9 White Lion Street, London N1 9PO ☎ 01 837 8808
Alan Haydon, Amanda King, Visual Arts/Performance Art/Photography

►Lincolnshire & Humberside Arts

Covers: Lincolnshire & Humberside
St Hughs, Newport, Lincoln LN1 3ND ☎ 0522 533555
Alan Humberstone: Visual Arts, Crafts, Performance Art; Kevin Moore: Assistant Visual Arts

WESTERN ISLES
Inverness
HIGHLAND
GRAMPIAN
Aberdeen
Fort William
TAYSIDE
Dundee
Perth
Scottish Arts Council
Scottish Development Agency
FIFE
CENTRAL
Stirling
Kirkaldy
Edinburgh
LOTHIAN
Glasgow
Berwick
Arts Council of
Northern Ireland
STRATHCLYDE
Galashiels
BORDERS
Ayr
DUMFRIES AND GALLOWAY
Dumfries
NORTHUMBERLAND
Northern Arts
Derry (Londonderry)
NORTHERN IRELAND
Stranraer
TYNE AND WEAR
Newcastle
Sunderland
Carlisle
Belfast
Durham
DURHAM
Darlington
Hartlepool
CLEVELAND
Teesside
CUMBRIA
Yorkshire Arts
Scarborough
NORTH YORKSHIRE
Barrow
Harrogate
Lincolnshire
& Humberside
Arts
Lancaster
North West
Arts
LANCASHIRE
York
HUMBERSIDE
W. YORKSHIRE
Hull
Blackpool
Preston
Burnley
Leeds
Bradford
Blackburn
Huddersfield
Southport
MERSEYSIDE
Merseyside
Arts
MANCHESTER
Doncaster
Grimsby
St. Helens
Manchester
Barnsley
S. YORKSHIRE
East
Midlands
Arts
Arts
Council
(Eire)
Liverpool
Sheffield
Warrington
NOTTINGHAMSHIRE
LINCOLNSHIRE
Colwyn Bay
CHESHIRE
DERBYSHIRE
Lincoln
Caernarfon
Chester
CLWYD
GWYNEDD
Stoke
Derby
Nottingham
STAFFS
NORFOLK
Norwich
North Wales Arts
Shrewsbury
LEICESTERSHIRE
Leicester
Birmingham
SHROPSHIRE
W. MIDLANDS
NORTHAMPTONSHIRE
Peterborough
Aberystwyth
Coventry
CAMBS
West Midlands
Arts
POWYS
HEREFORD AND WORCESTER
Warwick
WARWICK
Northampton
Cambridge
SUFFOLK
Ipswich
Worcester
Bedford
DYFED
BEDS
Hereford
Milton Keynes
Luton
ESSEX
Colchester
GLOUCESTER
Cheltenham
OXON
HERTS
Eastern
Arts
West Wales Arts
Gloucester
Chelmsford
Pembroke
W. GLAM
Swansea
GWENT
Oxford
Watford
Newport
BUCKS
M. GLAM
LONDON
Southend
AVON
Swindon
Cardiff
S. GLAM
South East Wales Arts
Bristol
BERKSHIRE
Slough
Reading
Bath
WILTSHIRE
SURREY
Guildford
Canterbury
KENT
SOMERSET
Salisbury
HAMPSHIRE
Taunton
W. SUSSEX
E. SUSSEX
South West Arts
Southampton
DEVON
Portsmouth
Worthing
Brighton
DORSET
Exeter
Bournemouth
Eastbourne
South
East Arts
ISLE OF WIGHT
Weymouth
Southern Arts
Greater London Arts
CORNWALL
Plymouth
Torquay
Truro
Buckinghamshire Arts

►Merseyside Arts
Covers: Merseyside and West Lancashire
Graphic House, Duke Street, Liverpool L1 4JL ☎ 051 709 0671
Tony Woof: Visual Arts, Performance Art, Photography; Rachel Sherratt: Crafts

►North West Arts
Covers: Lancashire (except W. Lancs), Cheshire, Greater Manchester and the High Peak District of Derbyshire
12 Harter Street, Manchester M1 6HY ☎ 061 228 3062
Virginia Tandy: Visual Arts, Photography; Lyn Barbour: Crafts

►Northern Arts
Covers: Cumbria, Durham, Northumberland, Cleveland and Tyne & Wear
10 Osborne Terrace, Newcastle upon Tyne NE2 1NZ ☎ 091 281 6334
Peter Davies: Visual Arts, Performance Art; Laurie Short: Crafts; John Bradshaw: Photography

►South East Arts
Covers: East Sussex, Kent and Surrey (excluding Greater London areas)
10 Mount Ephraim, Tunbridge Wells TN4 8AS ☎ 0892 41666
Frances Smith: Visual Arts & Crafts; Tim Cornish: Photography

►South West Arts
Covers: Avon, Cornwall, Devon, Dorset (except Bournemouth, Christchurch & Poole), Gloucestershire and Somerset
Bradninch Place, Gandy Street, Exeter EX4 3LS ☎ 0392 218188
Val Millington, Anne Dundon: Visual Art, Crafts, Photography, Performance Art

►Southern Arts
Covers: Berkshire, Hampshire, Oxfordshire, West Sussex, Wiltshire, the Isle of Wight and the Poole, Bournmouth and Christchurch areas of Dorset
19 Southgate Street, Winchester, Hants ☎ 0962 55099
Hugh Adams: Visual Arts, Photography, Performance Art; David Kay: Crafts

►West Midlands Arts
Covers: West Midlands, Hereford, Worcestershire, Staffordshire, Shropshire and Warwickshire
82 Granville Street, Birmingham B1 2LH ☎ 021 631 3121
Julie Seddon Jones: Visual Arts, Craft, Performance Art; Helen Doherty: Photography, Media and Film; Muriel Fry: Crafts

►Yorkshire Arts
Covers: North, South and West Yorkshire
Glyde House, Glydegate, Bradford BD5 0BQ ☎ 0274 723051
Yvonne Deane: Visual Arts, Performance Art; Olivia Stross: Crafts; Paul Brookes: Photography

►Crafts Council
Covers: England and Wales
12 Waterloo Place, London SW1Y 4AU ☎ 01 930 4811
Barclay Price: Regional Officer

►Ireland◄

►Arts Council of Northern Ireland
181A Stranmillis Road, Belfast BT9 5DU ☎ 0232 381591
Brian Ferran: Visual Arts Director

►Arts Council (Eire)
70 Merrion Square, Dublin 2 ☎ 0001 611840
Medb Ruane: Visual Arts Officer

►Crafts Council of Ireland
Covers: Crafts in Ireland and Northern Ireland
The Powers Court, Town House Centre, South William Street, Dublin 2
☎ 0001 797368
Sean O'Farrell: Crafts Officer

►Scotland◄

►Scottish Arts Council
12 Manor Place, Edinburgh EH3 7DO ☎ 031 226 6051
Fiona Logue, Assistant Art Director: Visual Art, Photography, Performance Art

►Scottish Development Agency
Covers: Crafts in Scotland
Rosebery House, Haymarket Terrace, Edinburgh ☎ 031 337 9595
Susan Mackinnon: Crafts Officer
(Negotiations are not yet concluded as to whether the Scottish Arts Council will assume responsibility for crafts in Scotland).

►Wales◄

►Welsh Arts Council
Museum Place, Cardiff CF1 3NX ☎ 0222 394711
Vacancy: Art Marketing; Roger Le Fevre: Crafts; Alison Scott; Commissions

►North Wales Arts
Covers: North Wales
10 Wellfield House, Bangor, Gwynedd ☎ 0248 353248
V. Clifford Jones, Deputy Director

►South-East Wales Art
Covers: Mid-Glamorgan, South Glamorgan, Gwent and S. Powys
Victoria Street, Cwmbran NP44 3YT ☎ 06333 75075
Richard Cox: Visual Arts, Crafts, Photography, Performance Art

►West Wales Arts
Covers: West Glamorgan and Dyfed
3 Red Street, Carmarthen, Dyfed SA31 1QL ☎ 0267 234248
Sybil Crouch: Deputy Director

Advertisers'

SCOTTISH SCULPTURE WORKSHOP & GALLERY

Provides facilities for sculptors with large workshops and equipment for traditional and modern techniques. Self-catering accommodation available.

SSW, 1 Main Street, Lumsden, Huntly, Aberdeenshire AB5 4JN
Tel No. 046 46 372

photo: Tracy McKenna at work.

Established 12 years, offering a fine printmaking workshop with a wide range of resources

stone lithography
plate lithography
intaglio
screen printing
relief printing
print sales
editioning
co-publishing
materials sales
slide index
Thomas Bewick prints
exhibitions

Charlotte Press (formerly known as Northern Print)
5 Charlotte Square, Newcastle upon Tyne NE1 4XF
telephone 091 232 7531

GLASGOW SCULPTURE STUDIOS

** large open-plan studio space*
** fully equipped workshops for all media*
** spaces for installation work, etc.*
** available for short- or long-term rental*
** regular commissions, projects and opportunities*
** foreign exchange programme*
** resource library and slide index*
** information mailings to all members*
** membership is open to all*

- for further details please contact:

The Co-ordinator
Glasgow Sculpture Studios Ltd
85 Hanson Street
Glasgow G31 2HF
Tel: 041-551 0562

BERLLANDERI SCULPTURE WORKSHOP

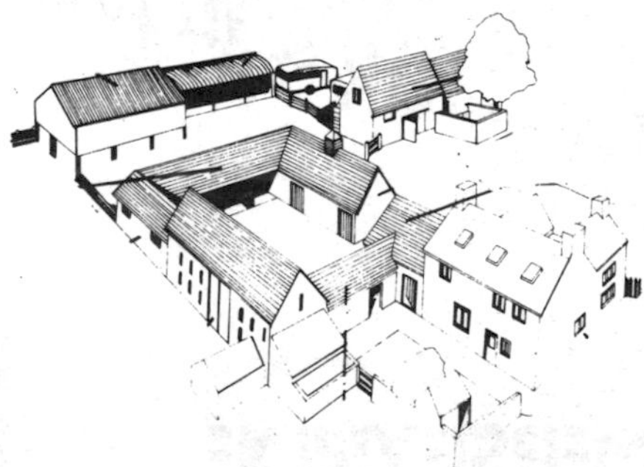

Berllanderi offers a retreat for practising sculptors from Britain and abroad.

For more information please apply to
Berllanderi Sculpture Workshop, Usk Road, Raglan, Gwent NP5 2HR
Telephone: 0291 690268

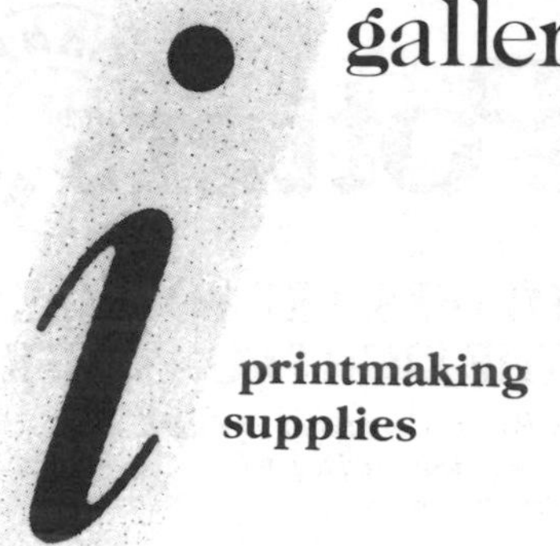

The Fulham Pottery
Est 1671

A Code of Practice for Independent Photography

Amust for all photographers, organisations, funders and sponsors. Guidelines to assist in negotiations and contractual agreements, covering employment, equal oportunities, copyright, exhibiting, commissions, residencies and placements, publications, purchases.

Ed Vince Wade. 32 A5 pages
£2.60 UK, £3 Eire/Europe, £3.95 elsewhere

Independent Photography Directory

Essential resource on over 250 independent photography organisations detailing darkroom facilities, exhibition and education activities.... Also listing awards, fellowships, magazines, press lists, training, unions, professional associations, funding bodies.

Ed Mike Hallett & Barry Lane, Arts Council
224 A5 pages
£7.50 UK, £8.25 Eire/Europe, £10.75 elsewhere

Organising Your Own Exhibition

A practical guide to all aspects of setting up and organising exhibitions. Finding space, finances, setting out a timetable, dealing with publicity, framing and mounting work, organising the private view, selling work and making the best of the exhibition.

By Debbie Duffin, published by ACME
100 A5 pages
£3.95 UK, £4.25 Eire/Europe, £6.45 elsewhere

Books for Artists by Post Order Form

Name ______________________________

Address ______________________________

____

Postcode ______________________________

- ❑ A Code of Practice for Independent Photography
- ❑ Independent Photography Directory
- ❑ Organising Your Own Exhibition

Please tick appropriate box and send with acheque/postal order made payable to AN Publications to:
AN Publications, PO Box 23, Sunderland SR4 6DG
Payments for overseas orders must be in Sterling.
Overseas order sent by Airmail

Looking for good places to exhibit?
Save time, money and avoid frustration by using the 1989 edition of the **Directory of Exhibition Spaces.**

Over 2,000 entries, the most comprehensive and up-to-date listing of galleries, museums, arts centres, theatre and bar spaces, libraries, colleges... in fact anywhere showing temporary exhibitions of artists' work.

The easy-to-use layout tells you who wants applications and how to apply; whether you'll get a fee; what commission the gallery charges; descriptions of the spaces; disabled access; programming policy....

Directory of Exhibition Spaces Order Form

Name ______________________________

Address ______________________________

____

Postcode ______________________________

Mail order prices including postage:

- ❑ UK £13.95
- ❑ Europe/Eire £14.75
- ❑ Elsewhere £19.45

Please tick appropriate box and send with a cheque/postal order made payable to AN Publications to:
AN Publications, PO Box 23, Sunderland SR4 6DG
Payments for overseas orders must be in Sterling.
Overseas order sent by Airmail

Contributors

►Articles◄

►**Adrian Barr-Smith:** is a solicitor with Denton, Hall, Burgin & Warrens and one-time Director of Artlaw Services Ltd.

►**Oliver Bevan:** is an artist working in London.

►**David Briers:** lives in Cardiff, and is a freelance writer on visual arts and crafts, and an area contributor to *Artists Newsletter.*

►**David Butler:** is an artist and editor of *Artists Newsletter.*

►**Tim Challis** and **Gary Roberts:** researched and compiled *Caution: A Guide to Safe Practice in the Arts & Crafts.*

►**Rosemary Christmas:** is an artist and Director of Merseyside Exhibitions.

►**Lee Corner:** has been the Co-ordinator of Art Link in the West Midlands since 1979.

►**Nick Clements:** is an artist and administrator for the Pioneers, a Cardiff-based co-operative which works in areas of high social need.

►**Daniel Dahl:** is an artist and a freelance writer and researcher.

►**Sarah Eckersley:** lives and works in Oxford and is a freelance writer on visual arts.

►**Peter Fink:** is a sculptor who has undertaken a number of public commissions and residencies who was a member of an Art and Architecture research team for the Department of the Environment.

►**Peter Hill:** is an artist living in Edinburgh and the editor of *Alba.*

►**Susan Jones:** is an artist, member of Sunderland Artists Group and a freelance writer and researcher.

►**Bill Laws:** is a writer on the visual arts.

►**Charles Maclean:** is a literary agent in Edinburgh.

►**Richard Padwick:** was until 1980 an exhibition organiser and undertook research into temporary exhibition provision for East Midlands Arts. He is now publications editor for *Artic Producers.*

►**Carole Pemberton:** was Careers Counsellor at the Faculty of Art and Design at Brighton Polytechnic until 1988 and is now Principal Training and Development Officer for the London Borough of Kingston.

►**Cameron Scott:** is an artist working in assemblage, collage and papermaking and is Head of the Department of Art and Design at Burnley College.

►**Nick Sharp:** is a company solicitor, a director of Artic Producers and also a director of the Barbican Arts Trust

►**Tom Smith:** is Co-ordinator of Creative Studies at Bolton Metropolitan College and undertook research on methods of conveying information to artists and craftspeople on 'survival'.

►**Geoff Staden** and **Paul Donnelly:** are members of Artists Support Peace, an organisation raising the issue of peace in the arts. They campaign against unethical business sponsorship.

►**Annie Wheeler:** was an editor of *Artists Newsletter* during 1985/86.

►**Stewart Young:** is an accountant with Dodd and Co in Carlisle which handles accounts for many artists and craftspeople.

►Cartoons◄

►**Natalie d'Arbeloff:** is a painter, writer, cartoonist, book artist and part-time teacher. She runs NdA Press, a one-person enterprise which publishes, among other things, *Small Packages*, a series of booklets where her cartoon creature 'Augustine' first appeared.

►**Damon Burnard:** is a painter and cartoonist/illustrator providing drawings for a number of periodicals and publications including *New Statesman*.

Index

►A◄

►B◄

►C◄

►H◄

►I◄

►J◄

►L◄

►M◄

►N◄

►O◄

▶T◀

▶U◀

▶V◀

▶W◀

▶Y◀

133657